Expert
Oracle JDBC
Programming

R. M. MENON

Apress®

Expert Oracle JDBC Programming
Copyright © 2005 by R. M. Menon

ISBN (pbk): 1-59059-407-X

Printed and bound in the United States of America 9 8 7 6 5 4 3 2 1

Lead Editor: Tony Davis
Technical Reviewers: Rob Harrop, Thomas Kyte, Torben Holm, Julian Dyke
Editorial Board: Steve Anglin, Dan Appleman, Ewan Buckingham, Gary Cornell, Tony Davis,
    Jason Gilmore, Jonathan Hassell, Chris Mills, Dominic Shakeshaft, Jim Sumser
Associate Publisher: Grace Wong
Project Manager: Sofia Marchant
Copy Editor: Nicole LeClerc
Production Manager: Kari Brooks-Copony
Production Editor: Kelly Winquist
Compositor: Van Winkle Design Group
Proofreader: Nancy Sixsmith
Indexer: Broccoli Information Management
Artist: Diana Van Winkle, Van Winkle Design Group
Interior Design: Diana Van Winkle, Van Winkle Design Group
Cover Designer: Kurt Krames
Manufacturing Manager: Tom Debolski

Distributed to the book trade in the United States by Springer-Verlag New York, Inc., 233 Spring Street, 6th Floor, New York, NY 10013, and outside the United States by Springer-Verlag GmbH & Co. KG, Tiergartenstr. 17, 69112 Heidelberg, Germany.

In the United States: phone 1-800-SPRINGER, fax 201-348-4505, e-mail orders@springer-ny.com, or visit http://www.springer-ny.com. Outside the United States: fax +49 6221 345229, e-mail orders@springer.de, or visit http://www.springer.de.

For information on translations, please contact Apress directly at 2560 Ninth Street, Suite 219, Berkeley, CA 94710. Phone 510-549-5930, fax 510-549-5939, e-mail info@apress.com, or visit http://www.apress.com.

The source code for this book is available to readers at http://www.apress.com in the Downloads section. You will need to answer questions pertaining to this book in order to successfully download the code.

I dedicate this book to the fond memories of my beloved sister, Manjula Menon, and my dear nephew, Anil Menon.

Contents at a Glance

Contents

About the Author

■**R.M. MENON** has worked with the Oracle database for over nine years, the last six of which have been at Oracle Corporation, where he is currently Project Lead in the Server Technologies division. For the past five years, he has used JDBC and other J2EE technologies extensively as part of his work. When he is not doing research on Oracle, Menon learns Indian classical vocal music and performs at local cultural events as a singer. Occasionally, he also dabbles in sketching portraits, and drawing paintings and cartoons.

About the Technical Reviewers

ROB HARROP is Principal Consultant for Interface21, specializing in delivering high-performance, highly scalable enterprise applications. He is an experienced architect with a particular flair for understanding and solving complex design issues. With a thorough knowledge of both Java and .NET, Rob has successfully deployed projects across both platforms. He has extensive experience across a variety of sectors, in particular retail and government. Rob is the author of five books, including *Pro Spring* (Apress, 2005), a widely acclaimed, comprehensive resource on the Spring Framework.

Rob has been a core developer of the Spring Framework since June 2004 and currently leads the JMX and AOP efforts. He cofounded UK-based software company Cake Solutions Limited in May 2001, having spent the previous two years working as Lead Developer for a successful dot-com startup. Rob is a member of the JCP and is involved in the JSR-255 Expert Group for JMX 2.0. Rob can be reached at `rob.harrop@interface21.com`.

TOM KYTE is a Vice President in Oracle's Public Sector division. Before starting at Oracle, Kyte worked as a systems integrator building large-scale, heterogeneous databases and applications, mostly for military and government customers. Kyte spends a great deal of time working with the Oracle database and, more specifically, working with people who are working with the Oracle database. In addition, Kyte is the Tom behind the "Ask Tom" column (`http://asktom.oracle.com`) in *Oracle Magazine*, answering people's questions about the Oracle database and its tools. Kyte is also the author of *Expert One-on-One Oracle* (Apress, 2004) and *Effective Oracle by Design* (Osborne McGraw-Hill/Oracle Press, 2003), and a coauthor of *Beginning Oracle Programming* (Apress, 2004). These are books about the general use of the database and how to develop successful Oracle applications.

TORBEN HOLM has been in the computer business since 1987, and he has been working with Oracle as a developer and DBA since 1992. He worked for four years in the Royal Danish Airforce as a systems analyst, application developer, and DBA. Later he moved on to work at Oracle Denmark in the Premium Services group as Senior Principal Consultant, where he performed application development and DBA tasks. He has taught PL/SQL, SQL, DBA, and WebDB courses as well. For the last four years he has worked for Miracle A/S as a consultant. He is Developer 6*i* Certified (and partly 8*i* Certified, for what it's worth). He is also a member of the OakTable network.

Acknowledgments

I would like to thank many people who helped me in writing my first book. To begin with, I want to thank Thomas Kyte of Oracle Corporation, from whose books and site (http://asktom.oracle.com) I have learned many Oracle concepts. Thank you, Tom, for generously agreeing to review this book, for patiently answering many of my questions on Oracle (several times on weekends), and for being such a tremendous inspiration to me and to the Oracle community at large. This book would not have happened without your support and generosity.

I would also like to express my deepest gratitude to Rob Harrop, whose meticulous review comments made this book that much better and technically accurate. My sincere thanks are also due to the reviewers Torben Holm and Julian Dyke.

Several other folks at Oracle Corporation have also helped me a lot. In particular, I would like to thank Douglas Surber of the JDBC group, who always responded promptly to my queries. I also appreciate the timely help Quan Wang extended to me on issues related to the JPublisher utility. In the same vein, I am grateful to Debu Chatterjee, Kuassi Mensah, and Rajkumar Iruda-yaraj for clarifying some of the connection pooling–related concepts. I would also like to express my gratitude to John Beresniewicz for kindly reviewing the chapter on PL/SQL.

My sincere thanks to Apress for giving me the opportunity to write this book. Many thanks to Tony Davis for the patient and untiring application of his exceptional editorial skills on this book. My heartfelt thanks to Sofia Marchant for keeping this project on track, to Nicole LeClerc for her scrupulous copy editing, to Kelly Winquist for doing an excellent production-editing job, and to all others at Apress who worked hard behind the scenes to make this book a reality.

On a personal note, I would like to express my deepest gratitude to my family and friends. In particular, I thank my dear parents, P.K.R. Menon and Padma Menon, my ever-supportive brother, Madhu, and my delightful in-laws, Mr. and Mrs. Raveendran, without whose constant love and tireless support I would be completely lost. I would also like to thank my dear cousin brother, Vishwanathan Menon, for giving me some excellent feedback on my writing style. Last, but not least, many thanks go to my wonderful and darling wife, Shyamala Raveendran, who has endured the countless hours I spent on this book that should otherwise have been spent in her company.

Introduction

With the popularity of Java language, JDBC is now perhaps the most commonly used API to access databases. Oracle is one of the premium databases of the world. This book is about accessing and manipulating data in Oracle using JDBC, with a focus on performance and scalability.

Why another book on JDBC and Oracle, you may ask? I wrote this book because I realized that most of the other JDBC books available today more or less regurgitate the JDBC specification and the Oracle JDBC documentation that is freely available on the Internet. This book is different. The central aim of this book is to complement the available documentation on JDBC and Oracle, and to teach you how to use JDBC with Oracle *effectively*. This book is also different from other JDBC books because of its focus on performance and scalability of applications. Using this book, you will discover the following, among other things:

- How to use all the major features of standard JDBC and its Oracle extensions (Oracle 10*g* and 9*i*)

- The most important architectural features of Oracle, an understanding of which will enable you to write solid Oracle applications

- How to write and run your own benchmarks to validate (or invalidate) various performance claims, using invaluable Oracle performance tools such as `tkprof`, SQL trace, etc.

- The importance of understanding how to effectively exploit SQL and PL/SQL in your applications

Please note that this book does not cover related technologies such as OC4J, JSP, Spring Framework, and so on. Instead, it maintains focus on the JDBC API and the database tier. Within the JDBC API, I have skipped some of the less commonly used JDBC features such as distributed transactions, some of the RAC-related topics, and rowsets. The section "Overview of JDBC API" in Chapter 3 explains in detail the different interfaces of the JDBC API and the chapters that cover them (and it provides appropriate references if a topic is not covered).

Who This Book Is For

This book is for those who want to learn how to write effective JDBC code when developing an Oracle application. The book assumes that you are familiar with Java and have some basic knowledge of SQL and PL/SQL. The book does not assume any prior knowledge of JDBC. All concepts are illustrated with detailed examples accompanied by interspersed comments explaining the examples. Your best bet to make the most out of this book is to run the examples while you are reading along.

What This Book Covers

The book consists of 17 chapters covering a wide range of topics. The following sections present chapter-by-chapter breakdowns.

Chapter 1: Performance Toolkit

The very first chapter introduces you to the various performance tools you'll use throughout the book. These include tools such as `tkprof` that come bundled with Oracle, as well as tools I wrote in Java for your convenience. This is a reference chapter that I recommend you revisit whenever you need to refresh your memory about a tool used elsewhere in the book.

Chapter 2: Oracle Fundamentals

This chapter explores some of the fundamental architectural features of Oracle that you as a developer should know. You'll be introduced to topics such as multiversioning read consistency, the locking mechanism used by Oracle, shared pool, latches, undo, redo, and so on, with illustrative examples. I also provide performance guidelines applicable in general when developing an application. I recommend that you read this chapter before you read any other remaining chapters in this book.

Chapter 3: Introduction to JDBC

In this chapter, you'll learn the software you need to install to develop and run JDBC programs on either UNIX or the Windows platform. You'll examine the various types of JDBC drivers, and which ones to use when. You'll also get a good overview of the JDBC API and learn how to connect to a database. You'll then go on to write your first JDBC program.

Chapter 4: Transactions

Transactions form the basis of any database. In this chapter, you'll take a brief look at transactions in the context of JDBC. You'll see how to commit and roll back a transaction in JDBC. You'll learn what transaction isolation levels are and which ones are supported by Oracle. You'll learn about some important principles you need to follow when writing transactions for an Oracle application. You'll also examine transaction savepoints, a feature exposed to Java programs in JDBC 3.0.

Chapter 5: Statement and PreparedStatement

In this chapter, you'll first be introduced to the mechanics of how Oracle processes SQL statements. You'll then examine two of the fundamental statement interfaces of JDBC: `Statement` and `PreparedStatement`. You'll look at why you should almost always prefer `PreparedStatement` over `Statement`. You'll learn about how using `PreparedStatement` can help avoid SQL injection (a security hacking technique) attacks. You'll also learn about standard and Oracle update batching, and compare the two in terms of performance and other features.

Chapter 6: CallableStatement

In this chapter, you'll explore in detail how to invoke stored SQL procedures from JDBC using the `CallableStatement` interface. You'll learn how to use SQL92 syntax or Oracle syntax when invoking a stored procedure using the `CallableStatement` interface.

Chapter 7: Result Sets Explored

This chapter describes the advanced features of the `ResultSet` interface, including prefetching, scrollability, positioning, sensitivity, and updatability. You'll learn the various strengths and weaknesses of these features, and you'll examine how to paginate through the results of a query efficiently. You'll learn how you can dynamically build query statements with unknown number of bind variables using either the `PreparedStatement` or `CallableStatement` interface. The `ResultSetMetaData` and `DatabaseMetaData` interfaces are also covered.

Chapter 8: Oracle Objects: An Objective Analysis

This chapter introduces Oracle objects and collections. You'll critically examine how these features should be used in Oracle applications in general. Note that this chapter doesn't discuss how to access objects and collections from JDBC; those topics are covered in the next three chapters. I strongly recommend you read this chapter, though, since it forms the basis of the following three chapters that discuss Oracle objects and collections.

Chapter 9: Using Weakly Typed Struct Objects

In this chapter, you'll learn how to materialize Oracle objects as *weakly typed* objects in Java. A weakly typed object refers to a Java object that represents objects using an array of attributes.

Chapter 10: Using Strongly Typed Interfaces with JPublisher

Here, you'll learn how to materialize objects as *strongly typed* objects in Java. A strongly typed object refers to an object belonging to a custom Java class specifically created to represent a given database object type in Java. Along the way, you'll learn how to use the JPublisher utility to generate custom classes representing Oracle objects.

Chapter 11: Using Oracle Collections and References

This chapter explains how to retrieve the collections in Oracle as either a weakly typed or strongly typed array of custom class objects (generated using the JPublisher utility). You'll critically examine some of the performance extensions Oracle provides you with, and you'll also study suitable benchmarks evaluating the effectiveness of these extensions. You'll then move on to learn about references, and how to access and manipulate them using JDBC.

Chapter 12: Using LOBs and BFILEs

In this chapter, you'll learn what LOBs (large objects) are and how they're stored in Oracle. You'll then examine how to retrieve and manipulate them. You'll also compare various alternatives when manipulating LOBs through the JDBC API.

Chapter 13: Statement Caching

In this chapter, you'll learn about statement caching, its different flavors in JDBC, and how it improves the performance of JDBC programs. As a background to the statement-caching concept, you'll also examine cursors and ref cursors in detail. In addition, you'll look at two other related caches Oracle provides you with: the PL/SQL cursor cache (which is the PL/SQL equivalent of the JDBC statement cache) and session cached cursors.

Chapter 14: Connection Pooling and Caching

In this chapter, you'll learn about connection pooling and caching, and how they can improve the performance of your application. You'll look at the 9*i* and 10*g* implementations separately. Finally, you'll examine Oracle's OCI driver connection pooling feature.

Chapter 15: Security-Related Issues

This chapter examines some of the security issues involved in a three-tier architecture that uses connection pooling. In particular, it delves into various alternatives of mapping an application end user to a database end user, and different ways in which an application can authenticate to the database on behalf of an end user. You'll also learn about the proxy authentication feature.

Chapter 16: Locking-Related Issues

In this chapter, you'll look at some of the issues related to locking in Oracle. In particular, you'll learn about the infamous *lost update* problem and various ways to address it. Along the way, you'll examine different strategies to implement two solutions to the lost update problem, namely optimistic locking and pessimistic locking. You'll also compare these two solutions and determine when to use each strategy.

Chapter 17: Selected PL/SQL Techniques

In the final chapter, you'll learn why it is critical for a JDBC programmer working with Oracle databases to learn and master PL/SQL. You'll also examine a few selected PL/SQL techniques that will help you in writing high-performance and maintainable PL/SQL code.

Appendix

The Appendix includes two reference tables that list mappings between SQL object types and Java types.

Recommended Reading Order

The book is best read in sequential order. If you do want some flexibility in the order in which you read the book, then please follow these guidelines.

To begin with, I recommend you read Chapters 1 through 7 in sequential order. The remainder of the book is divided into two (more or less) self-contained parts. The first part consists of Chapters 8 through 11, which describe Oracle objects and how to use them in JDBC. You should read these chapters in sequential order. The second part consists of Chapters 12 through 17, which are fairly self-contained and can be read in any order, except for the fact that you may want to read Chapter 13 before Chapter 14.

Contacting the Author

I welcome any comments or questions you may have about the book. You may contact me at rmenon.us@gmail.com.

About the OakTable Network

In and by itself, the OakTable network is just a bunch of people who would like to talk to and be in contact with like-minded people—that is, people with a scientific approach (and inquiring mind) regarding Oracle's database technology.

It all started sometime in 1998 when a group of Oracle experts, including Anjo Kolk, Cary Millsap, James Morle, and a few others, started meeting once or twice a year, on various pretexts. Each would bring a bottle of Scotch or Bourbon and in return earn the right to sleep on the floor somewhere in my house.

We spent most of our time sitting around my dining table, with computers, cabling, paper, and other stuff all over the place, discussing Oracle, relaying anecdotes, and experimenting with new and better ways of working with the database. By the spring of 2002, the whole thing had grown. One evening, I realized that I had 16 world-renowned Oracle scientists sitting around my dining table. We were sleeping three or four to a room and even had to borrow the neighbor's shower in the mornings. Anjo Kolk suggested we call ourselves the "OakTable network" (after my dining table), and about 2 minutes later, http://www.OakTable.net was registered.

James Morle now maintains the website along with his wife Elaine, and although it doesn't get updated with new content perhaps as often as it should, it is useful at least for providing the links, names, and such. We also use it for the Challenge questions and answers.

The Challenge is something we occasionally run during conferences. Ask us anything (technical) about Oracle, and if we can't find the answer (whether it be yes, no, or a solution) within 24 hours, the person who asked the question gets a T-shirt stating that he or she beat the OakTable.

The Challenge, though, is not used as much as we'd like, probably because it looks as if we want to be challenged with questions to which we cannot find answers. The opposite is actually true—the purpose is to answer questions from anybody, regardless how "simple" or "easy" they might seem.

The Members

I recently read the book *Operation Certain Death*, about an operation in Sierre Leone by the British Special Forces. I want to make perfectly clear that in no way can the physical abilities of the OakTable members be compared to those of the Special Forces. In fact, not at all.

But somewhere in the book the author makes the observation that the Special Forces soldiers are all totally convinced of the maxim that anything can be done with two elastic bands and a piece of rope, if you think long and hard enough about it. In other words, never, ever give up.

That struck me as something I also have observed with the OakTable members: they all believe that there's always one more option, always one more way of looking at things. It might take a chat with another member, maybe even a Chinese parliament, but the idea of giving up on a problem really is not acceptable, unless you're ordered to.

So imagine bringing a bunch of people with that attitude (and a tremendous respect for each other) together for even just a few days. It's never boring, and you very rarely see them waiting on an idle wait event, as we put it.

Imagine standing on the cold, gray cement in the exhibition hall at Oracle World in Copenhagen, realizing that we hadn't paid for carpeting or anything, just 6×6 meters of cement floor. Well, it turned out the Intel guys had some spare super-quality AstroTurf carpet, but needed beer. It was Gary Goodman who brokered that deal within half an hour.

Then Johannes Djernes saw the BMC guys bringing all their advanced exhibition stuff in, placed in two crates that each measured $2.5 \times 1 \times 1$ meters. Two cases of beers later we had borrowed the empty crates. Then Johannes went out and bought various bits and pieces, and within a few hours we had the tallest tower (5 meters high) in the whole exhibition area. It was possibly also the ugliest, but people noticed it.

During the same event, James Morle fought like a lion to establish the World's Biggest Laptop RAC Cluster, using a NetApp filer, a Linux boot CD, and the laptops of anybody who happened to pass by. It was a huge success, but without the *Never Give Up* attitude of James and of others like Michael Möller and Morten Egan, it would never have happened.

A committee, consisting of James Morle, Cary Millsap, Anjo Kolk, Steve Adams, Jonathan Lewis, and myself, review suggestions for new OakTable members. At the time of this writing, the number of members is approaching 50, and I have no doubt we will continue to add members with the inquiring, scientific, never-give-up attitude that is the hallmark of this extraordinary group of humans.

The Politics

How often have you heard the phrase "Oracle says that . . ." or "Oracle Support promised . . ."? Well, most of the time it isn't Oracle as a corporation that "says" something, but an individual who has an opinion or an idea. I know, because I spent 10 years working for Oracle Support, and it is indeed a strange feeling to hear one's own words later repeated as the words of Oracle Corporation (or at least Oracle Denmark).

It is the same with the OakTable. We don't act as a single body, but as individuals. Some (technical) views might be shared, but that's just lucky coincidence. There are no guidelines regarding the individual member's conduct or attitudes, except that ideas should be shared and guessing should be eliminated by constantly testing and pushing boundaries.

Sharing ideas openly between peers and striving for scientific methods is what the OakTable network is all about. On those aims there can and will be no compromise.

The Books

One day in Kenilworth, UK, during an Oracle SIG meeting, James Morle came up with the idea of the BAARF Party (Battle Against Any RAID Five/Four/and err . . . Free) while having a Larsen cognac. That same evening we had dinner with Tony Davis from Apress, and that's when James came up with this idea of a press label called **OakTable Press**. Tony thought that was a splendid idea, and a few days later it was a reality.

The idea was to let OakTable members either write books or at least review books before they were published under this label. At least two OakTable members must review and OK a book before it can be published.

Along with the book you have in your hands now, the current catalog consists of the following:

- *Mastering Oracle PL/SQL: Practical Solutions*: Connor McDonald et al. show you how to write PL/SQL code that will run quickly and won't break in high load, multiuser environments.

- *Oracle Insights: Tales of the Oak Table*: A bunch of OakTable members (including me) present a series of stories about our experiences (good and bad) using the Oracle software: where it's been, where it's going, how (and how not) to use it successfully, and some frightening tales of what can happen when fundamental design principles are ignored.

- *PeopleSoft for the Oracle DBA*: David Kurtz provides a "survival guide" for any Oracle DBA charged with maintaining a PeopleSoft application. The book shows you how to effectively implement common Oracle database administration techniques using the PeopleSoft toolset, how to analyze application activity, and how to obtain the critical data that will allow you to track down the causes of poor performance.

- *Mastering Oracle SQL and SQL*Plus*: Lex de Haan covers the SQL fundamentals in complete and accurate detail with a wealth of nontrivial examples that clearly illustrate how to use the SQL language in an effective manner. Lex has knowledge you can trust: he has 14 years of experience with the Oracle database and 25 years of teaching experience, and he is a member of the ANSI/ISO SQL standardization national body.

We hope that every book published by OakTable Press will be imbued by the qualities that we admire: they will be scientific, rigorous, accurate, innovative, and fun to read. Ultimately, we hope that each book is as useful a tool as it can possibly be in helping make your life easier.

—Best,
Mogens Nørgaard
Managing Director of Miracle A/S
(http://www.miracleas.dk)
and cofounder of the OakTable network

CHAPTER 1

■■■

Performance Toolkit

In this chapter, you'll learn how to set up an environment so that you can test the example code in this book. You'll also learn about some common utilities for benchmarking performance used throughout this book. The chapter covers the following topics:

- Setting up your SQL*Plus environment

- Setting up the SCOTT/TIGER demonstration schema

- Setting up the BENCHMARK/BENCHMARK schema, which we'll use throughout the book for executing some of our code examples

- Setting up sql_trace, timed_statistics, and tkprof, two parameters and a command-line tool that will tell you what SQL your application executed and how that SQL performed

- Setting up and using various performance tools, including the runstats utility and its Java counterpart, JRunstats

- Using the JBenchmark class to time Java programs in general

Note that I provide only basic setup instructions here for the various performance tools, so that you may quickly configure your environment to run the examples in this book. For full instructions and information on how to interpret the data that these tools provide, refer to the Oracle documentation set or a relevant book, such as Thomas Kyte's *Expert One-on-One Oracle* (Apress, ISBN: 1-59059-243-3). The Java utility JRunstats invokes stored procedures from the Java program using the JDBC API—you will learn about stored procedures in detail in the Chapter 6.

Setting Up the SQL*Plus Environment

Some of the examples in this book are designed to run in the SQL*Plus environment. SQL*Plus provides many handy options and commands that we'll use frequently throughout this book. For example, some of the examples in this book use dbms_output. For dbms_output to work, the following SQL*Plus command must be issued:

```
SQL> set serveroutput on
```

Alternatively, SQL*Plus allows you to set up a `login.sql` file, a script that is executed each and every time you start a SQL*Plus session. In this file, you can set parameters such as serveroutput automatically. An example of a `login.sql` script (taken from Chapter 2, "Your Performance Toolkit," of Tom Kyte's *Effective Oracle by Design* [Osborne McGraw-Hill, ISBN: 0-07-223065-7]) with self-explanatory comments is as follows (you can edit it to suit your own particular environment):

```
REM turn off the terminal output - make it so SQLPlus does not
REM print out anything when we log in
set termout off
set head off

REM default your editor here.  SQLPlus has many individual settings
REM This is one of the most important ones
REM define _editor=vi

REM serveroutput controls whether your DBMS_OUTPUT.PUT_LINE calls
REM go into the bit bucket (serveroutput off) or get displayed
REM on screen.  I always want serveroutput set on and as big
REM as possible - this does that.  The format wrapped elements
REM causes SQLPlus to preserve leading whitespace - very useful
set serveroutput on size 1000000

REM Here I set some default column widths for commonly queried
REM columns - columns I find myself setting frequently, day after day
column object_name format a30
column segment_name format a30
column file_name format a40
column name format a30
column file_name format a30
column what format a30 word_wrapped
column plan_plus_exp format a100

REM by default, a spool file is a fixed width file with lots of
REM trailing blanks.  Trimspool removes these trailing blanks
REM making the spool file significantly smaller
set trimspool on

REM LONG controls how much of a LONG or CLOB sqlplus displays
REM by default.  It defaults to 80 characters which in general
REM is far too small.  I use the first 5000 characters by default
set long 5000

REM This sets the default width at which sqlplus wraps output.
REM I use a telnet client that can go up to 131 characters wide -
REM hence this is my preferred setting.
set linesize 131

REM SQLplus will print column headings every N lines of output
```

```
REM this defaults to 14 lines.  I find that they just clutter my
REM screen so this setting effectively disables them for all
REM intents and purposes - except for the first page of course
set pagesize 9999

REM here is how I set my signature prompt in sqlplus to
REM username@database>   I use the NEW_VALUE concept to format
REM a nice prompt string that defaults to IDLE (useful for those
REM of you that use sqlplus to startup their databases - the
REM prompt will default to idle> if your database isn't started)
define gname=idle
column global_name new_value gname
select lower(user) || '@' ||
       substr( global_name, 1, decode( dot,
                                        0, length(global_name),
                                        dot-1) ) global_name
  from (select global_name, instr(global_name,'.') dot
          from global_name );
set sqlprompt '&gname> '

REM and lastly, we'll put termout back on so sqlplus prints
REM to the screen
set termout on
```

Furthermore, you can use this script to format the SQL*Plus prompt so you always know who you're logged in as and on which database. For example, as you work through this book, you'll encounter prompts of the following format:

```
scott@ORA10G>
```

This tells you that you're logged into the SCOTT schema on the ORA10G database. The following is the code in the login.sql script that achieves this:

```
REM here is how I set my signature prompt in sqlplus to
REM username@database>   I use the NEW_VALUE concept to format
REM a nice prompt string that defaults to IDLE (useful for those
REM of you who use sqlplus to start up your databases - the
REM prompt will default to idle> if your database isn't started)
define gname=idle
column global_name new_value gname
select lower(user) || '@' ||
       substr( global_name, 1, decode( dot,
                                        0, length(global_name),
                                        dot-1) ) global_name
  from (select global_name, instr(global_name,'.') dot
          from global_name );
set sqlprompt '&gname> '

REM and lastly, we'll put termout back on so sqlplus prints
REM to the screen
set termout on
```

When you use SQL*Plus 9*i* and before, this login script will be run only once, at startup. So, if you log in at startup as SCOTT and then change to a different account, this won't register on your prompt (this isn't an issue if you're using a 10*g* database):

```
ora92  33> sqlplus scott/tiger

SQL*Plus: Release 9.2.0.1.0 - Production on Wed Dec 8 20:38:31 2004

Copyright (c) 1982, 2002, Oracle Corporation.  All rights reserved.


Connected to:
Oracle9i Enterprise Edition Release 9.2.0.1.0 - Production
With the Partitioning, OLAP and Oracle Data Mining options
JServer Release 9.2.0.1.0 - Production
```

Note in the following code that the prompt still shows SCOTT even though you are connected as the user BENCHMARK:

```
scott@ORA92I> conn benchmark/benchmark
Connected.
scott@ORA92I>
```

The following connect.sql script will solve this:

```
set termout off
connect &1
@login
set termout on
```

Then you simply run this script (which connects and then runs the login script) every time you want to change accounts:

```
scott@ ORA92I> @connect benchmark/benchmark
benchmark@ORA92I>
```

To get SQL*Plus to run the login script automatically on startup, you need to save it in a directory (put connect.sql in the same directory) and then set the SQLPATH environment variable to point at that directory. On UNIX, the command to set the environment variable is different, depending on the shell you use. For example, in tcsh shell, you would use

```
setenv SQLPATH /home/rmenon/mysqlscripts
```

In Windows, there are many ways to run the login script automatically on startup, but the easiest is to set it in the Environment Variables section of the System Properties. In Windows XP, follow this procedure:

1. Right-click the My Computers icon and select Properties.

2. Select the Advanced tab and then click the Environment Variables button. Create a new variable as required (or edit it if it already exists).

In Windows you can also use the set command and put the script in your autoexec.bat file:

```
set SQLPATH=C:\MYSQLSCRIPTS
```

Setting Up autotrace in SQL*Plus

Throughout the book, it will be useful for us to monitor the performance of the queries we execute. SQL*Plus provides an autotrace facility that allows us to see the execution plans of the queries we've executed and the resources they used. The report is generated after the successful execution of a SQL Data Manipulation Language (DML) statement. There is more than one way to configure the autotrace facility; the following is a recommended method.

1. Execute cd $ORACLE_HOME/rdbms/admin.

2. Log into SQL*Plus as any user with create table and create public synonym privileges.

3. Run @utlxplan to create a plan_table for use by autotrace.

4. Run create public synonym plan_table for plan_table, so that everyone can access this table without specifying a schema.

5. Run grant all on plan_table to public, so that everyone can use this table.

6. Exit SQL*Plus and change directories as follows: cd $ORACLE_HOME/sqlplus/admin.

7. Log into SQL*Plus as SYSDBA.

8. Run @plustrce.

9. Run grant plustrace to public.

You can test your setup by enabling autotrace and executing a simple query:

```
SQL> set AUTOTRACE traceonly
SQL> select * from emp, dept
  2   where emp.deptno=dept.deptno;

14 rows selected.

Execution Plan
----------------------------------------------------------
   0      SELECT STATEMENT Optimizer=CHOOSE
   1    0   MERGE JOIN
   2    1     SORT (JOIN)
   3    2       TABLE ACCESS (FULL) OF 'DEPT'
   4    1     SORT (JOIN)
   5    4       TABLE ACCESS (FULL) OF 'EMP'

Statistics
----------------------------------------------------------
        0  recursive calls
        8  db block gets
```

```
       2  consistent gets
       0  physical reads
       0  redo size
    2144  bytes sent via SQL*Net to client
     425  bytes received via SQL*Net from client
       2  SQL*Net roundtrips to/from client
       2  sorts (memory)
       0  sorts (disk)
      14  rows processed
```

```
SQL> set AUTOTRACE off
```

For full details on the use of autotrace and interpretation of the data it provides, see the chapter titled "Using Application Tracing Tools" of *Oracle Database Performance Tuning Guide and Reference (10g Release 1)* in the Oracle documentation set or the chapter titled "Tuning SQL*Plus" of *SQL*Plus User's Guide and Reference (10g Release 1)*.

Effect of Setting echo on in SQL*Plus

Prior to running the SQL*Plus code examples in this book, the script issues the set echo on command:

```
SQL> set echo on
```

The effect of this on SQL*Plus output can be explained by the following simple example. Suppose we are running a script, demo_echo_option.sql, the contents of which are as follows:

```
set echo on
drop table t1;
create table t1
(
  x number,
  y varchar2(30),
  z date
);
```

The output of the preceding script when executed as the user SCOTT looks like this:

```
scott@ORA10G> set echo on
scott@ORA10G> drop table t1;

Table dropped.

scott@ORA10G> create table t1
  2  (
  3    x number,
  4    y varchar2(30),
  5    z date
  6  );

Table created.
```

Note in particular the SQL prompt (due to the `login.sql` script) and the fact that the line numbers are shown. You need to be familiar with the preceding form of output, as all SQL*Plus examples in this book use it.

Setting Up the SCOTT/TIGER Schema

Many of the examples in this book draw on the `emp/dept` tables in the SCOTT schema. I recommend that you install your own copy of these tables in some account other than SCOTT to avoid side effects caused by other users using and modifying the same data. In Oracle9*i* and earlier, follow these steps to create the SCOTT demonstration tables in your own schema:

1. From the command line, run `cd [ORACLE_HOME]/sqlplus/demo`.

2. Log into SQL*Plus as the required user.

3. Run `@demobld.sql`.

The `demobld.sql` script will create and populate five tables for you. When the script is complete, it exits SQL*Plus automatically, so don't be surprised when SQL*Plus disappears after running the script. If you would like to drop this schema at any time to clean up, simply execute `[ORACLE_HOME]/sqlplus/demo/demodrop.sql`.

In 10*g*, you install the SCOTT schema by executing `[ORACLE_HOME]/rdbms/admin/utlsampl.sql`.

Setting Up the BENCHMARK/BENCHMARK Schema

Some of the code examples in this book have a user called BENCHMARK with the password BENCHMARK. You can install this user by executing the script `cr_benchmark_user.sql` in the directory `code\mysqlscripts`. You can find this script in the code download area for this book at `http://www.apress.com`. The content of the script follows. As you can see, the script also contains various grants and privileges used when I discuss concepts in different chapters, and also required by some utilities that we execute as the user BENCHMARK:

```
create user benchmark identified by benchmark default tablespace users quota
unlimited on users;

grant create any directory,
      create session,
      create table,
      create view,
      create synonym,
      create materialized view,
      create procedure,
      create trigger,
      create sequence,
      create type to benchmark;

grant select on v_$session_cursor_cache  to benchmark;
```

```
grant select on v_$sesstat to benchmark;
grant select on v_$open_cursor  to benchmark;
grant select on v_$sql  to benchmark;
grant select on  v_$sqlarea to benchmark;
grant create any context to benchmark;
grant drop any context to benchmark;
grant select on sys.col$ to benchmark; -- query data dict
grant select on sys.dba_segments to benchmark; -- for block dump
grant select on v_$process to benchmark
```

Performance Tools

We'll also make use of other performance tools throughout the book. This section presents brief setup instructions for these tools.

timed_statistics

The timed_statistics parameter specifies whether Oracle should measure the execution time for various internal operations. Without this parameter set, there is much less value to the trace file output. As with other parameters, you can set timed_statistics either on an instance level (in init.ora) or on a session level. The former shouldn't affect performance, so it's generally recommended. Simply add the following line to your init.ora file, and the next time you restart the database, timed_statistics will be enabled:

```
timed_statistics=true
```

On a session level, you would issue this

```
SQL> alter session set timed_statistics=true;
```

Use the preceding method to set this parameter from your JDBC programs when required.

sql_trace and tkprof

Together, the sql_trace facility and the tkprof command-line utility enable detailed tracing of the activity that takes place within the database. In short, sql_trace is used to write performance information on individual SQL statements down to trace files in the file system of the database server. Under normal circumstances, these trace files are hard to comprehend directly. For that purpose, you use the tkprof utility to generate text-based report files from the input of a given trace file.

sql_trace

The sql_trace facility is used to trace all SQL activity of a specified database session or instance down to a trace file in the database server operating system. Each entry in the trace file records a specific operation performed while the Oracle server process is processing a SQL statement. sql_trace was originally intended for debugging, and it's still well suited for that purpose, but it can just as easily be used to analyze the SQL activity of the database for tuning purposes.

Setting Up sql_trace

sql_trace can be enabled for either a single session or a whole database instance. It is, however, rarely enabled at a database level, because that would cause serious performance problems. Remember that sql_trace writes down every SQL statement processed down to a log file, with accompanying input/output (I/O) activity.

To enable tracing for the current session, issue alter session, as shown here:

```
SQL> alter session set sql_trace=true;
```

Enable tracing for a session at a selected interval and avoid having tracing in effect for long periods of time. To disable the current trace operation, execute the following:

```
SQL> alter session set sql_trace=false;
```

In this book, I use the following command to set SQL tracing; this gives the maximum level of tracing output. You can read more about it in Cary Millsap's article at http://www.oracle.com/technology/oramag/oracle/04-jan/o14tech_perf.html.

```
SQL> alter session set events '10046 trace name context forever, level 12';
```

Controlling the Trace Files

The trace files generated by sql_trace can eventually grow quite large. A few global initialization parameters, set in init.ora for the database instance or session settings, affect the trace files. If enabled, sql_trace will write to a file in the operating system directory indicated by the user_dump_dest initialization parameter. You should note that trace files for user processes (dedicated servers) go to the user_dump_dest directory. Trace files generated by Oracle background processes, such as the shared servers used with a multithreaded server (MTS) and job queue processes used with the job queues, will go to background_dump_dest. Use of sql_trace with a shared server configuration isn't recommended—it will result in your session hopping from shared server to shared server, generating trace information in not one, but many trace files, rendering it useless.

Trace files are usually named ora<spid>.trc, where <spid> is the server process ID of the session for which the trace was enabled. On Windows, you may use the following query to retrieve your session's trace file name (you may have to tweak the query since Oracle changes the naming scheme sometimes; also the parameter tracefile_identifier affects a trace file name, as you will see shortly):

```
SQL> select c.value || '\ORA' || to_char(a.spid,'fm00000') || '.trc'
  2    from v$process a, v$session b, v$parameter c
  3   where a.addr = b.paddr
  4     and b.audsid = userenv('sessionid')
  5     and c.name = 'user_dump_dest';
```

On UNIX, this query can be used to retrieve the session's trace file name:

```
SQL> select c.value || '/' || d.instance_name || '_ora_' ||
  2                to_char(a.spid,'fm99999') || '.trc'
```

```
3    from v$process a, v$session b, v$parameter c, v$instance d
4   where a.addr = b.paddr
5     and b.audsid = userenv('sessionid')
6     and c.name = 'user_dump_dest';
```

You can also set an identifier that would be part of the trace file name by issuing the following command:

```
SQL> alter session set tracefile_identifier='my_trace_file';

Session altered.
```

The size of the trace files is restricted by the value of the max_dump_file_size initialization parameter set in init.ora for the database instance. You may also alter this at the session level using the alter session command, for example:

```
SQL> alter session set max_dump_file_size = unlimited;
Session altered.
```

tkprof

The tkprof utility takes a sql_trace trace file as input and produces a text-based report file as output. It's a simple utility that summarizes a large set of detailed information in a given trace file so that it can be understood for performance tuning. This section explains briefly how to use this very useful utility.

In its simplest form, tkprof can be invoked as shown here:

```
tkprof <trace-file-name> <report-file-name>
```

To illustrate the joint use of tkprof and sql_trace, we'll set up a simple example. Specifically, we'll trace the query used previously in the autotrace example and generate a report from the resulting trace file. First, we log into SQL*Plus as the intended user, and then execute the following code:

```
SQL> select c.value || '\ORA' || to_char(a.spid,'fm00000') || '.trc'
2      from v$process a, v$session b, v$parameter c
3     where a.addr = b.paddr
4       and b.audsid = userenv('sessionid')
5       and c.name = 'user_dump_dest';

C.VALUE||'\ORA'||TO_CHAR(A.SPID,'FM00000')||'.TRC'
--------------------------------------------------------------------------------
---------------------------------------------------
C:\oracle\admin\oratest\udump\ORA01528.trc

SQL> alter session set timed_statistics=true;

Session altered.
```

```
SQL> alter session set sql_trace=true;

Session altered.

SQL> select * from emp, dept
  2   where emp.deptno=dept.deptno;

SQL> alter session set sql_trace=false;

SQL> exit
```

Now we simply format our trace file from the command line using tkprof, as follows:

```
C:\oracle\admin\oratest\udump>tkprof ORA01528.TRC tkprof_rep1.txt
```

We can open the tkprof_rep1.txt file and view the report. I don't intend to discuss the output in detail here, but briefly, at the top of the report we should see the actual SQL statement issued. Next, we get the execution report for the statement.

call	count	cpu	elapsed	disk	query	current	rows
Parse	1	0.01	0.02	0	0	0	0
Execute	1	0.00	0.00	0	0	0	0
Fetch	2	0.00	0.00	0	2	8	14
total	4	0.01	0.02	0	2	8	14

This report illustrates the three different phases of Oracle SQL processing: parse, execute, and fetch. For each processing phase, we see the following:

- The number of times that phase occurred

- The CPU time elapsed for the phase

- The real-world time that elapsed

- The number of physical I/O operations that took place on the disk

- The number of blocks processed in "consistent-read" mode

- The number of blocks read in "current" mode (reads that occur when the data is changed by an external process during the execution of the statement)

- The number of blocks that were affected by the statement

■**Note** If you are not familiar with physical I/O, and "consistent-read" and "current" mode of blocks, see the section "Logical I/O and Physical I/O" in Chapter 2 for more details.

Following the execution report, we can see the optimizer approach used and the user ID of the session that enabled the trace (we can match this ID against the all_users table to get the actual username):

```
Misses in library cache during parse: 0
Optimizer goal: CHOOSE
Parsing user id: 52
```

Additionally, we see the number of times the statement wasn't found in the library cache. The first time a statement is executed, this count should be 1, but it should be 0 in subsequent calls if bind variables are used. Again, watch for the absence of bind variables—a large number of library cache misses would indicate that.

Finally, the report displays the execution plan used for this statement. This information is similar to that provided by autotrace, with the important difference that the number of actual rows flowing out of each step in the plan is revealed:

```
Rows    Row Source Operation
-------  ---------------------------------------------------
    14  MERGE JOIN
     5   SORT JOIN
     4    TABLE ACCESS FULL DEPT
    14   SORT JOIN
    14    TABLE ACCESS FULL EMP
```

For full details on the use of sql_trace and tkprof, and interpretation of the trace data, see Chapter 10 of *Oracle9i Database Performance Tuning Guide and Reference*. Another excellent reference is Chapter 10, "Tuning Strategies and Tools," in Tom Kyte's *Expert One-on-One Oracle* (Apress, ISBN: 1-59059-243-3). The most comprehensive (and an eminently readable) book on tracing in general is Cary Millsap's *Optimizing Oracle Performance* (O'Reilly, ISBN: 0-596-00527-X).

runstats

runstats is a simple test harness that allows comparison of two executions of code and displays the costs of each in terms of the elapsed time, session-level statistics (such as parse calls), and latching differences. The latter of these, latching, is the key piece of information that this tool provides.

■**Note** The runstats tool was originally built by Tom Kyte, the man behind the http://asktom.oracle.com website. You can find full information and an example usage of runstats at http://asktom.oracle.com/~tkyte/runstats.html.

■**Note** *Latches* are lightweight serialization resources Oracle uses when accessing shared memory structures. See the section titled "Locks and Latches" in Chapter 2 of this book for more details. You can also read more about latches in *Oracle Database Concepts Guide (10g Release 1).*

To run this test harness, you must have access to V$STATNAME, V$MYSTAT, and V$LATCH. You must be granted *direct* select privileges (not via a role) on SYS.V_$STATNAME, SYS.V_$MYSTAT, and SYS.V_$LATCH. You can then create the following view:

```
SQL> create or replace view stats
  2  as select 'STAT...' || a.name name, b.value
  3         from v$statname a, v$mystat b
  4        where a.statistic# = b.statistic#
  5       union all
  6       select 'LATCH.' || name,  gets
  7          from v$latch;

View created.
```

All you need then is a small table to store the statistics:

```
create global temporary table run_stats
( runid varchar2(15),
  name varchar2(80),
  value int )
on commit preserve rows;
```

The code for the test harness package is as follows:

```
create or replace package runstats_pkg
as
    procedure rs_start;
    procedure rs_middle;
    procedure rs_stop( p_difference_threshold in number default 0 );
end;
/

create or replace package body runstats_pkg
as

g_start number;
g_run1  number;
g_run2  number;

procedure rs_start
is
begin
    delete from run_stats;
```

```
    insert into run_stats
    select 'before', stats.* from stats;

    g_start := dbms_utility.get_time;
end;

procedure rs_middle
is
begin
    g_run1 := (dbms_utility.get_time-g_start);

    insert into run_stats
    select 'after 1', stats.* from stats;
    g_start := dbms_utility.get_time;

end;

procedure rs_stop(p_difference_threshold in number default 0)
is
begin
    g_run2 := (dbms_utility.get_time-g_start);

    dbms_output.put_line
    ( 'Run1 ran in ' || g_run1 || ' hsecs' );
    dbms_output.put_line
    ( 'Run2 ran in ' || g_run2 || ' hsecs' );
    dbms_output.put_line
    ( 'run 1 ran in ' || round(g_run1/g_run2*100,2) ||
      '% of the time' );
    dbms_output.put_line( chr(9) );

    insert into run_stats
    select 'after 2', stats.* from stats;

    dbms_output.put_line
    ( rpad( 'Name', 30 ) || lpad( 'Run1', 10 ) ||
      lpad( 'Run2', 10 ) || lpad( 'Diff', 10 ) );

    for x in
    ( select rpad( a.name, 30 ) ||
             to_char( b.value-a.value, '9,999,999' ) ||
             to_char( c.value-b.value, '9,999,999' ) ||
             to_char( ( (c.value-b.value)-(b.value-a.value)), '9,999,999' ) data
        from run_stats a, run_stats b, run_stats c
       where a.name = b.name
         and b.name = c.name
         and a.runid = 'before'
```

```
            and b.runid = 'after 1'
            and c.runid = 'after 2'
            and (c.value-a.value) > 0
            and abs( (c.value-b.value) - (b.value-a.value) )
                  > p_difference_threshold
       order by abs( (c.value-b.value)-(b.value-a.value))
    ) loop
        dbms_output.put_line( x.data );
    end loop;

    dbms_output.put_line( chr(9) );
    dbms_output.put_line
    ( 'Run1 latches total versus runs -- difference and pct' );
    dbms_output.put_line
    ( lpad( 'Run1', 10 ) || lpad( 'Run2', 10 ) ||
      lpad( 'Diff', 10 ) || lpad( 'Pct', 8 ) );

    for x in
    ( select to_char( run1, '9,999,999' ) ||
             to_char( run2, '9,999,999' ) ||
             to_char( diff, '9,999,999' ) ||
             to_char( round( run1/run2*100,2 ), '999.99' ) || '%' data
        from ( select sum(b.value-a.value) run1, sum(c.value-b.value) run2,
                      sum( (c.value-b.value)-(b.value-a.value)) diff
                 from run_stats a, run_stats b, run_stats c
                where a.name = b.name
                  and b.name = c.name
                  and a.runid = 'before'
                  and b.runid = 'after 1'
                  and c.runid = 'after 2'
                  and a.name like 'LATCH%'
             )
    ) loop
        dbms_output.put_line( x.data );
    end loop;
end;

end;
/
```

Using runstats

To demonstrate the information we can get out of runstats, we'll compare the performance of a query in the following two cases:

- *Using the cost-based optimizer (CBO)*: The CBO is the engine that generates an execution plan for SQL statements in Oracle based on statistics gathered on our schema objects. It is the only optimizer that is supported starting with 10*g*.

- *Using the rule-based optimizer (RBO)*: The RBO is no longer supported, starting with 10*g*. It is an alternative optimizer that generates plans based on a set of rules (and hence is not very intelligent). We can still use hints to force the use of the RBO in our SQL statements. Of course, this should not be done in production code.

Note If you aren't familiar with the CBO, it's a good idea to read up on it in the section "Overview of the Optimizer" in the chapter "SQL, PL/SQL, and Java" in *Oracle Database Concepts Guide (10*g *Release 1)*.

Let's now create the tables on which we'll run the query. First we create a table, t, with just one number column, x:

```
benchmark@ORA10G> create table t ( x number );
```

```
Table created.
```

Then we insert 10,000 0s and 10,000 1s into table t. For this, we use the mod function on the rownum pseudo column in a query from a Cartesian product of the views all_objects and all_users:

```
benchmark@ORA10G> insert into t select mod(rownum, 2 )
  from all_objects, all_users where rownum <= 20000;
```

```
20000 rows created.
```

```
benchmark@ORA10G> select count(*) from t where x = 0;
```

```
    10000
```

```
benchmark@ORA10G> select count(*) from t where x = 1;
```

```
    10000
benchmark@ORA10G> commit;
```

```
Commit complete.
```

Next, we create an index on column x:

```
benchmark@ORA10G> create index t_idx on t(x);
```

```
Index created.
```

We then create an identical table, t1, with identical data in it. We also create an index, t1_idx, on t1:

```
benchmark@ORA10G> create table t1 ( x number );
```

```
Table created.
```

```
benchmark@ORA10G> insert into t1 select mod(rownum, 2 )
  from all_objects, all_users where rownum <= 20000;

20000 rows created.

benchmark@ORA10G> select count(*) from t1 where x = 0;

    10000

benchmark@ORA10G> select count(*) from t1 where x = 1;

    10000

benchmark@ORA10G> commit;

Commit complete.

benchmark@ORA10G> create index t1_idx on t1(x);

Index created.
```

The CBO works on statistics gathered on a table's data. We collect statistics on both tables and indexes next:

```
benchmark@ORA10G> begin
  2    dbms_stats.gather_table_stats(
  3      ownname => 'BENCHMARK',
  4      tabname => 'T',
  5      cascade => true );
  6    dbms_stats.gather_table_stats(
  7      ownname => 'BENCHMARK',
  8      tabname => 'T1',
  9      cascade => true );
 10  end;
 11  /
PL/SQL procedure successfully completed.
```

We'll compare the following two queries now (we execute them along the way so that Oracle's cache gets warmed up):

```
benchmark@ORA10G> select count(*)
  2  from t1, t
  3  where t1.x = t.x
  4  and t1.x = 0;

  100000000
```

```
benchmark@ORA10G> select /*+ RULE */count(*)
  2   from t1, t
  3   where t1.x = t.x
  4   and t1.x = 0;

100000000
```

Note that the queries are the same except that in the second query, we give the RULE hint to force Oracle to use the RBO to generate its execution plan.

Let's now use the RUNSTATS package to compare these two queries. The first step when using RUNSTATS is to mark the beginning of the comparison by invoking the rs_start procedure. This procedure takes a snapshot of all database statistics that we want to compare in our two approaches:

```
benchmark@ORA10G> exec runstats_pkg.rs_start;

PL/SQL procedure successfully completed.
```

We execute our first query:

```
benchmark@ORA10G> select count(*)
  2   from t1, t
  3   where t1.x = t.x
  4   and t1.x = 0;

100000000
```

We now mark the middle of our benchmark to take another snapshot of the database statistics:

```
benchmark@ORA10G> exec runstats_pkg.rs_middle;

PL/SQL procedure successfully completed.
```

and execute the second query:

```
benchmark@ORA10G> select /*+ RULE */count(*)
  2   from t1, t
  3   where t1.x = t.x
  4   and t1.x = 0;

100000000
```

Finally, we end the benchmarking by invoking the rs_stop method, which also prints out our comparison results:

```
benchmark@ORA10G> exec runstats_pkg.rs_stop;
Run1 ran in 1199 hsecs
Run2 ran in 2687 hsecs
run 1 ran in 44.62% of the time
```

Name	Run1	Run2	Diff
STAT...buffer is not pinned co	0	1	1
LATCH.session switching	1	0	-1
LATCH.ksuosstats global area	1	2	1
STAT...session cursor cache co	0	1	1
LATCH.sort extent pool	1	0	-1
STAT...sorts (memory)	2	1	-1
STAT...parse count (hard)	0	1	1
STAT...active txn count during	5	6	1
STAT...enqueue releases	0	1	1
<- trimmed to conserve space ->			
STAT...table scan rows gotten	40,000	0	-40,000
STAT...no work - consistent re	70	180,019	179,949
STAT...consistent gets from ca	81	190,028	189,947
STAT...consistent gets	81	190,028	189,947
STAT...session logical reads	765	190,71	189,951
LATCH.cache buffers chains	3,663	383,485	379,822

```
Run1 latches total versus runs -- difference and pct
Run1          Run2         Diff        Pct
4,941         396,481      391,540     1.25%.
```

In this book, we'll focus on two numbers that runstats displays:

- *Difference in execution times*: In the example, notice that the first query ran in 12 seconds (1199 hsecs and 1 hsec = 1/100 of a second) and the second query ran in 27 seconds. The first query ran in 44.62% of the time that the second query took.

- *Difference in latches consumed*: Another number to focus on is the difference in latches consumed at the end of the output. For the preceding comparison, the first query consumed only 1.25% of the latches compared to the second query. Latch consumption is a good indicator of the scalability of an approach—the fewer number of latches an approach takes, the more scalable it will be. This implies that in the preceding case, the first query is *much* more scalable than the second one.

Thus, in the previous comparison case, runstats showed that the CBO generated an execution plan that ran the query in less than half the time while consuming a fraction of the resources as compared to the RBO plan.

Overall, I hope that this section has demonstrated how useful runstats can be in benchmarking two approaches. Please note that for runstats results to be accurate, you should run it in a database in isolation. This is because you're measuring latches and other statistics as just shown, and you don't want other database activities to influence your benchmark results.

JDBC Wrapper for runstats

Since this is a book on JDBC, it makes sense to have a JDBC wrapper on the runstats utility so that we can use it in our Java programs. The runstats utility uses the PL/SQL procedure dbms_output to print its final results. To get these results in Java (without modifying runstats in any way), we need a way to get the dbms_output results in the Java layer. The following class, DbmsOutput (written originally by Tom Kyte), does exactly that. I explain the workings of this program in comments interspersed throughout the code. However, since the program uses JDBC concepts that I will cover later in Chapter 6, you may want to revisit this section after having read that chapter. You can also find an explanation of this program in the section "DBMS_OUTPUT" in Appendix A of Tom Kyte's *Expert One-on-One Oracle* (Apress, ISBN: 1-59059-243-3):

```
package book.util;
// originally written by Tom Kyte - I have made some minor modifications
import java.sql.CallableStatement;
import java.sql.SQLException;
import java.sql.Connection;
public class DbmsOutput
{
```

We declare the instance variables as shown in the following code. We use the CallableStatement JDBC class to invoke PL/SQL code in this class. We use three statements in this class. The first statement enables dbms_output, which is equivalent to set serveroutput on in SQL*Plus. The second statement disables dbms_output in a similar way to how we do it in SQL*Plus using set serveroutput off. The last statement displays the results of DBMS_OUTPUT using the System.out method in Java.

```
private CallableStatement enable_stmt;
private CallableStatement disable_stmt;
private CallableStatement show_stmt;
```

The constructor simply prepares the three statements we plan on executing. Preparing a statement is a step that creates a statement with placeholders for us to bind input parameters and register output parameters. The statement we prepare for SHOW is a block of code to return a string of dbms_output output.

```
public DbmsOutput( Connection conn ) throws SQLException
{
  enable_stmt  = conn.prepareCall( "begin dbms_output.enable(:1); end;" );
  disable_stmt = conn.prepareCall( "begin dbms_output.disable; end;" );
  show_stmt = conn.prepareCall(
    "declare " +
    "    l_line varchar2(255); " +
    "    l_done number; " +
    "    l_buffer long; " +
    "begin " +
    "  loop " +
    "    exit when length(l_buffer)+255 > :1 OR l_done = 1; " +
    "    dbms_output.get_line( l_line, l_done ); " +
    "    l_buffer := l_buffer || l_line || chr(10); " +
    "  end loop; " +
    " :2 := l_done; " +
    " :buffer := l_buffer; " +
```

```
    "end;" );
}
```

The method enable() simply sets the dbms_output size and executes the dbms_output.enable call:

```
public void enable( int size ) throws SQLException
{
  enable_stmt.setInt( 1, size );
  enable_stmt.executeUpdate();
}
```

The method disable() executes the dbms_output.disable call:

```
public void disable() throws SQLException
{
  disable_stmt.executeUpdate();
}
```

The method show() does most of the work. It loops over all of the dbms_output data, fetching it in this case 32,000 bytes at a time (give or take 255 bytes). It then prints this output on stdout:

```
public void show() throws SQLException
{
  int done = 0;
  show_stmt.registerOutParameter( 2, java.sql.Types.INTEGER );
  show_stmt.registerOutParameter( 3, java.sql.Types.VARCHAR );
  for(;;)
  {
    show_stmt.setInt( 1, 32000 );
    show_stmt.executeUpdate();
    System.out.print( show_stmt.getString(3) );
    if ( (done = show_stmt.getInt(2)) == 1 ) break;
  }
}
```

The method close() closes the callable statements associated with the DbmsOutput class:

```
public void close() throws SQLException
{
  enable_stmt.close();
  disable_stmt.close();
  show_stmt.close();
}
}
```

Now we're ready to write a Java program that invokes runstats. The class JRunstats shown shortly is a wrapper around runstats. This program does the following:

- Invokes runstats and prints out the resulting comparison results

- Prints out the runtime difference between the two approaches being compared, as seen from the Java client (using the System.currentTimeMillis() method)

Usually, the runtime difference shown as a result of runstats and the one printed separately by JRunstats should be the same, but the two may differ if a PL/SQL optimization is used that is not available in JDBC layer.

Once again the class uses the CallableStatement JDBC class, which is explained in detail in Chapter 6:

```
/* This program is a Java wrapper around the runstats utility written
 * by Tom Kyte and available at http://asktom.oracle.com/~tkyte/runstats.html.
 */
package book.util;
import java.sql.Connection;
import java.sql.CallableStatement;
import java.sql.SQLException;
import java.sql.Statement;
public class JRunstats
{
```

The method markStart() invokes the method rs_start in the runstats utility. We invoke this method before starting the first of the two approaches we're comparing in a given benchmark run:

```
  public static void markStart( Connection connection )
    throws SQLException
  {
    _startTime = System.currentTimeMillis();
    _benchmarkStatementArray[BENCHMARK_START_INDEX].execute();
  }
```

The method markMiddle() invokes the method rs_middle in the runstats utility. We invoke this method before starting the second of the two approaches we're comparing in a given benchmark run:

```
  public static void markMiddle( Connection connection )
    throws SQLException
  {
    _middleTime = System.currentTimeMillis();
    _benchmarkStatementArray[BENCHMARK_MIDDLE_INDEX].execute();
  }
```

The method markEnd() invokes the method rs_stop in the runstats utility. We invoke this method at the end of the benchmark run. The method also takes a threshold that controls the amount of data printed. It results in JRunstats printing only latches and statistics whose absolute difference value between the two benchmarked approaches is greater than this threshold:

```
public static void markEnd( Connection connection,
  int benchmarkDifferenceThreshold )
  throws SQLException
{
  _markEnd( connection, benchmarkDifferenceThreshold );
}
```

The method markEnd() is an overloaded method that invokes the method rs_stop in the runstats utility with a default value for the threshold mentioned earlier:

```
public static void markEnd( Connection connection ) throws SQLException
{
  _markEnd( connection, DEFAULT_BENCHMARK_DIFFERENCE_THRESHOLD );
}
```

The method closeBenchmarkStatements() closes all benchmark-related statements and is invoked before the program ends:

```
public static void closeBenchmarkStatements (
  Connection connection )  throws SQLException
{
  for( int i=0; i < _benchmarkStatementArray.length; i++)
  {
    _benchmarkStatementArray[i].close();
  }
}
```

The method prepareBenchmarkStatements() prepares all benchmark-related statements:

```
public static void prepareBenchmarkStatements (
  Connection connection ) throws SQLException
{
  _benchmarkStatementArray[BENCHMARK_START_INDEX]=
    connection.prepareCall( BENCHMARK_START );

  _benchmarkStatementArray[BENCHMARK_MIDDLE_INDEX]=
    connection.prepareCall( BENCHMARK_MIDDLE );

  _benchmarkStatementArray[BENCHMARK_STOP_INDEX]=
    connection.prepareCall( BENCHMARK_STOP );
  _dbmsOutput = new DbmsOutput ( connection );
  _dbmsOutput.enable ( DBMS_OUTPUT_BUFFER_SIZE );
}
///////////////////////////// PRIVATE SECTION ///////////////
```

The private method _printBenchmarkResults() prints the benchmark results (I follow a coding convention of starting a private method with an underscore character in this book):

```
private static void _printBenchmarkResults() throws SQLException
{
  System.out.println( "------- Benchmark Results --------" );
  System.out.println( "Results from RUNSTATS utility" );
  _dbmsOutput.show();
  _dbmsOutput.close();
  System.out.println( "" );
  System.out.println( "Runtime Execution Time Differences " +
    "as seen by the client" );
  long run1 = _middleTime-_startTime;
  long run2 = _endTime-_middleTime;
  System.out.println( "Run1 ran in " + run1/10 + " hsecs");
  System.out.println( "Run2 ran in " + run2/10 + " hsecs");
  System.out.println( "Run1 ran in " +
    Math.round((run1*100.00)/(run2)) + "% of the time" );

}
```

The method _markEnd is a helper method invoked by the overloaded versions of the public method markEnd():

```
private static void _markEnd( Connection connection,
  int benchmarkDifferenceThreshold )
  throws SQLException
{

  _endTime = System.currentTimeMillis();
  _benchmarkStatementArray[BENCHMARK_STOP_INDEX].setInt(1,
    benchmarkDifferenceThreshold);
  _benchmarkStatementArray[BENCHMARK_STOP_INDEX].execute();
  printBenchmarkResults();
}
```

At the end, we declare all the variables used by the program:

```
private static long _startTime;
private static long _middleTime;
private static long _endTime;
private static String BENCHMARK_START = "begin runstats_pkg.rs_start; end;";
private static String BENCHMARK_MIDDLE = "begin runstats_pkg.rs_middle; end;";
private static String BENCHMARK_STOP = "begin runstats_pkg.rs_stop(?); end;";
private static CallableStatement[] _benchmarkStatementArray =
  new CallableStatement[3];
private static DbmsOutput _dbmsOutput;
private static final int DBMS_OUTPUT_BUFFER_SIZE = 1000000;
private static final int BENCHMARK_START_INDEX = 0;
```

```
  private static final int BENCHMARK_MIDDLE_INDEX = 1;
  private static final int BENCHMARK_STOP_INDEX = 2;
  private static final int DEFAULT_BENCHMARK_DIFFERENCE_THRESHOLD = 0;
}
```

Once again, you should revisit this class to understand the mechanics of it after reading Chapter 6. For now, let's focus on how to invoke this program to compare the same two queries compared in the section "Using runstats." The following program, DemoJRunstats, does just that. It uses the PreparedStatement class to execute the queries (you'll learn about the PreparedStatement classes in Chapter 5). The program begins by importing JDBC classes:

```
/* This program demonstrates how to use the JRunstats utility */
package book.util;
import java.sql.ResultSet;
import java.sql.SQLException;
import java.sql.PreparedStatement;
import java.sql.Connection;
public class DemoJRunstats
{
  public static void main(String[] args) throws Exception
  {
```

Then we define two query statements in string variables:

```
    String queryUsingCBO = "select count(*) " +
                           "from t1, t " +
                           "where t1.x = t.x " +
                           "and t1.x = ?";
    String queryUsingRBO = "select /*+ RULE */ count(*) " +
                           "from t1, t " +
                           "where t1.x = t.x " +
                           "and t1.x = ?";
```

Next, we obtain the JDBC connection as the user BENCHMARK using the utility class JDBCUtil (the logic of how to get a JDBC connection is explained in Chapter 3):

```
    Connection conn = null;
    try
    {
      conn = JDBCUtil.getConnection("benchmark", "benchmark", "ora10g");
```

We prepare all the benchmarking statements in JRunstats:

```
      JRunstats.prepareBenchmarkStatements( conn );
```

Then we mark the beginning of the runstats run (this internally invokes runstats_pkg.rs_start):

```
      JRunstats.markStart( conn );
```

We execute our first query by invoking a private method defined later:

```
_executeQuery( conn, queryUsingCBO );
```

We mark the middle of the benchmark (this internally invokes runstats_pkg.rs_middle()):

```
JRunstats.markMiddle( conn );
```

Now we execute the second query by invoking the private method _executeQuery() again:

```
_executeQuery( conn, queryUsingRBO );
```

We mark the middle of the benchmark (this internally invokes runstats_pkg.rs_stop):

```
      JRunstats.markEnd( conn );
    }
    catch (SQLException e)
    {
      // handle the exception properly - in this case, we just
      // print the stack trace.
      JDBCUtil.printException ( e );
    }
    finally
    {
      // release the JDBC resources in the finally clause.
      JRunstats.closeBenchmarkStatements( conn );
      JDBCUtil.close( conn );
    }
  }
```

The following private method uses PreparedStatement to execute a given query:

```
private static void _executeQuery( Connection conn,
  String query ) throws SQLException
{
  PreparedStatement pstmt = null;
  ResultSet rset = null;
  try
  {
    pstmt = conn.prepareStatement( query );
    pstmt.setInt( 1, 0 );
    rset = pstmt.executeQuery();
    System.out.println( "printing query results ...\n");
    while (rset.next())
    {
      int count = rset.getInt ( 1 );
      System.out.println( "count = " + count );
    }
  }
  finally
  {
```

```
      // release JDBC related resources in the finally clause.
      JDBCUtil.close( rset );
      JDBCUtil.close( pstmt );
    }
  }
}
```

Once again, don't worry if you don't completely understand the mechanics of this program (or that of JRunstats)—at this stage, you aren't expected to. Once you've learned about the PreparedStatement and CallableStatement classes, the workings of this program should be clear to you. Right now, simply focus on how to use this program and how to interpret its results. The output of the preceding program DemoJRunstats is as follows:

```
URL:jdbc:oracle:thin:@(DESCRIPTION=(ADDRESS=(PROTOCOL=tcp)
(PORT=1521)(HOST=rmenon-lap))(CONNECT_DATA=(SID=ora10g)))
printing query results ...

count = 100000000

printing query results ...

count = 100000000

------- Benchmark Results --------

Results from RUNSTATS utility

Run1 ran in 1009 hsecs
Run2 ran in 2524 hsecs
run 1 ran in 39.98% of the time
```

Name	Run1	Run2	Diff
STAT...free buffer requested	11	10	-1
STAT...active txn count during	2	1	-1
<- trimmed to conserve space ->			
STAT...session uga memory max	196,392	0	-196,392
LATCH.cache buffers chains	3,626	383,533	379,907

```
Run1 latches total versus runs -- difference and pct
    Run1     Run2     Diff    Pct
    4,691    396,076  391,38  1.18%

Runtime Execution Time Differences as seen by the client

Run1 ran in 1011 hsecs

Run2 ran in 2525 hsecs

Run1 ran in 40% of the time
```

As you can see, the program first prints the results of the `runstats` utility under the line `Results from RUNSTATS utility`. At the end, after the line `Runtime Execution Time Differences as seen by the client`, we also print out the execution time differences as seen by your Java client (in this case, they are pretty much the same as the ones shown by `runstats`). The results are slightly different from the original run, which indicates that we should run these benchmarks multiple times and average their results.

Timing Java Programs

When benchmarking Java programs, it's a good idea to let the Java Virtual Machine (JVM) reach a steady state, which takes a few minutes. One way to achieve this is to make sure that we run the program (or method) being benchmarked enough times for the entire benchmark to take around five minutes. For this, we first find out how many runs it takes for the method being benchmarked to consume five minutes. Then, we run the method that number of times and find out the average time per run by dividing the total time by the number of runs. Since we'll benchmark many times, I wrote a simple program called JBenchmark.java for this purpose. This section explains the program workings—as usual, you can get the actual code from the Downloads section of http://www.apress.com.

JBenchmark allows up to three methods to be timed at a time; we can, of course, modify it to enable more methods. Following is the program listing interspersed with explanations.

First, we import the relevant classes and declare methods that need to be benchmarked:

```
package book.util;
import java.sql.Connection;
public class JBenchmark
{
  // classes must override the method that they are
  // timing - by default these methods don't do anything.
  public void firstMethod( Connection conn, Object[] parameters )
    throws Exception{ }
  public void secondMethod( Connection conn, Object[] parameters )
    throws Exception { }
  public void thirdMethod( Connection conn, Object[] parameters )
    throws Exception{ }
  public void firstMethod() throws Exception{ }
  public void secondMethod() throws Exception{ }
  public void thirdMethod() throws Exception{ }
```

A program that wants to use the preceding utility program for benchmarking would extend it and override the correct number of methods. For example, if we want to time two methods, we'll override the methods firstMethod() and secondMethod() of JBenchmark in our program. By default the methods don't do anything. Note that each of the methods firstMethod(), secondMethod(), and thirdMethod() is overloaded to take a connection and an array of objects since most of our benchmarks require a connection to be passed. The object array is useful if we want to pass additional parameters to each method.

The following `timeMethod()` method runs the actual timing of the method being bench-marked. It takes as parameters a method number indicating which method to benchmark (`firstMethod()`, `secondMethod()`, or `thirdMethod()`), a connection, an array of optional object parameters, and a message to print before the benchmark is run.

```
public final void timeMethod( int methodNumber,
  Connection conn, Object[] parameters, String message ) throws Exception
{
  System.out.println( message );
```

In the same method, we first find out how many times we need to run the method so that it runs for five minutes. The following `_runMethod()` method (I explain it when we look at its definition soon) simply runs the appropriate method depending on the method number passed.

```
// find out how many runs it takes to run for 5 minutes
long startTime = System.currentTimeMillis();
_runMethod( methodNumber, conn, parameters );
long endTime = System.currentTimeMillis();
long numOfRuns = (long)( (5*60*1000)/( endTime-startTime ) );
```

If the number of runs is 0, it means that the method being benchmarked took more than five minutes in the first run, so we need to run it only once for benchmarking purposes; hence we set the number of runs to 1 in this special case.

```
if( numOfRuns == 0 )
{
  System.out.println( "One run took more than 5 minutes." );
  numOfRuns = 1;
}
```

Finally, we take the average time it takes to run the method being benchmarked for the number of runs we just established, and print the results.

```
// average over the number of runs calculated above
startTime = System.currentTimeMillis();
for(int i=0; i < numOfRuns; i++ )
{
  _runMethod( methodNumber, conn, parameters );
}
endTime = System.currentTimeMillis();
long averageRunTime = (endTime-startTime)/numOfRuns;
System.out.println( "\tOn an average it took " +
  averageRunTime + " ms (number of runs = " + numOfRuns + ".)");
}
```

The following _runMethod() method simply selects the correct method to invoke based on the method number. If the connection is null, invoke the versions of firstMethod() and so on that don't take any parameters.

```java
private void _runMethod( int methodNumber,
  Connection conn, Object[] parameters ) throws Exception
{
  if( conn != null )
  {
    if( methodNumber == FIRST_METHOD )
      firstMethod( conn, parameters );
    else if( methodNumber == SECOND_METHOD )
      secondMethod( conn, parameters );
    else if( methodNumber == THIRD_METHOD )
      thirdMethod( conn, parameters );
    else
    {
      System.err.println( "Invalid method number: " + methodNumber );
      System.exit( 1 );
    }
  }
  else
  {
    if( methodNumber == FIRST_METHOD )
      firstMethod( );
    else if( methodNumber == SECOND_METHOD )
      secondMethod( );
    else if( methodNumber == THIRD_METHOD )
      thirdMethod( );
    else
    {
      System.err.println( "Invalid method number: " + methodNumber );
      System.exit( 1 );
    }
  }
}
```

At the end of the program, we declare three constants denoting method numbers to be passed as parameters to runMethod() by the program that overrides JBenchmark.

```java
public static final int FIRST_METHOD = 1;
public static final int SECOND_METHOD = 2;
public static final int THIRD_METHOD = 3;
}// end of class
```

The program DemoJBenchmark compares the time taken by two methods by overriding firstMethod() and secondMethod() of JBenchmark. The first method concatenates 1,000 strings using the string concatenation approach, and the second does the same using the String-Buffer class's append method.

```java
import book.util.JBenchmark;
public class DemoJBenchmark extends JBenchmark
{
  public static void main(String[] args) throws Exception
  {
    new DemoJBenchmark()._runBenchmark();
  }

  public void firstMethod() throws Exception
  {
    String x = "";
    for( int i=0; i < 1000; i++ )
      x  = x + Integer.toString(i);
  }

  public void secondMethod() throws Exception
  {
    StringBuffer x = new StringBuffer();
    for( int i=0; i < 1000; i++ )
      x.append( Integer.toString(i) );
    String y = x.toString();
  }

  private void _runBenchmark() throws Exception
  {
    timeMethod( JBenchmark.FIRST_METHOD, null, null, "Concatenating Using String");
    timeMethod( JBenchmark.SECOND_METHOD, null, null,
      "Concatenating Using StringBuffer");
  }
}
```

Sample output when I ran the program DemoJBenchmark is as follows. It indicates (as expected) that StringBuffer-based concatenation outperforms string concatenation.

```
Concatenating Using String
  On an average it took 66 ms (number of runs = 1910.)
Concatenating Using StringBuffer
  On an average it took 1 ms (number of runs = 150000.)
```

A Utility to Pause in a Java Program

Listing 1-1 shows a utility that I use in some of my programs to generate a *pause*. I use it when I want to run something separately (e.g., a query to some tables being modified by the program), but want to do so at intermediate stages in the program. The program uses standard Java I/O classes in the overloaded method waitTillUserPressesEnter().

Listing 1-1. *The* InputUtil *class generates a pause in Java programs*

```java
package book.util;

import java.io.IOException;
import java.io.BufferedReader;
import java.io.InputStreamReader;

public class InputUtil
{
  public static void main(String[] args)
    throws Exception
  {
    String line = waitTillUserHitsEnter();
    System.out.println( line );
  }

  public static String waitTillUserHitsEnter( String message )
    throws IOException
  {
    System.out.println( message );
    return waitTillUserHitsEnter();
  }

  public static String waitTillUserHitsEnter()
    throws IOException
  {
    System.out.println("Press Enter to continue..." );
    BufferedReader standardInput = new BufferedReader(
      new InputStreamReader( System.in ) );
    String line = null;
    line = standardInput.readLine();

    return line;
  }
}
```

Summary

This chapter covered some of the tools that we will use throughout this book, mainly in our performance benchmark programs. Many of these tools involve concepts that are explained in the references provided where the tool was mentioned. Some of these tools are written using JDBC concepts, which are explained elsewhere in this book. I recommend revisiting the code for these utilities once you've grasped the underlying concepts from the later chapters.

In the next chapter, we'll look at some of the fundamental concepts related to Oracle that every Oracle application programmer (including JDBC programmers) should be familiar with.

CHAPTER 2

■ ■ ■

Oracle Fundamentals

This is one of the most important chapters of the book, even though it is not directly about JDBC. My objective here is to convince you, through examples, that there is more to writing effective Java database applications than an in-depth understanding of the JDBC API. Furthermore, I want to convey that to write correct, robust, and high-performance Oracle applications using JDBC (or any other API for that matter), you need to

- *Understand how Oracle works.* You should understand the fundamentals of Oracle's architecture and how to design your application accordingly.

- *Learn and master SQL and PL/SQL.* JDBC on Oracle works on top of SQL and PL/SQL. If your SQL and PL/SQL code is suboptimal, your application will run in a suboptimal fashion. I use these languages, where appropriate, throughout the book.

- *Know what features Oracle offers.* Unless you are familiar with the features offered by Oracle, you will end up developing, debugging, and maintaining code that is already available to you in Oracle.

If you are interested in jumping directly to JDBC mechanics, you should start with the next chapter. However, I strongly recommend that you read this chapter first or at least skim through it. The reason for this is that, in my opinion, if you don't understand how Oracle works and what features it offers, more often than not *you'll write incorrect and/or nonperforming code.* This statement may come as a surprise to you, but by the time you've finished this chapter, I hope to have convinced you of its validity.

Of course, in a single chapter, we can only really scratch the surface of Oracle and its features, although we will cover enough so that their significance and their impact on the way in which you write your Java programs will be apparent.

■**Note** If you wish to learn more, I strongly urge you to get hold of the following two books: *Expert One-on-One Oracle* (Apress, ISBN: 1-59059-243-3) and *Effective Oracle by Design* (Osborne McGraw-Hill, ISBN: 0-07-223065-7), both written by the well-known Oracle expert Tom Kyte. Additionally, Tom's site, http://asktom.oracle.com, is a treasure trove of information on Oracle. You can ask questions on most Oracle-related topics on this site and get well-researched, correct answers unbelievably fast and for free.

Let's now look at some selected Oracle concepts that you need to be aware of to build applications on top of Oracle.

Selected Oracle Concepts

Although it is not necessary to know the intimate details of how the Oracle kernel works, it is very useful to be familiar with certain Oracle architectural details, such as its concurrency model, how it manages data in its memory and disk, and so on.

Database vs. Instance

Two terms that are commonly used in reference to basic Oracle architecture, and that often cause confusion, are "database" and "instance." In simple terms,

- A *database* is a collection of physical data files (operating system files) that reside on disk.

- An *instance* is a set of Oracle processes along with their shared memory area. These processes (referred to as *background processes*) are what actually operate on the database files, performing such tasks as storing and retrieving the data.

So, a database is a collection of physical storage files, and an instance is set of processes and an area of memory that allows you to operate on those files. You do not have to do anything special in your JDBC code to account for this distinction, but it is useful to be aware of it.

Schemas

A *schema* is simply the collection of objects (tables, indexes, views, stored procedures, and so on) owned by a database user. A database user can *own* exactly one schema, though the same user may have *access* to multiple schemas.

Included in the database are two important users/schemas: the SYS and SYSTEM users. The SYS user/schema contains, among other things, the *data dictionary* for the database. The data dictionary consists of various tables and views that contain all the metadata for the rest of the database, including definitions for all of the objects in a schema (as well as the database as a whole).

For example, the user_tables view contains a great deal of information about each of the tables in the schema for the current user. You may need to occasionally look up information about objects in the database such as size, location, or creation date, for example, and the data dictionary is the place to do it. Accessing the information in the data dictionary is performed in the same manner as accessing any other information in the database. However, since the data dictionary is read-only, only select statements are permitted.

■**Note**   See *Oracle Database Concepts Guide (10g Release 1)* or the *Oracle Database Reference (10g Release 1)* in the Oracle-supplied documentation for complete details on the tables and views in the data dictionary.

The SYS user is the user with the highest privileges in an Oracle database and may be viewed as the database equivalent of the "Administrator" or "root" operating system accounts. Second in command to the SYS user is the SYSTEM user. This user contains important schema objects that are used internally by Oracle in much the same way as those belonging to the SYS schema. Under normal circumstances, these users should not be used for anything other than database administration tasks.

Tablespaces

Tablespaces are used to logically group functionally related schema objects. For example, the system tablespace contains all the objects for the SYS and SYSTEM schemas.

A schema object that requires physical storage must belong to a tablespace. When a schema object is created, you may specify a tablespace in which to create the object or you may allow it to be created in the default tablespace for that user. The default tablespace for a user is defined when the user is initially created, and it may be altered after the user has been created if needed or desired. If the default tablespace for a user is altered after creation, any objects previously created for the user will not automatically move or migrate to the new default tablespace; only new objects created after the new default tablespace has been assigned will be created in that tablespace.

■**Caution** You should *never* specify the system tablespace as the default tablespace for a "normal" user. The SYS and SYSTEM users use the system tablespace, and this tablespace "belongs" to Oracle. Consider it off-limits.

Data Blocks

Oracle manages the storage space in the data files of a database in units called *data blocks* (aka *DB blocks* or *database blocks*). A data block is the smallest unit of data used by Oracle during its I/O operations. As you are probably aware, each operating system itself has a *block size*. Oracle requests data in multiples of Oracle data blocks, not operating system blocks. The standard block size is specified by the db_block_size initialization parameter. A table's data is stored in data blocks. Note that one data block may contain more than one row of a table.

It is important to understand data blocks, as any discussion about performance measurement in Oracle invariably includes this concept. For example, when we measure performance, the number of data blocks accessed forms an important criterion in deciding between two approaches, as you will learn later in the section "Logical and Physical I/O."

■**Note** See the section "Overview of Data Blocks" in Chapter 2 of the *Oracle Database Concepts Guide (10g Release 1)* document for more details on this topic.

What Makes Oracle Different?

There are, of course, many ways in which Oracle differs from other RDBMSs, but from a developer's perspective, possibly the two major concepts to understand are Oracle's *locking* mechanism and its *multiversion read consistency* model.

Oracle's Locking Mechanism

Locks (and latches) are constructs used to regulate concurrent access to a shared resource within Oracle. These constructs play a crucial role in maintaining data integrity during concurrent modification of the shared resources. In Oracle, a shared resource is not just your data; it could also be your code (e.g., a PL/SQL package procedure cannot be altered when it is being executed).

Oracle automatically obtains necessary locks to execute SQL statements; in general, users need not be concerned with managing locks in Oracle. The following are some important facts about Oracle's locking policy:

- Oracle uses row-level locking, as appropriate, to ensure that only one transaction can modify (write) a piece of data at a given time. Oracle does not lock data during reads (selects).

- There is no significant overhead to locking in Oracle. Oracle stores the lock status of a row in the data block holding the row, rather than in the data dictionary or a "lock manager," thus avoiding contention on a "row lock status" table.

- Oracle never escalates locks to the table level. Even if you are modifying every row of a 1,000-row table, Oracle will place a row-level lock on each row.

■**Note** See the section "How Oracle Locks Data" of Chapter 13 in *Oracle Database Concepts Guide (10g Release 1)* for a detailed explanation of how locks work in Oracle.

The consequence of this row-level locking scheme is that writes don't block writes unless the contending write operations are "writing" a common set of rows. For example, if two sessions are updating the same table but update a mutually exclusive set of rows, they don't block each other. Only when they try to update the same row(s) does one of the sessions get blocked until the other session issues a commit or a rollback to end its transaction.

Furthermore,

- Reads don't block writes.

- Writes don't block reads.

Reads (selects) don't block writes (inserts, updates, deletes, etc.). If you're reading a piece of data, don't assume that another transaction can't modify that same piece of data. After all, Oracle doesn't, by default, place any locks during reads. A user can be updating a row of data at the same time as another user is querying that row. If you really want your read to block other writes, you have to "lock" the selected row with the `for update` clause of the `select` statement. For example, if you want to lock the row in the table `emp` corresponding to the employee `BLAKE`, you would issue the following statement:

```
select ename from emp where ename = 'BLAKE' for update;
```

This statement will block any `update` statement trying to update the row corresponding to the employee `BLAKE` in the table `emp` until the current session completes its transaction.

What may seem even more surprising is that writes don't block reads. Consider a query that starts at time `t1` and will read 10,000 rows. While this query is reading row number 5,000, a second SQL statement is executed that modifies row number 7,000 in the set of rows that the query is reading, changing the value of a column being read in that row from 1 to 2. What happens when the query hits row number 7,000 may surprise you:

- If the update has been committed, the query will simply read the data in row number 7,000. Oracle performs a check to find out if the value in the row has changed since time `t1`. When Oracle finds that the value has changed, it retrieves and uses the value as it was at time `t1`.

- If the update has not been committed, a lock will still be in place on row number 7,000. However, this is only to prevent other writers from modifying that same data; it does not prevent us from reading it. Thus, Oracle reads through the lock, reconstructs the value as it was at time `t1`, and uses this value.

What this effectively means is that, without using any unnecessary locking, Oracle can present a consistent view of the data with respect to a given point in time—in this case with respect to the time the query started, `t1`. The reason Oracle is able to do this relates to its ability to maintain multiple versions of the data based on a concept called multiversion read consistency, which we'll examine next.

Multiversion Read Consistency

When you make a change to a block of Oracle data, Oracle makes a copy of that block and stores it in an *undo* (or *rollback*) segment. This undo segment contains enough information about the block of data to undo (hence the name) the changes made to it and make it look like it did at the beginning of the transaction. Oracle has a special internal "clock" known as the *system change number* (*SCN*). Oracle is able to compare the current SCN with the SCN that existed at the start of a transaction. If you are querying data that is (or was) being updated at the time your query started, Oracle is able to look through the undo segment(s) to find the proper copy of the data as it existed at the time your query began. This feature of Oracle is known as *multiversion read consistency*.

So, in Oracle, in the default transaction mode of READ COMMITTED (you'll learn about transactions and transaction modes in Chapter 4), the data a query sees and returns comes from a single point in time. In other words, the results are consistent with respect to the point in time at which the query began execution. This phenomenon is called *statement-level read consistency*. The vast majority of Oracle applications use the default transaction mode of READ COMMITTED.

Oracle can also provide *transaction-level read consistency*, which means all queries within a transaction see and return data from a single point of time—the point at which the *transaction* began. Transaction-level read consistency is triggered when you set the transaction mode to either SERIALIZABLE or READ ONLY. The term "multiversion read consistency" encapsulates both statement-level and transaction-level read consistency.

Because multiversion read consistency directly impacts the results of a query that developers write, you must take it into account when designing your system.

Let's now look at an example that illustrates statement-level read consistency. In this example, we first create a simple table, t1, with one number column, x, as follows:

```
benchmark@ORA10G> create table t1
  2  (
  3    x number
  4  );

Table created.
```

We insert and commit a record in this table next:

```
benchmark@ORA10G> insert into t1 values ( 1 );

1 row created.

benchmark@ORA10G> commit;

Commit complete.
```

We then create a PL/SQL procedure, p, which returns in its out parameter, p_cursor, a ref cursor pointing to a query that selects all records from table t1. In the same procedure, we insert and commit four more records into table t1 *after* opening the cursor:

```
benchmark@ORA10G> create or replace procedure p ( p_cursor out sys_refcursor ) is
  2  begin
  3    open p_cursor for
  4    select * from t1;
  5    insert into t1 values ( 5 );
  6    insert into t1 values ( 2 );
  7    insert into t1 values ( 3 );
  8    insert into t1 values ( 4 );
  9    commit;
 10  end;
 11  /

Procedure created.
```

We then execute the procedure and print the results of the ref cursor we opened (representing the result set of the query):

```
benchmark@ORA10G> variable c refcursor;
benchmark@ORA10G> exec p( :c )

PL/SQL procedure successfully completed.

benchmark@ORA10G> print c;

        1
```

If we were not aware of the multiversion read consistency feature, we might expect the cursor to print all five records that we know exist in table t1 at this point of time. After all, at the point where we retrieve the cursor values, there are five records inserted and committed in table t1. But the results show that only one record is printed. This demonstrates the concept of multiversion read consistency, due to which our query's result set was preordained at the time its execution began (or in this case, at the time we opened the cursor pointing to the query).

■**Note** For further details on this very important concept, please see Chapters 4 and 13 of *Oracle Database Concepts Guide (10g Release 1)*.

Writing Effective Code

By "writing effective code," I mean writing application code that uses the Oracle database in the most efficient manner. It is quite easy to write code that "works" with the Oracle database, but you will often find, if you investigate, that your code is performing much slower than with other available alternatives, is hogging shared resources in the database (thus affecting performance and scalability), or is simply making the database do unnecessary work in achieving a particular task.

The mantra in this book is that we should not just produce code that "works"; we should produce code that works *well*. We test our code rigorously at every stage, using the tools described in Chapter 1, and we *prove* that it doesn't consume too many system resources, and that it doesn't make the database perform more work than is necessary to complete a given task.

The following sections cover techniques to help you achieve these goals.

Use Bind Variables

We now come to the first architectural feature that directly affects the way in which you should write your JDBC programs, namely that of the shared pool and the use of bind variables.

An Oracle instance consists of certain memory structures that allow you to operate on a physical database. Possibly the most important memory structure associated with an instance is the *shared global area* (*SGA*), and the most important component of the SGA for a JDBC programmer is the *shared pool*, because the manner in which you use the shared pool via your code has an enormous bearing on the performance of your code.

The shared pool is an Oracle memory structure that consists of shared program constructs accessed and executed on your behalf by Oracle. These include stored PL/SQL procedures and packages, shared cursors, data dictionary objects, etc. When you submit a SQL statement (such as select, insert, update, delete, or merge) to Oracle, it has to parse the statement and generate an execution plan to execute it.

■**Note** I cover the topic of SQL statement parsing in more detail in the section "Overview of How Oracle Processes SQL Statements (DML)" of Chapter 5.

Since the step of generating the execution plan is very CPU-intensive, Oracle stores the results of this step in the shared pool to avoid reparsing a statement if it is submitted again.

It follows from the previous discussion that, in general, you should strive to improve reuse of the shared code in the shared pool so that overall parsing overhead is kept to a minimum. Using bind variables is an excellent way of achieving this goal.

A *bind variable* is a variable (or a parameter) in a SQL statement that is replaced (or bound) at runtime with a valid value in order for the statement to successfully execute. The following code shows a SQL statement with and without a bind variable:

```
-- SQL with a literal
select ename from emp where empno = 7788;

-- The same SQL with a bind variable in place of the literal
select ename from emp where empno = ?;
```

In the former case, every time this statement is submitted with a different empno value in the where clause, it will be treated as a completely new statement and it will have to be parsed, an execution plan will have to be generated, and so on. In the latter case, all subsequent executions of similar SQL statements after the first one will reuse the existing execution plan for the statement from the shared pool.

You can use bind variables in virtually all languages that can talk to Oracle (JDBC in Java, Pro*C, C++, and, of course, PL/SQL). As you'll see, in general, the performance of a system degrades rapidly if you don't use bind variables.

Let's look at an example. First we need to create a simple table, t1:

```
benchmark@ORA10G> create table t1
  2  (
  3    x number
  4  );

Table created.
```

The following JDBC class, DemoBind, compares two approaches of inserting 10,000 records into table t1, first without using bind variables and then using bind variables.

■**Note** I cover the JDBC concepts used in this example in much more detail in Chapter 5, where I also discuss bind variables in more depth. Don't worry if you aren't able to fully understand the mechanics of this program for now—the focus at this stage is to demonstrate the importance of bind variables to the performance of your JDBC programs.

We'll use the JRunstatsprogram described in the previous chapter to compare the two approaches. The program first uses the PreparedStatement class to execute the insert state-ments with bind variables. It then uses the Statement class to execute the insert statements without bind variables. The program begins by importing relevant Java classes and getting a connection to our 10g database:

```
/* This program demonstrates the importance of using bind variables*/
import java.sql.SQLException;
import java.sql.PreparedStatement;
import java.sql.Statement;
import java.sql.Connection;
import book.util.JDBCUtil;
import book.util.JRunstats;
public class DemoBind
{
  public static void main(String[] args) throws Exception
  {
    Connection conn = null;
    try
    {
      conn = JDBCUtil.getConnection("benchmark", "benchmark", "ora10g");
```

We then prepare all the statements used by the JRunstats program:

```
    JRunstats.prepareBenchmarkStatements( conn );
```

We follow this up by marking the beginning of the benchmark run. We then invoke _insertWithBinds() (a private method that inserts 10,000 records with bind variables), mark the middle of the benchmark run, and invoke _insertWithoutBinds() (a private method that inserts 10,000 records without bind variables):

```
      JRunstats.markStart( conn );
      _insertWithBind( conn );
      JRunstats.markMiddle( conn );
      _insertWithoutBind( conn );
```

Finally, we invoke the JRunstats methodthat marks the end of the benchmarking and prints out the benchmarking results:

```
      JRunstats.markEnd( conn );
    }
    catch (SQLException e)
```

```
  {
    // handle the exception properly - in this case, we just
    // print the stack trace.
    JDBCUtil.printException ( e );
  }
  finally
  {
    // release the JDBC resources in the finally clause.
    JRunstats.closeBenchmarkStatements( conn );
    JDBCUtil.close( conn );
  }
}
```

The _insertWithBind() method uses the PreparedStatement interface to execute the 10,000 inserts:

```
private static void _insertWithBind( Connection conn ) throws SQLException
{
  PreparedStatement pstmt = null;
  try
  {
    pstmt = conn.prepareStatement( "insert into t1(x) values( ? ) " );
    for( int i=0; i < 10000; i++ )
    {
      pstmt.setInt( 1, i );
      pstmt.executeUpdate();
    }
  }
  finally
  {
    // release JDBC-related resources in the finally clause.
    JDBCUtil.close( pstmt );
  }
}
```

The _insertWithoutBind() method uses the Statement interface to execute the 10,000 inserts without using bind variables:

```
private static void _insertWithoutBind( Connection conn ) throws SQLException
{
  Statement stmt = null;
  try
  {
    stmt = conn.createStatement();
    for( int i=0; i < 10000; i++ )
    {
      stmt.executeUpdate( "insert into t1( x ) values( " + i + ")" );
    }
  }
}
```

```
    finally
    {
      // release JDBC-related resources in the finally clause.
      JDBCUtil.close( stmt );
    }
  }
}
```

The important thing to note in the DemoBind class is that in the case where we use bind variables, *only one* statement string is submitted to Oracle: insert into t1 (x) values (?). Here, ? is the bind variable that is bound at runtime to the values 1, 2, . . . 10,000 in the loop. In the case where we don't use bind variables, Oracle sees a different insert statement for each value being inserted (insert into t1 (x) values (0) for a value of 0, insert into t1 (x) values (1) for a value of 1, and so on). Since Oracle has to parse each new query and generate a query execution plan, this approach doesn't scale well at all. In our example, Oracle has to process 10,000 spuriously different statements when we don't use bind variables. Let's run the program to see how these two approaches compare:

```
URL:jdbc:oracle:thin:@(DESCRIPTION=(ADDRESS=(PROTOCOL=tcp)(PORT=1521)
(HOST=rmenon-lap))(CONNECT_DATA=(SID=ora10g)))

------- Benchmark Results --------

Results from RUNSTATS utility

Run1 ran in 43 hsecs
Run2 ran in 214 hsecs
run 1 ran in 20.09% of the time
```

As you can see, the approach that uses bind variables runs substantially faster. It completes in about 1/5 the time of the alternative that does not use bind variables. This in itself is a very good reason to use bind variables in your code. However, it is even more critical to understand the importance of differences in consumption of latches in the two approaches. You can see this from the next section of the JRunstatsreport:

```
Name                            Run1      Run2       Diff
STAT...messages sent              3         4          1
STAT...calls to kcmgcs            5         6          1
<-- trimmed to conserve space -->
STAT...session pga memory max   131,072     0      -131,072

Run1 latches total versus runs -- difference and pct
     Run1      Run2      Diff     Pct
    16,883   126,673   109,790   13.33%
```

The approach that uses bind variables consumes approximately *13% of the latches* as compared to the alternative that does not use bind variables.

Latches are lightweight serialization resources Oracle uses when accessing shared memory structures. While one session is parsing, Oracle will place latches on common resources in the shared pool so that no other sessions may modify them. The more latches there are in place, and the longer they are held, the longer the subsequent sessions have to wait in order to gain access to these resources. When approach 1 consumes 13% of the latches consumed by approach 2, as is true in the preceding example, the scalability of the system that uses approach 1 is substantially superior to the one that employs approach 2. In other words, as more and more users start using the system concurrently, the performance of the system employing approach 2 will degrade rapidly.

To demonstrate this point in terms of its impact on elapsed time when multiple users are using the system, I ran the preceding program simultaneously for two, three, four, and five sessions separately. For example, to run it simultaneously in three sessions, I opened three windows on my PC and ran the program in each window simultaneously. The result is plotted in the graph shown in Figure 2-1.

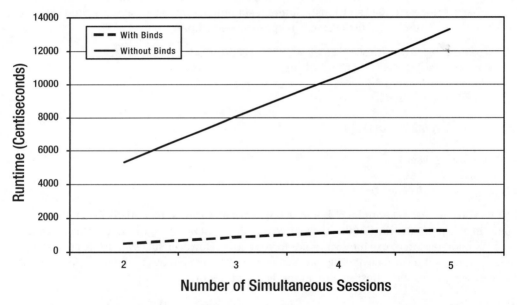

Figure 2-1. *This graph compares runtimes with and without bind variables for simultaneous sessions. I did the comparison for two, three, four, and five simultaneous sessions each.*

From the graph in Figure 2-1, we can conclude that as the number of sessions increases, the performance of the approach that doesn't use bind variables deteriorates rapidly and at a much faster rate as compared to the approach that uses bind variables. This is mainly because Oracle is unable to reuse the work it did in generating a query's execution plan for different input values for the same query when we don't use bind variables. Thus, when you write an application on Oracle, your goal typically is to choose an approach that consumes the minimum amount of latches. Using bind variables is one of the most fundamental techniques that can help you achieve this goal in most cases.

Note You can set `CURSOR_SHARING` to `SIMILAR` or `FORCE` to force all queries in your database to use bind variables. Generally, this technique is useful in cases where a third-party application you have isn't using bind variables and you don't have access to the code to change it. Note that setting `CURSOR_SHARING` to `SIMILAR` or `FORCE` has its own drawbacks; you should use it only as a temporary solution. The best and cleanest approach at the end of the day is to use bind variables in the first place. For more details on this topic, see the section "Cursor Sharing for Applications" of Chapter 7 in *Oracle Database Performance Tuning Guide and Reference (10g Release 1)*.

Minimize I/O, Undo, and Redo

Unfortunately, the trigger for many performance investigations is a complaint from its users that the application is running too slowly. In most cases, the root cause is poorly written SQL code or poorly written database access code (e.g., absence of bind variables). In the previous examples, this caused unnecessary parsing and unnecessary latching, resulting in poor performance and poor scalability. The following sections cover other types of work that the database performs and some techniques for minimizing such work.

Logical and Physical I/O

When Oracle executes a query, it needs to perform I/O, either to its shared pool to retrieve cached data or to the disk. This section discusses the types of I/O Oracle performs and how you should incorporate these in your application development strategy.

Oracle stores frequently used data in a memory cache called the *database buffer cache*.

- A *logical I/O* (*LIO* for short) occurs whenever the database buffer cache is accessed to satisfy a request from the Oracle kernel. If the kernel does not find the data in the cache, it asks the operating system to get the data from the disk.

- A *physical I/O* (*PIO* for short) occurs whenever the Oracle kernel asks the operating system to fulfill a request, since it cannot fulfill the request from the database buffer cache. Please note that not all PIOs translate to a disk read, as many of them can be satisfied from the operating system's internal buffer cache, but from Oracle's point of view they are all disk reads or PIOs.

Although it may seem counterintuitive, in general, your goal should be to focus on reducing LIOs rather than PIOs, for the following reasons:

- Typically, LIOs require use of latches and/or serialization devices, which can have a seriously negative impact on the scalability of the system.

- If you reduce LIOs, PIOs take care of themselves naturally because most PIOs are preceded by LIO calls in the first place.

- PIOs may not be as costly as they seem, since many times they can be satisfied by operating system's internal data buffer cache.

■**Tip** See http://www.hotsos.com/downloads/registered/00000006.pdf for an excellent article on this topic by Cary Millsap (Please note that to access the article, you need to be a registered member of the website.)

■**Tip** In general, you should focus on reducing Logical I/Os as opposed to Physical I/Os generated by your system.

Logical I/Os are of two types:

- **Consistent gets:** These are logical I/Os that occur *typically* when you execute a query. Recall that when a query is executed in Oracle, in the default transaction mode, Oracle gets the data *as of* the time the query started (i.e., the data retrieved is *consistent* with the time the query started). This mode of retrieval of data is called *consistent-read* mode.

- **DB block gets or current gets:** These are logical I/Os in which the database gets the data as it exists right now (not as of a point of time in the past). This LIO mode is called *current* mode. During data modification, Oracle reads the database blocks being modified in the current mode before modifying them.

Measuring Logical I/O

The total number of logical I/Os performed is the sum of consistent gets and DB block gets. For a single SQL statement, you can use the autotrace facility to easily find out the number of database blocks read in consistent-read mode and the number of blocks read in current mode. In the following query, 25 blocks were read in consistent get mode (25 consistent gets) and zero blocks were read in current mode (0 db block gets). There were zero physical reads or PIOs.

```
benchmark@ORA10G> set autotrace traceonly statistics
benchmark@ORA10G> select count(*)
  2  from all_users;

Statistics
----------------------------------------------------------
          0  recursive calls
          0  db block gets
         25  consistent gets
          0  physical reads
          0  redo size
        393  bytes sent via SQL*Net to client
        508  bytes received via SQL*Net from client
          2  SQL*Net roundtrips to/from client
          0  sorts (memory)
          0  sorts (disk)
          1  rows processed
```

You can also use the performance tool `tkprof` (discussed in the section "tkprof" of Chapter 1) to find out the LIOs and PIOs of one or more SQL or PL/SQL statements. Note that in a `tkprof` report, the consistent gets are shown under the total value of the column `query`, and DB block gets are shown under the total value of the column `current`, as shown in the following `tkprof` report for the preceding query:

```
select count(*)
from
 all_users
```

call	count	cpu	elapsed	disk	query	current	rows
Parse	1	0.00	0.00	0	0	0	0
Execute	1	0.00	0.00	0	0	0	0
Fetch	2	0.00	0.00	0	25	0	1
total	4	0.00	0.00	0	**25**	**0**	1

Reducing Logical I/O

There are many ways to reduce LIOs in your system.

- *Eliminate work being done in the system that is not being used by the end user.* It is amazing how a large portion of your system may not actually be doing anything useful for the end user. Get rid of these activities, and you can reduce the burden on the database considerably. Cary Millsap, a famous Oracle performance analyst, puts it well when he says, "The fastest way to speed up something is to not do it at all!"

- *Tune individual queries that are bottleneck in your system.* Tuning queries can appear to be an "art" or "magic" if you don't have a full command of SQL, but doing so is vital to the performance of your applications, and it becomes much easier once you understand your basic goals and have knowledge of various tools at your disposal.

  You should always benchmark your tuning results to prove that you've actually improved the performance of a query (e.g., by using `runstats` or its JDBC equivalent, `JRunstats`). Don't blindly follow any advice you get from others. Myths abound in the SQL tuning area, so ask for proof or examples of where something does or does not work. Besides, a piece of advice, even if it is sound, may not directly apply to your application. For example, a common myth is that full table scans are always bad, and using an index to retrieve data is always good. You'll see an example that proves this isn't the case shortly.

- *Employ array processing techniques to improve performance. Array processing* refers to the idea of reducing network round-trips and LIOs by processing more than one row at a time in your SQL statements. You'll learn how to do array processing in JDBC in the section "Prefetching" of Chapter 7. In PL/SQL, you can achieve these objectives by using bulk operations, which are covered in the section "Using Bulk Operations to Boost Performance" of Chapter 17.

Example: Index Access vs. Full Table Scan

Let's look at a simple example of how reducing LIOs can help you tune your system. In many ways, the actual example used isn't as important as the demonstration of how drastically unnecessary I/O can affect performance and how to measure that. In addition, this example serves to debunk the myth that index-based data access is "always best." Of course, indexing is an important component in ensuring optimal data access, but many developers are shocked to find that the database isn't actually using a particular index and take steps (such as using hints) to force it to do so. This example demonstrates that, in fact, a full table scan can sometimes perform much better than an index access; the reason being that the index access causes more LIOs.

We first create a table, t, using data from the all_objects view:

```
benchmark@ORA10G> create table t as select object_name as x,
mod(rownum, 2) as y, owner as z from all_objects
 where rownum <= 5000;

Table created.
```

Note that the table will have 2,500 rows with a value of 1 and 2,500 rows with a value of 0 in the column y. We then create an index on the y column:

```
benchmark@ORA10G> create index t_idx on t(y);

Index created.
```

We create another identical table, t1, with identical data:

```
benchmark@ORA10G> create table t1 as select object_name as x,
mod( rownum, 2) as y, owner as z from all_objects
where rownum <= 5000;

Table created.
```

Next, we gather statistics for the Oracle optimizer to use:

```
benchmark@ORA10G> begin
  2     dbms_stats.gather_table_stats(
  3     ownname => 'BENCHMARK',
  4     tabname => 'T' );
  5     dbms_stats.gather_index_stats(
  6     ownname => 'BENCHMARK',
  7     indname => 'T_IDX' );
  8     dbms_stats.gather_table_stats(
  9     ownname => 'BENCHMARK',
 10     tabname => 'T1' );
 11  end;
 12  /

PL/SQL procedure successfully completed.
```

We then set the autotrace option that would show us the query plans and the statistics. We also set the timing on so we can see elapsed time for each query.

```
benchmark@ORA10G> set autotrace traceonly;
benchmark@ORA10G> set timing on
```

Our first query is a simple join between the two tables:

```
benchmark@ORA10G> select *
  2  from t, t1
  3  where t.y = t1.y
  4    and t.y = 0;

6250000 rows selected.

Elapsed: 00:01:15.83

Execution Plan
----------------------------------------------------------
   0      SELECT STATEMENT Optimizer=ALL_ROWS (Cost=15084
Card=6250000 Bytes=337500000)
   1    0   MERGE JOIN (CARTESIAN) (Cost=15084 Card=6250000
 Bytes=337500000)
   2    1     TABLE ACCESS (FULL) OF 'T' (TABLE) (Cost=8 Card=2500
Bytes=67500)
   3    1     BUFFER (SORT) (Cost=15076 Card=2500 Bytes=67500)
   4    3      TABLE ACCESS (FULL) OF 'T1' (TABLE) (Cost=6 Card=2500
Bytes=67500)

Statistics
----------------------------------------------------------
         0   recursive calls
         0   db block gets
      2542   consistent gets
         0   physical reads
         0   redo size
 209911567   bytes sent via SQL*Net to client
   4583834   bytes received via SQL*Net from client
    416668   SQL*Net roundtrips to/from client
         1   sorts (memory)
         0   sorts (disk)
   6250000   rows processed
```

As you can see, the optimizer uses a full table scan on both tables for this query. The query took 2,542 LIOs (2,542 consistent gets + 0 DB block gets) and completed in 1 minute 16 seconds as shown by the highlighted elapsed time.

In the second query, we give the RULE hint, which will force Oracle to use the rule-based optimizer (RBO). RBO uses an index blindly whenever one is available, as follows:

```
benchmark@ORA10G> select /*+ RULE*/*
  2  from t, t1
  3  where t.y = t1.y
  4    and t.y = 0;

6250000 rows selected.

Elapsed: 00:01:55.67

Execution Plan
----------------------------------------------------------
   0      SELECT STATEMENT Optimizer=HINT: RULE
   1    0   TABLE ACCESS (BY INDEX ROWID) OF 'T' (TABLE)
   2    1     NESTED LOOPS
   3    2       TABLE ACCESS (FULL) OF 'T1' (TABLE)
   4    2       INDEX (RANGE SCAN) OF 'T_IDX' (INDEX)


Statistics
----------------------------------------------------------
          1  recursive calls
          0  db block gets
     918352  consistent gets
          0  physical reads
          0  redo size
  209911567  bytes sent via SQL*Net to client
    4583834  bytes received via SQL*Net from client
     416668  SQL*Net roundtrips to/from client
          0  sorts (memory)
          0  sorts (disk)
    6250000  rows processed
```

The same query, when using the index, takes 918,352 LIOs (918,352 consistent gets + 0 DB block gets). This is *360* times the LIOs taken by the execution plan that used the full table scan. As you can see, it consumes 1 minute 56 seconds (roughly *1.50* times more than the first query). In a multiuser environment, this query will perform even worse since it consumes many more latches due to the additional LIOs it incurs.

■Note The number of LIOs increases when you use an index in the earlier example, because indexes read one block at a time in the sorted order of the data in the index key columns (not in the order in which the blocks are physically stored on the disk). Thus, when using an index, you might end up rereading the same block many times, since different rows being accessed may very well reside on the same block.

For example, if the index is reading 100 rows in the order of row 1, row 2, . . . row 100, and the rows 1, 20, and 30 are on the database block `block1`, then it would read `block1` three times during the course of execution of the query. A full table scan, on the other hand, reads large chunks of data sequentially and does not need to reread the same block. So when you are retrieving a large set of rows of a table, a full table scan *usually* performs much better.

More important, perhaps, in general, when you're comparing the performance of two queries that get you the same answer, make sure you render your judgment based on the number of LIOs, not on whether a particular index is being used or not.

Undo (or Rollback)

Undo was introduced earlier as the information that Oracle maintains to create a multiversion read consistent image of the data. Oracle uses information stored in *undo segments* (referred to as *rollback segments* before 9*i*) to reconstruct a data block as required to give you data as of the point of time the query (or the transaction) started.

   Undo information is generated by Oracle whenever a statement that changes something (user data or an internal Oracle structure) in the database is issued. Oracle also uses this information when you roll back a transaction. In this case, Oracle uses the undo segments to retrieve the "pretransaction" state of the system. So, if you insert ten rows into table t and issue a rollback, Oracle gets back to the pretransaction state by using the transaction's undo stored in undo segments.

Measuring Undo

In general, the more undo your transaction generates, the more resources Oracle consumes in terms of disk space and CPU. Hence, at the minimum, you need to be able to measure the undo generated and know what you can do to minimize it. For measuring the undo used by a transaction, you can look at the column used_ublk of the view v$transaction, which gives the undo held by your transaction in the number of database blocks. For example, if your database block size is 8,192, the undo size (in bytes) used by your transaction at any given time can be measured by running the following query:

```
select used_ublk *8192 as "Undo in Bytes"
from v$transaction;
```

The following function returns the undo generated at a given point of time (it requires direct select privileges on the views v_$transaction and v_$instance; the underscores are relevant):

```
benchmark@ORA10G> create or replace function get_undo
  2   return number
  3   is
  4     l_undo number := 0;
  5   begin
  6     begin
  7       select used_ublk * (select value from v$parameter
where name='db_block_size')
  8         into l_undo
  9         from v$transaction;
 10     exception
 11     when no_data_found then
 12        null; -- ignore - return 0
 13     when others then
 14        raise;
 15     end;
 16     return l_undo;
 17   end;
 18   /
```

```
Function created.
```

To measure the undo generated for any code block, you have to take a snapshot of the undo generated before and after the code block, and subtract them to get the undo generated by the code block.

Minimizing Undo

Many times, you can rewrite the same piece of code in a way that the undo generated is minimized. There are no fixed rules in general to achieve this. One common technique of reducing the undo generated is to use SQL if possible instead of procedural code. We'll look at an example of this technique in the next section.

Example: Procedural Processing vs. SQL

Again, at this stage, the specific example is less important than the measurement technique and the understanding that suboptimal code can result in the generation of excessive undo in the database, causing performance degradation.

However, this example does emphasize a point that recurs several times in this book: although using procedural code is often necessary, using a SQL alternative (if available) will often increase performance.

To demonstrate this concept, we'll insert into a table, t1 (which has one number column, x), 100,000 numbers (from 1 to 100,000). We'll first do this a row at a time using procedural code, and then we'll compare that (in terms of the undo generated) with performing the same task with a simple SQL statement.

In the row-by-row procedure, we open a cursor that selects the 100,000 rows from all_objects. We fetch each row and insert the row into t1:

```
benchmark@ORA92I> create or replace procedure row_by_row
  2  as
  3  begin
  4    for i in ( select rownum from all_objects, all_users where rownum <= 100000 )
  5    loop
  6      insert into t1(x) values(i.rownum);
  7    end loop;
  8  end;
  9  /

Procedure created.
```

In the single_stmt_insert procedure, we do the same thing using a single insert into select clause:

```
benchmark@ORA92I> create or replace procedure single_stmt_insert
  2  as
  3  begin
  4    insert into t1
  5    select rownum
  6    from all_objects, all_users
  7    where rownum <= 100000;
  8  end;
  9  /

Procedure created.
```

We first execute the row_by_row procedure:

```
benchmark@ORA92I> exec row_by_row

PL/SQL procedure successfully completed.
```

We next print out the undo generated by this procedure by invoking the function get_undo, which was discussed earlier:

```
benchmark@ORA92I> exec dbms_output.put_line( get_undo );
7069696

PL/SQL procedure successfully completed.

benchmark@ORA92I> select count(*) from t1;

    100000
```

We roll back to end this transaction:

```
benchmark@ORA92I> rollback;

Rollback complete.
```

We execute our second procedure in a new transaction, printing out the undo generated afterward:

```
benchmark@ORA92I> exec single_stmt_insert

PL/SQL procedure successfully completed.

benchmark@ORA92I> exec dbms_output.put_line( get_undo );
253952

PL/SQL procedure successfully completed.

benchmark@ORA92I> select count(*) from t1;

    100000
```

■**Note** From the SQL prompt in the preceding example, you may have noticed that I ran the preceding code against Oracle9*i* (instead of 10*g*). This is because of a bug in Oracle 10*g* Release 1, due to which the undo information generated is more than actually is required, which in turn makes it difficult to demonstrate the concept on 10*g*. The bug is being worked on at the time of this writing.

As you can see, the procedure row_by_row generates only 7,069,696 bytes of undo, which is around 28 times the 253,952 bytes of undo generated by the procedure single_stmt_insert. In general, if you use single SQL statement instead of doing row-by-row procedural processing, your code will generate less undo, run faster, and be more scalable.

■**Tip** All things being equal, you should choose an approach that generates the least amount of undo.

■**Tip** In general, row-by-row processing (as is done by the previous row_by_row procedure) is almost always slower than a single SQL statement approach (as is done by single_stmt_insert).

Let's look at the concept of redo next.

Redo

Redo refers to information stored in redo log files by Oracle for use in recovering a database after a crash. During the recovery of a database instance after a crash, Oracle "replays" the actions in redo log files to get back to the point in the system before the crash. An important thing for developers to remember is that Oracle updates the redo log files very frequently to minimize data loss in the event of a recovery. The redo log file data is written at least

- Every three seconds

- When the memory structure maintaining redo information (called the *redo log buffer*) is one-third or 1MB full

- Whenever a transaction is committed

Since the frequency with which redo log files are written to is necessarily high by design, the process that does this job can easily become a systemwide bottleneck if the following conditions are true:

- The redo log files have not been optimally sized or configured to minimize systemwide contention. This is, strictly speaking, a DBA's job.

- The code written by you as the developer is generating more redo than necessary.

The second point highlights the fact that the more redo your code generates, the more time it takes to complete your operation and, perhaps more importantly, the slower the *entire* system becomes, since redo log synchronization is a systemwide point of contention. So, at a minimum, you need to be able to measure the redo generated by your code and know what you can do in general to minimize it.

Measuring Redo

For a single SQL statement, you can easily measure the redo generated by using the SQL*Plus autotrace facility, as shown in the following code snippet:

```
benchmark@ORA92I> set autotrace on statistics
benchmark@ORA92I> insert into t1
  2  select rownum
  3  from all_objects;
23554 rows created.
Statistics
----------------------------------------------------------
results snipped for clarity …
   …
    367656  redo size
   …
results snipped for clarity …
     23554  rows processed
```

In the `insert` statement, 367,656 bytes of redo information was generated. For PL/SQL code blocks, `autotrace` does not work. For such cases, the following PL/SQL function gives you the redo generated by your session at a given point in time (note that you need to have direct `select` privileges on the views `v_$mystat` and `v_$statname` for the following code to compile):

```
benchmark@ORA10G> create or replace function get_redo_size
  2  return number
  3  as
  4    l_redo_size number;
  5  begin
  6    select value
  7    into l_redo_size
  8    from v$mystat m, v$statname s
  9    where s.name like 'redo size'
 10      and m.statistic# = s.statistic#;
 11    return l_redo_size;
 12  end;
 13  /
```

```
Function created.
```

For example, the following code snippet shows that we generated 60,092 bytes of redo at this point in time in our session:

```
benchmark@ORA10G> exec dbms_output.put_line( get_redo_size );
60092
```

To measure redo generated for any code block, you have to take a snapshot of the redo size generated before and after the code block, and subtract them to get the redo generated by the code block. For example, to find out the redo generated by the procedure `single_stmt_insert` defined earlier, we first store the current amount of redo generated in a variable:

```
benchmark@ORA10G> variable value number;
benchmark@ORA10G> exec :value := get_redo_size;
```

```
PL/SQL procedure successfully completed.
```

And execute our procedure:

```
benchmark@ORA10G> exec single_stmt_insert
```

```
PL/SQL procedure successfully completed.
```

Then we print out the redo generated by the procedure by subtracting the previously stored redo size value from the current amount of redo generated:

```
benchmark@ORA10G> exec dbms_output.put_line( 'redo consumed = ' ||
(get_redo_size - :value) );
redo consumed = 23738012
```

```
PL/SQL procedure successfully completed.
```

In general, you should choose the approach that generates the least amount of redo.

Minimizing Redo

One technique for reducing the overall amount of redo generated is to avoid committing more frequently than required by your transaction semantics. I discuss this scenario in more detail in the section "Sizing Your Transaction Resources According to Your Business Needs" in Chapter 4.

Understand SQL and PL/SQL

In the previous sections, we looked at some selected topics and examples and covered how it is important for you to understand the inner workings of Oracle. In this section, I will demonstrate why you need to have a solid grasp of SQL and PL/SQL in your quest for writing high-performance applications.

First, let's look at a straightforward logical argument. Listed here are the high-level steps a typical JDBC program goes through:

1. Obtain an Oracle connection to the database.

2. Set up resources required to execute SQL statements.

3. *Execute a set of SQL and/or PL/SQL statements.*

4. Give back (or close) resources required to execute SQL statements.

5. Give back (or close) the connection to the database.

The total time spent in your JDBC program will be the sum of the time spent in all the preceding steps. In a typical, well-written, nontrivial JDBC program, the majority of time is spent on step 3. From this simple observation, we conclude that there are two main aspects of writing a high-performance JDBC program:

- Optimal use of JDBC API (involves all the previously listed steps)

- Optimal use of SQL and/or PL/SQL code executed by the JDBC layer (involves step 3)

Even if you have written your application so that the use of the JDBC layer is optimal, if the SQL or PL/SQL code that gets invoked is poorly written, your program is bound to operate at a suboptimal (read: dog-slow in many cases) level.

However, before we explore further the topic of optimal SQL, I'd like to discuss the perhaps controversial idea that the best environment from which to execute SQL in your applications is PL/SQL, rather than Java (so in step 3 you would call a PL/SQL program to execute SQL, rather than executing SQL directly from within JDBC).

Why Use PL/SQL?

The following sections contain the arguments put forward in favor of avoiding PL/SQL, along with my counter arguments:

Using PL/SQL Locks My Application into Using Oracle

An equivalent argument is the one that promotes the idea of writing database-independent code. The idea of writing database-independent code by avoiding the use of database features, such as the use of PL/SQL, is foolhardy in my opinion because

- In the majority of cases, your code really does not need to be run against different databases. In such cases, this requirement is bogus.

- If you try to write code that is supposed to work on more than one database by avoiding database features, you would be rewriting, debugging, and maintaining code for features that are already available in the database, which can lead to skyrocketing costs in terms of developer time.

- In order for your code to perform and scale well, you have to understand and exploit features exposed in the database anyway, as you have already witnessed to a large extent in this chapter.

- In many cases, you will still end up using database-specific features unknowingly (such as the `connect` by feature in SQL written against Oracle).

- When porting code from one database to another (assuming it comes to that), you will end up rewriting most of the code anyway, because a solution that works well in the original database may well work poorly (or even incorrectly) in the second database to which your application is being ported.

Using PL/SQL Doesn't Give Me Anything That I Couldn't Get from Java

This is not true for the following reasons (among others):

- PL/SQL code can create a layer of code above which the code can truly be database-independent (in the rare case when database independence is a genuine requirement). The code within PL/SQL is free to exploit all features of Oracle. If you want to move to a different database, you need to typically just replace the implementation of the stored procedure layer with an implementation of the layer in the stored procedure language of the new database.

- The PL/SQL code can be invoked by any language that can talk to Oracle (e.g., C, C++, Perl, etc.). Thus, your central logic that deals with data is not locked into a particular layer of code written in one language or technology stack (such as Java/J2EE), which is inaccessible from other languages.

- Writing code in PL/SQL allows you to write code that exploits many of the PL/SQL features, such as

  - Benefits of static SQL caching (as discussed in the section "PL/SQL Cursor Cache" of Chapter 13)

  - Code compactness and robustness

  - Bulk bind, bulk collect, etc. (as explained in the section "Using Bulk Operations to Boost Performance" of Chapter 17)

  - Ability to write more secure code (since you only need to grant the execute privilege on the PL/SQL procedures instead of having to grant direct select, insert, and update privileges on the underlying schema to the database user)

- It is much easier to tune SQL written in PL/SQL code.

■**Note** We'll look at many more reasons to use PL/SQL extensively when writing an Oracle application in later chapters (especially Chapters 6 and 17). Also, Chapter 1 of *Mastering Oracle PL/SQL* by Connor McDonald (Apress, ISBN: 1-59059-217-4) provides useful discussion on this topic.

Use PL/SQL Effectively

Once you've decided to exploit PL/SQL in your applications, it makes sense that, as with SQL, you should understand it in enough depth to write it efficiently. The next section presents an example that shows how having good knowledge of PL/SQL can improve the performance of your code considerably.

Example: Row-by-Row Processing vs. Bulk Binding

The example in this section makes use of the *bulk binding* feature of PL/SQL to improve perform-ance of code that needs to copy data from one table to another while dealing appropriately with any bad records in the source table. Very briefly, bulk binding allows you to improve performance of inserts, updates, and deletes in a loop. With bulk binding, you insert, delete, or update tables using values from an initialized collection (such as a varray, a nested table, or associative arrays).

Say we want to copy data from the table source_table to another table, destination_table, in our JDBC program. source_table may contain some bad records, which would result in errors when we insert them into destination_table.

Let's first create and populate source_table with some data to simulate this scenario. We create a table with just the column x, which contains numbers. We assume that a zero or nega-tive number in the table represents a bad record. In the following SQL, we create source_table with numbers ranging from –10 to –1 (representing ten bad records), and from 1 to 100,000 (representing 100,000 good records):

```
benchmark@ORA10G> create table source_table
  2  as select rownum x
  3  from all_objects, all_users
  4  where rownum <= 100000
  5  --10 bad records - a negative number
  6  union all
  7  select rownum * -1
  8  from all_objects
  9  where rownum <= 10;

Table created.
```

Next, we create the destination_table table, to which the data will be copied. Note that the table has constraint checks, so that it accepts only non-negative numbers greater than 0:

```
benchmark@ORA10G> create table destination_table (
x number constraint check_nonnegative check( x > 0 ) );

Table created.
```

We create a third table, bad_records_table, where our code will insert any bad records, with the record value (the bad number) and an appropriate error message:

```
benchmark@ORA10G> create table bad_records_table (
x number, error_message varchar2(4000 ));
```

```
Table created.
```

One solution that comes to mind is to write procedural code that loops through the records of the table source_table and filters out the bad records, inserting the bad records into bad_records_table while inserting the valid records into destination_table. The following row_by_row procedure does just that. It inserts the records into destination_table, and if there is an exception raised, it inserts the appropriate information into bad_records_table:

```
benchmark@ORA10G> create or replace procedure row_by_row
  2   as
  3     cursor c is select x from source_table;
  4     l_x source_table.x%type;
  5     l_error_message long;
  6   begin
  7     open c;
  8     loop
  9       fetch c into l_x;
 10       exit when c%notfound;
 11       begin
 12         insert into destination_table(x) values( l_x );
 13       exception
 14         when others then
 15           l_error_message := sqlerrm;
 16           insert into bad_records_table( x, error_message )
 17           values( l_x, l_error_message );
 18       end;
 19     end loop;
 20     commit;
 21   end;
 22   /
```

```
Procedure created.
```

To test the code, let's execute it:

```
benchmark@ORA10G> exec row_by_row;
```

```
PL/SQL procedure successfully completed.
```

and select out records from bad_records_table:

```
benchmark@ORA10G> select * from bad_records_table;
```

```
      -1
ORA-02290: check constraint (BENCHMARK.CHECK_NONNEGATIVE) violated

      -2
<-- trimmed to save space -->
ORA-02290: check constraint (BENCHMARK.CHECK_NONNEGATIVE) violated

      -10
```

Although the procedure row_by_row does the job, it turns out that we can do much better in PL/SQL in terms of performance at the cost of a little bit more code complexity. We will use the PL/SQL feature known as bulk binding (this feature is discussed at length in the section "Using Bulk Binding" of Chapter 17; here we just focus on its impact on performance).

We first create a SQL nested table type that can store numbers:

```
benchmark@ORA10G> create or replace type number_table as table of number;
  2  /

Type created.
```

In the following bulk_bind procedure, we first collect all the records into the nested table using the bulk collect clause. We then use the forall clause to insert the records into the table destination_table. Finally, we use the save_exceptions clause to save any exceptions that may have occurred, and we insert these exceptions into bad_records_table.

```
benchmark@ORA10G> create or replace procedure bulk_bind
  2  as
  3    l_number_table number_table;
  4    l_error_message long;
  5    l_error_row_number number;
  6    l_error_code number;
  7  begin
  8    select x
  9    bulk collect into l_number_table
 10    from source_table;
 11    begin
 12      forall i in 1..l_number_table.count save exceptions
 13        insert into destination_table( x ) values( l_number_table(i) );
 14    exception
 15     when others then
 16        for j in 1..sql%bulk_exceptions.count loop
 17          l_error_row_number := sql%bulk_exceptions(j).error_index;
 18          l_error_code := sql%bulk_exceptions(j).error_code;
 19          l_error_message := sqlerrm( -1 * l_error_code );
 20          insert into bad_records_table( x, error_message )
 21          values( l_number_table(l_error_row_number),
 22              l_error_message );
 23        end loop;
 24    end;
```

```
25    commit;
26  end;
27  /
```

Procedure created.

After deleting all records from destination_table and bad_records_table, we find that the procedure does its job correctly:

```
benchmark@ORA10G> exec bulk_bind;

PL/SQL procedure successfully completed.

benchmark@ORA10G> select * from bad_records_table;

       -1
ORA-02290: check constraint (.) violated

       -2
ORA-02290: check constraint (.) violated

       -3
ORA-02290: check constraint (.) violated

<-- trimmed to save space -->
      -10
ORA-02290: check constraint (.) violated

10 rows selected.
```

■**Note** You may point out that the error message in the procedure bulk_bind is not as complete as in the case of row_by_row (the constraint name is missing). I am assuming that this is an acceptable trade-off for the performance gain achieved by using bulk bind in this example.

In my tests with JRunstats for invoking the preceding two JDBC procedures, I found that the procedure row_by_row took around *19 times* the time and consumed about *99 times* the number of latches as compared to the procedure bulk_bind. Clearly, even if we had optimized our JDBC layer, we would have written a severely suboptimal program had we not used PL/SQL efficiently in this case.

This example underlines the fact that you have to know PL/SQL well to write a high-performance JDBC application using PL/SQL (which is very common). In Chapter 6, I present strong arguments for using PL/SQL extensively in your code and using CallableStatement to invoke the PL/SQL code from your Java programs.

Use SQL Effectively

You have just seen that PL/SQL bulk binding can be more effective than processing one row at a time. However, the fact is that if an equivalent pure SQL solution exists, then there is a good chance that this solution will provide better performance still.

It's a good idea to use PL/SQL, as appropriate, in your applications, but don't use it to do the job of SQL. In the following examples, you'll learn how, with good knowledge of SQL, you can improve performance even further.

Example 1: PL/SQL Bulk Bind vs. SQL Multitable Insert

We compare two approaches in this section:

- In the first approach, we use the bulk_bind method defined in the previous section (see the example in the previous section).

- In the second approach, we use a single *multitable* insert statement to accomplish the same goal (please see section "INSERT" of *Oracle Database SQL Reference (10g Release 1)* if you are not familiar with multitable insert syntax).

As part of our SQL solution, we define a second procedure called single_sql_statement as follows:

```
benchmark@ORA10G> create or replace procedure single_sql_statement
  2  as
  3  begin
  4    insert all
  5      when ( x > 0 ) then
  6    into destination_table(x) values (x)
  7      when ( x <= 0 ) then
  8    into bad_records_table( x, error_message ) values ( x, error_message )
  9    select x, case
 10          when x > 0 then null
 11          when x <= 0 then 'invalid record: negative or zero number'
 12        end error_message
 13    from source_table;
 14    commit;
 15  end;
 16  /
Procedure created.
```

In my tests using JRunstats, on average, the SQL-based approach ran in *50%* of the time and consumed *75%* of the latches as compared to the PL/SQL bulk bind approach. In general, you will find that a SQL-based solution, if available, will almost always outperform an equivalent PL/SQL procedural solution, often by a wide margin.

■**Tip** In general, a SQL solution will outperform a PL/SQL solution. SQL is a very powerful language, and the more you master it, the more you will be able to exploit it, thereby improving the performance and scalability of your code tremendously.

Example 2: Using the Power of Analytic Functions

Let's end this section with another example that illustrates the power of SQL. We first implement a small specification in PL/SQL. Next, we improve upon our PL/SQL solution by using SQL. Finally, we further improve our SQL solution by using SQL *analytic* functions.

If you are unfamiliar with SQL analytic functions, you have been missing out on one of the greatest innovations of the Oracle SQL engine. SQL analytic functions have been available since version 8.1.6, and they have improved in functionality and features with each subsequent release.

■**Note** Analytic functions are documented in Chapter 21 of *Oracle Database Data Warehousing Guide (10g Release 1)*. Don't be misled by the fact that they are documented in the *Data Warehousing Guide* document; they are very useful in any application that uses SQL on Oracle.

Now, on to our example. Suppose the requirement of our code is as follows:

For each department, get all the employees who earn an above average or average salary for the department, and insert these records into a table called above_avg_emp. *Insert the remaining employee records into the* below_avg_emp *table.*

Let's create the schema for this scenario. We first create a table called emp in our schema and populate it with 20,000 employees (dummy data) who work in three departments (department numbers 10, 20, and 30):

```
benchmark@ORA10G> create table emp as
  2  select 'name' ||rownum as ename,
  3         (mod( rownum, 3 ) + 1)*10 as deptno,
  4         trunc(dbms_random.value(1000, 6000)) as sal
  5  from all_objects
  6  where rownum <= 20000;

Table created.

benchmark@ORA10G> select count(*), count(distinct deptno) from emp;

    20000                      3
```

```
benchmark@ORA10G> select distinct deptno from emp;

    10
    20
    30.
```

We also create two tables, above_avg_emp and below_avg_emp, which are essentially copies of table emp with no data:

```
benchmark@ORA10G> create table above_avg_emp as select * from emp where 1!=1;

Table created.

benchmark@ORA10G> create table below_avg_emp as select * from emp where 1!=1;

Table created.
```

Our requirement specification can be directly translated into a PL/SQL procedure, insert_emp_plsql, which we will define soon. First, we create an object type, dept_avg_sal, that can hold a department number and its average salary. We also create a nested table of the preceding type called dept_avg_sal_list:

```
benchmark@ORA10G> create or replace type dept_avg_sal as object
  2  (
  3    deptno number(2),
  4    avg_sal number
  5  );
  6  /

Type created.

benchmark@ORA10G> create or replace type dept_avg_sal_list as table of dept_avg_sal;
  2  /

Type created.
```

We are now ready to define our PL/SQL procedure called insert_emp_plsql, which will implement our requirements. In this procedure (defined in the following code), we first bulk collect the department-wide average salary into a variable of type dept_avg_sal_list (please see the section "Using Bulk Operations to Boost Performance" of Chapter 17 if you are not familiar with the bulk collect clause). We then loop through a join between the emp table and the nested table variable l_dept_avg_sal_list (see Chapter 8 if you are not familiar with the table clause we use), and insert the data into the appropriate table based on our requirements:

```
benchmark@ORA10G> create or replace procedure insert_emp_plsql
  2  as
  3    l_dept_avg_sal_list dept_avg_sal_list;
  4  begin
  5    -- first store the average salary
  6    select dept_avg_sal( deptno, avg(sal) )
```

```
 7     bulk collect into l_dept_avg_sal_list
 8     from emp
 9     group by deptno;
10
11     for i in ( select emp.deptno, ename, sal, t.avg_sal as avg_sal
12              from emp, table( l_dept_avg_sal_list ) t
13              where emp.deptno = t.deptno )
14     loop
15       if( i.sal >= i.avg_sal ) then
16         insert into above_avg_emp( deptno, ename, sal)
values( i.deptno, i.ename, i.sal );
17       else
18         insert into below_avg_emp( deptno, ename, sal)
values( i.deptno, i.ename, i.sal );
19       end if;
20     end loop;
21   end;
22   /
```

```
Procedure created.
```

This procedure works, but can we use our SQL knowledge to improve upon it? Yes, indeed we can (we will compare performance of all these alternatives later). We need a SQL statement that selects the department name, employee name, and salary, and a flag that indicates whether or not the employee salary is above the average salary for the department. We can then use the multitable insert technique to write a single SQL statement that does our job. We will test our SQL statement in the SCOTT schema. We will also set autotrace on to measure the LIOs incurred.

The following SQL statement uses a co-related subquery to achieve our objective (note again that we run it in the SCOTT schema). Apart from the required columns, it computes a flag called above_avg_flag, which has the value Y for employees with above average salaries, and the value N otherwise:

```
scott@ORA10G> select deptno, ename, sal, 'Y' as above_avg_flag
  2       from emp e1
  3     where e1.sal >= (select avg(sal)
  4           from emp e2
  5           where e1.deptno = e2.deptno)
  6     union all
  7     select deptno, ename, sal, 'N'
  8     from emp e1
  9     where e1.sal < (select avg(sal)
 10           from emp e2
 11           where e1.deptno = e2.deptno)
 12   order by deptno, ename, sal;
```

```
    DEPTNO ENAME             SAL ABOVE_AVG_FLAG
---------- ---------- ---------- ----------------
        10 CLARK            2450 N
        10 KING             5000 Y
        10 MILLER           1573 N
        20 ADAMS            1100 N
        20 FORD             3000 Y
        20 JONES            2975 Y
        20 SCOTT            3000 Y
        20 SMITH             800 N
        30 ALLEN            1600 Y
        30 BLAKE            2850 Y
        30 JAMES             950 N
        30 MARTIN           1350 N
        30 TURNER           1500 N
        30 WARD             1250 N

14 rows selected.

Statistics
----------------------------------------------------------
          …
          0  db block gets
         28  consistent gets
          0  physical reads
          ….
         14  rows processed
```

As you can see, the query required 28 LIOs to complete. It turns out that we can do even better if we use the SQL analytic function–based approach. The following query uses the SQL analytic function–based approach to achieve the same objective in seven LIOs (half of that used by the previous query):

```
scott@ORA10G> select deptno, ename, sal,
  2         case when sal >= avg_sal then 'Y' else 'N' end above_avg_flag
  3      from
  4      (
  5        select deptno, ename, sal, avg( sal ) over( partition by deptno ) avg_sal
  6        from emp
  7      );

    DEPTNO ENAME             SAL ABOVE_AVG_FLAG
---------- ---------- ---------- ----------------
        10 CLARK            2450 N
        10 KING             5000 Y
        10 MILLER           1573 N
        20 SMITH             800 N
        20 ADAMS            1100 N
```

```
20 FORD              3000 Y
20 SCOTT             3000 Y
20 JONES             2975 Y
30 ALLEN             1600 Y
30 BLAKE             2850 Y
30 MARTIN            1350 N
30 JAMES              950 N
30 TURNER            1500 N
30 WARD              1250 N
```

14 rows selected.

Statistics

...
          0 db block gets
          7 consistent gets
          0 physical reads
...
         14 rows processed
```

The following insert_emp_sql procedure implements our requirements using a multitable insert statement and our first SQL solution:

```
benchmark@ORA10G> create or replace procedure insert_emp_sql
  2 as
  3 begin
  4   insert
  5   when above_avg_flag = 'Y' then
  6   into above_avg_emp(deptno, ename, sal) values(deptno, ename, sal)
  7   when above_avg_flag = 'N' then
  8   into below_avg_emp(deptno, ename, sal) values(deptno, ename, sal)
  9   select deptno, ename, sal, 'Y' as above_avg_flag
 10   from emp e1
 11   where e1.sal >= (select avg(sal)
 12   from emp e2
 13   where e1.deptno = e2.deptno)
 14   union all
 15   select deptno, ename, sal, 'N'
 16   from emp e1
 17   where e1.sal < (select avg(sal)
 18   from emp e2
 19   where e1.deptno = e2.deptno);
 20 end;
 21 /

Procedure created.
```
```

The following procedure, insert_emp_sql_analytics, encapsulates our SQL analytic function–based solution in a procedure using multitable insert again:

```
benchmark@ORA10G> create or replace procedure insert_emp_sql_analytics
  2  as
  3  begin
  4    insert
  5      when sal >= avg_sal then
  6        into above_avg_emp( deptno, ename, sal) values( deptno, ename, sal)
  7      when sal < avg_sal then
  8        into below_avg_emp( deptno, ename, sal) values( deptno, ename, sal)
  9      select deptno, ename, sal, avg_sal
 10      from
 11      (
 12        select deptno, ename, sal, avg( sal ) over( partition by deptno ) avg_sal
 13        from emp
 14      );
 15  end;
 16  /

Procedure created.
```

I compared the elapsed times and latches of all three solutions (one PL/SQL-based and two SQL-based) that we discussed on the schema that we created in the benchmark schema. Table 2-1 shows the results.

Table 2-1. *Comparing the PL/SQL Solution with Two SQL Solutions (with and Without the Use of SQL Analytic Functions)*

Approach	Average Elapsed Time (Seconds)	Relative Number of Latches
PL/SQL solution in procedure insert_emp_plsql	1.87	7 times that of insert_emp_sql
SQL solution in procedure insert_emp_sql_analytics	0.23	1.5 times that of insert_emp_sql
SQL solution based on analytic function in procedure insert_emp_sql_analytics	0.17	

Once again, we see that SQL-based solutions outperformed the PL/SQL solution. Within the SQL-based solutions, we were able to further improve performance and scalability by using analytic function–based techniques. Overall, our best SQL-based solution ran in less than 10% of the time and consumed around 10% of the latches our PL/SQL solution took. These performance improvements will, of course, directly translate to performance improvements in JDBC programs that invoke them.

The examples we went through in this and the previous section have hopefully convinced you that that you need to have a solid grasp of performance improvement techniques and approaches in PL/SQL and SQL to write high-performance and scalable JDBC applications. In the next section, we will look at the importance of getting your database schema design right.

Get Your Database Schema Design Right

Like everything else, your database schema should also be designed according to your application's business needs. From a developer's point of view, the database schema typically includes tables, indexes, views, and various constraints, among other things. As a developer, you will write SQL that works against database tables. Hence, you need to understand how these tables are designed, since schema design has a direct impact on your SQL.

One of the central themes of table design is that you should design tables with prioritized performance requirements in mind from day one. Various aspects of table design include choosing the appropriate normalization level, table organization type (heap, index-organized, etc.), indexing strategy, integrity checks, constraints, and column data types for your tables. In this section, we will consider just one aspect of table design: choosing the appropriate table type based on your requirements. We will see how this single factor can significantly affect the performance of an application.

Tip I strongly urge you to read Chapter 7 of the book *Effective Oracle by Design* by Tom Kyte (Osborne McGraw-Hill, ISBN: 0-07-223065-7) for a very interesting discussion on this topic. Similarly, I suggest you read Chapters 6 and 7 of *Expert One-on-One Oracle* (Apress, ISBN: 1-59059-243-3), also by Tom Kyte, to understand how to use indexes and constraints as part of your database schema design.

Say the requirement is that of a table that will be loaded with a large amount of data once during night, but queried lots of times during the day. Furthermore, the most frequently used queries select based on the table's primary key. We have the following facts:

- Our queries (based on primary keys) should be fast (since they are used frequently).

- Somewhat slower inserts are acceptable (since data is loaded once during off-peak hours).

- It would be a bonus if we can save space on the large amount of data.

This is an ideal design scenario to try out an index-organized table structure. Normally when you create a table in Oracle, it is organized as a *heap* by default. In a heap-organized table, data is managed as a heap—that is, the inserts fill up the first available free space with no particular maintained order. The primary key of a heap table uses a separate index structure. By contrast, in an *index-organized table* (*IOT* for short), the table data is stored in the primary key index structure itself in a sorted order according to the primary key values. This has the following implications:

- In an IOT, since the data is stored sorted by the primary key, we need fewer logical I/Os compared to a heap table to get the same data for primary key–based lookups. This is because, in a heap table, typical data access by index occurs in two steps:

    1. Index access to get the ROWID.

    2. Table data access by the ROWID obtained in step 1.

In the case of an IOT, step 2 is not required, since the index and table are in the same structure.

- We require less storage in an IOT because the primary key values are stored only once in an IOT (in the index structure). In the case of a heap table, primary key values are stored as part of the table and again as part of the index structure.

- Inserts, deletes, and updates on an IOT may be slower since the data has to be inserted in the correct place in the IOT index structure.

For more details on IOTs (and all the other types of tables Oracle provides), please see the section "Overview of Tables" in *Oracle Database Concepts Guide (10g Release 1)*.

Let's compare the performance of queries on these two types of tables for our design case using `tkprof`. First, we create a heap-organized table called `heap`:

```
benchmark@ORA10G> create table heap
  2  (
  3    a varchar2(30),
  4    b varchar2(30),
  5    c varchar2(30),
  6    constraint heap_pk primary key (a, b )
  7  );

Table created.
```

Next, we create another table, `iot`, with same column information, but we create it with the organization index (as shown by the highlighted `organization` clause):

```
benchmark@ORA10G> create table iot
  2  (
  3    a varchar2(30),
  4    b varchar2(30),
  5    c varchar2(30),
  6    constraint iot_pk primary key (a, b )
  7  )
  8  organization index;

Table created.
```

We then create the procedures `insert_heap` and `insert_iot` to insert data into the heap and the IOT tables, respectively:

```
benchmark@ORA10G> create or replace procedure insert_heap
  2  is
  5  begin
  6    for i in 1 .. 100 loop
  7      for j in 1 .. 1000 loop
  8        insert into heap values ( 'a'||i, 'a'||i||j, 'cccc' );
  9      end loop;
 10    end loop;
```

```
11    commit;
12  end;
13  /
```

Procedure created.

```
benchmark@ORA10G> create or replace procedure insert_iot
  2  is
  3  begin
  4    for i in 1 .. 100 loop
  5      for j in 1 .. 1000 loop
  6        insert into iot values ( 'a'||i, 'a'||i||j, 'cccc' );
  7      end loop;
  8    end loop;
  9    commit;
 10  end;
 11  /
```

Procedure created.

Finally, we create the procedures select_heap and select_iot:

```
benchmark@ORA10G> create or replace procedure select_heap
  2  is
  3    l_a heap.a%type;
  4  begin
  5    for i in 1 .. 100 loop
  6      l_a := 'a'||i;
  7      for x in (select * from heap where a=l_a) loop
  8        null;
  9      end loop;
 10    end loop;
 11  end;
 12  /
```

Procedure created.

```
benchmark@ORA10G> create or replace procedure select_iot
  2  is
  3    l_a iot.a%type;
  4  begin
  5    for i in 1 .. 100 loop
  6      l_a := 'a'||i;
  7      for x in (select * from iot where a=l_a) loop
  8        null;
  9      end loop;
 10    end loop;
 11  end;
 12  /
```

Procedure created.

We now populate both tables by invoking the procedures insert_heap and insert_iot:

```
benchmark@ORA10G> show errors;
No errors.
benchmark@ORA10G>
benchmark@ORA10G> begin
  2      insert_heap;
  3      insert_iot;
  4   end;
  5   /

PL/SQL procedure successfully completed.
```

I compared invocation of select_heap and select_iot from a JDBC program using JRun-stats. In my benchmark runs, the heap table–based solution took almost *twice the amount of time* and, more important perhaps, consumed more than *five times the latches* as compared to the IOT-based solution. We can further improve our IOT solution by using the compress option available in IOT to reduce space consumption (I leave this as an exercise for the reader).

In this section we demonstrated how a single aspect of database table design, when combined with our knowledge of the different database types offered by Oracle, allowed us to significantly improve our application's performance.

This chapter concludes by summarizing some general guidelines for writing high-performance code in the next section.

General Guidelines for Writing High-Performance Code

Up to now, we have discussed the need to write application code that performs well and does not make the database do unnecessary work. We have also seen how a solid grasp of PL/SQL and SQL will help you succeed in your quest to write high-performance applications. In this section, we will look at some general guidelines for achieving high performance in your applications.

Know the Features Offered by Oracle

Time and again, I have seen that developers don't take enough time to gain knowledge about the features offered by Oracle. This proves very costly as we reinvent the wheel by rewriting what has already been written by Oracle for us. In the past, I myself have been guilty of this.

For example, in one of the systems I worked on, I needed to maintain a history of changes to records in a set of tables. It took my team about a man-month to write procedural code for this purpose before we realized that there is a feature called Workspace Management in Oracle that will do this for us already (see *Oracle Application Developer's Guide – Workspace Manager [10g Release 1]* for more details). I was able to write pretty much the same code in half a day using the Workspace Management feature! Had I known about this feature earlier, I could have potentially saved the team at least that one man-month's worth of effort (assuming that the restrictions that this feature imposed were acceptable to our system).

I have seen people routinely coding for features that are part of the Oracle database offering. Some common examples are

- Coding referential integrity in the application instead of using database features such as foreign keys

- Not using materialized views when applicable

- Creating query joins in the application layer (a very bad idea indeed)

People recode features already available in Oracle for one or more of the following reasons:

- *Unawareness of these features*: This can be avoided by actively learning about Oracle. See Appendix B for a list of resources I recommend strongly. You can also learn a lot by attending conferences, joining Oracle user groups in your area, and reading the articles at `http://otn.oracle.com`.

- *Fear of new features*: Some people are wary of a new feature from a release-stability point of view. However, it's still worth reading up on and learning about new features and using them actively; otherwise, you'll continue to write the same code. (And don't forget that you may also introduce your own bugs.) In general, if you're about to write an application feature that seems like something that might already be present in Oracle, do some research on what Oracle offers before you jump in and start coding.

- *"Attitude problem" (i.e., the mistaken belief that you could do a better job than Oracle)*: My philosophy is to trust the database to do its job well. If you reinvent code already written by Oracle, you'll inevitably spend lots of effort in writing code that performs terribly, is incorrect, and is hard to maintain. The time and effort you spend in learning a new Oracle feature will pay off many times over later on.

Design to Optimize the Most Important Business Functions First

Performance is all about making conscious trade-offs between various resources such as development time, hardware and software resources, customer requirements, etc. You should design in a way that the most important business needs of a user are given the highest priority in terms of meeting performance expectations. An excellent book that discusses this theme in great detail is Cary Millsap's *Optimizing Oracle Performance* (O'Reilly, ISBN: 0-596-00527-X).

■**Tip** Design in a way that the most important business needs of a user are given the highest priority in terms of meeting performance expectations.

Incorporate Performance from Day One

Many developers start the tuning process toward the end of the development cycle—or worse still, after deployment! This approach is a recipe for disaster, especially if you have overlooked the scalability aspect of performance in your design. The following are some reasons why you should consider performance from day one.

- Performance is part of your end user's requirements; it is an important feature that the user demands (implicitly or explicitly). For an end user, bad performance implies that you have not delivered the desired functionality or that your code is buggy.

- Fixing something in the performance area as an afterthought can lead to expensive code rewrites, customer dissatisfaction and, many times, a failed project.

- Considering performance early in the process gives you a better idea of various trade-offs and choices that you can present to the user, who can then make informed decisions.

Instrument Your Code Extensively

The process of writing the code so that you can find out (by messages emitted by the code in an output stream such as a file or screen) what the code does at any point of time is called *instrumentation*. Instrumenting your code is critical for you to be able to diagnose performance (and even nonperformance) problems in your code during development and after deployment. Effectively instrumenting your code gives the following benefits:

- It enables faster development since you identify logical errors and performance bottlenecks much more easily and early on based on diagnostic outputs.

- It enables you to debug any performance issues much faster and more efficiently, even after deployment. This increases the supportability of your product and saves tremendously on overall resources.

An example of the power of instrumentation is the Oracle kernel. You can enable it to emit extremely useful information in a trace file during a diagnostic session. You can then use utilities such as tkprof to format these trace files and analyze them. Trace file–based diagnosis is one of the most powerful features used by performance analysts today. It would be *impossible* to tune an Oracle-based system without the trace file generation feature.

Note that your instrumentation code should be designed in such a way that it is possible to turn it on and off at will. This way, the users don't pay a performance penalty during normal business operations, and the code is right there when you need it to diagnose a problem later. Recall that the Oracle kernel instrumentation also needs to be turned on specifically to emit information in the trace files. In the section "Seamless Instrumentation of PL/SQL and JDBC Code" of Chapter 17, you will learn about a powerful PL/SQL and JDBC instrumentation technique.

Test for Performance

There are two types of performance tests that form the core of the strategy of writing high-performance applications:

- Testing code in isolation using utilities such as JRunstats for scientifically proving which approach out of a set of approaches is suitable for your system. You have already seen how useful this test harness is in some of the previous examples.

- A suite of tests for systemwide testing that enables the following:

  - A way to load the system with typical representative data sets. The data loading logic should be maintained and enhanced as you learn more about the system later on. The code that does this should also be an inherent part of the rest of your checked-in source code.

  - A set of tests that test out the performance of the most important business functions of your end user.

  - A way to preserve the systemwide performance data in the test and production systems. This enables you to compare your current code with how it did in the past, and to identify new performance bottlenecks as soon as they are introduced in the system. One way to do this for an Oracle-based system is to use the statspack utility (in 10*g*, the feature Automatic Workload Repository has replaced statspack; see *Oracle Database Performance Tuning Guide and Reference [10*g* Release 1]* for more details).

Elapsed Time Is Less Than Half the Story

You have already seen this principle in action in previous sections. If approach 1 works 10% faster than approach 2 in a single-user environment, but it consumes 100% more resources (in terms of latches, etc.), then approach 2 is much more likely to be suitable for a multiuser environment. In this book, we will always consider scalability of an approach as well as the response time before coming to a conclusion on which approach is better. We will use the runstats utility and its Java version, JRunstats, for this purpose throughout the book.

Beware of Universal Truths

Perhaps the only universal truth when it comes to performance guidelines is that there are no universal truths! A sound approach in one situation often turns out to be a lousy one in another. The only sane approach is to know the tools at your disposal, know how to use them, and benchmark to prove that your approach is the appropriate one in your particular case. Beware of guidelines that tell you to "always" take an approach, because more often than not there will be situations when that approach will not be the best one at hand (and it could easily be the worst one!).

For example, take the guideline that says, "Always use bind variables." It is true that in the majority of systems, this guideline holds true. However, if you are writing a data warehouse system, using bind variables may not be a good approach. This is because, in a data warehouse system, the execution time of queries is much higher than the parsing time, and the number of queries executed by the system per second is very small. In this case, it may make sense not to use bind variables so that the Oracle query optimizer gets more information to arrive at a better query plan based on the input data.

Summary

In this chapter, you looked at some examples that demonstrate why it is critical for an Oracle application developer to know about Oracle's features and the Oracle architecture. You learned some important Oracle concepts, such as multiversion read consistency, undo, redo, and so on, that should whet your appetite and motivate you to learn more about Oracle. You also learned why mastering SQL and PL/SQL is crucial in achieving your goal of being an effective JDBC programmer. You may need to put in some additional effort to learn more about the concepts touched on in this chapter from the many references I gave throughout. In the next chapter, you will consider the JDBC API and write your first JDBC program.

CHAPTER 3

■ ■ ■

Introduction to JDBC

This chapter discusses the fundamentals of JDBC. It provides an overview of the JDBC interface and explains the different types of JDBC drivers that implement JDBC API and how to choose between these drivers.

The chapter largely focuses on writing JDBC connection code, both using the old-style `DriverManager`, and the more elegant and flexible technique that employs data sources and, optionally, the Java Naming and Directory Interface (JNDI).

The chapter wraps up by demonstrating a fully working JDBC program that executes a query against an Oracle database and prints out the query results. This program uses some of the key JDBC interfaces (`Statement`, `ResultSet`, etc.) that we will investigate fully in subsequent chapters.

What Is JDBC?

JDBC is a standard *Application Programming Interface* (API) in Java you use to access a relational database. The API itself was developed by Sun Microsystems.

■**Note** Officially, JDBC is a trademarked name and not an abbreviation, but for all intents and purposes we can assume it is shorthand for *Java Database Connectivity*.

Various relational database vendors such as Oracle Corporation, Sybase Inc., and so on provide the underlying JDBC drivers that implement the standard JDBC API, and offer vendor-specific extensions. The standard JDBC API consists of two packages:

- `java.sql`: This package contains the core JDBC API to access and manipulate information stored in a database.

- `javax.sql`: This package contains APIs for accessing server-side data sources from JDBC clients.

Oracle's core JDBC implementation lies in the following two packages:

- `oracle.jdbc`: This package implements and extends functionality provided by the `java.sql` and `javax.sql` interfaces (e.g., `OraclePreparedStatement` and `OracleCallableStatement`)..

- `oracle.sql`: This package contains classes and interfaces that provide Java mappings to SQL data types (e.g., `OracleTypes`).

You can browse through the standard JDBC packages on the `http://java.sun.com` site. Currently, the exact URL is `http://java.sun.com/j2se/1.4.2/docs/api/index.html` (this may change in the future).

JDBC Driver Types

A *JDBC driver* is the code that implements the JDBC API. Many vendors supply implementations of JDBC drivers (obviously, we will use the ones supplied by Oracle in this book). JDBC driver implementations are categorized into following four types:

- *Type 1* drivers implement the JDBC API as a mapping to another data access API, such as ODBC. These drivers are generally dependent on a native client library, which limits their portability. Sun's JDBC-ODBC Bridge driver is an example of a Type 1 driver. This driver has many limitations, including limited support for JDBC 3.0 and the fact that it is not multithreaded.

- *Type 2* drivers are written partly in the Java programming language and partly in native code. These drivers require a native client library specific to the data source to which they connect and are therefore often referred to as *thick* drivers. Again, due to the native code, their portability is limited.

- *Type 3* drivers use a pure Java client and communicate with a middleware server using a database-independent protocol. The middleware server then translates the client's requests to the data source using the database-dependent protocol.

- *Type 4* drivers are implemented completely in Java (hence, they are platform independent). They communicate directly with the data source using a standard Java socket and require no extra client-side software. They are commonly referred to as *thin* drivers.

Oracle JDBC Drivers

Oracle currently provides four JDBC drivers, two client-side and two server-side:

- *Client side*: JDBC thin driver (Type 4) and JDBC OCI driver (Type 2)

- *Server side*: JDBC server-side thin driver (Type 4) and JDBC server-side internal driver (Type 2)

The client-side drivers are used for JDBC code running *outside* the database (e.g., in an application, an applet, a servlet, etc.), and the server-side drivers are for JDBC code running *inside* the database.

The 10*g* Release 1 JDBC drivers can access Oracle 8.1.7 and higher version of database. While all Oracle JDBC drivers are similar, some features apply only to JDBC OCI drivers and some apply only to the JDBC thin driver.

Besides implementing all the interfaces in the JDBC standard `java.sql` package, all four drivers implement Oracle's own extensions in the `oracle.jdbc` package. The following sections detail each of the Oracle driver types and help you choose an appropriate driver for your application.

JDBC Thin Driver

Oracle's JDBC thin driver is used for accessing a database from a Java program running on an application or an applet. This driver is written 100% in Java and hence is platform independent. It does not require any additional Oracle software on the client (i.e., the machine from which you run your JDBC program). This driver supports only TCP/IP-based communication. This means that this driver requires the server to be configured with a TCP/IP listener.

JDBC OCI Driver

Oracle's JDBC OCI driver (also known as the *thick driver*) is meant for accessing a database from an application (i.e., not an applet). OCI stands for *Oracle Call Interface*, an API that allows you to access and manipulate data in the Oracle database server using a third-generation language (3GL) such as C/C++. The JDBC OCI driver is a wrapper around the OCI layer and is Oracle platform–specific since it requires the OCI C libraries, Oracle Net libraries, CORE libraries, and other necessary files to be present on the client machine on which the JDBC program runs.

Until 9*i* Release 2, this driver required the entire Oracle client installation to be present on the machine on which the JDBC program using this driver runs. Starting with 10*g*, there is an option called Instant Client that simplifies the use of this driver by significantly reducing the number of files it requires on the client machine. The OCI driver supports all installed Oracle Net adapters, including IPC, named pipes, and TCP/IP.

JDBC Server-Side Thin Driver

The JDBC server-side thin driver is the same as JDBC thin driver, except it runs inside a database server. It can also be used to access a remote database server or a different database session from within the database it runs on. The code written for a JDBC thin driver is the same as that for a JDBC server-side thin driver for a given application.

JDBC Server-Side Internal Driver

The JDBC server-side internal driver supports code running inside the database such as in Java stored procedures. Since it runs in the same process space as the database, SQL calls executed from code using the JDBC server-side internal driver do not incur any network round-trip overhead.

Choosing the Right Driver

You should consider the following factors before choosing a JDBC driver for your application:

- If your code runs inside the Oracle database that acts as a middle tier (implying it accesses other remote databases), then you could use the JDBC server-side thin driver. Note that you should also consider other database features such as using database links as an alternative when dealing with such a scenario (for more details on database links, see the "Database Links" section of the chapter titled "Distributed Database Concept" in the *Oracle Database Administrator's Guide [10g Release 1]* document).

- If your code runs inside the Oracle database server and accesses only that server, then you should use the JDBC server-side internal driver.

- If you want to use JDBC in applets, the JDBC thin driver is your only option.

- If you are using any of the following features specific to the JDBC OCI driver (as of Oracle 10g Release 1), you need to use the JDBC OCI driver:

  - You want to connect to Oracle using a network protocol other than TCP/IP.

  - You want to use OCI connection pooling (see the section "OCI Connection Pooling" of Chapter 14 for more information).

  - You want to use Transparent Application Failover (TAF), which is relevant if you are using the Oracle Real Application Cluster (RAC) technology. We don't cover RAC-specific features in this book (see the chapter titled "OCI Driver Transparent Application Failover" of *Oracle Database JDBC Developer's Guide and Reference [10g Release 1]*).

  - You want to use the `HeteroRM XA` feature related to distributed transactions (i.e., transactions that span multiple databases). We don't cover distributed transactions in this book (see the chapter titled "Distributed Transactions" of *Oracle Database JDBC Developer's Guide and Reference [10g Release 1]*).

  - You want to use third-party authentication features supported by Oracle Advanced Security, such as those provided by RADIUS, Kerberos, or SecureID (see *Oracle Advanced Security Administrator's Guide [10g Release 1]*).

- If you have many clients from which your JDBC program would be accessing the Oracle database, you should use the JDBC thin driver. This is because you won't need to install or maintain any additional client-side software (required by the JDBC OCI driver) on each of the client machines, thus saving you from the associated administrative hassles. Please note that starting with 10g, you no longer need to install the entire Oracle client software—the special installation option OCI Instant Client lets you download only files relevant for programming with OCI drivers.

- If portability across platforms is important for your application, use the JDBC thin driver, since it is written in 100% Java.

- If you are using JDBC in your server code (e.g., the code running in your middle tier hosted on an application server), then the JDBC OCI driver may be a better choice in some cases because of its extra features and slight edge in performance (see the next point). The downside associated with the JDBC OCI driver of having to maintain additional software may be mitigated in this case by the fact that the number of middle-tier machines is usually small.

- Performance-wise, the JDBC thin driver has been catching up with the JDBC OCI driver over the years. Before 9*i*, the OCI driver used to be considerably faster than the thin driver in many cases. In 9*i* and 10g, most of the time the performance between the two drivers is comparable. Thus, performance may no longer be an important criterion when choosing a driver.

Note that the feature list specific to the JDBC OCI and thin drivers changes from release to release, and you should consult the Oracle JDBC documentation to find this information for your particular Oracle database and driver release. A comprehensive list of such features is available at `http://www.oracle.com/technology/tech/java/sqlj_jdbc/htdocs/jdbc_faq.htm`. In any case, it is easy to switch between the two drivers (and you should be ready to do so) since, barring the centralized code to connect to the database and the code that uses a driver-specific feature, the majority of the JDBC code in a typical application is independent of the driver you choose. In this book, most examples will use the JDBC thin driver simply because it requires less software to set up.

Software Requirements and Setup Instructions

All code examples in this book have been tested against Oracle Database 10g Enterprise Edition Release 10.1.0.2.0. The examples should also run successfully on all platforms supported by Oracle running the same or higher versions of Oracle software. Unless otherwise stated, these examples have also been tested successfully against Oracle9*i* Enterprise Edition Release 9.2.0.1.0. Examples using Oracle 10g–specific features will be highlighted as we encounter them.

■Note At the time of this writing, you can download 10g Oracle software from `http://www.oracle.com/technology/software/products/database/oracle10g/index.html`. The link may change, but the download should be easy enough to locate from Oracle's home page (`http://www.oracle.com`). Be sure to review the licensing terms carefully before downloading and using the software.

This section covers the setup instructions for the JDBC thin and OCI drivers, as we use these drivers in this book. If you do need to use the JDBC server-side internal and server-side thin drivers, note that no separate classes files are available or needed since both of these drivers run only in the Oracle Server JVM and their classes are installed as part of installing the JVM.

> **■Tip** For more information on the different files used by the different JDBC drivers, please see the official Oracle JDBC FAQ at `http://www.oracle.com/technology/tech/java/sqlj_jdbc/htdocs/jdbc_faq.htm`.

You will also need JDK 1.4 installed on your machine. The book's examples have been run using Sun's JDK 1.4.2, which you can download from `http://java.sun.com`.

JDBC Thin Driver on UNIX

Assuming you have installed 10*g* Release 1 (or 9*i* Release 2) and Sun's JDK 1.4.2, Table 3-1 shows how to set the required environment variables for running examples in this book based on the JDBC thin driver on a UNIX machine (e.g., Solaris or Linux).

Table 3-1. *Environment Variables for JDBC Thin Driver Applications on Oracle 10*g *and* 9i *Release 2 on UNIX (Solaris, Linux, Etc.)*

Environment Variable	Oracle 10*g* (10.1.0.2.0)	Oracle9*i* Release 2 (9.2.0.1.0)

CLASSPATH	`.:$ORACLE_HOME/jdbc/lib/`
	`ojdbc14.jar:$ORACLE_HOME/`
	`jdbc/lib/orai18n.jar`
		`.:$ORACLE_HOME/jdbc/lib/`
		`ojdbc14.jar:$ORACLE_HOME/`
		`jdbc/lib/nls_charset12.jar`

PATH	`$ORACLE_HOME/bin:$JAVA_HOME/bin`	`$ORACLE_HOME/bin:$JAVA_HOME/bin`

Please note the following:

- The environment variable JAVA_HOME points to your JDK 1.4 installation directory.

- You don't need to have ORACLE_HOME or ORACLE_SID environment variables set to use the thin driver; your code just needs the correct JAR files in your CLASSPATH.

- The JAR files ojdbc14.jar and classes12.jar represent the same classes, except that ojdbc14.jar contains only those classes compatible with JDK 1.4. Oracle JDBC class files are now named ojdcbXX.jar, where XX is the Java version number. Note that this naming convention does not apply to the classes12 files. Also, Oracle will not provide ZIP files version of classes12 files (i.e., classes12.zip) for Java 1.4 and beyond.

- The JAR file nls_charset12.jar for the 9*i* database contains classes to support all Oracle character sets in Advanced Data Types (objects) when using a Java 1.4 (or Java 1.2 or Java 1.3 VM). If the database character set is one other than US7ASCII, W8DEC, or ShiftJIS, and the application uses objects, then you must include this class in your CLASSPATH. Note that this JAR file is replaced in 10*g* by the file orai18n.jar.

- The CLASSPATH has the present working directory represented by a period (.).

- In addition to the previously mentioned JAR files, you may need to add the JAR file corresponding to this book's code in your CLASSPATH if you are using any of the examples or generic utilities written as part of this book's code. The code is available from the Downloads area of the Apress website (http://www.apress.com).

- Additional JAR files may be required in your CLASSPATH for certain functionalities. Such information will be provided as and when required.

JDBC Thin Driver on Windows

Table 3-2 shows how to set the required environment variables for running the JDBC thin driver examples in this book on a Windows machine.

Table 3-2. *Environment Variables for JDBC Thin Driver Applications on Oracle 10*g *and 9*i *Release 2 on Windows*

Environment Variable	Oracle 10*g* (10.1.0.2.0)	Oracle9*i* Release 2 (9.2.0.1.0)
CLASSPATH	.;%ORACLE_HOME%\jdbc\lib\ ojdbc14.jar;%ORACLE_HOME%\ jdbc\lib\orai18n.jar	.;%ORACLE_HOME%\jdbc\lib\ ojdbc14.jar;%ORACLE_HOME%\ jdbc\lib\nls_charset12.jar
PATH	%ORACLE_HOME%\bin;%JAVA_HOME%\bin	%ORACLE_HOME%\bin;%JAVA_HOME%\bin

Note that the environment requirements for JDBC programs using thin drivers on Windows are essentially the same as that on UNIX (as explained in the previous section), except for how the Windows variables are specified. In particular, note that the separator between different directories is a semicolon (;) in Windows; in UNIX it is a colon (:).

JDBC OCI Driver on UNIX and Windows (10*g* Only)

For 10*g* JDBC OCI driver–based examples, we will set up the environment using the new Instant Client option (see Chapter 20 of *Oracle Database JDBC Developer's Guide and Reference [10*g* Release 1]*). Table 3-3 shows the files we need for this purpose. These files can be downloaded from http://www.oracle.com/technology/tech/oci/instantclient/instantclient.html.

Table 3-3. *Additional Files Required to Set Up the OCI Instant Client for 10*g *to Use the JDBC OCI Driver**

UNIX	Windows	Description
libclntsh.so.10.1	oci.dll	Client code library
libociei.so	oraociei10.dll	OCI Instant Client data shared library
libnnz10.so	orannzsbb10.dll	Security library
libocijdbc10.so	oraocijdbc10.dll	OCI Instant Client JDBC library

* Table information from Oracle Database JDBC Developer's Guide and Reference (10*g* Release 1).

You can set up the Instant Client as follows:

1. Create a directory called `ociclient` in a convenient place.

2. Put all the files listed in Table 3-3 (and available as part of the Instant Client installation) in the `ociclient` directory.

3. On UNIX, set the environment variable `LD_LIBRARY_PATH` to the directory `ociclient` you created in step 1. On Windows, set the environment variable `PATH` to include the `ociclient` directory.

4. You also need to set `NLS_LANG` to the appropriate National Language Support (NLS) language setting for using the OCI driver. For example, in my case I set it to `AMERICAN`. If you are not sure which setting to use, you can query `NLS_LANG` from your database as follows:

```
scott@ORA10G> select * from nls_session_parameters
where parameter='NLS_LANGUAGE
';

PARAMETER                        VALUE
-----------------------------    --------------
NLS_LANGUAGE                     AMERICAN
```

5. As a reminder, you also need to set the environment variables defined earlier in Table 3-1 (for UNIX) and Table 3-2 (for Windows).

JDBC OCI Driver on UNIX and Windows (9*i*)

To run the OCI examples in 9*i* Release 2, you need to install Oracle client software on your machine. Please see the Oracle client installation details in *Oracle Database Installation Guide Release 2 (9.2.0.1.0)* for more details. After installing the Oracle client software, you need to do the following:

- On UNIX (Solaris/Linux), add the directory `$ORACLE_HOME/lib` to your `LD_LIBRARY_PATH` environment variable.

- On Windows, add the directory `%ORACLE_HOME%\lib` to your `PATH` environment variable.

Let's now go through an overview of the JDBC API.

Overview of JDBC API

This section provides a brief overview of the JDBC API, which consists mainly of interfaces that are implemented by the JDBC drivers. Figure 3-1 shows the main interfaces and classes in the `java.sql`, `oracle.jdbc`, and `oracle.sql` packages. Interfaces in the figure are shown in italics, and classes are displayed in bold. For each standard interface, the Oracle extension of the same interface is shown in brackets.

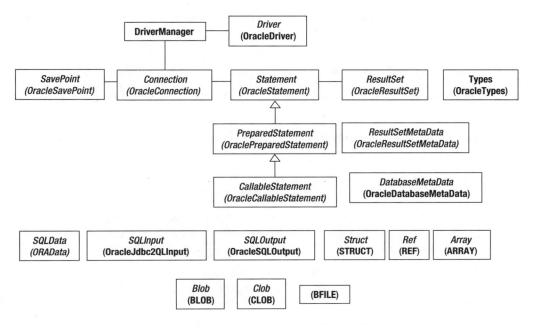

Figure 3-1. *List of the main JDBC interfaces and classes in the* `java.sql`, `oracle.jdbc`, *and* `oracle.sql` *packages*

Following is a brief description of the main JDBC interfaces and classes in the `java.sql` package, along with their Oracle extension in the `oracle.jdbc` package (Oracle extension interfaces and classes are shown in parentheses, while all classes are shown in bold):

- `Connection` (`OracleConnection`): This interface encapsulates a connection (or session) with a specific database. A JDBC program executes all SQL statements within the context of a connection (introduced in this chapter and discussed in later chapters whenever we use different methods in this interface related to the topic under discussion).

- `Savepoint` (`OracleSavepoint`): This interface represents a savepoint within a transaction to which the transaction can be rolled back (discussed in Chapter 4).

- `Statement` (`OracleStatement`): This interface allows you to execute SQL statements (including stored procedures) without using bind variables. You should avoid using this interface since it does not support bind variables (discussed in Chapter 5).

- `PreparedStatement` (`OraclePreparedStatement`): This extends the `Statement` interface to add methods that allow you to execute SQL statements using bind variables (discussed in Chapter 5).

- `CallableStatement` (`OracleCallableStatement`): This extends the `PreparedStatement` interface to add methods that allow you to execute and retrieve data from stored procedures (discussed in Chapter 6).

- ResultSet (OracleResultSet): This encapsulates results returned by a query (discussed in this chapter and Chapter 7).

- ResultSetMetaData (**OracleResultSetMetaData**): This encapsulates information about the types and properties of the columns in a ResultSet object (discussed in Chapter 7).

- DatabaseMetaData (OracleDatabaseMetaData): This encapsulates information about the database as a whole (discussed in Chapter 7).

- **Types** (**oracle.sql.OracleTypes**): This defines constants for SQL data types (discussed as and when required in this book).

- SQLData (oracle.sql.ORAData): This interface is used for the custom mapping of a SQL user-defined type (UDT) or object type to a class in Java (discussed in Chapter 10).

- SQLInput (**oracle.sql.OracleJdbc2SQLInput**): This interface encapsulates an input stream that contains values representing an instance of a SQL structured type (discussed in Chapter 10).

- SQLOutput (**oracle.sql.OracleSQLOutput**): This interface encapsulates the output stream for writing the attributes of a UDT (or object types) back to the database (discussed in Chapter 10).

- Struct (**oracle.sql.STRUCT**): This interface encapsulates standard mapping in Java for a SQL structured type (discussed in Chapter 9).

- Ref (**oracle.sql.REF**): This interface encapsulates mapping in Java of a SQL REF value, which is a reference to a SQL structured type value in the database (discussed in Chapter 11).

- Array (**oracle.sql.ARRAY**): This interface encapsulates mapping in Java for the SQL type ARRAY (discussed in Chapter 11).

- Blob (**oracle.sql.BLOB**): This interface encapsulates mapping in Java for the SQL type BLOB (discussed in Chapter 12).

- Clob (**oracle.sql.CLOB**): This interface encapsulates mapping in Java for the SQL type CLOB (discussed in Chapter 12).

- BFILE (**oracle.sql.BFILE**): This class represents the Oracle-specific data type BFILE (discussed in Chapter 12). There is no corresponding class or interface in the standard JDBC API at the time of this writing.

Not shown in Figure 3-1 are the classes in the package javax.sql, of which the following are the main classes:

- javax.sql.DataSource (**oracle.jdbc.pool.OracleDataSource**): This interface encapsulates a set of methods to connect to a data source (discussed in this chapter and in Chapter 14).

- `javax.sql.RowSet` (**oracle.jdbc.rowset.OracleRowSet**): This interface adds support to a JavaBeans-style interface for the JDBC API. (This topic is not covered in this book; see the chapter titled "Row Set" in *Oracle Database JDBC Developer's Guide and Reference [10g Release 1]*).

Now that we have gone through an overview of the JDBC API, let's move on to discuss how to perform the first step in a JDBC program: establishing a connection to the database.

Connecting to a Database

Before we write our first JDBC program, we need to understand how to connect to a database. To connect to a database, an application may use either of the following:

- The `DriverManager` class working with one or more `Driver` interface implementations

- A `DataSource` implementation optionally using the JNDI naming service

Using the `DataSource` method is preferred over the method using the `DriverManager` class for the following reasons:

- Using `DataSource` makes it possible for an application to transparently make use of connection pooling and distributed transactions. You'll learn how connection pooling is vital for your application's scalability and performance in Chapter 14.

- In the future, Sun Microsystems may deprecate `DriverManager` and its related classes.

- Using the `DataSource` method enhances application portability over different databases, assuming your application needs to be designed with this requirement in mind. This is because the JDBC programmer doesn't need to specify any vendor-specific driver class names in the code. This is more of a convenience than a major advantage since even in the case of using `DriverManager`, you can achieve this by using property files containing driver class names that are loaded dynamically in your Java code. Besides, the logic of obtaining a connection to a database should be designed as a centralized piece of code and hence should be relatively easy to modify when required.

- Using `DataSource` with JNDI can improve the maintenance of your code since your application obtains a connection through a logical name—the physical implementation encapsulated by the `DataSource` is hidden and can be changed dynamically at runtime. Again, in the old-fashioned `DriverManager`, this can be achieved using property files.

You are likely to encounter the `DriverManager` approach in the code you read for some time in the future, so we'll examine that approach first, and then we'll move on to cover the new recommended way of connecting using a `DataSource`.

Using DriverManager

To connect to the Oracle database using this technique, follow these steps:

1. Import the required classes.

2. Register the appropriate JDBC driver. This causes the driver class to be loaded into the JVM.

3. Formulate the database URL to which you will connect.

4. Establish the connection.

The following sections describe these four steps in turn, in the creation of the JDBCOldStyleConnection Java class that is used to connect to the Oracle database. Also covered are potential errors when compiling or executing the JDBCOldStyleConnection Java class.

Importing Classes

The first step in the creation of the JDBCOldStyleConnection class is to import the appropriate Java classes before the main() method declaration:

```
/* This class demonstrates how to connect to a database using DriverManager.
 * COMPATIBLITY NOTE: tested against 10.1.0.2.0. and 9.2.0.1.0 */
import java.sql.Connection;
import java.sql.DriverManager;
import java.sql.SQLException;
import oracle.jdbc.OracleDriver;

class JDBCOldStyleConnection
{
  public static void main (String args[])
  {
```

■**Note** I recommend that you avoid using the code syntax import java.sql.*. Instead, always explicitly import each class the code depends on. Explicitly importing packages makes your dependencies completely clear, and it also helps avoid ambiguities that come from two classes with the same name in different packages.

Registering the JDBC Driver (Thin or OCI)

This step registers the JDBC driver that we'll use and causes the JVM to load the driver in memory. We need to perform this step only once in our program. Continuing with the class JDBCOldStyleConnection, the following code loads and registers the driver by calling the registerDriver method of the DriverManager class:

```
try
{
  DriverManager.registerDriver( new OracleDriver());
}
catch (SQLException e)
{
  // handle the exception properly - in this case, we just
  // print a message and stack trace and exit the application
  System.err.println ("ERROR: Could not register the driver! Exiting .." );
  e.printStackTrace();
  Runtime.getRuntime().exit(1);
}
```

Alternatively, we can use the forName() method of the java.lang.Class class to load the JDBC drivers as well, for example:

```
Class.forName ("oracle.jdbc.OracleDriver").newInstance();.
```

Formulating a Database URL and Establishing a Connection

A database URL is a string that defines the address of the Oracle database to which you wish to connect (using JDBC in our case). It is of the following form:

jdbc:oracle:driver_type:@database

where

- driver_type specifies the type of JDBC driver to use for the connection. The following options exist:

    - oci is for the Oracle9*i* and 10*g* OCI driver.

    - thin is for the Oracle thin driver.

    - kprb is for the Oracle internal driver.

- database specifies the address of the database to which to connect. The following options exist:

    - host:port:sid: This option works for the thin and OCI drivers. Here, host is the host name or IP address of the database server, port is the port number of the Oracle listener, and sid is the Oracle system identifier or Oracle service name of the database (discussed shortly).

    - *Net service name*: This is only used for the OCI driver. It is a tnsnames.ora file entry that resolves to a connect descriptor (discussed shortly).

    - *Connect descriptor*: This is only used for the OCI or thin driver. This is the Net8 address specification (discussed shortly).

Please note the following:

- SID is an Oracle term that stands for *system identifier*. The SID, represented by the environment variable `ORACLE_SID` combined with the directory pointed to by the environment variable `ORACLE_HOME` and the host name, uniquely identifies an Oracle instance.

- `tnsnames.ora` is a configuration file that contains net service names mapped to connect descriptors for the local naming method, or net service names mapped to listener protocol addresses.

- A *net service name* is an alias mapped to a database network address contained in a connect descriptor.

- A *connect descriptor* contains the location of the listener through a protocol address and the service name of the database to which to connect. Simply put, it has information to completely identify a database instance. Clients and database servers (that are clients of other database servers) use the net service name when making a connection to the database. By default, the `tnsnames.ora` file is located in the `$ORACLE_HOME/network/admin` directory on UNIX and in the `%ORACLE_HOME%\network\admin` directory on Windows. It may also be stored in the directory pointed to by the `TNS_ADMIN` environment variable on UNIX or Windows.

■**Note** For more information on the topics discussed in this section, please see *Oracle Database Net Services Administrator's Guide (10*g *Release 1).*

Table 3-4 lists examples containing various combinations of choices in a JDBC URL. For these examples, we assume the following:

- The database server name is `rmenon-lap` (on my laptop machine with 10*g* and 9*i* installed on it).

- The listener port is 1521.

- The Oracle SID is `ora10g`.

- The net service name is `ora10g.us.oracle.com`.

- The connect descriptor is as follows:

  ```
  (DESCRIPTION = (ADDRESS_LIST =(ADDRESS = (PROTOCOL = TCP)(HOST = rmenon-lap)
  (PORT = 1521)))(CONNECT_DATA =(SERVER = DEDICATED)(SERVICE_NAME =
  ora10g.us.oracle.com)))
  ```

  As you can see, the connect descriptor has all the information to identify a database instance.

Table 3-4. *Examples of Formulating Database URLs for Establishing a JDBC Connection to the Oracle Database*

Type of Connection	Database URL
Thin driver using `host:port:sid`	`jdbc:oracle:thin:@rmenon-lap:1521:ora10g`
Thin driver using connect descriptor	`jdbc:oracle:thin:@(DESCRIPTION =(ADDRESS_LIST =(ADDRESS = (PROTOCOL = TCP)(HOST = rmenon-lap) (PORT = 1521)))(CONNECT_DATA =(SERVER = DEDICATED) (SERVICE_NAME = ora10g.us.oracle.com)))`
OCI driver using net service name of `ora10g`	`jdbc:oracle:oci:@ora10g`
OCI driver using connect descriptor	`jdbc:oracle:oci:@(DESCRIPTION =(ADDRESS_LIST = (ADDRESS = (PROTOCOL = TCP)(HOST = rmenon-lap) (PORT = 1521)))(CONNECT_DATA =(SERVER = DEDICATED) (SERVICE_NAME = ora10g.us.oracle.com)))`

■**Caution** For code that uses the OCI driver, make sure that you have an `instantclient` directory, where you installed the OCI Instant Client files, in the beginning of the `PATH` environment variable. Otherwise, on Windows you may get an error something to effect of "The procedure entry point kpuhhalo could not be located in the dynamic link library oci.dll." In my case, this happened once because my Oracle 9*i* `%ORACLE_HOME%\bin` directory was before the `instantclient` directory in the `PATH` environment variable on my PC.

Connecting Using the Thin Driver

To get a thin driver connection using the format `host:port:sid`, we initialize the database URL and establish the connection (assume that the username is `SCOTT` and the password is `TIGER`) as follows:

```
Connection thinDriverConnection = null;
try
{
  String thinDriverURL = "jdbc:oracle:thin:@rmenon-lap:1521:ora10g";
  thinDriverConnection = DriverManager.getConnection (
    thinDriverURL, "scott", "tiger" );
}
catch (SQLException e)
{
  // handle the exception properly - in this case, we just
  // print a message and stack trace and exit the application
  System.err.println ("ERROR: Could not get connection! Exiting .." );
  e.printStackTrace();
  Runtime.getRuntime().exit(1);
}
finally
```

```
{
  try
  {
    if( thinDriverConnection != null )
      thinDriverConnection.close();
  }
  catch (SQLException ignore ) {}
}
```

The preceding code snippet also shows how to close a connection in the finally clause once we're done using the connection (e.g., for querying data from the database). Next, we obtain a thin driver connection using a connect descriptor:

```
String connectDescriptor = "(DESCRIPTION = (ADDRESS_LIST = (ADDRESS =
(PROTOCOL = TCP)(HOST = rmenon-lap)(PORT = 1521))) (CONNECT_DATA =
(SERVER = DEDICATED) (SERVICE_NAME = ora10g.us.oracle.com)))";
// Thin driver connection using a connect descriptor
try
{
  String thinDriverConnectDescriptorURL =
    "jdbc:oracle:thin:@" + connectDescriptor;

  thinDriverConnection = DriverManager.getConnection (
    thinDriverConnectDescriptorURL, "scott", "tiger" );
}
catch (SQLException e)
{
  // handle the exception properly - in this case, we just
  // print a message and stack trace and exit the application
  System.err.println ("ERROR: Could not get connection! Exiting .." );
  e.printStackTrace();
  Runtime.getRuntime().exit(1);
}
finally
{
  try
  {
    if( thinDriverConnection != null )
      thinDriverConnection.close();
  }
  catch (SQLException ignore ) { }
}
```

Connecting Using the OCI Driver

We next obtain a connection using the OCI driver and the net service name specified in the file tnsnames.ora:

```java
// OCI driver connection using net service name of ora10g
Connection ociDriverConnection = null;
try
{
  String ociDriverURL = "jdbc:oracle:oci:@ora10g";

  ociDriverConnection = DriverManager.getConnection (
    ociDriverURL, "scott", "tiger" );
}
catch (SQLException e)
{
  // handle the exception properly - in this case, we just
  // print a message and stack trace and exit the application
  System.err.println ("ERROR: Could not get connection! Exiting .." );
  e.printStackTrace();
  Runtime.getRuntime().exit(1);
}
finally
{
  try
  {
    if( ociDriverConnection != null )
      ociDriverConnection.close();
  }
  catch (SQLException ignore ) { }
}
```

Finally, we use the connect descriptor we defined earlier in the variable connectDescriptor to get a connection, this time with an OCI driver:

```java
// OCI driver connection using a connect descriptor
try
{
  String ociDriverConnectDescriptorURL =
    "jdbc:oracle:oci:@" + connectDescriptor;

  ociDriverConnection = DriverManager.getConnection (
    ociDriverConnectDescriptorURL, "scott", "tiger" );
}
catch (SQLException e)
{
  // handle the exception properly - in this case, we just
  // print a message and stack trace and exit the application
  System.err.println ("ERROR: Could not get connection! Exiting .." );
  e.printStackTrace();
  Runtime.getRuntime().exit(1);
}
finally
```

```
        {
          try
          {
            if( ociDriverConnection != null )
              ociDriverConnection.close();
          }
          catch (SQLException ignore ) { }
        }
      }//end of main
    }// end of program
```

Potential Errors When Compiling or Executing JDBCOldStyleConnection

You may encounter some problems when compiling or executing JDBCOldStyleConnection. If this happens, please ensure that you have the correct version of the JDK (JDK 1.4.1 or above) and that your PATH environment variable points to the correct version of the JDK. In particular, you can check the version of your JDK as follows:

```
B:\>java -version
java version "1.4.2_05"
Java(TM) 2 Runtime Environment, Standard Edition (build 1.4.2_05-b04)
Java HotSpot(TM) Client VM (build 1.4.2_05-b04, mixed mode)
```

You should also be working with the correct version of Oracle (10*g* or 9*i* Release 2). Table 3-5, on the following page, lists some other errors that you may encounter when compiling or executing the program JDBCOldStyleConnection, along with the possible causes and actions you can take to remedy the errors.

Using a Data Source

JDBC 2.0 introduced the concept of data sources that are standard objects for specifying a source of data such as an Oracle database. As mentioned earlier, this is a more flexible way of establishing a database connection than the method using DriverManager discussed in the previous section. Let's look at the DataSource interface and its properties.

DataSource Interface and Properties

In JDBC, a *data source* is a class that implements the interface javax.sql.DataSource, the main two methods of which are as follows. (In case of Oracle, the class that implements this interface is oracle.jdbc.pool.OracleDataSource.)

```
public interface DataSource
{
  Connection getConnection() throws SQLException;
  Connection getConnection(String username, String password)
    throws SQLException;
...
}
```

Table 3-5. *Potential Errors While Compiling or Executing* JDBCOldStyleConnection *and Their Fixes*

Step	Error Message (Trimmed)	Possible Cause	Fix

Compilation	`> javac JDBCOldStyleConnection.java`
	`JDBCOldStyleConnection.java:6: package oracle.jdbc does not exist`
	`import oracle.jdbc.OracleDriver;`
	`. . .`
		Your CLASSPATH is not set properly.	See earlier sections on setting up the required environment variables.

Execution	`ERROR: Could not get connection! Exiting ..`
	`java.sql.SQLException: ORA-12154: TNS:could not resolve the` ←
	`connect identifier specified at`
	`oracle.jdbc.driver.DatabaseError.throwSqlException←`
	`(DatabaseError.java:125)`
	
	`. . .` `at JDBCOldStyleConnection.main(JDBCOldStyleConnection.java:106)`
		ORACLE_HOME and/or ORACLE_SID is not set.	Set ORACLE_HOME and ORACLE_SID appropriately (required for the OCI driver only).

Execution	`ERROR: Could not get connection! Exiting ..`
	`java.sql.SQLException: Io exception: The Network Adapter could not`
	`establish the connection at . . .`
		The Oracle listener may be down, or the database may be down.	Start the database if it is down; start the listener using the following command (see *Oracle Database Net Services Administrator's Guide* [10g Release 1] for more details): `$ORACLE_HOME/bin/lsnrctl start`

Execution	`ERROR: Could not get connection! Exiting ..`
	`java.sql.SQLException: ORA-12705: invalid or unknown NLS` ←
	`parameter value specified . . .`
		NLS_LANG is not set and is required for the OCI driver connection to work	Set the NLS_LANG environment variable as discussed in the section "JDBC OCI Driver on UNIX and Windows (10g Only)."

Execution	`ORA-01017: invalid username/password; logon denied`
	`java.sql.SQLException: ORA-01017: invalid username/password; logon`
	`denied at oracle.jdbc.driver.DatabaseError.throwSqlException`
		The username or password is invalid.	Double-check the username or password; try connecting using the same username and password through SQL*Plus. If the SCOTT user does not exist, install it by running %ORACLE_HOME/ sqlplus/demo/demobld.sql as the sys user (or see the section "Setting Up the SCOTT/TIGER Schema" of Chapter 1).

The OracleDataSource class provides a set of properties that can be used to specify a database to connect to (we will cover this topic shortly). Table 3-6 shows the standard JDBC data source properties implemented by OracleDataSource.

Table 3-6. *Standard* DataSource *Properties*

Name	Data Type	Description
databaseName	String	Name of the particular database on the server; also known as the SID in Oracle terminology.
dataSourceName	String	Name of the underlying data source class (for connection pooling, this is an underlying pooled connection data source class).
description	String	Description of the data source.
networkProtocol	String	Network protocol for communicating with the server. For Oracle, this applies only to the OCI drivers and defaults to tcp (other possible settings include ipc; see *Oracle Database Net Services Administrator's Guide [10g Release 1]* for more information).
password	String	Login password for the username.
portNumber	int	Number of the port where the server listens for requests.
serverName	String	Name of the database server.
user	String	Name for the login account.

For each property in Table 3-6, OracleDataSource implements a getter and a setter method (there is no getter method for password property for security reasons). For example, for the property databaseName these methods are

```
public synchronized void setDatabaseName(String dbname);
public synchronized String getDatabaseName();
```

Apart from implementing the preceding standard properties, Oracle also implements the properties specific to the Oracle database (called the Oracle extended data source properties). Table 3-7 lists these properties. (Please note that only the properties covered in this book are listed in Table 3-7. For a complete list of these properties, please see *Oracle Database JDBC Developer's Guide and Reference [10g Release 1]*).

The getter and setter methods are based on the JavaBeans naming style. For example, for the property connectionCacheProperties, these methods are

```
void setConnectionCacheProperties( java.util.Properties properties );
java.util.Properties getConnectionCacheProperties();
```

Table 3-7. *Oracle Extended Data Source Properties**

Name	Data Type	Description
connectionCacheName	String	Name of the cache. This cannot be changed after the cache has been created (see Chapter 14).
connectionCacheProperties	java.util.Properties	Properties for Implicit Connection Cache (see Chapter 14).
connectionCachingEnabled	Boolean	Specifies whether Implicit Connection Cache is in use (see Chapter 14).
connectionProperties	java.util.Properties	Connection properties. See Javadoc for a complete list.
DriverType	String	Oracle JDBC driver type: oci, thin, or kprb (server-side internal).
ImplicitCachingEnabled	Boolean	Whether the implicit connection cache is enabled (see Chapter 14).
loginTimeout	int	Maximum time in seconds that this data source will wait while attempting to connect to a database.
LogWriter	java.io.PrintWriter	Log writer for this data source.
maxStatements	int	Maximum number of statements in the application cache (see Chapter 14).
serviceName	String	Database service name for this data source.
url	String	URL of the database connect string. Provided as a convenience, it can help you migrate from an older Oracle database. You can use this property in place of the Oracle tnsEntry and driverType properties, and the standard portNumber, networkProtocol, serverName, and databaseName properties.

* Table information from Oracle Database JDBC Developer's Guide and Reference (10g Release 1).

We will use many of these methods in subsequent examples. Please note the following (quoted verbatim from *Oracle Database JDBC Developer's Guide and Reference [10g Release 1]*):

> *If you are using the server-side internal driver—i.e., the* driverType *property is set to* kprb—*then any other property settings are ignored. If you are using the thin or OCI drivers then:*
>
> - *A URL setting can include settings for* user *and* password, *as in the following example, in which case this takes precedence over individual* user *and* password *property settings:*
>
>   jdbc:oracle:thin:scott/tiger@localhost:1521:orcl
>
> - *Settings for user and password are required, either directly, through the URL setting, or through the* getConnection() *call. The user and password settings in a* getConnection() *call take precedence over any property settings.*
>
> - *If the* url *property is set, then any* tnsEntry, driverType, portNumber, networkProtocol, serverName, *and* databaseName *property settings are ignored.*
>
> - *If the* tnsEntry *property is set (which presumes the* url *property is not set), then any* databaseName, serverName, portNumber, *and* networkProtocol *settings are ignored.*
>
> - *If you are using an OCI driver (which presumes the* driverType *property is set to* oci) *and the* networkProtocol *is set to* ipc, *then any other property settings are ignored.*

Before we move on, you need to understand briefly the JNDI standard API. JNDI allows an application to use logical names in accessing remote services, thus removing vendor-specific syntax from application code. For a JDBC application, a remote service would typically be a database connection. There are two alternatives to using data sources to connect to an Oracle database: One uses JNDI and the other does not. The following sections explain each method.

Using a Data Source Without JNDI

The process of connecting to an Oracle database without JNDI involves creating an OracleDataSource instance, initializing it with one or more of the properties (standard or Oracle-extended) that we saw in the previous section, and using the getConnection() method. This process is illustrated by the class JDBCDataSourceConnectionWithoutJNDI, which begins with import statements followed by the declaration of the main() method:

```
/* This class demonstrates how to connect to a database using the
   DataSource interface without using JNDI.
 * COMPATIBLITY NOTE: tested against 10.1.0.2.0. and 9.2.0.1.0 */
import java.sql.Connection;
import java.sql.SQLException;
```

```
import java.util.Properties;
import oracle.jdbc.pool.OracleDataSource;
class JDBCDataSourceConnectionWithoutJNDI
{
  public static void main (String args[])
  {
```

We declare a variable of type OracleDataSource. Note that to set any data source property (standard or vendor-specific), you have to use the vendor-specific interface (OracleDataSource in our case). This is because the DataSource interface does not define any getter or setter methods for these properties:

```
// Connecting to Oracle using DataSource without JNDI
OracleDataSource ods = null;
```

Next, we instantiate the OracleDataSource object:

```
try
{
  ods = new OracleDataSource();
}
catch (SQLException e)
{
  // handle the exception properly - in this case, we just
  // print a message and stack trace and exit the application
  System.err.println ("ERROR: Could not instantiate data source! Exiting .." );
  System.err.println ( e.getMessage() );
  e.printStackTrace();
  Runtime.getRuntime().exit (1);
}
```

and set the data source properties that define our connection:

```
// set the properties that define the connection
ods.setDriverType ( "thin" );        // type of driver
ods.setServerName ( "rmenon-lap" ); // database server name
ods.setNetworkProtocol("tcp");       // tcp is the default anyway
ods.setDatabaseName("ora10g");       // Oracle SID
ods.setPortNumber(1521);             // listener port number
ods.setUser("scott");                // username
ods.setPassword("tiger");            // password
```

Finally, we obtain our connection using the getConnection() method. This part of the program depends only on the methods of the standard DataSource interface:

```
// get the connection without JNDI
Connection connection = null;
try
{
  connection = ods.getConnection();
  System.out.println( "SUCCESS!");
```

```
      // do some work with the connection
    }
    catch (SQLException e)
    {
      // handle the exception properly - in this case, we just
      // print a message and stack trace and exit the application
      System.err.println ("ERROR: Could not get the connection! Exiting .." );
      System.err.println ( e.getMessage() );
      e.printStackTrace();
      Runtime.getRuntime().exit (1);
    }
    finally
    {
      try
      {
        if( connection != null )
          connection.close();
      }
      catch (SQLException ignore ) {}
    }
  }// end of main
}// end of class
```

Note that we could also use the overloaded version of getConnection() of the standard
DataSource interface to connect with a different username and password:

```
Connection conn = ods.getConnection("benchmark", "benchmark");
```

If you run this program, you should get the following output:

```
B:\>java JDBCDataSourceConnectionWithoutJNDI
SUCCESS!
```

Using a Data Source with JNDI

This involves initializing an OracleDataSource instance with appropriate properties, registering with JNDI to associate a logical name with the connection resource, and then obtaining
the connection in the rest of the application using the logical name. If you use this method,
the vendor-dependent part of the code is present only in the portion of code that binds a data
source instance to a JNDI logical name. From that point onward, you can create maintainable
code by using the logical name in creating data sources from which you will get your connection instances. If later the data source or information about it changes, the properties of the
DataSource object can simply be modified to reflect the changes; no change in application
code is necessary. This method can be used if your code already is using JNDI in the context
of a database access layer (e.g., to access users stored in a centralized LDAP directory that is
accessed using JNDI). In other cases, using DataSource without JNDI is easier and is recommended. In both cases, you should design your application such that the portion of the code
that retrieves the connection is separated from the portion of the code that sets the connection properties (since the latter uses a vendor-specific interface).

For running the example in this section, you will need to get a JNDI reference implementation that can be used to store the connection properties and logical mapping of the data source and its name. I ran my example on Sun's JNDI file systems reference implementation.

■**NOTE** You can download the classes for Sun's JNDI file systems implementation from `http://java.sun.com/products/jndi/downloads/index.html`, although please note that this URL might change in the future.

After downloading a reference implementation (I used JNDI 1.2.1, File Systems Service Provider 1.2, Beta 3), unzip the files into any directory. Then add the full path of the two JAR files in the directory, `fscontext.jar` and `providerutil.jar`, in your `CLASSPATH` (the path should include the JAR file name). You also need to add `$ORACLE_HOME/jlib/jndi.jar` to your `CLASSPATH` for the example in this section to work. You then create a directory (in my example, `B:\code\book\ch03\jndi_test`) for specifying the root of the JNDI context.

The class `JDBCDataSourceConnectionWithJNDI` demonstrates this. It begins with the import statements followed by the `main()` method declaration:

```
/* This class demonstrates how to connect to a database using the
   DataSource interface using JNDI.
 * COMPATIBLITY NOTE: tested against 10.1.0.2.0. and 9.2.0.1.0 */
import java.sql.Connection;
import java.sql.SQLException;
import java.util.Properties;
import oracle.jdbc.pool.OracleDataSource;
import javax.sql.DataSource;
import javax.naming.Context;
import javax.naming.InitialContext;
import javax.naming.NamingException;
class JDBCDataSourceConnectionWithJNDI
{
  public static void main (String args[])
  {
    OracleDataSource ods = null;
    Connection connection = null;
    try
    {
```

First, we initialize a `Properties` object with two properties. The first property, `Context.INITIAL_CONTEXT_FACTORY`, is initialized to the fully qualified class name of the factory class that will create an initial context (in our case, Sun's file systems reference implementation's factory class):

```
      Properties properties = new Properties();
      properties.setProperty( Context.INITIAL_CONTEXT_FACTORY,
        "com.sun.jndi.fscontext.RefFSContextFactory");
```

Then, we specify the value of the property `Context.PROVIDER_URL`, which specifies the configuration information for the service provider to use. (Note that the directory you specify should exist in your machine where the program is running, and you should have read/write/execute permissions on this directory.)

```
properties.setProperty( Context.PROVIDER_URL,
 "file:B:/code/book/ch03/jndi_test");
```

We create the `javax.naming.Context` object that will define the JNDI context for our program:

```
Context context = new InitialContext(properties);
```

We then create an `OracleDataSource` object in the same way we did in the previous section, initializing it with properties defining our connection:

```
// create the data source
ods = new OracleDataSource();
ods.setDriverType ( "thin" );        // type of driver
ods.setServerName ( "rmenon-lap" ); // database server name
ods.setNetworkProtocol("tcp");       // tcp is the default anyway
ods.setDatabaseName("ora10g");       // Oracle SID
ods.setPortNumber(1521);             // listener port number
```

Finally, we associate the data source with a name of our choice (in my case, I chose `jdbc/testdb`). This name can be used in other programs to look up the data source later.

```
// associate a logical name with the connection service.
// Following recommended convention, we use a subcontext,
// jdbc, and put our name under it as jdbc/testdb
context.bind ( "jdbc/testdb", ods );
```

In a real-world application, you would perform the steps listed so far only once. (In fact, if you try to reuse a logical name to bind some other data source, you'll get a `javax.naming.NameAlreadyBoundException`.)

You can then obtain the connection from any other program by looking up the data source using JNDI and using it to get the connection as follows. Note that we can now use the standard `DataSource` interface to obtain the connection.

```
DataSource dsUsingJNDI = (DataSource) context.lookup("jdbc/testdb");
connection = dsUsingJNDI.getConnection("scott", "tiger");
System.out.println( "SUCCESS!");
}
catch (NamingException e)
{
  // handle the exception properly - in this case, we just
  // print a message and stack trace and exit the application
  System.out.println ("ERROR: in registering with JNDI! Exiting .." );
  System.out.println (e.getMessage() );
  e.printStackTrace();
  System.exit (1);
}
```

```
    catch (SQLException e)
    {
      // handle the exception properly - in this case, we just
      // print a message and stack trace and exit the application
      System.err.println ("ERROR: Could not get the connection! Exiting .." );
      System.err.println ( e.getMessage() );
      e.printStackTrace();
      Runtime.getRuntime().exit (1);
    }
    finally
    {
      try
      {
        if( connection != null )
          connection.close();
      }
      catch (SQLException ignore ) {}
    }
  }// end of main
}// end of program
```

The program JDBCDataSourceConnectionWithJNDI prints "SUCCESS!" on a successful run. Please note that after a successful run, you would find a "hidden" text file called .bindings in the directory corresponding to the property Context.PROVIDER_URL (B:/code/book/ch03/jndi_test in the preceding example). This file stores all the data source properties, along with other information. Note that if in the preceding example we had configured the username and password also as part of the data source property (instead of passing them as arguments to the getConnection() method invocation), the text would contain this sensitive information in plain text. So, you need to be careful about where your data source properties get stored.

A Complete JDBC Program

This section assumes that you have set up the software and environment successfully as described in the previous section(s). We are now ready to run our first JDBC program! Our aim in this program is to run a query against the database and print out the results. We run the query against the SCOTT user to select the employee number, name, and job from the emp table of all employees. First, we run the query using SQL*Plus as follows to see what results to expect in our JDBC program:

```
scott@ORA10G> select empno, ename, job from emp;
     EMPNO ENAME      JOB
---------- ---------- ---------
      7369 SMITH      CLERK
      7499 ALLEN      SALESMAN
      7521 WARD       SALESMAN
      7566 JONES      MANAGER
      7654 MARTIN     SALESMAN
```

```
7698 BLAKE       MANAGER
7782 CLARK       MANAGER
7788 SCOTT       ANALYST
7839 KING        PRESIDENT
7844 TURNER      SALESMAN
7876 ADAMS       CLERK
7900 JAMES       CLERK
7902 FORD        ANALYST
7934 MILLER      CLERK
14 rows selected.
```

Then we run the same query in our first JDBC program. This program illustrates the following:

- How to connect to Oracle (covered in the previous section)

- How to execute a query against Oracle and retrieve data

- How to release the various resources that we acquired

The complete listing of the class GetEmpDetails, interspersed with comments, follows. The main() method comes up after the import statements:

```
/* This class runs a query against the SCOTT schema.
* COMPATIBLITY NOTE: tested against 10.1.0.2.0. and 9.2.0.1.0 */
import java.sql.ResultSet;
import java.sql.SQLException;
import java.sql.Statement;
import java.sql.Connection;
import oracle.jdbc.pool.OracleDataSource;
class GetEmpDetails
{
  public static void main(String args[])
  {
```

We initialize variables holding the data source properties. Notice that we use the thin driver (also, remember to change the variables' values according to your environment):

```
String user = "scott"; // modify this value to your db user
String password = "tiger"; // modify this value to your db user password
String host = "rmenon-lap"; // modify this value to your db host
String port = "1521"; // modify this value to your db listener port
String dbService = "ora10g"; // modify this value to your db service name
```

Next, we concatenate the preceding variables to form a JDBC URL and print it out. This is another alternative to setting each of the properties separately, as we did in the earlier examples. Notice that we also put the username and password in the URL, though it is not necessary to do so.

```
String thinDriverPrefix = "jdbc:oracle:thin";
String thinConnectURL = thinDriverPrefix + ":" + user + "/" +
```

```
password + "@" + host + ":" + port + ":" + dbService;
// the string value = "jdbc:oracle:thin:scott/tiger@rmenon-lap:1521:ora10g";
System.out.println("Database connect url: " + thinConnectURL);
System.out.print("Establishing connection to the database...");
```

We declare the three variables that will hold JDBC data. The Connection object will hold
the connection, Statement will hold the SQL statement, and ResultSet will hold the query's
results:

```
ResultSet rset = null;
Connection conn = null;
Statement stmt = null;
try
{
```

Inside the try catch block, we first initialize the data source with the JDBC URL and
obtain the connection using the getConnection() method:

```
// instantiate and initialize OracleDataSource
OracleDataSource ods = new OracleDataSource();
ods.setURL(thinConnectURL );
// get the connection
conn = ods.getConnection();
System.out.println("Connected.\nPrinting query results ...\n");
```

Next, we create a Statement object:

```
// Create a stmt
stmt = conn.createStatement();
```

We execute the query by invoking the method executeQuery() on the Statement object.
The executeQuery() method executes the query in Oracle and returns the result of the query
as a java.sql.ResultSet object:

```
// execute the query
rset = stmt.executeQuery( "select empno, ename, job from emp" );
```

A ResultSet object is a data structure that represents rows and columns returned by any
query. It maintains a cursor pointing to its current row of data. Initially, the cursor is positioned before the first row. We use the next() method to move the cursor to the next row, thus
iterating through the result set as shown. The next() method returns false when there are no
more rows in the ResultSet object, at which point we exit the loop. Within the loop, we use the
appropriate getXXX() method of the ResultSet object, where XXX corresponds to an appropriate Java type. For example, we know that the data type for the columns ename and job of table
emp in our example is String, whereas for the empno column, it is int. Thus, we use getString()
method of the ResultSet object for the ename and job column values, and we use the getInt()
method of the ResultSet object for the empno column value, as shown in the following code.
These methods take an integer value that represents the index of the column in the select
clause. In our example, the indexes of the columns empno, ename, and job are 1, 2, and 3,
respectively. We first declare the column indexes as constants:

```
  // declare constants for column indexes in the query (indexes begin with 1)
  final int EMPNO_COLUMN_INDEX = 1;
  final int ENAME_COLUMN_INDEX = 2;
  final int JOB_COLUMN_INDEX = 3;
```

and loop through the result set, printing out the value in each column of a row:

```
  // print the results
  while (rset.next())
  {
    int empNo = rset.getInt ( EMPNO_COLUMN_INDEX );
    String empName = rset.getString ( ENAME_COLUMN_INDEX );
    String empJob = rset.getString ( JOB_COLUMN_INDEX );
    System.out.println( empNo + " " + empName + " " + empJob );
  }
}
catch (SQLException e)
{
  // handle the exception properly - in this case, we just
  // print a message and stack trace and exit the application
  System.err.println ("error message: " + e.getMessage() );
  e.printStackTrace();
  Runtime.getRuntime().exit(1);
}
```

■**Note** The preceding example uses the default ResultSet type. In Chapter 7, we cover other, more advanced features of the ResultSet interface, including prefetching and scrollability.

Once we are done printing the results, we use the close() method on the ResultSet, Statement, and Connection objects in the finally clause of the try catch block to end our program:

```
finally
{
  // close the result set, statement, and connection.
  // ignore any exceptions since we are in the
  // finally clause.
  try
  {
    if( rset != null )
      rset.close();
    if( stmt != null )
      stmt.close();
    if( conn != null )
      conn.close();
```

```
    }
    catch ( SQLException ignored ) {ignored.printStackTrace(); }
  }
 }
}
```

It is important to realize the need to close the ResultSet, Statement, and Connection objects explicitly in your JDBC application when you are done using them. Failure to do so can result in serious memory leaks and running out of cursors on the database server. Note that the cursor is not released until you close *both the* Statement *and* ResultSet *objects*. It is also critical to do the cleanup activities in the finally clause so that the resources are released, even if an exception is raised.

■**Tip** Remember to close the ResultSet, Statement, and Connection objects when you are done using them in the finally clause of the try catch block.

When you compile and run the code, you should see the following output:

```
B:\>java GetEmpDetails
Database connect url: jdbc:oracle:thin:scott/tiger@rmenon-lap:1521:ora10g
Establishing connection to the database...Connected.
Printing query results ...

7369 SMITH CLERK
7499 ALLEN SALESMAN
7521 WARD SALESMAN
7566 JONES MANAGER
7654 MARTIN SALESMAN
7698 BLAKE MANAGER
7782 CLARK MANAGER
7788 SCOTT ANALYST
7839 KING PRESIDENT
7844 TURNER SALESMAN
7876 ADAMS CLERK
7900 JAMES CLERK
7902 FORD ANALYST
7934 MILLER CLERK
```

Potential Errors When Executing Your First Program

If you were able to successfully run the GetEmpDetails program discussed in the previous section, you may skip to the next section. Otherwise, please read on, as it is vital for you to get this program working to proceed further. These are some of the checks you should make:

- Make sure you have taken care of all potential errors mentioned in the section "Potential Errors When Compiling or Executing JDBCOldStyleConnection." Many of these error conditions are applicable even though you get your connection using DataSource.

- When you run the program, you may get runtime exceptions. Table 3-8 summarizes some common scenarios (other than those mentioned in the section "Potential Errors When Compiling or Executing JDBCOldStyleConnection"), the probable cause, and the action you need to take to rectify the problem.

Table 3-8. *Common Runtime Exceptions When Running* GetEmpDetails *and Corresponding Remedial Actions*

Error Message (Trimmed)	Possible Cause	Fix
error message: ORA-00904: "EPNO": invalid identifier java.sql.SQLException: ORA-00904: "EPNO": invalid identifier . . .	Invalid column name in the query string	Correct your query statement string to ensure that all column names are valid.
java.sql.SQLException: ORA-00942: table or view does not exist	Invalid table name in your query	Correct the table name in your query. Ensure you have the database privilege to select from the table.

Exception Handling in JDBC

When an error occurs, Oracle throws an instance of the java.sql.SQLException object. You handle this exception just like any other Java exception. The errors can originate in the JDBC driver or in the database. You can retrieve basic error information with the following SQLException methods.

For errors originating in the JDBC driver, the following method returns the error message with no prefix. For errors originating in the RDBMS, it returns the error message prefixed with the corresponding ORA number.

getMessage()

For errors originating in either the JDBC driver or the RDBMS, this method returns the five-digit ORA number:

getErrorCode()

For errors originating in the database, this method returns a five-digit code indicating the SQL state:

getSQLState()

Like any exception, this method prints out the exception stack trace:

printStackTrace()

Introducing JDBCUtil

JDBCUtil is a class I wrote that contains useful utility methods that you will add to as and when you learn different concepts in this book. In this chapter, you learned how to obtain a connection to a database and release resources associated with Connection, Statement, and ResultSet objects. These are ideal candidates for being incorporated in the JDBCUtil class for use in code written in later chapters.

I have put the JDBCUtil class in the package book.util. You can download this class from the Downloads area of the Apress website (http://www.apress.com). Let's look at the method getConnection() in this class, which takes as parameters a username, password, and database name (SID or service name):

```
public static Connection getConnection( String username,
   String password, String dbName)
   throws SQLException
{
   OracleDataSource ods = null;
   Connection connection = null;
   ods = new OracleDataSource();
   // set the properties that define the connection
   ods.setDriverType ( "thin" );        // type of driver
   ods.setServerName ( "rmenon-lap" ); // database server name
   ods.setNetworkProtocol("tcp");       // tcp is the default anyway
   ods.setDatabaseName(dbName);       // Oracle SID
   ods.setPortNumber(1521);        // my 10g listener port number
   ods.setUser(username);          // username
   ods.setPassword(password);        // password
   System.out.println( "URL:" + ods.getURL());System.out.flush();
   connection = ods.getConnection();
   connection.setAutoCommit( false );
   return connection;
}
```

The method should be self-explanatory. The only thing that I have not explained is the invocation of setAutoCommit(), which is explained in the next chapter in the section "The Autocommit Feature and Turning It Off."

The various overloaded versions of the following close() methods simply invoke the close() method on a ResultSet, Statement, or Connection object and are self-explanatory:

```
public static void close ( ResultSet resultSet, Statement statement,
   Connection connection )
{
   try
   {
      if( resultSet != null )
         resultSet.close();
      if( statement != null )
         statement.close();
      if( connection != null )
```

```
      connection.close();
    }
    catch ( SQLException ignored ) { }

}

public static void close ( ResultSet resultSet, Statement statement )
{
  try
  {
    if( resultSet != null )
      resultSet.close();
    if( statement != null )
      statement.close();
  }
  catch ( SQLException ignored ) { }
}

public static void close ( ResultSet resultSet )
{
  try
  {
    if( resultSet != null )
      resultSet.close();
  }
  catch ( SQLException ignored ) { }

}

public static void close ( Statement statement )
{
  try
  {
    if( statement != null )
      statement.close();
  }
  catch ( SQLException ignored ) { }

}

public static void close ( Connection connection )
{
  try
  {
    if( connection != null )
      connection.close();
  }
```

```
    catch ( SQLException ignored ) { }
}
```

Finally, the method `printException()` in the `JDBCUtil` class prints the `SQLException` error message along with the stack trace:

```
public static void printException ( Exception e )
{
  System.out.println ("Exception caught! Exiting .." );
  System.out.println ("error message: " + e.getMessage() );
  e.printStackTrace();
}
```

Summary

In this chapter, you were introduced to the JDBC API. You looked at different types of JDBC drivers and how to choose the one appropriate for your software development requirements. You discovered how to set up an environment for using the JDBC thin and OCI drivers, and you examined the various options of establishing a connection to the Oracle database and why you should consider using `DataSource` instead of `DriverManager` to establish such a connection. Finally, you wrote and analyzed your first JDBC program, which executes a query against Oracle database and prints out the query results. In the next chapter, you will look at the JDBC API associated with database transactions.

CHAPTER 4

■ ■ ■

Transactions

In this chapter, you'll take a brief look at transactions in the context of JDBC. You'll see how to commit and roll back a transaction in JDBC, and you'll learn what transaction isolation levels are and which ones are supported by Oracle. In addition, I'll explain why it's important to turn off the autocommit feature in JDBC in production code. Finally, you'll examine transaction savepoints, a feature exposed to Java programs in JDBC 3.0.

What Is a Transaction?

A *transaction* is a set of SQL statements that performs an *atomic* logical unit of work in the database. *Oracle Database Concepts Guide (10g Release 1)* states

> *According to the ANSI/ISO SQL standard, with which Oracle is compatible, a transaction begins with the user's first executable SQL statement.*

In practice, in Oracle, a transaction *usually* begins with the issue of a `select ... for update`, `insert`, `update`, `delete`, or `merge` statement, and ends with an explicit or implicit commit or rollback statement.

Note Other scenarios mark the beginning of a transaction in Oracle, some of which we'll look at in this chapter. For example, a transaction begins when we set the transaction to `READ ONLY` by using the command `set transaction read only`, as we will cover later in the section "Transaction Isolation Levels."

Committing a Transaction

Committing a transaction makes permanent in the database the effects of all statements (inserts, updates, deletes, etc.) issued since the previous commit or rollback. It's a way of saying, "OK, I'm sure that these changes to the database data are fine, and I want them to be made permanent in the database." Committing a transaction also releases all locks and other resources acquired by the database during the transaction. In JDBC, you commit a transaction by invoking the `commit()` method on the `Connection` object as follows (assume `connection` is an initialized variable of type `Connection`):

```
connection.commit();
```

Rolling Back a Transaction

Rolling back a transaction undoes all the changes to the database data made in the current transaction and releases any locks acquired by the database during the current transaction. In JDBC, you roll back a transaction by invoking the rollback() method on the Connection object as follows (assume connection is an initialized variable of type Connection):

```
connection.rollback();
```

Typically, a rollback is issued if you have encountered an error condition in your transaction.

Let's now look at the concept of transaction isolation levels.

Transaction Isolation Levels

Transaction isolation levels within a database specify what data is visible to our application within a transaction. Transaction isolation levels are defined in terms of three types of scenarios being permitted or not at a given isolation level:

Dirty read: A transaction with an isolation level that allows for dirty reads implies that within that transaction you can see changes to data not yet committed by other transactions. If the changes are rolled back later instead of being committed, it is possible for other transactions to have done work based on incorrect, transient data. Obviously, this is not conducive to maintaining data integrity in a database. Table 4-1 outlines a scenario that is possible if dirty reads are allowed.

Table 4-1. *Scenario Illustrating the Negative Impact of Dirty Reads on Data Integrity*

Point of Time	Transaction TXN1	Transaction TXN2
1	Execution of select sum(sal) from emp begins.	
2		Execution of update emp set sal = sal*1.50 where ename='BLAKE' begins and ends successfully.
3	Since TXN1 can see changes being made by TXN2, it sums up the salary based on the updated data for BLAKE.	
4		Issues a rollback.
5	Outputs incorrect information. The sum includes the incorrect salary of BLAKE based on data that no longer exists, and never actually existed, in the database.	

Nonrepeatable read: A nonrepeatable read occurs when

1. A transaction, TXN1, reads a row.

2. Another transaction, TXN2, updates (or deletes) the row and commits.

3. The transaction TXN1 rereads the row and is able to see the changes made by transaction TXN2 (the row is different or has been deleted).

Phantom read: A phantom read occurs when the following occur in sequential order:

1. A transaction, TXN1, executes a query against a table, table1, at a point of time, t1.

2. Another transaction, TXN2, inserts a new row in table table1 at point of time t2 and commits (or it does an update such that the same query will return additional rows).

3. The transaction TXN1 re-executes the query and sees the additional rows resulting from inserts or updates done by transaction TXN2, thus getting a different answer for the same query.

The difference between a nonrepeatable read and a phantom read is subtle. A nonrepeatable read refers to *changes* in rows propagated through updates and deletes in transaction TXN2 being visible in the re-execution of a query in transaction TXN1. On the other hand, a phantom read refers to *additional* rows being visible to transaction TXN1 when a query is re-executed—the additional rows resulting from inserts and updates done by another transaction, TXN2.

Based on the preceding three scenarios, the SQL92 standard defines four transaction isolation levels, and Oracle defines an additional one (READ ONLY). I discuss all five transaction isolation levels briefly here in order of increasing restrictiveness:

1. READ UNCOMMITTED: This isolation level allows transactions to see uncommitted data. This means dirty reads, nonrepeatable reads, and phantom reads are allowed. Data integrity is compromised severely in this isolation level, as explained earlier. Oracle does not support it. The constant TRANSACTION_READ_UNCOMMITTED defined in the Connection interface denotes this isolation level.

2. READ COMMITTED: This isolation level allows transactions to see only committed data. This prevents dirty reads, but nonrepeatable and phantom reads are still allowed. This is by far the most common isolation level used by applications. Oracle supports it. The constant TRANSACTION_READ_COMMITTED defined in the Connection interface denotes this isolation level.

3. REPEATABLE READ: This isolation level disallows dirty reads and nonrepeatable reads. Phantom reads are still allowed. Dirty reads being disallowed means that you can only see data committed by other transactions. Furthermore, since nonrepeatable reads are not allowed, you cannot see the updates and deletes done by other transactions (committed or uncommitted) to the same rows, but you *can* see any new data visible to the query due to inserts or updates done by other transactions, since phantom reads are allowed. The intent of allowing REPEATABLE READ is to solve the issue of *lost updates*. A lost update occurs when the following sequence of events happens:

   a. user1 queries a row.

   b. user2 queries the same row in a different session.

   c. user1 updates the row and commits.

d. user2 updates the row to a different value and commits, overwriting the updates done by user1. Updates done by user1 are "lost," hence the name "lost updates."

Later in Chapter 17, we will examine various alternatives to solve the lost update problem in Oracle. Oracle does not support this isolation level, which is denoted by the constant TRANSACTION_REPEATABLE_READ defined in the Connection interface.

■**Note** In Oracle, you can implement REPEATABLE READ, if required, by using the for update clause in your queries. However, this isolation level should be used only after careful consideration, since it locks up the relevant rows, thereby inhibiting concurrency.

---

4. SERIALIZABLE: This isolation level does not allow dirty reads, nonrepeatable reads, or phantom reads. This means that a transaction can see only those changes that were committed at the time the transaction began. When you set the transaction isolation level to SERIALIZABLE, all queries are read-consistent with respect to the beginning of the *transaction*. In other words, the answers to all queries are fixed as of the beginning of the transaction. A side effect of this behavior is that in a serializable transaction, if you attempt to update the same row that some other user is trying to update, you wait until the user commits and then get an error. This fact can be used to solve the lost updates problem just mentioned, as we will cover in Chapter 17 (the chapter also discusses other solutions to this problem). Oracle supports this isolation level, which is denoted by the constant TRANSACTION_SERIALIZABLE defined in the Connection interface.

5. READ ONLY: Apart from the aforementioned SQL92 standard transaction isolation levels, Oracle provides a transaction isolation level called READ ONLY. Read-only transactions see only those changes that were committed at the time the transaction began and *do not allow any statements that modify data* (such as insert, update, and delete statements). The READ ONLY transaction isolation level is more restrictive than the SERIALIZABLE transaction isolation level in that it doesn't allow any statement modifications from within a transaction. This transaction isolation level is useful in generating reports that

- Consist of multiple queries

- Require that all data shown be consistent from the point of time the report generation begins

Table 4-2 shows all five isolation levels, along with different scenarios allowed in each.

Table 4-2. *SQL92 Isolation Levels and the Oracle-Specific* READ ONLY *Isolation Level*

Isolation Level	Supported in Oracle?	Dirty Read	Nonrepeatable Read	Phantom Read	Data Modifying Statements (Inserts, Updates, Deletes, Etc.) Allowed?
READ UNCOMMITTED	No	Yes	Yes	Yes	Yes
READ COMMITTED	Yes (the default)	No	Yes	Yes	Yes
REPEATABLE READ	No	No	No	Yes	Yes
SERIALIZABLE	Yes	No	No	No	Yes
READ ONLY (Oracle-specific)	Yes	No	No	No	No

Transaction Isolation Levels in JDBC

To the four standard transaction isolation levels, JDBC adds a fifth nominal isolation level denoted by the constant Connection.TRANSACTION_NONE, which simply means that transactions are not supported within a database. The constants Connection.TRANSACTION_READ_COMMITTED, Connection.TRANSACTION_READ_UNCOMMITTED, Connection.TRANSACTION_REPEATABLE_READ, and Connection.TRANSACTION_SERIALIZABLE denote the various transaction isolation levels for a database. We set a transaction isolation level at a Connection object by invoking the method setTransactionIsolation() in the Connection interface:

```
public void setTransactionIsolation( int level ) throws SQLException;
```

In Oracle applications, only Connection.TRANSACTION_READ_COMMITTED and Connection.TRANSACTION_SERIALIZABLE are valid constants to use. We get a given transaction's isolation level by invoking the method getTransactionIsolation() in the Connection interface:

```
public int getTransactionIsolation() throws SQLException;
```

Since the JDBC standard does not allow for the transaction isolation level READ ONLY, we have to set it in a slightly different way, as we'll cover shortly.

We can set all three transaction levels allowed by Oracle using the set transaction command in the beginning of the transaction as follows (we'll look at how to do this from JDBC in a moment):

```
benchmark@ORA10G> set transaction isolation level read committed;

Transaction set.
```

Note that we cannot use the set transaction command in the middle of a transaction. For example, the preceding set transaction command has already started a transaction with an isolation level of READ COMMITTED. If we try to reset the transaction isolation level to SERIALIZABLE now in the middle of the transaction, we will get an error:

```
benchmark@ORA10G> set transaction isolation level serializable;
set transaction isolation level serializable
*
ERROR at line 1:
ORA-01453: SET TRANSACTION must be first statement of transaction
```

This means that we have to end this transaction by issuing either a rollback or a commit in the transaction before issuing any other set transaction statement that sets an isolation level:

```
benchmark@ORA10G> rollback;

Rollback complete.
```

Next, we set the transaction isolation level to SERIALIZABLE:

```
benchmark@ORA10G> set transaction isolation level serializable;

Transaction set.

benchmark@ORA10G> rollback;

Rollback complete.
```

Finally, we set the transaction to be READ ONLY. Note the difference in syntax; we don't use the isolation level keyword here.

```
benchmark@ORA10G> set transaction read only;

Transaction set.

benchmark@ORA10G> rollback;

Rollback complete.
```

We can also set the transaction isolation level to either READ COMMITTED or SERIALIZABLE (but not to READ ONLY) at a session level. In fact, this is what the Oracle JDBC driver's implementation of setTransactionIsolation() does internally:

```
benchmark@ORA10G> alter session set isolation_level=serializable;

Session altered.

benchmark@ORA10G> rollback;

Rollback complete.
```

```
benchmark@ORA10G> alter session set isolation_level=read committed;
```

Session altered.

The differences between using set transaction... and alter session set isolation_level... are as follows. The first difference, of course, is that when we use alter session set isolation_level, we can only change the isolation level to either SERIALIZABLE or READ COMMITTED (the default). Using set transaction..., we can change the isolation level to READ ONLY in addition to these isolation levels. The second, subtler difference is that set transaction... changes settings at a *transaction level only*. At the end of the transaction (i.e., after a commit or a rollback), the settings revert back to the default (READ COMMITTED). So if we are not using the default of READ COMMITTED, we have to reset the transaction again at the beginning of each transaction, incurring a round-trip even if we are in the same session. In contrast, alter session set isolation_level... works at the *session level*. Thus, all transactions for the same session are impacted by the change and retain the settings. It follows that if, using the same session, we need to have multiple transactions involving nondefault transaction mode, we save one round-trip per transaction if we use alter session set isolation_level.... Since JDBC implements the method setTransactionIsolation() internally using alter session set isolation_level..., this is the behavior we should expect. Thus, if we use set transaction... to set the transaction isolation level to READ ONLY via JDBC (as we will do soon), we should be aware that we will have to set it at the beginning of each transaction if required, even if we use the same Connection object for each such transaction.

The following DemoTransactionIsolationLevels class demonstrates how to set the transaction isolation level to different permissible values for an Oracle database transaction. Please see the interspersed comments for an explanation of the class.

```
/* This class demonstrates how to set different transaction levels in Oracle.
 * COMPATIBLITY NOTE: tested against 10.1.0.2.0. and 9.2.0.1.0 */
import java.sql.Connection;
import java.sql.CallableStatement;
import java.sql.SQLException;
import book.util.JDBCUtil;
class DemoTransactionIsolationLevels
{
  public static void main( String[] args ) throws Exception
  {
    Connection conn = null;
    try
    {
```

Inside the try catch block, we first get the connection using the JDBCUtil.getConnection() method (explained in the section "Introducing JDBCUtil" of Chapter 3):

```
      conn = JDBCUtil.getConnection( "scott", "tiger", args[0] );
```

Next, we get and print the transaction isolation level. Since we haven't changed it yet, this will be the default transaction level (i.e., READ COMMITTED). The method getTransactionIsolationDesc() simply translates each of the standard constants into a descriptive text (as you'll see in its definition at the end of this program):

```
int txnIsolationLevel = conn.getTransactionIsolation();
System.out.println( "Default transaction isolation level: " +
  _getTransactionIsolationDesc( txnIsolationLevel ) );
```

We then proceed to set the transaction isolation level to SERIALIZABLE, and print a description of it again to end the first try catch block. We close the connection in the finally clause:

```
conn.setTransactionIsolation( Connection.TRANSACTION_SERIALIZABLE );
txnIsolationLevel = conn.getTransactionIsolation();
System.out.println( "transaction isolation level is now " +
  _getTransactionIsolationDesc( txnIsolationLevel ) );
}
finally
{
  JDBCUtil.close( conn );
}
```

So far we have set the transaction isolation level to the two values that have direct JDBC API support (through the setTransactionIsolation() method and defined constants in the Connection interface). Since there is no constant in the Connection interface corresponding to the Oracle-specific isolation level of READ ONLY, we need to use a procedural call (a PL/SQL anonymous block) using the CallableStatement interface (the CallableStatement interface is discussed in detail in Chapter 6). In the anonymous block, we invoke the set transaction read only command discussed earlier. First, we declare a String variable containing the PL/SQL anonymous block, and then we declare a CallableStatement variable outside the try catch block:

```
String stmtString = "begin set transaction read only; end;";
CallableStatement cstmt = null;
try
{
```

We then obtain a connection:

```
conn = JDBCUtil.getConnection( "scott", "tiger", "ora10g" );
```

Next, we prepare and execute the CallableStatement, thus setting the transaction isolation level to READ ONLY:

```
System.out.println( "Setting the transaction isolation level to READ ONLY");
cstmt = conn.prepareCall( stmtString );
cstmt.execute();
```

We obtain the transaction level and print out its description to end the `main()` method:

```
    int txnIsolationLevel = conn.getTransactionIsolation();
    System.out.println( "transaction isolation level is now " +
      _getTransactionIsolationDesc( txnIsolationLevel ) );
  }
  finally
  {
    JDBCUtil.close( cstmt );
    JDBCUtil.close( conn );
  }
}
```

At the end of the program is the definition of the method `_getTransactionIsolationDesc`, which prints out the description of a given transaction isolation level:

```
  private static String _getTransactionIsolationDesc ( int txnIsolationLevel )
  {
    switch( txnIsolationLevel )
    {
      case Connection.TRANSACTION_READ_COMMITTED:
        return "READ_COMMITTED";
      case Connection.TRANSACTION_SERIALIZABLE:
        return "TRANSACTION_SERIALIZABLE";
      case Connection.TRANSACTION_READ_UNCOMMITTED:
        return "TRANSACTION_READ_UNCOMMITTED";
      case Connection.TRANSACTION_REPEATABLE_READ:
        return "TRANSACTION_REPEATABLE_READ";
      case Connection.TRANSACTION_NONE:
        return "TRANSACTION_NONE";
    }
    return "UNKNOWN";
  }
}
```

■**Note** Apart from invoking an anonymous PL/SQL block containing a `set transaction read only` command to make your transaction read-only, you can also invoke the method `read_only()` of the PL/SQL-supplied package `dbms_transaction` (see *PL/SQL Packages and Types Reference [10g Release 1]* for more details on this package).

> **Note** In 10*g* Release 1 and 9*i* Release 2, the method setReadOnly() of the Connection interface inter-
> nally does a set transaction read only. This is a bug, as it isn't the intended behavior of the method
> setReadOnly()—the intended behavior is a hint to the driver to possibly do some performance optimiza-
> tions. Oracle implementations don't really do any performance optimizations on the basis of this hint (except
> for issuing set transaction read only which, as just mentioned, turns out to be a bug).

The following is the output of the program DemoTransactionIsolations (note that it takes
the database name as a command-line parameter):

```
B:\>java DemoTransactionIsolationLevels ora10g
URL:jdbc:oracle:thin:@(DESCRIPTION=(ADDRESS=(PROTOCOL=tcp)(PORT=1521)(HOST=rmeno
n-lap))(CONNECT_DATA=(SID=ora10g)))
Default transaction isolation level: READ_COMMITTED
transaction isolation level is now TRANSACTION_SERIALIZABLE
URL:jdbc:oracle:thin:@(DESCRIPTION=(ADDRESS=(PROTOCOL=tcp)(PORT=1521)(HOST=rmeno
n-lap))(CONNECT_DATA=(SID=ora10g)))
Setting the transaction isolation level to READ ONLY
transaction isolation level is now READ_COMMITTED
```

Note that the transaction isolation level printed after we set the transaction isolation level
to READ ONLY is READ COMMITTED, which is incorrect. This happened because the getter method
getTransactionIsolation() does not actually query the database to find out the transaction
isolation level—it only looks at the Connection object in memory. Normally, this works, since
we go through the setter method setTransactionIsolation(), modifying the in-memory
Connection object as well, but if we want to set a transaction to READ ONLY, we have to
circumvent setTransactionIsolation(), which leads to the wrong result when you
invoke the getTransactionIsolation() method afterward.

Now that you have a good understanding of transaction isolation levels, let's look at an
important principal related to transactions that you should follow when developing an application on Oracle.

Sizing Your Transaction Resources According to Your Business Needs

Let's take a simple banking transaction. Say a wealthy bank customer wants to transfer
$1,000,000 from his savings account to his checking account. To satisfy this request, the data-
base may carry out the following steps (as instructed by the banking application):

1. Decrease the savings account balance by $1,000,000.

2. Increase the checking account balance by $1,000,000.

3. Do the banking application's financial transaction–related actions.

All the preceding steps may translate to any number of SQL statements, depending on how the banking application is implemented. Regardless, the atomicity of the transaction dictates that all three steps should either succeed or fail in their entirety. For example, say the customer gave a wrong checking account number by mistake. The second step would fail in that case. Now, if only the first step succeeds and the data in the database is committed at this point, then in technical jargon, the bank database's data integrity has been compromised (in practical terms, you have a really unhappy customer at hand!). A well-behaved application, on the other hand, would give a meaningful error message after rolling back the entire transaction. The customer then would get a chance to re-enter his information and proceed further.

As described in Chapter 2, when you create a transaction that modifies the database, Oracle internally generates undo data to maintain the pretransaction image of the database. This data needs to be retained in undo segments, at least until you issue a commit (at which point the data modifications become permanent) or a rollback (at which point the data modifications are undone). Once a commit or a rollback for a transaction, T1, is issued, the undo data generated by T1 is free to be overwritten by any other transaction. However, if you don't have sufficient undo space left before your transaction completes (meaning it commits or rolls back), you get an error message (specifically, ORA-30036: unable to extend segment ...) and you end up (typically) rolling back your transaction.

Now, say you have a large transaction, T1, that issues 1,000 SQL statements generating a lot of undo data. Suppose your database runs out of undo space when it is executing the five-hundredth SQL statement. As mentioned earlier, this would result in you typically issuing a rollback, thus undoing all the work done so far.

To solve this problem, the following solutions exist from a developer's point of view:

- Tune the SQL statements to reduce the overall resources consumed by them (including the undo space required). This is the best solution to the problem, is possible in the majority of cases, and is what you as a developer should consider first.

- Ask your DBA to allocate more undo space so that you don't run out of it in the midst of the transaction. This is a perfectly acceptable solution if you have already gone through step 1 and are still encountering the problem. Remember, disks are cheap nowadays— developer time is not!

- Divide the transaction into shorter transactions so that you issue intermittent commits to reduce the amount of undo space each of these transactions consumes. *Do not do this*! This is the worst solution for the problem, for the following reasons:

  - It compromises your data integrity. Remember the banking transaction? One equivalent of this solution would be issuing an intermittent commit after steps 1, 2, and 3 as shown.

    1. Decrease the savings account balance by $1,000,000.

    2. Issue a commit.

    3. Increase the checking amount in the checking account by $1,000,000.

    4. Issue another commit.

    5. Do the banking application's financial transaction–related actions.

    6. Issue the final commit.

Now imagine what happens if the bank's hotshot customer gave the wrong checking account number. Step 2 will fail, but this time the entire original transaction *will not* be rolled back because step 1 has already been committed to the database, thus compromising data integrity.

- The second reason you don't want to commit in the middle of your transaction is that doing so can increase the complexity of your code enormously. Since you have introduced commits in the middle of a transaction, you need to make sure that your code is able to restart in the event of a failure from any of those intermediate points where a commit has been issued. Depending on where you have placed these commits and how many such commits exist, this can soon lead to hugely complex code with multiple intermediate states from which you need to be able to reach the final state (after the last commit) to maintain the correctness of the logic. This means you need to develop, debug, and maintain more code.

- The last reason you don't want to issue intermittent commits in Oracle is that doing so slows down your entire system. This happens because each commit results in extra redo-log generation (see the "Redo" section of Chapter 2 for more details on redo), and redos are a systemwide point of contention.

To illustrate the last point of performance degradation due to intermittent commits just mentioned, let's run a simple benchmark using the JRunstats utility (see the section "JRunstats: The JDBC Wrapper for runstats" of Chapter 2 for more details on how to run this utility and interpret its results). This benchmark program will implement a transaction that inserts 10,000 records into a table, t1, created as shown here:

```
benchmark@ORA10G> create table t1 ( x number );
Table created.
```

In this example, we'll compare two different ways of inserting 10,000 records. One will commit inside the loop, and the other will commit at the end of the transaction. The program is as follows, with comments in between the code listings:

```
/* This class demonstrates why you should only commit at the end of your
transaction - it showcases the performance degradation when you issue a
commit in the middle of your transaction.
 * COMPATIBLITY NOTE: tested against 10.1.0.2.0. and 9.2.0.1.0 */
import java.sql.Connection;
import java.sql.PreparedStatement;
import java.sql.SQLException;
import book.util.JDBCUtil;
import book.util.JRunstats;
class BenchmarkIntermittentCommits
{
  public static void main( String[] args ) throws Exception
  {
```

In the main() method, we first get the connection inside the try catch block:

```
    Connection conn = null;
    try
    {
      conn = JDBCUtil.getConnection( "benchmark", "benchmark", "ora10g" );
```

We prepare our benchmarking statements in the JRunstats utility, and mark the beginning of the benchmark by invoking markStart():

```
JRunstats.prepareBenchmarkStatements( conn );
JRunstats.markStart( conn );
```

We invoke the procedure _doInsertCommitInLoop() (defined later in the program), which inserts the 10,000 records in a loop but commits within the loop:

```
_doInsertCommitInLoop( conn );
```

We then mark the middle of the program and invoke the procedure _doInsertCommitOutsideLoop()(defined later in the program), which commits outside the loop:

```
JRunstats.markMiddle( conn );
_doInsertCommitOutsideLoop( conn );
```

Finally, we end the benchmarking by calling the method markEnd() and closing all benchmarking statements in the JRunstats program:

```
    JRunstats.markEnd( conn );
  }
  finally
  {
    JRunstats.closeBenchmarkStatements( conn );
    JDBCUtil.close( conn );
  }
}
```

The following procedure, _doInsertCommitInLoop(), inserts 10,000 records into t1 in a loop and commits within the loop (shown in bold):

```
private static void _doInsertCommitInLoop( Connection conn ) throws SQLException
{
  String stmtString = "insert into t1( x ) values ( ? )";
  PreparedStatement pstmt = null;
  try
  {
    pstmt = conn.prepareStatement( stmtString );
    for( int i=0; i < NUM_OF_RECORDS; i++ )
    {
      pstmt.setInt( 1, 1 );
      pstmt.executeUpdate();
      conn.commit();
    }
  }
  finally
  {
    JDBCUtil.close( pstmt );
  }
}
```

The procedure _doInsertCommitOutsideLoop() does the same thing, except the commit is outside the loop (shown in bold):

```
private static void _doInsertCommitOutsideLoop( Connection conn )
  throws SQLException
{
  String stmtString = "insert into t1( x ) values ( ? )";
  PreparedStatement pstmt = null;
  try
  {
    pstmt = conn.prepareStatement( stmtString );
    for( int i=0; i < NUM_OF_RECORDS; i++ )
    {
      pstmt.setInt( 1, 1 );
      pstmt.executeUpdate();
    }
    conn.commit();
  }
  finally
  {
    JDBCUtil.close( pstmt );
  }
}

private static final int NUM_OF_RECORDS = 10000;
}
```

Note that the PreparedStatement interface just used is covered in more detail in Chapter 5. When we run the program BenchmarkIntermittentCommits, we get the following output:

```
B:\>java BenchmarkIntermittentCommits
URL:jdbc:oracle:thin:@(DESCRIPTION=(ADDRESS=(PROTOCOL=tcp)
(PORT=1521)(HOST=rmenon-lap))(CONNECT_DATA=(SID=ora10g)))

------- Benchmark Results --------

Results from RUNSTATS utility

Run1 ran in 1300 hsecs
Run2 ran in 363 hsecs
run 1 ran in 358.13% of the time
```

Name	Run1	Run2	Diff	
STAT...commit txn count during		0	1	1
<- trimmed to conserve space ->				
STAT...redo size	5,361,548	2,462,672	-2,898,876	

```
Run1 latches total versus runs -- difference and pct
     Run1      Run2      Diff     Pct
   585,190   126,639  -458,551    462.09%
```

```
Runtime Execution Time Differences as seen by the client
```

```
Run1 ran in 1318 hsecs
```

```
Run2 ran in 365 hsecs
```

```
Run1 ran in 361% of the time
```

As you can see, the method _doInsertCommitInLoop() took around 360% of the time and consumed approximately 460% of latches as compared to the method _doInsertCommitOutsideLoop().

From the previous discussion, we can conclude that in Oracle we should issue commits based on our transaction needs, not based on the amount of resources (such as disk space) that would be consumed. This is because issuing intermittent commits in the misguided attempt to save resources leads to compromised data integrity, an overall increase in resource consumption, and more complex and bug-ridden code that runs slowly and does not scale. Thus, we should adjust the Oracle resources consumed in a transaction according to our transaction needs (which, in turn, are based on business requirements), not the other way around. Of course, we should strive to use all Oracle resources optimally.

■**Note** Splitting a transaction seems to be a common (and possibly sound) performance optimization technique in many other databases, such as Microsoft SQL Server, since these databases have a large transaction overhead. Note, however, that even for these databases, other disadvantages such as compromised data integrity and increased code complexity still remain. Oracle was designed from the ground up to deal with large transactions and, as we've seen in this section, using this technique in Oracle isn't required and isn't a good idea.

The Autocommit Feature and Turning It Off

In JDBC, when we obtain a connection, by default it is in autocommit mode. This means that a commit is automatically issued after every SQL statement has been successfully executed. In other words, every SQL statement we issue is treated as a separate transaction. From the discussion in the previous section, you should know why this is not a good idea. Thus, after getting a connection, we should *always* turn this feature off by invoking the setAutoCommit() method on the Connection object, as highlighted in the following code snippet:

```
Connection connection = null;
  try
  {
```

```
    // ods is an initialized OracleDataSource object elsewhere
    connection = ods.getConnection();
    connection.setAutoCommit( false );
    . . .
  }
  . . .
```

In fact, we do this in the getConnection() method in the JDBCUtil class. One implication of turning off autocommit is that if we have made any changes, we need to explicitly commit them in case of success or roll them back in case of error (since we would be turning off the autocommit feature).

The commit and rollback methods could throw a SQLException, though this is a rare situation and cannot typically be handled by the application. Note that when autocommit is off, and a connection is closed without a commit or a rollback, an implicit commit is issued by Oracle, thus committing any uncommitted changes.

■**Note** There is an inconsistency in the Oracle JDBC driver (including the 10*g* driver) wherein if you commit once (with autocommit off), execute some other DMLs, and then forget to commit, the DMLs are rolled back (as opposed to being implicitly committed as the document *Oracle Database JDBC Developer's Guide and Reference* states).

However, we should always explicitly commit or roll back our transactions, since the default action may not be what we desire. Typically, we commit at the end of the transaction and roll back if there is an exception before reaching the commit statement in our program.

■**Tip** Turn off the JDBC autocommit feature right after you obtain a connection in your JDBC application running on Oracle. Explicitly issue a commit on a successful transaction or a rollback on failure.

Transaction Savepoints

The JDBC 3.0 specification exposes a database feature called *savepoints*. Savepoints offer finer demarcation within transactions. Without savepoints, a JDBC application (or any application, for that matter) has only two ways of controlling the effects of a transaction. The first way is to call the commit() method, as shown earlier, which causes *all* the modifications associated with the transaction to be saved. The second way is to call the rollback() method, which causes *all* unsaved modifications in the current transaction to be discarded. In other words, the only options are to save *all* the changes or abandon *all* the changes associated with the current transaction. Note that these options are not a bad thing and are in fact what we require most of the time.

■**Note** Savepoints have been around for quite some time in Oracle, but they were not exposed through a specific method in the JDBC API before JDBC 3.0. Even with pre-JDBC 3.0 drivers that support calling stored procedures, you can issue a savepoint by invoking either the savepoint command or the savepoint() method of the dbms_transaction PL/SQL-supplied package (see *PL/SQL Packages and Types Reference [10g Release 1]* for more details on this package).

With the introduction of savepoints in JDBC, applications can set a savepoint within a transaction using the standard JDBC API and then roll back to the savepoint. This implies that all work done up to the savepoint in the transaction is not discarded and can be committed later in the transaction. Code operating within the transaction is allowed to preserve partial states of the transaction.

■**Note** Savepoints are supported for local transactions only. Specifying a savepoint within a distributed transaction causes a SQLException to be thrown.

Using Savepoints in JDBC

Three steps are involved in using savepoints in a JDBC application:

1. Create a savepoint to mark a point in the transaction to which you may want to roll back later.

2. Roll back to the savepoint somewhere in your program.

3. Release the resources associated with the savepoint at the end of the transaction.

Let's look at each of these steps separately.

Creating a Savepoint

You create a savepoint either by using the setSavepoint() method of the Connection interface, which returns a java.sql.Savepoint object, or by invoking the oracleSetSavepoint() method of the OracleConnection interface, which returns an oracle.jdbc.OracleSavepoint object. The following line shows how to create a savepoint using the standard Connection interface, assuming you have a connection object in the conn variable:

```
Savepoint savepoint = conn.setSavepoint();
```

You can give a savepoint a name by supplying a string to the setSavepoint() method; if you do not specify a name, the savepoint is assigned an integer ID. You retrieve a name using the getSavepointName() method of the Savepoint interface, and you retrieve an ID using the getSavepointId() method of the Savepoint interface.

Rolling Back to a Savepoint

You roll back to a savepoint using the `rollback(Savepoint savepoint )` method of the `Connection` interface:

```
public void rollback(java.sql.Savepoint) throws SQLException;
```

You can also use the `oracleRollback()` method of the `OracleConnection` interface:

```
public abstract void oracleRollback(oracle.jdbc.OracleSavepoint)
throws SQLException;
```

Note that if you try to roll back to a savepoint that has been released, a `SQLException` is thrown.

Releasing the Resources Associated with a Savepoint

The method `releaseSavepoint()` in the `Connection` interface takes a `Savepoint` object as a parameter and removes it from the current transaction:

```
public void releaseSavepoint(java.sql.Savepoint) throws SQLException;
```

Note the following:

- Once a savepoint has been released, attempting to reference it in a rollback operation results in a `SQLException` being thrown.

- Rolling a transaction back to a savepoint automatically releases and makes invalid any other savepoints that were created after the savepoint in question.

- Any savepoints that have been created in a transaction are automatically released and become invalid when the transaction is committed or rolled back.

An Example of Using Savepoints

Savepoints have limited use in a JDBC application. This is because, in most cases, the requirement is to either commit the entire transaction or undo the effect of the entire transaction. However, savepoints may come in handy in some cases. Consider the requirement to log a transaction's identifying name and its success or failure in a table, `transaction_log`, which is created as follows:

```
benchmark@ORA10G> create table transaction_log
  2  (
  3    txn_name  varchar2(15),
  4    log_message varchar2(500)
  5  );

Table created.
```

If a transaction is successful, we want to insert a "success" message in this table. If a transaction fails, we want to log a message to the effect that the transaction has failed with a message indicating what caused the failure. Before any transaction, we also want to log a message indicating when the transaction began.

Consider the following pseudo code that tries to do this without savepoints:

```
Step 1: Log the message "beginning transaction at <timestamp>".
Step 2: Do the transaction. If there is an error then go to step 3. Otherwise go to
            Step 4.
Step 3: Since a rollback will undo the changes done by Step 1, we do the following:
        Step 3a. Redo the step 1 - hopefully, we have saved the original timestamp.
        Step 3b. Log the transaction failure message.
        Step 3c. Commit and raise an exception.
Step 4: Log the transaction success message.
Step 5: Commit the transaction.
```

Notice how in the case of a transaction failure, we need to redo the work done by step 1. Now if we use savepoints, the pseudo code changes to the following:

```
Step 1: Log the message "beginning transaction at <timestamp>".
Step 2: Create a savepoint save_point1.
Step 3: Do the transaction. If there is an error then go to Step 4. Otherwise go to
            Step 5.
    Step 4a. Roll back to save_point1.
    Step 4b. Log the transaction failure message.
    Step 4c. Commit and raise an exception.
Step 5: Log the transaction success message.
Step 6: Commit the transaction.
```

In case of success, the basic steps are the same. In case of an error in the transaction, we can simply roll back to the savepoint, log a failure message, commit, and raise an exception. Essentially, we did not have to redo the work done in step 1 because we used a savepoint. Let's see the same example in a working JDBC program. The transaction involves inserting three numbers into the table t1 created as follows:

```
benchmark@ORA10G> create table t1
  2  (
  3    x number primary key
  4  );
```

```
Table created.
```

Notice that column x in table t1 is a primary key. Thus, we cannot insert the same number twice in this table. The following DemoSavepoint program shows how to execute this simple transaction and use a savepoint to implement the pseudo code presented earlier. The class definition begins with the imports before the definition of the main() method:

```
/*This program demonstrates how to use the Savepoint feature
* that has been introduced in JDBC 3.0.
* COMPATIBLITY NOTE:
*    runs successfully on 10.1.0.2.0 and 9.2.0.1.0 */
import java.util.Date;
import java.sql.SQLException;
import java.sql.Savepoint;
```

```
import java.sql.PreparedStatement;
import java.sql.Connection;
import book.util.JDBCUtil;
public class DemoSavepoint
{
  public static void main(String args[]) throws SQLException
  {
```

Along with the usual connection variable, we also declare two PreparedStatement variables: one to insert the log statement and the other to insert into table t1 as part of the main transaction. We also declare a Savepoint variable:

```
Connection conn = null;
PreparedStatement pstmtLog = null;
PreparedStatement pstmt = null;
Savepoint savepoint = null;
```

The following insert statement would be used to log messages into the transaction_log table:

```
String insertTxnLogStmt =
  "insert into transaction_log(txn_name, log_message) " +
  "values( ?, ? )";
```

The following insert statement would be used to insert records into table t1:

```
String insertStmt = "insert into t1(x) values( ? )";
try
{
  try
  {
```

Inside the try catch block, we first get the connection:

```
    conn = JDBCUtil.getConnection("benchmark", "benchmark", args[0]);
```

Then we prepare the statement to insert the log messages and invoke the method _log() (defined later), which simply inserts a given transaction name and log message into the transaction_log table:

```
    pstmtLog = conn.prepareStatement( insertTxnLogStmt ) ;
    _log( pstmtLog, "demo_savepoint",
       "starting the txn to demo savepoints at: " + new Date() );
```

■**Note** Once again, don't worry if you're not yet comfortable with the PreparedStatement interface. Chapter 5 covers it in detail.

Next, we create a savepoint here because we don't want to lose the work done in logging in case of an error:

```
savepoint = conn.setSavepoint();
```

Then, we carry out the transaction of inserting three constant numbers—1, 2, and 3—in table t1:

```
    // our real transaction begins
    pstmt = conn.prepareStatement( insertStmt ) ;
    pstmt.setInt( 1, 1 );
    pstmt.executeUpdate();
    pstmt.setInt( 1, 2 );
    pstmt.executeUpdate();
    pstmt.setInt( 1, 3 );
    pstmt.executeUpdate();
}
```

In case of an error (which is indicated by a SQLException being thrown), we roll back to the savepoint, log a failure message, issue a commit, and rethrow the exception:

```
catch (SQLException e)
  {
    // an error occurred, we roll back to our savepoint
    conn.rollback( savepoint );
    // and log the error message
    _log( pstmtLog, "demo_savepoint", "Failed with error: " + e.getMessage());
    // we commit the log data
    conn.commit();
    // and throw the exception
    throw e;
  }
```

Otherwise, in case of success, we log a success message and commit the transaction:

```
    // if we reach here - it means transaction was successful
    // so we log the "success" message
    _log( pstmtLog, "demo_savepoint", "Successfully ended at: " + new Date() );
    // commit the changes to the database including the log message
    conn.commit();
  }
  finally
  {
    // release JDBC resources in the finally clause.
    JDBCUtil.close( pstmtLog );
    JDBCUtil.close( pstmt );
    JDBCUtil.close( conn );
  }
}
```

At the end of the program is the definition of the _log() method, which simply logs a message into transaction_log:

```
private static void _log( PreparedStatement pstmtLog, String txnName,
  String logMessage ) throws SQLException
{
  pstmtLog.setString( 1, txnName );
  pstmtLog.setString( 2, logMessage );
  pstmtLog.executeUpdate();
}
}
```

If we execute the program DemoSavepoint for the first time, we'll get the following results:

```
B:\code\book\ch04>java DemoSavepoint ora10g
URL:jdbc:oracle:thin:@(DESCRIPTION=(ADDRESS=(PROTOCOL=tcp)
(PORT=1521)(HOST=rmenon-lap))(CONNECT_DATA=(SID=ora10g)))
```

Let's look at the data in the tables t1 and transaction_log:

```
benchmark@ORA10G> column txn_name format a14
benchmark@ORA10G> column log_message format a30
benchmark@ORA10G> select * from transaction_log;

TXN_NAME       LOG_MESSAGE
-------------- ------------------------------
demo_savepoint starting the txn to demo savep
               oints at: Wed Dec 29 00:26:16
               PST 2004

demo_savepoint Successfully ended at: Wed Dec
                29 00:26:16 PST 2004


benchmark@ORA10G> select * from t1;

         X
----------
         1
         2
         3
```

As you can see, the transaction was successful, and the transaction start and success messages were logged in the table transaction_log as per the requirements.

If we rerun the DemoSavepoint program, we'll get an error since we're trying to reinsert the same value in column x of table t1, which is a primary key:

```
B:\code\book\ch04>java DemoSavepoint ora10g
URL:jdbc:oracle:thin:@(DESCRIPTION=(ADDRESS=(PROTOCOL=tcp)(PORT=1521)(HOST=rmeno
n-lap))(CONNECT_DATA=(SID=ora10g)))
Exception in thread "main" java.sql.SQLException: ORA-00001: unique constraint (
BENCHMARK.SYS_C005868) violated
...
```

When we execute a select from the tables t1 and transaction_log, we get the following:

```
benchmark@ORA10G> select * from transaction_log;

TXN_NAME        LOG_MESSAGE
--------------  ------------------------------
demo_savepoint  Failed with error: ORA-00001:
                unique constraint (BENCHMARK.S
                YS_C005868) violated

demo_savepoint  starting the txn to demo savep
                oints at: Wed Dec 29 00:26:16
                PST 2004

demo_savepoint  Successfully ended at: Wed Dec
                   29 00:26:16 PST 2004

demo_savepoint  starting the txn to demo savep
                oints at: Wed Dec 29 00:29:33
                PST 2004


benchmark@ORA10G> select * from t1;

         X
----------
         1
         2
         3
```

As you can see, the failure messages in transaction_log were also logged as required. Note that from a coding perspective, re-executing the statements before the savepoint may not be an issue, but doing so may be undesirable from a performance standpoint if these statements do a lot of work. Without savepoints, you may be potentially undoing a lot of work, only to redo it immediately afterward.

Summary

In this chapter, we briefly covered transactions, the different transaction isolation levels available, and the transaction isolation levels supported by Oracle. We discussed why we should commit a transaction based on business need, rather than on the amount of resources the transaction consumes. As you learned, breaking your transaction into smaller chunks with intermittent commits can lead to compromised data integrity, increased code complexity, and an overall slower system. You learned the importance of always turning off autocommit and explicitly executing a commit or rollback as required to end your transaction. You also examined transaction savepoints as applicable to JDBC applications, and you saw a use case illustrating savepoints.

In the next two chapters, we will look at statements that enable you to do all the work within your transaction.

CHAPTER 5

■■■

Statement and PreparedStatement

In this chapter, you'll briefly look at how Oracle processes SQL statements and then start your journey into the world of statements in JDBC. JDBC statements provide a mechanism for creating and executing SQL statements to query and modify the data stored in a database. As a quick introduction, JDBC offers the following flavors of statement interfaces:

- `Statement`: A `Statement` object lets you execute SQL statements, but does not allow you to vary input variables to the statement at runtime. An example of using this interface appears in Chapter 3.

- `PreparedStatement`: A `PreparedStatement` object represents a precompiled SQL statement that can be executed multiple times. It extends the `Statement` interface and adds the ability to use bind variables. *Bind variables* are parameter markers represented by ? in the SQL string, and they are used to specify input values to the statement that may vary at runtime.

- `CallableStatement`: This interface extends `PreparedStatement` with methods to execute and retrieve results from stored procedures.

You can browse the `javadoc` API for these and other JDBC classes and interfaces at `http://java.sun.com`. In this chapter, we'll focus on the `Statement` and `PreparedStatement` interfaces and their Oracle extensions. We'll cover `CallableStatement` and its Oracle extensions in the next chapter. By the end of this chapter, I hope to convince you that, in production code, you should *always* use `PreparedStatement` (or `CallableStatement`) objects instead of `Statement` objects. In fact, in the next chapter, I make a strong case for almost exclusively using `CallableStatement` in production code.

Before starting the discussion of the `Statement` objects, let's take a quick look at how Oracle processes SQL statements submitted by a client (through SQL*Plus, a JDBC application, etc.). This information will be useful in helping us arrive at certain performance-related conclusions later in this chapter.

Overview of How Oracle Processes SQL Statements (DML)

For this discussion, we only consider Data Manipulation Language (DML) statements. In particular, we exclude Data Definition Language (DDL) statements, as these are typically (and should be) done at install time and are not part of the application code.

DML statements are the statements that you will encounter most often, as you use them to query or manipulate data in existing schema objects. They include `select`, `insert`, `update`, `delete`, and `merge` statements. Oracle goes through the following stages to process a DML statement:

1. *Parsing*: In this step, the statement's syntax and semantics are parsed.

2. *Generating an execution plan*: For each statement, an execution plan is generated and stored in a shared memory area called the *shared pool* (see the section "Memory Structures: Shared Pool" in Chapter 2).

3. *Executing:* The statement executes, using the plan generated in step 2.

Step 2, generating the execution plan, can be very CPU-intensive. To skip this step in most cases, Oracle saves the results of the execution plan in a shared memory structure called the shared pool (see the section "Shared Pool and Bind Variables" of Chapter 2). When you submit a statement to Oracle, as part of the first step of parsing, it checks against the shared pool to see if the same statement was submitted by your session or some other, earlier session. If Oracle does not find the statement in the shared pool, it has to go through all three steps. This phenomenon is called a *hard parse*. On the other hand, if Oracle gets a hit in its shared pool cache, then it can skip the second step of generating the execution plan and directly go to the execution step. This phenomenon is called a *soft parse*.

■**Note** There is a third category of parsing loosely called *softer soft parse*. This happens if you have enabled your session to cache a set of cursors related to statements (we look at session cached cursors in more detail in Chapter 14). If there is a hit in a session cache, Oracle does a check in the shared pool to see if the cached cursor points to a valid SQL statement (the statement could become invalid for a variety of reasons, such as schema changes). If the entry is valid, then Oracle can reuse the results of an earlier soft parse done for this statement and go directly to execution step. Basically, this avoids repeated soft parses and saves Oracle resources, thus improving scalability of the applications even further.

Figure 5-1 shows the steps Oracle takes to execute a DML statement.

Oracle's Statement Processing Algorithm

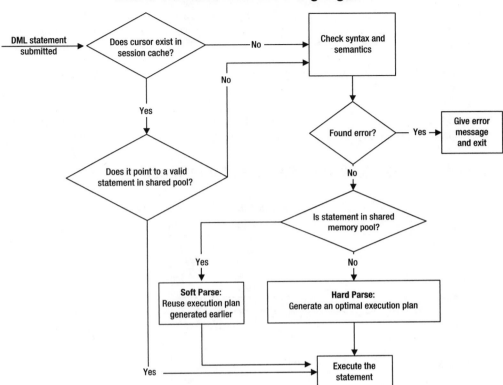

Figure 5-1. *The steps Oracle takes to process and execute a DML statement (see* http://asktom.oracle.com *and Chapter 5 of Tom Kyte's* Effective Oracle by Design *[Osborne McGraw-Hill, ISBN: 0-07-223065-7] for a detailed explanation of this algorithm)*

The goal when writing SQL statements in Oracle is to avoid repeated hard parsing and to minimize soft parsing. In this chapter, we'll focus on how to avoid hard parsing in JDBC programs. In Chapter 14, we'll cover techniques for minimizing soft parsing.

JDBC API for Statements

You're now ready to enter the exciting world of statements in JDBC. Recall that the standard JDBC API consists of two packages (see the section "Overview of JDBC API" in Chapter 3):

- `java.sql`: Contains the core JDBC API to access and manipulate information stored in a database, which includes the `Statement` interface and those that inherit from it (e.g., `PreparedStatement` and `CallableStatement`)

- `javax.sql`: Contains APIs for accessing server-side data sources from JDBC clients

Oracle's core JDBC implementation lies in the following two packages:

- `oracle.jdbc` *(and packages beneath it)*: Implements and extends functionality provided by `java.sql` and `javax.sql` interfaces (e.g., `OraclePreparedStatement` and `OracleCallableStatement`)

- `oracle.sql`: Contains classes and interfaces that provide Java mappings to SQL data types (e.g., `oracle.sql.OracleTypes`)

Figure 5-2 shows the JDBC classes pertinent to statements (also shown are the `Connection` and `ResultSet` interfaces, since they are relevant to most JDBC code using statements).

Connection, ResultSet, and Statement Interfaces

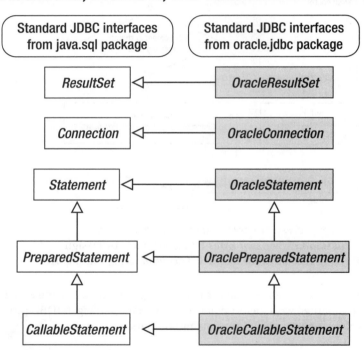

Figure 5-2. *JDBC* `Connection`, `ResultSet`, *and* `Statement` *interfaces and the implementing (or extending) Oracle interfaces*

On the left side of Figure 5-2 are JDBC interfaces in `java.sql` package, and on the right side are the corresponding Oracle interfaces in the `oracle.jdbc` package. Note that `OracleStatement` is an interface that extends `Statement`, `OraclePreparedStatement` is an interface that extends both `OracleStatement` and `PreparedStatement`, and so on.

■**Tip** I frequently use the command `javap` (available with the JDK) to examine the public methods of a class or an interface. For example, for finding out all public methods of the class `oracle.jdbc` `.OraclePreparedStatement`, you can execute the following command (after setting the environment and `CLASSPATH` as explained in Chapter 3):

```
javap oracle.jdbc.OraclePreparedStatement
```

In general, the prefix `Oracle` denotes an interface or a class that extends a JDBC standard interface or class, and provides its own Oracle-specific extensions in addition to the standard JDBC API functionality. For example, `java.sql.Connection` is a JDBC standard interface, and `oracle.jdbc.OracleConnection` is an interface that extends `java.sql.Connection`. Table 5-1 shows an overview of Oracle's key interfaces related to `Connection`, `Statement`, and `ResultSet` functionality.

Table 5-1. *JDBC Standard and Oracle Proprietary Interfaces Related to* `Connection`, `Statement`, *and* `ResultSet`

Class or Interface in the oracle.jdbc Package	Extends or Implements	Main Functionality
OracleConnection	java.sql.Connection	Encapsulates a database connection. It has methods to return Oracle statement objects and methods to set Oracle performance extensions for any statement executed by the current connection.
OracleStatement	java.sql.Statement	Has methods to execute SQL statements (including stored procedures) without bind variables.
OraclePreparedStatement	java.sql.PreparedStatement, OracleStatement	Has methods to execute SQL statements (including stored procedures) with bind variables. In the case of stored procedures, you cannot retrieve any result values back using PreparedStatement.
OracleCallableStatement	OraclePreparedStatement, java.sql.CallableStatement	Adds methods to PreparedStatement to execute and retrieve data from stored procedures.
OracleResultSet	java.sql.ResultSet	Contains data representing a data base result set, which is obtained by executing queries against a database.

The Statement Interface

The Statement interface is used to execute a SQL statement and return its results to the JDBC program. Chapter 3 presented an example of using this interface in the class GetEmpDetails. In this section, we will cover how to query and modify data using the Statement interface. For use in our example, we first create a simple table, t1, and a PL/SQL procedure, p2, that inserts a row in table t1 as shown:

```
scott@ORA10G> create table t1
  2  (
  3    x number
  4  );
Table created.
scott@ORA10G> create or replace procedure p2( p_x in number )
  2  as
  3  begin
  4    insert into t1 values( p_x );
  5  end;
  6  /
Procedure created.
```

Assuming you have a connection object initialized (as explained in Chapter 3), the steps involved in using a Statement interface are as follows:

1. Create a Statement object for the SQL statement:

   ```
   Statement stmt = conn.createStatement();
   ```

2a. The method used to execute a Statement object depends on the type of SQL statement being executed. If you want to execute a query using a select statement, then use the executeQuery() method:

   ```
   public ResultSet executeQuery(String sql) throws SQLException;
   ```

2b. If you want to execute a data-modifying statement such as insert, delete, update, etc., or a SQL statement that does not return anything, such as a DDL statement, use the executeUpdate() method of the Statement object. The method returns either the row count for the insert, update, delete, or merge statement, or 0 for SQL statements that return nothing. The signature of the method follows:

   ```
   public int executeUpdate(String sql) throws SQLException;
   ```

2c. If you don't know the statement type, you can use the execute() method of the Statement interface. For example, if the statement string is a query and you don't know that (because, for example, it is in a variable passed to you by some other program), you could use the execute() method:

   ```
   public boolean execute(String sql) throws SQLException;
   ```

2d. If you want to execute a stored procedure (without using bind variables and without being able to retrieve data returned from the procedure), you can use the execute() method.

■**Caution** As you may have already guessed, using the Statement interface for executing stored procedures is *not* a good idea. You should use CallableStatement, as explained in the next chapter, for this
purpose because it allows you to pass parameters as bind variables and it also allows you to retrieve
values returned by a stored procedure.

The following DemoStatement class illustrates the methods in the Statement interface. We
first look at the main() method after importing the requisite classes:

```
/* This program demonstrates how to use the Statement interface
* to query and modify data and execute stored procedures.
* Note that you should not use the Statement class for executing
* SQL in your production code since it does not allow you to
* use bind variables. You should use either the PreparedStatement
* or the CallableStatement class.
*   COMPATIBLITY NOTE: runs successfully against 9.2.0.1.0 and 10.1.0.2.0
*/
import java.sql.ResultSet;
import java.sql.Date;
import java.sql.SQLException;
import java.sql.Statement;
import java.sql.Connection;
import book.util.JDBCUtil;
public class DemoStatement
{
  public static void main(String args[])
  {
    Connection conn = null;
    try
    {
      conn = JDBCUtil.getConnection("scott", "tiger", args[0]);
      _demoQuery( conn );
      _demoInsert( conn );
      _demoExecute( conn, "select empno, ename from emp where job = 'CLERK'" );
      _demoExecute( conn, "insert into t1( x) values( 2 ) " );
      _demoInvokingSQLProcedure( conn );
      conn.commit();
    }
    catch (SQLException e)
    {
      // handle the exception - in this case, we
      // roll back the transaction and
      // print an error message and stack trace.
      JDBCUtil.printExceptionAndRollback ( conn, e );
    }
    finally
```

```
    {
        // release resources associated with JDBC
        // in the finally clause.
        JDBCUtil.close( conn );
    }
} // end of main
```

In the `main()` method, we get the connection as SCOTT, using the `JDBCUtil.getConnection()` method as explained in Chapter 3. We invoke the following methods, which I explain shortly:

- _demoQuery: Demonstrates executing a query using the Statement interface

- _demoInsert: Demonstrates executing an insert using the Statement interface

- _demoExecute: Demonstrates executing any DML (a query or an insert, update, etc.) using the Statement interface

- _demoInvokingSQLProcedure: Demonstrates invoking a SQL procedure without using bind variables and without being able to retrieve values back from the stored procedure

Let's look at each of these methods in detail now, starting with the first half of _demoQuery():

```
// execute a query using the Statement interface
private static void _demoQuery( Connection conn ) throws SQLException
{
    ResultSet rset = null;
    Statement stmt = null;
    try
    {
```

Inside the `try catch` block, we first create the statement:

```
    stmt = conn.createStatement();
```

Next, we use the `executeQuery()` method on the Statement object, passing the `select` statement that we want to execute. The invocation returns query results in the form of a ResultSet object.

```
    // execute the query
    rset = stmt.executeQuery(
        "select empno, ename, hiredate from emp where job = 'CLERK'" );
```

As explained in Chapter 3, a ResultSet object maintains a cursor pointing to its current row of data. Initially, the cursor is positioned before the first row. We use the next() method to move the cursor to the next row, thus iterating through the result set as shown in the following code. The next() method returns false when there are no more rows in the ResultSet object, at which point we exit the loop. Within the loop, we retrieve each column value of a row using the appropriate getXXX() method of the ResultSet interface. This means using getInt() with the integer column empno, getString() with the string column ename, and getDate() with the date column hiredate. The first parameter of these methods is the positional index of the column in the select clause in the query (the index starts from 1).

```
// loop through the result set and print
while (rset.next())
{
  int empNo = rset.getInt ( 1 );
  String empName = rset.getString ( 2 );
  Date hireDate = rset.getDate ( 3 );
  System.out.println( empNo + "," + empName + "," + hireDate );
}
```

We end the try catch block with a finally clause in which we close the result set and the statement objects. Putting these objects in the finally clause ensures that they always get called (e.g., even in the case of an exception); otherwise, the database can run out of cursor resources.

```
}
finally
{
  JDBCUtil.close( rset );
  JDBCUtil.close( stmt );
}
}
```

The next method, _demoInsert(), illustrates how to insert data using the executeUpdate() method of the Statement interface:

```
// demonstrate inserting record using the Statement interface
private static void _demoInsert( Connection conn ) throws SQLException
{
  Statement stmt = null;
  try
  {
    stmt = conn.createStatement();
    // execute the insert
    int numOfRowsInserted = stmt.executeUpdate(
       "insert into t1( x) values( 1 ) " );
    System.out.println( "Number of rows inserted = " + numOfRowsInserted );
  }
  finally
  {
    JDBCUtil.close( stmt );
  }
}
```

As you can see, most of the code is similar to the method _demoQuery() shown earlier. The only difference is that this time we use the executeUpdate() method to insert a row in the table t1 and print the number of rows inserted successfully as returned by executeUpdate(). The same technique can also be used to update and delete rows from a table.

The following method, _demoExecute(), takes a connection object and a SQL statement and executes the statement using the execute() method of the Statement interface. It can be invoked for a query statement as well as a nonquery DML statement, such as an insert, as illustrated in the main() program:

```java
// demonstrate the execute() method of the Statement interface
private static void _demoExecute( Connection conn, String sqlStmt )
  throws SQLException
{
  ResultSet rset = null;
  Statement stmt = null;
  try
  {
    stmt = conn.createStatement();
    // execute the query
```

After creating the statement, we execute it and get the boolean value that tells us if the statement was a query or a not.

```java
    boolean isQuery = stmt.execute( sqlStmt );
```

If it is a query, we get the ResultSet and print the results. In this example, we have to know the column type and position (or name) of the query to retrieve the results. Notice how we use the column names (instead of column's positional index) to get the results this time.

```java
    // if it is a query, get the result set and print the results
    if( isQuery )
    {
      rset = stmt.getResultSet();
      while (rset.next())
      {
        int empNo = rset.getInt ( "empno" );
        String empName = rset.getString ( "ename" );
        System.out.println( empNo + "," + empName );
      }
    }
```

If it is not a query, we assume it is an insert, update, or delete and get the number of rows affected using the getUpdateCount() method. We also close the statement and result set at the end of the method:

```java
    else
    {
      // we assume it is an insert, update, or delete statement
      int numOfRowsAffected = stmt.getUpdateCount();
      System.out.println( "Number of rows affected by execute() = " +
        numOfRowsAffected );
    }
  }
  finally
```

```
    {
      JDBCUtil.close( rset );
      JDBCUtil.close( stmt );
    }
  }
```

As mentioned earlier, we can also use the execute() method to execute a stored procedure, although we cannot use bind values, and we cannot retrieve any values returned by the
stored procedure. The method _demoInvokingSQLProcedure at the end of the program
DemoStatement illustrates this:

```
  private static void _demoInvokingSQLProcedure( Connection conn )
    throws SQLException
  {
    Statement stmt = null;
    try
    {
      stmt = conn.createStatement();
      // execute the sql procedure
      boolean ignore = stmt.execute( "begin p2( 3 ); end;" );
    }
    finally
    {
      JDBCUtil.close( stmt );
    }
  }
} // end of program
```

We use the Oracle style anonymous block enclosed in the begin/end block to invoke the
procedure. We will look at another style, called SQL92, in Chapter 6.

Now that you've learned about the Statement interface, let's look at why it isn't a good
idea to use it in your code. The basic problem with the Statement interface is that it accepts
only literal parameters. In the preceding example, the value of employee number would be
hard-coded into the query each time, and every variation of the query—even though it may
vary only by the value of supplied employee number—would be treated as a brand-new query
by Oracle and would be hard-parsed. For example, the query select ename from emp where
empno = 1234 is treated as distinct from the query select ename from emp where empno =
4321, whereas both queries are the same except for the user input of the employee number.
As already discussed, this is something to avoid. When we use a PreparedStatement object, we
replace the literal value with a placeholder (? in JDBC)—in other words, a *bind variable*—so
that Oracle will treat it as the same statement each time. The actual values (1234 and 4321 in
the example) are bound to the query at runtime. In this case, Oracle performs a hard parse the
first time it encounters the statement, and it performs much less expensive soft parses subsequently.

If you want to see proof of how much difference this can make in terms of performance,
I refer you to the example in the "Bind Variables Example" section of the Chapter 2, which
showed the vast decrease in execution time and resource uses obtained when inserting 10,000
records in a table with bind variables rather than without.

Another problem with using the Statement interface is that the program becomes vulnerable to SQL injection attacks by hackers. We'll look at SQL injection in more detail when we cover the PreparedStatement interface in the upcoming section titled "Using Bind Variables Makes Your Program More Secure."

Tip Never use the Statement class in your production code, as it does not allow you to use bind variables, which in turn makes your program slower, less scalable, and more vulnerable to SQL injection attacks. To use bind variables in JDBC, you have to use PreparedStatement/OraclePreparedStatement (or CallableStatement or OracleCallableStatement in the case of stored procedures, as we will see in the next chapter) instead of the Statement class.

The PreparedStatement Interface

A PreparedStatement object represents a precompiled SQL statement that lets you efficiently execute a statement multiple times using different bind variables. Using prepared statements lets Oracle compile the statement only once instead of having to compile it once with each call that changes one of the input parameters. An analogy would be a Java program that takes some input parameters.

The first option is to hard-code your input parameter values in the program. In this case, every time you need to deal with a different input value, you will have to change the program and recompile it. Using a Statement class is somewhat similar to this: Oracle has to compile your statement each time an input value changes, since the value is hard-coded in the statement itself.

A second, smarter option is to get the user input as a command-line parameter. In this case, you compile the program only once before invoking it many times with different values of the command-line parameters. Using PreparedStatement with bind values is similar to this scenario, in that you compile the statement only once and bind it at runtime with different values.

The next few sections discuss the PreparedStatement interface in detail.

Creating a PreparedStatement Object

The first step is to create a PreparedStatement object by invoking the prepareStatement() method of the Connection object, whose signature follows:

```
public PreparedStatement prepareStatement( String sql) throws SQLException
```

This method takes a statement and compiles it. Later, we can execute the same statement binding it with different values at runtime, for example:

```
PreparedStatement pstmt = conn.prepareStatement(
"select empno, ename, job from emp where empno = ? and hiredate < ?");
```

Notice how the actual values of the employee number and the hire date have been replaced by the literal ?. The ? in the query string acts as the placeholder for input variables that need to be bound subsequently in a statement. Let's now look at how we can use bind variables when working with a `PreparedStatement` object.

Using Bind Variables with PreparedStatements

There are two ways of binding parameters to the SQL statement:

- *By parameter index or ordinal position*: In this case, you use the parameter's index position to bind the parameter. The indexes begin with 1.

- *By parameter name*: In this case, you bind the parameter by its name. This requires the use of Oracle extension methods in the `OraclePreparedStatement` interface.

Binding Parameters by Index (or by Ordinal Position)

To bind a parameter by index, we use the appropriate `setXXX()` method depending on the data type of the input variable being bound. Here the index refers to the ordinal position of the ? value in the query string. For example, consider the SQL statement

```
select empno, ename, job from emp where empno = ? and hiredate < ?"
```

In the preceding statement, the first literal value has to be replaced by an integer representing the employee number, so we will use the `setInt()` method of the `PreparedStatement` interface:

```
public void setInt(int parameterIndex, int x) throws SQLException;
```

Similarly, the second literal value is a date, so we use the `setDate()` method to bind it with a date value:

```
public void setDate(int parameterIndex, java.sql.Date date ) throws SQLException
```

Next, we'll look at how to bind parameters by name.

Binding Parameters by Name (Oracle 10*g* Only)

An alternative to using ? as a placeholder for our bind variables is to bind by parameter name. This is an Oracle 10*g*-specific feature that improves the readability of the prepared statement string.

To use named parameters, we have to use the appropriate `setXXXAtName()` method of the `OraclePreparedStatement` interface. For example, if we want to bind the query discussed in the previous section by name, we would first use the following query string while preparing the statement:

```
select empno, ename, job from emp where empno = :empno and hiredate < :hiredate"
```

Notice that the literal placeholder ? has been replaced by a parameter name of our choice preceded with a colon (:). We then use setIntAtName() of the OraclePreparedStatement interface for the first parameter and setDataAtName() for the second parameter:

```
public void setIntAtName(java.lang.String parameterName,
  java.sql.Date value) throws SQLException;
public void setDateAtName(java.lang.String parameterName,
  java.sql.Date value) throws SQLException;
```

Executing a PreparedStatement

To execute a PreparedStatement, you can use one of the following three methods:

```
public boolean execute()throws SQLException
public ResultSet executeQuery()throws SQLException
public int executeUpdate()throws SQLException
```

The logic of when to use each method is the same as that for the methods with the same names in the Statement interface discussed in the section "The Statement Interface." Notice, however, that unlike their counterparts in Statement interface, these methods don't take a SQL string. This is because the SQL statement itself has already been precompiled at the time you invoke the prepareStatement() method of the Connection object.

It's time for some examples that illustrate all of the steps just described. Let's first look at an example that queries data.

Example of Using PreparedStatement to Query Data

The class DemoPreparedStatementQuery described in this section illustrates how to use the PreparedStatement interface in JDBC programs to select data from a database. It illustrates binding by parameter index and binding by parameter name. After the necessary imports, we have the main() method of the class:

```
/* This program demonstrates how to query data from a table
 * using the PreparedStatement interface. It illustrates
 * binding a parameter both by index and by name.
 * COMPATIBLITY NOTE: runs successfully against 10.1.0.2.0.
 *     against 9.2.0.1.0, you have to comment out the
 *     code using the binding by name feature to compile and
 *     run this, as bind by name is not supported in 9i.
 */
import java.sql.ResultSet;
import java.sql.SQLException;
import java.sql.PreparedStatement;
import java.sql.Connection;
import oracle.jdbc.OraclePreparedStatement;
import book.util.JDBCUtil;
import book.ch03.Util;
class DemoPreparedStatementQuery
{
```

```
public static void main(String args[])
{
  Util.checkProgramUsage( args );
  Connection conn = null;
  try
  {
    conn = JDBCUtil.getConnection("scott", "tiger", args[0]);
    _demoBindingByParameterIndex( conn );
    _demoBindingByParameterName( conn );
  }
  catch (SQLException e)
  {
    // handle the exception properly - in this case, we just
    // print the stack trace.
    JDBCUtil.printException ( e );
  }
  finally
  {
    // release the JDBC resources in the finally clause.
    JDBCUtil.close( conn );
  }
} // end of main()
```

In the main() method, after getting the JDBC connection, we invoke two methods:

- demoBindingByParameterIndex(): Demonstrates binding by parameter index

- demoBindingByParameterName(): Demonstrates binding by parameter name

We then close the connection in the finally clause to end the main() method.

The method _demoBindingByParameterIndex() starts by declaring required variables and beginning a try catch block (notice the constants declared for column indexes later):

```
/* demo parameter binding by index */
  private static void _demoBindingByParameterIndex( Connection conn )
    throws SQLException
  {
    String stmtString =
      "select empno, ename, job from emp where job = ? and hiredate < ?";
    System.out.println( "\nCase 1: bind parameter by index");
    System.out.println( "Statement: " + stmtString );
    PreparedStatement pstmt = null;
    ResultSet rset = null;
    final int JOB_COLUMN_INDEX = 1;
    final int HIREDATE_COLUMN_INDEX = 2;
    final int SELECT_CLAUSE_EMPNO_COLUMN_INDEX = 1;
    final int SELECT_CLAUSE_ENAME_COLUMN_INDEX = 2;
    final int SELECT_CLAUSE_JOB_COLUMN_INDEX = 3;
    try
    {
```

Notice how the select statement has ? for input parameters. The query will get us all employees of a given job title and hire date earlier than a given date. Next, we prepare the statement

```
pstmt = conn.prepareStatement( stmtString );
```

We then bind the parameters. The first parameter is a string for the job column of the emp table; hence we use the setString() method, passing the constant that defines the job column index value of 1 and the parameter value of CLERK.

```
pstmt.setString(JOB_COLUMN_INDEX, "CLERK" );
```

For the hiredate column, we pass the current date. The parameter index is the constant HIREDATE_COLUMN_INDEX with the value 2 in this case:

```
pstmt.setDate(HIREDATE_COLUMN_INDEX, new java.sql.Date(
    new java.util.Date().getTime()));
```

Notice that the date value is of type java.sql.Date, not java.util.Date.

We execute the statement next. Since it is a query, we use the executeQuery() method:

```
rset = pstmt.executeQuery();
```

Finally, we end the method after printing the results of the query and closing the result set and statement:

```
    // print the result
    System.out.println( "printing query results ...\n");
    while (rset.next())
    {
      int empNo = rset.getInt ( 1 );
      String empName = rset.getString ( 2 );
      String empJob = rset.getString ( 3 );
      System.out.println( empNo + " " + empName + " " + empJob );
    }
  }
  finally
  {
    // release JDBC-related resources in the finally clause.
    JDBCUtil.close( rset );
    JDBCUtil.close( pstmt );
  }
}
```

Let's look at how we can execute the same query, but this time binding parameters by name. The method _demoBindingByParameterName() begins by declaring variables and starting a try catch block:

```
private static void _demoBindingByParameterName( Connection conn )
  throws SQLException
{
  String stmtString = "select empno, ename, job " +
```

```
        "from emp where job = :job and hiredate < :hiredate";
    System.out.println( "\nCase 2: bind parameter by name\n");
    System.out.println( "Statement: " + stmtString );
    OraclePreparedStatement opstmt = null;
    ResultSet rset = null;
    final int SELECT_CLAUSE_EMPNO_COLUMN_INDEX = 1;
    final int SELECT_CLAUSE_ENAME_COLUMN_INDEX = 2;
    final int SELECT_CLAUSE_JOB_COLUMN_INDEX = 3;
    try
    {
```

Note that this time we use the parameter names :job and :hiredate for our input parameters. Notice also that we have to use the OraclePreparedStatement interface. The first step involves preparing the statement with the query:

```
    opstmt = (OraclePreparedStatement) conn.prepareStatement( stmtString );
```

Next, we bind the job parameter with the value CLERK using the setStringAtName() method of the OraclePreparedStatement interface (note that there is no : in the string we pass as the parameter name):

```
opstmt.setStringAtName("job", "CLERK" );
```

We bind the hiredate parameter with the current date value:

```
    opstmt.setDateAtName("hiredate", new java.sql.Date(
      new java.util.Date().getTime()));
```

The next steps of executing the query, printing the results, and releasing the resources are the same as in the previous example. This also ends our class listing.

```
        // execute the query
        rset = opstmt.executeQuery();
        // print the result
        System.out.println( "printing query results ...\n");
        while (rset.next())
        {
          int empNo = rset.getInt ( SELECT_CLAUSE_EMPNO_COLUMN_INDEX );
          String empName = rset.getString ( SELECT_CLAUSE_ENAME_COLUMN_INDEX );
          String empJob = rset.getString ( SELECT_CLAUSE_JOB_COLUMN_INDEX );
          System.out.println( empNo + " " + empName + " " + empJob );
        }
    }
    finally
    {
        // release JDBC-related resources in the finally clause.
        JDBCUtil.close( rset );
        JDBCUtil.close( opstmt );
    }
  }
} // end of program
```

This is the sample execution output of the `DemoPreparedStatementQuery` program:

```
B:\code\book\ch05>java DemoPreparedStatementQuery ora10g
URL:jdbc:oracle:thin:@(DESCRIPTION=(ADDRESS=(PROTOCOL=tcp)(PORT=1521)(HOST=rmeno
n-lap))(CONNECT_DATA=(SID=ora10g)))

Case 1: bind parameter by index
Statement: select empno, ename, job from emp where job = ? and hiredate < ?
printing query results ...

7369 SMITH CLERK
7876 ADAMS CLERK
7900 JAMES CLERK
7934 MILLER CLERK

Case 2: bind parameter by name

Statement: select empno, ename, job from emp where job = :job and hiredate < :hir
edate
printing query results ...

7369 SMITH CLERK
7876 ADAMS CLERK
7900 JAMES CLERK
7934 MILLER CLERK
```

So should you bind parameters by index or by name? This choice comes into play only if you are using Oracle 10*g*. In my benchmark tests, I found no material difference in performance between binding by index and binding by name. If portability across databases is critical for you, you should bind parameters by index. Otherwise, using `OraclePreparedStatement` and binding by parameter name can marginally improve the readability of your code. You can (and should) also improve readability in the case of binding by parameter index by defining meaningful constants for the parameter indexes as we did here (in other examples in this book, we may not follow this convention for simplicity). However, the SQL constants for statement strings still contain the not-so-readable ? in this case.

■**Caution** Under certain circumstances, previous versions of the Oracle JDBC drivers allowed binding `PreparedStatement` variables by name when using the standard `setXXX` methods. This capability to bind by name using the `setXXX` methods is *not* part of the JDBC specification, and Oracle *does not* support it. The JDBC drivers can throw a `SQLException` or produce unexpected results if you use this method, so I *strongly* recommend that you not use this technique.

Example of Using PreparedStatement to Modify Data

In this section, we'll look at how to make some modifications to existing data in our database. First, let's create a table, t1, and insert some data in it in the BENCHMARK schema as follows:

```
benchmark@ORA10G> create table t1 ( x number primary key,
  2   y varchar2(100),
  3   z date );
Table created.
benchmark@ORA10G> insert into t1 values ( 1, 'string 1', sysdate+1 );
1 row created.
benchmark@ORA10G> insert into t1 values ( 2, 'string 2', sysdate+2 );
1 row created.
benchmark@ORA10G> insert into t1 values ( 3, 'string 3', sysdate+3 );
1 row created.
benchmark@ORA10G> insert into t1 values ( 4, 'string 4', sysdate+4 );
1 row created.
benchmark@ORA10G> commit;
```

The following DemoInsUpdDelUsingPreparedStatement class illustrates how to use a prepared statement to insert, update, and delete data from table t1. The program begins by importing statements and defining the main() method that invokes other private methods:

```
/* This program shows how to insert, update, and delete data using
   the PreparedStatement interface.
* COMPATIBLITY NOTE: runs successfully against 10.1.0.2.0.
*     against 9.2.0.1.0, you have to comment out the
*     code using the binding by name feature to compile and
*     run this, as bind by name is not supported in 9i.
*/
import java.sql.SQLException;
import java.sql.PreparedStatement;
import java.sql.Connection;
import oracle.jdbc.OraclePreparedStatement;
import book.util.JDBCUtil;
import book.util.Util;
class DemoInsUpdDelUsingPreparedStatement_
{
  public static void main(String args[])
  {
    Util.checkProgramUsage( args );
    Connection conn = null;
    PreparedStatement pstmt = null;
    try
    {
      // get connection
      conn = JDBCUtil.getConnection("benchmark", "benchmark", args[0]);
      _demoInsert( conn );
      _demoUpdate( conn );
```

```
      _demoDelete( conn );
      conn.commit();
  }
  catch (SQLException e)
  {
      // handle the exception properly - in this case, we just
      // print a message and roll back
      JDBCUtil.printExceptionAndRollback( conn, e );
  }
  finally
  {
      // release JDBC resources in the finally clause.
      JDBCUtil.close( conn );
  }
}
```

After getting the connection, the main() method invokes three private methods:

- demoInsert(): Demonstrates inserting data

- demoUpdate(): Demonstrates updating data, and binds parameters by name

- demoDelete(): Demonstrates deleting data

The method _demoInsert() begins by preparing a statement to insert a row into t1:

```
// demo insert
private static void _demoInsert( Connection conn ) throws SQLException
{
  PreparedStatement pstmt = null;
  try
  {
      // prepare the statement
      pstmt = conn.prepareStatement( "insert into t1 values ( ?, ?, ? )");
```

Next, we bind the values for the three columns x, y, and z:

```
      pstmt.setInt(1, 5 ); // bind the value 5 to the first placeholder
      pstmt.setString(2, "string 5" );
      pstmt.setDate(3, new java.sql.Date( new java.util.Date().getTime()));
```

We execute the statement using the executeUpdate() method, which returns the number of rows inserted. We print out the number of rows inserted and close the prepared statement to end the method:

```
      int numOfRowsInserted = pstmt.executeUpdate();
      System.out.println( "Inserted " + numOfRowsInserted + " row(s)" );
  }
  finally
  {
      // release JDBC related resources in the finally clause.
```

```
    JDBCUtil.close( pstmt );
  }
}
```

The _demoUpdate() method updates one row of table t1. We use binding by parameter name this time. The method begins by creating a prepared statement and casting it to the OraclePreparedStatement interface:

```
// demo update use bind by name
private static void _demoUpdate( Connection conn ) throws SQLException
{
  OraclePreparedStatement opstmt = null;
  try
  {
    // prepare the statement
    opstmt = (OraclePreparedStatement)
      conn.prepareStatement( "update t1 set y = :y where x = :x");
```

We bind the two named parameters x and y next:

```
    // bind the values by name.
    opstmt.setStringAtName("y", "string 1 updated" );
    opstmt.setIntAtName("x", 1 );
```

The process of executing the statement is the same as that in the case of _demoInsert():

```
    // execute the statement
    int numOfRowsUpdated  = opstmt.executeUpdate();
    System.out.println( "Updated " + numOfRowsUpdated + " row(s)" );
  }
  finally
  {
    // release JDBC-related resources in the finally clause.
    JDBCUtil.close( opstmt );
  }
}
```

We end the program with the _demoDelete() method, which is similar to the _demoInsert() method:

```
// demo delete
private static void _demoDelete( Connection conn ) throws SQLException
{
  PreparedStatement pstmt = null;
  try
  {
    // prepare the statement
    pstmt = conn.prepareStatement( "delete from t1 where x = ?");
    // bind the values
    pstmt.setInt(1, 2 );
```

```
    // execute the statement
    int numOfRowsDeleted  = pstmt.executeUpdate();
    System.out.println( "Deleted " + numOfRowsDeleted + " row(s)" );
  }
  finally
  {
    // release JDBC-related resources in the finally clause.
    JDBCUtil.close( pstmt );
  }
 }
} // end of program
```

When we execute the program `DemoInsUpdDelUsingPreparedStatement`, we get the following output:

```
B:\code\book\ch05>java DemoInsUpdDelUsingPreparedStatement ora10g
URL:jdbc:oracle:thin:@(DESCRIPTION=(ADDRESS=(PROTOCOL=tcp)(PORT=1521)(HOST=rmeno
n-lap))(CONNECT_DATA=(SID=ora10g)))
Inserted 1 row(s)
Updated 1 row(s)
Deleted 1 row(s)
```

Using Bind Variables Makes Your Program More Secure

By now you should be convinced that using bind variables is critical for your program's performance and scalability. However, there is another equally important (in some cases, more important) reason to use bind variables. Using bind variables can protect your application from SQL injection attacks.

SQL injection is a technique that enables a hacker to execute unauthorized SQL statements by taking advantage of applications that use input criteria to dynamically build a SQL statement string and execute it. Let's look at an example. Consider an application that stores its username and password information in a table. For simplicity, we'll store this information in an unencrypted form, although in real-world applications better alternatives exist. We first create a table, `user_info`, with two columns, `username` and `password`:

```
benchmark@ORA10G> create table user_info
  2  (
  3    username varchar2(15) not null,
  4    password varchar2(15 ) not null
  5  );
```

We insert ten usernames and passwords. For illustration purposes, the data is such that the user `user1` has the password `password1`, the user `user2` has the password `password2`, and so on.

```
benchmark@ORA10G> begin
  2    for i in 1..10
  3    loop
```

```
4    insert into user_info( username, password )
5    values( 'user'||i, 'password'||i );
6    end loop;
7 end;
8 /
PL/SQL procedure successfully completed.
benchmark@ORA10G> select username, password from user_info;
USERNAME          PASSWORD
--------------    ---------------
user1             password1
user2             password2
user3             password3
user4             password4
user5             password5
user6             password6
user7             password7
user8             password8
user9             password9
user10            password10
```

Let's now look at DemoSQLInjection, a program that authenticates an application user by validating the combination of username and password input from the command line against table user_info's data. The usage of the program is

```
java DemoSQLInjection <bind|nobind> <username> <password>
```

The program takes three parameters from the command line. The first parameter can have two possible values: bind or nobind. If we give an option of nobind, the program verifies the username and password without using bind variables; otherwise, it does so using bind variables. The second parameter is the username, and the third parameter is the password. The class listing begins with import statements and declaration of the main() method:

```
/* This program demonstrates how using bind variables can prevent SQL
     injection attacks.
* COMPATIBLITY NOTE: runs successfully against 9.2.0.1.0 and 10.1.0.2.0.
*/
import java.sql.SQLException;
import java.sql.PreparedStatement;
import java.sql.Statement;
import java.sql.ResultSet;
import java.sql.Connection;
import book.util.JDBCUtil;
class DemoSQLInjection
{
  public static void main(String args[])
  {
```

Inside main(), we invoke _validateProgramInputs() (defined later), which performs simple input validation and prints program usage if required. We then store the three command-line parameters in string variables:

```
_validateProgramInputs( args );
String selectedOption = args[0];
String username = args[1];
String password = args[2];
```

The next step is to get the database connection within the try catch block.

```
Connection conn = null;
try
{
  // get connection
  conn = JDBCUtil.getConnection("benchmark", "benchmark", "ora10g");
```

If the first parameter is nobind, we invoke the method _authenticateWithoutUsingBind➥ Values(), which performs the authentication without using bind variables. Otherwise, it invokes _authenticateUsingBindValues(), which validates the username and password using bind variables. We end the main() method with the usual catch and finally clauses:

```
    if( NO_BIND.equals( selectedOption ) )
    {
      _authenticateWithoutUsingBindValues( conn, selectedOption,
        username, password );
    }
    else
    {
      _authenticateUsingBindValues( conn, selectedOption, username, password );
    }
  }
  catch (SQLException e)
  {
    // handle the exception properly - in this case, we just
    // print a message and roll back
    JDBCUtil.printExceptionAndRollback( conn, e );
  }
  finally
  {
    // release JDBC resources in the finally clause.
    JDBCUtil.close( conn );
  }
}
```

The definition of _authenticateWithoutUsingBindValues() follows. The main point to note is that the query statement string is computed by concatenating the input username and password to the query string. We use the Statement class to emphasize that we are not using bind variables in this case.

```
// authenticate without using bind values
private static void _authenticateWithoutUsingBindValues( Connection conn,
  String selectedOption, String username, String password ) throws SQLException
{
  Statement stmt = null;
  ResultSet rset = null;
  try
  {
    stmt = conn.createStatement();
    String verifyStmtString = "select count(*) from user_info " +
                              "where username = '" + username + "'" +
                              " and password = '" + password + "'";
    System.out.println("verify statement: " + verifyStmtString );
```

We execute the query next. If we find no records matching the input username and password, we print a message indicating that the authentication failed. Otherwise, authentication succeeds and a message to that effect is printed:

```
    rset = stmt.executeQuery( verifyStmtString );
    while( rset.next() )
    {
      int count = rset.getInt(1);
      if( count == 0 )
        System.out.println("Invalid username and password - access denied!");
      else
        System.out.println("Congratulations! You have been " +
          "authenticated successfully!");
    }
  }
  finally
  {
    // release JDBC-related resources in the finally clause.
    JDBCUtil.close( rset );
    JDBCUtil.close( stmt );
  }
}
```

The following method, authenticateUsingBindValues(), also executes the same select statement, except this time we use a PreparedStatement object and bind our input parameter values:

```
private static void _authenticateUsingBindValues( Connection conn,
  String selectedOption, String username, String password ) throws SQLException
{
  PreparedStatement pstmt = null;
  ResultSet rset = null;
  try
  {
```

```
      String verifyStmtString = "select count(*) from user_info " +
                                "where username = ? "+
                                " and password = ?";
    System.out.println("verify statement: " + verifyStmtString );
    // prepare the statement
    pstmt = conn.prepareStatement( verifyStmtString );
    // bind the values
    pstmt.setString(1, username );
    pstmt.setString(2, password );
    // execute the statement
    rset = pstmt.executeQuery();
    while( rset.next() )
    {
      int count = rset.getInt(1);
      if( count == 0 )
        System.out.println("Invalid username and password - access denied!");
      else
        System.out.println("Congratulations! You have been " +
          "authenticated successfully!");
    }
  }
  finally
  {
    // release JDBC related resources in the finally clause.
    JDBCUtil.close( rset );
    JDBCUtil.close( pstmt );
  }
}
```

The program ends after defining the _validateProgramInputs() method:

```
// check command-line parameters.
private static void _validateProgramInputs( String[] args )
{
  if( args.length != 3 )
  {
    System.out.println(" Usage: java <program_name> " +
      "<bind|nobind> <username> <password>");
    System.exit(1);
  }
  if( !( NO_BIND.equals( args[0] )  || BIND.equals( args[0] ) ) )
  {
    System.out.println(" Usage: java <program_name> " +
      "<bind|nobind> <username> <password>");
    System.exit(1);
  }
}
```

```
   private static final String NO_BIND= "nobind";
   private static final String BIND= "bind";
} // end of program
```

When we execute the preceding program with the nobind option while giving a valid username and password, it works fine:

```
B:\code\book\ch05>java DemoSQLInjection  nobind user1 password1
URL:jdbc:oracle:thin:@(DESCRIPTION=(ADDRESS=(PROTOCOL=tcp)(PORT=1521)(HOST=rmeno
n-lap))(CONNECT_DATA=(SID=ora10g)))
verify statement: select count(*) from user_info where username = 'user1' and pa
ssword = 'password1'
Congratulations! You have been authenticated successfully!
```

If we use the same option, but give a wrong username password combination, we are denied access, as expected:

```
B:\>java DemoSQLInjection  nobind user1 password2
URL:jdbc:oracle:thin:@(DESCRIPTION=(ADDRESS=(PROTOCOL=tcp)
(PORT=1521)(HOST=rmenon-lap))(CONNECT_DATA=(SID=ora10g)))
verify statement: select count(*) from user_info where username = 'user1' and pa
ssword = 'password2'
Invalid username and password - access denied!!
```

So far, the program looks rock-solid even if we don't use bind variables. Unfortunately, that is not really the case. Consider the following invocation with the option of nobind:

```
B:\> java DemoSQLInjection nobind invalid_user "junk_password' or 'x'='x"
URL:jdbc:oracle:thin:@(DESCRIPTION=(ADDRESS=(PROTOCOL=tcp)
(PORT=1521)(HOST=rmenon-lap))(CONNECT_DATA=(SID=ora10g)))
verify statement: select count(*) from user_info where username = 'invalid_user'
 and password = 'junk_password' or 'x'='x'
Congratulations! You have been authenticated successfully!
```

Even though an invalid username and password was given, the authentication was successful. What happened? A careful examination reveals that the input was engineered in such a way that the where clause of the query had the criterion " or 'x' = 'x'" appended to the end. And since this last criterion is always true, the executing select statement will always return a nonzero count, resulting in a successful authentication.

Let's see what happens if we use the same input parameters, but choose the bind option this time:

```
B:\code\book\ch05>java DemoSQLInjection bind invalid_user "junk_password' or 'x'
='x"
URL:jdbc:oracle:thin:@(DESCRIPTION=(ADDRESS=(PROTOCOL=tcp)
(PORT=1521)(HOST=localhost))(CONNECT_DATA=(SID=ora10g)))
verify statement: select count(*) from user_info
where username = ?  and password = ?
Invalid username and password - access denied!
```

The hacker would be disappointed in this case. When we use bind variables, the query itself remains the same, since we use ? in place of actual parameter values. Hence, it does not matter what the input parameter values are—the program will work as expected.

The SQL injection attack has caused a lot of grief at many websites that use relational databases. Note that the SQL injection attack is not specific to the Oracle database. Much has been written on this topic, as a simple search on Google will reveal. In Oracle, using bind variables can protect applications from this dangerous attack most of the time.

Now that you have seen how to use bind variables in the PreparedStatement and all the benefits of using bind variables, let's move on to look at some nuances related to bind variable usage.

Nuances of Bind Variable Usage

As you know by now, a bind variable is a parameter used in a SQL statement, the value of which is bound at runtime. So, for example, you could have the following statement, in which the values to be inserted into the emp table are bound at runtime:

```
PreparedStatement pstmt = conn.prepareStatement(
        "insert into emp values ( ?, ?, ? )");
```

However, can you run the following statement, in which the *table name* is bound at runtime?

```
PreparedStatement pstmt = conn.prepareStatement(
        "insert into ? values ( ?, ?, ? )");
```

The answer is no. If you try to run such code, you will get the exception java.sql.SQLException: ORA-00903: invalid table name.

Recall that the concept of bind variables exists so that Oracle can reuse the generated execution plans for a statement by substituting placeholders with literal values. Also, the parsing and query plan generation of a statement occur *before* the bind variables are evaluated. In the preceding case, for example, the parsing cannot be done because the optimizer needs to know the table name to generate a plan, to carry out the semantic checks (e.g., whether the user has the privilege to insert into the table), and so on. In other words, the optimizer does not have enough information to generate a query plan. A simple test to find out if something can be used as a bind variable is to ask, "Can I substitute a literal value (a string, an integer—whatever is appropriate) in its place and have SQL*Plus run it legally?" If the answer is yes, then you can use a bind variable there; otherwise, you cannot.

Table 5-2 gives some examples (with explanations) of correct and incorrect uses of ? as a bind variable placeholder.

Table 5-2. *Examples of Valid and Invalid Uses of Bind Variables in Statements*

Statement	Value(s) to Be Bound With	Valid?
`? into t1 values ( ?, ?, ? )`	insert	No

Explanation: `insert` is a keyword—you can't use bind variables for keywords.
(Try running `'insert' into t1 values (...)` in SQL*Plus.)

Statement	Value(s) to Be Bound With	Valid?
`update emp set job=? where ename = ?`	CLERK, KING	Yes

Explanation: You can legally run `update emp set job='CLERK' where ename = 'KING'`.

Statement	Value(s) to Be Bound With	Valid?
`delete emp where ename=?`	KING	Yes

Explanation: You can legally run `delete emp where ename='KING'`.

Statement	Value(s) to Be Bound With	Valid?
`select ?, ename from emp where empno=?`	1, 7629	Yes

Explanation: You can legally run `select 1, ename from emp where empno=7629`.

Statement	Value(s) to Be Bound With	Valid?
`select ?, ename from emp where empno=?`	empno, 7629	No

Explanation: You can bind values but not column names or table names in the `select` clause.
If you bind with a constant string value of empno, there won't be a runtime exception, though you
will get a constant string value of empno for all rows returned instead of the value of column empno,
which is most likely what you intended.

Update Batching

The update batching feature is relevant for data modification statements such as `insert`,
`delete`, and `update`. It allows you to submit multiple data modification statements in one
batch, thus saving network round-trips and improving performance significantly in many
cases. Oracle supports two models for batch updates:

- The standard model implements the JDBC 2.0 specification and is referred to as *standard update batching*.

- The Oracle-specific model is independent of the JDBC 2.0 specification and is referred
to as *Oracle update batching*. Note that to use Oracle update batching, you need to cast
the `PreparedStatement` object to the `OraclePreparedStatement` object.

Whether you use standard or Oracle update batching, you must disable autocommit
mode. In case an error occurs while you are executing a batch, this gives you the option to
commit or roll back the operations that executed successfully prior to the error. This is yet
another argument in favor of disabling autocommit.

Types of Statements Supported by Oracle's Batching Implementation

Oracle does not implement true batching for generic `Statement` and `CallableStatement` objects, even though it supports the *use* of standard update batching syntax for these objects. Thus, for Oracle databases using Oracle's JDBC drivers, update batching is relevant only for `PreparedStatement` objects. In other words, only `PreparedStatement` and, by extension, `OraclePreparedStatement` objects can gain performance benefits by using batch updates, regardless of whether we use standard or Oracle update batching. In a `CallableStatement` object, both the connection default batch value and the statement batch value are overridden with a value of 1. In a generic `Statement` object, there is no statement batch value, and the connection default batch value is overridden with a value of 1.

■**Tip** Whether you use standard update batching or Oracle update batching, you will gain performance benefits only when your code involves `PreparedStatement` objects.

Standard Update Batching

In standard update batching, you manually add operations to the batch and then explicitly choose when to execute the batch. This batching is recommended when JDBC code portability across different databases and JDBC drivers is a higher priority than performance. Instead of using the `executeUpdate()` method to execute an `insert`, `update`, or `delete`, you add an operation to a batch using the `addBatch()` method of the `Statement` interface:

```
public void addBatch( String sql) throws SQLException;
```

At the end, when you want to send the entire batch for execution, you manually execute the batch by invoking the `executeBatch()` method of the `Statement` interface:

```
public int[] executeBatch()  throws SQLException;
```

This method submits the batch of operations to the database for execution, and if they all execute successfully, the database returns an array of update counts. The elements of the returned array are ordered to correspond to the batch commands, which maintain the order in which they were added to the batch. In the Oracle implementation of standard update batching, the values of the array elements are as follows:

- For a prepared statement batch, it is not possible to know the number of rows affected in the database by each individual statement in the batch. Therefore, all array elements have a value of –2 (or the constant `Statement.SUCCESS_NO_INFO`). According to the JDBC 2.0 specification, a value of –2 indicates that the operation was successful but the number of rows affected is unknown.

- For a `Statement` batch or a `CallableStatement` batch, the array contains the actual update counts indicating the number of rows affected by each operation. The actual update counts can be provided because Oracle JDBC cannot use true batching for generic and callable statements in the Oracle implementation of standard update batching, as mentioned earlier.

If one of the batched operations fails during an executeBatch() call, then execution stops and a java.sql.BatchUpdateException (a subclass of java.sql.SQLException) is thrown. After a batch exception, the update counts array can be retrieved using the getUpdateCounts() method of the BatchUpdateException object. This returns an int array of update counts, just as the executeBatch() method does, the contents of which are as follows:

- For a prepared statement batch, each element has a value of –3 (or Statement.EXECUTE_FAILED), indicating that an operation did not complete successfully. In this case, presumably just one operation actually failed, but because the JDBC driver does not know which operation that was, it labels *all* the batched operations as failures.

- For a generic statement batch or callable statement batch, the update counts array is only a partial array that contains the actual update counts up to the point of the error. The actual update counts can be provided because Oracle JDBC *cannot* use true batching for generic and callable statements in the Oracle implementation of standard update batching.

If you want to clear the current batch of operations instead of executing it, simply use the clearBatch() method of the Statement interface. A clearBatch() essentially resets the batch contents to empty.

```
public void clearBatch();
```

Standard Update Batching Example

First, we create a simple table, t1, with one column, x, which is also the primary key:

```
scott@ORA10G> create table t1
  2  (
  3    x number primary key
  4  );
Table created.
```

The class DemoStandardBatching illustrates standard update batching:

```
/* This program illustrates the use of standard update batching.
 * COMPATIBLITY NOTE: runs successfully against 10.1.0.2.0. and  9.2.0.1.0.
 */
import java.sql.SQLException;
import java.sql.Connection;
import java.sql.BatchUpdateException;
import java.sql.PreparedStatement;
import java.sql.Statement; // for accessing constants only
import book.util.JDBCUtil;
import book.util.Util;
class DemoStandardUpdateBatching
{
  public static void main(String args[])
  {
```

Inside main(), we first validate program arguments, declare variables, and obtain a connection in the try catch block. Recall that autocommit is set to false in the JDBCUtil.getConnection() method:

```
Util.checkProgramUsage( args );
Connection conn = null;
PreparedStatement pstmt = null;
int[] updateCounts = null;
try
{
    // get connection, set autocommit to false in JDBCUtil method
    // Note: setting autocommit to false is required,
    // especially when you are using update batching.
    // of course, you should do this anyway for
    // transaction integrity and performance, especially
    // when developing applications on Oracle.
    conn = JDBCUtil.getConnection("benchmark", "benchmark", args[0]);
```

We prepare an insert statement next:

```
    // prepare a statement to insert data
    pstmt = conn.prepareStatement( "insert into t1( x ) values ( ? )");
```

The batching begins now. Instead of executing the statement after binding it with different values, we add it to a batch. We add three inserts to the batch, each with different values for column x:

```
    // first insert
    pstmt.setInt(1, 1 );
    pstmt.addBatch();
    // second insert
    pstmt.setInt(1, 2 );
    pstmt.addBatch();
    // third insert
    pstmt.setInt(1, 3 );
    pstmt.addBatch();
```

We then send the batch of three insert statements to be executed in one shot by using the sendBatch() method. The method returns an array of update counts. In the case of success, this count gives us the total number of successful insert operations. We conclude the transaction by committing it:

```
    // Manually execute the batch
    updateCounts = pstmt.executeBatch();
    System.out.println( "Inserted " + updateCounts.length + " rows successfully");
    conn.commit();
}
```

In case one of the insert operations fails, a BatchUpdateException is thrown. We handle this exception by obtaining the update count array from the exception object and printing out the values. In Oracle, there is not much value in the logic of this loop since it does not tell us which operation failed; it tells us only that *one* of the operations failed. After the loop, we print the exception and roll back:

```
catch (BatchUpdateException e)
{
  // Check if each of the statements in batch was
  // successful - if not, throw Exception
  updateCounts = e.getUpdateCounts();
  for( int k=0; k < updateCounts.length; k++ )
  {
    /*
       For a standard prepared statement batch, it is impossible
       to know the number of rows affected in the database by
       each individual statement in the batch.
       According to the JDBC 2.0 specification, a value of
       Statement.SUCCESS_NO_INFO indicates that the operation
       was successful but the number of rows affected is unknown.
    */
    if( updateCounts[k] != Statement.SUCCESS_NO_INFO )
    {
      String message = "Error in standard batch update - Found a value" +
        " of " + updateCounts[k] + " in the update count "+
        "array for statement number " + k;
      System.out.println( message );
    }
  }
  // print the exception error message and roll back
  JDBCUtil.printExceptionAndRollback( conn, e );
}
```

At the end of the class, we have the standard handling of the generic exception and the finally clause to release JDBC resources:

```
catch (Exception e)
{
  // handle the generic exception; print error message and roll back
  JDBCUtil.printExceptionAndRollback( conn, e );
}
finally
{
  // release JDBC resource in the finally clause.
  JDBCUtil.close( pstmt );
  JDBCUtil.close( conn );
}
  } // end of main
} // end of program
```

When we execute the preceding program with table t1 empty, we get the following output:

```
B:\>java DemoStandardUpdateBatching ora10g
URL:jdbc:oracle:thin:@(DESCRIPTION=(ADDRESS=(PROTOCOL=tcp)(PORT=1521)(HOST=rmeno
n-lap))(CONNECT_DATA=(SID=ora10g)))
Inserted 3 rows successfully
```

If we execute it again, we will get an error, because x is a primary key:

```
B:\>java DemoStandardUpdateBatching ora10g
URL:jdbc:oracle:thin:@(DESCRIPTION=(ADDRESS=(PROTOCOL=tcp)(PORT=1521)(HOST=rmeno
n-lap))(CONNECT_DATA=(SID=ora10g)))
Error in standard batch update - Found a value of -3 in the update count array f
or statement number 0
Error in standard batch update - Found a value of -3 in the update count array f
or statement number 1
Error in standard batch update - Found a value of -3 in the update count array f
or statement number 2
Exception caught! Exiting ..
error message: ORA-00001: unique constraint (BENCHMARK.SYS_C005873) violated

java.sql.BatchUpdateException: ORA-00001: unique constraint (BENCHMARK.SYS_C0058
73) violated…
```

Regardless of how many rows result in an error, the Oracle JDBC driver puts a value of –3 (indicating failure) in the update count for all of the rows.

Let's now turn our attention to Oracle update batching.

Oracle Update Batching

With Oracle update batching, the first step is to define a *batch value*, which is the number of operations you want to process per round-trip. You can set this batch value in two ways:

- By invoking the setDefaultExecuteBatch() method on the OracleConnection object:

  ```
  public void setDefaultExecuteBatch(int);
  ```

  This sets the batch size on all the statements associated with the connection to the specified value. As you may have guessed, there is a corresponding getDefault➡ ExecuteBatch() method available in the OracleConnection interface as well.

- By invoking the setExecuteBatch() method on the OraclePreparedStatement object:

  ```
  public void setExecuteBatch(int);
  ```

  This sets the batch size on a particular statement and is usually the way applications use the batching feature. A corresponding getExecuteBatch() method is available in the OraclePreparedStatement interface as well. Remember that the statement-level batch overrides the one set at the connection level.

If you want to explicitly execute accumulated operations before the batch value in effect is reached, then you can use the sendBatch() method of the OraclePreparedStatement interface, which returns the number of operations successfully completed:

```
public int sendBatch(int);
```

Just as in the case of standard update batching, you can clear the current batch of operations instead of executing it by using the clearBatch() method of the Statement interface. A clearBatch() essentially resets the batch contents to empty.

```
public void clearBatch();
```

Oracle Update Batching Example

In this section, we'll look at an example that illustrates Oracle update batching. The DemoOracleUpdateBatching class begins with the import statements and the main() method declaration. Within the main() method, we obtain the connection as usual:

```
/* This program illustrates use of Oracle update batching.
* COMPATIBLITY NOTE: runs successfully against 10.1.0.2.0. and 9.2.0.1.0.
*/
import java.sql.SQLException;
import java.sql.Statement; // for accessing constants only
import oracle.jdbc.OraclePreparedStatement;
import oracle.jdbc.OracleConnection;
import book.util.JDBCUtil;
import book.util.Util;
class DemoOracleUpdateBatching
{
  public static void main(String args[])
  {
    Util.checkProgramUsage( args );
    OracleConnection oconn = null;
    OraclePreparedStatement opstmt = null;
    try
    {
      // get connection, set it to autocommit within JDBCUtil.getConnection()
      oconn = (OracleConnection)JDBCUtil.getConnection(
        "benchmark", "benchmark", args[0]);
```

We prepare an insert statement, casting the returned object to the OraclePreparedStatement interface:

```
      // prepare a statement to insert data
      opstmt = (OraclePreparedStatement) oconn.prepareStatement(
        "insert into t1( x ) values ( ? )");
```

We set the batch size to 3 at the statement level:

```
      opstmt.setExecuteBatch( 3 );
```

We then insert three rows, printing out the number of rows returned each time. Since the batch size is 3, Oracle queues up the batches and executes them all together with the third insert.

```
// first insert
opstmt.setInt(1, 1 );
// following insert is queued for execution by JDBC
int numOfRowsInserted = opstmt.executeUpdate();
System.out.println("num of rows inserted: " + numOfRowsInserted );
// second insert
opstmt.setInt(1, 2 );
// following insert is queued for execution by JDBC
numOfRowsInserted = opstmt.executeUpdate();
System.out.println("num of rows inserted: " + numOfRowsInserted );
// third insert
opstmt.setInt(1, 3 );
// since batch size is 3, the following insert will result
// in JDBC sending all three inserts queued so far (including
// the one below) for execution
numOfRowsInserted = opstmt.executeUpdate();
System.out.println("num of rows inserted: " + numOfRowsInserted );
```

We next insert another row. This insert will get queued again in a fresh batch.

```
// fourth insert
opstmt.setInt(1, 4 );
// following insert is queued for execution by JDBC
numOfRowsInserted = opstmt.executeUpdate();
System.out.println("num of rows inserted: " + numOfRowsInserted );
```

We send this batch explicitly using the sendBatch() method:

```
// now if you want to explicitly send the batch, you can
// use the sendBatch() method as shown below.
numOfRowsInserted = opstmt.sendBatch();
System.out.println("num of rows sent for batch: " + numOfRowsInserted );
```

Finally, we commit our transaction and end the program:

```
    oconn.commit();
}
catch (Exception e)
{
  // handle the exception properly - in this case, we just
  // print a message and roll back
  JDBCUtil.printExceptionAndRollback( oconn, e );
}
finally
{
  // close the result set, statement, and connection.
```

```
        // ignore any exceptions since we are in the
        // finally clause.
        JDBCUtil.close( opstmt );
        JDBCUtil.close( oconn );
    }
  }
}
```

When we execute the preceding program (after deleting any pre-existing rows from t1), we get the following output:

```
B:\>java DemoOracleUpdateBatching ora10g
URL:jdbc:oracle:thin:@(DESCRIPTION=(ADDRESS=(PROTOCOL=tcp)(PORT=1521)(HOST=rmeno
n-lap))(CONNECT_DATA=(SID=ora10g)))
num of rows inserted: 0
num of rows inserted: 0
num of rows inserted: 3
num of rows inserted: 0
num of rows sent for batch: 1
```

As expected, the first two inserts were actually queued up and sent along with the third insert, as is evident from the number of rows inserted. The next insert is, however, executed explicitly when we use the sendBatch() method.

Now that you're familiar with both types of batching, next we'll cover a caveat regarding mixing interdependent statements in a batch.

Mixing Interdependent Statements in a Batch

Both update batching implementations generally work as expected. There are cases where the results may be surprising to you (especially when you use Oracle update batching). Intuitively, you would expect that changing the batch size should impact only the performance of the application, not the actual data inserted, deleted, and so on. However, this is not the case if you have multiple statements using batching in a loop, and some of these statements can have an impact on the rows manipulated by other statements in the loop.

Consider the following class (based on a test case supplied by Tom Kyte), which uses Oracle update batching. It takes a batch size as a command-line parameter and uses Oracle update batching to set the execution batch size on an insert and a delete from the same table t1 that we created in the earlier examples:

```
/* This program illustrates a special case of Oracle update batching
   where the results are nonintuitive although correct as per
   the JDBC specification.
* COMPATIBLITY NOTE: runs successfully against 10.1.0.2.0. and  9.2.0.1.0.
*/
import java.sql.Statement;
import java.sql.Connection;
import java.sql.PreparedStatement;
import oracle.jdbc.OraclePreparedStatement;
import book.util.JDBCUtil;
```

```
class TestUpdateBatching
{
  public static void main(String args[])throws Exception
  {
    if( args.length != 1 )
    {
      System.out.println("Usage: java TestUpdateBatching <batch_size>" );
    }
    int batchSize = Integer.parseInt( args[0] );
    Connection conn = null;
    Statement stmt = null;
    OraclePreparedStatement ipstmt = null;
    OraclePreparedStatement dpstmt = null;
    try
    {
      conn = JDBCUtil.getConnection("benchmark", "benchmark", "ora10g");
      stmt = conn.createStatement ();
      ipstmt = (OraclePreparedStatement) conn.prepareStatement(
          "insert into t1( x ) values ( ? )");
      ipstmt.setExecuteBatch( batchSize );
      dpstmt = (OraclePreparedStatement) conn.prepareStatement(
          "delete from t1 where x = ?" );
      dpstmt.setExecuteBatch( batchSize );
```

After creating the insert and delete statements and setting their batch size, we go in a loop where the insert statement inserts the loop index i, and the delete statement deletes the values matching 1 added to the loop index (i.e., i + 1).

```
      for( int i = 0; i < 2; i++ )
      {
        ipstmt.setInt(1, i );
        int numOfRowsInserted = ipstmt.executeUpdate();
        System.out.println("num of rows inserted: " + numOfRowsInserted );
        dpstmt.setInt(1, i+1 );
        int numOfRowsDeleted = dpstmt.executeUpdate();
        System.out.println("num of rows Deleted: " + numOfRowsDeleted );
      }
```

We send the batches for any remaining rows outside and commit the transaction at the end of the program:

```
      ipstmt.sendBatch();
      dpstmt.sendBatch();
      conn.commit();
    }
    catch (Exception e)
    {
      // handle the exception properly - in this case, we just
      // print a message and roll back
      JDBCUtil.printExceptionAndRollback( conn, e );
```

```
    }
    finally
    {
      // close the result set, statement, and connection.
      // ignore any exceptions since we are in the
      // finally clause.
      JDBCUtil.close( ipstmt );
      JDBCUtil.close( dpstmt );
      JDBCUtil.close( conn );
    }
  }
}
```

When we run the program with a batch size of 1, we get the following output:

```
B:\>java TestUpdateBatching 1
URL:jdbc:oracle:thin:@(DESCRIPTION=(ADDRESS=(PROTOCOL=tcp)(PORT=1521)(HOST=rmeno
n-lap))(CONNECT_DATA=(SID=ora10g)))
num of rows inserted: 1
num of rows Deleted: 0
num of rows inserted: 1
num of rows Deleted: 0
```

A select from table t1 gives

```
benchmark@ORA10G> select * from t1;
        0
        1
```

After deleting all rows from table t1, let's run the program with a batch size of 2:

```
B:\>java TestUpdateBatching 2
URL:jdbc:oracle:thin:@(DESCRIPTION=(ADDRESS=(PROTOCOL=tcp)(PORT=1521)
(HOST=rmenon-lap))(CONNECT_DATA=(SID=ora10g)))
num of rows inserted: 0
num of rows Deleted: 0
num of rows inserted: 2
num of rows Deleted: 1
```

When we do a select this time, we get a different result from the one we got when the batch size was 1:

```
benchmark@ORA10G> select * from t1;
        0
```

This is a case in which changing the batch size apparently changed the program's outcome! Although this looks like a bug, it turns out that this behavior is correct. Recall that in Oracle update batching, a batch is automatically sent to the database once the batch size is reached. When the batch size is 1, the delete statement does not affect any rows, since it attempts to delete values that do not exist in the database. So, we get two rows as expected. Table 5-3 lists the steps the JDBC driver goes through when the batch size is 2.

Table 5-3. *Steps in the* for *Loop When the Batch Size is 2 While Executing the* TestUpdateBatching *Class*

Loop Index Value (Value of i)	Statement	What Happens
0	insert	The batch size is 2. The statement gets queued up.
	delete	Since this is a new statement with a batch size of 2, it also gets queued up.
2	insert	This is the second insert, which implies we have reached the batch size limit. The JDBC driver sends both inserts inserting two rows, with column values of 0 and 1 for column x in table t1.
	delete	This is the second delete, which implies we have reached the batch size limit. The JDBC driver sends and executes both deletes. The first delete deletes the value of a row with a column value of 1. The second delete does not delete any rows since no rows match the criteria. Hence, we are left with just one row with a value of 0 for column x.

The key thing to note is that the delete statements in the loop directly affect the values inserted by the insert statement. In the case of a batch size of 1, the deletes worked on the data available after the inserts had been applied to the database. In the case of a batch size of 2, the state of the database on which deletes worked was different (since all deletes were sent after the two inserts were executed, not just the preceding ones). Since in the case of Oracle update batching this happens implicitly, it looks more confusing.

From this discussion, we can conclude that the batch size can impact the results when we mix different statements where the following statements affect the results of the preceding ones. In such cases, we should either ensure that our logic does not get impacted by the batch size or avoid using batches altogether. For example, we can change the loop structure of the program TestUpdateBatching to the following to get consistent results (assuming we want all inserts applied before all deletes):

```
for( int i = 0; i < 2; i++ )
{
  ipstmt.setInt(1, i );
  int numOfRowsInserted = ipstmt.executeUpdate();
  System.out.println("num of rows inserted: " + numOfRowsInserted );
}
ipstmt.sendBatch();
for( int i = 0; i < 2; i++ )
{
  dpstmt.setInt(1, i+1 );
  int numOfRowsDeleted = dpstmt.executeUpdate();
  System.out.println("num of rows Deleted: " + numOfRowsDeleted );
}
dpstmt.sendBatch();
conn.commit();
```

Oracle Update Batching vs. Standard Update Batching

In Oracle update batching, as soon as the number of statements added to the batch reaches the batch value, the batch is executed. Recall that

- You can set a default batch at the Connection object level, which applies to any prepared statement executed using that connection.

- You can set a statement batch value for any individual prepared statement. This value overrides any batch value set at the Connection object level.

- You can explicitly execute a batch at any time, overriding both the connection batch value and the statement batch value.

In contrast to Oracle update batching, standard update batching involves an explicit manual execution of the batch, as there is no batch value. You should choose standard update batching if you are concerned about the portability of your Java code across databases. Otherwise, choose Oracle update batching because you get better performance out of it (as you'll learn in the next section).

■**Caution** You can't mix and match the standard update batching syntax and Oracle update batching syntax. If you do so, you will get a SQLException.

Batching Performance Analysis

The following StandardVsOracleBatching class compares the elapsed time and the latches consumed for inserting 10,000 records for the case of standard update batching and Oracle update batching. The StandardVsOracleBatching class uses the utility class (discussed in the section "JDBC Wrapper for RUNSTATS" of Chapter 1) to compare the latches consumed and the time taken for the preceding three cases.

After the imports, the class begins by declaring some private variables:

```
/* This program compares standard update batching with Oracle update
   batching for elapsed times and latches consumed using the
   JRunstats utility.
* COMPATIBLITY NOTE: runs successfully against 10.1.0.2.0. and  9.2.0.1.0.
*/
import java.sql.SQLException;
import java.sql.Connection;
import java.sql.PreparedStatement;
import oracle.jdbc.OraclePreparedStatement;
import book.util.JDBCUtil;
import book.util.JRunstats;
class StandardVsOracleBatching
{
  private static int s_numberOfRecords = 0;
```

```
private static int s_batchSize = 1;
private static long s_start = 0;
private static long s_middle = 0;
private static long s_end = 0;
private static int[] s_batchSizeArr =
  { 1, 5, 10, 50, 75, 100, 150, 200, 300, 400, 500,
    750, 1000, 2000, 3000, 5000, 10000 };
```

In particular, the static variable s_batchSizeArr declares an array of batch sizes that we will run our three cases with. The following _checkUsage() method simply checks the program usage. The program takes the total number of records that we want to insert as a command-line parameter:

```
private static void _checkUsage (String[] args)
{
  int argc = args.length;
  if( argc != 1)
  {
    System.err.println(
      "Usage: java StandardVsOracleBatching <number of records>" );
    Runtime.getRuntime().exit(1);
  }
  s_numberOfRecords = Integer.parseInt( args[0] );
}
```

In the main() method, we invoke _checkUsage() and get the connection in the try catch block after declaring some variables:

```
public static void main(String args[])
  public static void main(String args[])
{
  _checkUsage( args );
  Connection conn = null;
  PreparedStatement pstmt = null;
  OraclePreparedStatement opstmt = null;
  String insertStmtStr = "insert into t1( x, y ) values ( ?, ?)";
  try
  {
    // get connection; set autocommit to false within JDBCUtil.
    conn = JDBCUtil.getConnection("benchmark", "benchmark", "ora10g");
```

We prepare the statements to be used for standard and Oracle update batching, respectively:

```
    pstmt = conn.prepareStatement( insertStmtStr );
    opstmt = (OraclePreparedStatement) conn.prepareStatement( insertStmtStr );
```

For each batch size, we execute the two cases, beginning with the case of standard update batching:

```
for(int x=0; x < s_batchSizeArr.length; x++ )
{
```

In the loop, we first prepare the benchmark statements in JRunstats:

```
JRunstats.prepareBenchmarkStatements( conn );
```

We set the current batch size in a variable:

```
s_batchSize = s_batchSizeArr[x];
```

Then we mark the beginning of the execution of the inserts based on standard update batching. We also mark our start time.

```
// mark beginning of execute with standard update batching
JRunstats.markStart( conn );
s_start = System.currentTimeMillis();
```

The following for loop inserts 10,000 records using the current batch size:

```
// execute with standard update batching
for( int i=0; i < s_numberOfRecords; i++)
{
  // batch s_batchSize number of statements
  // before sending them as one round-trip.
  int j = 0;
  for( j=0; j < s_batchSize; j++)
  {
    pstmt.setInt(1, i );
    pstmt.setString(2, "data" + i );
    pstmt.addBatch();
   // System.out.println( "Inserted " + numOfRowsInserted + " row(s)" );
  }
  i += (j-1);
  int[] updateCounts = pstmt.executeBatch();
  //System.out.println( "i = " + i );
}
```

Next, we insert the same number of records using Oracle update batching after marking the middle of our benchmark:

```
// mark beginning of execute with Oracle update batching
JRunstats.markMiddle( conn );
s_middle = System.currentTimeMillis();
// set the execute batch size
opstmt.setExecuteBatch( s_batchSize );
// bind the values
for( int i=0; i < s_numberOfRecords; i++)
{
```

```
            // bind the values
            opstmt.setInt(1, i );
            opstmt.setString(2, "data"+i );
            int numOfRowsInserted = opstmt.executeUpdate();
        }
```

We mark the end of the benchmark run, and then we print out the results followed by various close() statements being invoked to release JDBC resources in the finally clause:

```
            s_end = System.currentTimeMillis();
            JRunstats.markEnd( conn, 10000 );
            System.out.println( "Standard Update batching (recs="+
              s_numberOfRecords+ ", batch=" + s_batchSize + ") = "
              + (s_middle - s_start ) + " ms" );
            System.out.println( "Oracle Update batching (recs="+
              s_numberOfRecords+ ", batch=" + s_batchSize + ") = " +
              (s_end - s_middle ) + " ms");
            conn.commit();
            JRunstats.closeBenchmarkStatements( conn );
        }
    }
    catch (Exception e)
    {
      // handle the exception properly - in this case, we just
      // print a message and roll back
      JDBCUtil.printExceptionAndRollback( conn, e );
    }
    finally
    {
      // release JDBC resources in the finally clause.
      JDBCUtil.close( pstmt );
      JDBCUtil.close( opstmt );
      JDBCUtil.close( conn );
    }
  }
}
```

I ran the StandardVsOracleBatching program with multiple values of batch sizes for inserting 10,000 records into table t1 that I created as follows:

```
benchmark@ORA10G> create table t1 ( x number,  y varchar2(20));
Table created.
```

Table 5-4 and Figure 5-3 show the results of comparing elapsed times taken when I inserted 10,000 records for the cases of standard update batching and Oracle update batching. For no batching, it took an average of 13,201 milliseconds to insert 10,000 records.

Table 5-4. *Comparing Standard Update Batching with Oracle Update Batching for Inserting 10,000 Records*

Batch Size	Standard Update Batching (Milliseconds)	Oracle Update Batching (Milliseconds)
1	13,201	13,201
5	2,861	2,629
10	1,554	1,406
30	702	613
50	532	440
75	456	359
100	402	322
150	370	304
200	278	274
300	349	280
400	345	269
500	320	263
750	345	282
1,000	327	232
2,000	328	236
3,000	406	207
5,000	372	375
10,000	490	461

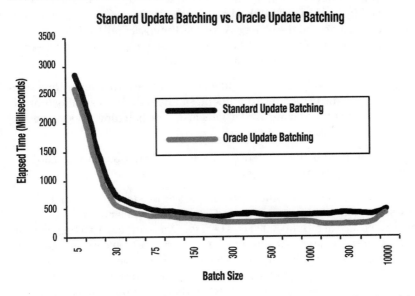

Figure 5-3. *Comparing standard update batching with Oracle update batching for inserting 10,000 records*

Figure 5-4 shows a comparison of latches consumed for standard versus Oracle update batching. The case of no batching is shown as batch size 1.

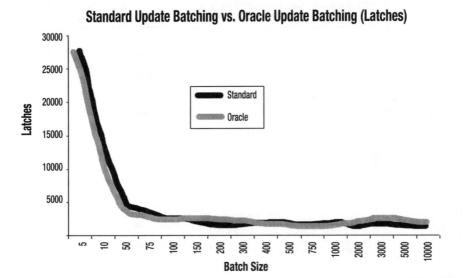

Figure 5-4. *Comparing standard update batching with Oracle update batching in terms of latches consumed*

We can make the following observations from the charts in Figure 5-3 and Figure 5-4:

- Batching makes a *huge* difference, both in elapsed time and in latches consumed. Without batching enabled (or equivalently with a batch size of 1), the average time taken is 13,201 milliseconds compared to the worst case of 2,861 milliseconds and the best case of 207 milliseconds when batching is used. Similarly, the latches consumed go down dramatically once batching is used, as shown in Figure 5-4.

- In general, in terms of elapsed time, Oracle update batching performs better than standard update batching. In the preceding experiment, standard update batching took between 1% to 30% more time as compared to Oracle update batching, depending on the batch size.

- In terms of latch consumption, the difference between Oracle update batching and standard update batching seems to be negligible.

- Although Oracle documentation recommends a batch size of 5 to 30 as optimal, the preceding case shows that a batch size of around 200 was best for standard update batching, and a batch size of around 3,000 was best for Oracle update batching in terms of elapsed times. In terms of latch consumption, a batch size of 2,000 was best for standard update batching, whereas a batch size of 750 resulted in the lowest number of latches consumed for Oracle update batching. Of course, this does not prove that these batch sizes are always optimal—it only demonstrates that you should benchmark critical portions of code using an experiment such as that just presented to find out what the optimal batch size is in your case.

- Notice that as the batch size increases, you gain in terms of elapsed time initially, and then you start witnessing a negative effect. For example, in the case of Oracle update batching, after a batch size of 3,000 you start seeing decreasing performance. This indicates that you cannot blindly set the batch size to the maximum number of records you modify; rather, you have to benchmark your particular scenario to arrive at an optimal batch size.

- It is a good idea to parameterize the batch size for an important set of operations so that you can easily change it.

Summary

In this chapter, you learned how to query and modify data using the JDBC classes `Statement`, `PreparedStatement`, and `OraclePreparedStatement`. You also learned the reasons you should not use the `Statement` class in production code, as it does not support using bind variables. By using bind variables in your program, you not only make your application more performant and scaleable, but you also make it more secure by preventing SQL injection attacks.

You discovered how to boost application performance tremendously by using update batching, which in Oracle is available only when you use prepared statements. You saw a comparison of standard and Oracle update batching in terms of elapsed times and latch consumption, and you observed that Oracle update batching outperforms standard update batching in terms of elapsed time (in terms of latches, the difference between the two is negligible). You also saw how batching can dramatically reduce the latch consumption, thus improving scalability. You looked at how mixing interdependent batch statements in your application can sometimes lead to unexpected results.

A major take-away message from this chapter is that, if you are embedding SQL statements in your JDBC code, you should use a `PreparedStatement` object and use bind variables wherever appropriate. However, a strong case can also be made for wrapping your DML statements in PL/SQL packaged procedures and invoking them from JDBC using `CallableStatement` objects. This is what we will examine in the next chapter.

■■■

CHAPTER 6

CallableStatement

A CallableStatement interface extends PreparedStatement to execute and retrieve data from stored SQL procedures. In this chapter, you'll explore in detail how to invoke stored SQL procedures from JDBC using the SQL92 syntax and Oracle syntax. Toward the end of the chapter, I'll make a strong case for almost always wrapping code in stored SQL procedures, and invoking the stored procedures using CallableStatement as opposed to embedding them in a JDBC program and using PreparedStatement to execute them.

A Brief Introduction to Stored Procedures and PL/SQL

Stored procedures allow you to perform certain tasks procedurally in the database that you can't perform using the set-oriented SQL language. When executing a stored procedure, you're already in the database, so network round-trips aren't an issue.

In Oracle, you can write stored procedures in either PL/SQL or Java. Since the syntax for calling Java stored procedures is the same as the syntax for calling PL/SQL stored procedures, we will deal only with PL/SQL procedures in this book. In particular, in this chapter the term "stored procedure" refers to PL/SQL stand-alone procedures, functions, packaged procedures, or packaged functions.

Please note that this section by no means presents a detailed introduction to stored procedures and PL/SQL—entire tomes have been written on this subject. I assume that you are reasonably familiar with PL/SQL; if not, I recommend reading *PL/SQL User's Guide and Reference* before you proceed further. I also highly recommend Connor McDonald's *Mastering Oracle PL/SQL* (Apress, ISBN: 1-59059-217-4) for advanced PL/SQL users. Having said that, let's briefly go through an example PL/SQL package that we'll subsequently invoke from Java in this chapter.

■**Note** For the uninitiated, a *PL/SQL package* is a schema object that groups logically related PL/SQL types, variables, and subprograms. A package has a specification that declares its subprograms and a body that actually implements these subprograms. You'll see the advantages of using packages in the section "Packaging Matters!" of Chapter 18.

The following code snippet shows the specification of our PL/SQL package:

```
scott@ORA10G> create or replace package callable_stmt_demo
  2   as
  3     function get_emp_details_func( p_empno in number )
  4        return sys_refcursor;
  5     procedure get_emp_details_proc( p_empno in number,
  6        p_emp_details_cursor out sys_refcursor );
  7     procedure get_emps_with_high_sal( p_deptno in number,
  8        p_sal_limit in number default 2000 ,
  9        p_emp_details_cursor out sys_refcursor );
 10     procedure give_raise( p_deptno in number );
 11   end;
 12   /
```

Package created.

As you can see, the PL/SQL package is called callable_stmt_demo. It defines three procedures, get_emp_details_proc, get_emps_with_high_sal, and give_raise, and a function, get_emp_details_func. The data type sys_refcursor used in these procedures refers to a *ref cursor*. Ref cursors are cursor variables typically used to return a query's result to a client program (e.g., one using JDBC). In a JDBC program, the ref cursor is seen as a ResultSet object (which you should be familiar with by now). The data type sys_refcursor is Oracle's built-in type (starting from 9*i*) that represents a ref cursor. Thus, when we invoke the function get_emp_details_func later using JDBC, we will get a ResultSet object that corresponds to the ref cursor returned by the function.

Let's now look at the package body that shows us the implementation of the package procedures and functions declared in the specification.

```
scott@ORA10G> create or replace package body callable_stmt_demo
  2   as
  3     function get_emp_details_func( p_empno in number )
  4        return sys_refcursor
  5     is
  6      l_emp_details_cursor sys_refcursor;
  7     begin
  8      open l_emp_details_cursor for
  9      select empno, ename, job
 10      from emp
 11      where empno = p_empno;
 12
 13      return l_emp_details_cursor;
 14     end;
 15     procedure get_emp_details_proc( p_empno in number,
 16       p_emp_details_cursor out sys_refcursor )
 17     is
 18     begin
 19      p_emp_details_cursor := get_emp_details_func(
```

```
20        p_empno => p_empno );
21    end;
22    procedure get_emps_with_high_sal( p_deptno in number,
23     p_sal_limit in number default 2000 ,
24     p_emp_details_cursor out sys_refcursor )
25    is
26    begin
27     open p_emp_details_cursor for
28     select empno, ename, job, sal
29     from emp
30     where deptno = p_deptno
31       and sal > p_sal_limit;
32    end;
33    procedure give_raise( p_deptno in number )
34    is
35    begin
36     update emp
37     set sal = sal * 1.5
38     where deptno = p_deptno;
39    end;
40  end;
41  /
```

Package body created.

As you can see, the function get_emp_details_func returns a cursor to a query that contains selected details of the employee whose employee number matches the function parameter p_empno. The procedure get_emp_details_proc returns a cursor to the same query in an out parameter. The procedure get_emps_with_high_sal gets the details of employees who earn a salary higher than the salary passed as a parameter to the procedure. And finally, the procedure give_raise gives a generous 50% raise to all employees of a given department.

In the next section, we discuss how to call these stored procedures using CallableStatement from JDBC.

Invoking Stored Procedures from JDBC

Calling a stored procedure from Java using JDBC involves the following steps:

1. Formulate the CallableStatement string.

2. Create a CallableStatement object.

3. Bind input parameters.

4. Register output parameters.

5. Execute CallableStatement and retrieve the results.

We'll go through each of these steps in the following sections.

Formulating the CallableStatement String

There are two syntaxes you can use to formulate a CallableStatement string: the SQL92 syntax and the Oracle syntax. The SQL92 syntax is more portable (note that it makes only your JDBC calls portable—the underlying stored procedures follow proprietary syntax). Since there is no cost associated with using one syntax over the other, you should use the SQL92 syntax in your production code. Let's look at the SQL92 syntax first.

SQL92 Syntax

For stand-alone procedures or packaged procedures, the SQL92 syntax is

```
{call [schema.][package.]procedure_name[ (?, ?, .. )]}
```

For stand-alone functions or packaged functions, the SQL92 syntax is

```
{? = call [schema.][package.]function_name[ (?, ?, .. )]}
```

Note the following points:

- The square brackets [ ] denote optionality of an element (e.g., the schema in which the procedure was created is optional). The curly braces {}, on the other hand, are part of the syntax—they don't denote optionality.

- The other elements break down as follows:

  - schema: The schema of the owner of the stored procedure.

  - package: The package name if the procedure is in a package.

  - procedure_name *or* function_name: The name of the procedure or function.

  - ?: The placeholder for the in, in out, and out parameters of the procedure, or the return value of a function. In 10*g*, you can also use binding by named parameters, in which case each ? can be replaced by the actual formal parameter name in the called procedure.

- When you call a procedure/function in PL/SQL, you include a semicolon ; at the end. Note, however, that there is no semicolon at the end of the SQL92 CallableStatement string.

If we apply the preceding syntaxes to call the callable_demo_package's procedure and function, we get the following string for the procedure:

```
{call callable_stmt_demo.get_emp_details_proc( ?, ?)}
```

and the following string for the function:

```
{? = call callable_stmt_demo.get_emp_details_func( ?, ?)}
```

Let's now look at the Oracle syntax.

Oracle Syntax

If you are familiar with anonymous blocks, then you should be comfortable with the following Oracle syntax. For stand-alone procedures or packaged procedures, the Oracle syntax is

```
begin [schema.][package.]procedure_name[ (?, ?, ... )]; end;
```

For stand-alone functions or packaged functions, the Oracle syntax is

```
begin ? := [schema.][package.]function_name[ (?, ?, ... )]; end;
```

The meaning of most elements is the same as explained in the previous section for the SQL92 syntax. Note in addition that begin appears at the beginning and end; (with a semi-colon) appears at the end. Also note that := is used instead of = (as in SQL92 syntax) when invoking a function.

For our example procedure and function in the package callable_demo_package, the preceding syntax yields the following CallableStatement string for the procedure:

```
"begin callable_stmt_demo.get_emp_details_proc( ?, ?) end;",
```

and this string for the function:

```
"begin ? := callable_stmt_demo.get_emp_details_func( ?, ?) end;",
```

Let's move on to create a CallableStatement using these strings next.

Creating a CallableStatement Object

We use the Connection object's prepareCall() method to create a CallableStatement object. For example, if we use the SQL92 syntax to invoke it, the creation of CallableStatement looks like

```
CallableStatement cstmt = null;
try
{
  String sql92Style =
    "{ call callable_stmt_demo.get_emp_details_proc(?,?) }";
  . . .
}
```

Now that we have the CallableStatement object, let's look at how to bind the input parameters.

Binding Input (in or in out) Parameters

For binding input parameters for a CallableStatement, we use the appropriate setXXX() method based on the type of the parameter to be bound. Recall the signature of the procedure get_emp_details_proc:

```
procedure get_emp_details_proc( p_empno in number,
  p_emp_details_cursor out sys_refcursor );
```

Here, the first parameter is an in (input) parameter, and the second parameter is an out (output) parameter. We can bind the input parameter (which is parameter number 1) by ordinal number (the index of the parameter) or by named parameter. The following snippet illustrates binding by parameter index:

```
CallableStatement cstmt = null;
try
{
  . . .
  String sql92Style =
    "{ call callable_stmt_demo.get_emp_details_proc(?,?) }";
  // create the CallableStatement object
  cstmt = conn.prepareCall( sql92Style );
  cstmt.setInt(1, inputEmpNo );
  . . .
}
```

The last line in the preceding code tells us that the first parameter is an int and its bind value is inputEmpNo.

In 10*g*, we can also use named parameters to bind input parameters.

■**Note** Binding or registering by named parameter is a new feature in 10*g*. Also, you can't mix named parameter binding and ordinal parameter binding for the same statement-related code.

To use named parameters in the preceding example, we replace the last statement in the code snippet with the following:

```
cstmt.setInt("p_empno", inputEmpNo );
```

Here, p_empno is the formal parameter name of the first parameter of the procedure get_emp_details_proc. This parameter name does not necessarily appear anywhere in the SQL string. This differs from the setXXXatName() method of the OraclePreparedStatement interface discussed in the previous chapter, whose first argument is a substring of the SQL string.

■**Note** As of 10*g* Release 1, there's no support for named parameters for a PL/SQL function, because there's no "name" of the returned parameter, and you can't mix and match binding by name and binding by ordinal parameter index.

Named parameters are especially useful if we have one or more parameters in a stored procedure with default values. In this case, we can specify only the parameters that do not have default values. For example, consider the following procedure in the package callable_stmt_demo:

```
procedure get_emps_with_high_sal( p_deptno in number,
  p_sal_limit in number default 2000 ,
  p_emp_details_cursor out sys_refcursor )
is
begin
  open p_emp_details_cursor for
  select empno, ename, job, sal
  from emp
  where deptno = p_deptno
    and sal > p_sal_limit;
end;
```

It returns a set of employees for a given department who earn a salary higher than a given limit as a ref cursor in its out parameter. The default value for the passed salary limit is 2,000. If we use ordinal parameter binding, we have to bind both input parameters (p_deptno and p_sal_limit), even if the default value of the p_sal_limit parameter is acceptable to us. However, if we use named parameters, we can just bind the input parameter p_deptno as follows (note that our SQL string has only the number of ?s that we are actually binding, which in this case is two: one for the in parameter p_deptno and the other for the out parameter p_emp_details_cursor):

```
try
{
  // formulate a CallableStatement string using SQL92
  // syntax
  String oracleStyle =
    "begin callable_stmt_demo.get_emps_with_high_sal(?, ?); end;";
  // create the CallableStatement object
  cstmt = conn.prepareCall( oracleStyle );
  // bind the input value by name
  cstmt.setInt("p_deptno", 10 );
  // no need to pass the second parameter "p_sal_limit"
  // which gets a default value of 2000
. . .
```

Registering Output (out or in out) Parameters

To get results back from a stored procedure, we have to register any output parameters (out or in out parameters) before executing the callable statement. Here, too, we can choose to use ordinal binding or named parameter binding (starting from Oracle 10g). We use the register-OutParameter() method. The following code snippet illustrates how to register the cursor output parameter for the procedure callable_stmt_demo.get_emp_details_proc:

```
CallableStatement cstmt = null;
try
{
  . . .
  // register the output value
```

```
    cstmt.registerOutParameter( 2, OracleTypes.CURSOR );
    . . .
}
```

As in the case of binding the input parameter, the first parameter in `registerOutParameter()` is the formal parameter index of the called procedure, and the second parameter is the type of the output parameter (in this case, a `ResultSet` that maps to `OracleTypes.CURSOR`). For binding by name, we would use the formal parameter name instead of the index number, as follows:

```
try
{
    . . .
    // register the output value
    cstmt.registerOutParameter( "p_emp_details_cursor", OracleTypes.CURSOR );
    . . .
}
```

NAMED PARAMETERS VS. ORDINAL PARAMETERS FOR CALLABLESTATEMENT

So should you use ordinal binding/registering or named parameter binding/registering? The decision is more of a style issue than anything else. Table 6-1 summarizes the pros and cons of using ordinal parameters versus using named parameters.

Table 6-1. *Ordinal Parameters vs. Named Parameters*

Ordinal Parameters: Binding or Registering	Named Parameters: Binding or Registering
You have to bind all input parameters even if the stored procedure has a default value.	You can skip the input parameters with default values.
There is no impact on the JDBC code if you change the name of a formal parameter (e.g., as part of a code cleanup).	This impacts the JDBC code if you change the formal parameter name, since you refer to it in JDBC.
The code is less readable since you have to know which parameter corresponds to which index. However, you can improve the readability of the calling code by using meaningful constants for the parameter indexes.	More readable since you use parameter names.
This impacts the JDBC code if you change the positions of the formal parameters, even if you retain their names.	There is no impact on the JDBC code if you change the positions of the formal parameters, as long as you retain their names.

Executing CallableStatement and Retrieving Results

After we have set the in, in out, and out parameters, we can execute CallableStatement using its execute() method, as follows:

```
try
{
  . . .
  cstmt.execute();
  . . .
}
```

■Note For CallableStatement objects that invoke PL/SQL procedures resulting in data modification (such as insert, delete, update, and merge), you could also use the executeUpdate() method. However, this method seems to always return 0 as the number of rows affected in my tests. I'll stick to using execute() in examples containing CallableStatement.

If we registered any out or in out parameters, we can get their returned values by calling the appropriate getXXX() method on the CallableStatement object. For example, to get a ResultSet object returned by the procedure callable_stmt_demo.get_emps_with_high_sal, we use the following (named parameter method):

```
try
{
  . . .
  cstmt.execute();
  rset = (ResultSet) cstmt.getObject( "p_emp_details_cursor" );
}
```

Putting It All Together in a Working Example

Now that you've gone through all the steps required to execute a callable statement, you're ready for a complete example that includes the relevant pieces of code you've studied so far. The following DemoCallableStatement class offers many examples of using CallableStatement. I provide explanatory comments in-between the code. I also list common errors and their resolutions in the next section, which should help you out when you encounter CallableStatement-related errors in your programs.

The class DemoCallableStatement demonstrates how to use

- SQL92 syntax for calling stored procedures

- Oracle syntax for calling stored procedures

- Binding by parameter index and binding by named parameters (including the case of PL/SQL procedures having parameters with default values)

The program begins by importing the requisite classes and checking the parameters (it accepts one parameter, which is the database name):

```
/** This program demonstrates how to use CallableStatement.
* COMPATIBLITY NOTE:
*    runs successfully against 10.1.0.2.0.
*    Against 9.2.0.1.0, you have to comment out the
*    code using the binding by name feature to compile and
*    run this, as bind by name is not supported in 9i.
*/
import java.sql.ResultSet;
import java.sql.SQLException;
import java.sql.CallableStatement;
import java.sql.Connection;
import oracle.jdbc.OracleTypes;
import book.util.JDBCUtil;
import book.util.Util;
class DemoCallableStatement
{
  public static void main(String args[])
  {
    Util.checkProgramUsage( args );
```

We declare some variables and get a connection inside the try catch block:

```
    ResultSet rset = null;
    Connection conn = null;
    CallableStatement cstmt = null;
    try
    {
      conn = JDBCUtil.getConnection("scott", "tiger", args[0]);
```

The first example invokes _demoSql92SyntaxProcedureBindByIndex(), which, as its name indicates, demonstrates how to use the SQL92 syntax to invoke a procedure with binding by parameter index:

```
      _demoSql92SyntaxProcedureBindByIndex( conn );
```

The second example invokes _demoOracleSyntaxFunctionBindByIndex(), which demonstrates how to use the Oracle syntax to invoke a procedure using binding by parameter index:

```
      _demoOracleSyntaxFunctionBindByIndex( conn );
```

The third example invokes _demoOracleSyntaxProcedureBindByName(), which demonstrates how to use the Oracle syntax to invoke a procedure using binding by named parameter:

```
      _demoOracleSyntaxProcedureBindByName( conn );
```

The fourth example invokes _demoOracleSyntaxProcedureBindByNameWithDefault(), which demonstrates how to use Oracle syntax to invoke a procedure using binding by named parameter, with one of the parameters having a default value:

```
_demoOracleSyntaxProcedureBindByNameWithDefault( conn );
```

The final example invokes _demoOracleSyntaxProcedureBindByNameUpdate(), which demonstrates how to use Oracle syntax to invoke a procedure that performs an update and uses binding by named parameter:

```
  _demoOracleSyntaxProcedureBindByNameUpdate( conn );
}
catch (SQLException e)
{
  // print stack trace.
  JDBCUtil.printException( e );
}
finally
{
  // close the connection in finally clause
  JDBCUtil.close( conn );
}
}
```

The definition of each of the procedures begins as follows, starting with _demoSql92SyntaxProcedureBindByIndex() (please see the interspersed comments for further details):

```
///////////// PRIVATE SECTION ////////////////
private static void _demoSql92SyntaxProcedureBindByIndex( Connection conn )
  throws SQLException
{
  System.out.println( "Example 1, SQL 92 syntax, calling a procedure, " +
    "binding by index" );
  int inputEmpNo = 7369;
  CallableStatement cstmt = null;
  ResultSet rset = null;
  try
  {
    // The procedure invoked below has a signature of:
    // procedure get_emp_details_proc( p_empno in number,
    //   p_emp_details_cursor out sys_refcursor )
```

First, we formulate a CallableStatement string using the SQL92 syntax:

```
String sql92Style =
  "{ call callable_stmt_demo.get_emp_details_proc(?,?) }";
```

Next, we create the CallableStatement object:

```
cstmt = conn.prepareCall( sql92Style );
```

Then we bind the input value using parameter by index:

```
cstmt.setInt(1, inputEmpNo );
```

We register the output value using the method registerOutParameter():

```
cstmt.registerOutParameter( 2, OracleTypes.CURSOR );
```

We are now ready to execute the procedure:

```
cstmt.execute();
```

Next, we retrieve the result set (which is the second parameter). We loop through the result set to print it out, followed by the finally clause, in which we release JDBC resources:

```
        rset = (ResultSet) cstmt.getObject( 2 );
        // print the result
        while (rset.next())
        {
          int empNo = rset.getInt ( 1 );
          String empName = rset.getString ( 2 );
          String empJob = rset.getString ( 3 );
          System.out.println( empNo + " " + empName + " " + empJob );
        }
      }
      finally
      {
        // release JDBC resources in finally clause.
        JDBCUtil.close( rset );
        JDBCUtil.close( cstmt );
      }
  }
```

Next is the definition of _demoOracleSyntaxFunctionBindByIndex():

```
private static void _demoOracleSyntaxFunctionBindByIndex( Connection conn )
  throws SQLException
{
  System.out.println( "\nExample 2, Oracle syntax,  calling a function," +
    " binding by index" );
  int inputEmpNo = 7369;
  ResultSet rset = null;
  CallableStatement cstmt = null;
  try
  {
    // The function invoked below has a signature of:
    // function get_emp_details_func( p_empno in number )
    //     return sys_refcursor
```

We formulate a `CallableStatement` string using the Oracle syntax:

```
String oracleStyle =
    "begin ? := callable_stmt_demo.get_emp_details_func(?); end;";
```

We create the `CallableStatement` object:

```
cstmt = conn.prepareCall( oracleStyle );
```

And then we bind the input variable and register the out parameter:

```
cstmt.setInt(2, inputEmpNo );
cstmt.registerOutParameter( 1, OracleTypes.CURSOR );
```

Next, we execute the query, get the result set, and print the query results:

```
cstmt.execute();
rset = (ResultSet) cstmt.getObject( 1 );
// print the result
while (rset.next())
{
  int empNo = rset.getInt ( 1 );
  String empName = rset.getString ( 2 );
  String empJob = rset.getString ( 3 );
  System.out.println( empNo + " " + empName + " " + empJob );
}
}
finally
{
  // release JDBC resources in finally clause.
  JDBCUtil.close( rset );
  JDBCUtil.close( cstmt );
}
}
```

The definition of `_demoOracleSyntaxProcedureBindByName()` follows:

```
private static void _demoOracleSyntaxProcedureBindByName( Connection conn )
  throws SQLException
{
  System.out.println( "\nExample 3, Oracle syntax, calling a procedure," +
    " bind by name" );
  int inputEmpNo = 7369;
  ResultSet rset = null;
  CallableStatement cstmt = null;
  try
  {
    // The procedure invoked below has a signature of:
    // procedure get_emp_details_proc( p_empno in number,
    //  p_emp_details_cursor out sys_refcursor )
```

```
// formulate a CallableStatement string using SQL92
// syntax
String oracleStyle =
  "begin callable_stmt_demo.get_emp_details_proc(?, ?); end;";
// create the CallableStatement object
cstmt = conn.prepareCall( oracleStyle );
```

Note how we use p_empno as the parameter name. This is the formal parameter name in the procedure:

```
// bind the input value by name
cstmt.setInt("p_empno", inputEmpNo );
// register the output value
cstmt.registerOutParameter( "p_emp_details_cursor", OracleTypes.CURSOR );
// execute the query
cstmt.execute();
```

We use the formal parameter again while retrieving results:

```
rset = (ResultSet) cstmt.getObject( "p_emp_details_cursor" );
// print the result
while (rset.next())
{
  int empNo = rset.getInt ( 1 );
  String empName = rset.getString ( 2 );
  String empJob = rset.getString ( 3 );
  System.out.println( empNo + " " + empName + " " + empJob );
}
}
finally
{
  // release JDBC resources in finally clause.
  JDBCUtil.close( rset );
  JDBCUtil.close( cstmt );
}
}
```

The definition of _demoOracleSyntaxProcedureBindByNameWithDefaul() demonstrates how binding by name makes it easier to invoke a procedure with default values:

```
private static void _demoOracleSyntaxProcedureBindByNameWithDefault(
  Connection conn )
  throws SQLException
{
  System.out.println( "\nExample 4, Oracle syntax, calling a procedure," +
    " named parameter (with default value)" );
  int inputEmpNo = 7369;
  ResultSet rset = null;
```

```
CallableStatement cstmt = null;
try
{
  // The procedure invoked below has a signature of:
  // procedure get_emps_with_high_sal( p_deptno in number,
  //   p_sal_limit in number default 2000 ,
  //   p_emp_details_cursor out sys_refcursor )
```

Note that while formulating the CallableStatement string, you should give only two parameter placeholders (there should not be a ? for the parameter with the default value in the statement string):

```
  // formulate a CallableStatement string using SQL92
  // syntax
  String oracleStyle =
    "begin callable_stmt_demo.get_emps_with_high_sal(?, ?); end;";
  // create the CallableStatement object
  cstmt = conn.prepareCall( oracleStyle );
  // bind the input value by name
  cstmt.setInt("p_deptno", 10 );
  // no need to pass the second parameter "p_sal_limit"
  // which gets a default value of 2000
  // register the output value
  cstmt.registerOutParameter( "p_emp_details_cursor",
    OracleTypes.CURSOR );
  // execute the query
  cstmt.execute();
  rset = (ResultSet) cstmt.getObject( "p_emp_details_cursor" );
  // print the result
  while (rset.next())
  {
    int empNo = rset.getInt ( 1 );
    String empName = rset.getString ( 2 );
    String empJob = rset.getString ( 3 );
    int empSal = rset.getInt ( 4 );
    System.out.println( empNo + " " + empName + " " + empJob + " " +
      empSal );
  }
}
finally
{
  // release JDBC resources in finally clause.
  JDBCUtil.close( rset );
  JDBCUtil.close( cstmt );
}
}
```

The procedure _demoOracleSyntaxProcedureBindByNameUpdate() simply does an update using binding by named parameters:

```
private static void _demoOracleSyntaxProcedureBindByNameUpdate( Connection conn )
  throws SQLException
{
  System.out.println( "\nExample 5, Oracle syntax, calling a procedure," +
    " update example" );
  CallableStatement cstmt = null;
  try
  {
    // The procedure invoked below has a signature of:
    //   procedure give_raise( p_deptno in number )

    // formulate a CallableStatement string using SQL92
    // syntax
    String oracleStyle =
      "begin callable_stmt_demo.give_raise( ? ); end;";
    // create the CallableStatement object
    cstmt = conn.prepareCall( oracleStyle );
    // bind the input value by name
    cstmt.setInt("p_deptno", 10 );
    // execute
    cstmt.execute();
    conn.commit();
  }
  catch (SQLException e)
  {
    // print a message and roll back.
    JDBCUtil.printExceptionAndRollback( conn, e );
  }
  finally
  {
    // release JDBC resources in finally clause.
    JDBCUtil.close( cstmt );
  }
}
```

CallableStatement Common Errors and Resolutions

Table 6-2 lists some common error conditions that you may encounter when using CallableStatement and their resolutions.

Table 6-2. *Common Errors While Using* CallableStatement *and Their Suggested Resolutions*

Exception Message*	Possible Cause(s)	Action(s)
`java.sql.SQLException: Malformed SQL92 string at position: 51 . . .`	The format of the callable string is incorrect.	Double-check your CallableStatement string. For SQL92-style strings, look for missing/ mismatched curly braces, for example.
`ORA-06550: line 1, column 60: of PLS-00103: Encountered the symbol "end-of-file" when expecting one of the following:` `; <an identifier> <a double-quoted delimited-identifier> . . .`	The format of the CallableStatement string is incorrect format.	You may have forgotten the semicolon at the end the Oracle-style CallableStatement string.
`Missing IN or OUT parameter at index:: 1` `java.sql.SQLException: Missing IN or OUT parameter at index:: 1 . . . .`	You did not bind all input parameters or register all output parameters.	Make sure you bind all input parameters and register all output parameters.
`ORA-06550: line 1, column 13: PLS-00382: expression is of wrong type`	There is a parameter type mismatch.	Make sure that you use the correct setXXX() method for binding input parameters and the correct type while registering output parameters.
`. . .operation not allowed: ordinal binding and Named binding cannot be combined!` `java.sql.SQLException: operation not allowed: Ordinal binding and Named binding cannot be combined! . . .`	You are using both ordinal and named parameter binding for the same statement execution.	Make sure you use only ordinal binding or named parameter binding—don't mix and match.
`ORA-06550: line 1, column 26:PLS-00302: component 'GET_EMPS_WITH_HIGH_SAL' must be declared`	Either the procedure does not exist or the user does not have the execute privilege on it.	Check the invoked procedure name. Make sure the database user has the execute privilege on the procedure.

Where Should Your SQL Statements Reside, in Java or PL/SQL?

In Chapter 5, we built a DemoPreparedStatementQuery class to fetch employee details given an employee number, using a PreparedStatement object. The relevant portion of the class is reproduced here:

```
try
{
  pstmt = conn.prepareStatement( stmtString );
  // bind the values
  pstmt.setString(JOB_COLUMN_INDEX, "CLERK" );
  pstmt.setDate(HIREDATE_COLUMN_INDEX, new java.sql.Date(
    new java.util.Date().getTime()));
  // execute the query
  rset = pstmt.executeQuery();
  // print the result
  System.out.println( "printing query results ...\n");
  while (rset.next())
  {
    int empNo = rset.getInt ( SELECT_CLAUSE_EMPNO_COLUMN_INDEX );
    String empName = rset.getString ( SELECT_CLAUSE_ENAME_COLUMN_INDEX );
    String empJob = rset.getString ( SELECT_CLAUSE_JOB_COLUMN_INDEX );
    System.out.println( empNo + " " + empName + " " + empJob );
  }
}
finally
{
  // release JDBC related resources in the finally clause.
  JDBCUtil.close( rset );
  JDBCUtil.close( pstmt );
}
```

Another way to achieve the same objective is to use CallableStatement (or OracleCallableStatement). We covered how to do this in the class DemoCallableStatement, the relevant portion of which is reproduced here:

```
try
{
  // The function invoked below has a signature of:
  // function get_emp_details_func( p_empno in number )
  //    return sys_refcursor

  // formulate a CallableStatement string using Oracle-style
  // syntax
  String oracleStyle =
    "begin ? := callable_stmt_demo.get_emp_details_func(?); end;";
  // create the CallableStatement object
```

```
    cstmt = conn.prepareCall( oracleStyle );
    // bind the input value
    cstmt.setInt(2, inputEmpNo );
    // register the output value
    cstmt.registerOutParameter( 1, OracleTypes.CURSOR );
    // execute the query
    cstmt.execute();
    rset = (ResultSet) cstmt.getObject( 1 );
    // print the result
    while (rset.next())
    {
      int empNo = rset.getInt ( 1 );
      String empName = rset.getString ( 2 );
      String empJob = rset.getString ( 3 );
      System.out.println( empNo + " " + empName + " " + empJob );
    }
  }
...
```

In this case, we wrap our select statement in a packaged function and invoke it from Java. Both alternatives achieve the same result, so which one should you prefer? In terms of performance, there is no material difference, since the hard parsing of the anonymous PL/SQL block that gets invoked should get done only once, and soft parsing can be controlled by the techniques mentioned in Chapter 14.

However, wrapping the select statements in PL/SQL and invoking them using CallableStatement has the following advantages:

- It creates a clear-cut work separation among developers. Those who love to do the middle-tier (or the front-end) code focus on the Java layer. They just invoke methods wrapped in PL/SQL interfaces when dealing with the database. Database experts, on the other hand, work on providing a robust and performant PL/SQL interface for the J2EE developers. Database developers using standard SQL tuning tools such as tkprof can do any tuning independently.

- Instead of giving select, insert, and other such privileges to the database user directly on tables, you can grant an execute privilege to the packages and procedures. This is a significant improvement in terms of security. Chapter 16 examines this further.

- If you want to extend your logic, add some additional validation, enable auditing, and so on, it is much easier to do so if your code resides in PL/SQL packages.

- It is much easier to tune, change, test, and deploy procedure queries (and inserts, etc.) in PL/SQL than in Java. You just need to update the database, and everyone sees the changes instantly. You don't need to update Java classes at multiple places where your middle-tier code is deployed. Also, the tuning process becomes infinitely easier. In most cases, you can just run the procedure (or the SQL statement) independent of the application, and use tkprof to tune it. You don't need to go through the compile/tune cycle on the middle-tier code in Java. I personally find this very convenient during development.

- If your code resides in PL/SQL, it is reusable by any application that can connect to a database. You have effectively put the logic inside the database, and your Java program accesses it through a well-defined PL/SQL interface. As a side effect, the system logic is open to access from *other* clients/applications using the same PL/SQL API (e.g., from an application written using Pro*C). For example, you could later on easily decide to expose the PL/SQL layer as an SDK API to your end users for customization purposes.

- If your logic resides in PL/SQL, you can take maximum advantage of all database features. Although it may seem a bit contradictory, this is the best way to make your code database-independent if your application needs to run against a database other than Oracle. (All major databases support a procedural language equivalent to Oracle's PL/SQL.) This way, you get the best of both worlds:

  - You exploit the database fully by using its proprietary technology, which exposes many powerful, database-specific features.

  - You have essentially only one layer of code to worry about when porting to a different database.

Of course, this assumes that you are using the SQL92 syntax to invoke stored procedures.

■**Note** A lot has been said and written about the fallacy of trying to make your application database-independent by not using the database proprietary features, so I won't repeat those arguments in this book. There's no harm in doing this if you can achieve it without any loss of functionality (e.g., by using the SQL92 syntax for invoking stored procedures instead of using the Oracle syntax). However, in the majority of cases, trying to make the code database-independent only leads to severe problems, especially in terms of performance. For more discussion on this topic, please see the section "Avoid the Black Box Syndrome" in Chapter 1 of *Effective Oracle by Design* (Osborne McGraw-Hill, ISBN: 0-07-223065-7), or read through Chapter 1 of *Expert One-on-One Oracle* (Apress, ISBN: 1-59059-243-3), both by Tom Kyte. You can also visit Tom's site at http://asktom.oracle.com to find discussions on this very important topic.

- You get all the other advantages that come with the PL/SQL. For example, PL/SQL is tightly integrated with SQL, so you can easily mix SQL statements in PL/SQL code. You also get the benefit of implicit cursor caching provided by PL/SQL (this feature is discussed in Chapter 14).

There is an exception where you may want to consider using PreparedStatement (or OraclePreparedStatement). This is when you bulk load a large amount of data into one or more tables from a source external to the database (e.g., a file visible to the client but not to the database server).

■**Note** If the external data source is visible to the database, other solutions such as using `bfile`, `utl_file`, and so on become viable (see Chapter 13). Of course, if the data source is within the database (e.g., in some other tables), or it is in some other database accessible to your database, you can and should use straight SQL-based solutions such as `insert into <table_name> select col1, co2 from ....`

In this case, you could use `PreparedStatement` with update batching (standard update batching or Oracle update batching) and gain performance. (Recall that in Oracle, update batching is effectively available only for `PreparedStatement` and `OraclePreparedStatement` objects.) You could conceivably implement a JDBC call to a stored procedure using array processing (which we'll cover in Chapter 12), where you take advantage of the bulk insert option in PL/SQL (see Chapter 18). However, in this case, your code becomes more complex (since you need to store the records in an array first and pass the array to the PL/SQL) and potentially less performant. Except for this case, my recommendation is to always wrap your code in PL/SQL packages (or in the procedural language equivalent to PL/SQL if you are using a non-Oracle database) and invoke them using `CallableStatement` (or `OracleCallableStatement`).

■**Tip** In general, it is a good idea to wrap your SQL statements in PL/SQL packages and use `CallableStatement` (or `OracleCallableStatement`) to invoke them, instead of putting your statements in Java and using `PreparedStatement` (or `OraclePreparedStatement`). One exception to this guideline is when you can take advantage of update batching to improve performance while bulk-loading a large amount of data from a data source that is external to database.

Summary

In this chapter, you looked at the `CallableStatement` and `OracleCallableStatement` interfaces and how you can use them to invoke stored SQL procedures using both the SQL92 syntax and the Oracle syntax. In addition, I made a strong case for almost exclusively using `CallableStatement` in programs to invoke logic that resides in PL/SQL packaged subprograms.

CHAPTER 7

■■■

Result Sets Explored

You've already seen how result sets work in their simplest form in the earlier chapters. In this chapter, you'll explore many other capabilities of the ResultSet object, most of which were introduced in JDBC 2.0. In particular, this chapter covers the following topics:

- *Prefetching*: The ability to set the number of rows to be retrieved with each trip to the database.

- *Scrollability*: The ability to scroll backward and forward through the rows of a result set. A ResultSet object with this ability is called a *scrollable result set*.

- *Positioning*: The ability of a scrollable result set to move to a particular row using a position number relative to the current row, or an absolute row number counting from the beginning or the end of the result set.

- *Sensitivity*: The ability to see *internal* and *external* changes made to the underlying tables in the result set rows.

- *Updatability*: The ability to update rows of a result set and propagate the changes to the underlying tables in the database.

Out of all these capabilities, prefetching is my favorite, as it can give excellent returns in terms of performance without imposing any artificial restrictions on the query itself. In my opinion, the remaining features can be considered "syntactic sugar" rather than useful because

- They impose various limitations on the query itself (see the section "Result Set Limitations" for a full list of these limitations). For example, for a result set to be updatable, the query can select from only a single table and can't contain any join operations, which severely limits the capabilities of your SQL code. The worst part is that in return you don't get anything that you can't achieve otherwise by using simple ResultSet objects.

- There are simpler alternatives to all these capabilities when it comes to using them in a real-world scenario. For example, instead of using the updatability feature to update data, you can use plain old SQL update statements in a PreparedStatement object. Another example is the use of a scrollable result set in scrolling through a fixed window of records, something that can be accomplished with SQL and a simple ResultSet much more efficiently (as you'll learn in the section "Paginating Through a Result Set").

Although the official Oracle JDBC documentation does not state it specifically, out of the preceding features, only prefetching is supported for result sets returned via stored procedures invoked by the CallableStatement interface. (Even this feature does not work in both 10*g* and 9*i* due to a bug at the CallableStatement level, but you can easily work around it by using the API at the ResultSet level, as you'll see later.)

■**Note** Scrollability, positioning, sensitivity, and updatability—*none* of these features is implemented for CallableStatement objects in Oracle JDBC drivers. If you need to use these features, you should use PreparedStatement.

Before we move on to cover these features, let's quickly look at how to deal with null values retrieved from the database and how to set a value to null using the ResultSet interface.

Handling Null Values

A Java variable that holds a reference to an object can hold a null value. But a primitive data type such as an int or a double can't hold a null value. So when you retrieve a null value into a primitive data type, the value retrieved is set to 0. However, you can use the method wasNull() of the ResultSet interface to check if the value you retrieved was a null or not. Note that you must first call one of the getter methods on a column to try to read its value and then call the method wasNull() to see if the value read was null or not:

```
public boolean wasNull() throws SQLException;
```

Similarly, to set any column value to null, you can use the setNull() method of the PreparedStatement interface, which also takes in the SQL type of the column as the second parameter:

```
public void setNull(int parameterIndex, int sqlType) throws SQLException;
```

The following program, DemoNullValues, starts with an empty table, t1, with just one number column, x. The program first inserts a null value into the table using the setNull() method. It then retrieves the null value into the Java primitive data type int and uses the wasNull() method to check if the value was null.

```
/* This program demonstrates how to deal with null values in JDBC.
* COMPATIBLITY NOTE: runs successfully against 10.1.0.2.0 and 9.2.0.1.0.
*/
import java.sql.ResultSet;
import java.sql.SQLException;
import java.sql.PreparedStatement;
import java.sql.Connection;
import oracle.jdbc.OracleTypes;
import book.util.JDBCUtil;
class DemoNullValues
{
```

```
public static void main(String args[]) throws Exception
{
  Connection conn = null;
  try
  {
    conn = JDBCUtil.getConnection("benchmark", "benchmark", "ora10g");
```

The method _insertNull() inserts a null value into column x of table t1. The method _retrieveNull() selects the same value later:

```
    _insertNull( conn );
    conn.commit();
    _retrieveNull( conn );
  }
  catch (SQLException e)
  {
    JDBCUtil.printException ( e );
  }
  finally
  {
    // release the JDBC resources in the finally clause.
    JDBCUtil.close( conn );
  }
} // end of main()
private static void _insertNull( Connection conn ) throws SQLException
{
  PreparedStatement pstmt = null;
  try
  {
    pstmt = conn.prepareStatement( "insert into t1 ( x ) values ( ? )" );
```

Notice how we pass the data type in our call to setNull():

```
    pstmt.setNull( 1, OracleTypes.NUMBER );
    int numOfRows = pstmt.executeUpdate();
    System.out.println( "Inserted " + numOfRows + " rows with null value" );
  }
  finally
  {
    JDBCUtil.close( pstmt );
  }
}
private static void _retrieveNull( Connection conn ) throws SQLException
{
  String queryStmt = "select x from t1 where x is null";
  ResultSet rset = null;
  PreparedStatement pstmt = null;
  try
  {
```

```
    pstmt = conn.prepareStatement( queryStmt );
    rset = pstmt.executeQuery();
    while( rset.next() )
    {
      int value = rset.getInt( 1 );
```

The call to wasNull() returns a boolean value indicating whether or not the getInt() method just executed was null:

```
    if( rset.wasNull() )
    {
      System.out.println( "got a null value..." );
    }
    System.out.println( "The value is retrieved as " + value );
  }
}
finally
{
  // release the JDBC resources in the finally clause.
  JDBCUtil.close( rset );
  JDBCUtil.close( pstmt );
}
}
} // end of program
```

On running the program, we get the following output:

```
B:\>java DemoNullValues
URL:jdbc:oracle:thin:@(DESCRIPTION=(ADDRESS=(PROTOCOL=tcp)
(PORT=1521)(HOST=rmenon-lap))(CONNECT_DATA=(SID=ora10g)))
Inserted 1 rows with null value
got a null value...
The value is retrieved as 0
```

Next, we'll look at the ability to prefetch values retrieved from the database and its impact on query performance.

Prefetching

JDBC 2.0 allows you to specify for a query the number of rows retrieved at a time with each database round-trip. This number is known as the *fetch size*, and the process of getting rows in advance is called *prefetching*. The default value of a fetch size in Oracle JDBC is 10. This means that by default, when you execute a query, the JDBC driver retrieves ten rows at a time per round-trip. By changing this number, you can control the number of round-trips your queries make to the database. For example, with the default fetch size value of 10, a query resulting in a total of 100 rows would actually make 11 round-trips (the eleventh round-trip is required to detect that the query has no more rows to return). But if you use a fetch size of, say, 50, the query would make only three round-trips to fetch 100 rows.

Note that the number of times you iterate through the result set loop is not affected by the fetch size you set; only the number of round-trips your application makes is affected. Consider a typical while loop iteration through an initialized ResultSet variable rset:

```
ResultSet rset = pstmt.executeQuery();
while( rset.next() )
{
    …
}
```

Assume that the preceding query returns 100 rows and the fetch size is 10. The very first fetch happens when you get the ResultSet object by invoking executeQuery(). The first ten iterations in the loop would get their data from the JDBC cache. When the program encounters the eleventh invocation of next(), JDBC would get ten more rows from the database (thus incurring a second network round-trip), and so on. Clearly, there is a trade-off in that for a higher fetch size you need more client-side memory to cache the rows. If fetchSize is the fetch size of the result set and rowSize is the size of a row, the JDBC cache size is proportional to fetchSize×rowSize. In this chapter, a large result set means a result set for which fetchSize×rowSize is large.

Setting and Getting Fetch Size

The following standard JDBC methods are available in the Statement, PreparedStatement, CallableStatement, and ResultSet interfaces for setting and getting the fetch size:

```
void setFetchSize(int rows) throws SQLException
int getFetchSize() throws SQLException
```

Oracle had the concept of prefetching before it came along in JDBC 2.0. This can lead to some confusion, as there are methods implemented as Oracle extension methods to set a fetch size, and those are still available. Thus, in addition to the preceding JDBC 2.0 API methods, if you use the Oracle extension class OracleConnection, you can get and set the default fetch size for all statements of a Connection object at the Connection level using the following methods (note that there is no equivalent method in the JDBC 2.0 Connection interface to set a default fetch size):

```
public int getDefaultRowPrefetch();
public void setDefaultRowPrefetch(int value) throws SQLException;
```

Finally, you can use the setRowPrefetch() and getRowPrefetch() methods in the OracleStatement interface (inherited by OraclePreparedStatement and OracleCallableStatement):

```
public int getRowPrefetch();
public void setRowPrefetch( int size ) throws SQLException;
```

The settings at the statement level override the settings at the Connection level (except for CallableStatement, which is due to a bug I'll cover soon), and the settings at the ResultSet level override those at the Statement level. Overriding the fetch size at the ResultSet level affects only *subsequent* trips (see the following note) to the database to get more rows for the original query or during *refetching* of the query results (see the upcoming section "Refetching Rows").

■**Note** As mentioned earlier, regardless of the fetch size you set at the `ResultSet` level, in the case of the Oracle implementation, the moment you execute a statement (e.g., by using the `executeQuery()` method on a `PreparedStatement` object), the JDBC driver silently does the first fetch. This first fetch will always use the fetch size set at the `Statement` level (or at the `OracleConnection` level if the `Statement`-level fetch size has not been set), since the `ResultSet` object is created only after the fact. This will become clearer shortly through an example.

Let's summarize the preceding discussion on setting and getting fetch size at different interface levels:

- JDBC 2.0 supports fetch size at the `Statement` and `ResultSet` levels with the methods `getFetchSize()` and `setFetchSize()`.

- Oracle supports, through its extension methods, setting a default fetch size at the `Connection` level in the `OracleConnection` interface using the methods `getDefaultRowPrefetch()` and `setDefaultRowPrefetch()`. The default value of a row prefetch in Oracle is 10. The values set at the `OracleConnection` level are used as the default values for the fetch size at the `Statement` and `ResultSet` interface levels. Oracle also supports getting and setting the fetch size in the `OracleStatement` and `OracleResultSet` interfaces using `getRowPrefetch()` and `setRowPrefetch()`.

- In general, you should not mix the JDBC 2.0 API with the Oracle extension APIs (see the next bullet point for an exception to this rule). I recommend that at the `Statement` and `ResultSet` levels you use JDBC 2.0 methods to set and get the fetch size for the simple reason that it improves portability across databases without any associated penalty.

- *However*, since JDBC does not support setting a default fetch size at the `Connection` level, to do so you can actually use the `getDefaultRowPrefetch()` and `setDefaultRowPrefetch()` methods of the `OracleConnection` interface if required.

- Finally, in the case of `CallableStatement`, due to a bug the `setFetchSize()` and `getFetchSize()` methods *seem* to work, but the returned result sets actually use the default fetch size set at the `OracleConnection` interface level (which is 10 by default). Fortunately, you can always set the fetch size on the `ResultSet` object itself using the preceding API, so this is not really an issue.

Prefetching Example

Let's look at an example that demonstrates the following:

- How to get and set fetch size at the `PreparedStatement` and `ResultSet` levels

- How any override of the `ResultSet` object's fetch size affects all fetches except the very first one

- The `CallableStatement` bug mentioned previously and its workaround

We first create a simple table, t1, populated with around 78,000 numbers:

```
benchmark@ORA10G> create table t1 as
  2  select rownum as x from all_objects
  3  union all
  4  select rownum as x from all_objects;

Table created.

benchmark@ORA10G> commit;

Commit complete.

benchmark@ORA10G> select count(*) from t1;

    78228
```

We use the rownum pseudo column on the table all_objects (which usually has a decent number of rows) to populate table t1 with numbers. The rownum pseudo column returns a number for each row, indicating the order in which Oracle selected the row. The first row selected has a rownum value of 1, the second has a value of 2, and so on.

Next, we create a PL/SQL package, prefetch_pkg, that contains a single procedure called get_details. We will use this package to demonstrate the CallableStatement bug and its workaround:

```
benchmark@ORA10G> create or replace package prefetch_pkg
  2  as
  3    procedure get_details( p_num_of_rows in number,
  4        p_sql_tag in varchar2, p_cursor in out sys_refcursor );
  5  end;
  6  /

Package created.
```

The package body defines the procedure get_details. It simply returns a ref cursor containing values of column x for a given number of rows. It uses the rownum pseudo column to restrict the number of rows returned. Note that we also have a SQL tag in the parameter p_sql_tag, using which we tag the SQL within the PL/SQL with the fetch size information we set at the OracleConnection, CallableStatement, and ResultSet interface levels. This helps us identify the SQL in the tkprof output, which is the tool we'll use to peek at what really goes on internally for a given prefetch size:

```
benchmark@ORA10G> create or replace package body prefetch_pkg
  2  as
  3    procedure get_details( p_num_of_rows in number, p_sql_tag in varchar2,
  4      p_cursor in out sys_refcursor )
  5    is
  6    begin
  7      open p_cursor for
```

```
 8          'select '|| p_sql_tag || 'x from t1 where rownum <= :p_fetch_size '
                using p_num_of_rows;
 9     end;
10   end;
11   /
```

Package body created.

The following program, DemoPrefetch, has explanatory comments interspersed with the code:

```
/* This program demonstrates how to set and get fetch size for your
 * queries using PreparedStatement.
 * COMPATIBLITY NOTE: runs successfully against 10.1.0.2.0, and 9.2.0.1.0
 */
import java.sql.ResultSet;
import java.sql.SQLException;
import java.sql.PreparedStatement;
import java.sql.CallableStatement;
import java.sql.Connection;
import oracle.jdbc.OracleConnection;
import oracle.jdbc.OracleTypes;
import book.util.JDBCUtil;

class DemoPrefetch
{
  public static void main(String[] args)
  {
```

This program takes three command-line parameters for fetch sizes that we need to set at the Connection, Statement, and ResultSet levels. The main() method begins with a check of these command-line parameters and puts them in three int variables:

```
    if( args.length != 3 )
    {
      System.err.println( "Usage: java DemoPrefetch " +
         "<connection level fetch size> <statement level fetch size>" +
         " <result set level fetch size>");
      Runtime.getRuntime().exit( 1 );
    }
    int connLevelDefaultPrefetch = Integer.parseInt( args[0] );
    int stmtLevelFetchSize = Integer.parseInt( args[1] );
    int rsetLevelFetchSize = Integer.parseInt( args[2] );
```

We then obtain the connection to our database:

```
    Connection conn = null;
    try
    {
      conn = JDBCUtil.getConnection("benchmark", "benchmark", "ora10g");
```

Next, we print out the default Connection-level fetch size and set it to the Connection level fetch size passed as the command-line parameter:

```
System.out.println( "\nDefault connection fetch size: " +
  ((OracleConnection) conn).getDefaultRowPrefetch() );
System.out.println( "setting the default fetch size at connection level to "
  + connLevelDefaultPrefetch );
((OracleConnection) conn).setDefaultRowPrefetch( connLevelDefaultPrefetch  );
System.out.println( "Now the connection fetch size: " +
  ((OracleConnection) conn).getDefaultRowPrefetch() );
```

We set the SQL trace so that we can generate tkprof output:

```
JDBCUtil.startTrace( conn );
```

We then invoke four methods. The first method, _demoPstmtFetchSize(), sets the fetch size on a PreparedStatement object, but doesn't override it at the ResultSet level:

```
_demoPstmtFetchSize( conn, connLevelDefaultPrefetch, stmtLevelFetchSize);
```

The second method, _demoPstmtFetchSizeWithRsetOverride(), sets the fetch size on a PreparedStatement object, but overrides it at the ResultSet level:

```
_demoPstmtFetchSizeWithRsetOverride( conn, connLevelDefaultPrefetch,
  stmtLevelFetchSize, rsetLevelFetchSize );
```

The third method, _demoCstmtFetchSize(), sets the fetch size on a CallableStatement object without overriding it at the ResultSet level:

```
_demoCstmtFetchSize( conn, connLevelDefaultPrefetch, stmtLevelFetchSize );
```

The final method, _demoCstmtFetchSizeWithRsetOverride(), sets the fetch size on a CallableStatement object, overriding it later at the ResultSet level:

```
  _demoCstmtFetchSizeWithRsetOverride( conn, connLevelDefaultPrefetch,
    stmtLevelFetchSize, rsetLevelFetchSize );
}
catch (SQLException e)
{
  // handle the exception properly - in this case, we just
  // print the stack trace.
  JDBCUtil.printException ( e );
}
finally
{
  // release the JDBC resources in the finally clause.
  JDBCUtil.close( conn );
}
} // end of main()
```

Let's look at the definition of the _demoPstmtFetchSize() method:

```
private static void _demoPstmtFetchSize( Connection conn,
   int connLevelDefaultPrefetch, int stmtLevelFetchSize ) throws SQLException
{
   System.out.println( "Inside _demoPstmtFetchSize" );
```

First, we create a SQL tag enclosed within the Oracle hint strings "/*+" and "*/" so that we can identify the statement within the tkprof output. Since the enclosed string is not a valid hint, Oracle will ignore it. Note that if you use "/*" instead of "/*+", Oracle will treat the hint string as a comment and strip it away in 10g (in 9i this is not the case). Within the dummy hint, we tuck away the fetch sizes set at the OracleConnection and PreparedStatement levels:

```
String sqlTag = "/*+" +
                "(CONN="  + connLevelDefaultPrefetch + ")" +
                "(PSTMT=" + stmtLevelFetchSize      + ")" +
          "*/";
```

Next, we form our SQL statement string, which selects a given number of rows. Note how we tag it with the sqlTag value we just created:

```
String stmtString = "select x "+ sqlTag + " from t1 where rownum <= ?";
```

We prepare our PreparedStatement object:

```
PreparedStatement pstmt = null;
ResultSet rset = null;

try
{
  pstmt = conn.prepareStatement( stmtString );
```

And we print the default statement fetch size, which is the one it inherits from the OracleConnection interface:

```
   System.out.println( "\tDefault statement fetch size: " +
     pstmt.getFetchSize());
```

We then set the fetch size at the PreparedStatement object and set the total number of rows to be retrieved as 100. Finally, we execute the statement and iterate through the result set, which is followed by the finally clause:

```
   pstmt.setFetchSize( stmtLevelFetchSize );
   System.out.println( "\tnew statement fetch size: " + pstmt.getFetchSize());
   pstmt.setInt( 1, 100 );
   rset = pstmt.executeQuery();
   System.out.println( "\tResult set fetch size: " + rset.getFetchSize());
   int i=0;
   while (rset.next())
   {
     i++;
   }
```

```
      System.out.println( "\tnumber of times in the loop: " + i );
    }
    finally
    {
      // release JDBC-related resources in the finally clause.
      JDBCUtil.close( rset );
      JDBCUtil.close( pstmt );
    }
  }
```

The method _demoPstmtFetchSizeWithRsetOverride() is exactly the same as the method
_demoPstmtFetchSize(), except that we override the fetch size at the ResultSet object as well.
Note that the SQL tag also has the ResultSet fetch size used in this case:

```
private static void _demoPstmtFetchSizeWithRsetOverride( Connection conn,
    int connLevelDefaultPrefetch, int stmtLevelFetchSize,
    int rsetLevelFetchSize ) throws SQLException
{
  System.out.println( "Inside _demoPstmtFetchSizeWithRsetOverride" );
  String sqlTag = "/*+" +
                  "(CONN=" + connLevelDefaultPrefetch + ")" +
                  "(PSTMT=" + stmtLevelFetchSize       + ")" +
                  "(RSET=" + rsetLevelFetchSize        + ")" +
              "*/";
  String stmtString = "select x "+ sqlTag + " from t1 where rownum <= ?";
  PreparedStatement pstmt = null;
  ResultSet rset = null;

  try
  {
    pstmt = conn.prepareStatement( stmtString );
    System.out.println( "\tDefault statement fetch size: " +
      pstmt.getFetchSize());
    pstmt.setFetchSize( stmtLevelFetchSize );
    System.out.println( "\tnew statement fetch size: " + pstmt.getFetchSize());
    pstmt.setInt( 1, 100 );
    rset = pstmt.executeQuery();
    rset.setFetchSize( rsetLevelFetchSize );
    System.out.println( "\tnew result set fetch size: " + rset.getFetchSize());
    int i=0;
    while (rset.next())
    {
      i++;
    }
    System.out.println( "\tnumber of times in the loop: " + i );
  }
  finally
  {
```

```
        // release JDBC-related resources in the finally clause.
        JDBCUtil.close( rset );
        JDBCUtil.close( pstmt );
    }
}
```

The method _demoCstmtFetchSize() is similar to the method _demoPstmtFetchSize(),
except that here we set the fetch size at the CallableStatement level by invoking our procedure
prefetch_pkg.get_details() (the setting of fetch size won't really work, as you'll see shortly).
Note also that we create the SQL tag with the Connection level and CallableStatement-level
fetch size information, and pass it to the PL/SQL procedure:

```
private static void _demoCstmtFetchSize( Connection conn,
    int connLevelDefaultPrefetch, int stmtLevelFetchSize )
    throws SQLException
{
    System.out.println( "Inside _demoCstmtFetchSize" );
    String sqlTag = "/*+" +
                    "(CONN="  + connLevelDefaultPrefetch + ")" +
                    "(CSTMT=" + stmtLevelFetchSize        + ")" +
                "*/";
    String stmtString = "{ call prefetch_pkg.get_details ( ?, ?, ? ) }";
    CallableStatement cstmt = null;
    ResultSet rset = null;
    try
    {
        cstmt = conn.prepareCall( stmtString );
        System.out.println( "\tDefault statement fetch size: " +
            cstmt.getFetchSize());
        cstmt.setFetchSize( stmtLevelFetchSize );
        System.out.println( "\tnew statement fetch size: " + cstmt.getFetchSize());
        cstmt.setInt( 1, 100); // number of rows to be fetched
        cstmt.setString( 2, sqlTag );
        cstmt.registerOutParameter( 3, OracleTypes.CURSOR );
        // execute the query
        cstmt.execute();
        rset = (ResultSet) cstmt.getObject( 3 );
        System.out.println( "\tresult set fetch size: " + rset.getFetchSize());
        System.out.println( "\tHowever, in case of callable statement, " +
            "the real fetch size for all result sets obtained from the statement" +
            " is the same as the one set at the connection level." );
        int i=0;
        while (rset.next())
        {
            i++;
        }
        System.out.println( "\tnumber of times in the loop: " + i );
    }
```

```
  finally
  {
    // release JDBC-related resources in the finally clause.
    JDBCUtil.close( rset );
    JDBCUtil.close( cstmt );
  }
}
```

Our final method of the class DemoPrefetch is the same as the previous method, except that we override the fetch size at the ResultSet level as well. The SQL tag this time will have information about fetch sizes at the Connection, Statement, and ResultSet levels:

```
private static void _demoCstmtFetchSizeWithRsetOverride( Connection conn,
   int connLevelDefaultPrefetch, int stmtLevelFetchSize,
   int rsetLevelFetchSize ) throws SQLException
{
   System.out.println( "Inside _demoCstmtFetchSizeWithRsetOverride" );
   String sqlTag = "/*+" +
                      "(CONN="  + connLevelDefaultPrefetch + ")" +
                      "(CSTMT=" + stmtLevelFetchSize        + ")" +
                      "(RSET="  + rsetLevelFetchSize         + ")" +
                  "*/";
   String stmtString = "{ call prefetch_pkg.get_details ( ?, ?, ? ) }";
   CallableStatement cstmt = null;
   ResultSet rset = null;
   try
   {
     cstmt = conn.prepareCall( stmtString );
     System.out.println( "\tDefault statement fetch size: " +
       cstmt.getFetchSize());
     cstmt.setFetchSize( stmtLevelFetchSize );
     System.out.println( "\tnew statement fetch size: " + cstmt.getFetchSize());
     cstmt.setInt( 1, 100); // number of rows to be fetched
     cstmt.setString( 2, sqlTag );
     cstmt.registerOutParameter( 3, OracleTypes.CURSOR );
     // execute the query
     cstmt.execute();
     rset = (ResultSet) cstmt.getObject( 3 );
     rset.setFetchSize( rsetLevelFetchSize );
     System.out.println( "\tnew result set fetch size: " + rset.getFetchSize());
     System.out.println( "\tHowever, in case of callable statement, " +
       "the real fetch size for all result sets obtained from the " +
       "statement is the same as the one set at the connection level." );
     int i=0;
     while (rset.next())
     {
       i++;
     }
```

```
      System.out.println( "\tnumber of times in the loop: " + i );
    }
    finally
    {
      // release JDBC-related resources in the finally clause.
      JDBCUtil.close( rset );
      JDBCUtil.close( cstmt );
    }
  }
} // end of program
```

In all four methods, we also increment a counter within the while loop pertaining to the ResultSet object and print it out at the end.

When we run the preceding program with values of 5, 20, and 50 for the Connection level, Statement level, ResultSet level fetch sizes, respectively, we get the following output:

```
B:\>java DemoPrefetch 5 20 50
URL:jdbc:oracle:thin:@(DESCRIPTION=(ADDRESS=(PROTOCOL=tcp)
  (PORT=1521)(HOST=rmenon-lap))(CONNECT_DATA=(SID=ora10g)))
Default connection fetch size: 10
setting the default fetch size at connection level to 5
Now the connection fetch size: 5
Inside _demoPstmtFetchSize
        Default statement fetch size: 5
        new statement fetch size: 20
        Result set fetch size: 20
        number of times in the loop: 100
Inside _demoPstmtFetchSizeWithRsetOverride 14.150
        Default statement fetch size: 5
        new statement fetch size: 20
        new result set fetch size: 50
        number of times in the loop: 100
Inside _demoCstmtFetchSize
        Default statement fetch size: 5
        new statement fetch size: 20
        result set fetch size: 5
        However, in case of callable statement, the real fetch size for all
result sets obtained from the statement is the same as the one set at the connection
 level.
        number of times in the loop: 100
Inside _demoCstmtFetchSizeWithRsetOverride
        Default statement fetch size: 5
        new statement fetch size: 20
        new result set fetch size: 50
        However, in case of callable statement, the real fetch size for all
result sets obtained from the statement is the same as the one set at the connection
 level.
        number of times in the loop: 100
```

The output confirms that in the case of PreparedStatement, the result set inherits the statement fetch size, whereas in the case of CallableStatement, though the Statement-level fetch size was changed to 12, the ResultSet-level fetch size was still 5 (as inherited from the Connection-level fetch size). In other words, the setting of fetch size at CallableStatement did not really do anything.

Let's now look at the tkprof of select statements for each of the four methods. The relevant portion of the tkprof output for _demoPstmtFetchSize() is as follows:

```
select x /*+(CONN=5)(PSTMT=20)*/
from
 t1 where rownum <= :1
```

call	count	cpu	elapsed	disk	query	current	rows
Parse	1	0.00	0.00	0	0	0	0
Execute	1	0.01	0.00	0	0	0	0
Fetch	6	0.00	0.01	0	8	0	100
total	8	0.01	0.01	0	8	0	100

Notice how the SQL tag containing the string "/*+CONN=5PSTMT=20*/ tells us that the fetch size at Connection level for this select was 5, and at the PreparedStatement level the fetch size was 20. Recall that we did not override it in this case at the ResultSet level.

The actual number of fetches is 6 (see column count of row Fetch in the tkprof output). This is because the very first fetch of 20 rows happened transparently with the executeQuery() method invocation on the PreparedStatement object and used the fetch size of 20 set at the PreparedStatement level. The remaining four fetches also used the fetch size of 20 set at the PreparedStatement object, since we did not override it at the ResultSet level. The last fetch is required to detect that there are no more records to fetch, as shown in Table 7-1.

Table 7-1. *Step-by-Step Account of the Number of Fetches for the* _demoPstmtFetchSize() *Method*

Fetch Number(s)	Fetch Size (Level Inherited From)	Total Records Fetched So Far
1	20 (PreparedStatement)	20
2, 3, 4, 5	20 (PreparedStatement)	100
6	20 (PreparedStatement)	100 (Last fetch to detect that no more records exist)

The number of logical I/Os (for a discussion on logical I/Os, see the section "Logical and Physical I/O" in Chapter 2) is 8 (the sum of totals for the current column, 0, and the query column, 8).

The relevant portion of the tkprof output for _demoPstmtFetchSizeWithRsetOverride() is as follows:

```
select x /*+(CONN=5)(PSTMT=20)(RSET=50)*/
from
 t1 where rownum <= :1
```

call	count	cpu	elapsed	disk	query	current	rows
Parse	1	0.00	0.00	0	0	0	0
Execute	1	0.00	0.00	0	0	0	0
Fetch	3	0.00	0.00	0	6	0	100
total	5	0.00	0.01	0	6	0	100

Note that the SQL tag containing the string "/*+CONN=5PSTMT=20(RSET=50)*/ tells us that the fetch size at the Connection level for this select was 5, at the PreparedStatement level it was 20, and at the ResultSet level it was overridden to 50.

The actual number of fetches is 3 (see column count of row Fetch in the tkprof output). This is because, once again, the very first fetch of 20 rows was based on the fetch size of 20 set at the PreparedStatement object. The second and third fetches used the fetch size of 50 set at the ResultSet object, as shown in Table 7-2.

Table 7-2. *Step-by-Step Account of the Number of Fetches for the* _demoPstmtFetchSizeWithRsetOverride() *Method*

Fetch Number(s)	Fetch Size (Level Inherited From)	Total Records Fetched So Far
1	20 (PreparedStatement)	20
2	50 (ResultSet)	70
3	50 (PreparedStatement)	100

The number of logical I/Os is 6. Note that the number of logical I/Os has decreased as the fetch size has increased.

The relevant portion of the tkprof output for _demoCstmtFetchSize() is as follows:

```
select /*+(CONN=5)(CSTMT=20)*/x
from
 t1 where rownum <= :p_fetch_size
```

call	count	cpu	elapsed	disk	query	current	rows
Parse	1	0.00	0.00	0	0	0	0
Execute	1	0.01	0.01	0	0	0	0
Fetch	21	0.01	0.02	0	23	0	100
total	23	0.03	0.03	0	23	0	100

Note that from the SQL tag string "/*+CONN=5CSTMT=20*/, we see that the fetch size at Connection level for this select was 5, at the CallableStatement level it was 20, and at the ResultSet level it was 20, since it was not overridden.

The actual number of fetches is 21 (see column count of row Fetch in the tkprof output). Note how the number of fetches is different from the corresponding result in the method _demoPstmtFetchSize(), where it was 3 for the same fetch size configuration. This is because the fetch size set at the CallableStatement level never really worked. All the fetches used the fetch size of 5 set at the Connection level, as shown in Table 7-3.

Table 7-3. *Step-by-Step Account of the Number of Fetches for the* _demoCstmtFetchSize() *Method*

Fetch Number(s)	Fetch Size (Level Inherited From)	Total Records Fetched So Far
1 through 20	5 (OracleConnection)	100
21	5 (OracleConnection)	100 (Last fetch to detect that no more records exist)

The number of logical I/Os has increased to 23 since the overall fetch size has decreased.

The relevant portion of the tkprof output for _demoCstmtFetchSizeWithRsetOverride() is as follows:

```
select /*+(CONN=5)(CSTMT=20)(RSET=50)*/x
from
t1 where rownum <= :p_fetch_size
```

call	count	cpu	elapsed	disk	query	current	rows
Parse	1	0.00	0.00	0	0	0	0
Execute	1	0.00	0.00	0	0	0	0
Fetch	3	0.00	0.00	0	5	0	100
total	5	0.00	0.00	0	5	0	100

Notice that the SQL tag containing the string "/*+CONN=5CSTMT=20(RSET=50)*/ tells us that the fetch size at the Connection level for this select was 5, at the CallableStatement level it was 20, and at the ResultSet level it was overridden to 50.

The actual number of fetches is 3 (see column count of row Fetch in the tkprof output). This is because the very first fetch of five rows in the while loop was based on the fetch size of 5 set at the Connection object (remember that the CallableStatement fetch size does not really work). The second and third fetches used the fetch size of 50 set at the ResultSet object, as shown in Table 7-4.

Table 7-4. *Step-by-Step Account of the Number of Fetches for the* _demoPstmtFetchSizeWithRsetOverride() *Method*

Fetch Number(s)	Fetch Size (Level Inherited From)	Total Records Fetched So Far
1	5 (OracleConnection)	5
2	50 (ResultSet)	55
3	50 (PreparedStatement)	100

The number of logical I/Os is 5 in this case.

The main points to note from the program `DemoPrefetch` are

- `PreparedStatement` inherits the fetch size set at the `OracleConnection` level.

- For `PreparedStatement`, we can change the fetch size at the `Statement` level (it works).

- For `CallableStatement`, we have to set the fetch size at the `ResultSet` level, since setting it at the `CallableStatement` level does not work due to a bug.

- If we override the fetch size at the `ResultSet` level, the very first fetch uses the fetch size set at the `PreparedStatement` level (or the `OracleConnection` level if it is not set at the `PreparedStatement` level). The subsequent fetches use the fetch size set at the `ResultSet` level.

- Fetch size does not have an impact on the total number of rows returned by query. It just sets the number of rows that would be transparently cached by the JDBC client. This is shown in our example by the fact that the number of iterations in the loop is always 100 because the query retrieves a total of 100 rows.

- Increasing the fetch size (to a certain limit) reduces the number of logical I/Os, which usually improves performance as demonstrated in the section "Logical and Physical I/Os" in Chapter 2. We'll measure this performance improvement in the next section.

Performance Impact of Fetch Size

To get an idea of the impact on performance of changing fetch size, I wrote a benchmark program, `BenchmarkPrefetch`, that finds the elapsed time of a query retrieving 50,000 rows from t1. This program extends the utility class `JBenchmark` discussed in the section "Timing Java Programs" in Chapter 1. The program begins with import statements, getting a connection and invoking the method `_runBenchmark()`:

```
/* This program benchmarks the impact of prefetch on a query.
 * COMPATIBLITY NOTE: runs successfully against 10.1.0.2.0, and 9.2.0.1.0
 */
import java.sql.ResultSet;
import java.sql.SQLException;
import java.sql.CallableStatement;
import java.sql.Connection;
import oracle.jdbc.OracleTypes;
import book.util.JDBCUtil;
import book.util.JBenchmark;

class BenchmarkPrefetch extends JBenchmark
{
  public static void main(String args[])
  {
    Connection conn = null;
    try
    {
      conn = JDBCUtil.getConnection("benchmark", "benchmark", "ora10g");
      new BenchmarkPrefetch()._runBenchmark( conn );
```

```
  }
  catch (Exception e)
  {
    // handle the exception properly - in this case, we just
    // print the stack trace.
    JDBCUtil.printException ( e );
  }
  finally
  {
    // release the JDBC resources in the finally clause.
    JDBCUtil.close( conn );
  }
} // end of main()
```

The following method, _runBenchmark(), prepares the statement to run our query that retrieves 50,000 rows. Before running the query, we start the SQL trace by invoking the method JDBCUtil.startTrace(). The query runs through a number of executions, each time retrieving a total of 50,000 rows using a given fetch size. The static array s_fetchSizes (declared later) defines all fetch sizes this program will benchmark our query on. Inside the loop, we find out the time taken by passing the fetch size information in an object array to the method timeMethod() inherited from JBenchmark:

```
private void _runBenchmark( Connection conn ) throws Exception
{
  String stmtString = "{ call prefetch_pkg.get_details ( ?, ?, ?) }";
  try
  {
    s_cstmt = conn.prepareCall( stmtString );
    JDBCUtil.startTrace( conn );
    for( int i=0; i < s_fetchSizes.length; i++ )
    {
      Integer fetchSize = new Integer ( s_fetchSizes[i] );
      timeMethod( JBenchmark.FIRST_METHOD, conn, new Object[]{fetchSize},
        "Fetch Size: " + fetchSize );
    }
  }
  finally
  {
    JDBCUtil.close( s_cstmt );
  }
}
```

We override the method firstMethod() to execute our query for a given fetch size. Note that we once again put the fetch size inside a dummy hint that acts as our SQL tag:

```
public void firstMethod( Connection conn, Object[] parameters )
    throws Exception
{
  ResultSet rset = null;
  Integer fetchSize = (Integer) parameters[0];
```

```
try
{
  String sqlTag = "/*+ FETCH_SIZE=" + fetchSize + "*/";
  s_cstmt.setInt( 1, 50000);
  s_cstmt.setString( 2, sqlTag );
  s_cstmt.registerOutParameter( 3, OracleTypes.CURSOR );
  s_cstmt.execute();
  rset = (ResultSet) s_cstmt.getObject( 3 );
  rset.setFetchSize( fetchSize.intValue() );
  int i=0;
  while (rset.next())
  {
    i++;
  }
}
finally
{
  // release JDBC-related resources in the finally clause.
  JDBCUtil.close( rset );
}
}
```

Finally, we declare the array containing fetch sizes for which this program was executed along with the static variable containing the CallableStatement object:

```
private static int[] s_fetchSizes = {10, 20, 50, 100, 500, 1000, 5000,
    10000, 30000};
private static CallableStatement s_cstmt;
} // end of program
```

The results of my run are shown in the chart in Figure 7-1.

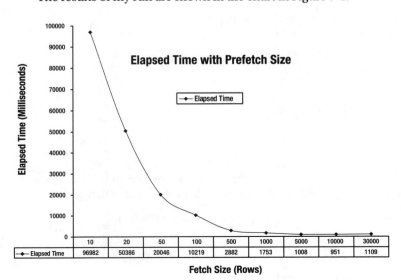

	10	20	50	100	500	1000	5000	10000	30000
Elapsed Time	96982	50386	20046	10219	2882	1753	1008	951	1109

Fetch Size (Rows)

Figure 7-1. *Elapsed times for a query with different fetch sizes*

Table 7-5 shows the actual data used in Figure 7-1. The third column shows the percentage of the elapsed time for the current fetch size as compared to the previous fetch size. For example, the elapsed time for a fetch size of 20 was 50.61% of the elapsed time for a fetch size of 10.

Table 7-5. *Elapsed Times with Changing Fetch Sizes*

Fetch Size	Elapsed Time (Milliseconds)	Percentage of Previous Time
10	96,982	--
20	50,386	51.95
50	20,046	39.78
100	10,219	50.98
500	2,882	28.20
1,000	1,753	60.83
5,000	1,008	57.50
10,000	951	94.35
30,000	1,109	116.61

As you can see, the elapsed time decreases dramatically as the fetch size increases. The optimal elapsed time corresponding to a fetch size of 10,000 in our run had an elapsed time that was only *0.98%* of the elapsed time corresponding to the default fetch size of 10. As is expected, though, after a certain point, diminishing returns set in (in this case because of the increase in memory required in the client-side cache that stores these prefetched results), and eventually the elapsed time starts showing an upward trend.

Next, we plot the number of logical I/Os for each fetch size, as shown in Figure 7-2.

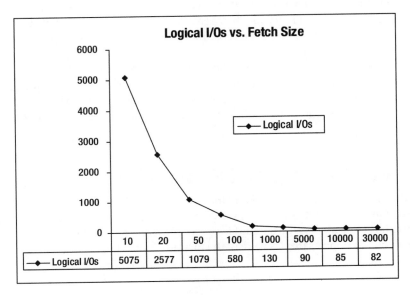

Figure 7-2. *Logical I/Os for a query with different fetch sizes*

Table 7-6 shows the logical I/Os performed with each fetch size. The third column shows the percentage of the logical I/Os for the current fetch size as compared to the previous fetch size. For example, logical I/Os for a fetch size of 20 were 50.78% of the logical I/Os for a fetch size of 10.

Table 7-6. *Logical I/Os with Changing Fetch Sizes*

Fetch Size	Logical I/Os	Percentage of Previous Time
10	5,075	
20	2,577	50.78
50	1,079	41.87
100	580	53.75
500	180	31.03
1,000	130	72.22
5,000	90	69.23
10,000	85	94.44
30,000	82	96.47

As Table 7-6 shows, the logical I/Os decrease in general with a decrease in fetch size. Toward the end, though, diminishing returns do set in as expected.

A critical fact to remember is that the preceding benchmark was run with the assumption that you want *all* rows to be returned as soon as possible. Many times that is not what you want. For example, a query may return a total of 50,000 rows, but you may be interested in getting only the first 15 rows as soon as possible. This could be your requirement if your query results are being displayed on a web page 15 rows at a time. In such cases, it does not make sense to set the fetch size for your query to a large value such as 1,000, even though that may be optimal in terms of getting *all* rows in your query as fast as possible; a smaller value of somewhere between 15 and 50 (or even retaining the default value of 10) may be more appropriate. Setting the fetch size becomes somewhat less critical in such a situation.

From the preceding discussion, we can conclude that tuning the fetch size can have a dramatic impact on the performance of your application, depending on the size of each row and how costly a network round-trip is to your application. You should be aware of what your goals are when you set this value for a given query (e.g., to get all rows as fast as possible or to get the first *n* rows as fast as possible).

Scrollability, Positioning, and Sensitivity

Scrollability refers to the ability to move backward and forward through the rows of a result set. A result set created with this ability to move backward and forward is called a *scrollable* result set. A result set without this ability (the default) is called a *forward-only* result set. The result sets in the earlier chapter code examples were of the forward-only type.

Within a scrollable result set, you can move your position using either *relative* or *absolute* positioning:

- *Relative* positioning allows you to move a given number of rows forward or backward from the current row.

- *Absolute* positioning allows you to move to a specified row number, counting from either the beginning or the end of the result set.

Note You cannot use positioning (relative or absolute) with forward-only result sets.

When creating a scrollable result set, you must also specify *sensitivity*:

- A *scroll-insensitive* result set is a scrollable result set that does not automatically detect certain changes made to the database while the result set is open, thus providing a static view of the underlying data. This is the default behavior. You would need to retrieve a new result set to see changes made to the database. Note that there are several limitations to the way this works in Oracle, as you will see in the section "Result Set Limitations and Downgrade Rules."

- A *scroll-sensitive* result set is a scrollable result set with a limited ability to detect certain changes made to the underlying result set data in the database from the current session or a different session while the result set is open.

Updatability

Updatability refers to the ability to insert, delete, or update rows in a result set and propagate these changes to the database. The updatability of a result set is determined by its *concurrency type*. Under JDBC 2.0, the following concurrency types are available:

- *Updatable*: Updates, inserts, and deletes can be performed on the result set and propagated to the database.

- *Read-only*: The result set cannot be modified in any way (the default behavior).

Note The updatability of a result set can be specified independently of the scrollability or sensitivity of the result set.

Table 7-7 lists six different combinations of result set categories available in Oracle, along with their capabilities.

Table 7-7. *Different Result Set Categories and Their Capabilities*

Result Set Category	Description
Forward-only/read-only (default)	Not scrollable. Cannot perform insert, update, and delete operations on the ResultSet object. Cannot detect any changes made to the database while the ResultSet is open.
Scroll-insensitive/read-only	Scrollable. Does not automatically detect certain changes made to the database while the ResultSet is open. Cannot perform insert, update, and delete operations on the ResultSet object.
Scroll-sensitive/read-only	Scrollable. Limited ability to detect certain changes made to the underlying ResultSet data in the database. Cannot perform insert, update, and delete operations on the ResultSet object.
Forward-only/updatable	Not scrollable. Can perform insert, update, and delete operations on the ResultSet object.
Scroll-insensitive/updatable	Scrollable. Does not automatically detect certain changes made to the database while the ResultSet is open. Can perform insert, update, and delete operations on the ResultSet object.
Scroll-sensitive/updatable	Scrollable. Limited ability to detect certain changes made to the underlying ResultSet data in the database. Cannot perform insert, update, and delete operations on the ResultSet object.

Creating Different Categories of Result Sets

To create any of the six combinations of result sets, you can use one of the following methods in the Connection object:

- Statement createStatement (int resultSetType, int resultSetConcurrency)

- PreparedStatement prepareStatement(String sql, int resultSetType, int resultSetConcurrency)

- CallableStatement prepareCall(String sql, int resultSetType, int resultSetConcurrency)

As mentioned earlier, although the Oracle JDBC documentation states that the result set scrollability and updatability are implemented in CallableStatement, I discovered that the current implementation does not work for result sets returned via stored procedures. This is not a real problem since updatability, as implemented currently, can be easily accomplished using standard SQL statements to update, insert, and delete rows. As far as scrollable result sets go, their most common use is to display a subset of rows at a time for a given result set and allow the user to scroll through it, say, ten rows at a time. For this scenario, as explained in the section "Paginating Through a Result Set," you can use an alternative implementation that uses forward-only result sets and yet accomplishes many of the goals of scrollable result sets more efficiently and without running into its limitations.

■**Caution** As of 10*g* Release 1, the Oracle JDBC implementation of scrollable and updatable result sets don't work with result sets returned by stored procedures via the `CallableStatement` interface.

In all the preceding methods, the first parameter, `resultSetType`, determines the scrollability and sensitivity of the result set, and the second parameter, `resultSetConcurrency`, determines if the result set is updatable or read-only.

You can specify one of the following constants defined in the `ResultSet` interface to set the scrollability/sensitivity attribute of the result set:

- `ResultSet.TYPE_FORWARD_ONLY` (the default)

- `ResultSet.TYPE_SCROLL_INSENSITIVE`

- `ResultSet.TYPE_SCROLL_SENSITIVE`

You can specify one of the following constants in the `ResultSet` interface to set the updatability attribute of the result set:

- `ResultSet.CONCUR_READ_ONLY` (the default)

- `ResultSet.CONCUR_UPDATABLE`

Result Set Limitations and Downgrade Rules

There are several limitations in the Oracle implementation of the result set's scrollability and updatability features to keep in mind. From a performance point of view, an important factor to consider is that scrollable/updatable result sets necessarily require a client-side cache. This means that if your result set contains many rows, many columns, or large columns, then it can have a severe performance impact on the JDBC application due to high memory consumption. Thus, the scrollability feature should be used only for small result sets.

■**Caution** Do not use the scrollability feature for large result sets.

Besides the performance implications of using a client-side cache, certain types of result sets are not feasible for certain kinds of queries. If you specify an infeasible result set type or concurrency type for the query you execute, the JDBC driver follows a set of downgrade rules to select "the next best" `ResultSet` type. In this section, we'll look at the various limitations of `ResultSet`.

Result Set Limitations

The following restrictions exist when you are trying to create an updatable `ResultSet`:

- The query can select from only a single table and cannot contain any join operations. In addition, for inserts to be feasible, the query must select all non-nullable columns and all columns that don't have a default value (unless a trigger or a default column value kicks in and populates the column value even if you don't explicitly specify it). This clearly is a considerable restriction and one of the main reasons I'm not a fan of this feature.

- The query can't use `select *`. However, you can easily work around this restriction by specifying table aliases. Thus, `select * from emp` won't work, but `select e.* from emp e` will give you an updatable result set.

- The query must select table columns only. It can't select derived columns or aggregates such as the `sum`, `count`, or `max` of a set of columns.

For an insert to work, you can't have an `order` by in the query for which the updateable result set is created. (This isn't noted in the official JDBC documentation.) If you try to perform an insert on a result set whose `select` statement has an `order` by clause, you'll get this `SQLException: java.sql.SQLException: ORA-01732: data manipulation operation not legal on this view`.

To create a scroll-sensitive result set

- A query cannot use `select *`. Once again, you can easily work around this by specifying table aliases.

- A query can select from only a single table.

These limitations mean that the scrollability and updatability features, as implemented currently, are useful only in very simple queries. The updatability feature in particular does not add any value over the regular way of doing updates using SQL statements—I have never found a need to use this feature.

Result Set Downgrade Rules

If you specify, for example, an updatable `ResultSet`, but the JDBC driver cannot fulfill this request due to the nature of the query, then the result set type will be silently downgraded to the nearest equivalent. These downgrade rules are as follows:

- If the specified result set type is `TYPE_SCROLL_SENSITIVE`, but the JDBC driver cannot fulfill that request, then the driver attempts a downgrade to `TYPE_SCROLL_INSENSITIVE`.

- If the specified (or downgraded) result set type is `TYPE_SCROLL_INSENSITIVE`, but the JDBC driver cannot fulfill that request, then the driver attempts a downgrade to `TYPE_FORWARD_ONLY`.

- If the specified (or downgraded) concurrency type is `CONCUR_UPDATABLE`, but the JDBC driver cannot fulfill that request, then the driver attempts a downgrade to `CONCUR_READ_ONLY`.

You can and always should verify the actual result set type and concurrency type by using the following two methods in the `ResultSet` interface (both throw a `SQLException`):

- `int getType()`: This method returns an `int` value for the result set type used for the query.

- `int getConcurrency()`: This method returns an `int` value for the concurrency type used for the query.

Note According to the documentation, in case of a downgrade, the driver should issue a `SQLWarning` on the statement object with information on the reason the downgrade occurred. However, this did not work during my tests. A simple workaround is to always check the type and concurrency type at the `ResultSet` level.

An easy way to find out if your result set can be scroll-sensitive or updatable is to run the same query in SQL*Plus but add the pseudo column `rowid` to the query's list of columns (the `rowid` pseudo column returns the address of the row in Oracle). If the query works, then most likely the request for a scrollable result set would succeed without a downgrade.

For example, if we add the pseudo column `rowid` to the query `select ename from emp`, it works as follows:

```
scott@ORA10G> select rowid, ename from emp;

ROWID               ENAME
------------------- ----------
AAAL+ZAAEAAAAAdAAA  SMITH
… <trimmed for saving space>

14 rows selected.
```

But if we add the pseudo column `rowid` to the query `select e.ename, d.deptno from emp e, dept d where e.deptno = d.deptno`, it does not work:

```
scott@ORA10G> select rowid, e.ename, d.deptno from emp e, dept d
  where e.deptno = d.deptno;
select rowid, e.ename, d.deptno from emp e, dept d where e.deptno = d.deptno
       *
ERROR at line 1:
ORA-00918: column ambiguously defined
```

Thus, the second query will go through a downgrade based on the rules stated earlier. The reason the preceding test works is that the JDBC driver silently (and blindly) adds a `rowid` pseudo column to the list of columns for such queries and uses the selected `rowid`s to perform various operations, such as updates on result sets, as you will see later.

■**Note** The fact that the JDBC driver silently (and blindly) adds a `rowid` pseudo column to the list of columns for such queries and uses the selected `rowid`s to perform various operations also explains why `select * from emp` does not work but `select e.* from emp` does.

Positioning in a Scrollable Result Set

As mentioned earlier, scrollable result sets (scroll-sensitive and scroll-insensitive) allow you to iterate through the result set either forward or backward, and to modify the current position in the result set to any desired row number using a relative or an absolute row number. This section covers some of these methods.

Methods to Move Within a Result Set

The following methods allow you to move to a new position in a scrollable result set (all of them throw a SQLException, although I don't show that specifically). The word "cursor" here refers to the current row position in the result set.

- `void beforeFirst()`: This method moves the cursor to a position before the first row of the result set, and it has no effect if there are no rows in the result set. This is the default initial position for any kind of result set. Note that after invoking this method, there is no valid current row, so you cannot position relatively from this point.

- `void afterLast()`: This method moves the cursor to a position after the last row of the result set, and it has no effect if there are no rows in the result set. You can use this method to position the current row of the result set after the final row to start process-ing the rows backward. Note that after invoking this method, you are outside the result set bounds. Thus, there is no valid current row, so you cannot position relatively from this point. Another implication of invoking this method is that Oracle has to read all the rows of the result set to reach the last row; it has performance implications that we will look at shortly.

- `boolean first()`: This method moves the cursor to the first row of the result set or returns `false` if there are no rows in the result set.

- `boolean last()`: This method moves the cursor to the last row of the result set or returns `false` if there are no rows in the result set.

- `boolean absolute(int row)`: This method moves the cursor to an absolute row from either the beginning or the end of the result set. If you input a positive number, it posi-tions from the beginning; if you input a negative number, it positions from the end. This method returns `false` if there are no rows in the result set.

■Note Attempting to move forward beyond the last row will move the cursor to after the last row and have the same effect as an `afterLast()` call. Similarly, attempting to move backward beyond the first row will move the cursor to before the first row and have the same effect as a `beforeFirst()` call. Also note that calling `absolute(1)` is equivalent to calling `first()`, and calling `absolute(-1)` is equivalent to calling `last()`.

- `boolean relative(int row)`: This method moves the cursor to a position relative to the current row, either forward if you input a positive number or backward if you input a negative number. It returns `false` if there are no rows in the result set.

■Caution Attempting to position relatively from before the first row (which is the default initial position) or after the last row will result in a `SQLException`.

- `boolean next()`: You are already familiar with this method. It moves the cursor to the next row and returns a `boolean` indicating if the new row is a valid row.

- `boolean previous()`: This method is similar to the `next` method, but it moves the cursor to the previous row instead and returns a `boolean` indicating if the new row is a valid row.

■Caution Attempting to use `previous()` in a nonscrollable (forward-only) result set will result in a `SQLException`.

Methods to Check Current Position Within a Result Set

The following `ResultSet` methods allow you to find out your current position in a scrollable result set (all of them throw a `SQLException`):

- `boolean isBeforeFirst()`: Returns `true` if the position is before the first row
- `boolean isAfterLast()`: Returns `true` if the position is after the last row
- `boolean isFirst()`: Returns `true` if the position is at the first row
- `boolean isLast()`: Returns `true` if the position is at the last row
- `int getRow()`: Returns the row number of the current row or `0` if there is no valid current row

Example of Positioning

The following DemoPositioning class demonstrates some of the positioning methods just described. The main() method in the class simply gets the connection and invokes _demoPositioning, which contains the main logic:

```
/* This program demonstrates positioning in a scrollable result set.
* COMPATIBLITY NOTE: runs successfully against 10.1.0.2.0 and 9.2.0.1.0.
*/
import java.sql.ResultSet;
import java.sql.SQLException;
import java.sql.PreparedStatement;
import java.sql.Connection;
import book.util.JDBCUtil;
class DemoPositioning
{
  public static void main(String args[]) throws Exception
  {
    Connection conn = null;
    try
    {
      conn = JDBCUtil.getConnection("scott", "tiger", "ora10g");
      _demoPositioning( conn );
    }
    catch (SQLException e)
    {
      // handle the exception properly - in this case, we just
      // print the stack trace.
      JDBCUtil.printException ( e );
    }
    finally
    {
      // release the JDBC resources in the finally clause.
      JDBCUtil.close( conn );
    }
  } // end of main()
```

The method _demoPositioning() first prepares a statement whose result sets will be scroll-insensitive and read-only. (Note that the example also works for scroll-insensitive result sets.)

```
  private static void _demoPositioning( Connection conn )
  throws SQLException
  {
    ResultSet rset = null;
    PreparedStatement pstmt = null;
    try
    {
      pstmt = conn.prepareStatement( "select x from t1 order by x",
        ResultSet.TYPE_SCROLL_INSENSITIVE, ResultSet.CONCUR_READ_ONLY);
```

We then invoke the utility method printRsetTypeAndConcurrencyType in the JDBCUtil class (shown right after this class code explanation), which simply prints out the statement's result set type and concurrency type based on the methods getResultSetType() and getResultSetConcurrencyType(), respectively:

```
JDBCUtil.printRsetTypeAndConcurrencyType( pstmt );
```

We next get the result set and use the overloaded version of printRsetTypeAnd➡
ConcurrencyType in the JDBCUtil class (shown right after this class code explanation), which prints out the result set type and concurrency type using the methods getType() and getConcurrencyType() in the ResultSet interface. This finds out if the result set was downgraded due to some JDBC driver limitations.

```
rset = (ResultSet) pstmt.executeQuery();
JDBCUtil.printRsetTypeAndConcurrencyType( rset );
```

We now start demonstrating the various positioning methods. First, we go to the last row and print out the row number:

```
rset.last(); // go to the last row
System.out.println( "current position: " + rset.getRow() );
```

We then go to the first row and print out a boolean indicating if it is the first row:

```
rset.first(); // go to the first row
System.out.println( "Is it the first row?: " + rset.isFirst());
```

Next, we go to the row number 4 and print out our current position:

```
rset.absolute( 4 ); // go to the row number 4
System.out.println( "current position: " + rset.getRow() );
```

We then move three rows forward, print the current position, move two rows backward, and print the current position:

```
rset.relative( +3 ); // go to the next 3 rows from current row
System.out.println( "current position: " + rset.getRow() );
rset.relative( -2 ); // go to the previous 2 rows from current row
System.out.println( "current position: " + rset.getRow() );
```

Next, we move to the row before the first row and move to the first row by executing the next() method. We print the current position:

```
rset.beforeFirst( ); // go to the position before the first row
rset.next(); // now go to first row
System.out.println( "current position: " + rset.getRow() );
```

Finally, we move to the row after the last row and move to the last row by executing the previous() method. We print the current position:

```
rset.afterLast( ); // go to the position after the last row
rset.previous(); // now go to last row
System.out.println( "current position: " + rset.getRow() );
```

```
    }
    finally
    {
      // release the JDBC resources in the finally clause.
      JDBCUtil.close( rset );
      JDBCUtil.close( pstmt );
    }
  }
} // end of program
```

The printRsetTypeAndConcurrencyType() method in the JDBCUtil class based on the Statement interface is as follows:

```
public static void printRsetTypeAndConcurrencyType( Statement stmt )
throws SQLException
{
  System.out.print( "\tResult set category (using Statement API): " );
  int resultSetType = stmt.getResultSetType();
  switch( resultSetType )
  {
    case ResultSet.TYPE_FORWARD_ONLY:
      System.out.print( "Forward only" );
      break;
    case ResultSet.TYPE_SCROLL_INSENSITIVE:
      System.out.print( "Scroll insensitive" );
      break;
    case ResultSet.TYPE_SCROLL_SENSITIVE:
      System.out.print( "Scroll sensitive" );
      break;
  }
  int resultSetConcurrency = stmt.getResultSetConcurrency();
  switch( resultSetConcurrency )
  {
    case ResultSet.CONCUR_READ_ONLY:
      System.out.println( ", Read only" );
      break;
    case ResultSet.CONCUR_UPDATABLE:
      System.out.println( ", Updatable" );
      break;
  }
}
```

The printRsetTypeAndConcurrencyType() method in the JDBCUtil class based on the ResultSet interface is as follows:

```
public static void printRsetTypeAndConcurrencyType( ResultSet rset)
throws SQLException
{
```

```
int resultSetType = rset.getType();
System.out.print( "\tResult set category (using ResultSet API): " );

switch( resultSetType )
{
  case ResultSet.TYPE_FORWARD_ONLY:
    System.out.print( "Forward only" );
    break;
  case ResultSet.TYPE_SCROLL_INSENSITIVE:
    System.out.print( "Scroll insensitive" );
    break;
  case ResultSet.TYPE_SCROLL_SENSITIVE:
    System.out.print( "Scroll sensitive" );
    break;
}
int resultSetConcurrency = rset.getConcurrency();
switch( resultSetConcurrency )
{
  case ResultSet.CONCUR_READ_ONLY:
    System.out.println( ", Read only" );
    break;
  case ResultSet.CONCUR_UPDATABLE:
    System.out.println( ", Updatable" );
    break;
}
}
```

This is the output of the program DemoPositioning:

```
java DemoPositioning
URL:jdbc:oracle:thin:@(DESCRIPTION=(ADDRESS=(PROTOCOL=tcp)(PORT=1521)
(HOST=rmenon-lap))(CONNECT_DATA=(SID=ora10g)))
        Result set category (using Statement API): Scroll insensitive, Read only
        Result set category (using ResultSet API): Scroll insensitive, Read only
current position: 30
Is it the first row?: true
current position: 4
current position: 7
current position: 5
current position: 1
current position: 30
```

Updating, Inserting, and Deleting Result Set Rows

Assuming that you have a result set with a concurrency type of ResultSet.CONCUR_UPDATABLE, you can directly update rows in the result set, insert rows into the result set, or delete rows from the result set.

After an update or insert operation in a result set, you propagate the changes to the database in a separate step that you can skip if you want to cancel the changes. A delete operation in a result set, however, is immediately executed (but not necessarily committed) in the database. Let's look at each of these, starting with the delete operation.

Deleting a Row

To delete the current row, you can invoke the method deleteRow() on the result set:

```
void deleteRow() throws SQLException;
```

Updating a Row

To update one or more columns of the current row, you can call the appropriate updateXXX() method for each column, based on the type of the column you want to update. A ResultSet object has an updateXXX() method for each data type. Each of these methods takes an int for the column number or a string for the column name, along with an item of the appropriate data type to set the new value. For example, if you want to update a column of type double in the current row, you can use one of the following methods:

```
public void updateDouble(int columnIndex, double x) throws SQLException;
public void updateDouble( String columnName, double x) throws SQLException;
```

Inserting a Row

To insert a row, perform the following steps:

1. Move to a blank row by invoking the moveToInsertRow() method:

   ```
   public void moveToInsertRow() throws SQLException
   ```

2. Update all the columns of the row using the updateXXX() methods discussed earlier in the context of the update operation. Note that you have to update all non-nullable columns to non-null values. The nullable columns, if left untouched, retain a null value after the insert is complete, unless a trigger or a default column value kicks in.

3. Propagate the changes to the database by invoking the method insertRow():

   ```
   public void insertRow() throws SQLException
   ```

Example of Updatability

The class DemoUpdatability illustrates how to update, insert, and delete rows from a table by performing these operations on the rows of the result set. Before running the program, re-create the table and populate it with numbers 1 to 30 in column x:

```
scott@ORA10G> drop table t1;

Table dropped.
```

```
scott@ORA10G> create table t1 as
  2  select rownum as x
  3  from all_objects
  4  where rownum <= 30;

Table created.

scott@ORA10G> select count(*) from t1;

  COUNT(*)
----------
        30

scott@ORA10G> commit;
```

The program DempUpdatability begins with the import statements followed by the main()
method, which invokes the _demoUpdatability() method containing the bulk of the logic:

```
/* This program demonstrates the updatability of a result set.
* COMPATIBLITY NOTE: runs successfully against 10.1.0.2.0, and 9.2.0.1.0 */
import java.sql.ResultSet;
import java.sql.SQLException;
import java.sql.PreparedStatement;
import java.sql.Connection;
import oracle.jdbc.OracleTypes;
import book.util.JDBCUtil;
class DemoUpdatability
{
  public static void main(String args[]) throws Exception
  {
    Connection conn = null;
    try
    {
      conn = JDBCUtil.getConnection("scott", "tiger", "ora10g");
      _demoUpdatability( conn );
    }
    catch (SQLException e)
    {
      // handle the exception properly - in this case, we just
      // print the stack trace.
      JDBCUtil.printException ( e );
    }
    finally
    {
      // release the JDBC resources in the finally clause.
      JDBCUtil.close( conn );
    }
  } // end of main()
```

The method _demoUpdatability() first obtains a scroll-insensitive and updatable result set. (Note that the example would also work for scroll-sensitive result sets.) It then prints out the result set's type and concurrency type:

```
private static void _demoUpdatability( Connection conn )
throws SQLException
{
  System.out.println("Inside _demoUpdatability");
  ResultSet rset = null;
  PreparedStatement pstmt = null;
  try
  {
    pstmt = conn.prepareStatement( "select  x  from  t1",
      ResultSet.TYPE_SCROLL_INSENSITIVE, ResultSet.CONCUR_UPDATABLE);
    JDBCUtil.printRsetTypeAndConcurrencyType( pstmt );
    rset = (ResultSet) pstmt.executeQuery();
    JDBCUtil.printRsetTypeAndConcurrencyType( rset );
```

Next, we move to row number 3 and update the value (originally 3) to 31:

```
    // demo update row
    rset.absolute( 3 );
    rset.updateInt(1, 31 );
    rset.updateRow();
```

We then move to row number 4 and delete it:

```
    // demo delete row
    rset.absolute( 4 );
    rset.deleteRow();
```

Finally, we insert a new row with a value of 35 for the x column. We also print the original row where we were before we did the insert. Finally, we commit and end the method with the usual finally clause:

```
    // demo insert row
    rset.moveToInsertRow();
    rset.updateInt(1, 35 );
    rset.insertRow();
    System.out.println("\tMoving to row where I was before inserting" );
    rset.moveToCurrentRow();
    System.out.println("\tThe row where I was before inserting: " +
      rset.getRow() );
    conn.commit();
  }
  finally
  {
    //  release the JDBC resources in the finally clause.
    JDBCUtil.close( rset );
    JDBCUtil.close( pstmt );
```

```
      }
   }
}// end of program
```

The output of the program is as follows:

```
>java DemoUpdatability
URL:jdbc:oracle:thin:@(DESCRIPTION=(ADDRESS=(PROTOCOL=tcp)(PORT=1521)
(HOST=rmenon-lap))(CONNECT_DATA=(SID=ora10g)))
Inside _demoScrollInsensitiveUpdatable
        Result set category (using Statement API): Scroll insensitive, Updatable

        Result set category (using ResultSet API): Scroll insensitive, Updatable

        Moving to row where I was before inserting
        The row where I was before inserting: 3
Inside _demoScrollSensitiveUpdatable
        Result set category (using Statement API): Scroll sensitive, Updatable
        Result set category (using ResultSet API): Scroll sensitive, Updatable
        Before delete current row number 4 has value: 5
        After delete current row number 3 has value: 31
```

Lost Updates

Whether you perform an update using the standard update statement or you use the update capability of a result set, JDBC (or Oracle) does not guarantee that someone else has not modified the row since the query was executed. Please see the section "Lost Updates" of Chapter 16 to read up on how to resolve the situation where your update operation conflicts with another transaction's DML operation.

Refetching Rows

Refetching of rows is defined as reobtaining the rows that correspond to *n* rows in a result set, starting with the current row, where *n* is the fetch size of the result set. As of 10g Release 1 (including 9i releases), you can refetch rows for the following types of result sets:

- Scroll-sensitive/read-only

- Scroll-sensitive/updatable

- Scroll-insensitive/updatable

To refetch the rows, you need to move to a valid row (not on a blank row created to perform an insert operation) and then invoke the refreshRow() method on the result set:

```
void refreshRow() throws SQLException;
```

Please note that you can only see any updates done on the *n* rows being refreshed. You won't see any new inserts or deletes that would be visible should you reissue the current query. For example, even if a row has been deleted from the database, if it existed in the result set originally, its value would be retained within the cached result set. This reduces the utility of the refreshRow() operation.

Example of Refetching Rows

First, we repopulate table t1 with numbers from 1 to 30 as we did in the beginning of the section "Example of Updatability." The following DemoRefreshRow program invokes the method _demoRefreshRow() in the main() method to illustrate the concept of refetching rows. Note that the query is ordered by column x, so we expect row number 1 to have a value of 1, row number 2 to have a value of 2, and so on.

```
/* This program demonstrates refetching of rows in a result set.
* COMPATIBLITY NOTE: runs successfully against 10.1.0.2.0 and 9.2.0.1.0.
*/
import java.io.IOException;
import java.sql.ResultSet;
import java.sql.SQLException;
import java.sql.PreparedStatement;
import java.sql.Connection;
import book.util.JDBCUtil;
import book.util.Benchmark;
import book.util.InputUtil;
class DemoRefreshRow
{
  public static void main(String args[]) throws Exception, IOException
  {
    Connection conn = null;
    try
    {
      conn = JDBCUtil.getConnection("scott", "tiger", "ora10g");
      _demoRefreshRow( conn, "select x from t1 order by x" );
    }
    catch (SQLException e)
    {
      // handle the exception properly - in this case, we just
      // print the stack trace.
      JDBCUtil.printException ( e );
    }
    finally
    {
      // release the JDBC resources in the finally clause.
      JDBCUtil.close( conn );
    }
  } // end of main()
```

The following _demoRefreshRow() method first obtains a scroll-insensitive, updatable result set, and prints the result set's type and concurrency type:

```
private static void _demoRefreshRow( Connection conn, String stmtString )
throws SQLException, IOException
{
  ResultSet rset = null;
  PreparedStatement pstmt = null;
  try
  {
    pstmt = conn.prepareStatement( stmtString,
      ResultSet.TYPE_SCROLL_INSENSITIVE, ResultSet.CONCUR_UPDATABLE);
    System.out.print( "For statement: " + stmtString + ", " );
    //JDBCUtil.printRsetTypeAndConcurrencyType( pstmt );
    rset = (ResultSet) pstmt.executeQuery();
    JDBCUtil.printRsetTypeAndConcurrencyType( rset );
```

Next, we set the fetch size to 7 and invoke the next() method to move to row number 1, which becomes our current row:

```
    rset.setFetchSize(7);
    rset.next(); // moves to first row
```

We then invoke the InputUtil.waitTillUserHitsEnter() method (see the section "A Utility to Pause in a Java Program" in Chapter 1 for a description of this method), which simply waits until the user presses Enter. We do this so we can go to another session as SCOTT and delete the first row (our current row) from t1. We also update the second row's value to something different. This is to verify that a delete operation indeed is not visible to our result set, whereas updates are visible. The next statement starts a SQL trace, which helps us understand how Oracle implements refetching. We then refetch the row using the refreshRow() method. We print out the current row value and end the program after the finally clause:

```
    InputUtil.waitTillUserHitsEnter( "Perform delete/update and " );
    //start trace
    Benchmark.startTrace( conn );
    rset.refreshRow();
    System.out.println( "Row number 1 has a value = " + rset.getInt( 1 ) );
    rset.next(); // moves to second row
    System.out.println( "Row number 2 has a value = " + rset.getInt( 1 ) );
  }
  finally
  {
    // release the JDBC resources in the finally clause.
    JDBCUtil.close( rset );
    JDBCUtil.close( pstmt );
  }
}
} // end of program
```

When we run the program, we see the following output:

```
>java DemoRefreshRow
URL:jdbc:oracle:thin:@(DESCRIPTION=(ADDRESS=(PROTOCOL=tcp)(PORT=1521)
   (HOST=rmenon-lap))(CONNECT_DATA=(SID=ora10g)))
For statement: select x from t1 order by x, Result set category (using
ResultSet API): Scroll insensitive, Updatable
Perform delete/update and
Press Enter to continue...
```

During this wait, in a different session we delete the first row, update the second row to a value of 222, and commit the transaction:

```
scott@ORA10G> delete from t1 where x = 1;

1 row deleted.

scott@ORA10G> update t1 set x= 222 where x = 2;

1 row updated.

scott@ORA10G> commit;

Commit complete.
```

We then come back to our running program and press Enter to see the following output:

```
Row number 1 has a value = 1
Row number 2 has a value = 222
```

As shown, the result set still displayed the deleted row value that contained a value of 1. However, the new updated value of the second row correctly contains the latest value. We then run tkprof on the trace file generated by this program (see Chapter 1 for details on how to use tkprof). The relevant section from the following tkprof output tells us what the JDBC driver did when we issued the refreshRow() method:

```
select rowid, x from t1
WHERE ( ROWID = :rowid0 OR ROWID = :rowid1 OR ROWID = :rowid2 OR ROWID =
   :rowid3 OR ROWID = :rowid4 OR ROWID = :rowid5 OR ROWID = :rowid6 )
order by   x
```

As you can see, JDBC silently added the pseudo column rowid to obtain the result set when we issued the query. When we did a refresh, JDBC issued a query that reselected all seven rows (remember, the fetch size was 7 in our case), starting from the current row, using their rowids. In the preceding select, :rowid0 stands for the bind variable with the value of first rowid, :rowid1 stands for the bind variable with the value of second rowid, and so on. From the results of this query, the JDBC driver repopulated its cache with the new set of rows.

■Note Since a deleted row will not get selected if we requery using a `rowid`, we can conclude that JDBC internally does not update its cache for a deleted row, even though the query would not fetch that row.

Refetching and Scroll-Sensitive Result Sets

Now that you understand the concept of refetching rows, you can look at how Oracle implements scroll-sensitive result sets. Oracle's implementation of scroll-sensitive result sets involves a window of rows. The window consists of n rows, starting with the current row where n is the fetch size. The window size affects how frequently the rows in the result set are refreshed to the latest rows.

As you scroll through the rows, as long as your current row remains within the window, no refresh takes place. As soon as your current row moves to a new window, you redefine the window to be n rows, starting with the new current row. Whenever the window is redefined, the n rows corresponding to the new window are automatically refreshed through an implicit call to `refreshRow()`. Thus, with scroll-sensitive result sets, you see external changes only when the window is refreshed. Obviously, this can have a performance impact depending on your network round-trip cost, your result set's fetch size, and the size of each row in the result set.

The class `DemoScrollSensitiveResultSet` shows how this works. The `main()` method simply invokes `_demoScrollSensitiveResultSet()`, passing in the connection and the familiar query from table t1.

```
/* This program demonstrates a scroll-sensitive result set.
* COMPATIBLITY NOTE: runs successfully against 10.1.0.2.0 and 9.2.0.1.0.
*/
import java.io.IOException;
import java.sql.ResultSet;
import java.sql.SQLException;
import java.sql.PreparedStatement;
import java.sql.Connection;
import book.util.JDBCUtil;
import book.util.InputUtil;
class DemoScrollSensitiveResultSet
{
  public static void main(String args[]) throws Exception, IOException
  {
    Connection conn = null;
    try
    {
      conn = JDBCUtil.getConnection("scott", "tiger", "ora10g");
      _demoScrollSensitiveResultSet( conn, "select x from t1 order by x" );
    }
    catch (SQLException e)
    {
      // handle the exception properly - in this case, we just
      // print the stack trace.
```

```
        JDBCUtil.printException ( e );
      }
      finally
      {
        // release the JDBC resources in the finally clause.
        JDBCUtil.close( conn );
      }
} // end of main()
```

The method _demoScrollSensitiveResultSet() gets a scroll-sensitive, read-only result set:

```
private static void _demoScrollSensitiveResultSet( Connection conn,
    String stmtString )
throws SQLException, IOException
{
    ResultSet rset = null;
    PreparedStatement pstmt = null;
    try
    {
      pstmt = conn.prepareStatement( stmtString,
        ResultSet.TYPE_SCROLL_SENSITIVE, ResultSet. CONCUR_READ_ONLY);
      System.out.print( "For statement: " + stmtString + ", " );
      rset = (ResultSet) pstmt.executeQuery();
      JDBCUtil.printRsetTypeAndConcurrencyType( rset );
```

After printing the result set type and concurrency type, we set the fetch size to 5. We move to the first row of the result set:

```
      rset.setFetchSize(5);
      System.out.println( "New fetch size: " + rset.getFetchSize() );
      rset.first(); // moves to first row
```

Next, we insert a program pause, during which we update the first row from SQL*Plus:

```
      System.out.println( "Row number " + rset.getRow() + " has a value = "
        + rset.getInt( 1 ) );
      InputUtil.waitTillUserHitsEnter( "Perform update on first row and " );
```

We then move to the last row; this will refresh just the last row. We move back to the first row; this will refresh the first five rows. We should see latest values of all these rows. To verify this, we print out the value of x in the first row, since we would have modified it during our pause:

```
      rset.last(); // moves to last row changing the window size
      rset.first(); // moves back to first row changing the window size
      System.out.println( "Row number " + rset.getRow() + " now has a value = "
        + rset.getInt( 1 ) );
    }
    finally
    {
```

```
    // release the JDBC resources in the finally clause.
    JDBCUtil.close( rset );
    JDBCUtil.close( pstmt );
  }
 }
} // end of program
```

We assume that t1 contains the numbers 1 to 30 in its column x before running this program. When we run the program, we get the following output:

```
>java DemoScrollSensitiveResultSet
URL:jdbc:oracle:thin:@(DESCRIPTION=(ADDRESS=(PROTOCOL=tcp)(PORT=1521)
(HOST=rmenon-lap))(CONNECT_DATA=(SID=ora10g)))
For statement: select x from t1 order by x, Result set category (using Resul
tSet API): Scroll sensitive, Read only
New fetch size: 5
Row number 1 has a value = 1
Perform update on first row and
Press Enter to continue...
```

We modify the first row as follows:

```
scott@ORA10G> update t1 set x = 111 where x = 1;

1 row updated.

scott@ORA10G> commit;

Commit complete.
```

When we press Enter, we should see the latest value as follows:

```
Press Enter to continue...

Row number 1 now has a value = 111
```

In the next section, we will look at the database changes visible to a ResultSet object.

Database Changes Visible to a Result Set

In this section, we briefly outline the ability of a result set to see two types of changes:

- *Internal changes*: Changes made within the result set by using the update, delete, or insert operation on the result set itself

- *External changes*: Changes made outside the result set, either from the current transaction or from a different session

A change being "visible" means that you can automatically (i.e., without refetching rows) see new data values from internal or external changes made to the result set rows. Table 7-8 summarizes the result set's visibility into different type of changes depending on the result set type.

Table 7-8. *Result Set's Visibility Depending on Type*

Result Set Type	Visibility of	Internal Delete	Internal Update	Internal Insert	External Delete	External Update	External Insert
Forward-only	No	Yes	No	No	No	No	
Scroll-insensitive	Yes	Yes	No	No	No	No	
Scroll-sensitive	Yes	Yes	No	No	Yes	No	

A Result Set's Ability to Detect Database Changes

A result set is said to be able to detect the database changes if it is aware that a particular row contains a new value since the result set was first populated. However, Oracle result sets cannot detect any operation (insert, update, or delete). Hence the following methods in the JDBC 2.0 would always return `false` in the case of an Oracle JDBC implementation (as of 10*g* Release 1):

```
boolean rowDeleted() throws SQLException
boolean rowInserted() throws SQLException
boolean rowUpdated()throws SQLException
```

Paginating Through a Result Set

A common scenario where you may think of using scrollable result sets is when you want to paginate through a query's results. By "paginate," I mean scrolling back and forth *n* rows out of a total number of *m* rows. For example, say *n* equals 10 and *m* equals 100. In this case, the first ten rows would be displayed to the user in the beginning. The user can navigate to the next ten rows by clicking a Next button (or its GUI equivalent). The user navigates to the previous ten rows by clicking a Previous button. At any given time, the user is looking at a window of ten rows out of a total of 100 rows. A typical requirement in this case is to also be able to sort the query results based on one or more of the columns. There are many approaches to solving this scenario.

- Use a scrollable result set and scroll back and forth *n* rows using one of the many positioning methods you learned about earlier. This approach has the following limitations:

  - Since a `ResultSet` is associated with a `Connection` object, you have to hold the connection across requests in the case of web applications. This is feasible only in the case of client/server applications and is not a recommended practice for web applications, as discussed in the section "Web Applications and Connection-Related Challenges" of Chapter 14.

  - For sorting on query columns, you will have to reissue the query.

- This would only work for small result sets, since caching a large result set can bring down your JVM due to excessive memory consumption.
  - This suffers from various limitations associated with scrollability, as discussed in the section "Result Set Limitations."
- Use a forward-only result set and cache all the rows in the middle tier. Subsequent user interactions work on the cached rows. This approach has the following limitations:
  - You can sort your rows in the middle-tier cache, but you have to write extra code for that. This gets more complicated if you want to sort multiple columns.
  - It has the drawback of excessive memory consumption in the middle tier in the case of large result sets.
- Use a forward-only result set and issue a query each time the user navigates to a new window. This is an interesting approach, and it is the one we look at in detail in this section.

At first glance, it may seem that issuing a query every time the user clicks Next or Previous would result in unnecessary network traffic. Though this is true, in many cases this disadvantage is more than compensated for by the following advantages:

- Your query doesn't need to hold the connection across requests in the case of web-based applications.
- Your query doesn't have any restrictions mentioned in the section "Result Set Limitations and Downgrade Rules" that a scrollable result set would impose.
- You don't need to cache the rows in the middle tier, so this approach scales far better with large result sets.

For sorting, you don't need to sort in the middle tier (which is required if you take the approach of caching in the middle tier). Instead of sorting in the middle tier, you can simply issue the same query with an appropriate order by clause. This means less code to write and fewer maintenance headaches. The sorting code in the middle tier can get pretty hairy if your requirement is to be able to sort on one or more columns in ascending or descending order.

We will use the following well-known template[1] for writing queries that gets *n* out of *m* rows for a given query:

```
select *
from
(
  select /*+ FIRST_ROWS */ a.*, rownum rnum
  from
  ( YOUR_QUERY_TEXT ) a
  where rownum <= :max_row_number
)
where rnum >= :min_row_number;
```

---

[1] Tom Kyte, *Effective Oracle by Design* (Emeryville, CA: Osborne McGraw-Hill, 2003), p. 496. This code is also available from http://asktom.oracle.com/~tkyte/paginate.html.

The template uses the pseudo column rownum to restrict the window of rows between the values :min_row_number and :max_row_number. The clause /*+ FIRST_ROWS */ is a hint to the optimizer to generate a plan of execution, the goal of which is to return the first rows as soon as possible. This is almost always the requirement, since you are trying to display *n* rows of the result set to the end user as soon as you can, instead of trying to get the entire set of rows and then displaying the window of *n* rows.

Let's walk through an example. First, we create and populate a table, t2, which has a number column, x, and a date column, y:

```
scott@ORA10G> create table t2 as
  2  select rownum as x, sysdate+rownum as y
  3  from all_objects;

Table created.

scott@ORA10G> commit;

Commit complete.

scott@ORA10G> desc t2
 Name      Null?    Type
 -------   -------- -----------
 X                  NUMBER
 Y                  DATE

scott@ORA10G> select count(*) from t2;

    41013
```

Assume that our user interface displays the columns x and y, and allows the user to paginate ten rows at a time. We also allow the user to sort by column x or y. The query that we issue using the preceding template would look like the following:

```
select *
from
(
  select /*+ FIRST_ROWS */ a.*, rownum rnum
  from
  ( select x, y from t2 order by x, y ) a
  where rownum <= :max_row_number
)
where rnum >= :min_row_number;
```

Using the preceding query form, we create a package, demo_pagination, with a single procedure, get_details, that fulfills our requirements. The procedure takes four parameters: two numbers representing minimum and maximum row numbers that need to be displayed, one string representing our order by clause, and a ref cursor out parameter that contains our result set with the rows.

```
scott@ORA10G> create or replace package demo_pagination
  2  as
  3    procedure get_details( p_min_row_number in number,
  4      p_max_row_number in number, p_order_by_clause in varchar2,
  5      p_cursor in out sys_refcursor );
  6  end;
  7  /
```

Package created.

The package body first declares a string with our query with the where clause appended to it:

```
scott@ORA10G> create or replace package body demo_pagination
  2  as
  3    procedure get_details( p_min_row_number in number,
  4      p_max_row_number in number, p_order_by_clause in varchar2,
  5      p_cursor in out sys_refcursor )
  6    is
  7      l_our_select_str long;
  8      l_pagination_select_str long;
  9    begin
 10      l_our_select_str := 'select x, y from t2 ' || p_order_by_clause;
```

We then declare the actual pagination query that we will construct dynamically:

```
 11      l_pagination_select_str := 'select x, y ' ||
 12              'from ' ||
 13              '( ' ||
 14              ' select /*+ FIRST_ROWS */ a.*, rownum rnum ' ||
 15              ' from ' ||
 16              ' (' || l_our_select_str ||
 17              ' ) a ' ||
 18              ' where rownum <= :max_row_number ' ||
 19              ') ' ||
 20              ' where rnum >= :min_row_number';
```

We print out the relevant variables in case we want to test them from SQL*Plus:

```
 21      dbms_output.put_line( l_our_select_str );
 22      dbms_output.put_line( l_pagination_select_str );
```

and open the cursor, returning it via the out parameter:

```
 23      open p_cursor for l_pagination_select_str using p_max_row_number,
            p_min_row_number;
 24    end;
 25  end;
 26  /
```

Package body created.

The following program, DemoPagination, simply invokes the procedure demo_pagination.get_details() using a callable statement. It takes three command-line parameters. The first two are the minimum and maximum row numbers, respectively, and the third parameter is the order by clause. These parameters are passed straight to our procedure, demo_pagination.get_details(). The program is fairly self-explanatory and is listed here without any further explanation:

```
/* This program demonstrates a generic solution for paginating through
     query results.
* COMPATIBLITY NOTE: runs successfully against 10.1.0.2.0 and 9.2.0.1.0.
*/
import java.sql.ResultSet;
import java.sql.SQLException;
import java.sql.CallableStatement;
import java.sql.Connection;
import oracle.jdbc.OracleTypes;
import book.util.JDBCUtil;
class DemoPagination
{
  public static void main(String args[]) throws Exception
  {
    if( args.length != 0 && args.length != 2 && args.length != 3 )
    {
      System.err.println( "Usage: java DemoPagination [<min_row_number> " +
        "<max_row_number> <order_by_clause>]" );
      System.exit( 1 );
    }
    if( args.length >= 2 )
    {
      s_minRowNumber = Integer.parseInt( args[0] );
      s_maxRowNumber = Integer.parseInt( args[1] );
    }
    if( args.length == 3 )
      s_orderByClause = args[ 2 ];
    Connection conn = null;
    try
    {
      conn = JDBCUtil.getConnection("scott", "tiger", "ora10g");
      long startTime = System.currentTimeMillis();
      _showCurrentSetOfRows( conn, s_minRowNumber, s_maxRowNumber,
        s_orderByClause );
      long endTime = System.currentTimeMillis();
      System.out.println( "time taken: " + (endTime-startTime) + " milliseconds" );
    }
    catch (SQLException e)
    {
      // handle the exception properly - in this case, we just
      // print the stack trace.
      JDBCUtil.printException ( e );
```

```
    }
    finally
    {
      // release the JDBC resources in the finally clause.
      JDBCUtil.close( conn );
    }
} // end of main()
private static void _showCurrentSetOfRows( Connection conn, int minRowNumber,
    int maxRowNumber, String orderByClause )
    throws SQLException
{
    ResultSet rset = null;
    CallableStatement cstmt = null;
    try
    {
      cstmt = conn.prepareCall( "{call demo_pagination.get_details( ?, ?, ?, ?)}" );
      cstmt.setInt( 1, minRowNumber );
      cstmt.setInt( 2, maxRowNumber );
      cstmt.setString( 3, orderByClause );
      cstmt.registerOutParameter( 4, OracleTypes.CURSOR );
      cstmt.execute();
      rset = (ResultSet) cstmt.getObject( 4 );
      rset.setFetchSize(10);
      while( rset.next() )
      {
        System.out.println( rset.getInt( 1 ) + ", " + rset.getDate( 2 ) );
      }
    }
    finally
    {
      // release the JDBC resources in the finally clause.
      JDBCUtil.close( rset );
      JDBCUtil.close( cstmt );
    }
}
private static int s_minRowNumber = 1;
private static int s_maxRowNumber = 10;
private static String s_orderByClause = "order by x, y";
} // end of program
```

When we run the program, we get the following results for the rows between row numbers 1 and 10:

```
>java DemoPagination 1 10
URL:jdbc:oracle:thin:@(DESCRIPTION=(ADDRESS=(PROTOCOL=tcp)(PORT=1521)
(HOST=rmenon-lap))(CONNECT_DATA=(SID=ora10g)))
1, 2004-11-23
2, 2004-11-24
3, 2004-11-25
4, 2004-11-26
```

```
5, 2004-11-27
6, 2004-11-28
7, 2004-11-29
8, 2004-11-30
9, 2004-12-01
10, 2004-12-02
time taken: 260 milliseconds
```

For the second run, we choose a window between rows 30,000 and 30,010:

```
>java DemoPagination 30000 30010
URL:jdbc:oracle:thin:@(DESCRIPTION=(ADDRESS=(PROTOCOL=tcp)(PORT=1521)
(HOST=rmenon-lap))(CONNECT_DATA=(SID=ora10g)))
30000, 2087-01-11
30001, 2087-01-12
30002, 2087-01-13
30003, 2087-01-14
30004, 2087-01-15
30005, 2087-01-16
30006, 2087-01-17
30007, 2087-01-18
30008, 2087-01-19
30009, 2087-01-20
30010, 2087-01-21
time taken: 271 milliseconds
```

Although in our example, the first window and the thirty-thousandth window take about the same time, in more complex queries, as you page through, each subsequent page takes a little more time than the previous one. That is OK, since users typically don't keep clicking the Next button for, say, 100 times.

I have found this solution to implement pagination very elegant and effective in that it avoids the middle-tier cache overhead and the inherent sorting hassles, doesn't have any artificial restrictions on the main query, and works efficiently.

■**Note** Some of you may wonder if the fact that you have an `order` by clause would not impact the performance adversely, since Oracle would presumably have to sort the entire query result set before it starts returning rows. Fortunately, Oracle does not have to sort the entire result set—it employs a clever algorithm to maintain just the n rows in memory in a sorted order. For more details on this sorting algorithm, I refer you to page 502 of Tom Kyte's book *Effective Oracle by Design* (Osborne McGraw-Hill, ISBN: 0-07-223065-7).

In the query template discussed previously, one challenge is to dynamically build the query that we substitute in place of YOUR_QUERY_TEXT, especially if we are dealing with an unknown number of bind variables. In the next section, we will examine two approaches for dealing with this problem.

Dynamically Building a Query with an Unknown Number of Bind Variables

In this section, we will cover how to dynamically build a query that has a where clause with the bind values known only at runtime. We will examine the problem by way of an example, and then we will look at a solution.

Imagine that we are developing a search page. The where clause of the query that retrieves the searched records changes depending on what the user selects. For example, the user may search for an employee by name, by department number, or both. Figure 7-3 shows a drawing of the relevant portion of the search page.

Employee Name [   ]

Department Name [   ]

(Go!)

Figure 7-3. *Portion of a search page where a user can search based on employee information*

Assume that the following four cases represent the expected behavior of the search page along with the query that would get us the search results (we use the scott.emp table for this example):

Case 1: If the user enters neither of the fields and clicks the Go! button, we should get records for all employees (the query is select ename, deptno, job, sal from emp).

Case 2: If the user enters a string to match the employee name and clicks the Go! button, we should get all records where the employee name begins with the entered value (the query is select ename, deptno, job, sal from emp where ename like ?).

Case 3: If the user enters only the department number and clicks the Go! button, we should get all records matching the department number (the query is select ename, deptno, job, sal from emp where deptno=?).

Case 4: If the user enters both a string to match the employee name and the department number before clicking the Go! button, we should get all records where the employee name begins with the entered value and the department number matches the entered value (the query is select ename, deptno, job, sal from emp where ename like ? and deptno = ?).

The problem boils down to creating dynamically the where clause of a query based on the user input and executing it. As you can see, the number of possible queries that need to be generated can explode depending on the number of fields. For two fields, we have four different queries; for three fields, there would be eight different queries; in general for n fields, there would be 2^n queries. Of course, we also want to use bind variables for performance and scalability, so simply creating a query that concatenates the query field values into the where clause will not work. We will look at two solutions for this problem—the first is based on the PreparedStatement interface, and the second uses the CallableStatement interface.

PreparedStatement-Based Solution

The PreparedStatement-based solution simply generates the PreparedStatement object with
the appropriate number of ? placeholders. We then bind the query based on the input values
and execute it. The following DemoDynamicQueryUsingPstmt class demonstrates this technique:

```
/* This program prepares dynamically a query where the number of binds are known
      only at runtime.
* COMPATIBLITY NOTE: runs successfully against 10.1.0.2.0 and 9.2.0.1.0.
*/
import java.sql.ResultSet;
import java.sql.SQLException;
import java.sql.PreparedStatement;
import java.sql.Connection;
import book.util.JDBCUtil;
class DemoDynamicQueryUsingPstmt
{
  public static void main(String args[]) throws Exception
  {
```

Our program can take two optional inputs: the first one for the employee name and the
second one for the department number. If we don't give either of them, the program assumes
the first case. If we give a value of null for the first parameter (ename) in the command line, the
program assumes we want to get records corresponding to all employee names and whatever
department number we specified. If we give a value of -1 in the second parameter (department
number) or omit it, the program assumes we want to get records corresponding to all department numbers and whatever employee name we specified. The following if statements
essentially implement this logic, and at the end of it, we have the two variables ename and
deptno initialized with the appropriate values based on which the query needs to be generated:

```
    if( args.length != 0 && args.length != 1 && args.length != 2)
    {
      System.err.println( "Usage: java DemoDynamicQueryUsingPstmt [ename_value] " +
        "[dept_no_value]. A value of \"null\" for first parameter will indicate " +
        "that you did not specify any value for ename . A value of -1 for the " +
        "second parameter indicates you did not specify any value for deptno" " );
      Runtime.getRuntime().exit( 1 );
    }

    if( ( args.length == 1 ) && ( !"null".equals(args[0] ) ) )
    {
      ename = args[0];
    }
    else if( args.length == 2 )
    {
      if( !"null".equals(args[0] ) )
      {
        ename = args[0];
      }
```

```
      deptno = Integer.parseInt( args[1] );
   }
   if( ename != null )
   {
      System.out.println( "ename = " + ename );
   }
   if( deptno != -1 )
   {
      System.out.println( "deptno = " + deptno );
   }
```

The next step is to get the connection:

```
Connection conn = null;
try
{
   conn = JDBCUtil.getConnection("scott", "tiger", "ora10g");
```

The method _buildDynamicQuery() builds the query, and the method executeDynamicQuery() executes it after binding the parameters appropriately:

```
      String queryStmt = _buildDynamicQuery( ename, deptno );
      _executeDynamicQuery( conn, queryStmt, ename, deptno );
   }
   catch (SQLException e)
   {
      JDBCUtil.printException ( e );
   }
   finally
   {
      // release the JDBC resources in the finally clause.
      JDBCUtil.close( conn );
   }
} // end of main()
```

The method _buildDynamicQuery() begins by initializing a default query string. Note that we have a where clause of where 0 = 0, which will always be true. We do this so that we don't have to worry about starting the where clause based on the input values later—we can simply append to it:

```
private static String _buildDynamicQuery( String ename, int deptno )
{
   StringBuffer queryStmt = new StringBuffer(
      "select ename, deptno, job, sal from emp where 0 = 0");
```

Next, we append as many binding placeholders as required based on the user input to generate our query string:

```
   if( ename != null )
   {
```

```
      queryStmt.append( " and ename like ?" );
    }
    if( deptno != -1 )
    {
      queryStmt.append( " and deptno = ?" );
    }
    return queryStmt.toString();
  }
```

We begin _executeDynamicQuery() by executing the query inside the try catch block:

```
private static void _executeDynamicQuery( Connection conn, String queryStmt,
  String ename, int deptno )
  throws SQLException
{
  ResultSet rset = null;
  PreparedStatement pstmt = null;
  try
  {
    pstmt = conn.prepareStatement( queryStmt );
```

We then dynamically bind values based on the input values and based on our knowledge of each input data type. Note that the percent sign (%) represents all employee names *beginning* with the given input value. Finally, we execute the query and print out the results:

```
    int colIndex = 1;
    if( ename != null )
    {
      pstmt.setString( colIndex++, ename+"%" );
    }
    if( deptno != -1 )
    {
      pstmt.setInt( colIndex, deptno );
    }
    rset = pstmt.executeQuery();
    while( rset.next() )
    {
      System.out.println( rset.getString( 1 ) + ", " +
        rset.getInt( 2 ) + ", " +
        rset.getString( 3 ) + ", " +
        rset.getInt( 4 ) );
    }
  }
  finally
  {
    // release the JDBC resources in the finally clause.
    JDBCUtil.close( rset );
    JDBCUtil.close( pstmt );
  }
```

```
    }
    private static String ename = null;
    private static int deptno = -1;
} // end of program
```

Let's run the program now. For Case 1, to retrieve all records, we execute the program as follows:

```
B:\>java DemoDynamicQueryUsingPstmt
URL:jdbc:oracle:thin:@(DESCRIPTION=(ADDRESS=(PROTOCOL=tcp)(PORT=1521)(HOST=rmeno
n-lap))(CONNECT_DATA=(SID=ora10g)))
SMITH, 20, CLERK, 800
ALLEN, 30, SALESMAN, 1600
<- trimmed to conserve space ->
FORD, 20, ANALYST, 3000
MILLER, 10, CLERK, 5308
```

To print employees whose name begins with "A" (Case 2), we execute the program as follows:

```
B:\>java DemoDynamicQueryUsingPstmt A
ename = A
URL:jdbc:oracle:thin:@(DESCRIPTION=(ADDRESS=(PROTOCOL=tcp)(PORT=1521)
(HOST=rmenon-lap))(CONNECT_DATA=(SID=ora10g)))
ALLEN, 30, SALESMAN, 1600
ADAMS, 20, CLERK, 1100
```

To print all records of department 10 (Case 3), we execute the program as follows:

```
B:\>java DemoDynamicQueryUsingPstmt null 10
deptno = 10
URL:jdbc:oracle:thin:@(DESCRIPTION=(ADDRESS=(PROTOCOL=tcp)(PORT=1521)(HOST=rmeno
n-lap))(CONNECT_DATA=(SID=ora10g)))
CLARK, 10, MANAGER, 8268
KING, 10, PRESIDENT, 16875
MILLER, 10, CLERK, 5308
```

And finally, to print all records of department 20 and for which the employee names begin with "A" (Case 4), we execute the program as follows:

```
B:\>java DemoDynamicQueryUsingPstmt A 20
ename = A
deptno = 20
URL:jdbc:oracle:thin:@(DESCRIPTION=(ADDRESS=(PROTOCOL=tcp)(PORT=1521)(HOST=rmeno
n-lap))(CONNECT_DATA=(SID=ora10g)))
ADAMS, 20, CLERK, 1100
```

Next, we'll look at an approach that solves the same problem, but this time using PL/SQL code in conjunction with the CallableStatement interface.

CallableStatement-Based Solution

The CallableStatement-based solution uses a PL/SQL stored procedure to dynamically generate the query and return a ref cursor to it to the Java program. There are two methods to
generate and execute a dynamic SQL statement in PL/SQL:

- *Use the* DBMS_SQL *PL/SQL package.* Please see the description of this package in the document *PL/SQL Packages and Types Reference (Oracle 10g Release 1).* Unfortunately, it is
  not possible to return a ref cursor using this PL/SQL package, which is what we need.

- *Use* execute immediate *(native dynamic SQL).* This category of dynamic SQL uses the
  execute immediate statement to dynamically execute an SQL command. Please see
  the section "Performing SQL Operations Using Native Dynamic SQL" in *PL/SQL User's
  Guide and Reference (Oracle 10g Release 1).* This technique to generate a query requires
  that the number of bind variables be known at compile time. Recall that in our particular scenario, the number of bind variables is only known at runtime. Fortunately, we
  can overcome this problem by combining the concept of application contexts and
  native dynamic SQL. Let's briefly look at application contexts next.

Application Contexts

An *application context* provides you with a namespace with which you can associate arbitrary
string name/value pairs. The application context itself is bound to a trusted PL/SQL package
or procedure. To set a name/value pair in an application context, you have to use the PL/SQL
package or procedure. This is for security reasons, to ensure that no one can set a value in the
application context because the values in these contexts may be driving query criteria and the
corresponding results. To get the value of a given name stored as a name/value pair in an
application context, use the sys_context() function, which works in both SQL and PL/SQL.
To create an application context, the user needs to have the create any context privilege
apart from the privileges connect and resource.

We will grant create any context to the SCOTT user first:

```
sys@ORA10G> grant create any context to scott;
Grant succeeded.
```

Next, we'll create the application context:

```
scott@ORA10G> create or replace context hr_app_ctx using hr_app_ctx_pkg;

Context created.
```

We create a context called HR_APP_CTX, which we can set using the PL/SQL package
HR_APP_CTX_PKG. To set a value in a context, we need to use the dbms_session.set_context
procedure (please see *PL/SQL Packages and Types Reference [10g Release 1]* for more details
on this package).

To verify that we can set the values in this context only via the package HR_APP_CTX_PKG,
we'll try to set the value in an anonymous PL/SQL block:

```
scott@ORA10G> begin
  2     dbms_session.set_context( 'HR_APP_CTX', 'ENAME', 'BLAKE');
  3  end;
```

```
  4  /
begin
*
ERROR at line 1:
ORA-01031: insufficient privileges
ORA-06512: at "SYS.DBMS_SESSION", line 82
ORA-06512: at line 2
```

We get an error as expected. Now we'll define the package. The package HR_APP_CTX_PKG has one procedure that builds the query dynamically and returns a ref cursor as an out parameter:

```
scott@ORA10G> create or replace package hr_app_ctx_pkg
  2  as
  3    procedure build_dynamic_query( p_ename in varchar2,
         p_deptno in number, p_cursor in out sys_refcursor );
  4  end;
  5  /

Package created.
```

The package body follows and has explanatory comments embedded within:

```
scott@ORA10G> create or replace package body hr_app_ctx_pkg
  2  as
  3    procedure build_dynamic_query( p_ename in varchar2,
         p_deptno in number, p_cursor in out sys_refcursor )
  4    is
  5      l_query long;
  6    begin
```

We begin our query with a where clause similar to the one in the earlier section in the Java program. The where clause always returns true and exists merely as a programming convenience.

```
  7      l_query := 'select ename, deptno, job, sal from emp where 0 = 0';
```

Next, we define our query string. This is where we use the dbms_session.set_context() method to set a value in the context. We set the employee name (if it is not null) in a name, ename, of the context. We append % to it also as required. Notice that the use of sys_context() in the query ensures that our values are actually bound at runtime. This is what enables us to dynamically bind any number of values in a query:

```
  8      if( p_ename is not null ) then
  9        dbms_session.set_context( 'HR_APP_CTX', 'ENAME', p_ename ||'%');
 10        l_query := l_query ||
 11             ' and ename like sys_context( ''HR_APP_CTX'', ''ENAME'')';
 12      end if;
```

Similarly, we bind the value of the p_deptno parameter as another name/value pair in the context. Notice that in this case we use the to_number() SQL function to convert the string value into a number value explicitly. At the end, we return a cursor to the query:

```
13     if( p_deptno is not null ) then
14        dbms_session.set_context( 'HR_APP_CTX', 'DEPT_NO', p_deptno );
15        l_query := l_query ||
16             ' and deptno = to_number(sys_context( ''HR_APP_CTX'',
                    ''DEPT_NO''))';
17     end if;
18     dbms_output.put_line( l_query );
19     open p_cursor for l_query;
20   end;
21 end;
22 /
```

```
Package body created.
```

The Java program DemoDynamicQueryUsingCstmt that invokes the preceding package to implement our functionality is relatively straightforward:

```
/* This program prepares dynamically a query where the number of binds are
    known only at runtime.
* COMPATIBLITY NOTE: runs successfully against 10.1.0.2.0 and 9.2.0.1.0.
*/
import java.sql.ResultSet;
import java.sql.SQLException;
import java.sql.CallableStatement;
import java.sql.Connection;
import oracle.jdbc.OracleTypes;
import book.util.JDBCUtil;
class DemoDynamicQueryUsingCstmt
{
  public static void main(String args[]) throws Exception
  {
```

The meaning of the command-line parameters and the associated processing is the same as that of the program DemoDynamicQueryUsingPstmt discussed in the previous section:

```
    if( args.length != 0 && args.length != 1 && args.length != 2)
    {
      System.err.println( "Usage: java DemoDynamicQueryUsingCstmt [ename_value] " +
        "[dept_no_value]. A value of \"null\" for first parameter will indicate " +
        "that you did not specify any value for ename. A value of -1 for the " +
        "second parameter indicates you did not specify any value for deptno" );
      Runtime.getRuntime().exit( 1 );
    }

    if( ( args.length == 1 ) && ( !"null".equals(args[0] ) ) )
```

```
{
  ename = args[0];
}
else if( args.length == 2 )
{
  if( !"null".equals(args[0] ) )
  {
    ename = args[0];
  }
  deptno = Integer.parseInt( args[1] );
}
if( ename != null )
{
  System.out.println( "ename = " + ename );
}
if( deptno != -1 )
{
  System.out.println( "deptno = " + deptno );
}
```

After getting the connection, we simply invoke the method _executeDynamicQuery():

```
Connection conn = null;
try
{
  conn = JDBCUtil.getConnection("scott", "tiger", "ora10g");
  _executeDynamicQuery( conn, ename, deptno );
}
catch (SQLException e)
{
  JDBCUtil.printException ( e );
}
finally
{
  // release the JDBC resources in the finally clause.
  JDBCUtil.close( conn );
}
} // end of main()
```

The _executeDynamicQuery() method simply invokes the method HR_APP_CTX_PKG.
EXECUTE_DYNAMIC_QUERY we defined earlier. Note how we use the setNull() method to pass
null values to the procedure when required:

```
private static void _executeDynamicQuery( Connection conn, String ename,
  int deptno )
  throws SQLException
{
  String stmtStr = "{call hr_app_ctx_pkg.execute_dynamic_query( ?, ?, ?)}";
  ResultSet rset = null;
```

```java
    CallableStatement cstmt = null;
    try
    {
      cstmt = conn.prepareCall( stmtStr );
      if( ename != null )
      {
        cstmt.setString( 1, ename );
      }
      else
      {
        cstmt.setNull(1, OracleTypes.VARCHAR);
      }
      if( deptno != -1 )
      {
        cstmt.setInt( 2, deptno );
      }
      else
      {
        cstmt.setNull(2, OracleTypes.NUMBER);
      }
      cstmt.registerOutParameter( 3, OracleTypes.CURSOR );
      cstmt.execute();
      rset = (ResultSet) cstmt.getObject( 3 );
      while( rset.next() )
      {
        System.out.println( rset.getString( 1 ) + ", " +
          rset.getInt( 2 ) + ", " +
          rset.getString( 3 ) + ", " +
          rset.getInt( 4 ) );
      }
    }
    finally
    {
      // release the JDBC resources in the finally clause.
      JDBCUtil.close( rset );
      JDBCUtil.close( cstmt );
    }
  }
  private static String ename = null;
  private static int deptno = -1;
} // end of program
```

As an example, to print employees whose names begin with "A" (Case 2), you would execute the program as follows:

```
B:\>java DemoDynamicQueryUsingCstmt A
ename = A
URL:jdbc:oracle:thin:@(DESCRIPTION=(ADDRESS=(PROTOCOL=tcp)(PORT=1521)(HOST=rmeno
n-lap))(CONNECT_DATA=(SID=ora10g)))
ALLEN, 30, SALESMAN, 1600
ADAMS, 20, CLERK, 1100
```

In the next section, we look at the ResultSetMetaData interface.

ResultSetMetaData

A ResultSetMetaData object can be used to get information about the types and properties of the columns in a ResultSet object. It represents the metadata about the ResultSet object. You can get a ResultSetMetaData object by invoking the method getMetaData() at the ResultSet interface level or at the PreparedStatement interface level:

```
public ResultSetMetaData getMetaData() throws SQLException;
```

Using the ResultSetMetaData interface, you can retrieve the number of columns, the data type of each column, and the column name, among other pieces of information, from a ResultSet object. For a full list of all methods of this interface, please see the JDK 1.4 API documentation at http://www.sun.com. Here are some of the more commonly used methods:

- int getColumnClassName(): Returns a fully qualified class name whose instances are created when you invoke the method getObject() to retrieve the value from a column

- int getColumnCount(): Returns the number of columns in the ResultSet object

- int getColumnDisplaySize(int column): Returns the display size of the column

- String getColumnName(int column): Returns the column name or column alias name of the column in the query

- int getColumnType(int column): Returns the SQL type of the column

- String getColumnTypeName(int column): Returns the name of the SQL type of the column

- String getTableName(int column): Returns the table name of the column (see the following note)

- String getSchemaName(int column): Returns the name of the schema to which the column's table belongs (see the following note)

Note The methods getTableName() and getSchemaName() currently return an empty string in the Oracle implementation. This is documented in *Oracle Database JDBC Developer's Guide and Reference*.

ResultSetMetaData is useful in writing applications and utilities that need to process a ResultSet in a generic manner. For example, say we want to write a generic utility that prints rows down the page with columns stacked vertically instead of across the page for a given ResultSet. This is useful if we're dealing with a query for which the results wrap around the computer screen. So instead of getting an output as

```
EMPNO ENAME
---------- ----------
      7369 SMITH
      7499 ALLEN
```

we want output in the following format:

```
----------------------------
EMPNO : 7369
ENAME : SMITH
----------------------------
----------------------------
EMPNO : 7499
ENAME : ALLEN
----------------------------
```

The following DemoResultSetMetaData class shows how to achieve this in principle:

```
/* This program demonstrates the use of the ResultSetMetaData interface.
* COMPATIBLITY NOTE: runs successfully against 10.1.0.2.0 and 9.2.0.1.0.
*/
import java.math.BigDecimal;
import java.sql.ResultSet;
import java.sql.ResultSetMetaData;
import java.sql.SQLException;
import java.sql.Date;
import java.sql.PreparedStatement;
import java.sql.Connection;
import book.util.JDBCUtil;
class DemoResultSetMetaData
{
  public static void main(String args[]) throws Exception
  {
    Connection conn = null;
    PreparedStatement pstmt = null;
    ResultSet rset = null;
    try
    {
```

The class takes a query as a command-line parameter so that we can test it easily with different queries. We check that we have at least one command-line parameter:

```
      if( args.length != 1 )
      {
```

```
    System.err.println( "Usage: java DemoResultSetMetaData <query>" );
    Runtime.getRuntime().exit( 1 );
}
```

Next, we get the connection and prepare a statement. For simplicity, let's assume that there is no where clause in the query statement itself (or at least no where clause that has bind variables). We can, of course, execute any other query (not passed from the command-line parameter) after binding any parameters as needed as well:

```
conn = JDBCUtil.getConnection("scott", "tiger", "ora10g");
pstmt = conn.prepareStatement( args[0] );
```

We execute the query:

```
rset = pstmt.executeQuery();
```

and pass the result to the method printResults(), which takes a ResultSet as parameter and prints the results with columns listed in a top-to-bottom fashion:

```
    printResults( rset );
}
catch (SQLException e)
{
    JDBCUtil.printException ( e );
}
finally
{
    // release the JDBC resources in the finally clause.
    JDBCUtil.close( rset );
    JDBCUtil.close( pstmt );
    JDBCUtil.close( conn );
}
} // end of main()
```

The definition of the method printResults() follows. We process the ResultSet rows in a while loop as usual:

```
public static void printResults( ResultSet rset ) throws SQLException
{
    while( rset.next() )
    {
```

The method getMetaData() of the ResultSet interface returns an object of type ResultSetMetaData:

```
    ResultSetMetaData rsetMetaData = rset.getMetaData();
    System.out.println( "---------------------------" );
```

We then loop through each column in the ResultSet:

```
    for( int i=0; i < rsetMetaData.getColumnCount(); i++ )
    {
```

We store the value of the column in an `Object` variable first:

```
Object columnValue = rset.getObject( i + 1 );
```

Just for demonstration purposes, we use `getClassName()` to get the class name to which the object belongs and use that to cast the object to the right class. This is useful if we want to use these objects later in our method. Note that we could have done this also by using the `instanceof` operator in Java. The only difference is that we would have to check for a `null` value separately, since `instanceof` always returns `false` when we compare a `null` object with any class.

```
String className = rsetMetaData.getColumnClassName( i + 1 );
if( "java.math.BigDecimal".equals( className ) )
{
  BigDecimal bigDecimalValue = (BigDecimal) columnValue;
}
else if( "java.lang.String".equals( className ) )
{
  String strValue = (String) columnValue;
}
else if( "java.sql.Timestamp".equals( className ) )
{
  // Due to a bug, class for a date is printed as java.sql.Timestamp
  // instead of "java.sql.Date"
  Date dateValue = (Date) columnValue;
}
```

Please note the following:

- We deal with only three SQL types here for brevity. We could add more data types to the preceding `if` statement.

- Due to a bug in the Oracle JDBC implementation, we get a wrong class value for a `date` column. It returns `java.sql.Timestamp` for a column that actually is manufactured as an object of type `java.sql.Date`. You can see this in the last `else if` clause in the preceding code.

Next, we get the column name from the `ResultSetMetaData` object and print it out after appending to it the column value:

```
String columnName = rsetMetaData.getColumnName( i + 1 );
StringBuffer columnInfo = new StringBuffer();
columnInfo.append( columnName ).append( ": " ).append( columnValue );
System.out.println( columnInfo.toString() );
}
System.out.println( "----------------------------" );
}
}
} // end of program
```

When I ran the program on my PC, I got the following output:

```
B:\>java DemoResultSetMetaData "select empno, ename from emp"
URL:jdbc:oracle:thin:@(DESCRIPTION=(ADDRESS=(PROTOCOL=tcp)(PORT=1521)
(HOST=rmenon-lap))(CONNECT_DATA=(SID=ora10g)))
---------------------------
EMPNO: 7369
ENAME: SMITH
---------------------------
---------------------------
EMPNO: 7499
ENAME: ALLEN
---------------------------
---------------------------
EMPNO: 7521
ENAME: WARD
---------------------------
<- trimmed to conserve space ->
```

DatabaseMetaData

The DatabaseMetaData interface is implemented by driver vendors to let users know the capabilities of a database in conjunction with the JDBC drivers being used to access it. Different relational databases implement and support different features in various ways, and use different data types. The DatabaseMetaData interface is mainly useful for tools that need to work with different databases and need to query the capabilities of the database/driver combination they use.

To get a DatabaseMetaData object, you need to invoke the getMetaData() method on the Connection object:

```
public DatabaseMetaData getMetaData() throws SQLException;
```

Close to 70 methods exist in this interface. For a detailed list of all methods, please consult the JDBC API at http://www.sun.com. The following DemoDatabaseMetaData program demonstrates invoking some of these methods. It is self-explanatory and is listed here without any further accompanying text:

```
/* This program demonstrates querying information about the database and JDBC
     driver using the DatabaseMetaData interface.
* COMPATIBLITY NOTE: runs successfully against 10.1.0.2.0 and 9.2.0.1.0.
*/
import java.sql.DatabaseMetaData;
import java.sql.SQLException;
import java.sql.Connection;
import book.util.JDBCUtil;
class DemoDatabaseMetaData
{
  public static void main(String args[]) throws Exception
```

```
    {
      Connection conn = null;
      try
      {
        conn = JDBCUtil.getConnection("scott", "tiger", "ora10g");
        DatabaseMetaData dbMetaData = conn.getMetaData();
        System.out.println("Database Major version: " +
          dbMetaData.getDatabaseMajorVersion() );
        System.out.println("Database Minor version: " +
            dbMetaData.getDatabaseMinorVersion() );
        System.out.println("Default Transaction isolation: " +
            dbMetaData.getDefaultTransactionIsolation() );
        System.out.println("Driver major Version: " +
            dbMetaData.getDriverMajorVersion() );
        System.out.println("Driver minor Version: " +
            dbMetaData.getDriverMinorVersion() );
        System.out.println( "JDBC major version: " +
            dbMetaData.getJDBCMajorVersion() );
        System.out.println( "JDBC minor version: " +
            dbMetaData.getJDBCMinorVersion() );
        System.out.println( "Maximum char literal length: " +
            dbMetaData.getMaxCharLiteralLength() );
        System.out.println( "Maximum column name length: " +
            dbMetaData.getMaxColumnNameLength() );
        System.out.println( "Maximum columns in group by: " +
            dbMetaData.getMaxColumnsInGroupBy() );
        System.out.println( "Maximum columns in select: " +
            dbMetaData.getMaxColumnsInSelect() );
        System.out.println( "Maximum columns in table: " +
            dbMetaData.getMaxColumnsInTable() );
        System.out.println( "Maximum tables in select: " +
            dbMetaData.getMaxTablesInSelect() );
      }
      catch (SQLException e)
      {
        JDBCUtil.printException ( e );
      }
      finally
      {
        // release the JDBC resources in the finally clause.
        JDBCUtil.close( conn );
      }
    } // end of main()
} // end of program
```

When I execute the preceding program on my PC, which uses a 10*g* database and Oracle 10*g* JDBC drivers, I get the following output:

```
B:\>java DemoDatabaseMetaData
URL:jdbc:oracle:thin:@(DESCRIPTION=(ADDRESS=(PROTOCOL=tcp)(PORT=1521)(HOST=rmeno
n-lap))(CONNECT_DATA=(SID=ora10g)))
Database Major version: 10
Database Minor version: 1
Default Transaction isolation: 2
Driver major Version: 10
Driver minor Version: 1
JDBC major version: 10
JDBC minor version: 1
Maximum char literal length: 2000
Maximum column name length: 30
Maximum columns in group by: 0
Maximum columns in select: 0
Maximum columns in table: 1000
Maximum tables in select: 0
```

Note that a 0 returned for any maximum limit denotes that the maximum limit is either unknown or there is no limit. For example, the value of 0 returned by the method getMaxColumnsInSelect() indicates that there are no known limits in the columns in a select clause in an Oracle 10*g* database when used in conjunction with Oracle 10*g* JDBC drivers.

Summary

In this chapter, you examined several ResultSet enhancements that came with JDBC 2.0. You began by learning how to deal with SQL null values in a ResultSet object. You then looked at prefetching, scrollability, positioning, and updatability of result sets. You covered a technique for the common scenario of paging through a query's results, and you learned two methods of building a query dynamically when you don't know the number of bind variables at compile time. You also examined the interfaces ResultSetMetaData and DatabaseMetaData.

Here's a summary of some of the key lessons you learned in this chapter:

- Prefetching can be a powerful tool to improve the performance of a query depending on how the query results are used. It is especially useful if you are trying to optimize the time required to retrieve all records of the query. It is less relevant if you are trying to optimize getting *n* rows out of a total of *m* rows in a query.

- I strongly recommend performing inserts, updates, and deletes using the Prepared↦ Statement and CallableStatement interfaces instead of using the updatability feature of a ResultSet. This is mainly because the updatability feature puts too many restrictions on a query.

- Consider using the pagination technique discussed in the section "Paginating Through a Result Set" to implement scrolling backward and forward using a normal forward-only ResultSet. Again, this is mainly because scrollability of a ResultSet also puts many restrictions on a query.

CHAPTER 8

■ ■ ■

Oracle Objects:
An Objective Analysis

Oracle is a relational database that supports objects. Objects within Oracle make it possible to model real-world objects such as Customer, Order, etc. as objects in a more intuitive fashion.

In this chapter, we'll first briefly cover Oracle objects and collections. Next, we'll examine how objects can be used in Oracle applications in general. Note that this chapter does not discuss how to access objects and collections from JDBC. We'll cover that topic in detail in the next three chapters. Instead, in this chapter, we'll look at the following topics:

- *Introduction to objects and collections*: We'll briefly walk through an introduction to the concepts of objects and collections. The main purpose of the introduction is to cover enough material so that you (hopefully) don't have to refer to the Oracle manuals to understand this chapter's examples. Please bear in mind, however, that there is no substitute for reading the Oracle document *Oracle Database Application Developer's Guide —Object Relational Features (10g Release 1)* to fully grasp the various capabilities of Oracle objects.

- *Guidelines on how to use Oracle objects*: We'll examine how we can meaningfully use objects within Oracle applications. The following are the three main ways of using objects within Oracle that we'll explore in this chapter:

  - *As programming constructs in any PL/SQL code you write*: In the sections "Why Use PL/SQL?" of Chapter 2 and "Where Should Your SQL Statements Reside, in Java or PL/SQL?" of Chapter 6, we explored many reasons why you might consider using PL/SQL code alongside your JDBC programs. In this scenario, you use objects to enhance the power of your PL/SQL code using object-oriented (OO) programming techniques. You can also use these constructs to boost the performance of PL/SQL code, as described in Chapter 17.

  - *As a mechanism to store data in object tables*: As you will learn shortly, in Oracle, you can create tables with one or more column of an *object type*, which is an equivalent of a Java class. As a Java programmer, you may be tempted to think that Oracle objects can be used to solve the problem of mapping the mismatch between Java objects and data stored in the relational schema by storing data as objects directly in object tables. Unfortunately, using Oracle objects to store data can result in overly complex code and performance-related issues, as you will see in this chapter. Therefore, I do not advocate the use of Oracle objects as a mechanism to store data in tables.

- *To access data by forming object views on top of existing relational schema*: *Object views* are views built on top of relational tables, such that the data in the view is accessed as if the underlying tables were defined as tables with object type columns. When you use object views, you can potentially get the best of both worlds: You can use queries against object views to retrieve data as objects directly, while retaining the flexibility of using SQL directly on the underlying relational tables when required.

Toward the end of this chapter, we'll compare relational tables, tables containing object types as columns, and object views when used to store data. We'll compare these three techniques in terms of performance and code maintainability. This chapter begins with a brief introduction to Oracle objects and collections in the next section.

Introducing Oracle Objects and Collections

Although Oracle terms the object features as "object-relational" (mainly in the context of using objects in tables to store data), Oracle objects support many traditional OO features. Chief among these are inheritance, polymorphism, and substitutability of types in an object type hierarchy. Oracle's implementation of the encapsulation feature, though, is undermined considerably by the fact that it does not support the equivalent of Java private or protected variables and methods in objects as of Oracle 10g Release 1.

This section will introduce you to objects and collections, and you'll examine the syntax of using these objects in your SQL and PL/SQL code. You'll also briefly look at how to use objects and collections in tables, and the associated syntax to access and manipulate data stored in object type columns in tables. First up is a discussion of the fundamental concept of object type.

Object Type (Equivalent of a Java Class)

An *object type* is a user-defined type (as opposed to a built-in data type, such as varchar2, number, and so on) that makes it possible to model real-world entities as objects. You can use object types in a fashion similar to how you use built-in types such as varchar2, date, and so on. In particular, you can declare variables of object types and also specify an object type as a data type of a table column.

An object type consists of *attributes* that contain object data and *methods* that implement the object interface. The object type definition consists of two parts: the *type definition* and the *type body*. The type definition lists all attributes of the objects and optionally declares any methods the object type may have. The type body (required only if you need to define any methods) consists of the implementation of any methods declared in the type definition itself. Let's look at an example.

Consider a Java class called Person defined as follows. The class consists of two attributes, _name and _dateOfBirth; the getter and setter methods corresponding to these attributes; and a static method, describe(), that prints a simple message describing the class:

```
import java.util.Date;
class Person
{
  private String _name;
```

```
private Date _dateOfBirth;
public Person()
{
}
public Person( String name, Date dateOfBirth )
{
  _name = name;
  _dateOfBirth = dateOfBirth;
}
public String getName()
{
  return _name;
}
public void setName( String name )
{
  _name = name;
}
public Date getDateOfBirth()
{
  return _dateOfBirth;
}
public void setDateOfBirth( Date dateOfBirth )
{
  _dateOfBirth = dateOfBirth;
}
public static void describe()
{
  System.out.println ( "This is a simple Java class that encapsulates a
person." );
}
public static void main( String[] args )
{
  Person person = new Person( "Varun", new Date() );
  System.out.println ( person.getName() + ", " + person.getDateOfBirth() );
}
}
```

To implement the preceding class using an Oracle object, we first create an object type definition called person as follows:

```
benchmark@ORA10G> create or replace type person as object
  2  (
```

We declare the attributes that an object belonging to the object type person would contain, in this case, the name and the date of birth:

```
  3    name varchar2(50),
  4    date_of_birth date,
```

Next, we declare a *user-defined* constructor that takes no arguments. Oracle provides, by default, such a constructor even if you don't supply one. The keyword self that is returned by the constructor represents an object instance and is equivalent to the keyword this in Java.

```
5    constructor function person return self as result,
```

On lines 6 and 7, we define an *overloaded* user-defined constructor that takes both the name and date_of_birth attributes as an argument. Oracle also provides a default constructor called an *attribute value* constructor. This constructor takes *all* the attributes as its arguments. Note that the constructor defined in line 6 replaces the attribute value constructor provided by the system since it takes the complete set of attributes as its arguments (name and date_of_birth).

```
6    constructor function person( name in varchar2,
7      date_of_birth in date )
8      return self as result,
```

On lines 9 to 12, we declare the member functions and procedures. These functions and procedures are equivalent to the nonstatic member methods in the Person class. These typically operate on (read/write) the attributes of the object.

```
9     member function get_name return varchar2,
10    member procedure set_name( p_name in varchar2 ),
11    member function get_date_of_birth return date,
12    member procedure set_date_of_birth( p_date_of_birth in date ),
```

On line 13, we declare the only static method, describe(), of the person object type. It is equivalent to the static method with the same name in the Person class. As you may have guessed, it is a method that operates at the object type itself (as opposed to instances of object types).

```
13    static procedure describe
```

On line 15, we declare the object type to be *not final*. Doing so implies that this object can have subtypes (just like a Java class can have subclasses, unless declared to be a final class).

```
14  )
15  not final;
16  /
```

```
Type created.
```

Next, we implement all the methods declared in the person object type in the object type body as follows:

```
benchmark@ORA10G> create or replace type body person
  2   as
```

First, we override the default no-arg constructor (a constructor with no arguments) with our own implementation:

```
3    constructor function person return self as result
4    is
5    begin
6      self.name := null;
7      self.date_of_birth := null;
8      return;
9    end;
```

Next, we override the attribute value constructor with our version:

```
11   constructor function person( name in varchar2,
12     date_of_birth in date )
13     return self as result
14   is
15   begin
16     self.name := name;
17     self.date_of_birth := date_of_birth;
18     return;
19   end;
```

We implement the getter and setter methods for the two attributes next:

```
21   member function get_name return varchar2
22   is
23   begin
24     return name;
25   end;
26
27   member procedure set_name( p_name in varchar2 )
28   is
29   begin
30     name := p_name;
31   end;
32
33   member function get_date_of_birth return date
34   is
35   begin
36     return date_of_birth;
37   end;
38
39   member procedure set_date_of_birth( p_date_of_birth in date )
40   is
41   begin
42     date_of_birth := p_date_of_birth;
43   end;
```

Finally, our static method, describe, simply prints a message using the dbms_output built-in PL/SQL package:

```
45    static procedure describe
46    is
47    begin
48      dbms_output.put_line ( 'This is a simple Oracle object type
that encapsulates a person.');
49      end;
50    end;
51    /
```

Type body created.

Declaring and Using Object Variables in PL/SQL

In this section, we will look at a simple example that demonstrates how to declare and use a variable of an object type in PL/SQL. Note that a variable of an object type, just like any other variable, is stored in the Oracle memory corresponding to your user session. The following is our example using a PL/SQL anonymous block:

benchmark@ORA10G> declare

We first declare a variable, l_person, of type person:

```
2      l_person_obj person;
3    begin
```

We then use the person constructor that takes all arguments to initialize the variable:

```
5      l_person_obj := person('Varun', sysdate - (12*365) );
```

Next, we print out the value in the object created:

```
7      dbms_output.put_line ( 'Name = ' || l_person_obj.name );
8      dbms_output.put_line ( 'Name (using getter method) = ' ||
9        l_person_obj.get_name() );
10     dbms_output.put_line ( 'Date of birth = ' ||
11       l_person_obj.date_of_birth );
```

Finally, we invoke the static method describe in the person object type:

```
12     person.describe;
13   end;
14   /
Name = Varun
Name (using getter method) = Varun
Date of birth = 22-MAR-93
This is a simple Oracle object type that encapsulates a person.
```

PL/SQL procedure successfully completed.

Collections (Nested Tables and Varrays)

Collections represent a data type that allows you to store more than one element of a built-in data type or an object type. Oracle supports two types of collection data types:

- *Varray*: A varray is an *ordered* collection of a fixed number of elements of the same data type (very similar to arrays in Java).

- *Nested table*: A nested table is an *unordered* set of data elements, all of the same data type.

Let's look at each of these collection types in detail.

Varrays

A varray is an ordered set of data elements, belonging to the same data type, with the maximum number of elements defined at the time of creation. The elements are accessed based on their index positions (an index starts from 1). The maximum number of elements and even the data type (with some limitations) can be changed later.

Creating a Varray Type

You create a varray type once in Oracle, typically as part of your application schema installation (as is the case with tables in your schema). For example, the following code creates a varray type that can store up to 25 numbers:

```
benchmark@ORA10G> create or replace type varray_of_numbers as varray(25) of number;
  2  /

Type created.
```

The following code creates a varray type that can store up to ten objects of type person that we created in the earlier examples:

```
benchmark@ORA10G> create or replace type varray_of_persons as varray(10) of person;
  2  /

Type created.
```

Declaring and Using Variables of Type Varray in PL/SQL

You can declare variables of type varray and store elements in them. For example, in the following PL/SQL code, we initialize and use the variable varray_of_numbers of type varray, each member of which is of type number:

```
benchmark@ORA10G> declare
  2     l_varray_of_numbers varray_of_numbers;
  3  begin
```

We first initialize the varray variable using the Oracle-supplied default constructor:

```
  5     l_varray_of_numbers := varray_of_numbers();
  6     -- extend it to store 3 numbers.
```

```
 7     l_varray_of_numbers.extend(3);
 8     l_varray_of_numbers(1) := 1;
 9     l_varray_of_numbers(2) := 2;
```

Next, we loop through it, printing each element:

```
10     for i in 1..l_varray_of_numbers.count
11     loop
12        dbms_output.put_line( l_varray_of_numbers(i) );
13     end loop;
14  end;
15  /
 1
 2
```

PL/SQL procedure successfully completed.

Let's look at another example. This time, we declare a varray of type varray_of_persons:

```
benchmark@ORA10G> declare
 2     l_varray_of_persons varray_of_persons;
 3  begin
```

We initialize the variable with three person objects, this time using a different syntax:

```
 4     l_varray_of_persons :=
 5       varray_of_persons( person( 'Joe', sysdate-23*365),
 6                          person( 'John Doe', sysdate-25*365),
 7                          person( 'Tim Drake', sysdate-27*365)
 8                        );
```

The next part of this example might expose a possibly surprising capability to you. In this example, we loop through the members of the varray variable l_varray_of_persons. However, we do that by running a select on the variable. Look at the select statement in the following implicit for loop carefully. The table keyword instructs the Oracle database to treat the collection as a table value that can be used in the from clause of a query. Note that we need to give this "in-memory table" an alias (such as the alias vp given in the following example) for the query to work. This amazing and very useful capability allows us to exploit all our SQL skills on collection variables of type varray and of type nested table (examples for nested tables follow shortly). For example, we use a where clause in the following example to filter out the contents of the varray variable:

```
 9     for i in(
10              select vp.name, vp.date_of_birth
11              from table(l_varray_of_persons) vp
12              where vp.name like 'J%'
13             )
14     loop
15        dbms_output.put_line( i.name || ', ' || i.date_of_birth );
16     end loop;
```

```
17  end;
18  /
Joe, 25-MAR-82
John Doe, 25-MAR-80
```

```
PL/SQL procedure successfully completed.
```

We can also declare a column type in a table as varray. We'll cover this capability later in the section "Using Varrays to Store Data." Let's now look at nested tables.

Nested Tables

A *nested table* is an unordered set of data elements, all of the same data type. Unlike varrays, there is no maximum limit on the number of elements, and the order of the elements is not preserved. You can declare variables of type nested table in your PL/SQL in a fashion similar to varray variables. You can also use them as part of a database table, as you'll see in the section "Using Nested Tables to Store Data." In this section, we'll look at how to create a nested table type and how we can use nested tables in our PL/SQL code.

Creating a Nested Table Type

You create a nested table type once in Oracle, typically as part of your application schema installation (as is the case with tables in your schema). The following code shows how to create a nested table type of type varchar2(50):

```
benchmark@ORA10G> create or replace type varchar_nt as table of varchar2(50);
  2  /
```

```
Type created.
```

This code shows how to create a nested table type, each element of which is of type person:

```
benchmark@ORA10G> create or replace type person_nt as table of person;
  2  /
```

```
Type created.
```

Declaring and Using Variables of the Nested Table Type in PL/SQL

You can declare variables of the nested table type and store elements in them. For example, in the following PL/SQL code, we initialize and use a variable of nested table type varchar2_nt:

```
benchmark@ORA10G> declare
  2    l_nt_variable varchar_nt;
  3  begin
```

First, we initialize the varchar2_nt variable with some values:

```
  5    l_nt_variable := varchar_nt( 'A', 'B','C');
```

Next, we carry out a select on the nested table variable. The select uses the table construct introduced earlier to display the contents of the variable. Note the use of the keyword column_value to get the value of the built-in type varchar2. The keyword column_value is useful when you are selecting a nested table (or a varray) whose inner type itself is a built-in type and hence does not have a corresponding attribute name, using which we could refer to it.

```
11    for i in ( select nt.column_value
12                 from table( l_nt_variable) nt )
13    loop
14      dbms_output.put_line( 'i = ' || i.column_value );
15    end loop;
16  end;
17  /
i = A
i = B
i = C

PL/SQL procedure successfully completed.
```

The following example initializes and uses a variable of nested table type person_nt. The example is very similar to the earlier example using a varray of the person type:

```
benchmark@ORA10G> declare
  2    l_person_nt person_nt;
  3  begin
  4    /* initializing the nested table variable with some values */
  5    l_person_nt := person_nt
  6                 ( person( 'Joe', sysdate-23*365),
  7                   person( 'John Doe', sysdate-25*365),
  8                   person( 'Tim Drake', sysdate-27*365)
  9                 );
 10    for i in(
 11           select nt.name, nt.date_of_birth
 12           from table( l_person_nt ) nt
 13           where nt.name like 'J%'
 14           )
 15    loop
 16      dbms_output.put_line( i.name || ', ' || i.date_of_birth );
 17    end loop;
 18  end;
 19  /
Joe, 25-MAR-82
John Doe, 25-MAR-80

PL/SQL procedure successfully completed.
```

Now that you're familiar with objects and collections, let's look at how to use them as programming constructs.

Using Objects As Programming Constructs

When I talk of using objects as programming constructs, I am referring to using the object types and collections (nested tables and varrays) to enhance the power of your PL/SQL code. This section illustrates some of these techniques.

There are two main ways in which you can exploit object capabilities in your code:

- *Use the object-oriented features of Oracle objects.* As mentioned earlier, Oracle objects support many OO capabilities, such as inheritance, polymorphism, etc. Using these features, you can create sophisticated OO business logic.

- *Use objects to improve the performance of PL/SQL.* This is perhaps the most common and useful way in which you can use Oracle objects. This technique involves using collections (usually nested tables) in conjunction with techniques such as bulk collect and bulk bind within your PL/SQL code to significantly improve its performance. I don't cover this topic in this chapter; I cover it in detail in the section "Using Bulk Operations to Boost Performance" in Chapter 17.

In the next section, we'll look at an example that demonstrates how to exploit the OO features of objects.

Using the Object-Oriented Features of Oracle Objects

This section illustrates the concept of inheritance when using objects. For this, we create an object type, employee, that inherits from the person object type introduced earlier. The employee object type adds a third attribute, employee_id, that will store an employee's ID. The inheritance itself is signified by the under person phrase in the first line of the following code:

```
benchmark@ORA10G> create or replace type employee under person
  2  (
```

We declare the new attribute employee_id:

```
  3    employee_id number,
```

We declare a getter and setter for the new attribute:

```
  4    member function get_employee_id return number,
  5    member procedure set_employee_id( p_employee_id in number ),
```

Just for illustration purposes, we override the member function get_name() that is inherited from the person object type (the keyword overriding signifies that we are overriding an inherited method):

```
  6    overriding member function get_name return varchar2
  7  )
  8  not final;
  9  /
```

```
Type created.
```

The methods declared in the employee object type are defined in the type body as follows (the code should be self-explanatory). Please note that we put a message using the dbms_output package inside the overriding function get_name().

```
benchmark@ORA10G> create or replace type body employee
  2  as
  3    member function get_employee_id return number
  4    is
  5    begin
  6      return employee_id;
  7    end;
  8
  9    member procedure set_employee_id( p_employee_id in number )
 10    is
 11    begin
 12      employee_id := p_employee_id;
 13    end;
 14    -- an example of overriding
 15
 16    overriding member function get_name return varchar2
 17    is
 18    begin
 19      dbms_output.put_line( 'In employee get_name() method');
 20      return name;
 21    end;
 22
 23  end;
 24  /

Type body created.
```

Next, we instantiate the employee objects in PL/SQL using the default constructor supplied by Oracle, and invoke the overridden method:

```
benchmark@ORA10G> declare
  2    l_employee employee;
  3  begin
  4    l_employee := employee( 'John the King', sysdate - 43*365, 1);
  5    dbms_output.put_line( l_employee.get_name() );
  6  end;
  7  /
In employee get_name() method
John the King

PL/SQL procedure successfully completed.
```

As confirmed by the output, the overridden version of the method get_name() was invoked. This example demonstrates how to use inheritance in code using Oracle objects. Using the concept of inheritance and other similar OO features of Oracle objects, you can write sophisticated PL/SQL programs that can then be invoked by the JDBC layer. Note that in the preceding example, the objects were not being used to store persistent data as part of tables. We'll cover that topic in the next section.

Using Objects to Store Data (Not Recommended)

As mentioned earlier, Oracle allows you to declare a table with one or more columns, the data type of which is an object type or a collection type. There are two categories of such tables:

- *Object table*: An object table is a special kind of table in which each row represents an entire object. Essentially, this type of table consists of only one column, the data type of which is an object type. In the following code snippet, we create an object table of type person:

  ```
  benchmark@ORA10G> create table person_table of person;

  Table created.
  ```

- *Table with column objects*: A table in which at least one column is of an object type or collection type is called (for lack of a better name) a *table with column objects*. A *column object* is an object stored as a column of a table in a row that contains at least one more attribute. For example, the table contacts defined as follows falls under this category:

  ```
  benchmark@ORA10G> create table contacts
    2  (
    3      contact_person person,
    4      contact_type varchar2(20)
    5  );

  Table created.
  ```

Tables can also have columns whose data type is a varray or a nested table. These are typically used in lieu of storing a parent/child relationship.

In this section, we'll first discuss how objects can be stored, retrieved, and updated in tables in Oracle in the form of nested tables and varrays. We'll then discuss the reasons this is *not*, in general, a recommended practice (mainly because it leads to poor performance and increases code complexity). Let's begin with a discussion of how to store varrays in tables.

Using Varrays to Store Data

In this section, we'll walk through the various steps involved in creating and populating a table with a varray column. While examining some of the techniques involved in populating and retrieving data from a table that contains a varray column, you'll likely start to appreciate the increased code complexity that using objects and collections in tables introduces. Using varrays in tables involves the following steps:

1. Create the varray type.

2. Create the table containing a column of the varray type.

3. Perform Data Manipulation Language (DML) statements on the table containing a column of the varray type.

Let's look at each of these steps separately.

Creating a Varray Type

The first step is to create the varray type itself. The following code creates a varray of varchar2 variables called varray_of_varchars that can store up to ten varchar2(50) entries:

```
benchmark@ORA10G> create or replace type varray_of_varchars as
  2      varray(10) of varchar2(50);
  3  /

Type created.
```

Creating a Table Containing a Column of the Varray Type

The next step is to create the table with the varray column. In the following code, we create a table, dep_email_addresses, that stores up to ten e-mail addresses of a department in the column email_addresses of type varray_of_varchars:

```
benchmark@ORA10G> create table dep_email_addresses
  2  (
  3    dep_no number,
  4    email_addresses  varray_of_varchars
  5  );

Table created.
```

Performing DML on a Table Containing a Column of the Varray Type

We insert some values into the table dep_email_addresses next. Notice how we initialize the varray column using the Oracle-supplied constructor:

```
benchmark@ORA10G>    insert into dep_email_addresses( dep_no, email_addresses)
  2      values( 10, varray_of_varchars('king@mycompany.com',
  3        'joe@mycompany.com', 'john@mycompany.com') );

1 row created.
```

We query the values we inserted so far to get one row we inserted. The result shows the column email_addresses as a single entity representing all the e-mail addresses nested within:

```
benchmark@ORA10G> select * from dep_email_addresses;
DEP_NO  EMAIL_ADDRESSES
------  ------------------------------------------------------------------
    10  VARRAY_OF_VARCHARS('king@mycompany.com', 'joe@mycompany.com',
        'john@mycompany.com')
```

To "unnest" the individual e-mail address values tucked away in the varray column into separate rows, we can use the table clause along with the keyword column_value in our query as follows. Essentially, we have to do a join of the table dep_email_addresses with our varray column cast as a table using the table clause. As you can see, what would be a simple select joining a parent/child table looks more complicated when we use objects to store data in tables:

```
benchmark@ORA10G> select c.dep_no, a.column_value
  2  from dep_email_addresses c, table(c.email_addresses) a;


DEP_NO COLUMN_VALUE
------ -------------------------------------------------
    10 king@mycompany.com
    10 joe@mycompany.com
    10 john@mycompany.com

3 rows selected.
```

Next, we insert another row into dep_email_addresses. This row is obtained as the result of a query from the same table (this shows how to use the syntax for insert into <table_name> <select from>-type statements with tables containing columns of the collection type). The code is even more complicated in this case. The innermost select uses the syntax to unnest the varray column values, as you saw in the previous example. The keyword multiset is used to specify that the subquery can return more than a row (without it, Oracle will give an error if the subquery returns more than one row). The cast function casts a value from one type to another. We use it here to cast the resulting query rows into our varray type:

```
benchmark@ORA10G>  insert into dep_email_addresses
  2    select 20,
  3    cast
  4    (
  5      multiset
  6      (
  7        select a.column_value
  8        from dep_email_addresses c, TABLE(c.email_addresses) a
  9      )
 10      as varray_of_varchars
 11    )
 12    from dep_email_addresses
 13    where dep_no = 10;

1 row created.
```

To update a value in the varray column, you have to replace the entire varray with a new varray value—you cannot selectively replace or add an element. Thus for a simple update, you will have to use procedural code. This is a huge limitation that should more or less convince you that using varrays in tables is not a good idea in general. Not only does the code complexity increase, but also the performance of an update decreases since you are now forced to use procedural code instead of SQL.

As an example of a procedural update, see the following code for the procedure add_email_address. The procedure adds a new a e-mail address to a given department number in the dep_email_addresses table:

```
benchmark@ORA10G> create or replace procedure add_email_address(
  2      p_dep_no in number, p_email_address in varchar2)
  3  is
  4      l_prev_email_addresses dep_email_addresses.email_addresses%type;
  5  begin
  6
```

First, we select the old varray column value into a varray variable:

```
  8      select c.email_addresses
  9      into l_prev_email_addresses
 10      from dep_email_addresses c
 11      where dep_no = p_dep_no;
 12
```

Next, we extend the varray variable to store the new e-mail address:

```
 14      l_prev_email_addresses.extend(1);
```

We then store the new e-mail address as the last element of the varray variable:

```
 16      l_prev_email_addresses( l_prev_email_addresses.count)
 17          := p_email_address;
```

Finally, we replace the varray column in the table with the new varray variable value:

```
 20      update dep_email_addresses d
 21      set d.email_addresses = l_prev_email_addresses
 22      where dep_no = p_dep_no;
 23  end add_email_address;
 24  /
```

```
Procedure created.
```

We invoke the procedure to add an e-mail address to the department number 10:

```
benchmark@ORA10G> exec add_email_address( 10, 'new_contact@mycompany.com')
```

```
PL/SQL procedure successfully completed.
```

We run a query to verify that the "update" went through successfully:

```
benchmark@ORA10G> select a.column_value
  2  from dep_email_addresses c, TABLE(c.email_addresses) a
  3  where dep_no=10;
```

```
king@mycompany.com
joe@mycompany.com
john@mycompany.com
new_contact@mycompany.com
```

Next, we'll take a quick peek at how Oracle internally stores a `varray` column.

Storage Considerations for Varray Columns

Oracle decides how to store the `varray` based on the maximum possible size of the `varray` computed using the limit of the declared array. According to the official Oracle documentation, if the size exceeds approximately 4,000 bytes, Oracle stores the `varray` as a LOB; otherwise, Oracle stores it as a `raw` value. However, it turns out that a `raw` data type can store only a maximum of 2,000 bytes. Thus it is highly likely that Oracle actually stores the `varray` as a `varchar2` (not as a `raw`) when the size is less than 4,000 bytes.

Now that we have discussed varrays in tables and their associated disadvantages in terms of increased code complexity and potential performance issues, let's move on to look at how we can use nested tables to store data.

Using Nested Tables to Store Data

In this section, I'll illustrate how to use nested tables to store data. You can use a nested table column in a table as an alternative to creating separate parent/child tables (I'll discuss the pros and cons of both approaches subsequently). To compare and contrast methods, we'll also create a relational schema for the same example.

The Application Scenario

Our simple example consists of creating a schema for the scenario illustrated in Figure 8-1. The entity Component consists of zero or more parts.

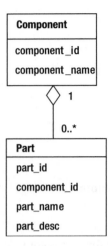

Figure 8-1. *The components and parts relationship*

Relational Tables–Based Approach

Using the traditional relational schema–based approach, this scenario can be modeled as a parent table, components_rel, and a child table, parts_rel, with a foreign key relationship as shown in the following code. First, we create the parent table components_rel (the prefix rel reminds us that this is part of a pure relational approach):

```
benchmark@ORA10G> create table components_rel
  2  (
  3    component_id number primary key,
  4    component_name varchar2(50)
  5  );

Table created.
```

Next, we create the child table parts_rel. For simplicity, assume that one part can belong to at most one component.

```
benchmark@ORA10G> create table parts_rel
  2  (
  3    component_id number references components_rel on delete cascade,
  4    part_id   number primary key,
  5    part_name varchar2(50),
  6    part_desc varchar2(500)
  7  );

Table created.
```

We also create an index on the foreign key column in the child table `parts_rel`. Almost always, this index is required in real-life applications to speed up the access to queries on child tables and to avoid unnecessary locking and even deadlocks during a `delete cascade` operation (see `http://asktom.oracle.com/~tkyte/unindex/index.html` for more details).

```
benchmark@ORA10G> create index parts_id_rel_idx on parts_rel(component_id );
```

Nested Tables–Based Approach

Let's now look at an alternative solution that uses nested tables to store the same data. Using nested tables to store data involves the following steps:

1. Create the nested table type.

2. Create the table containing a column of the nested table type.

3. Perform DMLs on the table containing a column of the nested table type.

Let's look at each of these steps separately.

Creating a Nested Table Type

The first step is to create an object type, `part_type`, to represent the child table columns:

```
benchmark@ORA10G> create or replace type part_type as object
  2  (
  3     component_id number,
  4     part_id number,
  5     part_name varchar2(50),
  6     part_desc varchar2(500)
  7  );
  8  /

Type created.
```

Then we can create the nested table type, `part_type_tab`, representing a collection of `part_type` objects:

```
benchmark@ORA10G> create or replace type part_type_tab as table of part_type;
  2  /

Type created.
```

Creating a Table Containing a Column of the Nested Table Type

Finally, we create the components table called `components_nt`, wherein we have the `parts` column of the nested table type representing the parts of a component. Thus the child table is embedded or "nested" within the parent table in this approach. The nested table column data is actually stored in a real, physical table called `parts_nt`, as specified by the `nested table parts stored as parts_nt` clause:

```
benchmark@ORA10G> create table components_nt
  2  (
  3     component_id number primary key,
  4     component_name varchar2(50),
  5     parts part_type_tab
  6  )
  7  nested table parts store as parts_nt;
```

```
Table created.
```

Attempting to create a foreign key constraint on the nested table does not work because nested tables do not allow referential integrity constraints, as shown in the following code. We will address this issue shortly.

```
benchmark@ORA10G> alter table parts_nt add constraint
  parts_nt_fk foreign key(component_id)
  2  references components_nt(component_id);
alter table parts_nt add constraint parts_nt_fk foreign key(component_id)
*
ERROR at line 1:
ORA-30730: referential constraint not allowed on nested table column
```

Performing DML on a Table Containing a Column of the Nested Table Type

Let's now look at how to carry out DML operations on a table containing a nested table column. We can insert a row in the table components_nt as follows:

```
benchmark@ORA10G> insert into components_nt values
  2  ( 1, 'component 1',
  3    part_type_tab( (part_type(1,1, 'part1', 'part1 description')),
  4                   (part_type(1,2, 'part2', 'part2 description') )
  5                 )
  6  );
```

```
1 row created.
```

The syntax should be familiar to you by now: It uses nested table constructors, which we have already covered. The following example runs a simple select on table components_nt:

```
benchmark@ORA10G> select * from components_nt;
```

```
COMPONENT_ID COMPONENT_NAME  PARTS(COMPONENT_ID, PART_ID, PART_NAME, PART_DESC)
------------ --------------- --------------------------------------------------
           1 component 1     PART_TYPE_TAB(PART_TYPE(1, 1, 'part1', 'part1
                             description'), PART_TYPE(1, 2, 'part2', 'part2
                             description'))
```

If we want to "unnest" the nested table contents, we can run the following `select` using the `table` construct to "join" the nested table with its parent table (very similar to the case of varrays):

```
benchmark@ORA10G> select p.*
  2  from components_nt c, TABLE( c.parts ) p;

COMPONENT_ID    PART_ID PART_NA PART_DESC
------------ ---------- ------- --------------------
           1          1 part1   part1 description
           1          2 part2   part2 description
```

This provides a way to treat the nested table contents as any relational table contents when writing queries (which should make you wonder why, instead of using a relational child table, you would ever use nested table in the first place). Notice that we don't have to give a where clause to join the two tables; Oracle internally does that for us. Alternatively, we could also use the hint `nested_table_get_refs` to get the same results as follows:

```
benchmark@ORA10G> select /*+ nested_table_get_refs */ part_id, part_name, part_desc
  2  from parts_nt;

   PART_ID PART_NA PART_DESC
---------- ------- --------------------
         1 part1   part1 description
         2 part2   part2 description
```

Let's look at some more DML examples. The first one inserts into the `components_nt` table with a `select` from the same table. This example is similar to the earlier example presented during the varrays discussion. Here again, the `multiset` keyword is used to specify that the subquery inside can return one row (without it, Oracle will give an error if the subquery returns more than one row). Similarly, the `cast` keyword casts a value from one type to another; we use it here to cast the resulting query value to our nested table type. Note that we use the hint `nested_table_get_refs` to unnest the nested table data in the inner `select`. Once again, the code is complicated for what would be a simple SQL statement in the case of a relational approach:

```
benchmark@ORA10G> insert into components_nt
  2  select 2, 'component 2',
  3    cast
  4    (
  5      multiset
  6      (
  7        select /*+ nested_table_get_refs */ 2,3, part_name, part_desc
  8        from parts_nt
  9        where component_id = 1
 10      ) as part_type_tab
 11    )
 12  from components_nt c
 13  where c.component_id = 1;

1 row created.
```

By now, you are perhaps convinced at least that the code complexity of tables containing object types or collections as columns is, in general, higher than that of the equivalent relational tables.

Next, we'll examine in more detail how Oracle internally stores a nested table in a table. This should give you some additional reasons to avoid using nested tables as a storage mechanism.

Storage Considerations for Nested Table Columns

A peek into the internal mechanism that Oracle uses to store nested tables reveals some additional issues with using nested tables to store data. To discover the internal "magic" that Oracle does behind the scenes to store tables with nested table columns, we run the following query that selects the column names and their maximum lengths for the table components_nt. Note that for this query to work, we need the select privilege on table col$, which is owned by the SYS user.

```
benchmark@ORA10G> select name, length
  2  from sys.col$ c, user_objects uo
  3  where uo.object_id = c.obj#
  4    and uo.object_name = 'COMPONENTS_NT';
```

NAME	LENGTH
COMPONENT_ID	22
COMPONENT_NAME	50
PARTS	16
SYS_NC0000300004$	**16**

Note that Oracle stores a hidden column called SYS_NC0000300004$ (these columns are system-generated, and the names may be different in your database runs). This column contains a key generated internally by Oracle, as shown by the following select on the two rows we inserted earlier:

```
benchmark@ORA10G> select component_id, SYS_NC0000300004$
  2  from components_nt;
```

```
COMPONENT_ID SYS_NC0000300004$
------------ --------------------------------
           1 450F0E036B3D4AD39F1026235CDBA8C6
           2 FE2F3FD8316A4EAA949A1D90A1286CFB
```

The purpose of storing the hidden column SYS_NC0000300004$ will be clear in a moment. First, let's look at how Oracle stores internally the nested table parts_nt:

```
benchmark@ORA10G> select name, length
  2  from sys.col$ c, user_objects uo
  3  where uo.object_id = c.obj#
  4    and uo.object_name = 'PARTS_NT';
```

NAME	LENGTH
NESTED_TABLE_ID	16
SYS_NC_ROWINFO$	1
COMPONENT_ID	22
PART_ID	22
PART_NAME	50
PART_DESC	500

As shown, the nested table itself has two hidden internal columns: nested_table_id and sys_nc_rowinfo$. A quick select reveals the values in these two columns as follows:

```
benchmark@ORA10G> select /*+ nested_table_get_refs */ nested_table_id,
  2           sys_nc_rowinfo$
  3  from parts_nt;
```

```
NESTED_TABLE_ID                      SYS_NC_ROWINFO$(COMPONENT_ID, PART_ID, PART_NAME,
-------------------------------      -------------------------------------------------
450F0E036B3D4AD39F1026235CDBA8C6 PART_TYPE(1, 2, 'part2', 'part2 description')
FE2F3FD8316A4EAA949A1D90A1286CFB PART_TYPE(2, 3, 'part1', 'part1 description')
FE2F3FD8316A4EAA949A1D90A1286CFB PART_TYPE(2, 3, 'part2', 'part2 description')
                                     PART_TYPE(1, 4, 'part3', 'part3 description
                                     updated')
```

From the preceding select we can see that the hidden column sys_nc0000300004$ in the parent table components_nt has the same key values that the hidden column nested_table_id in the child table parts_nt. Thus the hidden column sys_nc0000300004$ in the parent table is the foreign key to the column nested_table_id in the nested child table. Also, as shown in the preceding select, the column sys_nc_rowinfo$ is another hidden column in the nested table that Oracle uses to internally reference the entire nested table row as a single object.

We can see that behind the scenes Oracle internally works on two different tables (a parent table and a child table) with an internally generated foreign key that connects the two tables. This mitigates the shortcoming of not being able to create a referential integrity constraint on nested tables that we encountered earlier. Let's look at the constraints and indexes that Oracle creates for us internally on the parent table components_nt and the child table parts_nt:

```
benchmark@ORA10G> select c.table_name,
  2           c.constraint_name,
  3           case
  4             when c.constraint_type = 'P'
  5             then 'Primary Key'
  6             when c.constraint_type = 'U'
  7             then 'Unique Key'
  8           end constraint_type_desc,
  9          i.index_name, i.column_name
 10  from all_ind_columns i, user_constraints c
 11  where i.index_name = c.index_name
 12    and c.table_name in( 'COMPONENTS_NT', 'PARTS_NT' );
```

TABLE_NAME	CONSTRAINT_NAME	CONSTRAINT_TYPE	INDEX_NAME	COLUMN_NAME
COMPONENTS_NT	SYS_C006271	Primary Key	SYS_C006271	COMPONENT_ID
COMPONENTS_NT	SYS_C006272	Unique Key	SYS_C006272	PARTS

As you can see, Oracle created a unique index, sys_c006272, on the hidden column sys_nc0000300004$ (shown as being against the column parts in the result of the first query). However, as of Oracle 10.1.0.2.0, Oracle *does not create the index on the corresponding child table column* nested_table_id. As discussed earlier, it is imperative to create an index on this column in most cases. If you do use nested tables in your schema for storing data, you *must remember to create an index on the* nested_table_id *column yourself*. For example, in our case, we create an index as follows:

```
benchmark@ORA10G> create index parts_nt_idx on
parts_nt(nested_table_id);

Index created.
```

Thus you can see that behind the scenes Oracle works in terms of relational tables, which adds to code complexity as well. In the next section, we summarize these and other reasons that we have uncovered so far justifying the recommendation to avoid objects as a way to store data in tables.

Why It Is Not Recommended to Use Objects to Store Data

Now that we've looked at how we can use either varrays or nested tables to store data, let's summarize the various reasons for not doing so in the first place. In the case of nested tables, the following are the major disadvantages of using them to store data in tables:

- *Oracle ultimately stores nested tables data in the relational tables.* The overhead of doing so comes in the form of hidden columns, which may be mostly extraneous had we decided to use simple relational schema. For example, Oracle internally created two hidden columns of 16 bytes each in the parent table and the hidden nested tables as part of its attempt to simulate the foreign key relationship. These two columns are thrust upon the user. In the equivalent relational schema, you would simply have created a foreign key on the child table. You also have the flexibility of creating a sequence-based column as a primary key if need be. The bottom line is that the two hidden columns take additional (unnecessary, in most cases) space in your schema and constrain your design choices.

■Note You can improve the nested table performance and reduce the overall storage incurred by creating the nested tables as index-organized tables with the compress option in the first place. However, all other disadvantages mentioned in this section still hold true. For more details on using index-organized tables for creating nested tables, please see section "Nested Table in an Index-Organized Table (IOT)" in *Oracle Database Application Developer's Guide – Object Relational Features (10g Release 1)*.

- *The code becomes overly complex if you use nested tables.* You have to be aware of the nested table type, the nested table column in the parent table, and the internally created relational table where the nested table column data is actually stored. Moreover, the syntax of retrieving, inserting, and modifying data becomes more complicated, as you saw in the examples presented in earlier sections of this chapter.

- *The hint* nested_table_get_refs *(or the equivalent exotic syntax using a combination of the* table *and* cast *keywords) needs to be used if you want to select, insert, delete, or update the individual columns.* The fact that in the majority of cases you do need to manipulate the child table contents independent of the parent tables and end up using this hint really begs the question as to why you need to use nested tables in the first place. Why not simply create a relational parent and child table instead?

- *The data stored in tables containing nested table columns may not be accessible to many third-party tools that don't understand the syntax to retrieve and store data in them.* Your application may become less "open" and accessible from third-party tools that understand only the more standard relational SQL.

- *DMLs can run substantially slower and scale much less when you use nested tables rather than relational tables.* We will do a comparison of different alternatives later in section "Object Views vs. Relational Tables vs. Nested Tables" to establish this fact.

Most of the preceding arguments hold true in principle when you use varrays in tables as well. In addition, varrays are even less flexible when it comes to updating them, since they don't allow selective updates; you have to replace the entire varray even if you want to change only one value in the varray. Besides, you can't create indexes on individual varray object columns. Thus, you can conclude that using nested tables or varrays as a mechanism to persist your data isn't really a good idea. The question becomes, is there a middle ground? In other words, can you have the flexibility of storing data in relational tables, and yet access them as objects when needed? Object views, covered in the next section, may provide you with one such mechanism.

Using Object Views on Top of Relational Tables

Object views allow you to access and manipulate relational data as if the data were stored in tables containing object type or collection columns. Object views give you the flexibility to store data in relational tables. Thus you can selectively choose to use object features when it makes sense (e.g., to retrieve data directly as objects for your Java applications). For the most part, you can use relational SQL directly on the underlying relational schema, thus avoiding the code complexity and performance problems associated with storing data in tables containing objects.

The process of creating object views on relational tables involves the following steps:

1. Define an object type. In this step, we define an object type where each attribute corresponds to a relational table column. This object type will be used in creating the object view.

2. Define an object view. Next, we define an object view with a query that represents the object-oriented view we have in mind.

3. Define the `instead of` triggers. In this step, we write `instead of` triggers on the view to support required DML statements such as `insert`, `update`, and `delete` that work directly on the object view. This step is required only if we want to insert, delete, and update directly on the object view. The alternative is to do these operations directly on the underlying tables. As you'll see shortly, the `instead of` triggers can be quite complex, and the resulting DMLs on the object view can result in very poor performance. Hence I recommend that you avoid creating these triggers and instead use object views only to perform selects on them.

We'll look at each of the preceding steps in the following sections. We will demonstrate the use of object views by creating an object view on top of the relational tables, `components_rel` and `parts_rel`, that we created in the earlier section "Relational Tables–Based Approach." We assume that our relational schema consisting of the tables `components_rel` and `parts_rel` has the following data to begin with:

```
benchmark@ORA10G> select * from components_rel;

COMPONENT_ID COMPONENT_NAME
------------ --------------
           1 component1
           2 component2

benchmark@ORA10G> select * from parts_rel;

COMPONENT_ID PART_ID PART_NAME  PART_DESC
------------ ------- ---------- --------------------
           1       1 part11     part 11 desc
           1       2 part12     part 12 desc
           2       3 part21     part 21 desc
           2       4 part22     part 22 desc
```

Now, let's look at each of the previous three steps involved in creating an object view on top of the tables `components_rel` and `parts_rel`.

Defining an Object Type

The first step is to define an object type based on which we will create an object view. Since we want our view to be equivalent in functionality to table `components_nt` created in the section "Using Nested Tables to Store Data," we create an object type as follows:

```
benchmark@ORA10G> create or replace type components_nt_tab as object
  2  (
  3    component_id number,
  4    component_name varchar2(50),
  5    parts part_type_tab
  6  );
  7  /

Type created.
```

Defining an Object View

The next step is to define an object view called `components_or_view` on top of our relational tables `components_rel` and `parts_rel`, based on the object type `components_nt_tab` created in the previous section, as illustrated in the following code. Notice how we give the object identifier to be the primary key column, `component_id`, to indicate that the `component_id` column uniquely identifies one row in the object view. (The syntax using `cast` and `multiset` was explained in earlier sections. For a more detailed explanation of this syntax, please see the *Oracle Database Application Developer's Guide – Object Relational Features [10g Release 1]*.)

```
benchmark@ORA10G> create or replace view components_or_view of
  2    components_nt_tab with object identifier( component_id )
  3    as
  4    select component_id, component_name,
  5      cast
  6      (
  7        multiset
  8        (
  9          select component_id, part_id, part_name, part_desc
 10          from parts_rel p
 11          where p.component_id = c.component_id
 12        )
 13        as part_type_tab
 14      )
 15    from components_rel c;

View created.
```

In the next section, we'll examine examples of how to query data from the object view.

Performing Queries on the Object View

Using the object view, we can directly materialize the rows of the underlying relational tables as an object. Let's look at some examples of this. The first example performs a `select` that returns all rows in our object view. Notice how the data inserted into the underlying relational tables is materialized as objects:

```
benchmark@ORA10G> select * from components_or_view;

COMPONENT_ID COMPONENT_NAME PARTS(COMPONENT_ID, PART_ID, PART_NAME, PART_DESC)
-------------------------------------------------------
           1 component1     PART_TYPE_TAB(PART_TYPE(1, 1,'part11','part 11 desc'),
                                          PART_TYPE(1, 2, 'part12', 'part 12 desc'))
           2 component2     PART_TYPE_TAB(PART_TYPE(2, 3,'part21','part 21 desc'),
                                          PART_TYPE(2, 4, 'part22', 'part 22 desc'))
```

Thus the queries on the object view `components_or_view` give results similar to our equivalent object table, `components_nt`. The following is another `select` statement from the object view as an illustration. Notice that we no longer need to use the `nested_table_get_refs` hint here, as there is no nested table in our object view! If we do supply the hint, it will be ignored.

```
benchmark@ORA10G> select p.*
  2  from  components_or_view c, TABLE (c.parts) p;

COMPONENT_ID PART_ID PART_NAME  PART_DESC
------------ ------- ---------- --------------------
           1       1 part11     part 11 desc
           1       2 part12     part 12 desc
           2       3 part21     part 21 desc
           2       4 part22     part 22 desc
```

If our inserts, updates, and deletes are done *directly* on the underlying tables `components_rel` and `parts_rel` (not on the view `components_or_view`), then we are done as far as the object view solution goes. But what if we wanted to carry out inserts, updates, and deletes directly on the object view (instead of on the relational tables on which it is based)? In such situations, we need to define `instead of` triggers on the object view.

■**Note** `instead of` triggers provide a transparent way of performing DMLs on views. These triggers are called `instead of` triggers because, unlike other types of triggers, Oracle fires the trigger *instead of* executing the triggering statement. For more information on this and other types of triggers, see the section "Types of Triggers" in Chapter 22 of *Oracle Database Concepts (10g Release 1)*.

Defining instead of Triggers

In this section, we'll explore the various `instead of` triggers required to perform inserts, updates, and deletes. Our approach is to perform a particular DML on the object view without the trigger and note its failure. Then we'll define a trigger that will make the DML succeed. The code presented in this section is adapted largely from the code in the section "The O-R View" of Chapter 20 of the book *Expert One-on-One Oracle* (Apress, ISBN: 1-59059-243-3) written by Tom Kyte. We begin with defining `instead of` triggers that enable updates on the object view.

Updating on an Object View

As mentioned earlier, our approach is to demonstrate the need for a trigger by first running an operation that fails, and then writing a trigger to make the operation succeed.

■**Caution** Use of `instead of` triggers on object views can get fairly complex, especially when enabling updates on the view. You may want to read this section with either a fresh mind or a fresh cup of coffee—or both!

Let's begin this section by trying to run a simple update on the view as it is. In this update, we change the column `component_name` of the view. Notice, in particular, that none of the columns that belong to the child table are involved in this update.

```
benchmark@ORA10G> update components_or_view
  2  set component_name = component_name || 'modified';

2 rows updated.
```

So this update seems to work. Let's now try to run another update wherein we update a column of the child table `parts` in the following manner:

```
benchmark@ORA10G> update table
  2         (
  3             select parts
  4             from components_or_view
  5             where component_id = 1
  6         )
  7  set part_desc = part_desc || ' or';
set part_desc = part_desc || ' or'
    *
ERROR at line 7:
ORA-25015: cannot perform DML on this nested table view column
```

This operation fails with an exception. To make the preceding update work, we need to use an `instead of` trigger on the object view that enables updates on the columns in the child table `parts` as accessed from the object view. The following is the definition of the trigger that achieves this. Note that the trigger is on the nested table `parts` of the object view as signified by the phrase `on nested table parts of components_or_view`. This is because we want to enable updates on the attributes of the nested table in the view. Explanatory comments are interspersed within the code.

```
benchmark@ORA10G> create or replace trigger parts_io_update
  2  instead of update on nested table parts of components_or_view
  3  begin
```

If the primary key part_id has not been updated, then we update the underlying relational table part_rel instead as per our requirement. If the primary key part_id is modified, then we raise an error since updating primary keys of a table is not a good practice.

```
4    if( :new.part_id = :old.part_id ) then
5      update parts_rel
6      set part_name = :new.part_name, part_desc =  :new.part_desc
7      where part_id = :new.part_id;
8    else
9      raise_application_error( -20001,
10        'Updating the primary key part_id is not allowed' );
11   end if;
12 end;
13 /
```

```
Trigger created.
```

The update that failed earlier works now as follows:

```
benchmark@ORA10G> update table
2          (
3            select parts
4            from components_or_view
5            where component_id = 1
6          )
7  set part_desc = part_desc || ' or';
```

```
2 rows updated.
```

However, there is more to come. What if we want to replace all parts of a component? The following update replaces the entire parts column of the view components_or_view. This fails because we still do not have a trigger on the object view per se (remember, the previous trigger was on the nested table column parts of the object view—the difference will be clear in a moment).

```
benchmark@ORA10G> declare
2    l_parts part_type_tab;
3  begin
4    select parts
5    into l_parts
6    from components_or_view
7    where component_id = 1;
8
9    for i in 1 .. l_parts.count
10   loop
11     l_parts(i).part_desc := l_parts(i).part_desc || 'changed';
12   end loop;
13
14   update components_or_view
```

```
15    set parts = l_parts
16      where component_id = 1;
17  end;
18  /
declare
*
ERROR at line 1:
ORA-01732: data manipulation operation not legal on this view
ORA-06512: at line 14
```

For this update to work, we need to create an instead of trigger on the object view that enables update on the object view itself. The logic of the trigger is explained in the interspersed comments.

```
benchmark@ORA10G> create or replace trigger components_or_view_io_update
  2  instead of update on  components_or_view
  3  begin
  4    --dbms_output.put_line( 'old component_id: ' ||:old.component_id );
  5    --dbms_output.put_line( 'new component_id: ' ||:new.component_id );
```

If we are updating the column component_name, we simply update the corresponding relational table component_rel as follows:

```
  6    case
  7      when( updating('COMPONENT_NAME') ) then
  8        update components_rel
  9        set component_name = (:new.component_name )
 10        where component_id = :old.component_id;
 11      when( updating( 'PARTS' ) ) then
```

On the other hand, if we are updating the column parts, then the logic is slightly more complex. Our first step is to remove all records from parts such that they were in the old set but are not there in the new set of records:

```
 16
 17        delete from parts_rel
 18        where part_id in
 19        (
 20          select part_id
 21          from TABLE( cast( :old.parts as part_type_tab ) )
 22          minus
 23          select part_id
 24          from TABLE( cast( :new.parts as part_type_tab ) )
 25        );
```

The next step is to update those records in parts_rel such that their part_id exists in both the old and new set of records, and they have undergone a change in the remaining columns. To do this, we need to use the table and cast syntax, both of which were briefly explained in earlier sections.

```
32        update parts_rel rp
33        set ( component_id, part_name, part_desc ) =
34        (
35          select :new.component_id, part_name, part_desc
36          from TABLE( cast( :new.parts as part_type_tab ) ) np
37          where np.part_id = rp.part_id
38        )
39        where rp.part_id in
40        (
41          select part_id
42          from
43          (
44            select *
45            from TABLE( cast( :old.parts as part_type_tab ) )
46            minus
47            select *
48            from TABLE( cast( :new.parts as part_type_tab ) )
49          )
50        );
```

Finally, we insert any records in parts_rel that were newly added to the nested table column parts:

```
54        insert into parts_rel
55        select component_id, part_id, part_name, part_desc
56        from
57        (
58          select *
59          from TABLE( cast( :new.parts as part_type_tab ) ) p
60          where part_id in
61          (
62            select part_id
63            from TABLE( cast( :new.parts as part_type_tab ) )
64            minus
65            select part_id
66            from TABLE( cast( :old.parts as part_type_tab ) )
67          )
68        );
69        --dbms_output.put_line( 'inserted ' || sql%rowcount );
70    end case;
71  end;
72  /
```

```
Trigger created.
```

With the preceding, fairly complex trigger in place, we can proceed to successfully carry out updates on the object view. The following is the update that failed earlier, now shown to be running successfully:

```
benchmark@ORA10G> declare
  2    l_parts part_type_tab;
  3  begin
  4    select parts
  5    into l_parts
  6    from components_or_view
  7    where component_id = 1;
  8
  9    for i in 1 .. l_parts.count
 10    loop
 11      l_parts(i).part_desc := l_parts(i).part_desc || 'changed';
 12    end loop;
 13
 14    update components_or_view
 15    set parts = l_parts
 16    where component_id = 1;
 17  end;
 18  /

PL/SQL procedure successfully completed.
```

We are finished with enabling updates. As you can see, the code is fairly complex. Next, we'll look at how to enable inserts directly on the view.

Inserting on an Object View

In this section, we'll enable inserts on the object view. If we try to insert data without having created any instead of triggers, the insert operation fails as follows:

```
benchmark@ORA10G> insert into components_or_view values
  2  (
  3    3, 'component 3',
  4    part_type_tab(part_type(3,6,'part 11', 'part 11 description'))
  5  );
insert into components_or_view values
*
ERROR at line 1:
ORA-01733: virtual column not allowed here
```

For the preceding insert to work, we need to write an instead of insert trigger on the components_or_view itself as follows:

```
benchmark@ORA10G> create or replace trigger components_or_view_io_insert
  2  instead of insert on components_or_view
  3  begin
```

First, we insert into the parent relational table components_rel:

```
  5    insert into components_rel( component_id, component_name )
  6    values ( :new.component_id, :new.component_name );
  7
```

Then we insert into the child table `parts_rel` any new child records. Any duplicate records are filtered out based on the primary key of the child table (in this case, the primary key of the child table `parts_rel` is the column `part_id`):

```
 9    insert into parts_rel
10    select *
11    from TABLE( cast( :new.parts as part_type_tab ) )
12    where part_id not in
13    ( select part_id from parts_rel );
14  end;
15  /
```

```
Trigger created.
```

Now the insert should work:

```
benchmark@ORA10G> insert into components_or_view values
 2  (
 3     3, 'component 3',
 4     part_type_tab(part_type(3,6,'part 11', 'part 11 description'))
 5  );
```

```
1 row created.
```

But how about if we just want to insert data into the `parts` table? One way to do so is to use `update`, in which case our update trigger takes care of it. However, what if we want to use the insert only on the nested table `parts` of the object view as follows?

```
benchmark@ORA10G> insert into
 2    TABLE
 3    (
 4       select c.parts
 5       from components_or_view c
 6       where c.component_id=1
 7    )
 8  values
 9  (
10    1, 7, 'part 17','part 17 description'
11  );
   from components_or_view c
       *
ERROR at line 5:
ORA-25015: cannot perform DML on this nested table view column
```

As you may have guessed by now, for this insert to work, we need another `instead of` trigger on insert; this time it will be on the nested table column `parts`.

```
benchmark@ORA10G> create or replace trigger parts_io_insert
 2  instead of insert on nested table parts of components_or_view
 3  begin
```

```
4    -- Insert into the underlying relational child table
5    insert into parts_rel ( component_id, part_id, part_name, part_desc )
6    values( :new.component_id, :new.part_id, :new.part_name, :new.part_desc );
7
8  end;
9  /
```

Trigger created.

Now the same insert should work as follows:

```
benchmark@ORA10G> insert into
  2    TABLE
  3    (
  4       select c.parts
  5       from components_or_view c
  6       where c.component_id=1
  7    )
  8  values
  9  (
 10    1, 7, 'part 17','part 17 description'
 11  );
```

1 row created.

We are finished with all triggers required to enable inserts. Next, we'll move on to the topic of enabling deletes.

Deleting on an Object View

As before, we begin by trying to delete a part from a given component without having created any triggers:

```
benchmark@ORA10G> delete TABLE
  2    (
  3       select c.parts
  4       from components_or_view c
  5       where c.component_id=1
  6    ) t
  7  where t.part_id = 1;
    from components_or_view c
         *
ERROR at line 4:
ORA-25015: cannot perform DML on this nested table view column
```

Well, by now you may have guessed that we need an `instead` of trigger on the nested table column `parts` to make the preceding delete work. The trigger code is as follows:

```
benchmark@ORA10G> create or replace trigger parts_io_delete
  2  instead of delete on nested table parts of components_or_view
  3  begin
  4    -- delete from the underlying relational child table
  5    delete parts_rel
  6    where part_id = :old.part_id;
  7    --dbms_output.put_line( sql%rowcount || ' rows deleted');
  8  end;
  9  /
```

```
Trigger created.
```

We are not finished yet. How about if we issue a `delete` based on the non-nested table columns (i.e., the columns that come from the parent table on which the view is based)?

```
benchmark@ORA10G> delete components_or_view
  2  where component_id = 1;
delete components_or_view
       *
ERROR at line 1:
ORA-01732: data manipulation operation not legal on this view
```

For the preceding `delete` to work, we need a trigger on `components_or_view` itself. The trigger first deletes the records from the child table `parts_rel` and then proceeds to delete the parent record in `components_rel`:

```
benchmark@ORA10G> create or replace trigger components_or_view_io_delete
  2  instead of delete on  components_or_view
  3  begin
  4    -- First delete from the child table
  5    delete parts_rel
  6    where part_id in
  7    (
  8      select part_id
  9      from TABLE( cast( :old.parts as part_type_tab ) )
 10    );
 11
 12    -- then delete from the parent table
 13    delete components_rel
 14    where component_id = :old.component_id;
 15  end;
 16  /
```

```
Trigger created.
```

Now the same delete should work as follows:

```
benchmark@ORA10G> delete components_or_view
  2  where component_id = 1;
```

```
1 row deleted.
```

Phew! That completes our section on instead of triggers to enable DMLs on object views. They are complicated (especially the ones enabling updates); however, the fact that they need to be written only once per object view is a bit encouraging from the maintainability point of view. Once the triggers have been written, the calling code can work transparently on them. Of course, you still need to maintain them as the schema changes, but schema changes are relatively rare, in general.

In the next section, we will compare the performance of DML statements on solutions that use object views, relational tables, and nested tables to store parent child data.

Object Views vs. Nested Tables vs. Relational Tables

You now know three approaches of storing parent/child type of data: good old relational tables, nested tables, and object views on top of relational tables. Which ones should you use? Since this book is focused on performance, we will compare these three methods to see which ones fare better as far as performance goes. Intuitively, an approach based on relational tables should outperform the other two approaches. However, we still need to ascertain by approximately how much. Also, it would be interesting to know the difference in performance between the nested table–based approach and the object view–based approach, as they are more or less equivalent in functionality and expressiveness (once all the instead of triggers on the object view are in place).

So without further ado, let's look at the package that compares insert, delete, and update on the three approaches based on the schema that we created earlier. The package will perform various DML operations on the relational schema, the schema that used nested tables to store data, and the object view–based schema that we examined earlier. I explain the code in comments interspersed within the package code.

```
benchmark@ORA10G> create or replace package or_nt_rel_pkg
  2  as
  3    g_num_of_select_runs constant number := 10000;
  4    g_num_of_child_updates constant number := 10000;
  5    part_rel_id  number := 1;
  6    part_or_id   number := 1;
  7    part_nt_id   number := 1;
  8
  9    procedure do_or_select;
 10    procedure do_nt_select;
 11    procedure do_rel_select;
 12    procedure do_or_insert( p_num_of_parents in int := 50,
 13      p_num_of_children in int := 500 );
 14    procedure do_nt_insert( p_num_of_parents in int := 50,
 15      p_num_of_children in int := 500 );
```

```
16    procedure do_or_update;
17    procedure do_or_child_update;
18    procedure do_rel_update;
19    procedure do_rel_child_update;
20    procedure do_nt_update;
21    procedure do_nt_child_update;
22    procedure do_or_delete;
23    procedure do_rel_delete;
24    procedure do_nt_delete;
25    procedure do_rel_bulk_insert( p_num_of_parents in int := 50,
26       p_num_of_children in int := 500 );
27  end;
28  /
```

Package created.

The actual implementation in the package body explains each procedure in detail:

```
benchmark@ORA10G> create or replace package body or_nt_rel_pkg
  2  as
```

The procedure do_or_select repeats 10,000 times a query that selects one child record based on the child table primary key (part_id) on the object view:

```
3     procedure do_or_select
4     as
5        l_x number := 0;
6     begin
7        for i in 1..g_num_of_select_runs
8        loop
9          for x in ( select p.*
10                       from   components_or_view c, TABLE (c.parts) p
11                       where p.part_id = i
12                    )
13          loop
14             l_x := l_x + 1;
15          end loop;
16        end loop;
17        dbms_output.put_line( l_x );
18     end do_or_select;
```

The procedure do_nt_select repeats 10,000 times a query that selects one child record based on the child table primary key (part_id) on the table components_nt:

```
20     procedure do_nt_select
21     as
22        l_x number := 0;
23     begin
24        for i in 1..g_num_of_select_runs
25          loop
```

```
26        for x in ( select p.*
27                    from   components_nt c, TABLE (c.parts) p
28                    where p.part_id = i
29                  )
30        loop
31          l_x := l_x + 1;
32        end loop;
33      end loop;
34      dbms_output.put_line( l_x );
35    end do_nt_select;
```

The procedure do_rel_select repeats 10,000 times a query that selects one child record based on the child table primary key (part_id) on the relational table part_rel:

```
37    procedure do_rel_select
38    as
39      l_x number := 0;
40    begin
41      for i in 1..g_num_of_select_runs
42      loop
43        for x in ( select p.*
44                    from   parts_rel p
45                    where p.part_id = i
46                  )
47        loop
48          l_x := l_x + 1;
49        end loop;
50      end loop;
51      dbms_output.put_line( l_x );
52    end do_rel_select;
53
```

The procedure do_or_insert inserts a given number of parent records and a given number of children for each parent record into the object view components_or_view:

```
54    procedure do_or_insert ( p_num_of_parents in int := 50,
55      p_num_of_children in int := 500 )
56    as
57      l_part_type_tab part_type_tab;
58      l_part_type part_type;
59      l_part_or_id number := 1;
60    begin
61      l_part_type_tab := part_type_tab();
62      l_part_type_tab.extend( p_num_of_children );
63
64      for i in 1..p_num_of_parents
65      loop
66        for j in 1..p_num_of_children
67        loop
```

```
68        l_part_type_tab(j) :=
69           part_type( i, l_part_or_id, 'part'||i||j, 'part desc '||i||j );
70        l_part_or_id := l_part_or_id + 1;
71      end loop;
72      insert into components_or_view values
73         ( i, 'component'||i, l_part_type_tab );
74    end loop;
75    commit;
76   end do_or_insert;
77
```

The procedure do_nt_insert inserts a given number of parent records and a given number of children for each parent record into the table components_nt:

```
78    procedure do_nt_insert( p_num_of_parents in int := 50,
79      p_num_of_children in int := 500 )
80    as
81      l_part_type_tab part_type_tab;
82      l_part_type part_type;
83      l_part_or_id number := 1;
84    begin
85      l_part_type_tab := part_type_tab();
86      l_part_type_tab.extend( p_num_of_children );
87
88      for i in 1..p_num_of_parents
89      loop
90        for j in 1..p_num_of_children
91        loop
92          l_part_type_tab(j) :=
93             part_type( i, l_part_or_id, 'part'||i||j, 'part desc '||i||j );
94          l_part_or_id := l_part_or_id + 1;
95        end loop;
96        insert into components_nt values
97        ( i, 'component'||i, l_part_type_tab );
98      end loop;
99      commit;
100   end do_nt_insert;
```

The procedure do_or_update updates one column of all rows in the object view components_or_view:

```
102   procedure do_or_update
103   as
104   begin
105     update components_or_view
106     set component_name = component_name || ' or update';
107   end;
109   procedure do_or_child_update
110   as
```

```
111      l_component_id components_or_view.component_id%type;
112    begin
113      for i in 1..g_num_of_child_updates
114      loop
115        l_component_id := mod(i,500);
116        update table
117          ( select parts
118            from components_or_view
119            where component_id = l_component_id
120          )
121        set part_desc = part_desc || ' updated'
122        where part_id = i;
123      end loop;
124    end do_or_update;
```

The procedure do_rel_update updates one column of all rows in the table
components_rel:

```
126    procedure do_rel_update
127    as
128    begin
129      update components_rel
130        set component_name = component_name || ' or update';
131    end do_rel_update;
```

The procedure do_rel_child_update updates one column of all rows in the child table
parts_rel:

```
133    procedure do_rel_child_update
134    as
135    begin
136      for i in 1..g_num_of_child_updates
137      loop
138        update parts_rel
139        set part_desc = part_desc || ' updated'
140        where part_id = i;
141      end loop;
142    end do_rel_child_update;
```

The procedure do_nt_update updates one column of all rows in the table components_nt:

```
144    procedure do_nt_update
145    as
146    begin
147      update components_nt
148        set component_name = component_name || ' or update';
149    end do_nt_update;
```

The procedure do_nt_child_update updates one column of all rows in the child table parts_nt (the hidden table containing the nested table data). Note that owing to a bug in Oracle 10g Release 1 and Oracle9i Release 2, because of which the nested_table_get_refs hint does not work in static SQL, the update fails unless you use dynamic SQL, as follows:

```
151    procedure do_nt_child_update
152    as
153    begin
154      for i in 1..g_num_of_child_updates
155      loop
156        execute immediate 'update /*+ nested_table_get_refs */ parts_nt' ||
157        ' set part_desc = part_desc|| :1 ' ||
158        ' where part_id = :2 '
159        using 'updated', i;
160      end loop;
161    end do_nt_child_update;
```

The procedure do_or_delete deletes all rows in components_or_view:

```
163    procedure do_or_delete
164    as
165    begin
166      delete components_or_view;
167    end do_or_delete;
```

The procedure do_rel_delete deletes all rows in components_rel and implicitly in parts_rel:

```
169    procedure do_rel_delete
170    as
171    begin
172      delete components_rel;
173    end do_rel_delete;
```

The procedure do_nt_delete deletes all rows in components_nt and implicitly in parts_nt:

```
175    procedure do_nt_delete
176    as
177    begin
178      delete components_nt;
179    end do_nt_delete;
```

The procedure do_rel_bulk_insert inserts a given number of parent records and a given number of children for each parent record into the tables components_rel and parts_rel using PL/SQL bulk binding technique. When using bulk binding, you first store all rows to be inserted in a collection, and then insert it in one shot using the special forall syntax, thus avoiding the overhead of switching contexts between the SQL engine and the PL/SQL engine. Bulk binding is discussed in detail in the section "Using Bulk Binding" of Chapter 17.

```
181   procedure do_rel_bulk_insert( p_num_of_parents in int := 50,
182     p_num_of_children in int := 500 )
183   as
184     l_tmp_comp  number;
185     type array is table of parts_rel%rowtype index by binary_integer;
186     l_childdata array;
187     l_part_rel_id  number := 1;
188   begin
189     for i in 1..p_num_of_parents
190     loop
191       insert into components_rel values ( i, 'component'||i );
192       for j in 1..p_num_of_children
193       loop
194         l_childdata(j).component_id := i;
195         l_childdata(j).part_id := l_part_rel_id;
196         l_childdata(j).part_name := 'part'||i||j;
197         l_childdata(j).part_desc := 'part desc' || i||j;
198         l_part_rel_id := l_part_rel_id + 1;
199       end loop;
200       forall X in 1 .. p_num_of_children
201         insert into parts_rel values l_childdata(X);
202     end loop;
203     commit;
204   end do_rel_bulk_insert;
205 end ;
206 /
```

Package body created.

I must point out that the preceding performance benchmark suffers from the drawback that, of necessity, I had to choose specific scenarios for updates, deletes, and selects, among other things. In particular, for comparing updates, I ran my tests on the case where I update all records of rows in the child table, which may not represent reality in general. Also, the nested tables–based approach can be improved by storing the nested tables as an index-organized table as mentioned in an earlier note. Having said that, the conclusions drawn from the benchmark should more or less hold true.

I used the runstats utility to measure the differences between the elapsed time for inserting 50 parents, each having 500 child records, for each of the three cases compared. To conserve space, I do not show the actual program runs, but that should not be an issue since I give the details of the package I used to run the various comparisons.

Table 8-1 summarizes the elapsed times and latches for various scenarios that I observed in my runs. For each case I show in bold and within parentheses, the values normalized to the lowest value of the elapsed time or the latches for a given DML. For example, inserts in the nested tables–based approach took 2.86 times the elapsed time and consumed 16.20 times the latches as compared to the relational approach.

Table 8-1. *Comparing Elapsed Times (in Hundredths of Seconds) and Latches for Relational Solution, Nested Table–Based Solution, And Object View–Based Solution for Insert, Update, and Delete*

DML	Relational		Nested Table		Object View	
	Elapsed Time (1/100 of Second)	Latches	Elapsed Time (1/100 of Second)	Latches	Elapsed Time (1/100 of Second)	Latches
Insert	171 (**1.00**)	19,592 (**1.00**)	489 (**2.86**)	317,433 (**16.20**)	8942 (**52.29**)	6,267,036 (**319.00**)
Update	215 (**1.05**)	221,839 (**1.00**)	3633 (**17.90**)	224,739 (**1.01**)	270 (**1.25**)	620,001 (**2.80**)
Delete	380 (**1.00**)	460,808 (**1.00**)	396 (**1.04**)	475,312 (**1.03**)	546 (**1.44**)	1,700,907 (**3.69**)
Select	61 (**1.00**)	87,075 (**1.00**)	3890 (**63.77**)	6,469,635 (**74.30**)	190 (**3.11**)	95,190 (**1.10**)

From Table 8-1, we can draw the following performance-related conclusions:

- In general, the relational tables–based solution outperforms the other two solutions (in many cases by orders of magnitudes, both in terms of elapsed times and latches).

- The object views–based solution performs rather poorly when compared to the nested tables–based solution when it comes to inserts, deletes, and updates. This can be attributed to the overhead of the `instead of` triggers that do all the work behind the scenes.

- When it comes to selects, object views perform much better than the nested tables–based solution.

From the discussion we have had so far in this chapter, we can conclude the following about the code maintenance of all three approaches:

- In general, the code written on top of the relational schema is much more maintainable and also more open to be accessed from various tools that work using SQL as compared to schema that uses objects as storage mechanism.

- The code complexity increases tremendously for both object views and the nested tables–based schema.

On the whole, it is a good idea to always give preference to a pure relational tables–based approach given the performance benefits and the other benefits, as discussed in the earlier sections. If you do have a good reason to choose otherwise, then the second choice, in general, may be the object views–based solution, especially if the inserts, deletes, and updates are done directly on the underlying tables and only selects, when required, are done on the object view itself.

Summary

In this chapter, you learned about different ways in which objects are useful in Oracle. In particular, you learned about three different ways in which objects are useful:

- Purely as a programming construct

- As a mechanism to store data in object tables

- In the form of object views that work on top of relational tables

You discovered that it is best to use objects as a programming construct to enhance the power of your PL/SQL code. Storing data in object tables that contain varrays or nested table columns can lead to complex code that does not perform well, as you learned from the performance study done at the end of the chapter. In particular, you discovered that DMLs on relational tables perform much better in general when compared to DMLs carried out on object views and tables containing nested tables. In the next chapter, we will look at how to access objects from JDBC.

CHAPTER 9

■■■

Using Weakly Typed Struct Objects

In the previous chapter, you learned how to make the best use of objects in Oracle. In particular, you learned that you should avoid using objects to store data in a table. Object views, on the other hand, allow you to create a layer of abstraction on top of relational tables, giving you the option of accessing objects directly from your code, while also retaining the flexibility of writing code that works on the underlying relational tables using traditional SQL. Even though it is not, in general, advisable to store data in object tables, it still makes sense to discuss how to work with objects using JDBC, for the following reasons:

- Even if you don't store objects in tables, you may have to pass Oracle objects back and forth between Java and your stored procedures that take objects as parameters. Since this would be also true for stored procedures that use objects as programming constructs rather than as a storage mechanism, it is useful to learn these concepts.

- The idea of accessing and manipulating objects is an integral part of the JDBC API, and this book would be incomplete without a discussion of this topic.

- You need to be familiar with accessing objects from object tables, in case you encounter code that uses the concepts involved.

In this chapter and the next two chapters, you will learn different options available for mapping Oracle database objects and collections to objects in Java.

In this chapter, we will discuss how to materialize database objects as *weakly typed* objects in Java. A weakly typed object refers to a Java object that implements the java.sql.Struct interface. A java.sql.Struct object represents in a uniform fashion, in Java, database objects belonging to any given database object type. It represents the database object as an array of attributes, which are stored in an array of Java objects (i.e., Object[]). For example, using this technique, a database object of type person and a database object of type address can both be mapped to a single java.sql.Struct object and initialized with an appropriate set of attributes.

In Chapter 10, we will discuss how to materialize objects as *strongly typed* objects in Java. A strongly typed object refers to an object belonging to a custom Java class specifically created to represent a given database object type in Java. For example, when we use strongly typed Java objects, a database object of type person object would map to a Java object of a custom class, say `Person`, whereas a database object of type `address` would map to, for instance, a Java object of custom class `Address`.

In Chapter 11, we will discuss how to materialize a database collection of built-in types (such as a `varray` of `varchar2`), a database collection of object types (such as a nested table of `person` objects), and database object references (references are defined in Chapter 11) as either weakly typed `java.sql.Struct` objects or as strongly typed custom class objects in Java.

In addition, in this chapter and in Chapters 10 and 11, we will cover how to manipulate data stored in tables containing objects or collections using either weakly typed or strongly typed Java objects. Although we will use tables with object columns in our examples for simplicity, the same code should work with object views as well, with appropriate triggers, as explained in Chapter 8 (regardless of whether we use weakly typed or strongly typed objects).

■**Note** There are many tools and frameworks available outside the realm of JDBC that address the issue of mapping data in relational schema to Java objects (without using Oracle database object types or collections). Some of the popular ones are TopLink, Hibernate, and the Spring framework. Discussion of these tools is beyond the scope of this book. However, I do strongly encourage you to consider and evaluate these tools when working with relational data that needs to be materialized as objects in Java.

Weakly Typed Struct Objects

The term "weakly typed object" in Java refers to an object that implements the JDBC standard interface `java.sql.Struct` (referred to as simply `Struct` going forward). A `Struct` object represents a database object of any given object type (such as `person`) in a generic fashion, namely as a collection of attributes. The object attributes are stored in an `Object` array that contains individual attributes as Java objects. By default, an attribute class is based on the mapping between the SQL data type and Java class, as specified in Table A-1 in this book's appendix. For example, an object attribute of type `number` materializes in Java as a `java.math.BigDecimal` object.

■**Note** In the next chapter, you'll see how you can change this default mapping by supplying a type map in the `Connection` object (a mapping that informs the JDBC driver which Java class you want to use to manifest a given database type).

The order of these attribute objects in the `Object` array is the same order in which they were specified at the time of the creation of the object type that they represent. For example, a `Struct` Java object that corresponds to the database `person` object type (defined in section "Object Type [Equivalent of a Java Class]" of Chapter 8 and containing the attributes `name` and `date_of_birth`, in that order) would be stored in an internal array of `Object` elements (i.e., an `Object[]` object) containing two elements:

- The first attribute would be a String object (since the database type varchar2 maps to a String object in Java, by default) that contains the value in the name attribute of the person object.

- The second attribute would be a java.sql.Timestamp object (since the database type date, by default, maps to a java.sql.Timestamp object in Java) that contains the value in the date_of_birth attribute of the person object.

Note that you may need to cast each of these attributes manually into an object of the appropriate data type in Java. For example, while manipulating the second element of the Object[] structure in the previous example (corresponding to the date_of_birth attribute), you may need to cast the second array element to the interface java.sql.Timestamp type in order to access any methods specific to the interface java.sql.Timestamp.

Weakly typed Struct objects are useful in the following scenarios:

- If your program needs to work with an arbitrary object type in a generic fashion without really needing to materialize it as a custom class object. This may be true, for example, if you are building a utility that needs to deal with an object of an arbitrary object type in a generic fashion as a collection of attributes.

- If your end user application doesn't need to do a lot of manipulation of objects in memory. If you need to do a lot of manipulation in memory, then it is much more intuitive to use strongly typed objects, where a custom class that has appropriate getter and setter methods for the object attributes represents the database object type.

Oracle implements the Struct interface as an object of type oracle.sql.STRUCT class which, in a typical fashion, implements the standard methods in the Struct interface and also adds Oracle extension methods. We briefly discuss the Struct interface and its Oracle implementation class, oracle.sql.STRUCT, in the next two sections.

The Struct Interface

The Struct interface is the standard JDBC interface that defines the mapping in Java for a SQL structured type (Oracle object types in this chapter). A Struct object contains a value for each attribute of the SQL structured type that it represents. You can use the Struct interface as the container for your objects if you want to stick to standard JDBC. The Struct interface has the three methods whose signatures follow:

```
public Object[] getAttributes(Map map) throws SQLException;
```

This method retrieves the values of the attributes, using entries in the specified *type map* associated with the Connection object to determine the Java classes to use in materializing any attribute that is a structured object type. The type map refers to a mapping between a database type and the Java class to which it is mapped. If there is no entry in the connection's type map that matches the structured type that this Struct object represents, the driver uses the standard mapping as defined in Table A-1 of the Appendix. The Java types for other attribute values would be the same as for a getObject() call on data of the underlying SQL type (the default JDBC types). You will learn more about using type maps in the next chapter.

Note that the JDBC driver seamlessly handles embedded objects in the same way that it normally handles objects. When the JDBC driver retrieves an attribute that is an object, it follows the same rules of conversion, using the type map if it is available, and using default mapping if it is not.

```
public Object[] getAttributes() throws SQLException;
```

This method is the same as the preceding getAttributes(map) method, except it uses the default type map provided by the driver.

```
public String getSQLTypeName() throws SQLException;
```

This method returns a Java String that represents the fully qualified name (schema.sql_type_name) of the Oracle object type this Struct represents.

The Struct interface does not expose any methods to instantiate Struct objects in our Java program to insert or update objects in the database. Hence, for inserting or updating data, we have to use the extended Oracle functionality exposed by the class oracle.sql.STRUCT (unless we use relational DML, which is always a possibility).

The oracle.sql.STRUCT Class

The oracle.sql.STRUCT class implements the Struct interface and provides extended functionality beyond the JDBC 3.0 standard. Unlike the Struct interface, which can be used only to query data, the Oracle extension oracle.sql.STRUCT class can also be used to insert or update data. The following are the signatures of some of the common methods defined in the oracle.sql.STRUCT class:

```
public oracle.sql.Datum[] getOracleAttributes() throws SQLException;
```

This method retrieves the values of the values array as oracle.sql.* objects. The interface oracle.sql.Datum is implemented by classes in the oracle.sql package. An oracle.sql.Datum object represents a data type in Oracle's native format (e.g., oracle.sql.NUMBER).

```
public oracle.sql.StructDescriptor getDescriptor() throws SQLException;
```

This method returns the oracle.sql.StructDescriptor object for the SQL type that corresponds to this oracle.sql.STRUCT object. An oracle.sql.StructDescriptor object represents the details of a database object type. It is used in instantiating an oracle.sql.STRUCT object, as you will see shortly.

We will examine how to use some of the extension methods of this class in the upcoming sections. In the next section, we will discuss how to use the Struct interface to select data, and how to use the oracle.sql.STRUCT class to insert and update data in tables containing object columns. Deleting data from such tables uses straightforward relational SQL.

Performing DML Operations Using Struct Objects

In this section, we will examine how to use Struct objects to perform DML operations on data held in object type columns stored in object tables. Specifically, we will demonstrate

- How to retrieve Oracle objects using Struct objects in conjunction with the PreparedStatement and CallableStatement interfaces

- How to insert data into Oracle objects using Struct in conjunction with the PreparedStatement and CallableStatement interfaces

- How to update data in Oracle objects in conjunction with the PreparedStatement and CallableStatement interfaces

Before delving into our example, we need to create our object types and tables, and store some data in them, along with a stored procedure that will return our object when called from the CallableStatement interface in our JDBC example. We'll do that in the next section.

Creating the Example Database Schema

First, we create an object type, item, as follows:

```
benchmark@ORA10G> create or replace type item as object
  2  (
  3    id number,
  4    name varchar2(20),
  5    description varchar2(50)
  6  )
  7  /
```

```
Type created.
```

We then create a table, item_table, that contains item objects, and we insert one row into it (later, we will select this row from our JDBC program):

```
benchmark@ORA10G> create table item_table of item;
```

```
Table created.
```

```
benchmark@ORA10G> insert into item_table values ( 1, 'item1', 'item1 desc' );
```

```
1 row created.
```

```
benchmark@ORA10G> commit;
```

```
Commit complete.
```

There are some differences when manipulating data in tables such as item_table that contain only one object column and other tables where the object column is not the only column. To show these distinctions when required, we create another table, manufactured_item_table, that can store objects as well as relational data in a row. We then insert and commit a row in it as follows:

```
benchmark@ORA10G> create table manufactured_item_table
  2  (
  3    manufactured_item item,
  4    manufactured_date date
  5  );

Table created.

benchmark@ORA10G> insert into manufactured_item_table values (
  2    item(1, 'manu_item1', 'manu_item1 desc'), sysdate -1 );

1 row created.

benchmark@ORA10G> commit;

Commit complete.
```

To demonstrate the use of a weakly typed Struct object when using CallableStatement, we create a PL/SQL package called item_pkg:

```
benchmark@ORA10G> create or replace package item_pkg
  2  as
  3    procedure get_item( p_item in out item ) ;
  4    procedure get_items( p_items out sys_refcursor ) ;
  5    procedure insert_item( p_item in item ) ;
  6  end item_pkg;
  7  /

Package created.
```

Note that the data type sys_refcursor refers to a ref cursor data type that corresponds to a ResultSet in our JDBC code; for more information on the ref cursor data type, please see the section "Ref Cursors (or Cursor Variables)" of Chapter 13. The package body with explanatory comments follows:

```
benchmark@ORA10G> create or replace package body item_pkg
  2  as
```

The first procedure, get_item(), simply selects an item object in a row of the table and returns it in the out parameter p_item.

■Note Due to a bug, executing a stored procedure and retrieving an object returned via an `out` parameter does not work as expected when you use `CallableStatement` with `Struct`. The workaround, as you will see shortly, is to return the object as a ref cursor column, from which you can retrieve the `Struct` object.

```
 3    procedure get_item( p_item in out item  )
 4    is
 5    begin
 6      select value(i)
 7      into p_item
 8      from item_table i
 9      where rownum <= 1;
10    end get_item;
```

The procedure `get_items()` simply returns a ref cursor to all rows in the object table `item_table`. This form of procedure that returns a ref cursor works with the `CallableStatement` and `Struct` interfaces. Note that since the only column of the object table is an object, we need to use the in-built function `value()` to extract the object from the row:

```
11    procedure get_items( p_items out sys_refcursor  )
12    is
13    begin
14      open p_items for
15        select value(c)
16        from item_table c;
17    end get_items;
```

We will use the procedure `insert_item` to demonstrate inserting a row using `CallableStatement`:

```
18    procedure insert_item( p_item in item  )
19    is
20    begin
21      insert into item_table values( p_item );
22    end insert_item;
23
24  end item_pkg;
25  /
```

`Package body created.`

In the remainder of this chapter, we'll explore the capabilities of the standard `Struct` interface and the Oracle extension `oracle.sql.STRUCT` class.

Using the Struct Interface to Select Oracle Objects

The following steps are involved in selecting objects from a database into a Struct object using the PreparedStatement or CallableStatement interface:

1. Obtain a result set that points to one or more rows containing objects.

2. For the object column value in each row, do the following:

   a. Retrieve the object using the getObject() method, and cast it to a Struct variable.

   b. Retrieve the attributes from the Struct object into an object array using the getAttributes() method. The order in which these attributes are retrieved will be the order in which the attributes were created in the corresponding object type.

   c. Retrieve each attribute and cast it to an appropriate Java class. If an attribute of the object is another object itself, then we cast that attribute as a Struct and go through the same steps to get the attributes of the embedded object. See Table A-1 of the Appendix for the actual classes to which the JDBC driver materializes.

3. Release JDBC resources by closing the result set, etc.

We will explore the preceding steps in the context of PreparedStatement and Callable→ Statement in separate sections. Both concepts are explained as part of the class StructQuery→ Example described over the next two sections, with explanatory comments interspersed.

Using Struct Objects with PreparedStatement

In this section, we examine how to select an object as Struct using the PreparedStatement interface as part of the definition of the class StructQueryExample. We'll first go through the main() method that invokes the methods described in this and the next section:

```
/** This program demonstrates how to use the java.sql.Struct class
* to retrieve objects.
* COMPATIBLITY NOTE: runs successfully against 10.1.0.2.0, and 9.2.0.1.0
*/
import java.sql.ResultSet;
import java.sql.SQLException;
import java.sql.CallableStatement;
import java.sql.PreparedStatement;
import java.sql.Connection;
import java.sql.Struct;
import java.sql.Types;
import oracle.jdbc.OracleTypes;
import book.util.JDBCUtil;
class StructQueryExample
{
  public static void main(String args[]) throws SQLException
  {
```

We begin by checking the program usage:

```
if( args.length != 1 )
{
  System.err.println( "Usage: java <program_name> <database_name>");
  Runtime.getRuntime().exit(1);
}
Connection conn = null;
try
{
```

Inside the try catch block, the first thing we do is get a connection to the database (the first command-line parameter is the database SID):

```
conn = JDBCUtil.getConnection("benchmark", "benchmark", args[0] );
```

The function _demoQueryWithPreparedStmt() takes a connection object and a query string that selects an item from the object table item_table. Because in this table there is only one column, and that column is an object type, we need to use the value() function to extract the object value:

```
_demoQueryWithPreparedStmt( conn,
  "select value(it) from item_table it" );
```

Next, we invoke the same function, but this time with a query string that selects an item from the table manufactured_item_table. Because in this table the object column is not the only one, we do not need to use the value() function to extract the object value:

```
_demoQueryWithPreparedStmt( conn,
  "select m.manufactured_item from manufactured_item_table m" );
```

The next function simply invokes the procedure get_items, which returns a ref cursor, from which we extract objects as Struct Java objects:

```
_demoQueryWithCallableStmt( conn,
  "begin item_pkg.get_items( ? ); end;" );
```

The final commented code invokes the procedure get_item(), which returns an item object as an out parameter. As noted earlier, this won't work as expected due to a bug in both Oracle 10g Release 1 and 9i Release 2:

```
/* the following gives an error in both 10g Release 1 and 9i Release 2.
_demoStructWithCallableStmtGivesError( conn,
  "begin item_pkg.get_item( ? ); end;" );
*/
}
finally
{
  // release resources in the finally clause.
  JDBCUtil.close( conn );
}
}
```

The definition of the first function, _demoQueryWithPreparedStmt(), is as follows:

```
private static void _demoQueryWithPreparedStmt( Connection conn,
  String stmtStr )
throws SQLException
{
  PreparedStatement pstmt = null;
  ResultSet rset = null;
  try
  {
    pstmt = conn.prepareStatement( stmtStr );
    rset = pstmt.executeQuery();
    // print the result
    while (rset.next())
    {
```

Inside the while loop, for each object column of a row, we first retrieve the object using the getObject() method of ResultSet interface and cast it to the Struct object:

```
      Struct itemStruct = (Struct) rset.getObject ( 1 );
```

The next step retrieves all attributes from the Struct object into an object array. Notice how all attributes of the object type person materialize as a collection of attributes in an Object array:

```
      Object[] attributes = itemStruct.getAttributes();
```

Finally, we print out the number of attributes and loop through them, printing their class names and their values when converted to a String object:

```
      System.out.println ( "num of attributes: " + attributes.length );
      for(int i=0; i < attributes.length; i++ )
      {
        System.out.println ( "class of attribute " + i + " = " +
          (attributes[i]).getClass().getName() +
          ", value = " + attributes[i] );
      }
    }
  }
  finally
  {
    // release resources in the finally clause.
    JDBCUtil.close( rset, pstmt);
  }
}
```

In the next section, we define and explain the methods that use Struct objects in conjunction with CallableStatement.

Using Struct Objects with CallableStatement

The next method, _demoQueryWithCallableStmt(), retrieves a ref cursor that contains the object column values. All the steps for converting the object into a Struct and retrieving individual values are exactly the same as in the case of the method _demoQueryWithPreparedStmt() discussed earlier.

```
private static void _demoQueryWithCallableStmt( Connection conn,
  String stmtStr ) throws SQLException
{
  CallableStatement cstmt = null;
  ResultSet rset = null;
  try
  {
    cstmt = conn.prepareCall( stmtStr );
    cstmt.registerOutParameter( 1, OracleTypes.CURSOR );
    cstmt.execute();
    rset = (ResultSet) cstmt.getObject(1);
    while( rset.next() )
    {
      Struct itemStruct = (Struct) rset.getObject ( 1 );
      Object[] attributes = itemStruct.getAttributes();
      System.out.println ( "num of attributes: " + attributes.length );
      for(int i=0; i < attributes.length; i++ )
      {
        System.out.println ( "class of attribute " + i + " = " +
          (attributes[i]).getClass().getName() +
          ", value = " + attributes[i] );
      }
    }
  }
  finally
  {
    // release resources in the finally clause.
    JDBCUtil.close( rset);
    JDBCUtil.close( cstmt);
  }
}
```

The method _demoStructWithCallableStmtGivesError() tries to invoke a procedure that returns an item object directly as an out parameter (using the procedure item_pkg.get_item()) instead of returning it as a column of a ref cursor. It gives an error, as you will see shortly:

```
private static void _demoStructWithCallableStmtGivesError(
  Connection conn, String stmtStr ) throws SQLException
{
  CallableStatement cstmt = null;
  try
  {
    cstmt = conn.prepareCall( stmtStr );
    cstmt.registerOutParameter( 1, OracleTypes.STRUCT );
    cstmt.execute();
    // get the "item" object and its attributes
    Struct itemStruct = (Struct) cstmt.getObject ( 1 );
    Object[] attributes = itemStruct.getAttributes();
    System.out.println ( "num of attributes: " + attributes.length );
    for(int i=0; i < attributes.length; i++ )
    {
      System.out.println ( "class of attribute " + i + " = " +
        (attributes[i]).getClass().getName() +
        ", value = " + attributes[i] );
    }
  }
  finally
  {
    // release resources in the finally clause.
    JDBCUtil.close( cstmt );
  }
}
} // end of program
```

Running the Example

When we execute the preceding program, we get the following output, showing the data we populated earlier:

```
B:\>java StructQueryExample ora10g
URL:jdbc:oracle:thin:@(DESCRIPTION=(ADDRESS=(PROTOCOL=tcp)(PORT=1521)
(HOST=rmenon-lap))(CONNECT_DATA=(SID=ora10g)))
num of attributes: 3
class of attribute 0 = java.math.BigDecimal, value = 1
class of attribute 1 = java.lang.String, value = item1
class of attribute 2 = java.lang.String, value = item1 desc
num of attributes: 3
class of attribute 0 = java.math.BigDecimal, value = 1
class of attribute 1 = java.lang.String, value = manu_item1
class of attribute 2 = java.lang.String, value = manu_item1 desc
num of attributes: 3
```

```
class of attribute 0 = java.math.BigDecimal, value = 1
class of attribute 1 = java.lang.String, value = item1
class of attribute 2 = java.lang.String, value = item1 desc
```

As you can see, the number attributes are converted into java.math.BigDecimal by default (this is specified in Table A-1 of the Appendix). If we change the program to comment out all method invocations in the main() method except for the method _demoStructWithCallable➥ StmtGivesError(), we get the following error (as mentioned earlier, this is a bug in the Oracle implementation):

```
URL:jdbc:oracle:thin:@(DESCRIPTION=(ADDRESS=(PROTOCOL=tcp)(PORT=1521)
(HOST=rmenon-lap))(CONNECT_DATA=(SID=ora10g)))
Exception in thread "main" java.sql.SQLException: ORA-03115: unsupported network
 datatype or representation
...
```

To summarize, we get a SQLException when we return an object as an out parameter in a PL/SQL procedure. The workaround is to retrieve object column data as a ResultSet and then extract the column as a Struct object, as discussed alongside the description of the method _demoQueryWithCallableStmt() in the previous section.

Using the oracle.sql.STRUCT Class to Insert Oracle Objects

The Struct interface does not expose any methods to create Struct objects in your Java program so that you can insert or update objects in the database. Thus, for inserting and/or updating data, you have to use the extended Oracle functionality exposed by the class oracle.sql.STRUCT. Inserting an object using oracle.sql.STRUCT in conjunction with either the PreparedStatement interface or the CallableStatement interface involves the following steps:

1. Create an oracle.sql.StructDescriptor object for the database object type. The StructDescriptor object contains information about the object type required to manually construct a STRUCT object later. You need only one StructDescriptor object for any number of STRUCT objects that correspond to the same SQL type. For example, to create a new StructDescriptor object for the object type item, assuming that conn is an initialized Connection object, you can use the following code:

   ```
   StructDescriptor itemDescriptor =
     StructDescriptor.createDescriptor( "BENCHMARK.ITEM", conn );;
   ```

2. Create an array of objects with the same number of elements as the number of attributes of the object type. Each element must be of the appropriate data type representing the object attribute (as per Table A-1 in the Appendix). If the object type consists of nested objects, you need to create a corresponding oracle.sql.STRUCT object in its place.

3. Construct an oracle.sql.STRUCT object, passing in the StructDescriptor you created in step 1, a Connection object, and the array of objects you created in step 2 as the object attribute values.

4. Use the setObject() method in the PreparedStatement or CallableStatement interface to set the value of the object and then insert it into the table containing the object.

The following StructInsertExample class, along with the interspersed explanatory comments, illustrates how to insert data using the Struct class into a table containing object columns. We demonstrate the concept using both the PreparedStatement and CallableStatement interfaces.

```
/** This program demonstrates how to use the java.sql.Struct class
* to insert data into a table containing object columns.
* COMPATIBLITY NOTE: runs successfully against 10.1.0.2.0, and 9.2.0.1.0
*/
import java.sql.SQLException;
import java.sql.PreparedStatement;
import java.sql.CallableStatement;
import java.sql.Connection;
import java.sql.Struct;
import java.sql.Types;
import java.math.BigDecimal;
import oracle.sql.STRUCT;
import oracle.sql.StructDescriptor;
import book.util.JDBCUtil;
class StructInsertExample
{
  public static void main(String args[]) throws SQLException
  {
    Connection conn = null;
    try
    {
      conn = JDBCUtil.getConnection("benchmark", "benchmark", "ora10g");
```

After getting the connection, we invoke the first method that uses the PreparedStatement interface to insert objects into the table item_table:

```
      _demoInsertUsingPreparedStmt( conn );
```

Next, we invoke the method that uses the CallableStatement interface to insert objects into the table item_table by invoking the method item_pkg.insert_item:

```
      _demoInsertUsingCallableStmt( conn );

    }
    finally
    {
      // release resources in the finally clause.
      JDBCUtil.close( conn );
    }
  }
```

Using PreparedStatement to Insert an oracle.sql.STRUCT Object

In this section, we describe how to use PreparedStatement to insert an oracle.sql.STRUCT object as part of the definition of the method _demoInsertUsingPreparedStmt(), which follows:

```
private static void _demoInsertUsingPreparedStmt( Connection conn )
  throws SQLException
{
  PreparedStatement pstmt = null;
  try
  {
```

The first step is to create a StructDescriptor for the object type item. Note that for a given object type, we need to create the StructDescriptor only once. Also note that we should always qualify the object type with the user that owns it (e.g., benchmark in the following example).

```
      StructDescriptor itemDescriptor =
        StructDescriptor.createDescriptor( "BENCHMARK.ITEM", conn );
```

The next step is to create and initialize the object array that contains values of attributes of the item object that we want to insert. Note how we create the attributes in the order in which we specified them during the object type creation (in this example, the first attribute is id, the second attribute is name, and the third attribute is description). We also use the appropriate class to create an attribute (java.math.BigDecimal for number and String for varchar2):

```
      Object[] itemAttributes = new Object[ itemDescriptor.getLength()];
      itemAttributes[0] = new BigDecimal(2);
      itemAttributes[1] = "item2";
      itemAttributes[2] = "item2 desc using prepared statement";
```

Next, we create an oracle.sql.STRUCT object using the descriptor and the object array containing the attribute values:

```
      // Next we create the STRUCT object
      Struct itemObject = new STRUCT ( itemDescriptor, conn,
        itemAttributes );
```

The remaining steps are the usual ones required to insert a record using the PreparedStatement interface:

```
      pstmt = conn.prepareStatement( "insert into item_table values( ? )");
      pstmt.setObject(1, itemObject, Types.STRUCT );
      int numOfRowsInserted = pstmt.executeUpdate();
      System.out.println( "Inserted " + numOfRowsInserted + " rows");
      conn.commit();
  }
  finally
  {
    // release resources in the finally clause.
    JDBCUtil.close( pstmt);
  }
}
```

Using CallableStatement to Insert an oracle.sql.STRUCT Object

The definition of the method _demoInsertUsingCallableStmt() is very similar to that of
the method _demoInsertUsingPreparedStmt(), the only difference being that we use the
CallableStatement interface to invoke the stored procedure method item_pkg.insert_item
to insert our record in this case:

```
private static void _demoInsertUsingCallableStmt( Connection conn )
  throws SQLException
{
  CallableStatement cstmt = null;
  try
  {
    StructDescriptor itemDescriptor =
      StructDescriptor.createDescriptor( "BENCHMARK.ITEM", conn );
    Object[] itemAttributes = new Object[ itemDescriptor.getLength()];
    itemAttributes[0] = new BigDecimal(3);
    itemAttributes[1] = "item2";
    itemAttributes[2] = "item2 desc using callable stmt";
    // Next we create the STRUCT object
    Struct itemObject = new STRUCT ( itemDescriptor, conn,
      itemAttributes );
    cstmt = conn.prepareCall( "{call item_pkg.insert_item(?)}");
    cstmt.setObject(1, itemObject, Types.STRUCT );
    cstmt.execute();
    conn.commit();
  }
  finally
  {
    // release resources in the finally clause.
    JDBCUtil.close( cstmt );
  }
}
}
```

Using the oracle.sql.STRUCT Class to Update Oracle Objects

In the previous section, you learned how to insert objects using the oracle.sql.STRUCT class
methods. You can see that the process is inherently more complex than a simple relational
SQL insert. However, more than an insert or a delete, the process of updating an object attribute using STRUCT highlights the difference in usability when you use DML on objects (instead
of relational SQL). This is because when you insert or delete a row containing objects, you
insert or delete the entire object along with all its attributes. However, when updating an
object, more often than not you are interested in modifying only a subset of object attributes.
Now, if you use relational SQL, you can update just the required columns of a table (or, equivalently, the attributes of the object) in a table that you need to change, and you are done. If,
however, you use the oracle.sql.STRUCT interface to do the same, there are two levels of complexity you need to deal with:

- No matter how many attributes you want to modify, you have to select the *entire* object, materialize it as an oracle.sql.STRUCT object, change the attributes that you need to change, and update the object. If an object has ten attributes and you want to change only one of them, you still need to materialize the entire object, change just that one attribute, and perform the update.

- The second level of complexity arises because you need to break your update operation into two steps: the first step selects the original object, and the second updates with the new object values. Furthermore, since in Oracle a select does not block an update from another session, you also need to lock the object during your select by using the for update clause.

Thus, performing an update using an oracle.sql.STRUCT object is fairly complicated. In this section, we'll illustrate this fact in the example. We'll demonstrate how to perform an update using a PreparedStatement, first using the oracle.sql.STRUCT object and then using straightforward relational SQL. Since the CallableStatement interface essentially uses the same technique as PreparedStatement, we do not go through an example using the CallableStatement interface in this section.

The following steps are required to update an Oracle object using the STRUCT interface:

1. Retrieve the object's value into a Struct object and lock it using the for update clause.

2. Retrieve the Struct object attributes into an Object array.

3. Modify the object attributes as desired.

4. Get the StructDescriptor from the original Struct object.

5. Instantiate a new Struct object using the object using the StructDescriptor and the modified Object array.

6. Finally, use a PreparedStatement object's setObject() method to set the value of the object, and then update the table containing the object with the modified value.

The following listing contains an example illustrating these steps. Before executing the program, the database had the following three entries in the table item_table:

```
benchmark@ORA10G> select * from item_table it order by it.id;

ID NAME       DESCRIPTION
--- ---------- ----------------------------------
  1 item1      item1 desc
  2 item2      item2 desc using prepared statement
  3 item2      item2 desc using callable stmt
```

The program StructUpdateExample retrieves one item object and updates its description attribute. We do this using the oracle.sql.STRUCT object first, and then we use relational SQL to achieve the same objective. The program listing follows, with explanatory comments interspersed.

```
/** This program demonstrates how to use the java.sql.Struct class
 * to update data in a table containing object columns.
 * COMPATIBLITY NOTE: runs successfully against 10.1.0.2.0, and 9.2.0.1.0
 */
import java.sql.SQLException;
import java.sql.PreparedStatement;
import java.sql.ResultSet;
import java.sql.Connection;
import java.sql.Struct;
import java.sql.Types;
import java.math.BigDecimal;
import oracle.sql.STRUCT;
import oracle.sql.StructDescriptor;
import book.util.JDBCUtil;
class StructUpdateExample
{
  public static void main(String args[]) throws SQLException
  {
    Connection conn = null;
    try
    {
      conn = JDBCUtil.getConnection("benchmark", "benchmark", "ora10g");
```

To carry out the update that uses the oracle.sql.STRUCT class, we first select an item with the id value of 2 as a Struct by invoking the method _getItem() (explained shortly):

```
      Struct itemStruct = _getItem( conn, 2 );
```

Next, we pass it on to the method _demoUpdateUsingSTRUCT(), which will update its description attribute using the oracle.sql.STRUCT class:

```
      _demoUpdateUsingSTRUCT( conn, 2, itemStruct );
```

Finally, we demonstrate how, by using relational SQL, we can not only update just the attribute we need to but also do it in one step without having to select the object into memory first:

```
      _demoUpdateUsingRelationalSQL( conn, 3 );
    }
    finally
    {
      // release resources in the finally clause.
      JDBCUtil.close( conn );
    }
  }
```

Performing Updates Using the oracle.sql.STRUCT Object

The first step is to select the object that needs to be updated. The method _getItem() selects an object that matches the passed item id in the variable itemID:

```
private static Struct _getItem( Connection conn,
    int itemID ) throws SQLException
{
  PreparedStatement pstmt = null;
  ResultSet rset = null;
  try
  {
```

The main thing to note in this method is that we use a for update nowait clause. This means that the select will lock the table row if it succeeds, preventing any other user from updating the same row before we update it. If someone else has locked the row already, we will get an error message. The locking issues associated with this situation are discussed in much more detail in Chapter 16. The remainder of the method should be self-explanatory.

```
      pstmt = conn.prepareStatement(
        "select value(it) from item_table it" +
        " where it.id = ? and for update NOWAIT" );
      pstmt.setInt( 1, itemID );
      rset = pstmt.executeQuery();
      Struct itemStruct = null;
      if (rset.next())
      {
        // get the "item" object and its attributes
        itemStruct = (Struct) rset.getObject ( 1 );
      }
      return itemStruct;
  }
  finally
  {
    // release resources in the finally clause.
    JDBCUtil.close( rset, pstmt);
  }
}
```

The method _demoUpdateUsingSTRUCT() that actually performs the update follows. It updates a supplied item object (that was selected in the form of a Struct using the method _getItem() presented earlier):

```
private static void _demoUpdateUsingSTRUCT( Connection conn,
    int itemID, Struct itemStruct ) throws SQLException
{
  PreparedStatement pstmt = null;
  STRUCT itemSTRUCT = (STRUCT) itemStruct;
  try
  {
```

As the first step, we retrieve the attributes of the object we selected earlier by invoking the method _getItem():

```
Object[] itemAttributes = itemStruct.getAttributes();
```

We modify the third attribute (the description) to a new value. This change happens only in memory.

```
itemAttributes[2] = "item2 desc updated using prepared statement";
```

Next, we need to create the modified Struct object for which the first step is to retrieve the StructDescriptor from the object already selected:

```
StructDescriptor itemDescriptor = itemSTRUCT.getDescriptor();
```

Then we create the STRUCT object with the modified attributes:

```
Struct itemObject = new STRUCT ( itemDescriptor, conn, itemAttributes );
```

and use the standard update statement (note the use of the value() function again) to carry out the update:

```
      pstmt = conn.prepareStatement(
        "update item_table it set value(it) = ? " +
        " where it.id = ?" );
      pstmt.setObject(1, itemObject );
      pstmt.setInt(2, itemID );
      int numOfRowsUpdated = pstmt.executeUpdate();
      System.out.println( "Updated " + numOfRowsUpdated + " rows");
      conn.commit();
    }
    finally
    {
      // release resources in the finally clause.
      JDBCUtil.close( pstmt);
    }
  }
}
```

Performing Updates Using Relational SQL

The method _demoUpdateUsingRelationalSQL() uses a relational SQL to carry out the same update in one step:

```
private static void _demoUpdateUsingRelationalSQL( Connection conn,
  int itemID) throws SQLException
{
  PreparedStatement pstmt = null;
  try
  {
```

The main difference in this case is the relational SQL, which directly changes the description attribute in the table as presented here. The rest of the code is straightforward.

```
pstmt = conn.prepareStatement(
  "update item_table it set it.description= ? " +
  " where it.id = ?" );
pstmt.setString(1, "item desc updated using relational SQL" );
pstmt.setInt(2, itemID );
int numOfRowsUpdated = pstmt.executeUpdate();
System.out.println( "Updated " + numOfRowsUpdated + " rows");
conn.commit();
}
finally
{
  // release resources in the finally clause.
  JDBCUtil.close( pstmt);
}
}
}
```

If we run the program, we get the following output:

```
B:\>java StructUpdateExample
URL:jdbc:oracle:thin:@(DESCRIPTION=(ADDRESS=(PROTOCOL=tcp)(PORT=1521)
(HOST=rmenon-lap))(CONNECT_DATA=(SID=ora10g)))
printing query results ...

Updated 1 rows
Updated 1 rows
```

Using the following query, we verify that our updates have been successful:

```
benchmark@ORA10G> select * from item_table it order by it.id;
```

ID	NAME	DESCRIPTION
1	item1	item1 desc
2	item2	item2 desc updated using prepared s tatement
3	item2	item desc updated using relational SQL

As this section demonstrated, performing an update using an `oracle.sql.STRUCT` object is complicated. The fact that the update is carried out in two operations (a `select for update` followed by an `update` operation) means that it is also slower as compared to its relational SQL counterpart.

Deleting Objects

The process of deleting objects typically is the same as in a normal relational delete case, for example:

```
"delete from item_table it where it.id = ?"
```

I encourage you to write code for deleting a value from the table item_table yourself.

Summary

This chapter defined weakly typed and strongly typed objects. You learned how to use the Struct interface to select objects as a collection of attributes. You also learned how to insert and update objects stored in tables using oracle.sql.STRUCT class methods. The steps involved in these operations tend to be more complicated than the straightforward relational alternative. You saw that this is particularly true when performing updates. In the next chapter, you will learn how to access and manipulate objects in tables using strongly typed objects.

CHAPTER 10

■■■

Using Strongly Typed Interfaces with JPublisher

In the previous chapter, we examined the technique of using the Struct interface to material-ize database objects as a generic collection of attributes. This technique works well for a small set of applications that needs to treat different object types in a generic manner. However, this technique does not satisfy the requirements of the majority of object-oriented applications that require you to work in terms of actual objects instead of a loose collection of attributes.

In this chapter, we discuss the alternative of using *strongly typed interfaces* to create cus-tom Java classes that correspond to Oracle objects in the database. Using this technique, you can generate a custom class for each object type in the database, making it possible to manip-ulate the contents in memory in a more natural fashion (i.e., using proper getter and setter methods for the attributes instead of indexing into a generic Object[ ]).

You will first consider what strongly typed interfaces are. Then, you will learn how to use JPublisher, a utility that allows you to generate custom classes corresponding to Oracle object types. You will use JPublisher to generate custom classes that implement either the standard interface SQLData or the Oracle extension interfaces ORAData and ORADataFactory. Let's begin with an introduction to strongly typed interfaces.

Strongly Typed Interfaces

Strongly typed interfaces represent the attributes of a database object using a custom class. This means that a Java class Person, for example, would represent an Oracle object type person and so on. In other words, each database object type is represented by its own custom Java class.

To create a custom class for an object type, there must be a mechanism by which you inform the JDBC driver of the following:

- Which Java class should you convert the object type to?

- Which Java classes would each of the attributes map to by default, and how do you change the default mapping?

The driver must be able to read from and write to these custom Java classes. To create and populate the custom classes and provide them with read/write capabilities, you have to implement one of the following two interfaces:

- The JDBC standard `java.sql.SQLData` interface (referred to as `SQLData` from here onward)

- The `oracle.sql.ORAData` (referred to as `ORAData` from here onward) and `oracle.sql.ORADataFactory` (referred to as `ORADataFactory` from here onward) interfaces provided by Oracle

You can create the custom object classes that implement one of these interfaces yourself, but the most convenient way is to use the Oracle JPublisher utility to create them for you. JPublisher supports generating classes that implement the standard `SQLData` interface or the Oracle-specific `ORAData` interface. I recommend using JPublisher to create the custom classes since creating them manually is tedious and error-prone. We will use the JPublisher utility to create the custom classes in this book.

In the next section, we'll walk through an introduction to the JPublisher utility and its most commonly used options. After that, we'll study JPublisher examples of generating custom classes that implement the `SQLData` interface, followed by examples of generating classes that implement the `ORAData` and `ORADataFactory` interfaces. We'll then finish up by comparing these two alternatives.

An Introduction to JPublisher

JPublisher is a utility that generates Java classes to represent database entities such as SQL objects and PL/SQL packages in your Java client program. It also provides support for publishing from SQL, PL/SQL, or server-side Java to web services, and for enabling invocation of external web services from inside the database. JPublisher can create classes to represent the following types of database entities:

- User-defined SQL object types

- Object reference types (`REF` types)

- User-defined SQL collection types (`varray` types or nested table types)

- PL/SQL packages

- Server-side Java classes

- SQL queries and DML statements

We'll focus on the first three types in this book. In this chapter, we'll cover SQL object types. We'll cover `REF` types and SQL collection types in the next chapter. For a complete discussion of all the capabilities and options offered by JPublisher—and there are quite a few—please see *Oracle Database JPublisher User's Guide (10g Release 1)* supplied by Oracle. Let's now move on to an overview of setting up the environment to use the JPublisher utility.

Setting Up the JPublisher Environment

As of Oracle 10.0.1.0, JPublisher requires you to have SQLJ set up. SQLJ is another standard for accessing data in relational databases. For more information on SQLJ, please see the section "Overview of SQLJ Concepts" in Chapter 1 of *Oracle Database JPublisher User's Guide (10g Release 1)*. You can download and install the SQLJ (with the JPublisher utility) separately from the OTN website (`http://otn.oracle.com`).

■**Note** Oracle had earlier decided to move away from the use of SQLJ and had even officially announced the end of support for SQLJ on all platforms. However, as per the note under the heading "SQLJ is Back!" at `http://www.oracle.com/technology/tech/java/sqlj_jdbc/index.html`, Oracle has since decided to reverse its decision.

To use JPublisher, you need to add the following JAR files to your `CLASSPATH` environment variable (in addition to the JDBC environment–related JAR files):

- `$ORACLE_HOME/sqlj/lib/translator.jar` contains the JPublisher and SQLJ translator classes.

- `$ORACLE_HOME/sqlj/lib/runtime12.jar` contains the SQLJ runtime library.

Also, you can add the JPublisher invocation script `jpub` (for UNIX) or `jpub.exe` for Windows in your `PATH` environment variable to avoid having to specify the full path name for these scripts while running them.

JPublisher Commonly Used Options

A JPublisher script is invoked from the command line as follows:

```
jpub <options>
```

The following is an alphabetically sorted list of some commonly used options with valid values (default values are underlined wherever possible) and brief explanations. For a complete list of JPublisher options, please see the Oracle document *Oracle Database JPublisher User's Guide (10g Release 1)*. In particular, you may want to focus on the following options, which are the most commonly used and which we discuss in this book: builtintypes, input, methods, numbertypes, package, props, sql, user, usertypes, usertypes, and input.

- `-builtintypes` (jdbc|oracle): Specifies the data type mappings (jdbc or oracle) for built-in data types (e.g., a standard Java class such as String or an Oracle Java class such as VARCHAR) that are non-numeric and non-LOB.

- `-case` (lower|mixed|same|upper): Specifies the case of Java identifiers that JPublisher generates.

- `-classpath`: Adds to the Java CLASSPATH for JPublisher to use in resolving Java source and classes during translation.

- -d: Specifies the root directory for placement of compiled class files.

- -dir: Specifies the root directory where generated Java files are placed.

- -driver (driver_name): Specifies the JDBC driver used for the JDBC connection in generated classes. The default is `oracle.driver.OracleDriver`.

- -encoding (encoding_of_character_set): Specifies the Java encoding of JPublisher input files and output files. The default is the value of the system property `file.encoding`.

- -generatebean (true|false): Specifies whether or not generated code should comply with the JavaBeans specification.

- -input or -i (input_file_name): Specifies a mapping file that allows you to specify the data type mapping between SQL and Java in a file rather than on the command line (equivalent of using the -sql command-line option).

- -lobtypes (jdbc|oracle): Specifies the data type mappings that JPublisher uses for BLOB and CLOB types.

- -methods (all|none|named|always|overload|unique): This option determines whether JPublisher generates wrapper methods for methods in SQL object types and PL/SQL packages (through a setting of all, none, named, or always), or whether overloaded method names are allowed (through a setting of overload or unique).

  - -methods=all: This is the default among the first group of settings. In this case, JPublisher generates wrapper methods for all the methods in the object types and PL/SQL packages it processes. This results in generation of a SQLJ class if the underlying SQL object or package actually defines methods, and a non-SQLJ class if not.

  - -methods=none: JPublisher does not generate any wrapper methods. If you want to have wrapper methods in this case you have to handcraft them (typically in a subclass of the generated class).

  - -methods=named: JPublisher generates wrapper methods only for the methods explicitly named in the input file.

  - -methods=always: This also results in wrapper methods being generated. However, for backward compatibility with Oracle8*i* and Oracle9*i* JPublisher versions, this setting always results in SQLJ classes being generated for all SQL object types, regardless of whether the types define any methods.

■Note For backward compatibility, JPublisher also supports the setting true as equivalent to all, the setting false as equivalent to none, and the setting some as equivalent to named.

- -numbertypes (jdbc|objectjdbc|bigdecimal|oracle): This option controls data type mappings for numeric SQL and PL/SQL types.

- jdbc: In this case, most numeric data types are mapped to Java primitive types such as int and float; DECIMAL and NUMBER are mapped to java.math.BigDecimal.

- objectjdbc: In this mapping (the default), most numeric data types are mapped to Java wrapper classes such as java.lang.Integer and java.lang.Double; DECIMAL and NUMBER are mapped to java.math.BigDecimal.

- bigdecimal: In this mapping, all numeric data types are mapped to java.math.BigDecimal.

- oracle: In this mapping, all numeric data types are mapped to oracle.sql.NUMBER.

- omit_schema_names: This option controls if schema name is used in generated classes (disabled by default.)

- outarguments (array|holder|return): This option specifies how to treat mapping of the in, out, or in out designations in Java. You can specify one of three alternatives for holders:

  - Arrays (the default)

  - JAX-RPC holder types

  - Function returns

- package: Specifies the name of the package for generated Java classes.

- props or -p (properties_file_name): Specifies a file that contains JPublisher options in addition to those listed on the command line.

- sql or -s
  (toplevel|type_name:super_class_name:map_class_name|type_name:map_class_name):
  Specifies the name of a Java object, an optional superclass name, and a Java class name to which the sql object or package is mapped.

  - toplevel: Translates all top-level PL/SQL subprograms in a schema

  - type_name: Name of the sql object type, collection, or package

  - super_class_name: Name of an intermediate class file that the developer extends

  - map_class_name: Name of the class that is used in the type map

- -tostring (false|true): Specifies whether to generate a toString() method for generated Java classes.

- url (database_url): Specifies the database URL. The default is jdbc:oracle:oci:@.

- user (username/password): The username and password for connecting to the database—this is mandatory for using JPublisher.

- usertypes (oracle|jdbc): This option controls whether JPublisher implements the Oracle ORAData interface or the standard SQLData interface in the generated classes for the user-defined types.

- When -usertypes=oracle (the default), JPublisher generates ORAData classes for objects, collections, and object reference types.

- When -usertypes=jdbc, JPublisher generates SQLData classes for object types. JPublisher does not generate classes for collection or object reference types in this case; you must use java.sql.Array for all collection types and java.sql.Ref for all object reference types.

Next, we'll look at how to use a JPublisher property file, which allows you to specify your JPublisher options in a text file.

JPublisher Property File Syntax

Let's assume we execute the following command (don't worry about what this command does for now—we'll delve into that soon):

```
jpub -user=benchmark/benchmark -methods=none -builtintypes=jdbc
-numbertypes=objectjdbc -usertypes=jdbc -sql address:Address
```

Instead of using command-line options as just shown, we can put these options in a properties file and specify the properties filename instead of the command line, by using the -props command-line option. (You have to prefix an option with jpub. in the properties file.) We'll use this technique throughout the book, as it is convenient and less error-prone. For example, the following prop_address.txt properties file contains all command-line options specified in the preceding JPublisher command:

```
jpub.user=benchmark/benchmark
jpub.methods=none
jpub.builtintypes=jdbc
jpub.numbertypes=objectjdbc
jpub.usertypes=jdbc
jpub.sql=address:Address:MyAddress
jpub.package=book.ch10.jpub
```

We can now execute a JPublisher command equivalent to the previous one that uses the command-line options specified in prop_address.txt:

```
jpub -props=prop_address.txt
```

JPublisher Input File Syntax

Instead of specifying the class generation option (see the -sql option in the section "JPublisher Commonly Used Options") on the command line, we can specify them in an input file, which in turn can be specified on the command line using the -input command-line option. We could also specify the input file option itself in the properties file with the property jpub.input. An input file consists of one or more *translation statements* (statements that specify which database object type would map to which Java class) that adhere to the following syntax (from *Oracle Database JPublisher User's Guide [10g Release 1]*) :

```
( SQL name
| SQL [ schema_name.]toplevel [( name_list)]
| TYPE type_name)
[GENERATE java_name_1]
[AS java_name_2]
[TRANSLATE
database_member_name AS simple_java_name
{ , database_member_name AS simple_java_name}*
]
```

The commonly used translation line elements are provided in the sections that follow. For more details on the syntax and a host of other useful options related to the input file, please see Chapter 5 of *Oracle Database JPublisher User's Guide (10g Release 1)*.

Specifying the Object Type Name or Package Name to Be Materialized in Java

The SQL name | TYPE type_name clause identifies a SQL type or a PL/SQL package that you want JPublisher to translate (i.e., publish a Java class)—for example, SQL BENCHMARK.PERSON.

Specifying the Target Java Class Name and/or Subclass Name to Be Generated

The GENERATE clause essentially determines the name of the generated class and any subclasses that you may want to generate and eventually override. When you use only the AS clause (i.e., without a GENERATE clause), JPublisher generates the specified class and maps it to the SQL type or the PL/SQL package. When you use both the GENERATE clause and the AS clause for a SQL user-defined type, the GENERATE clause specifies the name of the base Java class that JPublisher generates, and the AS clause specifies the name of the derived Java class that extends the generated base class. For example, the following line instructs JPublisher to generate a class named Address in a file called Address.java for the object type address:

```
SQL address as Address
```

Suppose you want to generate a class named MyAddress corresponding to the object type address. You would also like to generate a base class Address that the class MyAddress class extends. The following translation line does it for you:

```
SQL address GENERATE Address as MyAddress
```

Customizing the Generated Java Object Attribute Names

The TRANSLATE database_member_name AS simple_java_name clause optionally specifies a different name for an attribute or method. For example, if you want to change the name of the attribute hire_date in database to HireDate in Java, you can specify the following TRANSLATION clause: TRANSLATE HIRE_DATE AS HireDate. This is useful in ensuring that the generated Java attribute names follow your desired naming convention.

Using the SQLData Interface

It's now time to take a look at the SQLData interface. We'll use JPublisher to generate classes implementing this interface.

The SQLData interface is used for the custom mapping of a SQL object type to a class in the Java programming language. It consists of three methods:

```
public String getSQLTypeName() throws SQLException
```

This method returns the fully qualified name of the SQL object type that this object represents (e.g., BENCHMARK.PERSON). It is called by the JDBC driver to get the name of the object type mapped to this instance of SQLData.

```
public void readSQL(SQLInput stream, String typeName)
throws SQLException
```

This method populates this object with data read from the database. Here, SQLInput is an input stream that contains a stream of values representing an instance of a SQL object. This interface is used only for custom mapping and is used by the driver behind the scenes.

```
public void writeSQL(SQLOutput stream) throws SQLException
```

This method writes the object to the given SQL data stream, converting it back to its SQL value in the data source. Here, the SQLOutput object represents the output stream for writing the attributes of a user-defined type back to the database.

Generating Custom Classes That Implement SQLData

We are finally ready to use JPublisher. In this section, we will use JPublisher to create a custom class that represents an object type we will create. The classes generated in this section implement SQLData interface. The steps involved in creating and using a custom class, MyAddress, that implements SQLData and represents the object type address are as follows:

1. Generate custom classes using JPublisher. In this step, we use JPublisher to generate a custom class that implements the SQLData interface.

2. Extend generated classes to add functionality (if required). If you want to add to the functionality of the generated classes, extend the class and make any changes. (Changing the generated class directly itself is not recommended since your changes will be overwritten the next time you generate these classes again using JPublisher.)

3. Add the generated class to the type map of the connection. Add the custom class that represents the object type to the *type map*. The type map is a mapping that informs the JDBC driver of which Java class a specific object type should be mapped to.

4. Perform DML using custom classes. Use the generated classes in your calling program to select, insert, update, or delete objects.

Before we can perform these steps, however, we need to create our schema and object tables that we'll use in this example. We'll then walk through each of the four steps in turn.

Creating the Schema Containing an Object Type and Object Table

The first step is to create the schema that we will use in our examples. The following code begins this process by defining an object type address that can hold the address of a house or apartment in the United States. The map function get_address() (signified by the keywords map member function preceding the function name) may be a new concept to many of you. Very briefly, a *map method* is an optional method that provides a basis for comparing objects by mapping object instances to one of the scalar types DATE, NUMBER, or VARCHAR2, or to an ANSI SQL type such as CHARACTER or REAL. Please see the section "Methods for Comparing Objects" of Chapter 1 in the Oracle document *Oracle Database Application Developer's Guide – Object Relational Features (10g Release 1)* for more details.

```
benchmark@ORA10G> create or replace type address as object
  2  (
  3    line1 varchar2(50),
  4    line2 varchar2(50),
  5    street varchar2(50),
  6    city varchar2(30),
  7    state varchar2(2),
  8    zip   varchar2(10),
  9    map member function get_address return varchar2
 10  )
 11  not final;
 12  /

Type created.
```

We create the type body that contains the implementation of the function get_address(). Note how we map the address to a varchar2 by concatenating different attributes of the address separated by a space:

```
benchmark@ORA10G> create or replace type body address
  2    as
  3      map member function get_address
  4      return varchar2
  5      is
  6      l_address varchar2(200);
  7      begin
  8      l_address := line1|| ' ' ||
  9                   line2 || ' ' ||
 10                   street || ' ' ||
 11                   city || ' ' ||
 12                   state || ' ' ||
 13                   zip;
 14
 15      return l_address;
 16      end;
 17  end;
 18  /

Type body created.
```

Now that we have an object type, we need to create a table that will store the data contained in the object type. In the following code snippet, we create an object table, address_table, that contains rows of type address:

```
benchmark@ORA10G> create table address_table of address;

Table created.
```

We end the section with a piece of code that inserts an address object into the table address_table:

```
benchmark@ORA10G> declare
  2      l_address address;
  3  begin
  4      l_address := address( '145 Apt # 7','', 'Wander St',
  5                    'Mountain View', 'CA', '94055' );
  6      insert into address_table values ( l_address );
  7      commit;
  8      dbms_output.put_line ( l_address.get_address() );
  9  end;
 10  /
145 Apt # 7  Wander St Mountain View CA 94055

PL/SQL procedure successfully completed.
```

Generating a Custom Class Using JPublisher

I assume that you've set up your environment as specified in the earlier section "Setting Up the JPublisher Environment." We'll now create custom classes for the object type address using JPublisher. First, we'll pass command-line parameters to JPublisher. We'll then repeat the process by using the JPublisher properties file and input file.

Using JPublisher Command-Line Parameters

The following command generates a class called book.ch10.jpub.MyAddress that extends another generated class, book.ch10.jpub.Address, to add a Java method corresponding to the method get_address() in the object type address. The object type itself will be mapped to the MyAddress class. (Note that the final line is the output of the program run and is not part of the command itself. It lists the object types for which JPublisher is generating Java classes.)

```
B:\code\book\ch10\jpub>jpub -user=benchmark/benchmark -methods=none
 -builtintypes=jdbc -numbertypes=objectjdbc -usertypes=jdbc
-sql address:Address:MyAddress -package=book.ch10.jpub

BENCHMARK.ADDRESS
```

The meaning of each command-line option is as follows:

- -user=benchmark/benchmark: The username and password for connecting to the database.

- `-methods=none`: Do not generate any wrapper methods in the Java class that implement the corresponding method in the object type. This means that we will not get a wrapper method for the only method, `get_address()`, in the object type address for example. Instead, we will implement this functionality in the class `MyAddress` that extends the class `Address`, which will also serve to demonstrate the concept of extending a JPublisher-generated class to enhance its functionality. In a real-world scenario, you would probably use `-methods=all` if you wanted to generate a wrapper method for the methods in the object type.

- `-builtintypes=jdbc`: Use the standard Java classes for mapping object attributes.

- `-numbertypes=objectjdbc`: Numeric data types should be mapped to Java wrapper classes such as `java.lang.Integer` and `java.lang.Double`, and `NUMBER` should be mapped to `java.math.BigDecimal`. Alternatively, we could set this option to the value `jdbc`, in which case most numeric data types are mapped to Java primitive types such as `int` and `float`. Note that the data type `number` is still mapped to `java.math.BigDecimal`.

- `-usertypes=jdbc`: Generate classes that implement the standard `SQLData` interface.

- `-sql address:Address:MyAddress`: Map the address object type to the Java class `MyAddress` that extends the generated class `Address`. We could have hand-coded the extended class completely, but JPublisher gives us a "stub" that makes life a little easier.

- `-package book.ch10.jpub`: Generate classes such that they belong to the package `book.ch10.jpub`.

Using the JPublisher Input File and Properties File

Let's now create the properties file and the input files that give instructions to JPublisher equivalent to the command-line options we discussed in the previous section.

The following file, `input_address.txt`, contains one line that is equivalent to the `-sql` options in the previous command. This one line tells JPublisher to generate a parent class `Address` and also to generate a class `MyAddress` that extends the `Address` class and is mapped to the address object type:

```
SQL ADDRESS GENERATE Address AS MyAddress
```

The following properties file, `prop_address.txt`, represents the command-line options, including the reference to the input file `input_address.txt`:

```
jpub.user=benchmark/benchmark
jpub.methods=none
jpub.builtintypes=jdbc
jpub.numbertypes=objectjdbc
jpub.usertypes=jdbc
jpub.package=book.ch10.jpub
jpub.input=input_address.txt
```

Finally, we run the equivalent command using the previous properties files as follows:

```
jpub -props=prop_address.txt
```

When we run this command, we should have two files containing our generated Java classes, Address.java and MyAddress.java, in the current directory. The generated Address.java file contents are as follows (trimmed to conserve space and for clarity):

```
package book.ch10.jpub;

import java.sql.SQLException;
import java.sql.Connection;
import oracle.jdbc.OracleConnection;
import oracle.jdbc.OracleTypes;
import java.sql.SQLData;
import java.sql.SQLInput;
import java.sql.SQLOutput;
import oracle.sql.STRUCT;
import oracle.jpub.runtime.MutableStruct;

public class Address implements SQLData
{
  public static final String _SQL_NAME = "BENCHMARK.ADDRESS";
  public static final int _SQL_TYPECODE = OracleTypes.STRUCT;

  private String m_line1;
  private String m_line2;
  private String m_street;
  private String m_city;
  private String m_state;
  private String m_zip;

  /* constructor */
  public Address()
  {
  }

  public Address(String line1, String line2, String street,
    String city, String state, String zip)
    throws SQLException
  {
    setLine1(line1);
    setLine2(line2);
    setStreet(street);
    setCity(city);
    setState(state);
    setZip(zip);
  }
```

```
public void readSQL(SQLInput stream, String type)
throws SQLException
{
    setLine1(stream.readString());
    setLine2(stream.readString());
    setStreet(stream.readString());
    setCity(stream.readString());
    setState(stream.readString());
    setZip(stream.readString());
}

public void writeSQL(SQLOutput stream)
throws SQLException
{
    stream.writeString(getLine1());
    stream.writeString(getLine2());
    stream.writeString(getStreet());
    stream.writeString(getCity());
    stream.writeString(getState());
    stream.writeString(getZip());
}

public String getSQLTypeName() throws SQLException
{
    return _SQL_NAME;
}

/* accessor methods */
public String getLine1()
{ return m_line1; }

public void setLine1(String line1)
{ m_line1 = line1; }
/* Other similar getter/setter methods for the remaining attributes
    deleted to conserve space */

}
```

Note the following points about the generated Address class:

- The Address class implements java.sql.SQLData as required by the option
  -usertypes=jdbc.

- The Address class *does not* implement the wrapper around the method get_address()
  in the object type address, as we specified -method=none.

Manually Adding a Method to a Generated Class

As discussed earlier, for the MyAddress class we didn't generate a method corresponding to the method get_address() in the object type address. Let's now extend the functionality to add this method. Later, we'll also look at automatically generating a wrapper method.

The following sections discuss the two ways you can add this functionality in the extended class MyAddress.

Reimplementing the Object Type Method

The first option is to write your own version of the get_address() method, called getAddress(), which implements the functionality already implemented in the object type method again in Java:

```java
public String getAddress()
{
  StringBuffer addressSB = new StringBuffer();
  addressSB.append( getLine1() ).append( " " ).
          append( getLine2() ).append( " " ).
          append( getStreet() ).append( " " ).
          append( getCity() ).append( " " ).
          append( getState() ).append( " " ).
          append( getZip() );
  return addressSB.toString();
}
```

This implementation has the advantage that it does not involve a network round-trip to the database. However, it has the disadvantage that it will result in two implementations of the method: one in the object type definition and the other in its Java version in the JDBC layer. Any changes in the logic would have to be maintained in both places. I recommend you avoid this approach *unless* the incurred round-trip results in measurable and significant perform-ance degradation. You should, however, consider using this approach if the performance gain of avoiding a network round-trip to the database more than compensates for the added code complexity.

Writing a Wrapper Method Around the Object Type Method

The second option is to create a wrapper method getAddress() that calls the get_address() method of the object type address. From the point of view of maintainability of the code, this is the recommended way.

We will extend the functionality of Address class in its subclass MyAddress by adding the wrapper method for the method get_address(). The generated class file MyAddress.java (edited for clarity) is as follows:

```java
package book.ch10.jpub;

import java.sql.SQLException;
import java.sql.Connection;
```

```
import oracle.jdbc.OracleConnection;
import oracle.jdbc.OracleTypes;
import java.sql.SQLData;
import java.sql.SQLInput;
import java.sql.SQLOutput;
import oracle.sql.STRUCT;
import oracle.jpub.runtime.MutableStruct;

public class MyAddress extends Address implements SQLData
{
    public MyAddress() { super(); }

  /* superclass accessors */

/*
  public void setLine1(String line1)
 { super.setLine1(line1); }

  public String getLine1()    { return super.getLine1(); }
 */
 /* Other similar accessor methods commented as setLine1 above have
    been deleted in this listing for clarity and to conserve space */
  }
}
```

Note that all the setters and getters are inherited from the superclass Address. The ones defined in MyAddress have been commented out by JPublisher. You can uncomment and enhance these methods if required. As noted in the final comment, I deleted the commented-out methods for brevity; if you are running the examples along with the chapter, you should see them.

We will now add the method called getAddress() to the generated file MyAddress.java, which in turn invokes the get_address() method of the address object type:

```
public String getAddress( Connection connection )
  throws SQLException
{
  String getAddressStmt =
    "begin ? := " + getSQLTypeName()+".get_address( ? ); end;";
  CallableStatement cstmt = null;
  try
  {
    cstmt = connection.prepareCall ( getAddressStmt );
    cstmt.registerOutParameter ( 1, OracleTypes.VARCHAR );
    // pass the second parameter corresponding to the
    // implicit parameter "self".
    cstmt.setObject( 2, this );
    cstmt.execute();
```

```
        String address = (String) cstmt.getObject( 1 );
        return address;
    }
    finally
    {
        JDBCUtil.close ( cstmt );
    }
}
```

Note the following:

- We need to import the classes book.util.JDBCUtil and java.sql.CallableStatement for the MyAddress class after adding the previous method, in order to compile the file MyAddress.java.

- We pass a Connection object in the wrapper method getAddress(). This is required to execute the object's get_address() method after connecting to the database.

- In the statement String of our CallableStatement, we have a parameter being passed to the method get_address() method of the address object type, whereas we did not have any parameters in the actual method get_address(), as shown in its signature reproduced below:

```
map member function get_address return varchar2;
```

- This extra parameter is used to tell the database the object instance whose get_address() method needs to be invoked. It turns out that Oracle invokes the object methods with an implicit parameter, self (which, if you remember, is the equivalent of the Java keyword this). This implies that when we invoke the method get_address(), Oracle implicitly passes the parameter self to the method, thus invoking the current object's method. In our Java method getAddress(), we bind this additional parameter explicitly with the this value (shown in bold font in the preceding definition of the method). The conversion of the this parameter of the MyAddress Java object to the self parameter of the database object type address is done automatically by the JDBC driver based on the type map information that we set up, as explained in the next section.

Using a Type Map to Map Object Types to Java Classes

Now that we have a JPublisher-generated class for the object type in the database, we need to tell the JDBC driver which object type maps to which Java class. We provide this information to the driver by adding a *type map* to the Connection object.

The type map for a connection is an object that implements the java.util.Map interface (similar to how java.util.HashMap does). It contains a key/value pair, with the database object name as the key and the class object of the corresponding custom class as the value. To add to the type map the mapping between the object type and the custom class, we need to first get the existing map, if any, from the Connection object using the following method of the Connection object:

```
public Map getTypeMap() throws SQLException
```

This method retrieves the `Map` object associated with a `Connection` object. Unless the application has added an entry, the type map returned will be empty. An example illustrating invocation of this method is

```
Map map = connection.getTypeMap();
```

Next, we need to add the entries to the `Connection` object's `Map` object. In this example, we map the Java class instance of the class `MyAddress` to the database object type `address` as follows:

```
myMap.put ( "BENCHMARK.ADDRESS",
        Class.forName( MyAddress.class.getName() ) );
```

We can set a `Map` object (containing the requisite mapping entries) on the `Connection` object by using the following method:

```
public void setTypeMap( Map typeMap) throws SQLException
```

For example, we can execute the following code:

```
connection.setType ( myMap );
```

Performing DML Using Custom SQLData Classes

In this section, we'll go through the steps of selecting, inserting, updating, or deleting objects using the custom classes generated in the previous section. The class `DemoSQLData` illustrates these steps for us and is explained in comments interspersed within the code:

```
/** This program demonstrates how to use the Java class
* MyAddress that maps to the address object type and uses
* the JDBC standard interface SQLData.
* COMPATIBLITY NOTE: runs successfully against 10.1.0.2.0. and  9.2.0.1.0.
*/
import java.util.Map;
import java.sql.SQLException;
import java.sql.Connection;
import java.sql.PreparedStatement;
import java.sql.ResultSet;
import book.util.JDBCUtil;
import book.ch10.jpub.MyAddress;
public class DemoSQLData
{
  public static void main(String[] args) throws Exception
  {
    Connection connection = null;
    try
    {
      connection = JDBCUtil.getConnection(
        "benchmark", "benchmark", "ora10g" );
```

After getting the connection, the first step is to retrieve the type map object from the Connection object:

```
Map myMap = connection.getTypeMap();
```

Then we map the address object type (notice the fully qualified object name including the schema name) to the MyAddress class object:

```
myMap.put ( "BENCHMARK.ADDRESS",
    Class.forName( MyAddress.class.getName() ) );
```

The methods demoSelect(), _demoInsert(), _demoUpdate(), and _demoDelete() demonstrate how to perform select, insert, update, and delete operations on the object table address_table using the custom class MyAddress. I explain each of these methods in separate sections shortly.

```
    // example demonstrating selecting object(s)
    _demoSelect( connection );
    // example demonstrating inserting object(s)
    _demoInsert( connection );
    // example demonstrating updating object(s)
    _demoUpdate( connection );
    // example demonstrating deleting object(s)
    _demoDelete( connection );
  }
  finally
  {
    JDBCUtil.close ( connection );
  }
}
```

Selecting Objects

For selecting an object, we use the getObject() method of the ResultSet interface. When we retrieve the object, the type map information set in the Connection object is used to automatically convert the database object into the corresponding Java object. The method _demoSelect() demonstrates this concept:

```
private static void _demoSelect( Connection connection )
throws SQLException
{
  PreparedStatement pstmt = null;
  ResultSet rset = null;
  try
  {
```

The first step is to initialize a string with the select statement. Notice how we use the function value() on the table alias to retrieve the address object value:

```
    String selectStmt = "select value(a) from address_table a";
    pstmt = connection.prepareStatement ( selectStmt );
    rset = pstmt.executeQuery();
```

```
while ( rset.next() )
{
```

Inside the result set loop, we cast the object retrieved to the MyAddress class. If, for some reason, the type map setting we did earlier is incorrect (e.g., if we erroneously put a different class in the mapping), then the following line of code would result in a ClassCastException being thrown:

```
MyAddress address = (MyAddress) rset.getObject(1);
```

Finally, we invoke the method getAddress() that we defined manually to obtain the address object in the form of the MyAddress Java object and print it out:

```
System.out.println( address.getAddress( connection ) );
    }
  }
  finally
  {
    JDBCUtil.close( rset );
    JDBCUtil.close( pstmt );
  }
}
```

Inserting Objects

To insert an object using a custom SQLData object, we first instantiate and set the attributes of the object using the Java object's constructor and setter methods. Once the object is ready in memory, we use the setObject() method to set the value in the placeholder of our CallableStatement or PreparedStatement strings. Finally, we execute the statement and do a commit. The method _demoInsert() illustrates these steps:

```
private static void _demoInsert( Connection connection )
throws SQLException
{
```

As a first step, we initialize the MyAddress object:

```
MyAddress myAddress = new MyAddress ();
myAddress.setLine1("133 Ferry Rd");
myAddress.setLine2( "Apt # 24");
myAddress.setStreet( "Crypton St." );
myAddress.setCity( "Dallas");
myAddress.setState( "TX" );
myAddress.setZip( "75201" );
PreparedStatement pstmt = null;
try
{
```

We use the setObject() method of the PreparedStatement interface to insert the object after creating the PreparedStatement object:

```
        String insertStmt = "insert into address_table values( ? )";
        pstmt = connection.prepareStatement ( insertStmt );
        pstmt.setObject (1, myAddress );
        int rows = pstmt.executeUpdate();
        System.out.println ( "Inserted " + rows + " row(s) " );
        connection.commit();
    }
    finally
    {
      JDBCUtil.close( pstmt );
    }
}
```

Updating Objects

We update an object by selecting it into memory, changing the in-memory Java object as required, and using the Java object to update the object value in the database. An important point to note is that when we select an object in memory, we *don't* have exclusive access to it, because in Oracle reads don't block writes. So it is possible that the changes we make are overridden by someone else who happens to be simultaneously updating the same set of rows using the same technique. This phenomenon is called *lost updates*. We will revisit and resolve this issue in detail in Chapter 16. To avoid lost updates, we need to lock any selected rows. We do that by using the for update nowait clause in our select statement. This tells Oracle to either lock the row for us or fail with an exception if the lock is already held by someone else updating the same row. The method _demoUpdate() illustrates this concept:

```
private static void _demoUpdate( Connection connection )
throws SQLException
{
```

As a first step, we need to select the object using the concepts discussed in the section "Selecting Objects" earlier. The only major difference is that the select statement has a phrase for update nowait at the end to indicate that we want to try and lock any rows that get selected:

```
    PreparedStatement pstmt = null;
    PreparedStatement pstmt1 = null;
    ResultSet rset = null;
    try
    {
      MyAddress myAddress = null;
      String selectStmt = "select value(a) from address_table a"+
                 " where line1 = ? for update nowait";
      pstmt = connection.prepareStatement ( selectStmt );
      pstmt.setString( 1, "145 Apt # 7" );
      rset = pstmt.executeQuery();
```

```
while( rset.next() )
{
  myAddress = (MyAddress) rset.getObject(1);
```

After obtaining the object, we modify the street attribute (you can, of course, change any other attribute as well):

```
myAddress.setStreet ( "Wonderful St" );
```

Then we update the corresponding row:

```
String updateStmt = "update address_table a" +
              " set value(a) = ?" +
              " where a.line1 = ?";
pstmt1 = connection.prepareStatement ( updateStmt );
pstmt1.setObject (1, myAddress );
pstmt1.setString (2, "145 Apt # 7" );
int rows = pstmt1.executeUpdate();
System.out.println ( "Updated " + rows + " rows " );
}
connection.commit();
}
finally
{
  JDBCUtil.close( rset );
  JDBCUtil.close( pstmt );
  JDBCUtil.close( pstmt1 );
}
}
```

Deleting Objects

There is nothing special about deleting an object. It is a simple relational statement, as illustrated in the following definition of the method _demoDelete():

```
private static void _demoDelete( Connection connection )
throws SQLException
{
  PreparedStatement pstmt = null;
  try
  {
    String deleteStmt = "delete address_table a" +
                " where a.line1 = ?";
    pstmt = connection.prepareStatement ( deleteStmt );
    pstmt.setString (1, "145 Apt # 7" );
    int rows = pstmt.executeUpdate();
    System.out.println ( "Deleted " + rows + " row(s) " );
    connection.commit();
  }
```

```
      finally
      {
        JDBCUtil.close( pstmt );
      }
    }
}
```

Generating Wrapper Method(s) Automatically

Previously, we manually created the wrapper method corresponding to the method `get_address()` of the object type `address`. In this section, we'll look at how to do this automatically using JPublisher.

To generate the wrapper method automatically, the only change we need to make is to modify the option `-methods=none` to `-methods=all` in `prop_address.txt`. This results in a new `prop_address.txt` file, the contents of which are as follows:.

```
jpub.user=benchmark/benchmark
jpub.methods=all
jpub.builtintypes=jdbc
jpub.numbertypes=objectjdbc
jpub.usertypes=jdbc
jpub.package=book.ch08.jpub
jpub.input=input_address.txt
```

For clarity, we specify the class names to be `AddressAuto` and `MyAddressAuto` in the file `input_address.txt`, which now looks as follows. `input_address.txt` results in two classes: a parent class called `AddressAuto` and a child class `MyAddressAuto`.

```
SQL ADDRESS GENERATE AddressAuto AS MyAddressAuto
```

The relevant portions of the generated parent class file `AddressAuto.java` (partially edited for clarity) are as follows:

```
/*@lineinfo:filename=AddressAuto*//*@lineinfo:user-code*//*@lineinfo:1^1*/
package book.ch10.jpub;
/* Some other imports deleted for clarity */

import oracle.jpub.runtime.MutableStruct;
import sqlj.runtime.ref.DefaultContext;
import sqlj.runtime.ConnectionContext;

public class AddressAuto implements SQLData
{
  public static final String _SQL_NAME = "BENCHMARK.ADDRESS";
  public static final int _SQL_TYPECODE = OracleTypes.STRUCT;

  /* connection management */
  protected DefaultContext __tx = null;
  protected Connection __onn = null;
```

```java
public void setConnectionContext(DefaultContext ctx) throws SQLException
{ release(); __tx = ctx; }
public DefaultContext getConnectionContext() throws SQLException
{ if (__tx==null)
  { __tx = (__onn==null) ? DefaultContext.getDefaultContext() :
        new DefaultContext(__onn); }
  return __tx;
};
public Connection getConnection() throws SQLException
{ return (__onn==null) ? ((__tx==null) ? null : __tx.getConnection()) : __onn; }
public void release() throws SQLException
{ if (__tx!=null && __onn!=null) __tx.close(ConnectionContext.KEEP_CONNECTION);
  __onn = null; __tx = null;
}

private String m_line1;
private String m_line2;
private String m_street;
private String m_city;
private String m_state;
private String m_zip;
/* constructors */
public AddressAuto()
{ __tx = DefaultContext.getDefaultContext(); }
public AddressAuto(DefaultContext c) /*throws SQLException*/
{ __tx = c; }
public AddressAuto(Connection c) /*throws SQLException*/
{ __onn = c;  }

public AddressAuto(String line1, String line2, String street,
String city, String state, String zip) throws SQLException
{
  setLine1(line1);
  setLine2(line2);
  setStreet(street);
  setCity(city);
  setState(state);
  setZip(zip);
}
public void readSQL(SQLInput stream, String type)
throws SQLException
{
    setLine1(stream.readString());
    setLine2(stream.readString());
    setStreet(stream.readString());
    setCity(stream.readString());
    setState(stream.readString());
```

```
        setZip(stream.readString());
    }

    public void writeSQL(SQLOutput stream)
    throws SQLException
    {
        stream.writeString(getLine1());
        stream.writeString(getLine2());
        stream.writeString(getStreet());
        stream.writeString(getCity());
        stream.writeString(getState());
        stream.writeString(getZip());
    }

    public String getSQLTypeName() throws SQLException
    {
      return _SQL_NAME;
    }

/* Code for accessor methods (setter and getter of various attributes)
   deleted for clarity */

    public String getAddress ()
    throws SQLException
    {
      AddressAuto __jPt_temp = this;
      String __jPt_result;
      /*@lineinfo:generated-code*//*@lineinfo:136^5*/

//   ************************************************************
//   #sql [getConnectionContext()] { BEGIN
//        :__jPt_result := :__jPt_temp.GET_ADDRESS();
//        END;
//        };
//   ************************************************************

{
  // declare temps
  oracle.jdbc.OracleCallableStatement __sJT_st = null;
  sqlj.runtime.ref.DefaultContext __sJT_cc = getConnectionContext(); if
(__sJT_cc==null) sqlj.runtime.error.RuntimeRefErrors.raise_NULL_CONN_CTX();
  sqlj.runtime.ExecutionContext.OracleContext __sJT_ec =
((__sJT_cc.getExecutionContext()==null) ?
sqlj.runtime.ExecutionContext.raiseNullExecCtx() :
  __sJT_cc.getExecutionContext().getOracleContext());
  try {
  String theSqlTS = "BEGIN\n        :1  :=  :2 .GET_ADDRESS();\n       END;";
```

```
  __sJT_st = __sJT_ec.prepareOracleCall(__sJT_cc,"Obook.ch10.jpub.AddressAuto",
    theSqlTS);
  if (__sJT_ec.isNew())
  {
     __sJT_st.registerOutParameter(1,oracle.jdbc.OracleTypes.VARCHAR);
  }
  // set IN parameters
  __sJT_st.setObject(2,__jPt_temp);
// execute statement
  __sJT_ec.oracleExecuteUpdate();
  // retrieve OUT parameters
  __jPt_result =  (String) __sJT_st.getString(1);
  } finally { __sJT_ec.oracleClose(); }
}

//   ********************************************************

/*@lineinfo:user-code*//*@lineinfo:140^5*/
    return __jPt_result;
  }
}/*@lineinfo:generated-code*/
```

Notice that the generated AddressAuto class code has additional code that employs SQLJ to get the connection information. It uses this connection to invoke the method get_address() of the object type address in the generated wrapper method getAddress(). The second generated Java file for the class MyAddressAuto (edited for clarity) is as follows:

```
/*@lineinfo:filename=MyAddressAuto*//*@lineinfo:user-code*//*@lineinfo:1^1*/
package book.ch10.jpub;

/* Some other imports deleted for clarity */
import oracle.jpub.runtime.MutableStruct;
import sqlj.runtime.ref.DefaultContext;
import sqlj.runtime.ConnectionContext;

public class MyAddressAuto extends AddressAuto implements SQLData
{
   public MyAddressAuto() { super(); }

   /* superclass accessors */
/* Code for accessor methods (setter and getter of various attributes)
are generated within comments by JPublisher - these have been deleted
for clarity */

   /* superclass methods */
   public String getAddress() throws SQLException
   {
     String __jRt_0 = null;
```

```
    __jRt_0 = super.getAddress();
    return __jRt_0;
  }
}/*@lineinfo:generated-code*/}
```

Note that the class now contains the getAddress() method, which is the wrapper equivalent of the get_address() method of the object type address.

The following listing presents the class DemoAddressAuto, which illustrates how to use the generated wrapper method:

```java
/** This program demonstrates how to use the Java class
 * MyAddressAuto that maps to the address object type with
 * its wrapper method generated automatically with
 * JPublisher.
 * COMPATIBLITY NOTE: runs successfully against 10.1.0.2.0. and  9.2.0.1.0.
 */
import java.util.Map;
import java.sql.SQLException;
import java.sql.Connection;
import java.sql.PreparedStatement;
import java.sql.ResultSet;
import book.util.JDBCUtil;
import book.ch10.jpub.MyAddressAuto;
public class DemoSQLDataAuto
{
  public static void main(String[] args) throws Exception
  {
    Connection connection = null;
    PreparedStatement pstmt = null; // select
    ResultSet rset = null;
    try
    {
      connection = JDBCUtil.getConnection (
        "benchmark", "benchmark", "ora10g" );
      Map myMap = connection.getTypeMap();
      myMap.put ( "BENCHMARK.ADDRESS",
        Class.forName("book.ch10.jpub.MyAddressAuto") );
      // select the object and invoke the wrapper method
      String selectStmt = "select value(a) from address_table a";
      pstmt = connection.prepareStatement ( selectStmt );
      rset = pstmt.executeQuery();
      while ( rset.next() )
      {
        MyAddressAuto address = (MyAddressAuto) rset.getObject(1);
```

The following statement sets up the SQLJ runtime context. As of 10g Release 1, if you try to invoke the wrapper method without executing this statement, you will get the following exception: `found null connection context`. Note that this problem does not exist if you use JPublisher to generate wrapper methods that implement the ORAData and ORADataFactory interfaces (as you will see shortly).

```
address.setConnectionContext(
    new sqlj.runtime.ref.DefaultContext(connection));
```

Note how we can use getAddress() without passing the Connection object. As shown earlier, JPublisher takes care of passing the connection object internally in its implementation using the SQLJ runtime context.

```
            System.out.println( address.getAddress() );
        }
    }
    finally
    {
        JDBCUtil.close ( rset, pstmt, connection );
    }
}
}
```

This concludes our discussion of using the SQLData interface. We will now discuss how to use the Oracle extension ORAData and ORADataFactory interfaces in JDBC programs. We will then compare the pros and cons of the SQLData and ORAData interfaces. The next section presents an overview of the interfaces ORAData and ORADataFactory.

Using the ORAData and ORADataFactory Interfaces

Instead of using custom classes that implement the standard SQLData interface, we can use custom classes that implement the Oracle proprietary interfaces ORAData and ORADataFactory. The ORAData interface provides more flexibility as compared to the SQLData interface. For example, it lets you provide a mapping between Java object types and any SQL type supported by the oracle.sql package. Later, we will examine a detailed comparison between using the standard SQLData interface and using the ORAData and ORADataFactory interfaces.

Let's start off with the definitions of ORAData and ORADataFactory:

```
public interface ORAData
{
    Datum toDatum (OracleConnection connection) throws SQLException;
}
public interface ORADataFactory
{
    ORAData create (Datum datum, int sqlTypeCode) throws SQLException;
}
```

Here, connection represents the Connection object, datum represents an object of type oracle.sql.Datum (an Oracle abstract class extended by oracle.sql.* objects such as oracle.sql.NUMBER), and sqlTypeCode represents the SQL typecode (from the standard java.sql.Types or oracle.sql.OracleTypes class) of the Datum object.

The ORAData and ORADataFactory interfaces do the following:

- The toDatum() method of the ORAData class converts the data into an oracle.sql.* representation.

- The create() method of ORADataFactory creates and returns an ORAData instance. The JDBC driver uses this method to return an instance of the custom object class to your Java application. It takes as input an oracle.sql.Datum object and an integer indicating the corresponding SQL typecode as specified in the OracleTypes class.

In the next section, we'll look at an example of using JPublisher to generate custom classes that implements the ORAData and ORADataFactory interfaces.

Generating Custom Classes that Implement the ORAData and ORADataFactory Interfaces

Using JPublisher, we will now generate custom classes for the address object type that implements the ORAData and ORADataFactory interfaces. The steps involved in creating and using a custom class called MyAddressORAData that implements the ORAData and ORADataFactory interfaces and represents the object type address are as follows:

1. Generate custom classes using JPublisher. In this step, we use JPublisher to generate a custom class that implements the ORAData and ORADataFactory interfaces.

2. Extend the generated classes to add functionality (if required). If you want to add to the functionality of the generated classes, extend the class and make any changes, since directly changing generated classes is error-prone.

3. Perform DMLs using the custom classes. Use the generated classes in your calling program to select, insert, update, or delete objects.

Notice that unlike the SQLData case, we don't need to add a type map to the Connection object because of the way the generated classes work. The following sections explain these steps further.

Generating Custom Classes Using JPublisher

We use the input file input_address_oradata.txt, which contains the following line:

```
SQL ADDRESS GENERATE AddressORAData AS MyAddressORAData
```

This line instructs JPublisher to generate a class, MyAddressORAData, that will extend the class AddressORAData.

We use the properties file `prop_address_oradata.txt`, the contents of which follow:

```
jpub.user=benchmark/benchmark
jpub.methods=all
jpub.builtintypes=jdbc
jpub.numbertypes=objectjdbc
jpub.usertypes=oracle
jpub.package=book.ch10.jpub
jpub.input=input_address_oradata.txt
```

Notice the use of `jpub.usertypes=oracle` here—this is the change in option that directs JPublisher to generate custom classes that implement the proprietary interfaces `ORAData` and `ORADataFactory`.

Next, we run the JPublisher command that uses the preceding properties file:

```
jpub -props=prop_address_oradata.txt
```

The following class files are generated in our directory:

- `AddressORAData.java`: The parent class extended by the `MyAddressORAData` class.

- `MyAddressORAData.java`: The child class mapped to the `address` object type. This is the class we should modify if required.

- `MyAddressORADataRef.java`: This represents a reference object.

Notice that apart from the two classes `AddressORAData` and `MyAddressORAData` that we specified, we also get a third class, `MyAddressORADataRef`. When using Oracle proprietary interfaces, JPublisher automatically generates a class that represents a reference to the database object type, in case we need to use it. For the time being, we will ignore the third class; we'll look at references to object types in the next chapter.

The following listing shows the content of the generated `AddressORAData.java` file (edited for clarity):

```
/*@lineinfo:filename=AddressORAData*//*@lineinfo:user-code*//*@lineinfo:1^1*/
package book.ch10.jpub;
/* All imports deleted for clarity */
public class AddressORAData implements ORAData, ORADataFactory
{
  public static final String _SQL_NAME = "BENCHMARK.ADDRESS";
  public static final int _SQL_TYPECODE = OracleTypes.STRUCT;

  /* connection management */
  protected DefaultContext __tx = null;
  protected Connection __onn = null;
  public void setConnectionContext(DefaultContext ctx)
    throws SQLException
  { release(); __tx = ctx; }
  public DefaultContext getConnectionContext() throws SQLException
```

```
{ if (__tx==null)
  { __tx = (__onn==null) ? DefaultContext.getDefaultContext() :
    new DefaultContext(__onn); }
  return __tx;
};
public Connection getConnection() throws SQLException
{ return (__onn==null) ? ((__tx==null) ? null :
    __tx.getConnection()) : __onn; }
public void release() throws SQLException
{ if (__tx!=null && __onn!=null) __tx.close(
  ConnectionContext.KEEP_CONNECTION);
  __onn = null; __tx = null;
}

protected MutableStruct _struct;

private static int[] _sqlType =  { 12,12,12,12,12,12 };
private static ORADataFactory[] _factory = new ORADataFactory[6];
protected static final AddressORAData _AddressORADataFactory =
  new AddressORAData();

public static ORADataFactory getORADataFactory()
{ return _AddressORADataFactory; }

protected static java.util.Hashtable _map = new java.util.Hashtable();
protected static boolean _initialized = false;
protected static synchronized void init()
{ if (!_initialized)
  { _initialized=true;
    _map.put("BENCHMARK.ADDRESS",
      book.ch10.jpub.MyAddressORAData.getORADataFactory());
} }

/* constructors */
protected void _init_struct(boolean init)
{ if (init) _struct = new MutableStruct(new Object[6],
  _sqlType, _factory); }
public AddressORAData()
{ _init_struct(true); __tx = DefaultContext.getDefaultContext(); }
public AddressORAData(DefaultContext c) /*throws SQLException*/
{ _init_struct(true); __tx = c; }
public AddressORAData(Connection c) /*throws SQLException*/
{ _init_struct(true); __onn = c; }
public AddressORAData(String line1, String line2,
  String street, String city, String state, String zip)
  throws SQLException
{
```

```
  _init_struct(true);
  setLine1(line1);
  setLine2(line2);
  setStreet(street);
  setCity(city);
  setState(state);
  setZip(zip);
}

/* ORAData interface */
public Datum toDatum(Connection c) throws SQLException
{
  if (__tx!=null && __onn!=c) release();
  __onn = c;
  return _struct.toDatum(c, _SQL_NAME);
}

/* ORADataFactory interface */
public ORAData create(Datum d, int sqlType) throws SQLException
{ return create(null, d, sqlType); }
public void setFrom(AddressORAData o) throws SQLException
{ setContextFrom(o); setValueFrom(o); }
protected void setContextFrom(AddressORAData o)
  throws SQLException
{ release(); __tx = o.__tx; __onn = o.__onn; }
protected void setValueFrom(AddressORAData o) { _struct = o._struct; }
protected ORAData create(AddressORAData o, Datum d, int sqlType)
  throws SQLException
{
  if (d == null) { if (o!=null) { o.release(); }; return null; }
  if (o == null) return createFromFactory("AddressORAData", d, sqlType);
  o._struct = new MutableStruct((STRUCT) d, _sqlType, _factory);
  o.__onn = ((STRUCT) d).getJavaSqlConnection();
  return o;
}
protected ORAData createExact(Datum d, int sqlType)
  throws SQLException
{
  AddressORAData o = new AddressORAData();
  o._struct = new MutableStruct((STRUCT) d, _sqlType, _factory);
  o.__onn = ((STRUCT) d).getJavaSqlConnection();
  return o;
}
protected ORAData createFromFactory(String s, Datum d, int sqlType)
  throws SQLException
{
  String sql = ((STRUCT) d).getSQLTypeName();
```

```
    init();
    AddressORAData factory = (AddressORAData)_map.get(sql);
    if (factory == null) {
        int p;
        if ((p=sql.indexOf(".")) >= 0) {
            factory = (AddressORAData)_map.get(sql.substring(p+1));
            if (factory!=null) _map.put(sql,factory); }
        if (factory == null) throw new SQLException
            ("Unable to convert a "+sql+" to a "+s+" or a subclass of "+s);
    }
    return factory.createExact(d,sqlType);
}
/* accessor methods */
public String getLine1() throws SQLException
{ return (String) _struct.getAttribute(0); }

public void setLine1(String line1) throws SQLException
{ _struct.setAttribute(0, line1); }
```

/* Code for remaining accessor methods deleted for clarity */

```
public String getAddress ()
throws SQLException
{
    AddressORAData __jPt_temp = this;
    String __jPt_result;
    /*@lineinfo:generated-code*//*@lineinfo:169^5*/
```

/* Some generated comments deleted for clarity */

```
{
    // declare temps
    oracle.jdbc.OracleCallableStatement __sJT_st = null;
    sqlj.runtime.ref.DefaultContext __sJT_cc = getConnectionContext();
    if (__sJT_cc==null) sqlj.runtime.error.RuntimeRefErrors.raise_NULL_CONN_CTX();
    sqlj.runtime.ExecutionContext.OracleContext __sJT_ec =
((__sJT_cc.getExecutionContext()==null) ?
    sqlj.runtime.ExecutionContext.raiseNullExecCtx() :
    __sJT_cc.getExecutionContext().getOracleContext());
    try {
    String theSqlTS = "BEGIN\n        :1  :=  :2 .GET_ADDRESS();\n      END;";
    __sJT_st = __sJT_ec.prepareOracleCall(__sJT_cc,"0book.ch10.jpub.AddressORAData",
        theSqlTS);
    if (__sJT_ec.isNew())
    {
        __sJT_st.registerOutParameter(1,oracle.jdbc.OracleTypes.VARCHAR);
    }
    // set IN parameters
    if (__jPt_temp==null) __sJT_st.setNull(2,2002,"BENCHMARK.ADDRESS");
```

```
    else __sJT_st.setORAData(2,__jPt_temp);
// execute statement
  __sJT_ec.oracleExecuteUpdate();
  // retrieve OUT parameters
  __jPt_result = (String) __sJT_st.getString(1);
  } finally { __sJT_ec.oracleClose(); }
}
//    ***********************************************************

/*@lineinfo:user-code*//*@lineinfo:173^5*/
    return __jPt_result;
  }
}/*@lineinfo:generated-code*/
```

Notice that the class extends the ORAData and ORADataFactory interfaces as expected and also generates a wrapper method getAddress() for the get_address method of the address object type. The following listing shows the contents of the generated MyAddressORAData.java file (edited for clarity).

```
/*@lineinfo:filename=MyAddressORAData*//*@lineinfo:user-code*//*@lineinfo:1^1*/
package book.ch10.jpub;
/* All imports deleted for clarity */
public class MyAddressORAData extends AddressORAData
  implements ORAData, ORADataFactory
{
  private static final MyAddressORAData _MyAddressORADataFactory =
    new MyAddressORAData();
  public static ORADataFactory getORADataFactory()
  { return _MyAddressORADataFactory; }

  public MyAddressORAData() { super(); }
  public MyAddressORAData(Connection conn) throws SQLException { super(conn); }
  public MyAddressORAData(DefaultContext ctx) throws SQLException { super(ctx); }
  public MyAddressORAData(String line1, String line2, String street,
    String city, String state, String zip)
    throws SQLException
  {
    setLine1(line1);
    setLine2(line2);
    setStreet(street);
    setCity(city);
    setState(state);
    setZip(zip);
  }
  /* ORAData interface */
  protected ORAData createExact(Datum d, int sqlType)
    throws SQLException
  { return create(new MyAddressORAData(), d, sqlType); }
```

```
/* Code for accessor methods (setter and getter of various attributes)
are generated within comments by JPublisher - they have been deleted
for clarity */
   /* superclass methods */
   public String getAddress() throws SQLException
   {
     String __jRt_0 = null;
     __jRt_0 = super.getAddress();
     return __jRt_0;
   }
}/*@lineinfo:generated-code*/
```

Please note that the step of extending generated custom classes to add functionality is very similar to the same step in the case of the SQLData interface, so I don't cover it again here. Please see the corresponding step in the section "Generating Custom Classes That Implement SQLData" for further details.

Performing DMLs Using Custom ORAData Classes

In this section, we go through the steps of selecting, inserting, updating, or deleting objects using the custom classes generated as described in the previous section. The class DemoORAData illustrates these steps for us and is explained in comments interspersed within the code:

```
/** This program demonstrates how to use the Java class
* MyAddressORAData to perform DMLs.
* COMPATIBLITY NOTE: runs successfully against 10.1.0.2.0.
* and  9.2.0.1.0.
*/
import java.util.HashMap;
import java.sql.SQLException;
import java.sql.ResultSet;
import java.sql.Connection;
import java.sql.PreparedStatement;
import oracle.jdbc.OracleResultSet;
import oracle.jdbc.OraclePreparedStatement;
import book.util.JDBCUtil;
import book.ch10.jpub.MyAddressORAData;
public class DemoORAData
{
  public static void main(String[] args) throws Exception
  {
    Connection connection = null;
    try
    {
      connection = JDBCUtil.getConnection (
        "benchmark", "benchmark", "ora10g" );
```

We invoke various methods in the following code that demonstrate DML operations. Each method is explained along with its definition in detail as part of the program comments:

```
      // example demonstrating first way of selecting object - we use
      // getORAData() method of OracleResultSet.
      _demoSelectUsingGetORAData( connection );
      // example demonstrating second way of selecting object - we use
      // getObject() method of ResultSet specifying a type map.
      _demoSelectUsingGetObject( connection );
      // example demonstrating inserting object(s)
      _demoInsertUsingSetORAData( connection );
      // example demonstrating inserting object(s)- second alternative
      _demoInsertUsingSetObject( connection );
      // example demonstrating updating object(s)
      _demoUpdate( connection );
      // example demonstrating deleting object(s)
   }
   finally
   {
      JDBCUtil.close ( connection );
   }
}
```

Selecting Objects Using the getORAData() Method of OracleResultSet

The method _demoSelectUsingGetORAData() uses the method getORAData() of the OracleResultSet interface. This method signature is

```
public ORAData getORAData (int col_index, ORADataFactory factory)
```

This method takes as input the column index of the data in our result set and an ORADataFactory instance. The method _demoSelectUsingGetORAData() follows:

```
private static void _demoSelectUsingGetORAData( Connection connection)
throws SQLException
{
   PreparedStatement pstmt = null;
   OracleResultSet orset = null;
   try
   {
      String selectStmt = "select value(a) from address_table a";
      pstmt = connection.prepareStatement ( selectStmt );
      orset = (OracleResultSet) pstmt.executeQuery();
      while ( orset.next() )
      {
```

Next, we invoke the getORAData() method of the OracleResultSet interface. Notice how we invoke the static method getORADataFactory() of the generated class MyAddressORAData:

```
    MyAddressORAData address = (MyAddressORAData) orset.getORAData(1,
      MyAddressORAData.getORADataFactory() );
    System.out.println( address.getAddress() );
  }
}
finally
{
  JDBCUtil.close( orset );
  JDBCUtil.close( pstmt );
}
}
```

Selecting Objects Using the getObject() Method of ResultSet

The second option for selecting objects is to use the standard getObject(index, map) method specified by the ResultSet interface to retrieve data as instances of ORAData. In this case, we must have an entry in the type map that identifies the factory class. This becomes clearer in the definition of the method _demoSelectUsingGetObject() as follows:

```
private static void _demoSelectUsingGetObject( Connection connection)
throws SQLException, ClassNotFoundException
{
  PreparedStatement pstmt = null;
  ResultSet rset = null;
  try
  {
```

In the following code, we populate a type map that maps the address object type to the class MyAddressORAData:

```
    HashMap myMap = new HashMap();
    myMap.put( "BENCHMARK.ADDRESS",
      Class.forName(MyAddressORAData.class.getName() ) );
    String selectStmt = "select value(a) from address_table a";
    pstmt = connection.prepareStatement ( selectStmt );
    rset = pstmt.executeQuery();
    while ( rset.next() )
    {
```

When retrieving the object using the getObject() method, we also pass the type map, which informs the JDBC driver which class the object type maps to:

```
    MyAddressORAData address = (MyAddressORAData)
      rset.getObject(1, myMap );
    System.out.println( address.getAddress() );
  }
}
```

```
    finally
    {
      JDBCUtil.close( rset );
      JDBCUtil.close( pstmt );
    }
  }
```

Inserting Objects Using the setORAData() Method of OraclePreparedStatement

There are two methods to insert objects. The first uses the setORAData() method of the Oracle extension interface OraclePreparedStatement (or OracleCallableStatement). The method signature is as follows. The method takes as input the column index of the data and an ORAData instance.

```
public void setORAData (int colIndex, ORAData oradata)
```

The method _demoInsertUsingSetORAData() defined as follows uses the setORAData() method as part of the process of inserting an object into address_table. The code is fairly self-explanatory.

```
    private static void _demoInsertUsingSetORAData( Connection connection)
    throws SQLException
    {
      OraclePreparedStatement opstmt = null;
      try
      {
        MyAddressORAData myAddress = new MyAddressORAData();
        myAddress.setLine1("133 Ferry Rd");
        myAddress.setLine2( "Apt # 24");
        myAddress.setStreet( "Crypton St." );
        myAddress.setCity( "Dallas");
        myAddress.setState( "TX" );
        myAddress.setZip( "75201" );
        String insertStmt = "insert into address_table values( ? )";
        opstmt = (OraclePreparedStatement)
          connection.prepareStatement ( insertStmt );
        opstmt.setORAData (1, myAddress );
        int rows = opstmt.executeUpdate();
        System.out.println ( "Inserted " + rows + " row(s) " );
        connection.commit();
      }
      finally
      {
        JDBCUtil.close( opstmt );
      }
    }
```

Inserting Objects Using the setObject() Method of PreparedStatement

The second method involves using the standard setObject() method of the Prepared➥
Statement interface (or the CallableStatement interface), as demonstrated by the following
_demoInsertUsingSetObject() method:

```
private static void _demoInsertUsingSetObject( Connection connection)
throws SQLException, ClassNotFoundException
{
  PreparedStatement pstmt = null;
  try
  {
    MyAddressORAData myAddress = new MyAddressORAData();
    myAddress.setLine1("134 Ferry Rd");
    myAddress.setLine2( "Apt # 24");
    myAddress.setStreet( "Crypton St." );
    myAddress.setCity( "Dallas");
    myAddress.setState( "TX" );
    myAddress.setZip( "75201" );
    String insertStmt = "insert into address_table values( ? )";
    pstmt = connection.prepareStatement ( insertStmt );
    pstmt.setObject (1, myAddress );
    int rows = pstmt.executeUpdate();
    System.out.println ( "Inserted " + rows + " row(s) " );
    connection.commit();
  }
  finally
  {
    JDBCUtil.close( pstmt );
  }
}
```

Updating Objects

As in the case of a SQLData-based implementation, you update an object by selecting it into
memory, changing the in-memory Java object as required, and using the Java object to update
the object value in the database, as shown in the following code. The phenomenon of lost
updates mentioned earlier is applicable here, too; hence we use the phrase for update nowait
during the select. The rest of the code uses concepts covered in earlier chapter sections.

```
private static void _demoUpdate( Connection connection)
throws SQLException, ClassNotFoundException
{
  OraclePreparedStatement opstmt = null;
  PreparedStatement pstmt = null;
  OracleResultSet orset = null;
  try
  {
    MyAddressORAData myAddress = null;
```

```
String selectStmt = "select value(a) from address_table a"+
              " where line1 = ? for update nowait";
pstmt = connection.prepareStatement ( selectStmt );
pstmt.setString( 1, "145 Apt # 7" );
orset = (OracleResultSet) pstmt.executeQuery();
if ( orset.next() )
{
  myAddress = (MyAddressORAData) orset.getORAData(1,
    MyAddressORAData.getORADataFactory() );
  myAddress.setStreet ( "Wonderful St" );
  String updateStmt = "update address_table a" +
                " set value(a) = ?" +
                " where a.line1 = ?";
  opstmt = (OraclePreparedStatement)
      connection.prepareStatement ( updateStmt );
  opstmt.setORAData (1, myAddress );
  opstmt.setString (2, "145 Apt # 7" );
  int rows = opstmt.executeUpdate();
  System.out.println ( "Updated " + rows + " rows " );
}
connection.commit();
}
finally
{
  JDBCUtil.close( orset );
  JDBCUtil.close( opstmt );
}
}
```

Deleting Objects

There is nothing special about deleting an object. It is a simple relational statement, as illustrated in the following _demoDelete() method:

```
private static void _demoDelete( Connection connection)
throws SQLException, ClassNotFoundException
{
  PreparedStatement pstmt = null;
  try
  {
    String deleteStmt = "delete address_table a" +
                " where a.line1 like ?";
    pstmt = connection.prepareStatement ( deleteStmt );
    pstmt.setString (1, "Mountain View" );
    int rows = pstmt.executeUpdate();
    System.out.println ( "Deleted " + rows + " row(s) " );
    connection.commit();
  }
```

```
    finally
    {
      JDBCUtil.close( pstmt );
    }
  }
}
```

Now that you know how to use the SQLData interface and the Oracle extension interfaces ORAData and ORADataFactory, let's compare the two approaches.

SQLData vs. ORAData and ORADataFactory

In this section, we'll highlight the differences between the SQLData and ORAData interfaces. Note that there may be times when you have to use ORAData—for example, if you want to create a custom class for a nonstandard Oracle-specific type. In practice, there are no *major* advantages or disadvantages to using either approach.

The main advantage of using the SQLData interface, at least in theory, is that it is a JDBC standard and makes your Java code more portable across databases. However, at the time of this writing, the implementation and use of objects in different databases varies so much that the majority of such code contains vendor-dependent code anyway.

Using the ORAData and ORADataFactory interfaces, on the other hand, has the following advantages (none of which is really earth-shattering):

- The ORAData interface has more flexibility than the SQLData interface. It lets you provide a mapping between Java object types and any SQL type supported by the oracle.sql package. For example, you can use it if you want to create a custom class for a nonstandard Oracle-specific type such as oracle.sql.BFILE.

- The ORAData interface does not require a type map to map the object type to Java classes.

- According to the documentation, using the ORAData interface leads to better performance since ORAData works directly with the internal format the driver uses to hold Oracle objects. This means there is no conversion required to hold the data. The tests I conducted to verify this statement were not conclusive, as in some cases, I actually found SQLData to be faster. So my advice is that you should use this criterion for choosing between the two approaches in your application only after running appropriate benchmarks in the context of your application.

A Note on Separating Domain Objects from the Persistence Mechanism

You may have noticed that regardless of whether you use SQLData or ORAData, the code generated by JPublisher suffers from what many would justifiably consider a serious drawback. The problem is that the custom classes (which are *domain* objects—that is, objects that represent end-user business entities such as an Address, a Person, and so on) are tightly coupled with the persistence mechanism. For example, the getAddress() method in the generated domain class MyAddressAuto executes the method get_address() to retrieve the data from the database.

Even if database independence is not a goal of your design, it is a good coding practice to separate out the persistence mechanism that you use to save and retrieve your domain objects from the domain objects themselves. This is a fairly involved topic in its own right, and it's beyond the scope of this book. Many well-documented frameworks (such as the Spring framework) are available, using which this objective can be achieved.

Summary

In this chapter, you learned what strongly typed interfaces are. You examined the JDBC standard interface, SQLData, and the Oracle extension interfaces, ORAData and ORADataFactory. You learned about the various options provided by JPublisher, a utility that generates custom classes mapping SQL objects to Java for you. You also learned, through examples, how to use JPublisher to generate custom classes that implement either SQLData or ORAData interfaces that allow you to retrieve and manipulate objects stored in the database. In the next chapter, we will examine how to use collections and references in a JDBC program.

CHAPTER 11

■■■

Using Oracle Collections and References

In Chapters 9 and 10, we discussed how to query and modify Oracle objects in JDBC either as weakly typed Struct (or its Oracle implementation STRUCT) objects or as strongly typed custom classes generated by JPublisher. In this chapter, we will continue the discussion for Oracle collections and references. I provided a brief introduction to Oracle collections in the section "Collections (Nested Tables and Varrays)" of Chapter 8 of this book. As far as references go, I will give a brief introduction to them in this chapter, along with how to access them using JDBC. Very briefly, *references* are pointers to already existing rows in an object table. For more detailed background information, I encourage you to consult *Oracle Database Application Developer's Guide – Object Relational Features (10g Release 1)*.

In this chapter, following the conventions of the Oracle documentation, the term "collection" is used when discussing nested tables and varrays in the database, and the term "array" is used when discussing their manifestation in JDBC programs. An important point to note is that inside the Oracle database, there may be many differences between nested tables and varrays (as discussed in Chapter 8), but there is no difference in terms of the JDBC code that we need to write in order to access or modify them. Both nested tables and varrays map to an array in JDBC, so the same code should work for both.

This chapter examines the following topics:

- How to retrieve collections in the database as a weakly typed java.sql.Array (or its Oracle extension, oracle.sql.ARRAY) object

- How to retrieve collections as a strongly typed array of custom class objects (generated using the JPublisher utility)

- Some of the Oracle extensions designed to improve performance with suitable benchmarks

- What references are and why they should, in general, be avoided

- How to access and manipulate references from JDBC

Weakly Typed Collection Classes

A *weakly typed* collection class is a manifestation of a collection in Java in the form of the Oracle extension class `oracle.sql.ARRAY` (which also implements the standard interface `java.sql.Array`). You can retrieve a database collection of built-in types (such as a nested table of `varchar2` elements) as an `oracle.sql.ARRAY` object in Java. You can also use the `oracle.sql.ARRAY` interface to retrieve a collection of object types (e.g., a `varray` of `person` objects, where `person` is an object type you created). In such cases, the collection is retrieved as an `oracle.sql.ARRAY` of `oracle.sql.STRUCT` objects (we covered the `oracle.sql.STRUCT` class in Chapter 9).

A weakly typed collection is mainly useful when, in Java, you don't need to carry out a lot of manipulation of the array object and its elements as objects in memory. In the next two sections, we'll look at the standard `Array` interface and its Oracle implementation: the `ARRAY` class.

The java.sql.Array Interface

The `java.sql.Array` (referred to as `Array` from here onward) interface provides methods to retrieve the database collection either as a generic `Object` or as a `ResultSet` from which you can retrieve the individual elements. An important fact to remember about the `Array` interface is that it has no setter methods, meaning it can't be used to modify the collection. Some of the more commonly used methods of this interface are presented in the sections that follow with brief descriptions.

getArray()

First up is the `getArray()` method, which is used to retrieve the contents of the database object in the form of an array in the Java programming language:

```
public Object getArray() throws SQLException;
public Object getArray( Map typeMap ) throws SQLException;
public Object getArray( long index, int count ) throws SQLException;
public Object getArray( long index, int count, Map typeMap ) throws SQLException;
```

These methods use the type map associated with the connection for defining which Java classes are used to represent a collection or its elements in Java. The two methods that take a type map use the passed type map to map the elements into Java objects instead of the type map associated with the `Connection` object. In the absence of a type map, the method converts the individual elements into various standard Java classes based on Table A-1 of the Appendix. For example, the individual elements of a nested table of `varchar2` elements are converted into `String` objects. Two overloaded versions (the last two methods in the preceding list) retrieve a slice of the database collection of a given `Array` object, beginning with the specified `index` and containing up to `count` successive elements of the SQL array. Note that the elements in the slice are not in a predictable order for a nested table since a nested table, if you recall, is an unordered collection of elements.

getResultSet()

The various overloaded versions of getResultSet() method retrieve a result set that contains the elements of the database collection (either all elements or a slice of elements as specified by index and count parameters) pointed to by a given Array object.

```
public ResultSet getResultSet() throws SQLException;
public ResultSet getResultSet( Map typeMap ) throws SQLException;
public ResultSet getResultSet( long index, int count ) throws SQLException;
public ResultSet getResultSet(long index, int count, int typeMap )
  throws SQLException;
```

The ResultSet contains two columns. The first column is the index of the element, and the second column is the element itself. The classes into which individual elements are materialized are based on a type map (either supplied in an overloaded version or the default values from Table A-1 of the Appendix). Again, the overloaded methods that take a type map as a parameter (the first and the third methods in the preceding list) use the supplied type map instead of the one associated with the Connection object to deduce the Java classes into which the elements are materialized.

getBaseTypeName()

This method returns the SQL type name of the elements of this array.

```
public synchronized String getBaseTypeName();
```

The oracle.sql.ARRAY Class

The oracle.sql.ARRAY class extends the Array interface to provide many additional useful methods. Some of the commonly used methods are described here.

The createDescriptor() and getDescriptor() methods are used to create and retrieve an oracle.sql.ArrayDescriptor object of the ARRAY object.

```
public static ArrayDescriptor createDescriptor(java.lang.String sqlType,
  Connection connection) throws SQLException;
public ArrayDescriptor getDescriptor()
  throws SQLException;
```

An ArrayDescriptor object describes the SQL type of an array. Only one array descriptor is necessary for any one SQL type. The driver caches ArrayDescriptor objects to avoid re-creating them if the SQL type has already been encountered. We will look at some examples of this class shortly.

The getOracleArray() method is identical to getArray(), but it retrieves the elements in oracle.sql.* format:

```
public synchronized oracle.sql.Datum[] getOracleArray():
```

The getBaseType() method returns the SQL type code for the array elements as defined in the oracle.jdbc.OracleTypes class:

```
public synchronized int getBaseType();
```

The getSQLTypeName() method returns the fully qualified SQL type name of the array as a whole:

```
public synchronized String getSQLTypeName();
```

Strongly Typed Collection Classes

Strongly typed collection classes are custom classes (typically generated using JPublisher) that represent the elements of a collection using a specific class based on the type of elements in the corresponding database collection. Since these objects store the attributes in a more convenient form (retrievable and modifiable through individual getter and setter methods), they are more suitable in cases where you need to manipulate the array elements in memory.

Now that you understand what weakly and strongly typed collection classes are, let's take a look at how to use them in JDBC programs. In the next section, we will look at how to materialize collections consisting of built-in type elements (such as number) as weakly typed ARRAY elements.

Materializing Collections of Built-in Types As Weakly Typed Objects

In this section, we will demonstrate different ways in which you can materialize collections made of built-in types as weakly typed objects. Specifically, in our examples, we will look at two different collections:

- A varray of varchar2 elements

- A varray of number elements

Note that the same programs should also work on a nested table composed of built-in types. We first need to create our schema elements, which our example programs will then access and manipulate.

Creating the Schema for Collections of Built-in Types

In this section, we'll create the schema elements on which our example JDBC programs, demonstrating access of collections of built-in types as weakly typed objects, will work.

We begin by creating a simple varray of varchar2 elements called varray_of_varchars:

```
benchmark@ORA10G> create or replace type varray_of_varchars as
  2    varray(20) of varchar2(50);
  3  /

Type created.
```

To demonstrate access and modification of a collection containing only numbers, we next create a varray of number elements called varray_of_numbers:

```
benchmark@ORA10G> create or replace type varray_of_numbers as
  2    varray(20) of number;
  3  /
```

Type created.

We follow it up by creating a table, varchar_varray_table, that contains the varchar2 varray as a column. We also create a table, number_varray_table, that contains the number varray as a column:

```
benchmark@ORA10G> create table varchar_varray_table
  2  (
  3    varray_column varray_of_varchars
  4  );
```

Table created.
```
benchmark@ORA10G> create table number_varray_table
  2  (
  3    varray_column varray_of_numbers
  4  );
```

Table created.

To illustrate how to access and manipulate collections from Java using the CallableStatement interface, we create a package called demo_varray_pkg that contains a single procedure, demo_passing_varray_param, which takes a parameter of type varray_of_varchars:

```
benchmark@ORA10G> create or replace package demo_varray_pkg
  2  as
  3    procedure demo_passing_varray_param( p_varchar_varray
          in varray_of_varchars );
  4  end;
  5  /
```

Package created.

```
benchmark@ORA10G> create or replace package body demo_varray_pkg
  2  as
```

Inside the procedure demo_passing_varray_param(), we insert a row into the table that contains the varray column. Later we can query this table from the SQL*Plus prompt to verify that our JDBC program worked as expected.

```
 11    procedure demo_passing_varray_param( p_varchar_varray in varray_of_varchars )
 12    is
 13    begin
 14      insert into varchar_varray_table values ( p_varchar_varray );
```

```
15    end;
16  end;
17  /
```

Package body created.

We next populate the table number_varray_table with some sample data and issue a commit:

```
benchmark@ORA10G> insert into number_varray_table values(
varray_of_numbers(1, 2, 3, 4, 5) );
```

1 row created.

```
benchmark@ORA10G> commit;
```

Commit complete.

The next section describes the JDBC code to access these varray elements as weakly typed ARRAY class objects.

Manifesting Collections of Built-in Types As ARRAY Objects

In this section, we'll look at how we can retrieve a collection of built-in type as an ARRAY object. We'll first examine how to pass a varray to a PL/SQL procedure. Then we'll look at how a varray can be materialized in Java as an ARRAY of built-in types, such as String, using a PreparedStatement. Let's begin by creating and passing an ARRAY to a procedure.

Creating and Passing an ARRAY to a PL/SQL Procedure

As discussed earlier, the ARRAY class implements the standard Array interface, using which you can retrieve the entire collection, a subset of the collection, the collection name, or the base SQL type name of the collection (you'll learn more about each of these soon). However, when using the ARRAY class, you can't modify the collection in the JDBC layer, as it does not provide any "setter" methods.

Creating and passing an ARRAY to a PL/SQL procedure involves three steps:

1. *Create an* ArrayDescriptor. An ArrayDescriptor is an object of type oracle.sql.ArrayDescriptor that describes the ARRAY object. As mentioned earlier, only one array descriptor is necessary for a particular collection type. For example, you can create an array descriptor object for the varray element varray_of_varchars and reuse it as many times as you want to create different ARRAY objects of the same collection type (assuming that the definition of the underlying collection has not changed).

2. *Create an* ARRAY *object.* The next step is to create the ARRAY object that we want to pass to our procedure using the constructor whose signature follows:

   ```
   public oracle.sql.ARRAY(oracle.sql.ArrayDescriptor descriptor,
       java.sql.Connection connection, java.lang.Object arrayElements );
   ```

3. *Pass the* ARRAY *object to the procedure.* The final step is to pass the ARRAY object to the CallableStatement object using the setArray() method of the CallableStatement interface.

We illustrate each of these steps as part of the description of the class DemoPassing➥
CollectionToProcedure as follows:

```
/** This program demonstrates how to pass a collection into a
* PL/SQL procedure from JDBC.
* COMPATIBLITY NOTE:
*   runs successfully against 9.2.0.1.0 and 10.1.0.2.0
*/
import java.sql.SQLException;
import java.sql.Connection;
import java.sql.CallableStatement;
import oracle.jdbc.OracleConnection;
import oracle.sql.ArrayDescriptor;
import oracle.sql.ARRAY;
import book.util.JDBCUtil;
import book.util.Util;
class DemoPassingCollectionToProcedure
{
```

The main() method invokes the method _doPassArrayToAProcedure(), passing the
Connection object and issuing a commit. The method _doPassArrayToAProcedure() contains
the bulk of the logic:

```
  public static void main(String args[]) throws Exception
  {
    Util.checkProgramUsage( args );
    Connection conn = null;
    try
    {
      conn = JDBCUtil.getConnection("benchmark", "benchmark", args[0]);
      _doPassArrayToAProcedure( conn );
      conn.commit();
    }
    finally
    {
      // release JDBC resources
      JDBCUtil.close( conn );
    }
  }
```

The method _doPassArrayToAProcedure() is defined as follows:

```
  private static void _doPassArrayToAProcedure( Connection conn )
  throws SQLException
  {
    CallableStatement cstmt = null;
    try
    {
```

The first step is to create the array descriptor. Note that we first check if the Connection object has a descriptor already populated with an array descriptor for our varray type. If it does, we can simply reuse the returned array descriptor. If it doesn't, we create one. Please note that the method getDescriptor() is an Oracle extension method, and to access it you need to cast the Connection object to the OracleConnection interface:

```
ArrayDescriptor arrayDescriptor = (ArrayDescriptor)
  ((OracleConnection) conn).getDescriptor(
    "BENCHMARK.VARRAY_OF_VARCHARS" );
if( arrayDescriptor == null )
{
  System.out.println("creating array descriptor");
  arrayDescriptor = ArrayDescriptor.createDescriptor(
    "BENCHMARK.VARRAY_OF_VARCHARS", conn );
}
```

As part of the second step, we first create the array contents. In our case, our varray element is made up of varchar2, so the corresponding Java elements would be String objects. Thus we simply create an array of String with two elements:

```
String[] elements = new String[] { "elem 1", "elem 2" };
```

We then create the ARRAY object, initializing it with the String array we created above:

```
ARRAY array = new ARRAY ( arrayDescriptor, conn, elements );
```

The third and final step is to invoke the procedure using the CallableStatement interface. In particular, note that we use the method setArray() to pass the array value to the procedure. We could also have used the method setObject() with the same result:

```
String stmtString =
  "begin demo_varray_pkg.demo_passing_varray_param(?); end;";
cstmt = conn.prepareCall( stmtString );
cstmt.setArray( 1, array );
cstmt.execute();
}
finally
{
  JDBCUtil.close( cstmt);
}
}
}
```

Invoking the preceding class should result in the following output:

```
B:\>java DemoPassingCollectionToProcedure ora10g
URL:jdbc:oracle:thin:@(DESCRIPTION=(ADDRESS=(PROTOCOL=tcp)(PORT=1521)
(HOST=rmenon-lap))(CONNECT_DATA=(SID=ora10g)))
creating array descriptor
```

A quick select verifies that the procedure invocation was successful (recall that we inserted the passed array into the table varchar_varray_table in the procedure):

```
benchmark@ORA10G> select * from varchar_varray_table;

VARRAY_COLUMN
----------------------------------------
VARRAY_OF_VARCHARS('elem 1', 'elem 2')
```

In the next section, we examine how we can use PreparedStatement in conjunction with the ARRAY class to materialize a collection of built-in types.

Using an ARRAY Class for Accessing Collections of Built-in Types

This section shows how to select a varray of built-in data types from the database using the ARRAY class. This process involves the following steps:

1. *Prepare and execute the statement.* This is the familiar step of preparing and executing a select statement that selects the Collection object.

2. *Retrieve the ARRAY object from the* ResultSet. In this step, we use the getArray() method on the ResultSet object to retrieve the ARRAY object. Note that if no rows are selected, we get a null ARRAY object returned.

3. *Retrieve individual elements from the ARRAY object.* Finally, we retrieve individual array elements. We will demonstrate the case of retrieving the array of varchar2 (varray_of_varchars type) and array of number (varray_of_numbers) separately. To retrieve the individual collection elements, we can use either the standard method getArray() of the Array interface, or one of the two methods getResultSet() or getOracleArray() of the ARRAY class. For numeric collections, we can, in addition to the aforementioned methods, use one of the many numeric extension methods (such as getIntArray()). Choosing between these methods is, to a large extent, a matter of convenience, although there are some performance implications as well. We will examine these methods along with examples shortly.

The following sections detail each of these steps as part of the explanation of the class DemoQueryingCollectionOfBuiltInTypes presented here:

```
/** This program demonstrates how to select a collection of built-in types
* into JDBC (we use varray of varchar2 and varray of number
* to demonstrate the concepts).
* COMPATIBLITY NOTE:
*  runs successfully against 9.2.0.1.0 and 10.1.0.2.0
*/
import java.math.BigDecimal;
import java.sql.SQLException;
import java.sql.Connection;
import java.sql.PreparedStatement;
import java.sql.Types;
import java.sql.ResultSet;
```

```
import oracle.sql.ArrayDescriptor;
import oracle.sql.ARRAY;
import oracle.sql.Datum;
import oracle.sql.NUMBER;
import oracle.sql.CHAR;
import book.util.JDBCUtil;
import book.util.Util;
class DemoQueryingCollectionOfBuiltInTypes
{
```

The `main()` method first invokes two functions passing the `Connection` object. The method `_doSelectVarchar2Array()` returns an `ARRAY` of varchar2 elements, whereas the method `_doSelectNumberArray()` returns an `ARRAY` of number elements. These two methods are explained along with their definitions as part of this listing. The method `_printArrayInfo()`, invoked once each for the two returned arrays, is used to print information about the passed array object as you will see shortly.

```
  public static void main(String args[]) throws Exception
  {
    Util.checkProgramUsage( args );
    Connection conn = null;
    try
    {
      conn = JDBCUtil.getConnection("benchmark", "benchmark", args[0]);
      ARRAY varcharArray = _doSelectVarchar2Array( conn );
      ARRAY numberArray = _doSelectNumberArray(conn );
      _printArrayInfo( varcharArray );
      _printArrayInfo( numberArray );
    }
    finally
    {
      // release JDBC resources
      JDBCUtil.close( conn );
    }
  }
}
```

Retrieving a Collection of Varchar2 Elements

The method `_doSelectVarchar2Array()` demonstrates how to retrieve members of a collection of varchar2 elements from a table.

```
  private static ARRAY _doSelectVarchar2Array( Connection conn )
  throws SQLException
  {
    PreparedStatement pstmt = null;
    ResultSet rset = null;
    ARRAY array = null;
    try
    {
```

As the first step, we prepare the statement that selects the varray column of varchar2 elements from the table varchar_varray_table. We then execute the statement and obtain the ResultSet:

```
String stmtString = "select varray_column from varchar_varray_table";
pstmt = conn.prepareStatement( stmtString );
// Step 2 - execute the statement and get the result set
rset = pstmt.executeQuery();
while( rset.next() )
{
```

We then use the getArray() method of the ResultSet interface to retrieve the array. Note that alternatively we could have used the Oracle extension method getARRAY(), also in the interface OracleResultSet. That makes your code ever so slightly more dependent on the Oracle proprietary interface; otherwise, there is no difference between the two methods.

```
array =( ARRAY ) rset.getArray(1);
```

The methods _doUseGetArray(), _doUseResultSet(), and _doUseGetOracleArray() use the methods getArray() of the Array interface, getResultSet() of the Array interface, and getOracleArray() of the ARRAY class, respectively. I explain each of these methods in more detail alongside their definition shortly.

```
    _doUseGetArray( array );
    _doUseResultSet( array );
    _doUseGetOracleArray( array );
  }
}
finally
{
  JDBCUtil.close( rset);
  JDBCUtil.close( pstmt);
}
}
```

Using the Standard getArray() Method of the Array Interface

In the definition of the method _doUseGetArray(), we use the method getArray() to retrieve the collection elements. In this case, Oracle automatically converts the database collection into an array in Java, the elements of which are Java objects of types based on the conversion in Table A-1 in the Appendix. For example, in our case we have a varray of varchar2 elements, so the array itself is returned as an array of String objects. In the case of the number array, the array is returned as an array of java.math.BigDecimal objects, and so on.

```
private static void _doUseGetArray( ARRAY array )
throws SQLException
{
  System.out.println("In _doUseGetArray");
  // Since varchar2 maps by default to String,
  // we can typecast the results to a String array.
  String[] arrayInJava = (String[])array.getArray();
```

```
    for( int i=0; i < arrayInJava.length; i++ )
    {
      System.out.println(arrayInJava[i]);
    }
    System.out.println("Exiting _doUseGetArray");
}
```

Using the Oracle Extension Method getOracleArray()

When you use the Oracle extension method getOracleArray(), the elements are retrieved into an oracle.sql.Datum[] array. A Datum is an interface in the oracle.sql package that represents the SQL data type stored in Java in Oracle internal format. This interface is implemented by all oracle.sql.* classes, such as oracle.sql.CHAR, etc. This is the format in which Oracle JDBC natively retrieves the database objects. If you use these objects as is, you can avoid the overhead of converting the objects into any other form. This can lead to performance improvement, as you'll see shortly. However, keep in mind that your application may become somewhat more complex since many standard utility classes don't recognize the Oracle proprietary classes such as oracle.sql.NUMBER. For example, to work with a utility in the java.lang.Math class that takes a double, you would have to use the method doubleValue() in oracle.sql.NUMBER.

```
private static void _doUseGetOracleArray( ARRAY array )
throws SQLException
{
  System.out.println("In _doUseGetOracleArray");
  Datum[] arrayElements = (Datum[])array.getOracleArray();
  for( int i=0; i < arrayElements.length; i++ )
  {
    System.out.println((CHAR)arrayElements[i]);
  }
  System.out.println("Exiting _doUseGetOracleArray");
}
```

Using the Standard Method getResultSet()

The getResultSet() method of the standard Array interface returns a result set, each row of which contains two columns. The first column is the array object's index, and the second column is the value. In the case of varrays, the index represents the object's position in the varray; in the case of a nested table, it represents the order in which the elements were returned for a given invocation (recall that the nested table is an unordered collection). The method _doUseResultSet() illustrates this:

```
private static void _doUseResultSet( ARRAY array )
throws SQLException
{
  System.out.println("In _doUseResultSet");
  ResultSet rset = null;
  try
  {
    rset = array.getResultSet();
    while( rset.next() )
    {
```

Inside the `ResultSet` loop, the first column is the array index, and the second column is the array element—in this case, a `String` object:

```
        int index = rset.getInt( 1 );
        String stringValue = rset.getString( 2 );
        System.out.println("element number " + index + " = " + stringValue);
    }
  }
  finally
  {
    JDBCUtil.close( rset);
  }
  System.out.println("Exiting _doUseResultSet");
}
```

Retrieving a Collection of NUMBER Elements

The method `_doSelectNumberArray()` demonstrates how to select a collection of number elements.

```
private static void _doSelectNumberArray( Connection conn )
throws SQLException
{
  PreparedStatement pstmt = null;
  ResultSet rset = null;
  try
  {
```

As the first step, we prepare the statement that selects the varray column of number elements from the table `number_varray_table`. We then execute the statement and obtain the `ResultSet`:

```
        String stmtString = "select varray_column from number_varray_table";
        pstmt = conn.prepareStatement( stmtString );
        rset = pstmt.executeQuery();
        while( rset.next() )
        {
```

In the next step, we retrieve the array by using the `getArray()` method:

```
        ARRAY array = (ARRAY) rset.getArray(1);
```

To retrieve the array elements, we could have used any of the three methods discussed earlier for the case of a collection of `varchar2` collections. These methods are the standard `getArray()` method of the `Array` interface, the Oracle extension method `getOracleArray()` of the `ARRAY` class, and the `getResultSet()` method of the standard `Array` interface. If we do that, we get each array element manifested as an object of type `java.math.BigDecimal` by default. It turns out that in the case of numeric collections, the `ARRAY` class provides a fourth choice that enables us to retrieve the collection as an array of primitive Java elements. This is demonstrated when we look at the definition of the method `_doUseNumericExtensionsForNumArray()` in a moment.

```
      _doUseNumericExtensionsForNumArray( array );
    }
  }
  finally
  {
    JDBCUtil.close( rset);
    JDBCUtil.close( pstmt);
  }
}
```

Accessing a Numeric Collection As an Array of Primitive Java Elements

The ARRAY class contains methods to retrieve array elements as Java primitive elements
directly. You should use this method when you need to work with an array of primitive elements in your application (otherwise, you have to convert the obtained array into an array
of primitive elements yourself). For arrays containing numbers, Oracle recommends this
method since it yields better performance (though, in my tests at least, I was not able to see
any noticeable performance improvement when using the numeric extension methods). A
list of methods that provides you with an array of appropriate Java primitive elements in the
ARRAY interface follows:

```
public int[] getIntArray()throws SQLException
public int[] getIntArray(long index, int count) throws SQLException
public long[] getLongArray()throws SQLException
public long[] getLongArray(long index, int count) throws SQLException
public float[] getFloatArray()throws SQLException
public float[] getFloatArray(long index, int count) throws SQLException
public double[] getDoubleArray()throws SQLException
public double[] getDoubleArray(long index, int count) throws SQLException
public short[] getShortArray()throws SQLException
public short[] getShortArray(long index, int count) throws SQLException
```

In the preceding list of methods, an overloaded version of a method without any parameters gives us an entire array, whereas an overloaded version of a method with the parameters
index and count gives us a slice of the array.

The definition of the method _doUseNumericExtensionsForNumArray() demonstrates how
we can retrieve the collection number_varray as an array of int elements:

```
private static void _doUseNumericExtensionsForNumArray( ARRAY array )
  throws SQLException
{
  System.out.println("In _doUseNumericExtensionsForNumArray");
```

For retrieving the collection elements as an int array, we simply invoke the Oracle extension method getIntArray() of the ARRAY class:

```
int[] arrayInJava = (int[])array.getIntArray();
for( int i=0; i < arrayInJava.length; i++ )
{
    System.out.println(arrayInJava[i]);
}
System.out.println("Exiting _doUseNumericExtensionsForNumArray");
}
```

In the next section, we define the method _printArrayInfo() of the class DemoQuerying➥CollectionOfBuiltInTypes. This method simply prints out some metadata about the supplied ARRAY object. For example, you could use the method getArrayType() of the ArrayDescriptor class to figure out if a particular collection is a varray or a nested table in your Java code.

Retrieving Information About the ARRAY Object

The method _printArrayInfo() uses some of the Array and ARRAY methods discussed earlier to print out some useful information about a given ARRAY object.

```
private static void _printArrayInfo( ARRAY array )
    throws SQLException
{
    //print some info from array for demo
    System.out.println( "\tbase type name: " + array.getBaseTypeName() );
    System.out.println( "\tsql type name: " + array.getSQLTypeName() );
    System.out.println( "\tlength: " + array.length() );
    ArrayDescriptor descriptor = array.getDescriptor();
```

The code presented here gives you one way of finding out if the underlying collection is a nested table or a varray:

```
    if( descriptor.getArrayType() == ArrayDescriptor.TYPE_NESTED_TABLE )
    {
        System.out.println( "\tit is a nested table." );
    }
    else
    {
        System.out.println( "\tit is a varray." );
    }
}
}// end of program
```

In the next section, we examine how much you gain in terms of performance when you retrieve a numeric collection, from an ARRAY object, using the Oracle's numeric extension methods (e.g., getIntArray()) instead of methods such as getArray() and so on.

Benchmarking the Use of Numeric Extensions for Retrieving Numeric Collection Elements

In this section we take a look at how much the elapsed time improves if we use the Oracle extension methods (such as getIntArray()) instead of the three alternative data retrieval methods (getArray(), getOracleArray(), and getResultSet()). As a first step, we create the schema on which the benchmark will be run. We begin by creating a nested table of number called number_table_type:

```
benchmark@ORA10G> create or replace type number_table_type as table of number;
  2  /

Type created.
```

Next, we create a table with a column of type number_table_type:

```
benchmark@ORA10G> create table number_table_nt
  2  (
  3    nt_col number_table_type
  4  )
  5  nested table nt_col store as number_nt;

Table created.
```

We then populate the table with one row in which the nested table contains 10,000 random numbers. (For details on the function cast and the keyword multiset, please see the section "Creating a Table Containing a Column of the Varray Type" of Chapter 8.) We then commit the data and query the nested table column data to verify the number of rows in the nested table:

```
benchmark@ORA10G> insert into number_table_nt
  2  select
  3    cast
  4    (
  5      multiset
  6      (
  7        select  round( dbms_random.value(), 2)*100
  8        from all_objects
  9        where rownum <= 10000
 10      ) as number_table_type
 11    )
 12  from dual;

1 row created.

benchmark@ORA10G> commit;

Commit complete.

benchmark@ORA10G> select count(*) from number_table_nt t, table( t.nt_col) v;

     10000
```

The following BenchmarkNumericExtension class extends the JBenchmark class (covered in the section "Timing Java Programs" of Chapter 1) to perform our comparison:

```
/** This program compares the effect of using ARRAY methods
* specific to numeric collections. We compare the following
* for a numeric collection.
*     1. Using getArray()
*     2. Using getOracleArray()
*     3. Using getResultSet()
*     3. Using getIntArray()
* COMPATIBLITY NOTE:
*   runs successfully against 9.2.0.1.0 and 10.1.0.2.0
*/
import java.math.BigDecimal;
import java.sql.SQLException;
import java.sql.Connection;
import java.sql.PreparedStatement;
import java.sql.ResultSet;
import oracle.sql.ArrayDescriptor;
import oracle.sql.ARRAY;
import oracle.sql.Datum;
import book.util.JDBCUtil;
import book.util.JBenchmark;
import book.util.Util;
class BenchmarkNumericExtension extends JBenchmark
{
  public static void main(String args[]) throws Exception
  {
    Util.checkProgramUsage( args );
    Connection conn = null;
    try
    {
      conn = JDBCUtil.getConnection("benchmark", "benchmark", args[0]);
```

The method _fetchArray() retrieves the array from the database using the techniques covered earlier:

```
      ARRAY array = _fetchArray( conn );
```

We then execute the benchmark by invoking the method _runBenchmark() explained shortly:

```
      new BenchmarkNumericExtension()._runBenchmark(
        conn, new Object[] { array } );
    }
    finally
    {
      // release JDBC resources in the finally clause.
      JDBCUtil.close( conn );
    }
  }
```

The method _fetchArray() retrieves the array elements from the database using techniques we covered in earlier sections:

```
private static ARRAY _fetchArray( Connection conn )
throws SQLException
{
  PreparedStatement pstmt = null;
  ResultSet rset = null;
  ARRAY array = null;
  try
  {
    // Step 1 - prepare and execute the statement
    String stmtString = "select nt_col from number_table_nt" +
                        " where rownum <= 1";
    pstmt = conn.prepareStatement( stmtString );
    rset = pstmt.executeQuery();
    if( rset.next() )
    {
      array = (ARRAY) rset.getArray(1);
    }
  }
  finally
  {
    JDBCUtil.close( rset);
    JDBCUtil.close( pstmt);
  }
  return array;
}
```

The method _runBenchmark() invokes the method timeMethod() (inherited from the JBenchmark class) to run the benchmark for each of the four cases. The first, second, third, and fourth methods are overridden to retrieve the array elements using the getArray(), getOracleArray(), getResultSet(), and getIntArray() methods, respectively.

```
private void _runBenchmark( Connection conn, Object[] parameters )
  throws Exception
{
  timeMethod( JBenchmark.FIRST_METHOD, conn, parameters,
    GET_ARRAY_DESC );
  timeMethod( JBenchmark.SECOND_METHOD, conn, parameters,
    GET_ORACLE_ARRAY_DESC );
  timeMethod( JBenchmark.THIRD_METHOD, conn, parameters,
    GET_RESULT_SET_DESC );
  timeMethod( JBenchmark.FOURTH_METHOD, conn, parameters,
    USE_NUMERIC_EXTENSION_DESC );
}
```

We implement the first method to use getArray() method:

```
public void firstMethod( Connection conn, Object[] parameters )
  throws Exception
{
  ARRAY array = (ARRAY) parameters [0];
  int numOfRecordsRetrieved = 0;
  Object[] arrayInJava = (Object[])array.getArray();
  for( int i=0; i < arrayInJava.length; i++ )
  {
    numOfRecordsRetrieved++;
  }
}
```

We implement the second method to use the getOracleArray() method:

```
public void secondMethod( Connection conn, Object[] parameters )
throws Exception
{
  ARRAY array = (ARRAY) parameters [0];
  int numOfRecordsRetrieved = 0;
  Datum[] arrayElements = (Datum[])array.getOracleArray();
  for( int i=0; i < arrayElements.length; i++ )
  {
    numOfRecordsRetrieved++;
  }
}
```

We implement the third method to use the getResultSet() method:

```
public void thirdMethod( Connection conn, Object[] parameters )
  throws Exception
{
  ARRAY array = (ARRAY) parameters [0];
  int numOfRecordsRetrieved = 0;
  ResultSet rset = null;
  try
  {
    rset = array.getResultSet();
    while( rset.next() )
    {
      Object object = rset.getObject(1);
      numOfRecordsRetrieved++;
    }
  }
  finally
  {
    JDBCUtil.close( rset);
  }
}
```

We implement the fourth method to use the getIntArray() method of the ARRAY class:

```
public void fourthMethod( Connection conn, Object[] parameters )
  throws Exception
{
  ARRAY array = (ARRAY) parameters [0];
  int numOfRecordsRetrieved = 0;
  int[] arrayElements = (int[])array.getIntArray();
  for( int i=0; i < arrayElements.length; i++ )
  {
    numOfRecordsRetrieved++;
  }
}
private static final String GET_ARRAY_DESC = "getArray()";
private static final String GET_ORACLE_ARRAY_DESC = "getOracleArray()";
private static final String GET_RESULT_SET_DESC = "getResultSet()";
private static final String USE_NUMERIC_EXTENSION_DESC = "Numeric Extensions";
}
```

The results of running the preceding class on my PC are shown in Table 11-1.

Table 11-1. *Comparison of Different Methods for Retrieving a Numeric Collection Containing 10,000 Records*

Method Used	Elapsed Time (Milliseconds)
getArray()	9
getOracleArray()	2
getResultSet()	14
getIntArray()	13

From Table 11-1, we can conclude the following:

- In my tests, there was no noticeable performance benefit in using the numeric extension getIntArray().

- The best performance was obtained when using getOracleArray().

- The method getResultSet() was the slowest; this could be attributed to the overhead of creating and destroying the ResultSet object.

An important fact to keep in mind is that our code compared retrieving 10,000 elements from a single collection in a tight loop. This is perhaps not a typical scenario in real-life applications. Given that the difference in performance in absolute terms between all four methods is not very high, considering that we are retrieving 10,000 elements. Thus, my advice is to, in general, choose a method based on nonperformance criteria such as usability, maintainability, portability, etc., unless you can prove to yourself that performance improvement of one method over the others is substantial in your particular scenario.

That concludes our section on retrieving collection of built-in types as ARRAY objects. In the next section, we look at how we can access and manipulate a collection of object types.

Materializing Collections of Object Types

In the previous section, our collection elements were built-in types such as varchar2 or number. In this section we will deal with collections whose elements are structured types (in our case, Oracle object types). Most of the topics covered in the previous section also apply to a collection of Oracle object types; the only difference is in how the member objects materialize in Java as objects.

We'll begin by creating schema elements on which our examples will work. We'll then demonstrate how to access a collection of Oracle objects as a weakly typed STRUCT object. Finally, we'll examine how, with the help of JPublisher, we can materialize these collections as objects of strongly typed custom classes.

Creating a Schema for a Collection of Object Types

Our first step is to create a new schema consisting of a collection of object types. This time we'll use nested tables as part of our schema instead of varrays. The first step is to create an object type, address, that stores a postal address in the United States.

```
benchmark@ORA10G> create or replace type address as object
  2  (
  3     line1 varchar2(50),
  4     line2 varchar2(50),
  5     street varchar2(50),
  6     city varchar2(30),
  7     state varchar2(2),
  8     zip  varchar2(10)
  9  )
 10  /

Type created.
```

Next, we create a nested table, nested_table_of_addresses, of address objects:

```
benchmark@ORA10G> create or replace type nested_table_of_addresses as
table of address;
  2  /

Type created.
```

We follow it up by creating a table called emp_table with one of the columns, namely emp_address_list, being of the nested table type nested_table_of_addresses. The table stores employee details, including a list of addresses stored as a nested table column.

```
benchmark@ORA10G> create table emp_table
  2  (
  3      empno number,
  4      ename varchar2(50),
  5      hiredate date,
  6      emp_address_list nested_table_of_addresses
  7  )
  8  nested table emp_address_list store as emp_address_list_table;

Table created.
```

Next we insert a row into the table emp_table. We first initialize a nested table variable of type nested_table_of_addresses using the built-in Oracle constructor, and then we proceed to insert it as part of a row into the table emp_table:

```
benchmark@ORA10G> declare
  2      l_address_list nested_table_of_addresses;
  3  begin
  4      l_address_list := nested_table_of_addresses
  5                  (
  6                      address( '145 Apt # 7','', 'Wander St',
  7                              'Mountain View', 'CA', '94055' ),
  8                      address( '333 Apt # 11','', 'Wonder St',
  9                              'Cupertino', 'CA', '94666' )
 10                  );
 11      insert into emp_table values ( 1, 'King', sysdate-47*365, l_address_list );
 12      commit;
 13  end;
 14  /

PL/SQL procedure successfully completed.
```

We issue a simple select on table emp_table to have a look at the row we inserted:

```
benchmark@ORA10G> select e.empno, e.ename, e.hiredate,
  2          e.emp_address_list as emp_address_list
  3  from emp_table e;

EMPNO ENAME  HIREDATE   EMP_ADDRESS_LIST(LINE1, LINE2, STREET, C
------ ------ ---------- ----------------------------------------
     1 King   06-APR-58  NESTED_TABLE_OF_ADDRESSES(ADDRESS('145 A
                         pt # 7', NULL, 'Wander St', 'Mountain Vi
                         ew', 'CA', '94055'), ADDRESS('333 Apt #
                         11', NULL, 'Wonder St', 'Cupertino', 'CA
                         ', '94666'))
```

In the next section, we will demonstrate how to select the nested table column emp_address_list in our Java program, with each object within the collection materializing as a STRUCT object.

Accessing a Collection of Oracle Objects As STRUCT Objects

By default, if you materialize a collection of Oracle objects in JDBC, each of the individual collection elements is retrieved as an instance of the oracle.sql.STRUCT class. The STRUCT class implements the standard java.sql.Struct interface. We have already delved into the details of this class in the Chapter 9; in this section, we will look at an example demonstrating the concept.

The following Java class, DemoCollectionOfObjectTypes, demonstrates how to retrieve the nested table column values of the single row inserted in the emp_table table that we created in the previous section, with individual elements manifesting as oracle.sql.STRUCT objects.

```java
/** This program demonstrates how to select a collection of objects into
* JDBC- and how by default they materialize in Java as
* oracle.sql.STRUCT objects.
* COMPATIBLITY NOTE:
*   runs successfully against 9.2.0.1.0 and 10.1.0.2.0
*/
import java.sql.Struct;
import java.sql.SQLException;
import java.sql.Connection;
import java.sql.Array;
import java.sql.PreparedStatement;
import java.sql.Types;
import java.sql.ResultSet;
import oracle.sql.ARRAY;
import oracle.jdbc.OracleConnection;
import oracle.jdbc.OracleResultSet;
import book.util.JDBCUtil;
import book.util.Util;

class DemoCollectionOfObjectTypes
{
  public static void main(String args[]) throws Exception
  {
    Util.checkProgramUsage( args );
    Connection conn = null;
    PreparedStatement pstmt = null;
    ResultSet rset = null;
    try
    {
      conn = JDBCUtil.getConnection("benchmark", "benchmark", args[0]);
```

After getting the connection, we prepare and execute a statement that selects just the nested table column emp_address_list of the table emp_table:

```
String stmtString = "select emp_address_list from emp_table";
pstmt = conn.prepareStatement( stmtString );
// Step 2 - execute the statement and get the result set
rset = pstmt.executeQuery();
while( rset.next() )
{
```

Inside the while loop of the ResultSet interface, we get the array using the getArray() method. You can use any of the methods getArray(), getOracleArray(), or getResultSet() to retrieve individual elements as discussed in the section "Retrieving a Collection of Varchar2 Elements" earlier. We will demonstrate the methods getArray() and getResultSet() in the definition of the methods _doUseGetArray() and doUseResultSet() invoked here:

```
    Array array = rset.getArray(1);
    _doUseGetArray( array );
    _doUseResultSet( array );
  }
}
finally
{
  // release JDBC resources
  JDBCUtil.close( rset);
  JDBCUtil.close( pstmt);
  JDBCUtil.close( conn );
}
}
```

The following code defines the method _doUseGetArray(). It uses the method getArray() to retrieve an array of objects. Then it loops through each element of the array, casting it as a Struct object and printing its attributes using the getAttributes() method of the Struct interface that we covered in Chapter 9.

```
private static void _doUseGetArray( Array array )
throws SQLException
{
  System.out.println("In _doUseGetArray");System.out.flush();
  Object[] arrayInJava = (Object[])array.getArray();
  for( int i=0; i < arrayInJava.length; i++ )
  {
    Struct empStruct = (Struct) (arrayInJava[i]);
    Object[] attributes = empStruct.getAttributes();
    for( int j=0; j < attributes.length; j++ )
    {
      System.out.println(attributes[j]);
    }
    System.out.println();
```

```
  }
  System.out.println("Exiting _doUseGetArray");System.out.flush();
}
```

The method _doUseResultSet(), defined as follows, uses the method getResultSet() to retrieve a ResultSet that contains array elements. It then loops through each element of the ResultSet interface, retrieving the Struct object and then printing out each attribute of these objects.

```
private static void _doUseResultSet( Array array )
throws SQLException
{
  System.out.println("In _doUseResultSet");
  ResultSet rset = null;
  try
  {
    rset = array.getResultSet();
    while( rset.next() )
    {
      int index = rset.getInt( 1 );
      Struct empStruct = (Struct) rset.getObject( 2 );
      Object[] attributes = empStruct.getAttributes();
      for( int j=0; j < attributes.length; j++ )
      {
        System.out.println(attributes[j]);
      }
      System.out.println();

    }
  }
  finally
  {
    JDBCUtil.close( rset);
  }
  System.out.println("Exiting _doUseResultSet");
  }
}
```

Accessing a Collection of Oracle Objects Using Custom Classes

In Chapter 10, you learned how to generate custom classes for object types using the JPublisher utility. In this section, we'll examine how to use the same technique to materialize the array member objects as custom class objects. The custom classes offer you the following advantages over the weakly typed alternative (Struct class) discussed in the previous section:

- They are strongly typed, meaning that many errors are checked at compilation time instead of at runtime (e.g., if you try to pass an array of persons as an array of addresses). This is possible because each collection is converted into its own custom Java class.

- Custom collection classes (produced by JPublisher) allow you to get and set individual elements using the getElement() and setElement() methods. Recall that the ARRAY class does not provide you with any setter methods for setting an array element.

A custom class must satisfy the following requirements:

- It must implement the oracle.sql.ORAData and oracle.sql.ORADataFactory interfaces, which we covered in Chapter 10.

- It must provide a means of storing the collection data (e.g., in a member ARRAY object).

We will use JPublisher to generate these classes for the object type emp_type and our varray, emp_type_varray. Please refer to Chapter 10 for details on how to use the JPublisher utility.

We use the following properties file (called prop.txt) for our JPublisher run:

```
jpub.user=benchmark/benchmark
jpub.methods=all
jpub.builtintypes=jdbc
jpub.numbertypes=objectjdbc
jpub.usertypes=oracle
jpub.package=book.ch11.jpub
jpub.input=input.txt
```

■**Note** You may need to modify the jpub.package property to give a package name according to your directory structure; this is the package to which the generated classes belong.

The file input.txt referred to in the property jpub.input contains the following lines:

```
SQL ADDRESS AS Address
SQL NESTED_TABLE_OF_ADDRESSES AS AddressList
```

As you can see, we plan to generate a class Address for our object type address and a class AddressList for our varray emp_table.

■**Note** When you use JPublisher to create a custom collection class, you must use the ORAData implementation. This is the case if JPublisher's -usertypes mapping option is set to oracle, as is the case in this section's example (as shown by the line jpib.usertypes=oracle). You can't use a SQLData implementation for a custom collection class (such an implementation is available for a custom object class only).

Once you have set up the prop.txt and input.txt files with the preceding contents in your directory, you can generate the classes by running the JPublisher command as follows:

```
jpub -props=prop.txt
```

When I executed the preceding command, it generated the following files in my directory:
Address.java, AddressList.java, and AddressRef.java (and their class files).

We will ignore AddressRef.java for now since for our purpose, we need only the classes
Address and AddressList. The class Address corresponds to a single database address object.
The generated Java file for the Address class (edited for clarity) is as follows:

```java
package book.ch11.jpub;

/* Some imports deleted for clarity */
import oracle.sql.Datum;
import oracle.sql.STRUCT;
import oracle.jpub.runtime.MutableStruct;

public class Address implements ORAData, ORADataFactory
{
  public static final String _SQL_NAME = "BENCHMARK.ADDRESS";
  public static final int _SQL_TYPECODE = OracleTypes.STRUCT;

  protected MutableStruct _struct;

  private static int[] _sqlType = { 12,12,12,12,12,12 };
  private static ORADataFactory[] _factory = new ORADataFactory[6];
  protected static final Address _AddressFactory = new Address();

  public static ORADataFactory getORADataFactory()
  { return _AddressFactory; }
  /* constructors */
  protected void _init_struct(boolean init)
  { if (init) _struct = new MutableStruct(new Object[6], _sqlType, _factory); }
  public Address()
  { _init_struct(true); }
  public Address(String line1, String line2, String street, String city,
    String state, String zip) throws SQLException
  { _init_struct(true);
    setLine1(line1);
    setLine2(line2);
    setStreet(street);
    setCity(city);
    setState(state);
    setZip(zip);
  }
  /* ORAData interface */
  public Datum toDatum(Connection c) throws SQLException
  {
    return _struct.toDatum(c, _SQL_NAME);
  }
```

```
/* ORADataFactory interface */
public ORAData create(Datum d, int sqlType) throws SQLException
{ return create(null, d, sqlType); }
protected ORAData create(Address o, Datum d, int sqlType) throws SQLException
{
  if (d == null) return null;
  if (o == null) o = new Address();
  o._struct = new MutableStruct((STRUCT) d, _sqlType, _factory);
  return o;
}
/* accessor methods */
public String getLine1() throws SQLException
{ return (String) _struct.getAttribute(0); }

public void setLine1(String line1) throws SQLException
{ _struct.setAttribute(0, line1); }

/* accessor methods for other attributes deleted for clarity */
}
```

The generated class AddressList (edited for clarity), which represents the nested table nested_table_of_addresses, is as follows:

```
package book.ch11.jpub;

/* imports deleted for clarity */

public class AddressList implements ORAData, ORADataFactory
{
  public static final String _SQL_NAME = "BENCHMARK.NESTED_TABLE_OF_ADDRESSES";
  public static final int _SQL_TYPECODE = OracleTypes.ARRAY;

  MutableArray _array;

  private static final AddressList _AddressListFactory = new AddressList();

  public static ORADataFactory getORADataFactory()
  { return _AddressListFactory; }
  /* constructors */
  public AddressList()
  {
    this((Address[])null);
  }
  public AddressList(Address[] a)
  {
    _array = new MutableArray(2002, a, Address.getORADataFactory());
  }
  /* ORAData interface */
```

```java
public Datum toDatum(Connection c) throws SQLException
{
  return _array.toDatum(c, _SQL_NAME);
}
/* ORADataFactory interface */
public ORAData create(Datum d, int sqlType) throws SQLException
{
  if (d == null) return null;
  AddressList a = new AddressList();
  a._array = new MutableArray(2002, (ARRAY) d,
    Address.getORADataFactory());
  return a;
}
public int length() throws SQLException
{
  return _array.length();
}
public int getBaseType() throws SQLException
{
  return _array.getBaseType();
}
public String getBaseTypeName() throws SQLException
{
  return _array.getBaseTypeName();
}
public ArrayDescriptor getDescriptor() throws SQLException
{
  return _array.getDescriptor();
}

/* array accessor methods */
public Address[] getArray() throws SQLException
{
  return (Address[]) _array.getObjectArray(
    new Address[_array.length()]);
}
public Address[] getArray(long index, int count) throws SQLException
{
  return (Address[]) _array.getObjectArray(index,
    new Address[_array.sliceLength(index, count)]);
}
public void setArray(Address[] a) throws SQLException
{
  _array.setObjectArray(a);
}
public void setArray(Address[] a, long index) throws SQLException
{
```

```
    _array.setObjectArray(a, index);
  }
  public Address getElement(long index) throws SQLException
  {
    return (Address) _array.getObjectElement(index);
  }
  public void setElement(Address a, long index) throws SQLException
  {
    _array.setObjectElement(a, index);
  }
}
```

Materializing the Collection and Its Member Elements

There are two options to select a collection and its member elements when using JPublisher-generated custom classes:

- *Select the collection as an* ARRAY *object and members as custom class objects.* In the context of our example, this would imply that we would materialize the collection as an ARRAY object whose members are of class Address.

- *Select the collection and members as custom class objects.* In the context of our example, this would imply that we would materialize the collection as an AddressList object whose members consist of Address objects.

The following DemoCollectionAsCustomObjects class demonstrates both options. In addition, it demonstrates how we can add an element to the collection. We begin with the import statements and obtain the connection in the main() method:

```
/** This program demonstrates how to select a collection of objects
 *   using custom collection classes. It also demonstrates how to modify
 *   an existing collection object.
 * COMPATIBLITY NOTE:
 *   runs successfully against 9.2.0.1.0 and 10.1.0.2.0
 */
import java.util.Map;
import java.sql.SQLException;
import java.sql.Connection;
import java.sql.PreparedStatement;
import java.sql.ResultSet;
import oracle.jdbc.OracleResultSet;
import oracle.sql.ARRAY;
import book.util.JDBCUtil;
import book.util.Util;
import book.ch11.jpub.Address;
import book.ch11.jpub.AddressList;
class DemoCollectionAsCustomObjects
{
```

```
public static void main(String args[]) throws Exception
{
  Util.checkProgramUsage( args );
  Connection conn = null;
  try
  {
    conn = JDBCUtil.getConnection("benchmark", "benchmark", args[0]);
```

The method _demoSelectAsARRAYAndCustomClassObject() invoked selects the nested table itself as an ARRAY object and its members as Address object.

```
    _demoSelectAsARRAYAndCustomClassObject( conn );
```

The method _demoSelectAsCustomCollectionClass() invoked selects the nested table itself as an AddressList object and its members as Address object.

```
    _demoSelectAsCustomCollectionClass( conn );
```

The method _doInsertAnEmployeeInCollection() inserts a member in the collection class. It involves first creating a modified collection object with a new member and then updating the table with the modified collection, as you will see shortly.

```
    _doInsertAnEmployeeInCollection( conn );
    conn.commit();
  }
  finally
  {
    // release JDBC resources
    JDBCUtil.close( conn );
  }
}
```

Selecting the Collection As an ARRAY Object and Members As Custom Class Objects

To select a collection as an ARRAY object and its members as custom class objects, we need to perform the following steps:

1. Populate the type map associated with the Connection object to map the object type of the collection member to the appropriate Java class. A type map is a mapping between a database entity and a Java class object to which it should be mapped by the JDBC driver.

2. Prepare and execute the statement that selects the collection object.

3. Use the method getArray() on the ResultSet object to obtain the collection as an ARRAY object.

4. Use the method getArray() on the ARRAY object to obtain the Object array, each element of which is of the class you specified in the type map in the first step.

We will now demonstrate each of these steps as part of the definition of the method _demoSelectAsARRAYAndCustomClassObject() presented here. The method _demoSelect➥AsARRAYAndCustomClassObject() materializes the collection as an ARRAY object and its members as Address objects as follows:

```
private static void _demoSelectAsARRAYAndCustomClassObject(
  Connection conn ) throws SQLException, ClassNotFoundException
{
  PreparedStatement pstmt = null;
  ResultSet rset = null;
  try
  {
```

The first step is to add an entry to the type map of the Connection object. In this case, we specify that the database object instance of object type address should be mapped to an object of the Address class:

```
    Map map = conn.getTypeMap();
  map.put( "BENCHMARK.ADDRESS",
        Class.forName(Address.class.getName()) );
```

The next step is to prepare and execute a statement that selects the nested table column emp_address_list from the table emp_table:

```
    String stmtString = "select emp_address_list from emp_table";
    pstmt = conn.prepareStatement( stmtString );
    rset = pstmt.executeQuery();
    while( rset.next() )
    {
```

We retrieve the collection as an ARRAY object by executing the getArray() method of the ResultSet interface:

```
      ARRAY array =( ARRAY ) rset.getArray(1);
```

Finally, we retrieve the entire array as an array of Address objects by executing the method getArray() of the ARRAY object. We can then loop through this array to access individual elements and their attributes (we print only two attributes of the Address attributes for demonstration purpose):

```
      Object[] arrayInJava = (Object[])array.getArray();
      for( int i=0; i < arrayInJava.length; i++ )
      {
        Address address = (Address) arrayInJava[i];
        System.out.println( address.getLine1() );
        System.out.println( address.getState() );
      }
    }
  }
  finally
  {
```

```
        JDBCUtil.close( rset);
        JDBCUtil.close( pstmt);
    }
}
```

Selecting the Collection and Members As Custom Class Objects

In this section, we will demonstrate the steps needed to select the collection and its elements as custom class objects. Oracle does not support the method that uses type map in this scenario (it gives a ClassCastException). The only correct and supported method is to invoke the Oracle extension method getORAData(). This does not require a type map, and it requires us to perform the following steps:

1. Prepare and execute the statement that selects the collection object.

2. Use the method getORAData() of the OracleResultSet interface to obtain the collection as an object belonging to the custom class.

3. Use the method getArray() on the custom collection object to obtain the Object array, each element of which is of the custom class that represents collection member element.

We will now demonstrate each of these steps as part of the definition of the method _demoSelectAsCustomCollectionClass() presented here. The method demoSelectAsCustom➡ CollectionClass() materializes the collection as an AddressList object and its members as Address objects as follows:

```
private static void _demoSelectAsCustomCollectionClass( Connection conn )
    throws SQLException, ClassNotFoundException
{
    PreparedStatement pstmt = null;
    ResultSet rset = null;
    try
    {
```

The first step is to prepare and execute a statement that selects the nested table column emp_address_list from the table emp_table:

```
        String stmtString = "select emp_address_list from emp_table";
        pstmt = conn.prepareStatement( stmtString );
        rset = pstmt.executeQuery();
        while( rset.next() )
        {
```

We retrieve the collection as an AddressList object by executing the getORAData() method of the OracleResultSet interface:

```
            AddressList addressList = (AddressList)((oracle.jdbc.OracleResultSet)
              rset).getORAData(1, AddressList.getORADataFactory());
```

Finally, we retrieve the entire array as an array of Address objects by executing the method getArray() of the AddressList object. We can then loop through this array to access individual elements and their attributes (we print only two attributes of the Address attributes for demonstration purpose):

```
        Address[] arrayInJava = addressList.getArray();
        for( int i=0; i < arrayInJava.length; i++ )
        {
          Address emp = arrayInJava[i];
          System.out.println( emp.getLine1() );
          System.out.println( emp.getState() );
        }
      }
    }
  finally
  {
    JDBCUtil.close( rset);
    JDBCUtil.close( pstmt);
  }
}
```

Modifying the Collection by Inserting a Member

In this section, we will demonstrate how to modify the collection itself. As part of this demonstration, we will insert a member into our collection. The process of deleting a member or updating a member should involve essentially the same steps:

1. Retrieve the collection as a Java object as explained in the earlier sections.

2. Create a new member element by using an appropriate constructor of the member class.

3. Add the new member to the array.

4. Update the table with the modified collection element.

Each of these steps is detailed as part of the method _demoAddingMemberToCollection() presented here:

```
 private static void _demoAddingMemberToCollection( Connection conn )
    throws SQLException, ClassNotFoundException
 {
```

The method _addMemberToArray() performs the first three steps, as you will see, as part of its definition. We invoke this method to obtain the modified array that contains the additional address object:

```
    AddressList modifiedCollection = _addMemberToArray(conn);
```

We then prepare and execute an update statement that updates emp_table with the new collection object:

```
String stmtString = "update emp_table e set e.emp_address_list = ?";
PreparedStatement pstmt = null;
try
{
  pstmt = conn.prepareStatement( stmtString );
  pstmt.setObject( 1, modifiedCollection );
  pstmt.execute();
}
finally
{
  JDBCUtil.close( pstmt);
}
}
```

The definition of the method _addMemberToArray() follows:

```
private static AddressList _addMemberToArray( Connection conn )
  throws SQLException, ClassNotFoundException
{
```

First, we instantiate an Address object in memory:

```
Address newAddress = new Address( "1177 Monica Lane", null,
  "Cryptic St", "Los Gatos", "CA", "94877");
```

Next, we retrieve the collection object from the table using the techniques presented earlier:

```
String stmtString = "select emp_address_list " +
                    " from emp_table where empno = ?";
PreparedStatement pstmt = null;
ResultSet rset = null;
AddressList addressList = null;
try
{
  pstmt = conn.prepareStatement( stmtString );
  pstmt.setInt( 1, 1 );
  rset = pstmt.executeQuery();
  if( rset.next() ) // assume only one row is updated
  {
    addressList = (AddressList)((oracle.jdbc.OracleResultSet)
      rset).getORAData(1, AddressList.getORADataFactory());
    Address[] arrayInJava = addressList.getArray();
```

At this point, we have an array of Address objects. We simply create a new array with space for one more element, copy the older array to it, and add the new element at the end:

```
Address[] updatedEmpList = new Address[ arrayInJava.length + 1];
System.arraycopy( arrayInJava, 0, updatedEmpList, 0,
  arrayInJava.length);
updatedEmpList[ arrayInJava.length ] = newAddress;
for( int i=0; i < updatedEmpList.length; i++ )
{
  System.out.println(updatedEmpList[i].getLine1());
}
```

We set the internal array of the AddressList object by invoking the method setArray() in it, passing our modified array as the parameter:

```
addressList.setArray( updatedEmpList );

    }
  }
  finally
  {
    JDBCUtil.close( rset);
    JDBCUtil.close( pstmt);
  }
  return addressList;
  }
} // end of program
```

ARRAY Class Performance Extensions

You have already seen one of the performance extensions for numeric element arrays, where you use methods such as getIntArray() to improve performance. There are two more performance extensions in the ARRAY class that you should be aware of, and these are covered in the sections that follow.

ARRAY Automatic Element Buffering

The Oracle JDBC driver provides the following methods to enable and disable buffering of ARRAY contents:

```
public void setAutoBuffering(boolean enable);
public boolean getAutoBuffering();
```

The setAutoBuffering() method enables or disables auto-buffering, and the getAuto➥ Buffering() method returns a boolean value indicating whether auto-buffering is enabled or not. By default, auto-buffering is disabled. When you enable auto-buffering, Oracle keeps a local copy of all converted elements. This avoids the data-conversion process for the second and subsequent access of the array elements. This can lead to substantial performance improvements, as you will see shortly in the benchmark. However, be aware that this could increase consumption of memory in your JDBC applications, which could have its own impact on performance and scalability.

■**Caution** There is a bug in 10*g* Release 1 (and 9*i* Release 2), due to which if you use the numeric extension method (e.g., getIntArray()) when auto-buffering is enabled, the program can sometimes give a NullPointerException. In particular, in my tests, I was able to reproduce this bug consistently when I first used the getArray() method and then used the getIntArray() method immediately on the same array to retrieve collection elements (with auto-buffering enabled).

ARRAY Automatic Indexing

When you enable the automatic indexing on an array, Oracle maintains an index structure to improve the access time of an element.

The ARRAY class contains the following methods to support automatic array indexing:

```
public synchronized void setAutoIndexing (boolean enable, int direction)
throws SQLException;
public synchronized void setAutoIndexing(boolean enable)
throws SQLException;
```

The direction parameter gives the array object a hint. You should specify this parameter to help the JDBC driver determine the best indexing scheme. It can take the following values:

```
ARRAY.ACCESS_FORWARD
ARRAY.ACCESS_REVERSE
ARRAY.ACCESS_UNKNOWN
```

The default value for the direction parameter is ARRAY.ACCESS_UNKNOWN.

Auto-indexing is disabled by default. It makes sense to enable auto-indexing for ARRAY objects when random access of array elements may occur.

In the next section, we will benchmark the impact of auto-indexing and auto-buffering on retrieval of array objects.

Benchmarking Auto-buffering and Auto-indexing

In this section, we compare the three methods of data retrieval (getArray(), getOracleArray(), and getResultSet()) we covered earlier with and without auto-buffering and auto-indexing. Note that, unfortunately, it not easy to compare memory consumption due to the way JVM works, so we will only compare elapsed times. In real life, you should use a tool such as JProbe (see http://www.quest.com/jprobe/index.asp) to compare the memory consumption of various alternatives as well to get a more balanced perspective.

For sample data for our benchmark, we will populate the table number_varray_table we created in the section "Creating the Schema for Collections of Built-in Types" with 10,000 numbers as follows:

```
benchmark@ORA10G> declare
  2    l_varray_of_numbers varray_of_numbers;
  3  begin
  4    l_varray_of_numbers := varray_of_numbers();
  5      l_varray_of_numbers.extend(10000);
```

```
 6    for i in 1..10000
 7    loop
 8       l_varray_of_numbers( i ) := i;
 9    end loop;
10    insert into number_varray_table values( l_varray_of_numbers );
11  end;
12  /
```

PL/SQLprocedure successfully completed.

benchmark@ORA10G> commit;

Commit complete.

benchmark@ORA10G> select count(*)   varray_num_of_rows
from number_varray_table t, table(t.varray_column) n;

```
VARRAY_NUM_OF_ROWS
------------------
             10000
```

The class BenchmarkCollectionRetrievalMethods extends the class JBenchmark to compare selecting the 10,000 elements of the varray using the various methods with and without auto-buffering and auto-indexing. The class takes three arguments. The first is the database service name to which you connect, the second is a flag value (true or false) that sets the automatic buffering mode, and the third is a flag value (true or false) that sets the automatic indexing mode.

```
/** This program compares the following three approaches
 * of retrieving array elements (after you have retrieved
 * the ARRAY object from the database) with and without
 * auto-indexing and auto-buffering on.
 *
 *     1. Using getArray()
 *     2. Using getOracleArray()
 *     3. Using getResultSet()
 * COMPATIBLITY NOTE:
 *   runs successfully against 9.2.0.1.0 and 10.1.0.2.0
 */
import java.sql.SQLException;
import java.sql.Connection;
import java.sql.PreparedStatement;
import java.sql.ResultSet;
import oracle.sql.ARRAY;
import oracle.sql.Datum;
import book.util.JDBCUtil;
import book.util.JBenchmark;
class BenchmarkCollectionRetrievalMethods extends JBenchmark
{
```

```
public static void main(String args[]) throws Exception
{
  _checkProgramUsage( args );
  Connection conn = null;
  try
  {
    conn = JDBCUtil.getConnection("benchmark", "benchmark", args[0]);
```

We first invoke the method _fetchArray(), which retrieves the array from the database using techniques covered earlier:

```
    ARRAY array = _fetchArray( conn );
```

We then set the auto-buffering and auto-indexing flag based on the values passed at the command line:

```
    array.setAutoBuffering( autoBufferingFlag );
    array.setAutoIndexing( autoIndexingFlag );
```

To identify which option we are running, we create a description of the option we chose (the setting of auto-buffering and auto-indexing). We will pass this to the individual methods we invoke later.

```
    String optionsDesc = " AutoBuffering: " + autoBufferingFlag +
                         " AutoIndexing: " + autoIndexingFlag;
```

Recall that auto-indexing makes sense only if the array members are being accessed randomly. To do that, we create 10,000 random indexes that range from 0 to 9999. We use the method random() in the java.lang.Math class to generate a number greater than or equal to 0.00 but less than 1.00. We multiply it by 9999 and then truncate it to an int to get random numbers within our desired range. We store these numbers in an int array.

```
    int[] indexes = new int[ 10000 ];
    for( int i=0; i < 10000; i++ )
    {
      int randomNumber = (int)(Math.random()* 9999);
      indexes[i] = randomNumber;
    }
```

We then invoke the method _runBenchmark(), passing the relevant information as parameters:

```
    new BenchmarkCollectionRetrievalMethods()._runBenchmark(
      conn, new Object[] { array, indexes }, optionsDesc );
  }
  finally
  {
    // release JDBC resources in the finally clause.
    JDBCUtil.close( conn );
  }
}
```

The method fetchArray() simply retrieves our varray collection as an ARRAY object using techniques we have already covered:

```
private static ARRAY _fetchArray( Connection conn )
throws SQLException
{
  PreparedStatement pstmt = null;
  ResultSet rset = null;
  ARRAY array = null;
  try
  {
    // Step 1 - prepare and execute the statement
    String stmtString = "select varray_column from number_varray_table" +
                        " where rownum <= 1";
    pstmt = conn.prepareStatement( stmtString );
    rset = pstmt.executeQuery();
    if( rset.next() )
    {
      array = (ARRAY) rset.getArray(1);
    }
  }
  finally
  {
    JDBCUtil.close( rset);
    JDBCUtil.close( pstmt);
  }
  return array;
}
```

The method _runBenchmark() simply invokes the method timeMethod() inherited from the JBenchmark class, passing in the relevant information to the method:

```
private void _runBenchmark( Connection conn,
  Object[] parameters, String optionsDesc)
  throws Exception
{
  timeMethod( JBenchmark.FIRST_METHOD, conn, parameters,
    GET_ARRAY_DESC + optionsDesc );
  timeMethod( JBenchmark.SECOND_METHOD, conn, parameters,
    GET_ORACLE_ARRAY_DESC + optionsDesc );
  timeMethod( JBenchmark.THIRD_METHOD, conn, parameters,
    GET_RESULT_SET_DESC + optionsDesc );
}
```

We override the first method to use the method getArray() of the ARRAY class. Notice how we retrieve each object based on the random indexes we generated in the int array:

```
public void firstMethod( Connection conn, Object[] parameters )
  throws Exception
```

```
{
  ARRAY array = (ARRAY) parameters [0];
  int[] indexes = (int[]) parameters [1];
  Object[] arrayInJava = (Object[])array.getArray();
  Object arrayElement = null;
  int i=0;
  for( i=0; i < arrayInJava.length; i++ )
  {
    arrayElement = arrayInJava[ indexes[i] ];
  }
}
```

We override the second method to use the method getOracleArray() of the ARRAY class. Again, we retrieve each object based on the random indexes we generated in the int array:

```
public void secondMethod( Connection conn, Object[] parameters )
  throws Exception
{
  ARRAY array = (ARRAY) parameters [0];
  int[] indexes = (int[]) parameters [1];
  Datum[] arrayElements = (Datum[])array.getOracleArray();
  int i=0;
  Object arrayElement = null;
  for( i=0; i < arrayElements.length; i++ )
  {
    arrayElement = arrayElements[ indexes[i] ];
  }
}
```

We override the third method to use the method getResultSet() of the ARRAY class. In this case, since the ResultSet does not allow us to index into an array element, we just retrieve the objects in sequence. Perhaps an improvement on the benchmark would be to use the positioning methods of the ResultSet interface to actually position the cursor on an element and then retrieve it.

```
public void thirdMethod( Connection conn, Object[] parameters )
  throws Exception
{
  ARRAY array = (ARRAY) parameters [0];
  int numOfRecordsRetrieved = 0;
  ResultSet rset = null;
  try
  {
    rset = array.getResultSet();
    while( rset.next() )
    {
      Object arrayElement = rset.getObject(2);
      numOfRecordsRetrieved++;
    }
```

```
    }
    finally
    {
      JDBCUtil.close( rset);
    }
  }
```

The method _checkProgramUsage() simply sets global variables based on passed command-line parameters. These global variables indicate if auto-indexing and auto-buffering are enabled or disabled for a given run:

```
  private static void _checkProgramUsage( String[] args )
  {
    if( args.length != 1 && args.length != 2 &&
        args.length != 3 )
    {
      System.out.println(
        "Usage: java <program_name> <database_name> [true|false][true|false]."
        + " The second parameter (optional) sets the autobuffering
 mode on or off"
        + " The third parameter (optional) sets the autoindexing mode
 on or off");
      System.exit(1);
    }
    if( args.length >= 2 )
    {
      autoBufferingFlag = Boolean.valueOf( args[1] ).booleanValue();
    }
    if( args.length == 3 )
    {
      autoIndexingFlag = Boolean.valueOf( args[2] ).booleanValue();
    }
    System.out.println( "auto buffering flag: " + autoBufferingFlag );
    System.out.println( "auto indexing flag: " + autoIndexingFlag );
  }
  private static boolean autoBufferingFlag = false;
  private static boolean autoIndexingFlag = false;
  private static final String GET_ARRAY_DESC = "getArray()";
  private static final String GET_ORACLE_ARRAY_DESC = "getOracleArray()";
  private static final String GET_RESULT_SET_DESC = "getResultSet()";
}
```

Table 11-2 shows the elapsed times for these three methods with auto-indexing and auto-buffering disabled.

Table 11-2. *Comparing* getArray(), getOracleArray(), *and* getResultSet() *Methods for Different Combinations of Auto-indexing and Auto-buffering*

Method to Retrieve 10,000 Elements	Auto-buffering On?	Auto-indexing On?	Average Elapsed Time (Milliseconds)
getArray()	No	No	6
getOracleArray()	No	No	2
getResultSet()	No	No	19
getArray()	No	Yes	9
getOracleArray()	No	Yes	4
getResultSet()	No	Yes	21
getArray()	Yes	No	0
getOracleArray()	Yes	No	0
getResultSet()	Yes	No	7
getArray()	Yes	Yes	0
getOracleArray()	Yes	Yes	0
getResultSet()	Yes	Yes	7

From the information in Table 11-2, we can make the following observations:

- Auto-buffering seems to make a tremendous difference. Notice how the elapsed time is 0 milliseconds (approximately) for the case of getArray() and getOracleArray() when auto-buffering is turned on. Remember, though, that this performance improvement comes at the cost of increased memory consumption.

- Auto-indexing does not seem to make a lot of difference. In fact, when it is turned on, performance goes down slightly (see rows 4 to 6 as compared to rows 1 to 3 in Table 11-2). This is presumably because of the overhead of creating the index structure when auto-indexing is turned on.

- getArray() and getOracleArray() fare better in general, as compared to getResultSet() (presumably because of the overhead in creating and destroying the ResultSet data structure).

With those observations, we conclude our discussions on collections. In the next section, we'll walk through an introduction to references and examine how to access and manipulate references using the JDBC API.

References

A *reference* in Oracle is a pointer to an already existing object row in a table. This section presents a brief introduction to references. We will then discuss how we can access and manipulate data using references in JDBC.

■**Note** For more background on references, I refer you to *Oracle Database Application Developer's Guide – Object Relational Features (10g Release 1)*.

A Brief Introduction to References

Let's begin by creating an object type containing a reference:

```
benchmark@ORA10G> create type emp_ref_type as object
  2  (
  3      emp_no number,
  4      name varchar2(20),
  5      manager ref emp_ref_type
  6  );
  7  /

Type created.
```

As shown, we have an object type emp_ref_type with the attribute manager (shown in bold) as a reference of type emp_ref_type. This means that the manager attribute can hold a reference to (or point to) a row of type emp_ref_type in a table.

Next, we create a table of this reference type and insert the first row corresponding to the CEO of the company, Larry. Notice that the value corresponding to the reference column manager is null, as this is the only row in the table at this point of time and a reference has to point to an *existing* table row. In other words, no one else manages Larry!

```
benchmark@ORA10G> create table emp_table_with_ref of emp_ref_type;

Table created.

benchmark@ORA10G> insert into emp_table_with_ref values( 1, 'Larry', null );

1 row created.
```

Now, we will add a second row for an employee named John, who works for Larry. The manager reference corresponding to John's row in the table points to Larry's row in the table. Notice how we create an object of type emp_ref_type and initialize the manager attribute by using the function ref(). The ref() function takes as its argument a table alias associated with a row of an object table or an object view, and returns a ref value for the object that is bound to the table row.

```
benchmark@ORA10G> insert into emp_table_with_ref
  2  select emp_ref_type( 2, 'John', ref(e))
  3  from emp_table_with_ref e
  4  where emp_no = 1;

1 row created.
```

Let's add another employee by the name of Jack, who works for John, and commit the data:

```
benchmark@ORA10G> insert into emp_table_with_ref
  2  select emp_ref_type( 3, 'Jack', ref(e))
  3  from emp_table_with_ref e
  4  where emp_no = 2;

1 row created.

benchmark@ORA10G> commit;

Commit complete.
```

A simple `select *` on the table `emp_table_with_ref` shows the following rows:

```
benchmark@ORA10G> select * from emp_table_with_ref;
EMP_NO NAME   MANAGER
------- ----- -----------------------------------------
      1 Larry
      2 John   0000220208529852ACD8C148BE9BE6A27D01FDA6
               5EF5DECA545DC24435820B9DB4F9A2BCD0
      3 Jack   00002202089B3B1CBC855A4038B15A4BE9788105
               E4F5DECA545DC24435820B9DB4F9A2BCD0
```

The value shown in the `manager` column of type `emp_ref_type` is the object ID of the reference value. The following `select` shows how to dereference the reference to get the underlying values by using the function `deref()` on the result of the `value()` function. The `value()` function takes as its argument a table alias associated with a row of an object table and returns object instances stored in the object table. The function `deref()` returns the object reference of its argument, which must return a `ref` to an object. The following query selects the manager of the employee Jack:

```
benchmark@ORA10G> select value(e).name Name, deref(value(e).manager) Manager
  2  from emp_table_with_ref e
  3  where e.name = 'Jack';

NAME   MANAGER(EMP_NO, NAME, MANAGER)
-----  ------------------------------------
Jack   EMP_REF_TYPE(2, 'John', 0000220208B40B43
       4961904E44AF83AC8FEE99EECEE983C5A859704C
       F6889D35D3862EDB06)
```

In the next section, we discuss an important issue related to *dangling references* (references that point to a row that has been deleted) and how to overcome it.

Dangling References and Data Integrity

The schema created in the preceding section can result in what are known as dangling references. A dangling reference is a pointer that points to a row that has been deleted. Having dangling references can thus result in data integrity issues with some of the references in your schema pointing to nonexistent rows.

For example, we can delete the record corresponding to John, even though the employee under him (Jack) still exists in the table:

```
benchmark@ORA10G> delete from emp_table_with_ref e
  2  where e.name = 'John';

1 row deleted.
```

The following query confirms that the reference in the row corresponding to Jack is now gone:

```
benchmark@ORA10G> select value(e).name Name, deref(value(e).manager) Manager
  2  from emp_table_with_ref e
  3  where e.name = 'Jack';

NAME   MANAGER(EMP_NO, NAME, MANAGER)
-----  ----------------------------------------
Jack
```

In fact, Oracle provides a way to select dangling references by using the is dangling (or the opposite version, is not dangling) predicate in where clause as follows:

```
benchmark@ORA10G> select value(e).name Name, deref(value(e).manager) Manager
  2  from emp_table_with_ref e
  3  where e.name = 'Jack'
  4    and value(e).manager is not dangling;

no rows selected
```

However, the best thing to do if you use references is to create a referential integrity constraint (a foreign key) and avoid dangling references in your application. To illustrate this, we drop the table emp_table_with_ref and re-create it as follows (notice the references clause, shown in bold, that creates the constraint):

```
benchmark@ORA10G> create table emp_table_with_ref of emp_ref_type
  2  ( manager references emp_table_with_ref );

Table created.
```

If we now repopulate the table with the same data and try to delete the row corresponding to John, we get the following error:

```
benchmark@ORA10G> delete from emp_table_with_ref e
  2  where e.name = 'John';
delete from emp_table_with_ref e
*
```

```
ERROR at line 1:
ORA-02292: integrity constraint (BENCHMARK.SYS_C006564) violated -
child record found
```

If you use references, you should always create a referential integrity constraint as just shown to avoid the problem of dangling references in your application data.

■Tip Always create a referential integrity constraints for any reference columns you use in your schema to avoid dangling references and the resulting data integrity issues.

Reasons for Not Using References

There are many reasons why you should avoid references, in general. Since references ultimately point to object rows in tables, all the reasons to avoid objects as a storage mechanism are applicable to references as well (as discussed in the section "Using Objects to Store Data [Not Recommended]" of Chapter 8). The following are some additional reasons for you to consider:

- References can complicate your code considerably. For example, if you want to write a hierarchical query that retrieves all child and parent records in a table, you can do so easily using the connect by clause for a traditional parent/child table. But if you use references instead, you will have to dereference each record separately, resulting in complicated and slow code.

- References result in extra information being stored in tables (see the section "Storage Size of Refs" in Chapter 8 of *Oracle Database Application Developer's Guide – Object Relational Features (10g Release 1)*. This takes up extra space, which you can avoid by adopting a design that uses simple parent/child relational tables.

- Performing DML operations with references can be complex and result in slow-running code, as you'll see shortly.

- In return for all the complexity and performance degradation, you don't get any particular benefit when using references.

That discussion concludes the brief introduction to references. Even though references are not a very useful feature for the reasons mentioned in this section, we'll cover JDBC access techniques for completeness and so that you can deal with them if you encounter them in code. In the next section, we'll examine how you can use references in your JDBC code.

Using References in JDBC

As in the case of object types and collections, Oracle gives you the option of using weakly typed reference classes (java.sql.Ref or oracle.sql.REF) in your JDBC application. You can also use custom classes created by the now familiar utility JPublisher. In the next two sections we'll look at both options. We'll begin with a discussion of how to use weakly typed Ref and REF interfaces to query references in your JDBC programs.

The Ref Interface and REF Class

The Ref interface is implemented (partially, as you will soon discover) and extended by the Oracle class oracle.sql.REF. The Ref interface consists of the following methods.

The following method gets the fully qualified base SQL name of the object type to which the reference points (e.g., BENCHMARK.EMP_REF_TYPE):

```
public String getBaseTypeName() throws SQLException;
```

The following method retrieves the SQL object type referenced by this Ref object:

```
public String getObject() throws SQLException;
```

If the connection's type map has an entry for the structured type, the instance will be custom-mapped to the Java class indicated in the type map. Otherwise, the structured type instance will be mapped to a Struct object. As you will see, this method does not work for Oracle 10*g* Release 1 or Oracle9*i* Release 2. Instead, you have to use the Oracle proprietary method get➡Value(), which is available in the REF class that extends the Ref interface.

The following method retrieves the referenced object and maps it to a Java type based on the supplied type map:

```
public String getObject( Map typeMap ) throws SQLException;
```

The following method sets the value pointed to by this Ref object to the supplied object:

```
public String setObject( Object refObject ) throws SQLException;
```

The REF class in the oracle.sql package implements the Ref interface partially and adds many proprietary methods. Some of the more commonly used methods are

```
public String getValue() throws SQLException;
public String getValue( Map typeMap ) throws SQLException;
```

As mentioned in the Ref section, the method getObject() in Oracle does not work as yet; it gives the unsupported feature exception. Instead, you need to use the REF counterpart getValue() or its overloaded version, which provides the same functionality.

In the next section, we provide an example of how to query and update Ref objects.

Using Weakly Typed Ref and REF Objects to Query References

The program DemoQueryAndUpdateUsingWeaklyTypedRefs demonstrates how to query or update reference objects from JDBC. The program begins with the import statements and obtaining the connection in the main() method as follows:

```
/** This program demonstrates how to
*    1. query a ref object
*    2. dereference it to get its value
*    3. update its value and store it back in the database
* COMPATIBLITY NOTE:
*    runs successfully against 9.2.0.1.0 and 10.1.0.2.0
*/
import java.sql.SQLException;
import java.sql.Connection;
```

```
import java.sql.PreparedStatement;
import java.sql.Ref;
import java.sql.ResultSet;
import oracle.sql.STRUCT;
import book.util.JDBCUtil;
import book.util.Util;
class DemoQueryAndUpdateUsingWeaklyTypedRefs
{
  public static void main(String args[]) throws SQLException
  {
    Util.checkProgramUsage( args );
    Connection conn = null;
    try
    {
      conn = JDBCUtil.getConnection("benchmark", "benchmark", args[0]);
```

The method _doSelectRef() demonstrates how to select a Ref object:

```
      _doSelectRef( conn );
```

The method _doUpdateRef() demonstrates how to update a Ref object so that it points to a different row after the update:

```
      _doUpdateRef( conn );
    }
    finally
    {
      // release resources associated with JDBC
      // in the finally clause.
      JDBCUtil.close( conn );
    }
  }
}
```

Querying a Ref Object

The method _doSelectRef() is defined as follows:

```
  private static void _doSelectRef( Connection conn )
    throws SQLException
  {
```

We define a query statement that selects all columns of the table emp_table_with_ref including the reference column manager:

```
    String stmtString = "select e.emp_no, e.name, e.manager" +
                        " from emp_table_with_ref e";
    PreparedStatement pstmt = null;
    ResultSet rset = null;
    try
    {
```

```
pstmt = conn.prepareStatement( stmtString );
rset = pstmt.executeQuery();
System.out.println("executed query");
while(rset.next())
{
```

We retrieve and print out the values in the columns emp_no and name first:

```
int empNo = rset.getInt( 1 );
String name = rset.getString( 2 );
System.out.println("emp no : " + empNo );
System.out.println("emp name : " + name );
```

We then use the method getRef() in the ResultSet interface to retrieve the reference object:

```
Ref managerRef = rset.getRef( 3 );
```

Next, we retrieve the object pointed to by the reference object. Since there is no type map specified, we will get the value as a STRUCT object. Note that the record corresponding to the top-level employee (Larry) has a null reference, so we need to check for that condition.

```
if( managerRef != null )
{
```

We print out the SQL object base type of this reference object:

```
System.out.println( "Reference SQL Type: " +
  managerRef.getBaseTypeName() );
```

As mentioned earlier, the getObject() method of java.sql.Ref interface gives an unsupported feature exception when working with either 9*i* Release 2 or 10*g* Release 1 databases. Hence, we have to use the getValue() method of the REF class:

```
// The following gives an Unsupported feature in 9i and 10g
//STRUCT manager = (STRUCT) ((oracle.sql.REF)managerRef).getObject();
STRUCT manager = (STRUCT) ((oracle.sql.REF)managerRef).getValue();
```

In the remainder of the method, we simply use the getAttributes() method of the Struct interface to print out the attribute values of the object to which the reference points:

```
Object attributes[] = manager.getAttributes();
System.out.println("no of manager attributes : " +
  attributes.length );
for(int i=0; i < attributes.length; i++ )
{
  if( attributes[i] != null )
  {
    System.out.println("\tattribute # " + i + " class name " +
      attributes[i].getClass().getName() + " value " +
      attributes[i]);
  }
```

```
        }
      }
    }
  }
  finally
  {
    JDBCUtil.close( rset);
    JDBCUtil.close( pstmt);
  }
}
```

Updating a Ref Object

Updating a Ref object simply means making it point to a different row in the table. The follow-ing _doUpdateRef() method does that by first invoking the method _getRefForUpdate() to retrieve the Ref object and then invoking the method _updateEmployeeRef() to update the reference object in the table:

```
private static void _doUpdateRef( Connection conn )
  throws SQLException
{
  Ref newManagerRef = _getRefForUpdate( conn, 1 );
  _updateEmployeeRef( conn, 3, newManagerRef );
  conn.commit();
}
```

The definition of the method _getRefForUpdate() basically is the same as that of the method _doSelectRef() covered in section "Querying a Ref Object" earlier. The only difference is that it uses the for update nowait clause to lock the row so that another session does not update the same row before we complete our update. This problem, known as the *lost update* problem, along with its suggested solutions, is discussed in detail in Chapter 16.

```
private static Ref _getRefForUpdate( Connection conn, int empNo )
  throws SQLException
{
  String stmtString =
    "select ref(e) " +
    " from emp_table_with_ref e " +
    " where e.emp_no = ? for update nowait";
  PreparedStatement pstmt = null;
  ResultSet rset = null;
  try
  {
    pstmt = conn.prepareStatement( stmtString );
    pstmt.setInt( 1, empNo );
    rset = pstmt.executeQuery();
    Ref managerRef = null;
    if(rset.next()) // only one row expected
    {
```

```
      managerRef = rset.getRef( 1 );
    }
    return managerRef;
  }
  finally
  {
    JDBCUtil.close( rset);
    JDBCUtil.close( pstmt);
  }
}
```

The method _updateEmployeeRef() takes the selected reference object and performs the actual update:

```
private static void _updateEmployeeRef( Connection conn, int empNo,
  Ref newManagerRef ) throws SQLException
{
```

The statement string for the update simply sets the reference column manager to the passed value. Later, we use the method setRef() of the PreparedStatement interface to carry out the actual update. In this case, we effectively change the data so that Jack reports directly to Larry instead of reporting to John (a huge promotion, considering Larry is the CEO!).

```
String updateStmtString =
    "update emp_table_with_ref e" +
    " set e.manager = ?" +
    " where e.emp_no = ?";
PreparedStatement pstmt = null;
try
{
  pstmt = conn.prepareStatement( updateStmtString );
  pstmt.setRef( 1, newManagerRef );
  pstmt.setInt( 2, empNo );
  pstmt.execute();
}
finally
{
  JDBCUtil.close( pstmt);
}
}
} // end of program
```

That wraps up our discussion of weakly typed Ref objects. In the next section, we look at how to use custom reference classes to query and update references.

Using Strongly Typed Custom Classes to Query References

As you may have guessed by now, we will use the JPublisher utility (see Chapter 7 for details on how to use this utility) to generate the custom classes for our reference objects.

A custom reference class must satisfy the following requirements:

- It must implement the `oracle.sql.ORAData` and `oracle.sql.ORADataFactory` interfaces.

- It must provide a way to refer to the underlying object's data (JPublisher does this by using an underlying `REF` attribute).

As in the case of collection classes, the standard `SQLData` interface supports only SQL object mappings; it does not support mappings for reference objects. Thus, if you instruct JPublisher to implement the standard `SQLData` interface in creating a custom object class, it will not generate a custom reference class. You must use the `ORAData` implementation for this purpose.

Generating Custom REF Classes Using JPublisher

In this section, we will use the JPublisher utility to generate the reference classes for the object type `emp_ref_type`. We will use the following properties file (called `prop.txt`) for this purpose:

```
jpub.user=benchmark/benchmark
jpub.methods=all
jpub.builtintypes=jdbc
jpub.numbertypes=objectjdbc
jpub.usertypes=oracle
jpub.package=book.ch08.ref.jpub
jpub.input=input.txt
```

Note that you may need to modify the `jpub.package` property to give a package name according to your directory structure; this is the package to which the generated classes belong.

The file `input.txt` referred to in the property `jpub.input` contains the following line:

```
SQLEMP_TYPE AS Employee
```

As you can see, we plan to generate a class `Employee` for our object type `emp_ref_type`. JPublisher will also generate the employee reference class (called `EmployeeRef`) automatically.

We finally generate the custom reference classes by running the following command:

```
Jpub -props=prop.txt
```

The following listing shows the generated code (edited for clarity) for the EmployeeRef class:

```
package book.ch11.ref.jpub;

/* imports deleted for clarity and conciseness */

public class EmployeeRef implements ORAData, ORADataFactory
{
  public static final String _SQL_BASETYPE = "BENCHMARK.EMP_REF_TYPE";
  public static final int _SQL_TYPECODE = OracleTypes.REF;

  REF _ref;

  private static final EmployeeRef _EmployeeRefFactory = new EmployeeRef();

  public static ORADataFactory getORADataFactory()
  { return _EmployeeRefFactory; }
  /* constructor */
  public EmployeeRef()
  {
  }


  /* ORAData interface */
  public Datum toDatum(Connection c) throws SQLException
  {
    return _ref;
  }


  /* ORADataFactory interface */
  public ORAData create(Datum d, int sqlType) throws SQLException
  {
    if (d == null) return null;
    EmployeeRef r = new EmployeeRef();
    r._ref = (REF) d;
    return r;
  }

  public static EmployeeRef cast(ORAData o) throws SQLException
  {
    if (o == null) return null;
    try { return (EmployeeRef) getORADataFactory().create(
      o.toDatum(null), OracleTypes.REF); }
    catch (Exception exn)
    { throw new SQLException("Unable to convert "+
      o.getClass().getName()+" to EmployeeRef: "+exn.toString()); }
}
```

```
  public Employee getValue() throws SQLException
  {
     return (Employee) Employee.getORADataFactory().create(
       _ref.getSTRUCT(), OracleTypes.REF);
  }

  public void setValue(Employee c) throws SQLException
  {
    _ref.setValue((STRUCT) c.toDatum(_ref.getJavaSqlConnection()));
  }
}
```

The following listing shows the generated Employee class (edited for clarity):

```
package book.ch11.ref.jpub;

/* imports deleted for clarity and conciseness */

public class Employee implements ORAData, ORADataFactory
{
  public static final String _SQL_NAME = "BENCHMARK.EMP_REF_TYPE";
  public static final int _SQL_TYPECODE = OracleTypes.STRUCT;

  protected MutableStruct _struct;

  private static int[] _sqlType = { 2,12,2006 };
  private static ORADataFactory[] _factory = new ORADataFactory[3];
  static
  {
    _factory[2] = EmployeeRef.getORADataFactory();
  }
  protected static final Employee _EmployeeFactory = new Employee();

  public static ORADataFactory getORADataFactory()
  { return _EmployeeFactory; }
  /* constructors */
  protected void _init_struct(boolean init)
  { if (init) _struct = new MutableStruct(new Object[3], _sqlType, _factory); }
  public Employee()
  { _init_struct(true); }
  public Employee(java.math.BigDecimal empNo, String name,
    EmployeeRef manager) throws SQLException
  { _init_struct(true);
    setEmpNo(empNo);
    setName(name);
    setManager(manager);
  }
```

```
   /* ORAData interface */
   public Datum toDatum(Connection c) throws SQLException
   {
     return _struct.toDatum(c, _SQL_NAME);
   }


   /* ORADataFactory interface */
   public ORAData create(Datum d, int sqlType) throws SQLException
   { return create(null, d, sqlType); }
   protected ORAData create(Employee o, Datum d, int sqlType) throws SQLException
   {
     if (d == null) return null;
     if (o == null) o = new Employee();
     o._struct = new MutableStruct((STRUCT) d, _sqlType, _factory);
     return o;
   }
   /* accessor methods */
   public java.math.BigDecimal getEmpNo() throws SQLException
   { return (java.math.BigDecimal) _struct.getAttribute(0); }

   public void setEmpNo(java.math.BigDecimal empNo) throws SQLException
   { _struct.setAttribute(0, empNo); }

   public String getName() throws SQLException
   { return (String) _struct.getAttribute(1); }

   public void setName(String name) throws SQLException
   { _struct.setAttribute(1, name); }

   public EmployeeRef getManager() throws SQLException
   { return (EmployeeRef) _struct.getAttribute(2); }

   public void setManager(EmployeeRef manager) throws SQLException
   { _struct.setAttribute(2, manager); }
}
```

Using Custom Classes to Query and Update Reference Objects

The following code listing is for the class DemoCustomRefQueryAndUpdate. It shows how to use the EmployeeRef and Employee classes to query and update the reference objects. I provided explanatory comments within the code where required.

```
/** This program demonstrates how, using custom classes, you can
*     1. query a ref object
*     2. dereference it to get its value
*     3. update its value and store it back in the database
* COMPATIBLITY NOTE:
*   runs successfully against 9.2.0.1.0 and 10.1.0.2.0
```

```
*/
import java.sql.SQLException;
import java.sql.Connection;
import java.sql.PreparedStatement;
import java.sql.Ref;
import oracle.jdbc.OracleConnection;
import oracle.jdbc.OracleResultSet;
import book.util.JDBCUtil;
import book.util.Util;
import book.ch11.ref.jpub.Employee;
import book.ch11.ref.jpub.EmployeeRef;
class DemoCustomRefQueryAndUpdate
{
  public static void main(String args[]) throws SQLException
  {
    Util.checkProgramUsage( args );
    Connection conn = null;
    try
    {
      conn = JDBCUtil.getConnection("benchmark", "benchmark", args[0]);
```

The method _doSelectRef() demonstrates how to select a Ref object:

```
      _doSelectRef( conn );
```

The method _doUpdateRef() demonstrates how to update a Ref object so that it points to a different row after the update:

```
      _doUpdateRef( conn );
    }
    finally
    {
      // release JDBC resources in the finally clause.
      JDBCUtil.close( conn );
    }
  }
```

Querying a Ref Object

The method _doSelectRef() is defined as follows:

```
  private static void _doSelectRef( Connection conn )
    throws SQLException
  {
```

We define a query statement that selects all columns of the table emp_table_with_ref including the reference column manager:

```
    String stmtString =
      "select e.emp_no, e.name, e.manager" +
      " from emp_table_with_ref e";
    PreparedStatement pstmt = null;
```

```
OracleResultSet orset = null;
try
{
  pstmt = conn.prepareStatement( stmtString );
  orset = (OracleResultSet) pstmt.executeQuery();
  while(orset.next())
  {
    int empNo = orset.getInt( 1 );
    String name = orset.getString( 2 );
    System.out.println("emp no : " + empNo );
    System.out.println("emp name : " + name );
```

We use the method getORAData() of the OracleResultSet interface to retrieve the reference object as an object of class EmployeeRef:

```
EmployeeRef managerRef = (EmployeeRef)
   orset.getORAData(3, EmployeeRef.getORADataFactory());
// retrieve the underlying object
if( managerRef != null )
{
```

We then use the method getValue() to retrieve the employee object to which this reference object points, and then print out all its attributes using the custom class generated methods:

```
Employee manager = managerRef.getValue();
System.out.println("\t manager emp no" + manager.getEmpNo());
System.out.println("\t manager emp name" + manager.getName());
System.out.println("\t manager's manager ref " +
   manager.getManager());
    }
  }
}
finally
{
  JDBCUtil.close( orset);
  JDBCUtil.close( pstmt);
}
}
```

Updating a Ref Object

Updating a Ref object simply means making it point to a different row in the table. The following _doUpdateRef() method does that by first invoking the method _getRefForUpdate() to retrieve the Ref object, and then invoking the method _updateEmployeeRef() to update the reference object in the table:

```
private static void _doUpdateRef( Connection conn )
  throws SQLException
{
```

```
    EmployeeRef newManagerRef = _getRefForUpdate( conn, 1 );
    _updateEmployeeRef( conn, 3, newManagerRef );
    conn.commit();
}
```

The definition of the method _getRefForUpdate() basically is the same as that of the method _doSelectRef() covered in the earlier section titled "Querying a Ref Object." The only difference is that it uses the for update nowait clause to lock the row so that another session does not update the same row before we complete our update. Again, this problem, known as the *lost update* problem, along with its suggested solutions, is discussed in detail in Chapter 16.

```
private static EmployeeRef _getRefForUpdate( Connection conn, int empNo )
    throws SQLException
{
    String stmtString =
        "select ref(e) " +
        " from emp_table_with_ref e " +
        " where e.emp_no = ? for update nowait";

    PreparedStatement pstmt = null;
    OracleResultSet orset = null;

    try
    {
        pstmt = conn.prepareStatement( stmtString );
        pstmt.setInt( 1, empNo );
        orset = (OracleResultSet) pstmt.executeQuery();
        orset.next();
        EmployeeRef managerRef = (EmployeeRef)
            orset.getORAData(1, EmployeeRef.getORADataFactory());

        return managerRef;
    }
    finally
    {
        JDBCUtil.close( orset);
        JDBCUtil.close( pstmt);
    }
}
```

The method _updateEmployeeRef() takes the selected reference object and performs the actual update:

```
private static void _updateEmployeeRef( Connection conn, int empNo,
    EmployeeRef newManagerRef ) throws SQLException
{
```

The statement string for the update simply sets the reference column manager to the passed value. Later, we use the method setRef() of the PreparedStatement interface to carry out the actual update. In this case, we effectively change the data so that Jack reports directly to Larry instead of reporting to John.

```
String updateStmtString =
  "update emp_table_with_ref e" +
  " set e.manager = ?" +
  " where e.emp_no = ?";
PreparedStatement pstmt = null;
try
{
  pstmt = conn.prepareStatement( updateStmtString  );
  pstmt.setRef( 1, newManagerRef );
  pstmt.setInt( 2, empNo );
  pstmt.execute();
}
finally
{
  JDBCUtil.close( pstmt);
}
}
} //end of program
```

Summary

In this chapter, we learned how to materialize collections (nested tables and varrays) in a JDBC application as Java objects. We looked at various JDBC standard classes and Oracle extensions. We learned how to use collections in JDBC program using weakly typed classes and strongly typed custom classes generated by JPublisher utility. We also learned about various performance extensions that Oracle provides you with and measured their effectiveness on data retrieval speeds. Finally we learned what references are, and why you should avoid them in general. We also learned how to query and update them using weakly typed Ref and REF classes or using strongly typed custom classes created either manually or using JPublisher utility.

Using LOBs and BFILEs

In this chapter, you'll learn what large objects (LOBs) are and how they're stored in Oracle. You'll also see how to retrieve and manipulate LOBs, and you'll explore some benchmarks comparing various alternatives when manipulating them through the JDBC API.

What Are LOBs?

Large objects (LOBs) are data types designed to hold large amounts of data. In 9*i*, a LOB can store up to 4GB of data. In 10*g*, a LOB can store up to a maximum range of 8TB to 128TB depending on how your database is configured. LOBs are typically used to store unstructured text data, such as text files, and binary data, such as GIFs, multimedia files, Microsoft Word documents, and so on.

LOBs vs. LONGs

Although Oracle supports the LONG data type as well for storing large objects, starting with Oracle 8.0, using LOB data types is strongly recommended for storing large amounts of unstructured data. LOB data types have several advantages over the LONG and LONG RAW types:

- *Larger capacity*: LOBs can store up to 4GB of data in 9*i* and up to a range of 8TB to 128TB of data in 10*g* depending on your system configuration. LONG and LONG RAW types can store only up to 2GB of data.

- *Restrictions on number of columns*: A table can have multiple LOB columns, but it can have only one LONG or LONG RAW column.

- *Random, piecemeal access*: LOBs support random access to data, but LONG data types support only sequential access.

- *Object attributes*: LOBs can also be object attributes, whereas LONG and LONG RAW cannot.

Types of LOBs

There are two types of LOBs: internal and external.

Internal LOBs are stored inside the database tablespaces. They consist of the following SQL data types: CLOB, NCLOB, and BLOB.

- CLOB: Typically used to store unstructured character text data in the database

- NCLOB: Typically used to store unstructured character text data in the database in the National Character Set format

- BLOB: Typically used to store unstructured binary data in the database

Internal LOBs can be further subcategorized into *persistent* and *temporary* LOBs. A persistent LOB is stored in a table column as part of a table row. A temporary LOB instance is created when you instantiate a LOB within the scope of your local application, and it is stored in the temporary tablespace associated with the user.

External LOBs are stored outside the database as operating system files. Oracle accesses them via the SQL data type BFILE. A BFILE is a read-only data type—you cannot write to the file pointed to by a BFILE from your application. The database stores a reference to an external file in form of a BFILE; the file itself is stored outside the database. Typically you use BFILEs to access large, unstructured, read-only data such as GIFs, multimedia files, and so on.

All LOBs are accessed by a locator (you will see how soon). The main difference between an internal LOB (CLOB, BLOB, and NCLOB) and an external LOB (BFILE) is that the BFILE is stored outside the database and the database does not give any transaction semantics over changes to the BFILE. The internal LOBs are stored within Oracle, and Oracle gives you the transaction semantics for them.

■**Note** I would like to emphasize that external LOBs (BFILEs) *do not* participate in transactions. Any support for integrity, data recovery, and so on must be provided by the underlying file system as governed by the operating system in which the actual data exists.

Table 12-1 summarizes the typical use of each of the LOB types.

Table 12-1. *Large Object Types and Their Descriptions*

SQL Data Type	Description
CLOB	Character Large Object. Typically used to store unstructured strings in the database character set format. Characters in the database character set are in a nonvarying width format.
NCLOB	National Character Set Large Object. Stores character strings in the National Character Set data format (supports characters of varying widths).
BLOB	Binary Large Object. Typically used to store binary data (graphic images, multimedia files, Microsoft Word documents, etc.).
BFILE	External Binary File. Useful for accessing read-only data stored outside the database from the database.

LOB Locator

A LOB consists of a locator and its value. A *LOB locator* is a reference to the LOB value. When you use a LOB in an operation such as passing a LOB as a parameter, you are actually passing a LOB locator. For the most part, you can work with a LOB instance in your application without being concerned with the semantics of LOB locators.

Note For the LOB types BLOB, CLOB, and NCLOB, each LOB instance stored in a column has its own distinct LOB locator and also a distinct copy of the LOB value. This is in contrast with the case of initialized BFILE columns, where the row stores a locator to the external operating system file that holds the value of the BFILE. Each BFILE instance in a given row has its own distinct locator; however, two different rows can contain a BFILE locator that points to the *same* operating system file.

Internal LOBs (CLOBs, NCLOBs, and BLOBs)

Internal LOBs can be accessed and manipulated from SQL, PL/SQL, and JDBC. Since SQL and PL/SQL are tools used extensively in JDBC, we will briefly look at how to manipulate LOBs in each of these environments in the next few sections. For a detailed discussion on these and other LOB-related topics, consult *Oracle Database Application Developer's Guide – Large Objects (10g Release 1)*. If you want to jump directly to the explanation of LOB usage in JDBC, please go to the section of this chapter titled "Using LOBs in JDBC."

Let's first create the schema to contain our CLOB data. The following table, clob_table, contains one CLOB column called clob_col:

```
benchmark@ORA10G> create table clob_table
  2  (
  3    x varchar2(30),
  4    id number,
  5    clob_col clob
  6  );

Table created.
```

Next, we insert one row using a simple insert statement and commit:

```
benchmark@ORA10G> insert into clob_table (clob_col)
  2  values ( 'A clob example' );

1 row created.
benchmark@ORA10G> commit;

Commit complete.
```

Using Internal LOBs in SQL

In Oracle8*i* and earlier, you had to use the PL/SQL package DBMS_LOB to access and manipulate LOBs. Starting with Oracle9*i*, you can access CLOBs (or NCLOBs) using the SQL varchar2 semantics. This is typically useful when performing operations with relatively smaller LOBs (e.g., up to 100,000 bytes). Many SQL functions that take varchar2 as a parameter will accept a CLOB instead. Let's go through some examples, starting with a simple select of the CLOB data we inserted:

```
benchmark@ORA10G> select clob_col from clob_table;
```

```
A clob example
```

Next, we apply some SQL functions that are known to work with varchar2 data. We use the functions substr, instr, and length, and the concatenation operator in these examples. The first example applies the substr function to the CLOB column of table clob_table:

```
benchmark@ORA10G> select substr( clob_col, 1, 3) from clob_table;
```

```
A c
```

Then we find the starting position of the string 'clob' in our CLOB column by using the intsr function:

```
benchmark@ORA10G> select instr( clob_col, 'clob') from clob_table;
```

```
                    3
```

In the next example, we select a string value concatenated with our CLOB column:

```
benchmark@ORA10G> select clob_col || '( concatenated to clob)'
  2  from clob_table;
```

```
A clob example( concatenated to clob)
```

We use the like operator to select rows matching a CLOB column's value:

```
benchmark@ORA10G> select clob_col
  2  from clob_table
  3  where clob_col like '%clob%';
```

```
A clob example
```

Finally, we use the LENGTH function to get the CLOB column's length:

```
benchmark@ORA10G> select length(clob_col) clob_length
  2  from clob_table;
```

```
           14
```

To insert a CLOB of zero length, we can use the function empty_clob() (or empty_blob() for BLOB; see the section "Empty LOBs" later in this chapter for more details). The following code updates our clob_col column to an empty_clob() and then verifies that the length of the CLOB value is now 0:

```
benchmark@ORA10G> update clob_table set clob_col = empty_clob();

1 row updated.

benchmark@ORA10G> commit;

Commit complete.

benchmark@ORA10G> select length( clob_col) length_clob from clob_table;

         0
```

Now for BLOBs. The following creates a blob_table table and inserts a row in it:

```
benchmark@ORA10G> create table blob_table
  2  (
  3      x varchar2(30),
  4      id number,
  5      blob_col blob
  6  );

Table created.

benchmark@ORA10G> insert into blob_table( blob_col) values ( '10101' );

1 row created.
```

However, you cannot do a select from the blob_table in SQL*Plus, as SQL*Plus is not equipped to display BLOB columns.

```
benchmark@ORA10G> select blob_col from blob_table;
SP2-0678: Column or attribute type can not be displayed by SQL*Plus
```

We will cover how to overcome this in PL/SQL and JDBC in the upcoming sections.

Using Internal LOBs in PL/SQL

In PL/SQL, the main mechanism of accessing and manipulating LOBs is through the DBMS_LOB package. We will briefly go through some examples in this section. You can explore this package functionality more fully by reading *PL/SQL Packages and Types Reference (10g Release 1)*.

Let's first look at the concepts of empty LOBs and temporary LOBs.

Empty LOBs

A LOB instance that is null *does not* have a locator. Before you can pass a LOB instance to any LOB API routine (PL/SQL or Java), the instance *must* contain a locator. You insert an empty locator by using the SQL function empty_clob() for CLOB columns and the SQL function empty_blob() for BLOB columns:

```
benchmark@ORA10G> insert into clob_table( clob_col) values ( empty_clob() );

1 row created.
```

You can also specify the CLOB column to have an empty value as a default value to ensure that you will always have API-friendly empty CLOB values in your tables.

Temporary LOBs

A temporary LOB is a BLOB, CLOB, or NCLOB that is accessible and persists only within the application scope in which it is declared. A temporary LOB does not exist in database tables and can be created explicitly as follows (setting CACHE to true means temporary LOBs are eligible to be read into the Oracle data buffer cache):

```
benchmark@ORA10G> declare
  2    l_clob clob;
  3  begin
  4    dbms_lob.createtemporary( lob_loc => l_clob,
  5      cache => true );
  6  end;
  7  /

PL/SQL procedure successfully completed.
```

Many SQL functions return temporary LOBs silently. You can also create temporary LOBs from JDBC, as you'll see later.

Let's now examine a quirk that may confuse you when inserting large data into a CLOB column from PL/SQL versus using pure SQL. We use our familiar clob_table in the examples that follow. Note that when we insert data directly using SQL, we are unable to insert data more than 4,000 bytes (the limit of varchar2 in SQL), regardless of the actual data size; Oracle silently truncates the column to 4,000 bytes.

```
benchmark@ORA10G> insert into clob_table( x, id, clob_col)
  2    values ( 'Insert from SQL', 1, rpad( '*',32000, '*' ) );

1 row created.
```

We insert a value of length 32,000 bytes, but verify the actual length of CLOB column inserted to be of 4,000 bytes by selecting the length of the CLOB value as follows:

```
benchmark@ORA10G> select x "Description", id,
  2          dbms_lob.getlength( clob_col ) "Length of clob"
  3  from clob_table;
```

```
Description                         ID Length of clob
------------------------------- ---------- ---------------
Insert from SQL                     1          4000
```

In PL/SQL, the maximum size for the VARCHAR2 variable is 32,760 bytes, so you can insert a string of length up to 32,760 bytes if you use PL/SQL as follows:

```
benchmark@ORA10G> declare
  2    l_big_string varchar2(32760) := rpad( '*',32760, '*' );
  3  begin
  4    insert into clob_table(x, id, clob_col)
  5    values ('Insert from PL/SQL', 2, l_big_string );
  6  end;
  7  /

PL/SQL procedure successfully completed.

benchmark@ORA10G> commit;

Commit complete.

benchmark@ORA10G> select x "Description", id,
  2          dbms_lob.getlength( clob_col ) "Length of clob"
  3  from clob_table;
```

```
Description                         ID Length of clob
------------------------------- ---------- ---------------
Insert from SQL                     1          4000
Insert from PL/SQL                  2          32760
```

We will soon cover how to insert values bigger than 32,760 bytes in PL/SQL. Let's now clean up and repopulate our clob_table data with a simple row.

```
benchmark@ORA10G> delete from clob_table;

0 rows deleted.

benchmark@ORA10G> insert into clob_table (clob_col)
  2  values ( 'A clob example' );

1 row created.
```

In PL/SQL, assigning a VARCHAR2 variable to a CLOB variable creates a temporary CLOB silently. The temporary variable is automatically freed at the end of the block. To find out the information about how many temporary LOBs exist, we can query the view V$TEMPORARY_LOBS. We do that in the procedure print_temporary_lob_info, which is defined as follows:

```
benchmark@ORA10G> create or replace procedure print_temporary_lob_info(
  p_msg in varchar2 default ' ' )
  2  is
```

```
 3  begin
 4    dbms_output.put_line ( p_msg );
 5    for i in ( select cache_lobs, nocache_lobs from v$temporary_lobs )
 6    loop
 7      dbms_output.put_line( 'cache lobs: ' || i.cache_lobs );
 8      dbms_output.put_line( 'nocache lobs: ' || i.nocache_lobs );
 9    end loop;
10  end;
11  /
```

Procedure created.

The procedure takes a message string, prints it out, and then loops through the records in the view V$TEMPORARY_LOBS, printing out the columns cache_lobs (number of cached temporary lobs) and nocache_lobs (the number of temporary lobs that are not cached). The following PL/SQL block creates a VARCHAR2 and assigns it to a CLOB variable. Right after that, it invokes the print_temporary_lob_info() method. It then invokes the same method once again after the PL/SQL block ends:

```
benchmark@ORA10G> declare
 2    varchar2_data varchar2(100) := 'value in varchar2';
 3    l_clob clob;
 4  begin
 5    l_clob := varchar2_data;
 6    print_temporary_lob_info ( 'after assignment' );
 7  end;
 8  /
after assignment
cache lobs: 1
nocache lobs: 0

PL/SQL procedure successfully completed.

benchmark@ORA10G> exec print_temporary_lob_info ( 'after PL/SQL block' );
after PL/SQL block
cache lobs: 0
nocache lobs: 0

PL/SQL procedure successfully completed.
```

As highlighted in the preceding code, a temporary LOB was created right after the assignment (note that the LOBs created thus are cached by default). There were no temporary LOBs after the PL/SQL block, as shown by the second execution of print_temporary_lob_info.

Let's now look at how to update LOBs in PL/SQL. Regardless of whether you use PL/SQL or Java, for updating a LOB an important thing to remember is that you need to lock the row containing the LOB data before updating it. Note that if you have just inserted the row that you need to update in the same session, then you don't need to explicitly lock it—Oracle already has a lock on the inserted row. The reason a lock is required in the first place is because of the way Oracle stores LOB data. Recall that LOB storage involves a LOB locator and a LOB value. When you select a LOB column, what you get is the LOB locator (not the LOB value). So an update typically involves two steps:

1. Get the LOB locator.

2. Update the LOB.

Now consider the following scenario:

1. User 1 selects a LOB column.

2. User 2 selects the same LOB column.

3. User 1 starts updating the selected LOB column.

4. User 2 updates the selected LOB column at the same time as user 1.

If the row is not locked, the users' actions would overwrite each other. Note that this is different from the lost update issue (discussed in Chapter 16), in that the contents are not just overwritten, but also can contain a "mixture" of the two writes at the end. In other words, if locking is not made mandatory, it is quite possible that two writes could interfere with each other, creating content that neither of them intended in the first place. Hence, the row needs to be locked.

The following code snippet first selects the clob_col value into a local variable and then uses the dbms_lob.writeappend procedure to append some text to it. It then updates the table with the new value.

```
benchmark@ORA10G> declare
   2    l_clob clob_table.clob_col%type;
   3    l_str_to_append varchar2(32760) :=  rpad('*',32760,'*');
   4  begin
```

We first select the LOB, taking care to lock the row by using the for update clause in the select statement:

```
   5    select clob_col into l_clob
   6    from clob_table
   7    where rownum <= 1
   8    for update; -- without this, you can't update the clob column
```

Next, we see how using dbms_lob.writeappend can create LOBs of a length more than 32,760 bytes in PL/SQL:

```
  12    for i in 1..3
  13    loop
  14      dbms_lob.writeappend( l_clob,
  15        length(l_str_to_append), l_str_to_append );
  16    end loop;
```

Finally, we update the LOB column and commit the data:

```
18    update clob_table set clob_col = l_clob
19    where rownum <= 1;
20    commit;
21  end;
22  /
```

PL/SQL procedure successfully completed.

Just as we wrote a LOB value of more than 32,000 in chunks, we can also read a CLOB of more than 32,000 bytes in PL/SQL. In the following snippet, we read the CLOB of 98,294 bytes we just created in chunks of 255 characters:

```
benchmark@ORA10G> declare
  2     l_read_buf varchar2(255);
  3     l_amount_to_read binary_integer := 255;
  4     l_clob clob;
  5     l_offset number := 1;
  6     begin
  7       select clob_col
  8       into l_clob
  9       from clob_table;
```

After selecting the CLOB in a variable, we read it in chunks of 255 bytes in a loop, as follows. We exit from the loop when the exception NO_DATA_FOUND indicates that there are no more bytes to read:

```
11        begin
12          loop
13            dbms_lob.read( l_clob, l_amount_to_read,
14              l_offset, l_read_buf );
15            l_offset := l_offset + l_amount_to_read;
16
17            dbms_output.put_line( l_read_buf );
18          end loop;
19        exception
20          when no_data_found then
21            null;
22        end;
23      end;
24  /
A clob example*************************...(truncated to conserve space)
```

That concludes our brief tour through internal LOBs in PL/SQL. I urge you to read *PL/SQL Packages and Types Reference (10g Release 1)* for more details on this very useful package. Next, we'll look at external LOBs in SQL and PL/SQL.

External LOBs (BFILEs) in SQL and PL/SQL

External LOBs, or BFILEs, contain a locator to a binary file that typically resides in the operating system. Let's quickly go through how to use BFILEs in SQL and/or PL/SQL first.

In the following example, the BFILE entry points to a text file called bfile_test.txt in the directory C:\TEMP, which contains the following four lines:

```
This is a test.
This is line number 2.
This is line number 3.
This is the final line.
```

To use a BFILE in SQL, we first need to create a directory object in SQL as follows:

```
benchmark@ORA10G> create or replace directory my_dir as 'C:\TEMP';

Directory created.
```

■**Note** A directory is a database object that serves as an alias for a full path name on the server's file system where the files are actually located. Note that you need to ensure that the directory you give as the argument is valid on your database server. In other words, the directory should be visible to your database server.

Now we'll look at an example in which we load a text file into a BLOB variable and print the contents of the file in SQL*Plus. This also demonstrates how you can print a BLOB column that actually contains text data. First, we declare some variables and initialize the BLOB variable by using the dbms_lob.createtemporary() method:

```
benchmark@ORA10G> declare
  2      l_blob blob;
  3      l_bfile bfile;
  4
  5      l_read_buf varchar2(200);
  6      l_amount_to_read binary_integer := 100;
  7      l_offset number := 1;
  8  begin
  9      dbms_lob.createtemporary( l_blob, true );
```

Next, we create the BFILE locator using the BFILENAME function as follows:

```
 10      l_bfile := bfilename( directory => 'MY_DIR', filename => 'test_bfile.txt' );
```

Note that as mentioned in the preceding comments, the directory argument should contain the directory object we created (my_dir) in capital letters and inside single quotes for the preceding code to work. Also, the bfilename argument should point to a real file, as it does in this case.

Note If you want to create a `directory` object with a name in mixed-case or lowercase letters, you should enclose the directory name in double quotes when creating it: or replace the directory `MY_DIR` with `C:\TEMP`.

The first step is to open the file using the `dbms_lob.fileopen()` function:

```
12    dbms_lob.fileopen( l_bfile );
```

Next, we use the `dbms_lob.loadfromfile()` function to load the file into our BLOB variable as follows:

```
14    dbms_lob.loadfromfile( l_blob, l_bfile,
15    dbms_lob.getlength( l_bfile) );
```

We now close the file:

```
17    dbms_lob.fileclose( l_bfile );
```

Finally, we read and print the BLOB that contains our file contents, as shown in the following code. We use the `dbms_lob.read()` function to read the BLOB in chunks of 100 bytes (the length of the variable `l_amount_to_read`). Notice how we need to use `utl_raw.cast_to_varchar2()` to cast the contents of the buffer in order to see the text output in SQL*Plus. This is how you can see text data stored in BLOB in SQL*Plus. When there is no more data left, we get a `NO_DATA_FOUND` exception that we catch and ignore to end the program:

```
20    dbms_output.put_line( 'blob contents -------' );
21    begin
22      loop
23        dbms_lob.read( l_blob, l_amount_to_read,
24          l_offset, l_read_buf );
25        l_offset := l_offset + l_amount_to_read;
26
27        -- output the line - note that we need to cast the
28        -- binary data into varchar2 using the
29        -- utl_raw.cast_to_varchar2 function.
30        dbms_output.put_line( utl_raw.cast_to_varchar2(l_read_buf) );
31      end loop;
32    exception
33      when no_data_found then
34        null;
35    end;
```

We then delete all rows from `blob_table` and insert the preceding BLOB value in it:

```
37    delete blob_table;
38    insert into blob_table( x, id, blob_col ) values( 'blob loaded from text',
39      1, l_blob );
40    commit;
```

```
41  end;
42  /
blob contents -------
This is a test.
This is line number 2.
This is line number 3.
This is the final line.

PL/SQL procedure successfully completed.
```

The following code shows how to display the text data in a BLOB column in SQL*Plus using utl_raw.cast_to_varchar2 in a select statement:

```
benchmark@ORA10G> select utl_raw.cast_to_varchar2( blob_col) blob_col
  2  from blob_table;

BLOB_COL
-------------------------------
This is a test.
This is line number 2.
This is line number 3.
This is the final line.
```

Using LOBs in JDBC

For the remainder of this chapter, we will discuss how to access and manipulate internal LOBs using the JDBC API. Figure 12-1 is a class diagram that shows the classes and interfaces involved.

LOB Interfaces and Implementing Classes

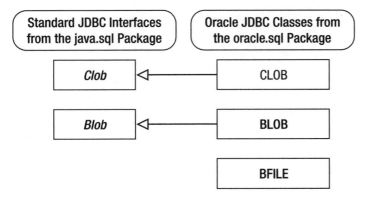

Figure 12-1. *JDBC standard interfaces and Oracle implementation classes providing LOB functionality*

JDBC has two standard interfaces, java.sql.Clob and java.sql.Blob, for supporting internal LOBs. The Oracle classes oracle.sql.CLOB and oracle.sql.BLOB implement these interfaces, respectively, in addition to adding some functionalities of their own. For the external LOB, there is no standard JDBC class; you have to use the Oracle class oracle.sql.BFILE.

Note that instances of the classes CLOB, BLOB, and BFILE contain only the locators of the LOB, but that is all you need to access and manipulate LOB data.

In the next few sections, we cover reading from and writing to CLOBs. Assume that we have the following data in our clob_table table:

```
benchmark@ORA10G> select x "Description", id,
  2           dbms_lob.getlength( clob_col ) "Length of clob"
  3  from clob_table;

Description                                      ID Length of clob
-----------------------------------  ----------  --------------
Insert from SQL                                   1          4000
Insert from PL/SQL                                2         32000
From PL/SQL Using chunks                          3         64000
```

Reading from and Writing to a CLOB

The class DemoClobOperations has different methods to read and write to a CLOB that are explained separately in the following sections. The class begins with import statements, and we first get the connection (recall that autocommit is turned off in the method JDBCUtil.getConnection()):

```
/* * This program demonstrates how to read from and write to a CLOB.
* COMPATIBLITY NOTE:
*    runs successfully against 9.2.0.1.0 and 10.1.0.2.0
*/
import java.util.Arrays;
import java.sql.SQLException;
import java.sql.Connection;
import java.sql.Clob;
import java.io.BufferedReader;
import java.io.BufferedWriter;
import java.io.OutputStreamWriter;
import java.io.Writer;
import java.io.OutputStream;
import java.io.InputStreamReader;
import java.io.IOException;
import java.sql.PreparedStatement;
import java.sql.CallableStatement;
import java.sql.ResultSet;
import oracle.sql.CLOB;
import book.util.JDBCUtil;
```

```
import book.util.Util;
class DemoClobOperations
{
  public static void main(String args[])
  {
    Util.checkProgramUsage( args );
    Connection conn = null;
    try
    {
      // following gets connection; sets autocommit to true
      conn = JDBCUtil.getConnection("benchmark", "benchmark", args[0]);
```

We invoke the following five methods in the main() method:

- readClob(): Reads a CLOB value

- readClobInChunks(): Reads a CLOB value piecemeal

- writeClob(): Writes to a CLOB value, replacing the characters from the beginning

- writeClobInChunks(): Writes to a CLOB value piecemeal, replacing the characters from the beginning

- appendToClob(): Appends a string value to a CLOB

At the end of the main() method, we commit the changes:

```
    _readClob( conn );
    _readClobInChunks( conn );
    _writeClob( conn );
    _writeClobInChunks( conn );
    _appendToClob( conn );
    conn.commit();
    }
    catch (Exception e)
    {
      JDBCUtil.printExceptionAndRollback(conn, e );
    }
    finally
    {
      // release resources associated with JDBC in the finally clause.
      JDBCUtil.close( conn );
    }
  }
}
```

The following section explains the method _readClob() in the class DemoClobOperations.

Reading CLOB Data

The method _readClob() is explained here, with comments interspersed:

```
/* demos how to read from a CLOB in the database.*/
  private static void _readClob( Connection conn )
  throws SQLException, IOException
  {
    PreparedStatement pstmt = null;
    ResultSet rset = null;
    BufferedReader reader = null;
    try
    {
```

In the try catch block, we first declare our query string to select the CLOB column, following which we prepare the query statement:

```
      String stmtString = "select clob_col from clob_table "+
        " where id = ?";
      pstmt = conn.prepareStatement( stmtString );
```

Next, we bind the value of the column id to 1 (the length of the CLOB column in this row is 4,000 bytes). We execute the query and begin the standard ResultSet while loop:

```
      pstmt.setInt( 1, 1 );
      rset = pstmt.executeQuery();
      while( rset.next() )
      {
```

We use the method getClob() to get the CLOB object:

```
        Clob clob = rset.getClob( 1 );
```

Next, we get the data from the CLOB object using the getAsciiStream() method. We then read the stream data using the standard Java I/O method and print the number of characters read:

```
        reader = new BufferedReader (
          new InputStreamReader ( clob.getAsciiStream() ) );
        int numOfCharactersRead = 0;
        String line = null;
        while( (line = reader.readLine()) != null )
        {
          //System.out.println( line );
          numOfCharactersRead += line.length();
        }
        System.out.println("num of characters read: " +
          numOfCharactersRead );
      }
    }
    finally
    {
```

Note that in the `finally` clause, we also close any stream-related objects we opened earlier:

```
if( reader != null )
  reader.close();
JDBCUtil.close( pstmt);
JDBCUtil.close( rset);
  }
}
```

In the next section, we'll cover how to read the `CLOB` data in small pieces.

Reading CLOB Data Piecemeal

Another mechanism of reading `CLOBs` is useful when you have to read big `CLOBs` and you want to control the chunk size in which you read the data into your client buffer. The following method, `_readClobInChunks()`, demonstrates how to do this:

```
/* demos how to read a CLOB in the database piecemeal. useful for large CLOBS.   */
  private static void _readClobInChunks( Connection conn )
  throws SQLException, IOException
  {
    PreparedStatement pstmt = null;
    ResultSet rset = null;
    BufferedReader reader = null;
    try
    {
      String stmtString =
        "select clob_col from clob_table " +
        " where id = ?";
      pstmt = conn.prepareStatement( stmtString );
      pstmt.setInt( 1, 2 );
      rset = pstmt.executeQuery();
      while( rset.next() )
      {
        System.out.println(": in _readClobInChunks");
        Clob clob = rset.getClob( 1 );
```

Until this point, the code is very similar to the method `_readClob()` we discussed earlier, except that this time we are selecting the `CLOB` column that has 32,000 bytes of data in it. After getting the `CLOB` data, we can read data in chunks equal to the *chunk size* obtained by the method getChunkSize() or the *ideal buffer size* obtained by the method getBufferSize(). We can use either the chunk size or the ideal buffer size calculated by JDBC. The ideal buffer size is a multiple of the chunk size and is usually close to 32KB. The important thing is to have a buffer size as a multiple of the chunk size for optimal performance:

```
        int chunkSize = ((CLOB) clob).getChunkSize();
        System.out.println( "Chunk Size:" + chunkSize );
        int idealBufferSize = ((CLOB) clob).getBufferSize();
        System.out.println( "Ideal buffer Size:" + idealBufferSize );
```

In this example, we use a chunk size for the size of our buffer, which we declare as a char array:

```
char[] buffer = new char[ chunkSize ];
```

Finally, we create a stream using the getAsciiStream() method on the Clob interface and read data in pieces of the size of our buffer just created:

```
        reader = new BufferedReader
          ( new InputStreamReader( clob.getAsciiStream()));
        int length = -1;
        int numOfCharactersRead = 0;
        while (( length = reader.read( buffer, 0, chunkSize)) != -1 )
        {
          //System.out.println( buffer );
          numOfCharactersRead += length;
        }
        System.out.println("num of characters read: " +
          numOfCharactersRead );
      }
    }
    finally
    {
      if( reader != null )
      {
        reader.close();
      }
      JDBCUtil.close( pstmt);
      JDBCUtil.close( rset);
    }
  }
```

In the next section, we'll look at how to write to a CLOB.

Writing to a CLOB (Overwriting at the Beginning)

While writing to a CLOB (or BLOB), you should ensure the following:

- You have to first select the CLOB (or BLOB) with a for update clause to lock the row, as discussed earlier in the section "Using Internal LOBs in PL/SQL."

- You must ensure that you have set autocommit to false in the connection you use. You should do this anyway to preserve transaction semantics (see the section "Sizing Your Transaction Resources According to Your Business Needs" in Chapter 4 for a detailed discussion on this topic). If you don't set autocommit to false, the database issues a commit right after the first select for update that you do to acquire the lock on LOB. The commit, of course, releases the lock, and you get a "fetch out of sequence" error when you try to write anything to the LOB later.

- As of Oracle 10g Release 1, you need to use the Oracle extension `oracle.sql.CLOB` to write the data, as the following standard methods in the `Clob` interface are *not supported* and give rise to an "Unsupported feature" exception. Note that at the time of this writing, Oracle 10g Release 1 documentation is incorrect in this regard.

```
public OutputStream setAsciiStream( long pos ) throws SQLException
Retrieves a stream to be used to write Ascii characters to the CLOB
value that this Clob object represents, starting at position pos.
```

```
public Writer setCharacterStream( long pos ) throws SQLException
Retrieves a stream to be used to write a stream of Unicode characters
to the CLOB value that this Clob object represents, at position pos.
```

Since the preceding two methods in the `Clob` interface *are not supported*, the alternative is to use either of the following two Oracle extension methods in the `CLOB` class:

```
public OutputStream getAsciiOutputStream() throws SQLException
public Writer getCharacterOutputStream() throws SQLException
```

We will use the second method in our example. Continuing with the code in our `DemoClobOperations` class, let's now look at the method `_writeClob()`, which demonstrates this concept:

```
private static void _writeClob( Connection conn ) throws SQLException, IOException
{
  PreparedStatement pstmt = null;
  ResultSet rset = null;
  Writer writer= null;
  //OutputStream writer = null;
  try
  {
    String stmtString =
      "select clob_col from clob_table " +
      " where id = ? for update";
    pstmt = conn.prepareStatement( stmtString );
    pstmt.setInt( 1, 2 );
    rset = pstmt.executeQuery();
    while( rset.next() )
    {
```

In this case, we cast the returned object into the `oracle.sql.CLOB` interface type:

```
      CLOB clob = (CLOB)rset.getClob( 1 );
```

We replace the first characters of the `CLOB` column with the following `String`:

```
      String newClobData = new String("NEW CLOB DATA");
```

We get the `Writer` object and write our `String` to the stream:

```
    writer= clob.getCharacterOutputStream();
    // You can also use the following to get an ASCII stream
    // OutStream writer= clob.getAsciiOutputStream();
    writer.write( newClobData );
  }
}
finally
{
  if( writer != null )
    writer.close();
  JDBCUtil.close( pstmt);
  JDBCUtil.close( rset);
}
}
```

Note that you *don't* need to execute an update to write the CLOB back to the database when using the stream operations—all stream "writes" write directly to the database. Of course, you still need to commit the transaction to make the changes permanent.

Writing to a CLOB Piecemeal (Overwriting at the Beginning)

Almost everything mentioned in the previous section for writing to a CLOB is applicable to this section. The only difference is in the step where we retrieve the stream data. We get the chunk size and set up a buffer of char of a size equal to the chunk size. In this example, we use the getAsciiStream() method of the CLOB class. The code is shown in the method _writeClobInChunks() of the class DemoClobOperations:

```
private static void _writeClobInChunks( Connection conn )
throws SQLException, IOException
{
  PreparedStatement pstmt = null;
  ResultSet rset = null;
  OutputStream out = null;
  try
  {
    String stmtString =
      "select clob_col from clob_table " +
      " where id = ? for update";
    pstmt = conn.prepareStatement( stmtString );
    pstmt.setInt( 1, 3 );
    rset = pstmt.executeQuery();
    while( rset.next() )
    {
      CLOB clob = (CLOB)rset.getClob( 1 );
      int chunkSize = clob.getChunkSize();
      byte[] buffer = new byte[ chunkSize];
```

In the next snippet, we use the `fill()` method of the class `java.util.Arrays` to fill all characters in our buffer with the same character ("a" in this example):

```
Arrays.fill( buffer, 0, chunkSize, (byte)'a' );
out = clob.getAsciiOutputStream();
```

In the `for` loop, we write the same buffer ten times serially into the stream:

```
for( int i=0; i < 10; i++ )
{
  out.write( buffer, 0, buffer.length );
}
}
}
finally
{
  if( out != null )
    out.close();
  JDBCUtil.close( pstmt);
  JDBCUtil.close( rset);
}
}
```

Appending to a CLOB

What if we need to append data to the end of a CLOB? Well, we can invoke `dbms_lob.writeappend` from JDBC to achieve this. The last method, `_appendToClob()`, of the class `DemoClobOperations` demonstrates this:

```
private static void _appendToClob( Connection conn )
  throws SQLException, IOException
{
  CallableStatement cstmt = null;
  try
  {
```

In the following code, we declare an anonymous PL/SQL block that takes three parameters. The first parameter is the ID of the row in the table `clob_table`. The second parameter is the number of bytes to append (the length of the string), and the third parameter is the string to append. Notice how we use the `dbms_lob.writeappend` method to accomplish our task (please see the Oracle document *PL/SQL Packages and Types Reference [10g Release 1]* for more details on this method):

```
String stmtString =
  "declare " +
  "  l_clob clob;" +
  "begin " +
  "  select clob_col into l_clob from clob_table " +
  "  where id = ? and rownum <= 1 for update;" +
  "  dbms_lob.writeappend( l_clob, ?, ? ); " +
  "end;";
```

We next create the string that we want to append to our CLOB column:

```
String newClobData = new String("data appended from JDBC");
```

The remaining code simply invokes the preceding anonymous PL/SQL block. This also ends our class, DemoClobOperations:

```
      cstmt = conn.prepareCall( stmtString );
      cstmt.setInt( 1, 1 );
      cstmt.setInt( 2, newClobData.length() );
      cstmt.setString( 3, newClobData );
      cstmt.execute();
    }
    finally
    {
      JDBCUtil.close( cstmt);
    }
  }
}
```

Reading from and Writing to a BLOB

We assume that our blob_table contains the following text data that we inserted earlier in section "External LOBs (BFILES) in SQL and PL/SQL." (The logic remains the same for binary data as well; we use text data in our examples because it makes it easier to verify the results of queries and updates.)

```
benchmark@ORA10G> select utl_raw.cast_to_varchar2( blob_col) blob_col
  2  from blob_table;

BLOB_COL
---------------------------
This is a test.
This is line number 2.
This is line number 3.
This is the final line.
```

The BLOB operations are demonstrated in the code in the class DemoBlobOperations. The class begins with import statements and getting the connection to the database:

```
/** This program demonstrates how to read from and write to a BLOB.
* COMPATIBLITY NOTE:
*    runs successfully against 9.2.0.1.0 and 10.1.0.2.0
*/
// importing standard JDBC classes under java.sql class hierarchy
import java.sql.SQLException;
import java.sql.Connection;
import java.sql.Blob;
```

```
import java.io.OutputStream;
import java.io.InputStream;
import java.io.IOException;
import java.sql.PreparedStatement;
import java.sql.CallableStatement;
import java.sql.ResultSet;
import oracle.sql.BLOB;
import book.util.JDBCUtil;
import book.util.Util;
class DemoBlobOperations
{
  public static void main(String args[])
  {
    Util.checkProgramUsage( args );
    Connection conn = null;
    try
    {
      // following gets connection; sets autocommit to true
      conn = JDBCUtil.getConnection("benchmark", "benchmark", args[0]);
```

We invoke the following three methods in the main() method:

- _readBlob(): Reads a BLOB value

- _writeBlob(): Writes to a BLOB value, replacing the characters from the beginning

- _appendToBlob(): Appends a string value to a BLOB

At the end of main() method, we commit the changes:

```
      _readBlob( conn );
      _writeBlob( conn );
      _appendToBlob( conn );
      conn.commit();
    }
    catch (Exception e)
    {
      JDBCUtil.printExceptionAndRollback(conn, e );
    }
    finally
    {
      // release resources associated with JDBC in the finally clause.
      JDBCUtil.close( conn );
    }
  }
```

Reading BLOB Data

The method _readBlob() begins by declaring variables outside the try catch block:

```
/* demos how to read from a BLOB in the database. */
private static void _readBlob( Connection conn ) throws SQLException, IOException
{
  PreparedStatement pstmt = null;
  ResultSet rset = null;
  InputStream byteStream = null;
  try
  {
```

We declare our query string that selects the BLOB column whose length is 4,000 bytes from the table blob_table:

```
    String stmtString = "select blob_col from blob_table "+
      " where id = ?";
    pstmt = conn.prepareStatement( stmtString );
    pstmt.setInt( 1, 1 );
    rset = pstmt.executeQuery();
    while( rset.next() )
    {
```

To read a BLOB, we first use the method getBlob() in the ResultSet interface. We then use the standard method getBinaryStream() in the Blob interface to get an InputStream. Finally, we use standard Java streams functionality to get the data as follows (note how we convert the resulting byte array to a String by using the appropriate String constructor to display the ASCII characters):

```
      BLOB blob = (BLOB) rset.getBlob( 1 );
      byteStream = blob.getBinaryStream();
      byte [] byteArray= new byte [10];
      int numOfBytesRead = 0;
      int bytesRead = -1;
      while( (bytesRead = byteStream.read( byteArray ) ) != -1 )
      {
        System.out.print( new String(byteArray, 0, bytesRead));
        numOfBytesRead += bytesRead;
      }
      System.out.println("total bytes read: " + numOfBytesRead );
    }
  }
  finally
  {
    if( byteStream != null )
      byteStream.close();
    JDBCUtil.close( pstmt);
    JDBCUtil.close( rset);
  }
}
```

Writing to a BLOB (Overwriting at the Beginning)

Let's now look at how to write to a BLOB, starting from the beginning and overwriting existing data. The first thing to remember is that as with CLOBs, we need to use a for update clause in our select to lock the row, and we also need to set autocommit to false. In addition, the following standard JDBC methods in the Blob interface for writing to a BLOB give an "Unsupported feature" exception in 10g Release 1 (and 9i Release 2):

```
OutputStream    setBinaryStream(long pos)
   Retrieves a stream that can be used to write to the BLOB value.
```

(Note that the 10g Release 1 documentation is once again erroneous in its explanation of this.)

Thus we need to use the method getBinaryOutputStream() in the CLOB class. The following method, _writeBlob(), demonstrates this:

```
/* demos how to write to a BLOB in the database (overwriting from the
   beginning). */
private static void _writeBlob( Connection conn )
   throws SQLException, IOException
{
   PreparedStatement pstmt = null;
   ResultSet rset = null;
   OutputStream out = null;
   try
   {
      String stmtString =
         "select blob_col from blob_table " +
         " where id = ? for update";
      pstmt = conn.prepareStatement( stmtString );
      pstmt.setInt( 1, 1 );
      rset = pstmt.executeQuery();
      while( rset.next() )
      {
```

We need to use the Oracle extension class BLOB as explained previously:

```
         BLOB blob = (BLOB)rset.getBlob( 1 );
         /* Following gives an "Unsupported feature"
            exception
            OutputStream ostream = blob.setBinaryStream(1L);
         */
```

We create a String object and convert it into a byte array. Next, we use the getBinary➡
OutputStream() method to retrieve the output stream and write to it using standard Java I/O functionality:

```
         String newBlobData = new String(
            "data to overwrite existing data in the beginning");
         byte[] byteArray = newBlobData.getBytes();
         out = blob.getBinaryOutputStream();
         out.write( byteArray );
```

```
      }
    }
    finally
    {
      if( out != null )
        out.close();
      JDBCUtil.close( pstmt);
      JDBCUtil.close( rset);
    }
  }
}
```

After the preceding code is executed, the BLOB data changes as follows:

```
benchmark@ORA10G> select utl_raw.cast_to_varchar2( blob_col) blob_col
  2   from blob_table;

BLOB_COL
----------------------------------------------------------------
data to overwrite existing data in the beginningine number 3.
This is the final line.
```

Notice how we overwrote the beginning of the BLOB data with our string data to overwrite existing data in the beginning.

Appending to a BLOB

What if we need to append data to the end of a BLOB? We've already seen how to do that for a CLOB by invoking the method dbms_lob.writeappend from JDBC. We do the same for a BLOB, with minor variations: this time, we need to pass an array of bytes using the setBytes() method of the CallableStatement object. The final method, _appendToBlob, of the class DemoBlobOperations does this:

```
/* demos how to append to a BLOB in the database.   */
  private static void _appendToBlob( Connection conn )
  throws SQLException, IOException
  {
    CallableStatement cstmt = null;
    try
    {
```

Once again, we declare an anonymous PL/SQL block that takes three parameters. The first parameter is the ID of the row in the table blob_table. The second parameter is the number of bytes to append (the length of the string). And the third parameter is the string to append. Notice how we use the dbms_lob.writeappend method to accomplish our task (please see *PL/SQL Packages and Types Reference [10g Release 1]* for more details on this method). We set all three parameters and invoke the procedure:

```
      String stmtString =
        "declare " +
        "  l_blob blob;" +
```

```
      "begin " +
      "   select blob_col into l_blob from blob_table " +
      "   where id = ? and rownum <= 1 for update;" +
      "   dbms_lob.writeappend( l_blob, ?, ? ); " +
      "end;";
    String newBlobData = new String("data to be appended");
    byte[] byteArray = newBlobData.getBytes();
    cstmt = conn.prepareCall( stmtString );
    cstmt.setInt( 1, 1 );
    cstmt.setInt( 2, byteArray.length );
    cstmt.setBytes( 3, byteArray );
    cstmt.execute();
  }
  finally
  {
    JDBCUtil.close( cstmt);
  }
 }
}
```

After the _appendToBlob method is executed, the string data to be appended gets appended to the end of the BLOB column:

```
benchmark@ORA10G> select utl_raw.cast_to_varchar2( blob_col) blob_col
  2  from blob_table;

BLOB_COL
--------------------------------------------------------------------------
---------------------------------------------------
data to overwrite existing data in the beginning line number 3.
This is the final line.
data to be appended
```

In the next section, we'll look at how to read data stored in a BFILE column.

Reading BFILE Data

To demonstrate how to read BFILE data, we first create a table, bfile_table, with a column of type BFILE:

```
benchmark@ORA10G> create table bfile_table
  2  (
  3     x varchar2(30),
  4     id number,
  5     bfile_col bfile
  6  );

Table created.
```

We create the `directory` object as shown in earlier sections of this chapter:

```
benchmark@ORA10G> create or replace directory my_dir as 'C:\TEMP';

Directory created.
```

We insert the first row with `bfile_col` pointing to the same file, `test_bfile.txt`, that we used in the earlier examples. The second row inserted points to an image file called `image.gif` in the same directory:

```
benchmark@ORA10G> insert into bfile_table( x, id, bfile_col )
  2  values ( 'Ascii text file', 1, bfilename( 'MY_DIR', 'test_bfile.txt' ));

1 row created.

benchmark@ORA10G> insert into bfile_table( x, id, bfile_col )
  2  values ( 'Binary Gif File', 2, bfilename( 'MY_DIR', 'image.gif' ));

1 row created.

benchmark@ORA10G> commit;

Commit complete.
```

The class `DemoBfileOperations` demonstrates how to read both the binary and text data in the table `bfile_table` just created. The class begins by importing requisite classes and getting a database connection:

```
/** This program demonstrates how to read from a BFILE.
* Note that BFILEs are read-only - you cannot write to
* them.
* COMPATIBLITY NOTE:
*    runs successfully against 9.2.0.1.0 and 10.1.0.2.0
*/
import java.sql.SQLException;
import java.sql.Connection;
import java.io.InputStream;
import java.io.IOException;
import java.sql.PreparedStatement;
import oracle.jdbc.OracleResultSet;
import oracle.sql.BFILE;
import book.util.JDBCUtil;
import book.util.Util;
class DemoBfileOperations
{
  public static void main(String args[]) throws Exception
  {
    Util.checkProgramUsage( args );
    Connection conn = null;
```

```
try
{
  // get connection (autocommit is set to false)
  conn = JDBCUtil.getConnection("benchmark", "benchmark", args[0]);
```

We invoke two methods:

- _readBfileAsBinaryData(): Demonstrates how to read the binary image from our table

- _readBfileAsTextData(): Demonstrates how to read the text file contents pointed to by our BFILE column

Reading BFILE Data As Binary Data

In the method _readBfileAsBinaryData(), we first use the getBFILE() method of the OracleResultSet object (remember that the BFILE is an Oracle-only feature; the standard JDBC API does not support this concept). We then use the getBinaryStream() method of the BFILE class to first get the InputStream. Finally, we use the Java stream functionality to extract data:

```
/* demos how to read from a BFILE from the database as a binary file. */
private static void _readBfileAsBinaryData( Connection conn )
  throws SQLException, IOException
{
  PreparedStatement pstmt = null;
  OracleResultSet orset = null;
  InputStream in = null;
  BFILE bfile = null;
  try
  {
    String stmtString = "select bfile_col from bfile_table "+
      " where id = ?";
    pstmt = conn.prepareStatement( stmtString );
    pstmt.setInt( 1, 2 );
    orset = (OracleResultSet) pstmt.executeQuery();
    while( orset.next() )
    {
      bfile = orset.getBfile( 1 );
      bfile.openFile();
      in = bfile.getBinaryStream();
      byte[] byteArray = new byte[100];
      int length = -1;
```

Next, we loop through to read chunks of 100 bytes of binary data into our byte array:

```
      int numOfBytesRead = 0;
      while (( length = in.read( byteArray)) != -1 )
      {
        //System.out.println( byteArray );
        numOfBytesRead += length;
      }
```

```
          System.out.println("binary file: num of bytes read: " + numOfBytesRead);
          System.out.println("");
      }
   }
   finally
   {
      if( in != null )
        in.close();
      if( bfile != null )
        bfile.closeFile();
      JDBCUtil.close( pstmt);
      JDBCUtil.close( orset);
   }
}
```

Reading BFILE Data As ASCII Text

Reading BFILE data as ASCII text follows the exact same procedure as presented in the previous section for reading binary data, except that we need to convert the bytes into a String before we use it in our Java code, as shown in the method _readBfileAsTextData:

```
/* demos how to read from a BFILE from the database as an ASCII file. */
private static void _readBfileAsAsciiData( Connection conn )
   throws SQLException, IOException
{
   PreparedStatement pstmt = null;
   OracleResultSet orset = null;
   BFILE bfile = null;
   InputStream in = null;
   try
   {
      String stmtString = "select bfile_col from bfile_table "+
        " where id = ?";
      pstmt = conn.prepareStatement( stmtString );
      pstmt.setInt( 1, 1 );
      orset = (OracleResultSet) pstmt.executeQuery();
      byte[] buffer = new byte[30];
      int numOfCharacersRead = 0;
      int length = -1;
      while( orset.next() )
      {
        bfile = orset.getBfile( 1 );
        bfile.openFile();
        in = bfile.getBinaryStream();
        while (( length = in.read( buffer)) != -1 )
        {
          System.out.print( new String( buffer, 0, length ) );
          numOfCharacersRead += length;
```

```
      }
      System.out.println("\ntext file: num of chars read: " + numOfCharacersRead);
    }
  }
  finally
  {
    if( in != null )
      in.close();
    if( bfile != null )
      bfile.closeFile();
    JDBCUtil.close( pstmt);
    JDBCUtil.close( orset);
  }
}
}// end of class
```

In the next section, we'll cover how to use temporary LOBs in JDBC. 29.380

Temporary LOBs in JDBC

Now you know what temporary LOBs are and how to use them to store transient data in PL/SQL. In this section, we will create a temporary CLOB in JDBC and insert the value in a table. To create a temporary CLOB, we use the static method createTemporary() defined in the BLOB and CLOB classes. The signature of this method in the CLOB and BLOB classes is as follows:

```
public static oracle.sql.CLOB createTemporary(Connection conn,
  boolean isCached, int duration)
public static oracle.sql.BLOB createTemporary(Connection conn,
  boolean isCached, int duration)
```

The duration must be either DURATION_SESSION or DURATION_CALL as defined in the BLOB or CLOB class. In client applications, DURATION_SESSION is appropriate. DURATION_CALL is relevant mainly in Java stored procedures.

After we have finished using the temporary LOB, we should free it with the freeTemporary() method defined in BLOB and CLOB classes:

```
public void freeTemporary()
```

We will now create a temporary CLOB and insert it into clob_table. The following DemoTemporaryLobs class illustrates this:

```
/** This program demonstrates how to use temporary LOBs.
* We work with temporary CLOBs, though the same concepts also
* apply to temporary BLOBs.
* COMPATIBLITY NOTE: In 9i you have to use the method
* getAsciiOutputStream() in the CLOB interface instead of the
* standard setAsciiStream() method as explained in the code:
*/
import java.util.Arrays;
import java.sql.SQLException;
```

```
import java.sql.Connection;
import java.io.OutputStream;
import java.io.IOException;
import java.sql.PreparedStatement;
import oracle.sql.CLOB;
import book.util.JDBCUtil;
import book.util.Util;
class DemoTemporaryLobs
{
```

The main() method simply invokes the method _insertClobUsingTemporaryClob() and commits. The method _insertClobUsingTemporaryClob() creates a temporary CLOB and inserts it into the table clob_table:

```
public static void main(String args[]) throws Exception
{
  Util.checkProgramUsage( args );
  Connection conn = null;
  try
  {
    // get connection (autocommit is set to false)
    conn = JDBCUtil.getConnection("benchmark", "benchmark", args[0]);
    _insertClobUsingTemporaryClob( conn );
    conn.commit();
  }
  finally
  {
    // release resources associated with JDBC in the finally clause.
    JDBCUtil.close( conn );
  }
}
```

In the method _insertClobUsingTemporaryClob(), we first declare variables before the try catch block begins:

```
/* demos how to insert a CLOB using temporary CLOBs.  */
  private static void _insertClobUsingTemporaryClob( Connection conn )
    throws SQLException, IOException
  {
    String insertStmt = "insert into clob_table(x, id, clob_col) " +
      " values( ?, ?, ? ) ";
    PreparedStatement pstmt = null;
    OutputStream out = null;
    CLOB tempClob = null;
    try
    {
```

We invoke the method createTemporary() to create a temporary CLOB:

```
    tempClob = CLOB.createTemporary( conn, true, CLOB.DURATION_SESSION );
```

We next open the CLOB. Opening and closing of LOBs in general improves performance when you do multiple writes to the LOB:

```
tempClob.open( CLOB.MODE_READWRITE);
```

We next get the chunk size and initialize a byte array of a size equal to the chunk size with the character "b":

```
int chunkSize = tempClob.getChunkSize();
System.out.println("chunk size for temporary lob: "
    + chunkSize);
byte[] buffer = new byte[ chunkSize ];
Arrays.fill( buffer, 0, chunkSize, (byte)'b' );
```

Then we initialize the OutputStream. In 10g, the standard method in the Clob interface works. In 9i, you have to use the Oracle extension method getAsciiOutputStream() in the CLOB interface:

```
out = tempClob.setAsciiStream( 0L );
// In 9i, you would have to use the following method instead
// of setAsciiStream()
// out = tempClob.getAsciiOutputStream();
```

We go in a loop and write data equal to ten chunks. Subsequently, we use the method setClob() to set the temporary CLOB value and insert it into the table:

```
for( int i=0; i < 10; i++ )
{
    out.write( buffer, 0, chunkSize );
}
pstmt = conn.prepareStatement( insertStmt );
pstmt.setString( 1, "Using temporary clob" );
pstmt.setInt( 2, 4 );
pstmt.setClob( 3, tempClob );
pstmt.executeUpdate();
}
finally
{
    try
    {
        if( out != null ) out.close();
        if( ( tempClob != null ) )
            CLOB.freeTemporary( tempClob );
    }
    catch (Exception e) { e.printStackTrace(); }
    JDBCUtil.close( pstmt);
    }
}
}// end of program
```

Notice how we use the freeTemporary() method in the finally clause to free the temporary CLOB.

Alternatives to BFILEs for File Operations

You've seen how you can read from a file (text or binary) using a BFILE in PL/SQL or JDBC. You can also use a BFILE along with the DBMS_LOB package to load a text or binary file directly into a CLOB or BLOB and access them from PL/SQL or JDBC. There are two alternatives to using a BFILE for file manipulations:

- *Use the* UTL_FILE *package.* The first alternative is to use the supplied PL/SQL package UTL_FILE to read from *and* write to a text or binary file accessible on a database server (remember, BFILEs do not allow you to write to a file; you can use the UTL_FILE package to work around that).

- *Use external tables.* The second alternative that allows you to read from an operating system text file directly using select statements is to use external tables. Note that you can only do a read using this alternative, and that too only on text files.

Both alternatives are Oracle-specific solutions and fall outside the scope of the JDBC API. However, since they form an alternative to the actual problem of file operations being achieved by the BFILE, I mention them briefly here.

Using the UTL_FILE PL/SQL Package to Read from and Write to a Text File

With the UTL_FILE package, PL/SQL programs (and JDBC programs that invoke these PL/SQL programs) can read from and write to text or binary files accessible to the database server. We will go through only a few subprograms of this package that allow us to read and write to a file. Please consult *PL/SQL Packages and Types Reference (10g Release 1)* (available from http://otn.oracle.com) for a detailed description of the package capabilities.

Note In the past, accessible directories for the UTL_FILE functions were specified in the initialization file using the UTL_FILE_DIR parameter. However, for Oracle9*i* and 10*g*, I recommend that you use the CREATE DIRECTORY feature, which replaces UTL_FILE_DIR. Directory objects offer more flexibility and granular control to the UTL_FILE application administrator and, more important, they can be maintained dynamically (i.e., without shutting down the database).

Following are brief descriptions of the package subprograms we will use in the examples:

- UTL_FILE.FOPEN: This function opens the file and returns a file handle that is used in subsequent operations on the file. The syntax is

```
UTL_FILE.FOPEN (location IN VARCHAR2, filename IN VARCHAR2,
open_mode IN VARCHAR2,max_linesize IN BINARY_INTEGER)
RETURN file_type;
```

The various parameters are as follows:

- location: The directory location of a file. This string is a directory object name and is case-sensitive. The default is uppercase. Read privileges must be granted on this directory object for the UTL_FILE user to run FOPEN.

- filename: The file name, including the extension (file type), without the directory path.

- open_mode: Specifies how the file is opened. Modes include

```
r - read text
w - write text
a - append text
rb - read byte mode
wb - write byte mode
ab - append byte mode
```

- max_linesize: The maximum number of characters for each line, including the newline character, for this file (the minimum value is 1; the maximum value is 32,767). If this parameter is unspecified, Oracle supplies a default value of 1,024.

- UTL_FILE.GET_LINE: This procedure reads text from the open file identified by the file handle and places the text in the output buffer parameter. Text is read up to, but not including, the line terminator, or up to the end of the file, or up to the end of the len parameter. It cannot exceed the max_linesize specified in FOPEN. The syntax is

```
UTL_FILE.GET_LINE ( file IN FILE_TYPE, buffer OUT VARCHAR2,
len IN PLS_INTEGER DEFAULT NULL);
```

The parameters are as follows:

- file: The file handle returned by FOPEN.

- buffer: The buffer in which the read data is populated.

- len: The maximum number of bytes to read from the file. The default is null. If this parameter is null, Oracle supplies the value of max_linesize.

- UTL_FILE.PUT_LINE: This procedure writes the text string stored in the buffer parameter to the open file identified by the file handle. The file must be open in write mode. PUT_LINE terminates the line with the platform-specific line terminator character or characters. The syntax is

```
UTL_FILE.PUT_LINE (file IN FILE_TYPE,buffer IN VARCHAR2,
  autoflush IN BOOLEAN DEFAULT FALSE);
```

The parameters are as follows:

- file: The active file handle returned by an FOPEN call

- buffer: The text buffer containing lines to be written to the file

- autoflush: Flushes the buffer to disk after the write

- UTL_FILE.FCLOSE: This procedure closes an open file. The syntax is

```
UTL_FILE.FCLOSE ( file IN OUT FILE_TYPE );
```

The parameter is as follows:

- file: An active file handle returned by an FOPEN call

Now we are ready to look at some working examples. First, we create a directory object under which the files will be manipulated by UTL_FILE:

```
benchmark@ORA10G> create or replace directory my_dir as 'C:\TEMP';
```

We then declare the buffer and file handle variables:

```
benchmark@ORA10G> declare
  2    l_buffer varchar2(32767);
  3    l_file_handle utl_file.file_type;
```

We open the file test_bfile.txt in read mode with a maximum line size of 256:

```
  4  begin
  5    l_file_handle := utl_file.fopen( 'MY_DIR', 'test_bfile.txt', 'R', 256 );
```

Then in a loop we invoke UTL_FILE.GET_LINE() to get each line and print it out. At the end of the file, the exception NO_DATA_FOUND is raised, at which point we invoke the UTL_FILE.FCLOSE() method to close the file.

```
  7    loop
  8      utl_file.get_line( l_file_handle, l_buffer );
  9      dbms_output.put_line( l_buffer );
 10    end loop;
 11  exception
 12    when no_data_found then
 13      utl_file.fclose( l_file_handle );
 14  end;
 15  /
This is a test.
This is line number 2.
This is line number 3.
This is the final line.

PL/SQL procedure successfully completed.
```

Next we write to a file. We create a new file called my_file.txt automatically by opening the file in write mode and use UTL_FILE.PUT_LINE to put some lines in the file. Finally, we close the file by invoking the UTL_FILE.FCLOSE() function. The code is as follows:

```
benchmark@ORA10G> declare
  2    l_buffer varchar2(32767);
  3    l_file_handle utl_file.file_type;
  4  begin
```

```
 5    -- open the file in write mode -- create one if
 6    -- file does not exist.
 7
 8    l_file_handle := utl_file.fopen( 'MY_DIR', 'my_file.txt', 'W',
 9      256 );
10    for i in 1 .. 10
11    loop
12      utl_file.put_line( l_file_handle, 'my line number ' || i );
13      dbms_output.put_line( l_buffer );
14    end loop;
15    utl_file.fclose( l_file_handle );
16  exception
17    when others then
18      raise;
19  end;
20  /
```

Our newly created file, my_file.txt, in the directory C:\TEMP looks as follows:

```
my line number 1
my line number 2
my line number 3
my line number 4
my line number 5
my line number 6
my line number 7
my line number 8
my line number 9
my line number 10
```

Using the UTL_FILE PL/SQL Package to Read from and Write to a Binary File

We will use the functions get_raw() and put_raw() described in this section for reading from and writing to a binary file.

Note The RAW data type stores data that is not to be interpreted (i.e., not explicitly converted when moving data between different systems) by the Oracle database. These data types are intended for binary data or byte strings.

- GET_RAW: This function reads a RAW value from a file and adjusts the file pointer ahead by the number of bytes read. It ignores line terminators and returns the actual number of bytes requested by the len parameter. The syntax is

```
UTL_FILE.GET_RAW (fid IN utl_file.file_type,
r OUT NOCOPY RAW,len IN PLS_INTEGER DEFAULT NULL);
```

The parameters are as follows:

- fid: The file ID.
- r: The raw binary data.
- len: The number of bytes read from the file. The default is null, in which case it is assumed to be the maximum length of RAW.

- PUT_RAW: This function accepts as input a RAW data value and writes the value to the output buffer. The syntax is

```
UTL_FILE.PUT_RAW ( fid IN utl_file.file_type, r IN RAW,
   autoflush IN BOOLEAN DEFAULT FALSE);
```

The parameters are as follows:

- fid: The file ID.
- r: The raw binary data.
- autoflush: If true, this parameter performs a flush after writing the value to the output buffer. The default is false.

In the following example, we open the GIF image in the file image.gif in the directory C:\TEMP, read it into the raw buffer, and write it back to another file called image1.gif that we open in write mode. Notice that we use 'RB' to open the first file in "read byte" mode and 'WB' to open the second file in "write byte" mode.

```
benchmark@ORA10G> declare
  2    l_buffer raw(32767);
  3    l_input_file utl_file.file_type;
  4    l_output_file utl_file.file_type;
  5  begin
  6    l_input_file := utl_file.fopen( 'MY_DIR', 'image.gif', 'RB',
  7      256 );
  8    l_output_file := utl_file.fopen( 'MY_DIR', 'image1.gif', 'WB',
  9      256 );
 10    loop
 11      utl_file.get_raw( l_input_file, l_buffer );
 12      utl_file.put_raw( l_output_file, l_buffer );
 13      --dbms_output.put_line( utl_raw.cast_to_varchar2(l_buffer) );
 14    end loop;
 15  exception
 16    when no_data_found then
 17      utl_file.fclose( l_input_file );
 18      utl_file.fclose( l_output_file );
 19  end;
 20  /

PL/SQL procedure successfully completed.
```

Using External Tables to Read Text Files

The external table feature (introduced in 9*i*) gives you the ability to query a flat file using a select statement. It is typically used to load huge amounts of data from files to tables in a data warehouse system. It can, however, be very useful in reading text data from PL/SQL or, for that matter, using JDBC. We'll go through a small example to read a text file, but you'll need to read through the Oracle documentation (see *Oracle Database SQL Reference [10*g *Release 1]*) for the detailed capabilities and options available with the external table feature. Just to emphasize again, you can use this feature only with text files, and you can only *read* from the operating system files—you cannot write to them using external tables.

First, we need to create a directory object in which our file exists as follows:

```
benchmark@ORA10G> create or replace directory my_dir as 'C:\TEMP';

Directory created.
```

Our example file, et_data.txt, exists in this directory and contains employee ID and employee number fields for some employees:

```
1, 'Varun Menon'
2, 'Chaandni Sneha'
3, 'John Edgar'
4, 'Jones Poe'
```

We now create an external table that points to the preceding file as follows:

```
benchmark@ORA10G> create table my_emp_et
  2  (
  3    empno number,
  4    ename varchar2(20)
  5  )
  6  organization external
  7  (
  8    type oracle_loader
  9    default directory my_dir
 10    access parameters
 11    (
 12      fields terminated by ','
 13      optionally enclosed by "'"
 14      missing field values are null
 15    )
 16    location( 'et_data.txt' )
 17  );

Table created.
```

The `organization external` keyword tells Oracle that this table actually is an external table. The `default directory` option specifies `my_dir` to be the directory under which the file for this table exists. The next three lines specify that the fields are terminated by a comma (`,`) are optionally enclosed by a single quote (`'`), and any fields that are missing should be treated as `null`. Finally, the `location` option specifies the file name to be `et_data.txt`. We are now ready to run a normal select on this table as follows:

```
benchmark@ORA10G> select * from my_emp_et;

    EMPNO ENAME
---------- --------------------
        1 Varun Menon
        2 Chaandni Sneha
        3 John Edgar
        4 Jones Poe

benchmark@ORA10G> select empno, ename
  2  from my_emp_et
  3  where empno <= 3;

    EMPNO ENAME
---------- --------------------
        1 Varun Menon
        2 Chaandni Sneha
        3 John Edgar
```

You can thus use this facility to do the following, among other things:

- Do a one-time load from files into databases using the `insert into select * from <external table>` syntax. This is the most common usage of external tables.

- Get the contents of a text file on the database server in your JDBC layer by using a simple `select` statement. Of course, all the amazing flexibility that comes along with the `select` statement is available for you to use.

- Treat a structured file as a table with individual columns (as we did previously) and run selects on them to get data, which can be filtered or transformed on its way to JDBC. If the file is not structured (it uses a free format) then, in most cases, you could use the new line as a separator to read the data in JDBC using simple selects.

BFILE vs. UTL_FILE vs. External Table

Table 12-2 shows a comparison of the features of three alternatives useful in server-side text and/or binary file reading and manipulation.

Table 12-2. *Comparison of Various Server-Side File Manipulation Alternatives*

BFILE	UTL_FILE	External Table
Can be used to read text and binary files.	Can be used to read *and* write text and binary files. It is the only alternative that supports both text and binary files.	Can be used to read text files.
Useful in reading text and binary files as streams that can be read in user-defined chunks.	Useful in reading and writing text and binary files in user-defined chunk sizes. You can also do random access using functions such as fseek (see the Oracle documentation for further details).	Useful in using selects to read text data. It is simple to use and allows you to transform/manipulate resulting data using the power that comes with the select statement. Also, the JDBC code is relatively simple and does not have to deal with streams (we use the ResultSet interface to get the data as strings). The maximum size of one "row" (or chunk) is limited to 4,000 bytes (the size of VARCHAR2 in SQL).
Works well in JDBC and PL/SQL for reading data.	Of limited use in JDBC if you want to read a file. Since there is no JDBC type corresponding to the file handle record type used by UTL_FILE, you will have to create a wrapper. Also, you will need to do multiple server calls per read while invoking the UTL_FILE.GET_LINE function, which can be a performance bottleneck. It works well in PL/SQL, as there are no round-trips involved.	Works well in JDBC for most text cases. In free-format texts, one text chunk bounded by the delimiter should not exceed 4,000 bytes (e.g., if the delimiter is a new line, then each line should be less than 4,000 bytes in size).

We'll now run a performance comparison between using BFILE and external tables to read a text file. (Using UTL_FILE is too cumbersome and is usually not a good option anyway, due to reasons mentioned in Table 12-2, so we won't bother to use UTL_FILE in this comparison.) First, we create the schema and the data on which the benchmark will run. We create the directory that will contain the benchmark file.

```
benchmark@ORA10G> create or replace directory my_dir as 'C:\TEMP';

Directory created.
```

Since you are now an expert in UTL_FILE, for fun let's create the benchmark file using the following UTL_FILE program:

```
benchmark@ORA10G> declare
  2      l_buffer varchar2(32767);
  3      l_file_handle utl_file.file_type;
  4  begin
  5      -- open the file in write mode -- create one if
  6      -- file does not exist.
  7
  8      l_file_handle := utl_file.fopen( 'MY_DIR', 'benchmark_input.txt', 'W',
```

```
 9       256 );
10     for i in 1 .. 10000
11     loop
12       utl_file.put_line( l_file_handle, 'my line number ' || i );
13     end loop;
14     utl_file.fclose( l_file_handle );
15   exception
16     when others then
17         raise;
18   end;
19   /
```

PL/SQL procedure successfully completed.

As you can see, the program simply writes 10,000 lines to a file called benchmark_input.txt.
The benchmark_input.txt file has a total of 188,894 characters; thus it has approximately 19
characters per line on average.

Next, we create a table containing a BFILE column and insert a row into the table:

```
benchmark@ORA10G> create table bfile_table
  2  (
  3    x varchar2(30),
  4    id number,
  5    bfile_col bfile
  6  );
```

Table created.

```
benchmark@ORA10G> insert into bfile_table( x, id, bfile_col )
  2  values ( 'benchmark text file', 1,
  3    bfilename( 'MY_DIR', 'benchmark_input.txt' ));
```

1 row created.

```
benchmark@ORA10G> commit;
```

Finally, we create an external table to point to our benchmark file (note that we use the
phrase records limited by newline to indicate that each "row" selected will be defined by the
newline delimiter):

```
benchmark@ORA10G> create table et_table
  2  (
  3    data varchar2(4000)
  4  )
  5  organization external
  6  (
  7    type oracle_loader
  8    default directory my_dir
  9    access parameters
```

```
10    (
11       records delimited by newline
12    )
13    location( 'benchmark_input.txt' )
14  );
```

Table created.

benchmark@ORA10G> select count(*) from et_table;

```
  COUNT(*)
----------
     10000
```

In our benchmark program, we do the following:

1. Take care to prepare the statements only once to avoid multiple soft parses of the statements.

2. Run the external table select with multiple fetch sizes.

3. To ensure that the JVM is in a steady state when the benchmark is run, we make sure we run each benchmark for five minutes (by finding out how many runs are required for running the benchmark for five minutes and then taking an average at the end).

Following is the class BenchmarkReadUsingBfileAndExternalTables that I used to run the benchmark. It extends the class JBenchmark covered in Chapter 1. It begins with the import statements:

```
/** This program compares read using a BFILE and external tables.
* COMPATIBLITY NOTE:
*    runs successfully against 9.2.0.1.0 and 10.1.0.2.0
*/
import java.sql.SQLException;
import java.sql.Connection;
import java.io.BufferedReader;
import java.io.InputStreamReader;
import java.io.InputStream;
import java.io.IOException;
import java.sql.PreparedStatement;
import java.sql.ResultSet;
import oracle.jdbc.OracleResultSet;
import oracle.sql.BFILE;
import book.util.JDBCUtil;
import book.util.JBenchmark;
class BenchmarkReadUsingBfileAndExternalTables extends JBenchmark
{
  public static void main(String args[]) throws Exception
  {
```

We check the command-line parameters. The first argument is the database name, and the second optional argument is the fetch size used in selects for the external tables:

```
if( args.length != 1 && args.length != 2 )
{
   System.err.println(" Usage: java <program_name> <database_name>
[prefetch_size]");
   Runtime.getRuntime().exit( 1 );
}
int prefetchSize = 20;
if( args.length == 2 )
{
   prefetchSize = Integer.parseInt( args[1] );
}
System.out.println( "Prefetch size for external table: " + prefetchSize );
Connection conn = null;
try
{
   // get connection (autocommit is off )
```

In the try catch block, we obtain the connection, prepare our benchmark statements, and invoke the method _runBenchmark(), which contains the bulk of the logic:

```
   conn = JDBCUtil.getConnection("benchmark", "benchmark", args[0]);
   _prepareBenchmarkStatements( conn );
   new BenchmarkReadUsingBfileAndExternalTables()._runBenchmark(
     conn, prefetchSize );
}
finally
{
   // release resources associated with JDBC in the finally clause.
   _closeBenchmarkStatements( conn );
   JDBCUtil.close( conn );
}
}
```

The method _runBenchmark() times the first and the second method of the JBenchmark passing the connection and the fetch size passed in (or a default fetch size of 20):

```
private void _runBenchmark( Connection conn, int prefetchSize ) throws Exception
{
   Object[] params = new Object[ 1 ];
   params[0] = new Integer( prefetchSize );
   timeMethod( JBenchmark.FIRST_METHOD, conn, params, BFILE_DESC );
   timeMethod( JBenchmark.SECOND_METHOD, conn, params, EXTERNAL_TABLE_DESC );
}
```

The method firstMethod() is overridden to implement the logic of reading the benchmark file line by line from the BFILE column in the table bfile_table:

```
/* reads an ASCII file using BFILE. */
public void firstMethod( Connection conn, Object[] params ) throws Exception
{
  OracleResultSet orset = null;
  BFILE bfile = null;
  BufferedReader reader = null;
  InputStream in = null;
  long numOfCharacersRead = 0;
  try
  {
    _bfilePstmt.setInt( 1, 1 );
    orset = (OracleResultSet) _bfilePstmt.executeQuery();
    String line = null;
    while( orset.next() )
    {
      bfile = orset.getBfile( 1 );
      bfile.openFile();
      in = bfile.getBinaryStream();
      reader = new BufferedReader(new InputStreamReader(in));
      numOfCharacersRead = 0;
      while (( line = reader.readLine() ) != null )
      {
        //System.out.println( line );
        numOfCharacersRead += line.length();
      }
    }
  }
  finally
  {
    if( in != null )
      in.close();
    if( bfile != null )
      bfile.closeFile();
    JDBCUtil.close( orset);
  }
  //System.out.println( "No of characters read: " + numOfCharacersRead );
}
```

The method secondMethod() is overridden to implement the logic of reading the benchmark file by selecting from the external table et_table:

```
/* reads from a text file using external tables.  */
public void secondMethod( Connection conn, Object[] parameters ) throws Exception
{
  ResultSet rset = null;
```

```
  long numOfCharacersRead = 0;
  int prefetchSize = ((Integer) parameters[0]).intValue();
  try
  {
    _externalTablePstmt.setFetchSize( prefetchSize );
    rset = _externalTablePstmt.executeQuery();
    numOfCharacersRead = 0;
    while( rset.next() )
    {
      String line1 = rset.getString(1);
      numOfCharacersRead += line1.length();
    }
  }
  finally
  {
    JDBCUtil.close( rset);
  }
  //System.out.println( "No of characters read: " + numOfCharacersRead );
}
```

The methods _prepareBenchmarkStatements() and _closeBenchmarkStatements() simply prepare and close the SQL statements used to run the appropriate query for the BFILE and external table cases:

```
private static void _prepareBenchmarkStatements( Connection conn )
  throws SQLException
{
  String stmtString = "select data from et_table";
  _externalTablePstmt = conn.prepareStatement( stmtString );
  stmtString = "select bfile_col from bfile_table "+
      " where id = ?";
  _bfilePstmt = conn.prepareStatement( stmtString );
}
private static void _closeBenchmarkStatements( Connection conn )
  throws SQLException
{
  JDBCUtil.close( _bfilePstmt );
  JDBCUtil.close( _externalTablePstmt );
}
private static final String BFILE_DESC = "Using Bfile";
private static final String EXTERNAL_TABLE_DESC = "Using external table";
private static PreparedStatement _bfilePstmt;
private static PreparedStatement _externalTablePstmt;
}
```

When I run the program for a fetch size of 100, for example, the results are as follows:

```
URL:jdbc:oracle:thin:@(DESCRIPTION=(ADDRESS=(PROTOCOL=tcp)(PORT=1521)
(HOST=rmenon-lap))(CONNECT_DATA=(SID=ora10g)))
Using Bfile
   On an average it took 30 ms (number of runs = 3225.)
Using external table
   On an average it took 158 ms (number of runs = 1063.)
```

As you can see, external tables run slower (they take around five times longer) in my test benchmarks compared to BFILEs. Runs for other fetch sizes yielded similar results. This does not mean that you should discard the idea of external tables. Remember that reading from a file such as this in a real production system is not a typical requirement. If you are indeed reading files regularly as this, you should consider loading them into the database anyway (external tables are an excellent tool for achieving a one-time load from files into tables). Loading files into the database also gives your application all the benefits that come from storing data in the database as opposed to retaining them in the operating system (e.g., the ability to recover data in the event of a crash). Also, external tables give you access to using SQL on the data to transform them on their way to the client. You should use all of these criteria in choosing the appropriate tool for your particular use case.

Summary

In this chapter, you learned what LOBs are and how they are useful in storing large text and binary data. You learned how to read from and write to CLOBs and BLOBs, and how to read from BFILEs. You then looked at some Oracle-specific alternatives to using BFILE: the UTL_FILE PL/SQL package and external tables. Also, you discovered that UTL_FILE can be used to read and write to text and binary files, whereas external tables can be used only to read from text files. Finally, you compared these alternatives in terms of features and performance.

■ ■ ■

Statement Caching

Statement caching is a JDBC 3.0 feature designed to improve performance by caching statements that are used repeatedly (e.g., in a loop) in the same session. By caching the statements, you prevent the overhead of repeated parsing of the cursor.

In this chapter, you'll learn about statement caching, its different flavors in JDBC, and how it improves the performance of JDBC programs. As a background to the statement caching concept, you'll first go through a detailed discussion of cursors and ref cursors. You'll also learn about two other related caches, namely the PL/SQL cursor cache (which is the equivalent of JDBC statement caching in PL/SQL code) and session cached cursors.

■Note We'll use the `tkprof` utility in this chapter, so if you aren't familiar with it I urge you to refer to the section on `tkprof` in Chapter 1 and the relevant section of *Oracle Database Performance Tuning Guide and Reference (10g Release 1)*. In this chapter, you'll also use the `runstats` utility and its JDBC wrapper, `JRunstats`, which is discussed in Chapter 1.

Cursors

A *cursor* is a handle to a private SQL area that points to an entry in the shared pool consisting of the parsed statement. It consists of session-specific information, such as bind variables, the cursor state, the current position in the row in the case of a `select` statement, and so on.

Cursors in PL/SQL (Explicit and Implicit)

Let's look at an example of a cursor in PL/SQL. Assume that we've already created a table, `t1`, and inserted numbers from 1 to 5 into it:

```
benchmark@ORA10G> create table t1 ( x number);

Table created.

benchmark@ORA10G> insert into t1
  2  select rownum
  3  from all_objects
  4  where rownum <= 5;
```

5 rows created.

benchmark@ORA10G> commit;

Commit complete.

Now we can declare a cursor explicitly in PL/SQL and retrieve its contents:

```
benchmark@ORA10G> -- open a cursor and select from it
benchmark@ORA10G> declare
  2     cursor l_cursor is select x from t1;
  3     l_dummy number;
  4  begin
  5     open l_cursor;
  6     loop
  7        fetch l_cursor into l_dummy;
  8        exit when l_cursor%notfound;
  9        dbms_output.put_line( l_dummy );
 10     end loop;
 11     close l_cursor;
 12  end;
 13  /
1
2
3
4
5

PL/SQL procedure successfully completed.
```

When PL/SQL encounters line 2 in the preceding code snippet, it creates a cursor handle and points it to the parsed select statement in the shared pool (if the statement doesn't exist yet in the shared pool, it needs to be hard-parsed before it's put into the shared pool; see the section "Overview of How Oracle Processes SQL Statements (DML)" of Chapter 5 for a brief discussion on hard parses and soft parses). Notice that there are two distinct data structures involved here:

- *The cursor itself,* which is specific to the session and consists of session-specific information, such as bind variables, the cursor state (whether it is open or closed), and so on, required in executing the statement

- *The parsed SQL statement,* which is in the shared pool and by definition can be shared among multiple sessions that execute the same statement

Line 5 in the code snippet opens the cursor, and then we loop through the cursor between lines 6 and 10. Notice how we use the PL/SQL construct cursor_variable%notfound to exit the loop when there are no more records to fetch. We then close the cursor outside the loop in line 11.

The preceding code is an example in which a cursor is *explicitly* declared in PL/SQL. The following code shows how to achieve the same results using an *implicit* cursor:

```
benchmark@ORA10G> begin
  2    for l_cursor in( select x from t1 )
  3    loop
  4       dbms_output.put_line( l_cursor.x );
  5    end loop;
  6  end;
  7  /
1
2
3
4
5

PL/SQL procedure successfully completed.
```

Notice how the code does not involve explicitly opening, closing, and fetching records from the cursor; PL/SQL does that for you. You will find that the code using implicit cursors is *usually* more concise, more readable, and slightly more performant compared to code using explicit cursors. Explicit cursors, on the other hand, give you more flexibility and control over when the open, fetch, and close of a cursor is done. This control can be used in techniques such as bulk collect to achieve better performance in certain cases, as you will see in Chapter 17.

Ref Cursors (or Cursor Variables)

A *ref cursor* or *cursor variable* is a pointer to a cursor. Unlike the implicit and explicit cursors that are hard-wired to specific queries at compile time, a ref cursor can be tied to different queries during the same execution of the program. For example, consider the following procedure created after we log in as the user SCOTT:

```
scott@ORA10G> create or replace procedure demo_refcursor(
      p_query_selector in varchar2,
  2      p_criterion in varchar2, p_ref_cursor in out sys_refcursor )
  3    is
  4      l_empno emp.empno%type;
  5      l_ename emp.ename%type;
  6      l_job emp.job%type;
  7    begin
  8      if( 'ename' = p_query_selector ) then
  9        open p_ref_cursor for
 10          select empno, ename, job
 11          from emp
 12          where ename like '%'||p_criterion||'%';
 13      elsif( 'job' = p_query_selector ) then
 14        open p_ref_cursor for
 15          select empno, ename, job
 16          from emp
```

```
17          where job like '%'||p_criterion||'%';
18      end if;
19  end;
20  /
```

Procedure created.

The procedure, demo_refcursor, demonstrates how the same ref cursor variable can be dynamically associated with a different cursor based on the user input. The procedure takes a query selector and a criterion, and returns a ref cursor in its third parameter, which is declared using the built-in PL/SQL data type sys_refcursor. In lines 4 through 6, we use the %type construct to declare variables whose types are anchored to the emp table column types. Based on the value of the query selector, the procedure opens and returns a different cursor, and uses the passed criterion in the query's where clause. We can now fetch these cursors as ResultSet objects using the CallableStatement interface in JDBC and print them out. The following DemoRefCursor class does this:

```
/** This program simply prints out a ref cursor, which points to a
    different query based on passed criteria
* COMPATIBLITY NOTE:
*    runs successfully against 9.2.0.1.0 and 10.1.0.2.0
*/
import java.sql.SQLException;
import java.sql.ResultSet;
import java.sql.Connection;
import java.sql.CallableStatement;
import oracle.jdbc.OracleTypes;
import book.util.JDBCUtil;
class DemoRefCursor
{
  public static void main(String args[]) throws Exception
  {
    Connection conn = null;
    CallableStatement cstmt = null;
    ResultSet rset = null;
```

The first command-line parameter to the class is the database name, the second parameter is the criterion (which becomes the first parameter of the procedure demo_refcursor), and the third parameter is the bind value to the dynamically generated ref cursor's query (which becomes the second parameter to the procedure demo_refcursor). We simply execute the procedure demo_refcursor in the following code, passing the appropriate parameters:

```
    try
    {
      // get connection - auto commit is off
      conn = (Connection) JDBCUtil. getConnection("scott", "tiger", args[0]);
      String stmtString = "{call demo_refcursor( ?, ?, ? ) }";
      cstmt = conn.prepareCall( stmtString );
      cstmt.setString( 1, args[1] ); // criterion
```

```
          cstmt.setString( 2, args[2] ); // bind value
          cstmt.registerOutParameter( 3, OracleTypes.CURSOR ); // returned cursor
          cstmt.execute();
          rset = (ResultSet) cstmt.getObject( 3 );
          while( rset.next() )
          {
            System.out.println( rset.getInt( 1 ) + ", " + rset.getString( 2 ) +
              ", " + rset.getString( 3 ) );
          }
        }
        finally
        {
          // release resources associated with JDBC in the finally clause.
          JDBCUtil.close( rset );
          JDBCUtil.close( cstmt );
          JDBCUtil.close( conn );
        }
      }
  }
}
```

We first invoke the program with the criterion ename and the bind value SCOTT to get the following output:

```
B:\>java DemoRefCursor ora10g ename SCOTT
URL:jdbc:oracle:thin:@(DESCRIPTION=(ADDRESS=(PROTOCOL=tcp)(PORT=1521)
(HOST=rmenon-lap))(CONNECT_DATA=(SID=ora10g)))
7788, SCOTT, ANALYST
```

Next, we invoke the program with the criterion job and the bind value CLERK to get the following output:

```
B:\>java DemoRefCursor ora10g job CLERK
URL:jdbc:oracle:thin:@(DESCRIPTION=(ADDRESS=(PROTOCOL=tcp)(PORT=1521)
(HOST=rmenon-lap))(CONNECT_DATA=(SID=ora10g)))
7369, SMITH, CLERK
7876, ADAMS, CLERK
7900, JAMES, CLERK
7934, MILLER, CLERK
```

The preceding program demonstrates that a ref cursor can be dynamically made to point to a different query at runtime. A ref cursor is typically used to return a query's result to client programs such as those written using JDBC/ODBC, Pro*C/Oracle Forms, and so on (as just demonstrated). This is a very powerful feature, because it allows the client and the server to transparently share the same result set. The ref cursor can be declared on the client (e.g., the ResultSet variable in our program, DemoRefCursor), it can be opened on the server, and the results can be fetched from the client.

The next few sections assume that you know the difference between a hard parse and a soft parse of a DML statement. If you're not familiar with these concepts, please review the section "Overview of How Oracle Processes SQL Statements (DML)" of Chapter 5.

Prepare Once, Bind and Execute Many Times

As you know by now, each time an application opens a cursor, Oracle hard-parses the statement on the first encounter (or if the statement is no longer in the shared pool), and then soft-parses it on subsequent encounters. In this section, we will look at how a statement is parsed within a loop.

To see the inner workings of our programs in this chapter, we will set SQL trace from Java by executing the method JDBCUtil.startTrace(). The method startTrace() of the JDBCUtil class is as follows:

```
/**
 * starts SQL trace for a JDBC program. The SQL trace is
 * automatically disabled when the program ends
 */
public static void startTrace ( Connection connection ) throws SQLException
{
  String setTimedStatisticsStmt = "alter session set timed_statistics=true";
  String setTraceStmt =
    "alter session set events '10046 trace name context forever, level 12'";
  Statement stmt = null;
  try
  {
    stmt = connection.createStatement();
    stmt.execute( setTimedStatisticsStmt );
    stmt.execute( setTraceStmt );
  }
  finally
  {
    stmt.close();
  }
}
```

As you can see, the method simply sets the timed statistics on and alters the session to enable SQL tracing. Subsequently, we will use tkprof to look at the trace file data.

The concept of soft and hard parses in a loop is illustrated by the following program, DemoParse, with interspersed explanatory comments:

```
import java.sql.SQLException;
import java.sql.ResultSet;
import java.sql.Connection;
import java.sql.PreparedStatement;
import oracle.jdbc.OracleTypes;
import book.util.JDBCUtil;
class DemoParse
{
  public static void main(String args[]) throws Exception
  {
    Connection conn = null;
    PreparedStatement pstmt = null;
```

```
PreparedStatement pstmt1 = null;
ResultSet rset = null;
ResultSet rset1 = null;
try
{
  // get connection - auto commit is off
  conn = (Connection) JDBCUtil. getConnection("scott", "tiger", args[0]);
```

We start the trace, as we will use `tkprof` to demonstrate the concepts:

```
JDBCUtil.startTrace( conn );
```

The first statement string has a "tag" enclosed within /*+ and */:

```
String stmtString = "select /*+ prepareStatement() within loop */" +
  " empno, job from emp where ename = ?";
```

Why do we need the tag? We need it because we will be comparing execution of the *same* statement (`select empno, job from emp where ename=?`) for two cases:

- *Case 1*: We execute `prepareStatement()` *within* a `for` loop that loops five times.

- *Case 2*: We execute `prepareStatement()` *outside* a `for` loop that loops five times.

When we look at the `tkprof` output, we need to distinguish between the two cases; otherwise, `tkprof` will combine the statistics for both at one place, since the statements will be identical. When we use a tag of the form /*+ *<some identifying string that is not a valid hint>*/, Oracle treats the tag as a no-op SQL hint (i.e., a `null` operation) and ignores it since it is not a valid hint, but still treats any two statements that have a different tag as "different." Using a tag like this is a very useful trick to compare identical statements in a SQL trace, but distinguish their alternative execution profiles in the trace file. This technique will become clearer once we look at the `tkprof` output.

■**Note** Instead of enclosing the tag between /*+ and */, you could enclose it within /* and */, which constitutes a comment. However, this works only in 9*i*; in 10*g*, as an optimization, Oracle strips out the comments before processing the statement, thus defeating the purpose of the tag.

From the tag value of `prepareStatement() within loop`, we can make out that we are going to execute case 1 first. We do that in the following code by executing our statement five times within the loop (note that the invocation of `prepareStatement()` is within the `for` loop):

```
for( int i=0; i < 5; i++ )
  {
    pstmt = conn.prepareStatement( stmtString );
    pstmt.setString( 1, "SCOTT" );
    rset = pstmt.executeQuery();
    while( rset.next() )
```

```
        {
        }
      }
```

Next, we prepare an identical statement except for the tag, which indicates that this time we prepare the statement outside the loop:

```
      stmtString = "select /*+ prepareStatement() outside loop */ " +
        "empno, job from emp where ename = ?";
      pstmt1 = conn.prepareStatement( stmtString );
      for( int i=0; i < 5; i++ )
      {
        pstmt1.setString( 1, "SCOTT" );
        rset1 = pstmt1.executeQuery();
        while( rset1.next() )
        {
        }
      }
    }
    finally
    {
      // release resources associated with JDBC in the finally clause.
      JDBCUtil.close( rset );
      JDBCUtil.close( pstmt );
      JDBCUtil.close( rset1 );
      JDBCUtil.close( pstmt1 );
      JDBCUtil.close( conn );
    }
  }
}
```

Following is the relevant portion of the tkprof output for case 1:

```
select /*+ prepareStatement() within loop */ empno, job
from
 emp where ename = :1
```

call	count	cpu	elapsed	disk	query	current	rows
Parse	5	0.00	0.00	0	0	0	0
Execute	5	0.18	0.19	0	0	0	0
Fetch	5	0.00	0.00	0	35	0	5
total	15	0.18	0.19	0	35	0	5

Misses in library cache during parse: **1**

The first thing to note is how the tag was retained by the SQL statement, thus enabling us to clearly see the profile of the statement separately. The tkprof output itself reveals the following:

- There were a total of five parses, which implies that the statement was parsed in every iteration of the loop.

- The 1 after the label Misses in library cache during parse indicates that the very first parse did not find the statement in the shared pool; hence, it was a hard parse. The remaining four parses were soft parses.

Looking at the tkprof output for our second loop, we see the following:

```
select /*+ prepareStatement() outside loop */ empno, job
from
 emp where ename = :1
```

call	count	cpu	elapsed	disk	query	current	rows
Parse	1	0.00	0.00	0	0	0	0
Execute	5	0.01	0.00	0	0	0	0
Fetch	5	0.00	0.00	0	35	0	5
total	11	0.01	0.00	0	35	0	5

Misses in library cache during parse: **1**

We can see that in case 2, Oracle needed to parse only once (a hard parse, as indicated by the misses in library cache being 1) for all five iterations.

We can conclude that whenever possible, we should prepare a statement only once, and bind or execute it many times to reduce the number of soft parses and the associated overhead. However, there are situations where this may not be straightforward. For example, I work in an environment where there are around 500 other developers all over the world working on the same product with different components. With each request, statements and result sets are created and closed using a centralized piece of code that implements connection pooling (connection pooling is covered in the next chapter). If I wanted to implement statement caching in such a scenario, I would have to implement and maintain my own centralized cache associated with a connection object, through which all code would need to be channeled. The closing of statements and cursors would also need to go through this piece of code, requiring a disciplined approach from all the developers. We would also have to manage the cache (aging out statements and so on). Fortunately, with JDBC 3.0, this functionality (called *statement caching*) is now available as part of JDBC, wherein this cache is created and managed transparently by the driver.

Before we look at statement caching, we will look at the related concept of *session cursor caching*, which is a mechanism Oracle provides to cache the cursors automatically in the session on the server side, to reduce the impact of soft parsing. We will then examine PL/SQL cursor caching, after which we will discuss JDBC statement caching.

Session Cursor Cache and "Softer" Soft Parses

In Oracle, when the opening and closing of cursors occurs repeatedly, the associated cursors can be cached in the *session cursor cache*. If you enable session cached cursors, the overhead of the soft parse decreases if you get a cache hit. Note that even if you get a hit in the session cache, Oracle still needs to validate that the opened cursor points to valid SQL in the shared pool (it could have been invalidated for some reason, such as schema changes since the last parse). Thus, it still needs to soft-parse the statement, although the soft parse in this case is less CPU-intensive and hence called a "softer" soft parse.

■**Note** If the session cache is enabled and you get a hit in the cache, the soft parse done is called a *softer soft parse* since it is less expensive compared to the case when session cache is disabled or when it is enabled but you don't get a hit in the cache.

Now that the JDBC driver provides you a mechanism to eliminate the soft parses automatically through statement caching (discussed later), the session cursor cache is less relevant for JDBC applications. It can still be useful in the following situations:

- As a temporary fix for an application until you enable statement caching on it.

- As a workaround to reduce the impact of soft parses for a JDBC application, when you don't have access to the application's code (hence, it isn't feasible to enable statement caching in it). This is feasible since session cached cursors can be controlled at the session level or instance level.

Let's next look at the session cursor cache in action.

Session Cursor Cache in Action

You enable session cached cursors by setting the parameter session_cached_cursors to the size of cache that you need (the default value is 0). Here "size" denotes the number of cursors you want to cache. You can do this either at the system level using the init.ora parameter session_cached_cursors, or at the session level using the alter session command. The public method setSessionCachedCursors() in the utility class JDBCUtil shown in the following code sets the session cursor cache size equal to the int parameter passed to it:

```
public static void setSessionCachedCursors ( Connection connection,
  int sessionCachedCursors ) throws SQLException
{
  String stmtStr = "alter session set session_cached_cursors=" +
    sessionCachedCursors ;
  Statement stmt = null;
  try
  {
    stmt = connection.createStatement();
```

```
    stmt.execute( stmtStr );
  }
  finally
  {
    stmt.close();
  }
}
```

We are now ready to demonstrate the impact of session cursor cache. First, we create a simple table, t1, with just one numeric column in which we insert the numbers 1 to 10,000:

```
benchmark@ORA10G> create table t1 as
  2  select rownum as x
  3  from all_objects
  4  where rownum <= 10000;

Table created.

benchmark@ORA10G> select count(*) from t1;

  COUNT(*)
----------
     10000
```

The following DemoSessionCachedCursors class compares two cases:

- *Case 1*: We run the select from table t1 10,000 times with session cached cursors set to 0.

- *Case 2*: We run the select from table t1 10,000 times with session cached cursors set to 500.

```
/** This program demonstrates the impact of session cursor cache.
* COMPATIBLITY NOTE:
*    runs successfully against 9.2.0.1.0 and 10.1.0.2.0 */
import java.sql.SQLException;
import java.sql.ResultSet;
import java.sql.Connection;
import java.sql.PreparedStatement;
import book.util.JDBCUtil;
import book.util.JRunstats;
class DemoSessionCachedCursors
{
  public static void main(String args[]) throws Exception
  {
    Connection conn = null;
    // first parameter: database name
    try
    {
      // get connection - auto commit is off
      conn = (Connection) JDBCUtil. getConnection("benchmark",
        "benchmark", args[0]);
```

We will use the JRunstats utility class (discussed in the section "JDBC Wrapper for runstats" of Chapter 1) for comparing the two cases. We begin by preparing the benchmark statements in the class JRunstats:

```
JRunstats.prepareBenchmarkStatements ( conn );
```

We mark the beginning of the benchmark run next:

```
JRunstats.markStart ( conn );
```

We set the session cached cursors to 0 in the first scenario, effectively disabling it:

```
JDBCUtil.setSessionCachedCursors( conn, 0 );
```

We execute the following query from t1 10,000 times (we don't need to retrieve the results for our test case):

```
String stmtString = "select x from t1";
PreparedStatement pstmt = null;
ResultSet rset = null;
for( int i=0; i < 10000; i++ )
{
  try
  {
    pstmt = conn.prepareStatement( stmtString );
    rset = pstmt.executeQuery();
  }
  finally
  {
    // release resources associated with JDBC in the finally clause.
    JDBCUtil.close( rset );
    JDBCUtil.close( pstmt );
  }
}
```

■Note As you'll learn later, you can't use a static cursor for this benchmark, as static cursors are cached by PL/SQL themselves, thus undermining the test results. You have to use a ref cursor.

We then mark the beginning of the second scenario by invoking the method markMiddle():

```
JRunstats.markMiddle ( conn );
```

We now set the session cached cursors to 500 and execute the second scenario. We finally print out the results by invoking JRunstats.markEnd() to end our program:

```
JDBCUtil.setSessionCachedCursors( conn, 500 );
stmtString = "select x from t1";
PreparedStatement pstmt1 = null;
```

```
          ResultSet rset1 = null;
          for( int i=0; i < 10000; i++ )
          {
            try
            {
              pstmt1 = conn.prepareStatement( stmtString );
              rset1 = pstmt1.executeQuery();
            }
            finally
            {
              // release resources associated with JDBC in the finally clause.
              JDBCUtil.close( rset1 );
              JDBCUtil.close( pstmt1 );
            }
          }
          JRunstats.markEnd ( conn );
        }
        finally
        {
          // release resources associated with JDBC in the finally clause.
          JRunstats.closeBenchmarkStatements ( conn );
          JDBCUtil.close( conn );
        }
      }
}// end of program
```

When we execute the program, we get the following results:

```
B:\>java DemoSessionCachedCursors
URL:jdbc:oracle:thin:@(DESCRIPTION=(ADDRESS=(PROTOCOL=tcp)(PORT=1521)
(HOST=rmenon-lap))(CONNECT_DATA=(SID=ora10g)))

------- Benchmark Results --------

Results from RUNSTATS utility

Run1 ran in 1311 hsecs
Run2 ran in 1230 hsecs
run 1 ran in 106.59% of the time

Name                                Run1      Run2      Diff
STAT...opened cursors current         0         1                    1
<-- trimmed to save space -->

Run1 latches total versus runs -- difference and pct
      Run1      Run2      Diff      Pct
        356,675         224,755         -131,920       158.70%
```

```
Runtime Execution Time Differences as seen by the client

Run1 ran in 1317 hsecs

Run2 ran in 1231 hsecs

Run1 ran in 107% of the time
```

You can see that when the session cache cursor was disabled, the program took *158%* times the amount of latches consumed when it was enabled to cache 500 cursors. Assuming the query was already in the shared pool, in both cases we soft-parsed 10,000 times (this can be verified using the tkprof utility); however, when the session cursor cache was on, due to softer soft parses, the parses that got a "hit" in the session cursor cache were less costly, resulting in significantly less latch consumption.

■**Note** From the results of this section's test, you should not conclude that you can set the session_cached_cursors parameter to a high value blindly. There is a point of diminishing returns, as you may expect. You should run benchmarks based on your application and set session_cached_cursors to an appropriate value accordingly.

PL/SQL Cursor Cache

In the previous section, you saw how you can make a soft parse softer by using session cursor cache. Before 10*g*, the PL/SQL language cached only *static* cursors (excluding ref cursors), thus allowing you to *avoid subsequent soft parses completely* in such cases. Starting with 10*g*, PL/SQL also caches native dynamic SQL (which uses execute immediate syntax) in a loop, assuming that the exact same statement is being executed for each iteration in the loop (i.e., the statement is not changing for different iterations) and the compiler can determine this at compile time.

PL/SQL avoids soft parses by performing a *soft close* on the cursor. In other words, when you close a cursor explicitly (e.g., by using the close command) or implicitly (e.g., when the cursor goes out of scope in the for loop in which it was defined), PL/SQL does not actually close the cursor—it caches it in its own separate cursor cache, hoping that your application will reuse the cursor in its next attempt. Of course, if the maximum limit for opened cursors is about to be reached, then it closes the cursor for real. The beauty of this feature is that for the class of cursors for which it is applicable, you can avoid soft parses completely!

■Note As of Oracle 10*g* Release 1, the PL/SQL cursor cache *does not* cache ref cursors. Ref cursors can be tricky to cache, since they can point to a different cursor during the same execution, as presented earlier. They can also "escape" to a client such as a JDBC program, in which case you no longer control the cursor (the JDBC client controls it). Recall, however, that ref cursors *are* cached by session cursor cache. Session cursor caches go through a softer soft parse during which they validate their cursor anyway; hence, it makes sense for ref cursors to be cached in session cache.

Let's now look at the PL/SQL cursor in action. We will, in fact, compare it to a loop similar to the one we executed earlier while benchmarking session cached cursors. We will use the same schema that we created: the one consisting of table t1 with one number column containing 10,000 rows, each a number from 1 to 10,000. This time, we will use the runstats package and PL/SQL code to demonstrate the concept.

First, we set session_cached_cursors to a value of 500 and execute the runstats_pkg.rs_↪ start() method, followed by the same loop that we executed in our tests for demonstrating session cached cursors. In this case, the PL/SQL cache does not come into the picture because we use a ref cursor.

```
benchmark@ORA10G> alter session set session_cached_cursors=500;

Session altered.

benchmark@ORA10G> exec runstats_pkg.rs_start

PL/SQL procedure successfully completed.

benchmark@ORA10G>
benchmark@ORA10G> declare
  2     l_cursor sys_refcursor;
  3  begin
  4     for i in 1..10000
  5     loop
  6       open l_cursor for
  7         select x
  8         from t1
  9         where x = i;
 10       close l_cursor;
 11     end loop;
 12  end;
 13  /

PL/SQL procedure successfully completed.
```

Next, we execute the `runstats_pkg.rs_middle()` method, followed by opening and closing the same `select` statement—but this time in a parameterized static cursor, which is a candidate for being cached by the PL/SQL cursor cache:

```
benchmark@ORA10G> exec runstats_pkg.rs_middle

PL/SQL procedure successfully completed.

benchmark@ORA10G> declare
  2    cursor l_cursor( p_x in number) is
  3    select x from t1 where x = p_x;
  4  begin
  5    for i in 1..10000
  6    loop
  7      open l_cursor( i );
  8      close l_cursor;
  9    end loop;
 10  end;
 11  /

PL/SQL procedure successfully completed.
```

Notice how in code lines 2 and 3, we declare a static parameterized cursor that allows us to pass bind values as parameters. We open the cursor and pass the bind value in line 7.

Finally, we execute the `runstats_pkg.rs_stop()` method to display the comparison results:

```
benchmark@ORA10G> exec runstats_pkg.rs_stop(80)
Run1 ran in 1461 hsecs
Run2 ran in 644 hsecs
run 1 ran in 226.86% of the time
```

Name	Run1	Run2	Diff
STAT...parse time elapsed	82	0	-82
<-- trimmed to save space -->			
LATCH.row cache objects	30,024	18	-30,006

```
Run1 latches total versus runs -- difference and pct
    Run1      Run2      Diff     Pct
  81,789    50,808   -30,981  160.98%
```

As you can see, the case where the PL/SQL cache was not in effect took more than twice the time and consumed *1.6* times the latches compared to the case where the PL/SQL cache was applicable. I ran the same test with SQL trace on. The following `tkprof` output shows the parse counts:

call	count	cpu	elapsed	disk	query	current	rows
Parse	10001	0.74	0.83	0	0	0	0

| Execute | 20000 | 6.97 | 6.87 | 0 | 0 | 0 | 0 |
Fetch	0	0.00	0.00	0	0	0	0
total	30001	7.71	7.70	0	0	0	0

As shown, the total soft parse count is 10,001: 10,000 in the ref cursor case and 1 in the static cursor case (that occurs the first time in the static cursor case loop).

Thus, we can conclude that the PL/SQL cursor cache significantly increases our performance transparently for static cursors (and native dynamic SQL cursors in 10*g*). This is another point in favor of using the combination of PL/SQL packaged procedures/functions and CallableStatement in JDBC programs (apart from the reasons discussed in Chapter 6).

■Note Prior to Oracle 9.2.0.5, the maximum number of the cursors in the PL/SQL cache was bounded by the value of the init.ora parameter open_cursors. The PL/SQL engine would start hard-closing the cursors once this limit was reached, so that you couldn't run out of cursors on account of the PL/SQL caching mechanism. However, starting with 9.2.0.5, this upper bound is defined by the session_cached_cursors parameter. When session_cached_cursors is either not set or set to 0, Oracle uses a PL/SQL cache of size 50. When session_cached_cursors is set to any nonzero value, the PL/SQL cursor cache size is bound by the session_cached_cursors size. This is critical to understand, since a low PL/SQL cache size can have a negative impact on your application's performance.

Statement Caching in JDBC

As mentioned in the beginning of this chapter, statement caching was introduced in JDBC 3.0. Put simply, statement caching improves performance by caching cursors associated with statements executed repeatedly in a loop. As you'll see soon, the performance improvement comes because statement caching prevents the overhead of repeated creation of cursors and repeated soft parses that a statement goes through when it is "prepared" using PreparedStatement or CallableStatement in a loop.

Statement Caching Fundamentals

A statement cache is associated with a particular connection (i.e., each distinct physical connection to the database) has its own statement cache. For a simple connection, statement caching is associated with the OracleConnection object. For a pooled connection, it is associated with the OraclePooledConnection object (you'll learn about pooled connections in Chapter 14).

Recall that the PL/SQL cursor cache does the actual caching of the cursor when you do an implicit or explicit "close" on a statement. In the same way, when statement caching is enabled, the JDBC driver caches a statement when the statement is closed. The next iteration picks the statement from the cache, thus avoiding the soft parse that would have otherwise been incurred in preparing the same statement again.

Implicit and Explicit Statement Caching

Oracle JDBC drivers provide you with two different flavors of statement caching: implicit and explicit. Each type of statement cache can be enabled or disabled independently, which means that you can have either, neither, or both in effect *simultaneously*. It is important to remember that both statement-caching types share the same cache. This information is relevant when you set the size of the statement cache.

Implicit Statement Caching

When you enable implicit statement caching, JDBC transparently caches the prepared or callable statement when you call the close() method of a statement object. Behind the scenes, the prepared and callable statements are cached and retrieved using the standard connection object and statement object methods.

The beauty of implicit caching is that only the isolated piece of code that retrieves the connection for an application needs to change to enable it. The bulk of the code that actually prepares and executes the statements remains the same. Note that plain Statement objects are *not* cached in an implicit cache because implicit statement caching uses the SQL statement string as a key, and plain statements are by definition created without a SQL string, as follows:

```
Statement stmt = conn.createStatement();
```

Therefore, implicit statement caching applies *only* to the PreparedStatement and CallableStatement objects (which are created with a SQL string). But hopefully this is a nonissue, because you should not use plain Statement objects for executing DML statements in production code anyway, for the numerous reasons covered in Chapter 5.

Assuming that implicit caching is enabled, when you prepare a PreparedStatement or CallableStatement object, the JDBC driver automatically searches the cache for the statement and gets a *hit* in the cache if the following are true:

- The statement type is the same (prepared or callable).
- The SQL string in the statement is identical (case sensitive) to the one in the cache.
- The scrollable type of result set produced by the statement is the same (forward-only or scrollable). You can determine the scrollability of the prepared or callable statement as explained in the Chapter 7.

If a match is found, the cached statement is returned and the rest of the code proceeds as usual. If no match is found, a new statement is created and returned. When you call the close() method of the statement, the new statement created along with its cursor and state is cached in the implicit statement cache.

Enabling and Disabling Implicit Statement Caching

You can enable or disable implicit statement caching by invoking appropriate methods on either the OracleConnection object or the OracleDataSource object from which the Connection object is obtained.

To enable implicit statement caching on the OracleConnection object, you need to perform the following steps:

1. Use the Oracle extension method setImplicitCachingEnabled(boolean flag) as follows:

   ```
   conn.setImplicitCachingEnabled( true );
   ```

2. Set the cache size (remember, the same cache is shared by implicit and explicit caching) by using the Oracle extension method setStatementCacheSize(int size) on the connection object as follows:

   ```
   conn.setStatementCacheSize( 10 );
   ```

To enable implicit statement caching on the OracleDataSource object, you need to perform the following steps:

1. Invoke OracleDataSource.getConnection() with the ImplicitCachingEnabled property set to true, or set ImplicitCachingEnabled on the OracleDataSource by calling Oracle➥ DataSource.setImplicitCachingEnabled(true) as follows (assume ods is an initialized variable of type OracleDataSource):

   ```
   ods.setImplicitCachingEnabled( true );
   ```

2. Set the cache size by invoking OracleDataSource.setMaxStatements(int maxNumber➥ OfStatements) as follows (assume ods is an initialized variable of type OracleDataSource):

   ```
   ods.setMaxStatements( 10 );
   ```

■**Note** It is not very clear from the Oracle 10*g* Release 1 JDBC documentation that setting the statement cache size to a nonzero value is required to enable the implicit statement cache (apart from the step of invoking setImplicitCachingEnabled(true)). From the documentation, you might get the impression that setting the cache size is a step required only to enable the *explicit* statement cache. However, my experiments show that you need to perform both steps to enable the implicit statement cache as well.

To find out the number of statements that you can cache, you can use the method getStatementCacheSize(), as follows:

```
System.out.println("cache size: " + conn.getStatementCacheSize() );
```

To disable implicit statement caching on a connection object, you need to use the Oracle extension method setImplicitCachingEnabled(boolean flag) as follows:

```
conn.setImplicitCachingEnabled( false );
```

To disable implicit statement caching on an OracleDataSource object, you need to invoke OracleDataSource.getConnection() with the ImplicitCachingEnabled property set to false, or set ImplicitCachingEnabled on the OracleDataSource by calling OracleDataSource. setImplicitCachingEnabled(false) as follows (assume ods is an initialized variable of type OracleDataSource):

```
ods.setImplicitCachingEnabled( false );
```

Disabling Implicit Caching for a Particular PreparedStatement or CallableStatement

When implicit statement caching is enabled for a connection, by default all callable and prepared statements of that connection are automatically cached. If you want to prevent a particular callable or prepared statement from being implicitly cached, use the Oracle extension method setDisableStatementCaching(), which is available in the interface OraclePreparedStatement (and also by extension in the interface OracleCallableStatement). This helps you disable caching on infrequently executed statements and manage the cache space better.

The following code disables implicit statement caching for an already initialized PreparedStatement object, pstmt:

```
((OraclePreparedStatement)pstmt).setDisableStmtCaching(true);
```

Physically Closing an Implicitly Cached PreparedStatement or CallableStatement

Recall that when you execute the close() method on an implicitly cached prepared or callable statement, the statement does not really get closed. The physical closing of the statement is not in your hands when implicit caching is enabled. The Oracle JDBC driver physically closes the statement automatically under one of the following three conditions:

- When the associated connection is closed

- When the cache reaches its size limit and the least recently used statement object is pre-empted from the cache by the Least Recently Used (LRU) scheme

- If you call the close() method on a statement for which statement caching is disabled at the Statement level

Implicit Statement Caching in Action

It is time to demonstrate implicit caching in action. We will do this by comparing the execution of a simple select statement in a for loop with implicit caching enabled and disabled. We will also demonstrate the implicit caching at work for a CallableStatement object, which will invoke the simple function f() defined in the following code (notice that we tag the select again since we will use tkprof subsequently and we need to identify where the SQL came from):

```
benchmark@ORA10G> create or replace function f return sys_refcursor
  2  as
  3    l_cursor sys_refcursor;
  4  begin
  5    open l_cursor for
  6    select /*+ to be called using callable statement */ dummy from dual;
  7    return l_cursor;
  8  end;
  9  /

Function created.
```

The following DemoImplicitCaching program, along with the explanatory comments, illustrates the concept of implicit caching:

```
/* * This program demonstrates implicit statement caching.
* COMPATIBLITY NOTE:
*    runs successfully against 9.2.0.1.0 and 10.1.0.2.0
*/
import java.sql.SQLException;
import java.sql.Connection;
import java.sql.PreparedStatement;
import java.sql.ResultSet;
import java.sql.CallableStatement;
import oracle.jdbc.OracleConnection;
import oracle.jdbc.OracleTypes;
import book.util.JDBCUtil;
import book.util.Util;
class DemoImplicitCaching
{
  public static void main(String args[]) throws SQLException
  {
    Util.checkProgramUsage( args );
    OracleConnection conn = null;
    try
    {
      // get connection
      conn = (OracleConnection) JDBCUtil.getConnection("benchmark",
        "benchmark", args[0]);
```

We print out the flag that indicates whether or not caching is enabled and the cache size (by default caching is disabled):

```
      System.out.println("implicit caching enabled: " +
        conn.getImplicitCachingEnabled() );
      System.out.println("cache size: " + conn.getStatementCacheSize() );
```

Next we start the SQL trace:

```
      JDBCUtil.startTrace( conn );
```

We invoke the method _doSelect() in a for loop 1,000 times. The method itself will be explained shortly.

```
      for( int i=0; i < 1000; i++ )
      {
        _doSelect ( conn, "/*+ implicit disabled */" );
      }
```

We invoke the same loop again after enabling implicit caching and setting the statement cache size to a positive number (10 in this case):

```
conn.setImplicitCachingEnabled( true );
conn.setStatementCacheSize( 10 );
System.out.println("implicit caching enabled: " +
  conn.getImplicitCachingEnabled() );
System.out.println("cache size: " +
  conn.getStatementCacheSize() );
for( int i=0; i < 1000; i++ )
{
  _doSelect ( conn, "/*+ implicit enabled */" );
}
```

We demonstrate the concept of implicit caching for a CallableStatement by invoking the method _doExecuteCallableStatement():

```
// demonstrating use of implicit caching with callable statement
for( int i=0; i < 1000; i++ )
{
  _doExecuteCallableStatement( conn,
"/*+ enabled implicit caching for callable statement */" );
 }
}
finally
{
  // release resources associated with JDBC in the finally clause.
  JDBCUtil.close( conn );
}
}
```

The method _doSelect() mentioned previously is as follows:

```
private static void _doSelect( Connection conn, String tag ) throws SQLException
{
  PreparedStatement pstmt = null;
  ResultSet rset = null;
```

The main point to note is that we tag the SQL string so that we can easily recognize it in the tkprof output. The rest of the code is a simple execution of the query using the PreparedStatement interface:

```
String stmtString = "select " + tag + " count(*) from dual";
try
{
  pstmt = conn.prepareStatement( stmtString );
  rset = pstmt.executeQuery();
}
finally
{
```

```
      JDBCUtil.close( rset );
      JDBCUtil.close( pstmt );
  }
}
```

We execute the function f() in the method _doExecuteCallableStatement(). Note how we tag the anonymous block.

```
  private static void _doExecuteCallableStatement( Connection conn, String tag )
    throws SQLException
  {
    CallableStatement cstmt = null;
    ResultSet rset = null;
    String stmtString = "begin" + tag + " ? := f; end;";
    try
    {
      cstmt = conn.prepareCall( stmtString );
      cstmt.registerOutParameter( 1, OracleTypes.CURSOR );
      cstmt.execute();
      rset = (ResultSet) cstmt.getObject( 1 );
    }
    finally
    {
      JDBCUtil.close( rset );
      JDBCUtil.close( cstmt );
    }
  }
}
```

The following snippet shows the relevant portion of the tkprof output of our statement execution profile for the case when implicit caching was disabled:

```
select /*+ implicit disabled */ count(*)
from
 dual
```

call	count	cpu	elapsed	disk	query	current	rows
Parse	1000	0.25	0.30	0	0	0	0
Execute	1000	0.23	0.23	0	0	0	0
Fetch	1000	0.20	0.27	0	0	0	1000
total	3000	0.68	**0.82**	0	0	0	1000

```
Misses in library cache during parse: 0
```

Notice how the statement was soft-parsed 1,000 times. This is because we prepared and closed the statement (and its cursor) in a loop 1,000 times, and since statement caching was disabled, each "close" of the statement physically closed the statement. Now take a look at the profile for the case when implicit caching was enabled:

```
select /*+ implicit enabled */ count(*)
from
 dual
```

call	count	cpu	elapsed	disk	query	current	rows
Parse	1	0.00	0.00	0	0	0	0
Execute	1000	0.29	0.26	0	0	0	0
Fetch	1000	0.14	0.15	0	0	0	1000
total	2001	0.43	**0.42**	0	0	0	1000

```
Misses in library cache during parse: 0
```

Notice how the statement was parsed only once. The rest of the time the prepared statement was obtained from the implicit cache, avoiding the soft parse. Also, implicit caching reduced the elapsed time by almost half (0.42 seconds versus 0.82 seconds).

The tkprof output for the CallableStatement case follows. It proves that the anonymous block gets soft-parsed only once due to implicit statement caching.

```
begin/*+ enabled implicit caching for callable statement */ :1 := f; end;
```

call	count	cpu	elapsed	disk	query	current	rows
Parse	1	0.01	0.00	0	0	0	0
Execute	1000	2.13	2.06	0	0	0	1000
Fetch	0	0.00	0.00	0	0	0	0
total	1001	2.14	2.06	0	0	0	1000

```
Misses in library cache during parse: 1
```

Explicit Statement Caching

Explicit statement caching enables you to cache selected prepared, callable, and plain statements. Explicit statement caching caches a statement with a key, an arbitrary Java string that you provide. The biggest difference between explicit and implicit caching is that with explicit caching, you have to use specialized Oracle methods that end with WithKey to cache and retrieve statements. This also implies that you have to use the interfaces OraclePreparedStatement and OracleCallableStatement, respectively, to use explicit statement caching. In the case of implicit caching, the JDBC driver automatically creates a statement if it is not there in the cache. In the case of explicit caching, the JDBC driver returns null for the statement; you have to check for null and explicitly create a statement using the createStatement() method, as we'll cover shortly. Toward the end of this section, we'll compare explicit and implicit caching in terms of features and when to use which technique.

Enabling and Disabling Explicit Statement Caching

You can enable or disable explicit statement caching by invoking appropriate methods on either the OracleConnection object or the OracleDataSource object from which the Connection object is obtained.

To enable explicit statement caching on the OracleConnection object, perform the following steps:

1. Use the Oracle extension method setExplicitCachingEnabled(boolean flag) on the Connection object as follows:

```
conn.setExplicitCachingEnabled( true );
```

2. Set the cache size by using the Oracle extension method setStatementCacheSize➥ (int size) on the Connection object as follows:

```
conn.setStatementCacheSize( 10 );
```

To enable explicit statement caching on the OracleDataSource object, perform the following steps:

1. Invoke OracleDataSource.getConnection() with the ExplicitCachingEnabled property set to true, or set ExplicitCachingEnabled on the OracleDataSource by calling Oracle➥ DataSource.setExplicitCachingEnabled(true) as follows (assume ods is an initialized variable of type OracleDataSource):

```
ods.setExplicitCachingEnabled( true );
```

2. Set the cache size by invoking OracleDataSource.setMaxStatements(int maxNumber➥ OfStatements) as follows (assume ods is an initialized variable of type OracleDataSource):

```
ods.setMaxStatements( 10 );
```

To determine whether explicit caching is enabled, invoke getExplicitCachingEnabled(), which returns true if explicit caching is enabled and false otherwise.

```
System.out.println("explicit caching enabled: " +
    conn.getExplicitCachingEnabled() );
```

■**Note** Remember that you can enable explicit and implicit caching separately—you can have either, neither, or both. Also remember that they both share the same cache for a given connection.

To disable explicit statement caching on a Connection object, use the Oracle extension method setExplicitCachingEnabled(boolean flag) as follows:

```
conn.setExplicitCachingEnabled( false );
```

To disable implicit statement caching on an `OracleDataSource` object, invoke `Oracle⟶DataSource.getConnection()` with the `ImplicitCachingEnabled` property set to false, or set `ExplicitCachingEnabled` on the `OracleDataSource` by calling `OracleDataSource.setImplicit⟶CachingEnabled( false)` as follows (assume ods is an initialized variable of type `OracleData⟶Source`):

```
ods.setExplicitCachingEnabled( false );
```

Explicit Statement Caching in Action

We will use the following program, `DemoExplicitCaching`, to see explicit statement caching in action. The program is very similar in structure to the program `DemoImplicitCaching` that we examined in the section "Implicit Caching in Action." Explanation of the program is interspersed with the code.

```
/** This program demonstrates explicit statement caching.
* COMPATIBLITY NOTE:
*    runs successfully against 9.2.0.1.0 and 10.1.0.2.0
*/
import java.sql.SQLException;
import java.sql.ResultSet;
import oracle.jdbc.OraclePreparedStatement;
import oracle.jdbc.OracleCallableStatement;
import oracle.jdbc.OracleConnection;
import oracle.jdbc.OracleTypes;
import book.util.JDBCUtil;
import book.util.Util;
class DemoExplicitCaching
{
  public static void main(String args[]) throws SQLException
  {
    Util.checkProgramUsage( args );
    OracleConnection conn = null;
    try
    {
      // get connection
      conn = (OracleConnection) JDBCUtil.getConnection("benchmark",
  "benchmark", args[0]);
```

We start the trace and then invoke the method _doSelect() with an appropriate SQL tag, one time without any caching enabled and the other time with explicit caching enabled. Then we invoke the PL/SQL function f() in the method _doExecuteCallableStatement():

```
      System.out.println("explicit caching enabled: " +
        conn.getExplicitCachingEnabled() );
      System.out.println("cache size: " + conn.getStatementCacheSize() );
      // enable trace
      JDBCUtil.startTrace( conn );
      for( int i=0; i < 1000; i++ )
      {
        _doSelect ( conn, "/*+ explicit disabled */" );
```

```
    }
    conn.setExplicitCachingEnabled( true );
    conn.setStatementCacheSize( 10 );
    System.out.println("explicit caching enabled: " +
      conn.getExplicitCachingEnabled() );
    System.out.println("cache size: " +
      conn.getStatementCacheSize() );
    for( int i=0; i < 1000; i++ )
    {
      _doSelect ( conn, "/*+ explicit enabled */" );
    }
    // demonstrating use of explicit caching with callable statement
    for( int i=0; i < 1000; i++ )
    {
      _doExecuteCallableStatement( conn,
  "/*+ enabled explicit caching for callable statement */" );
    }
  }
  finally
  {
    // release resources associated with JDBC in the finally clause.
    JDBCUtil.close( conn );
  }
}
```

The method _doSelect() invokes the select statement using explicit caching:

```
private static void _doSelect( OracleConnection conn, String tag )
  throws SQLException
{
  OraclePreparedStatement opstmt = null;
  ResultSet rset = null;
  String stmtString = "select " + tag + " count(*) from dual";
```

To cache the statement explicitly, we first create a string key as shown in the code that follows. In the try catch block, we use the Oracle extension method getStatementWithKey() to get the statement. If it is null, we create it using the standard prepareStatement() method in the connection object. Thus, the first time around, the OraclePreparedStatement object is explicitly created, and then for subsequent loop iterations, if explicit statement caching is enabled, we reuse the same OraclePreparedStatement object. Note how we close the statement with the method closeWithKey() in the finally clause, which actually puts the OraclePreparedStatement object in the cache.

```
  String stmtKey = EXPLICIT_CACHING_KEY_PREFIX + stmtString;
  try
  {
    opstmt = ( OraclePreparedStatement) conn.
      getStatementWithKey( stmtKey );
    if( opstmt == null )
    {
```

```
      opstmt = ( OraclePreparedStatement) conn.
        prepareStatement( stmtString );
    }
    rset = opstmt.executeQuery();
  }
  finally
  {
    JDBCUtil.close( rset );
    try
    {
      opstmt.closeWithKey( stmtKey );
    }
    catch ( Exception e) { e.printStackTrace();}
  }
}
```

The _doExecuteCallableStatement() method does the same thing using an Oracle➡ CallableStatement object:

```
private static void _doExecuteCallableStatement( OracleConnection conn,
  String tag ) throws SQLException
{
  OracleCallableStatement ocstmt = null;
  ResultSet rset = null;
  String stmtString = "begin" + tag + " ? := f; end;";
  String stmtKey = EXPLICIT_CACHING_KEY_PREFIX + stmtString;
  try
  {
    ocstmt = ( OracleCallableStatement) conn.
      getCallWithKey( stmtKey );
    if( ocstmt == null )
    {
      ocstmt = ( OracleCallableStatement) conn.  prepareCall( stmtString );
    }
    ocstmt.registerOutParameter( 1, OracleTypes.CURSOR );
    ocstmt.execute();
    rset = (ResultSet) ocstmt.getObject( 1 );
  }
  finally
  {
    JDBCUtil.close( rset );
    try
    {
      ocstmt.closeWithKey( stmtKey );
    }
    catch ( Exception e) { e.printStackTrace(); }
  }
}
private static final String EXPLICIT_CACHING_KEY_PREFIX =
  "EXPLICIT_CACHING_KEY_PREFIX";
}
```

The tkprof results for the case when explicit caching was disabled are as follows:

```
select /*+ explicit disabled */ count(*)
from
 dual
```

call	count	cpu	elapsed	disk	query	current	rows
Parse	1000	0.30	0.33	0	0	0	0
Execute	1000	0.25	0.23	0	0	0	0
Fetch	1000	0.27	0.21	0	0	0	1000
total	3000	0.82	0.78	0	0	0	1000

Misses in library cache during parse: 0

As expected, we soft-parse the statement 1,000 times. With explicit caching enabled, we parse the statement only once:

```
select /*+ explicit enabled */ count(*)
from
 dual
```

call	count	cpu	elapsed	disk	query	current	rows
Parse	1	0.00	0.00	0	0	0	0
Execute	1000	0.16	0.25	0	0	0	0
Fetch	1000	0.13	0.15	0	0	0	1000
total	2001	0.29	0.41	0	0	0	1000

Misses in library cache during parse: 0

Once again, we reduce the elapsed time to almost half using explicit caching (from 0.79 to 0.42).

The following tkprof output for the procedure invocation proves that the anonymous block gets soft-parsed only once due to explicit statement caching in the case of Oracle➥ CallableStatement as well:

```
begin/*+ enabled explicit caching for callable statement */ :1 := f; end;
```

call	count	cpu	elapsed	disk	query	current	rows
Parse	1	0.00	0.00	0	0	0	0
Execute	1000	2.03	2.06	0	0	0	1000
Fetch	0	0.00	0.00	0	0	0	0
total	1001	2.03	2.06	0	0	0	1000

Misses in library cache during parse: 0

■**Caution** When you retrieve an explicitly cached statement, make sure you use the method that matches your statement type when specifying the key—that is, use `getStatementWithKey()` for `PreparedState➥ment` and `getCallWithKey()` for `CallableStatement`. Otherwise, you may get unexpected results, such as a `NullPointerException`.

Implicit Caching vs. Explicit Caching

Table 13-1 summarizes the differences between implicit and explicit caching. Note that the assertion related to performance difference will be proved later in this section.

Table 13-1. *Differences Between Implicit and Explicit Statement Caching*

Implicit Statement Caching	Explicit Statement Caching
Designed to transparently enable caching in an entire application and then selectively disable it for infrequently used statements.	Designed to explicitly enable caching for specific statements.
Supports `PreparedStatement` and `CallableStatement`. Your code for executing statements does not change—only the portion of the code that retrieves the connection for your application changes when you enable implicit statement caching.	Supports `Statement`, `PreparedStatement`, and `CallableStatement`, although this is not a real advantage since you should mostly avoid using the `Statement` interface in production code anyway. Enabling explicit statement caching also introduces changes in the code that executes statements. This is because you need to supply the cache key, and you need to use Oracle extension methods that end with `WithKey`.
Methods used are `prepareStatement()` or `prepareCall()`, depending on whether you want to cache `PreparedStatement` or `CallableStatement`. To cache the statement, use the standard method `close()` on the statement. During implicit statement caching, if the JDBC driver cannot find a statement in the cache, it will automatically create one.	Methods used are `getStatementWithKey()` for `Statement` or `PreparedStatement` objects, and `getCallWithKey()` for `CallableStatement` objects. During explicit statement caching, if the JDBC driver cannot find a statement in cache, it will return `null`; you have to check for `null` and create a statement yourself.
Retains only the statement metadata, hence it runs slightly slower than explicit statement caching.	Retains statement data and state as well as metadata, hence it has a slight performance edge over implicit statement caching, which retains only metadata. In my tests, though, I could not find any material performance differences between the two caching mechanisms.

As promised, we will compare the performance of explicit caching with implicit caching. We will only do the comparison for `PreparedStatement`. The following class compares the performance of implicit statement caching with that of explicit statement caching for a simple count(*) from table t1, which has 10,000 rows. Since this code incorporates the same techniques previously discussed in this chapter, I did not provide any explanatory text within the code listing.

```java
/** This program compares implicit statement caching with
* explicit statement caching in terms of elapsed time.
* COMPATIBLITY NOTE:
*    runs successfully against 9.2.0.1.0 and 10.1.0.2.0
*/
import java.sql.SQLException;
import java.sql.PreparedStatement;
import java.sql.ResultSet;
import oracle.jdbc.OraclePreparedStatement;
import oracle.jdbc.OracleConnection;
import book.util.JDBCUtil;
import book.util.Util;
class ImplicitVsExplicitCaching
{
  public static void main(String args[]) throws SQLException
  {
    Util.checkProgramUsage( args );
    OracleConnection conn = null;
    try
    {
      // get connection
      conn = (OracleConnection) JDBCUtil.getConnection("benchmark",
    "benchmark", args[0]);
      conn.setExplicitCachingEnabled( true );
      conn.setImplicitCachingEnabled( true );
      conn.setStatementCacheSize( 10 );
      System.out.println("explicit caching enabled: " +
        conn.getExplicitCachingEnabled() );
      System.out.println("implicit caching enabled: " +
        conn.getImplicitCachingEnabled() );
      System.out.println("cache size: " +
        conn.getStatementCacheSize() );
      int numOfRuns = 5000;
      long startTime = System.currentTimeMillis();
      for( int i=0; i < numOfRuns; i++ )
      {
        _doSelectWithExplicitCachingEnabled( conn );
      }
      long endTime = System.currentTimeMillis();
      System.out.println("Implicit took: " + (endTime-startTime)+ " ms ");
      startTime = System.currentTimeMillis();
      for( int i=0; i < numOfRuns; i++ )
      {
```

```
        _doSelectWithImplicitCachingEnabled( conn );
      }
      endTime = System.currentTimeMillis();
      System.out.println("Explicit took: " + (endTime-startTime)+ " ms ");
    }
    finally
    {
      // release resources associated with JDBC in the finally clause.
      JDBCUtil.close( conn );
    }
  }
  /////////////////// PRIVATE SECTION ///////////////////
  private static void _doSelectWithExplicitCachingEnabled( OracleConnection conn )
throws SQLException
  {
    OraclePreparedStatement opstmt = null;
    ResultSet rset = null;
    String stmtString = "select count(*) from t1";
    String stmtKey = EXPLICIT_CACHING_KEY_PREFIX + stmtString;
    try
    {
      opstmt = ( OraclePreparedStatement) conn.
        getStatementWithKey( stmtKey );
      if( opstmt == null )
      {
        opstmt = ( OraclePreparedStatement) conn.
          prepareStatement( stmtString );
      }
      rset = opstmt.executeQuery();
    }
    finally
    {
      JDBCUtil.close( rset );
      try
      {
        opstmt.closeWithKey( stmtKey );
      }
      catch ( Exception e) { e.printStackTrace();}
    }
  }
  private static void _doSelectWithImplicitCachingEnabled( OracleConnection conn )
    throws SQLException
  {
    PreparedStatement pstmt = null;
    ResultSet rset = null;
    String stmtString = "select count(*) from t1";
    try
```

```
  {
    pstmt = conn.prepareStatement( stmtString );
    rset = pstmt.executeQuery();
  }
  finally
  {
    JDBCUtil.close( pstmt );
    JDBCUtil.close( rset );
  }
}
private static final String EXPLICIT_CACHING_KEY_PREFIX =
  "EXPLICIT_CACHING_KEY_PREFIX";
}
```

The program simply runs the same select statement 5,000 times in a loop, first with implicit caching enabled and then with explicit caching enabled. In my runs, I found very little difference between the two cases. Since most of the time the performance bottleneck is in the SQL statement itself, my suggestion is to ignore performance as a criterion when selecting the approach of implicit versus explicit caching. In general, I recommend going with implicit caching unless you have a strong reason to use explicit caching.

Session Cursor Cache vs. PL/SQL Cursor Cache vs. JDBC Statement Caching

Table 13-2 summarizes the main differences between these three caches.

Table 13-2. *Differences Between Session Cursor Cache, PL/SQL Cursor Cache, and JDBC Statement Caching*

Session Cursor Cache	PL/SQL Cursor Cache	JDBC Statement Caching
Server-side cache enabled and controlled by init.ora setting or session-level setting	Server-side cache enabled implicitly by the PL/SQL engine based on init.ora or session-level settings	Client-side cache enabled using the JDBC API
Does not eliminate soft parses, but makes them less resource-intensive	Eliminates soft parses altogether when applicable	Eliminates soft parses altogether when applicable
Caches SQL statements submitted by users as well as recursive SQL. Recursive SQL statements are ones generated by Oracle internally (e.g., to do a lookup in the data dictionary during a hard parse)	Caches only the statements in PL/SQL code, as explained earlier in this chapter	Caches only the statements in JDBC code, as explained earlier in this chapter

Summary

In this chapter, you revisited the concepts of cursors and ref cursors. You learned about session cursor cache and PL/SQL cursor cache, and you saw how they can improve the performance of your application. You then explored in detail the concept of JDBC statement caching. You learned about implicit and explicit statement caching, and how to use them in your JDBC programs to avoid unnecessary soft parses. You also compared implicit and explicit statement caches in terms of features and performance, and you discovered that in almost all cases implicit caching is the way to go. The chapter concluded with a summary of the differences between session cursor cache, PL/SQL cursor cache, and JDBC statement caching.

CHAPTER 14
■ ■ ■

Connection Pooling and Caching

In this chapter, you will learn about connection pooling and caching, and how they can improve performance of your application. We'll first look at Oracle9*i* connection pooling and the sample connection caching implementation provided by Oracle. We'll then cover the new and improved implicit connection caching in Oracle 10*g*. Finally, we'll examine the 10*g* implementation of OCI driver connection pooling, a feature also available with Oracle9*i*.

But first, let's start with a little background on connections and sessions that will help you better understand the remainder of this chapter.

Connections and Sessions in Oracle

Before we delve into connection pooling, you need to understand the difference between a connection and a session in the context of Oracle. This difference is particularly useful in understanding OCI connection pooling, which the upcoming section "OCI Connection Pooling" covers.

Most of us think of connections and sessions as being the same, but in reality they are not. A *connection* is a network connection or a physical pathway to the Oracle database. A *session* encapsulates a user's interaction with the Oracle database from the time the user has been authenticated to the time the user disconnects. A session connects to Oracle via a physical connection. Note that you could be connected to a database and yet have zero, one, or more sessions that use a given connection. In the most common case, one session corresponds to one connection—this explains why we tend to consider them the same.

Figure 14-1 illustrates a connection being shared by three sessions, two of which belong to the user SCOTT, and one of which belongs to the user BENCHMARK. The thick arrow represents the connection itself. Although the figure shows a two-tier system, the same concept applies to a three-tier system. You will learn in the section "OCI Connection Pooling" how you can open multiple sessions per physical connection.

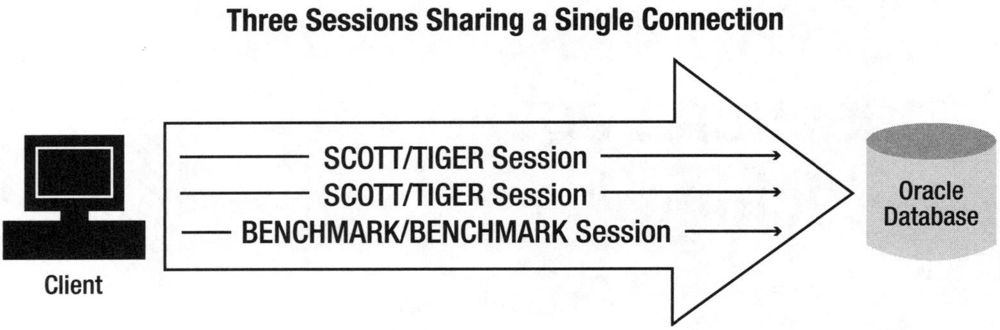

Three Sessions Sharing a Single Connection

Figure 14-1. *Three sessions sharing a single connection from a client to the database*

Let's look at a query that lists currently opened physical connections and sessions for us. The query assumes that we're connected to Oracle in a *dedicated server* mode as opposed to a *shared server* (previously known as *MTS*, or *multithreaded server*) mode.

■**Note** In dedicated server mode, each physical connection has a separate (or dedicated) process (or thread) associated with it, whereas in shared server mode, a pool of processes (or threads) is shared by all physical connections. Dedicated server is the more commonly used option. Please see the *Oracle Database Concepts Guide (10*g *Release 1)* document for more details.

```
sys@ORA10G> select s.program, s.server, p.spid server_pid, s.username
  2  from v$session s, v$process p
  3  where s.type = 'USER'
  4    and s.username != 'SYS'
  5    and p.addr(+) = s.paddr;
PROGRAM                         SERVER          SERVER_PID   USERNAME
------------------------------  --------------  -----------  ----------
sqlplus.exe                     DEDICATED       3648         SCOTT
sqlplus.exe                     DEDICATED       3028         BENCHMARK
```

Before running the preceding query, I logged off all users from my database and then logged in using SQL*Plus as the SCOTT and BENCHMARK users in two separate windows. Then I ran the query from a third session as the user SYS. You can run it as any other user as long as the user has been granted the select privilege on the underlying views v_$session and v_$process (v$session and v$process used in the preceding query are database synonyms to the views v_$session and v_$process, respectively). Note that I include a condition that precludes any rows for the user SYS in order to exclude the current SYS session from which I run the query. As you can see, at the time I ran this query, I had two sessions, one each for user, SCOTT, and BENCHMARK.

Also notice the process IDs under the column server_pid for the dedicated Oracle server processes that correspond to each of the connections. In this particular case, the query shows us that there are two sessions using two separate connections. We know that there are two separate connections because the process IDs for each row are different.

Now that you understand the difference between a connection and a session in Oracle, let's cover some background information that will help you understand the motivation for connection pooling. We'll then define the terms "connection pooling" and "connection caching."

Client/Server Applications and Connections

In a client/server application (such as a stand-alone Java application communicating directly to the database), a user has a dedicated, direct connection to the database for the entire duration of his interaction, as illustrated in Figure 14-2. Think of this as a phone connection that is dedicated to the two people talking to each other.

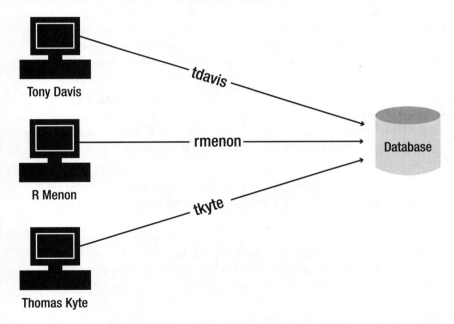

Figure 14-2. *In a client/server architecture, each end user has a dedicated database connection corresponding to a database user account.*

As shown in Figure 14-2, the end user Tony Davis authenticates himself using the database account tdavis. Once authenticated, Tony remains connected to the database for the entire duration of his interaction with the application. This has the following implications on the security and performance of the application Tony is using:

- *Security*: In terms of security, the database simply identifies Tony once in the beginning. As long as the dedicated network connection from Tony's client machine to the database server is secure, this is a safe approach.

- *Performance/scalability*: Since this connection is dedicated to Tony, the resources associated with the connection can't be used by anyone else until Tony logs off or his connection times out. Moreover, the connection has to be established and torn down each time Tony logs into or out of the application. If you increase the connection time-out period, there will be more idle time for the connection, resulting in more wasted resources. On the other hand, if you reduce the connection timeout, Tony would see performance problems associated with connection creation and destruction overhead that occurs after each timeout. Thus, the idea of dedicating one connection for one user for the lifetime of an application session can be a significant scalability inhibitor when we deal with a large number of users.

Web Applications and Connection-Related Challenges

With the advent of web applications, application servers mediate the interaction between the application and the database. Typically, a web application client uses the HTTP protocol to connect to an application server containing the middle-tier business logic. The application server in turn connects to the database to perform various functions. If we create a separate database account for each end user and maintain a dedicated connection, we run into two problems:

- *Performance*: The number of users in a large web application can easily run into the thousands (or more). Maintaining a dedicated connection for each user for the duration of one application session can rapidly exhaust the computing resources (memory and CPU) at the database and application server levels. It can also result in very poor usage of connection resources.

- *Security*: Maintaining separate database accounts for each user means that the application may have to know and maintain the database password of each user. This can result in password-management issues.

In this chapter, we will focus on tackling the performance issues just outlined using connection pooling. In the next chapter, we will examine how we can use proxy authentication to solve the security problem while maintaining good performance.

Cost of Opening and Closing a Connection

To quantify the cost of establishing and tearing down a database connection, I wrote a simple program. The following program, `CostOfConnection`, extends the `JBenchmark` class (explained in the section "Timing Java Programs" of Chapter 1) to time the process of creating and closing a connection.

First, we import the necessary classes and declare the requisite variables:

```
/** This program times the process of establishing and closing a connection.
* COMPATIBLITY NOTE: runs successfully against 9.2.0.1.0 and 10.1.0.2.0
*/
import java.sql.Connection;
```

```
import oracle.jdbc.pool.OracleDataSource;
import book.util.JBenchmark;
class CostOfConnection extends JBenchmark
{
  private static int _numOfConnections = 1;
  private OracleDataSource _ods;
```

Next, we override the method firstMethod() of the JBenchmark class to establish and close a given number of connections. The variable ods points to an initialized OracleDataSource instance, and the variable _numOfConnections points to the number of connections to be established and torn down for each iteration of the loop. _numOfConnections is passed as a command-line parameter:

```
public void firstMethod( ) throws Exception
{
  Connection connections[] = new Connection[ _numOfConnections ];
  for( int i=0; i < _numOfConnections; i++ )
  {
    try
    {
      connections[i] = _ods.getConnection();
    }
    catch( Exception e )
    {
      System.err.println( "failed in connection number: " + i );
      throw e;
    }
  }
  for( int i=0; i < _numOfConnections; i++ )
  {
    if( connections[i] != null )
    {
      connections[i].close();
    }
  }
}
```

The following _runBenchmark() method initializes the OracleDataSource instance variable and calls the method timeMethod() inherited from the JBenchmark class to run the benchmark. In this case, we time only one method.

```
private void _runBenchmark() throws Exception
{
  _ods = new OracleDataSource();
  _ods.setURL ( "jdbc:oracle:thin:@rmenon-lap:1521:ora10g" );
  _ods.setUser("scott");              // username
  _ods.setPassword("tiger");          // password
  // time the process of establishing a connection - method 1
  String msg = "Establishing " + _numOfConnections +
    " connection(s) and closing them";
  timeMethod( JBenchmark.FIRST_METHOD, null, null, msg );
}
```

Finally, in the `main()` method, we initialize the number of connections to establish, create an instance of our class, and invoke the `_runBenchmark()` method:

```
public static void main(String args[]) throws Exception
{
  if( args.length == 1 )
  {
    _numOfConnections = Integer.parseInt( args[0] );
  }
  new CostOfConnection()._runBenchmark();
}
}// end of program
```

Results of a run on my machine for ten connections are as follows:

```
B:\code\book\ch15>java CostOfConnection 10
Establishing 10 connection(s) and closing them
       On an average it took 1641 ms (number of runs = 130.)
```

As you can see, it took almost 164 milliseconds (approximately 1/6 of a second) to establish and close a connection. Closing a connection usually takes a negligible amount of time, so the entire time of 164 milliseconds can be approximately attributed to the act of establishing a connection. This can be very costly if you consider the case of thousands of users performing many small requests, with each request resulting in the creation and destruction of a connection. Also, since establishing a connection involves forking a process on UNIX and creating a new thread on Windows, it can quickly exhaust system resources. For example, on my PC, I could not establish more than 132 simultaneous connections at a time. The next section shows how the technique of connection pooling addresses this problem.

What Is Connection Pooling?

A *connection pool* is a pool of physical connections that can be reused across multiple client sessions. Instead of creating and destroying a connection each time the client needs one, we maintain a pool of connections. These connections are created typically once in the beginning (or on demand) and destroyed only when an application shutdown or an error occurs. Connection pooling enables multiple clients to share a small pool of pre-established connections, thus improving performance and scalability tremendously. In this way, for example, a pool of 50 to 100 physical database connections can be shared by 100, 500, 1,000, or more users.

In a three-tier architecture, the connection pool is maintained by the application server. When an application requests a connection, the application server takes a connection from the pre-established pool, marks it as "in use," and hands it over to the application. During the request, the application has effectively reserved (or checked out) this connection object. When the application "closes" a connection, the application server returns the connection back to the pool after clearing the connection state (it does not actually close the physical connection).

There are two performance advantages to this approach:

- Since we maintain a pool of connections (instead of creating and destroying connections with each request), the overhead of establishing database connections goes down dramatically for the case of a large number of users.

- Since the application "reserves" the connection only for the duration of the request, we don't waste connection resources when the application is idle (i.e., between requests). This again translates directly to improved performance and scalability.

Note that this solution scales only if you can map the large number of end users to a much smaller number of actual database users. On a popular website such as `http://www.amazon.com`, the number of users can run into the millions; creating a connection pool for these many different users is not feasible.

For example, imagine our website has 1,000,000 users, and for each user we have to connect as a separate database account. Say we have a connection pool of 100 connections. The connections in this pool are good for use only for the 100 users whose connections exist in the pool currently. The moment a new user tries to connect, the connection pool cannot serve that user, since each user requires connection to a different account. Thus, one of the connections will have to be aged out and a new connection established for this user. Clearly, the purpose of connection pool is defeated if you need to tear down and create a connection every time a new user whose connection is not currently in the pool tries to connect. Contrast this with a scenario where the 1,000,000 users can be "mapped" into 10 database users based on different privileges each user requires. Now the likelihood of a new user getting a "hit" in the connection pool is very high, thus allowing us to share the 100 connections among a much larger end-user population. So how do we map these many users to a manageable number of database users? We will look at this aspect in detail in the next chapter.

Let's now take a brief look at what the term "connection caching" means before we discuss Oracle9*i* connection pooling and caching, followed by Oracle 10*g* implicit connection caching.

What Is Connection Caching?

At the core, connection caching and connection pooling refer to the same concept: pooling physical database connections to be shared across multiple client sessions. *Connection caching*, usually implemented in the middle tier, refers to the concept of creating a cache of physical connections using the connection pooling framework provided by the JDBC driver. In Oracle9*i*, we need to create our own cache on top of the connection pooling framework provided by Oracle JDBC drivers. We can use a sample connection cache provided by Oracle as well. In Oracle 10*g*, the connection cache can be enabled implicitly at the data source level itself, thus obviating the need to maintain or manage our own cache.

The next section discusses in detail the Oracle9*i* implementation of connection pooling and caching.

Oracle9*i* Connection Pooling Framework

The Oracle9*i* connection pooling framework depends on the following key concepts:

- *Connection pool data source*: A connection pool data source is similar in concept and functionality to the data sources described in Chapter 3, but with methods to return *pooled connection* objects, instead of *normal connection* objects.

- *Pooled connection (or physical connection)*: A pooled connection instance represents a single connection to a database that remains open during use by a series of *logical connection* instances.

- *Logical connection*: A logical connection is a connection instance (such as a standard Connection instance or an OracleConnection instance) returned by a pooled connection instance. It is the pooled connection *checked out* by an application at a given point in time.

When we use connection pooling, we essentially introduce an intermediate step to enable reuse of a physical connection. The connection pool data source returns a pooled connection, which encapsulates the physical database connection. We then use the pooled connection to return JDBC connection instances (one at a time) that each act as a temporary handle (the logical connection).

When an application closes the logical connection, it does not result in the closing of the physical database connection. It does, however, clear the connection state, restore the defaults (e.g., it resets autocommit to true if you had set it to false), and mark the underlying physical connection (or pooled connection) as "available" for creating the next logical instance from the connection pool.

To actually close the physical connection, you must invoke the close() method of the pooled connection. This action is typically performed in the middle tier that manages the connection pool, and not by the application.

Related JDBC Standard and Oracle Interfaces

Figure 14-3 shows the JDBC interfaces related to connection pooling and their Oracle counterparts. Note that as an application developer, you will typically not deal with the PooledConnection and ConnectionPoolDataSource interfaces described in this section. These interfaces are implemented for you by the connection cache (either the sample Oracle9*i* connection cache or the implicit connection cache in 10*g*). So feel free to skip the section "Oracle9*i* Connection Caching" if you are not interested in this topic.

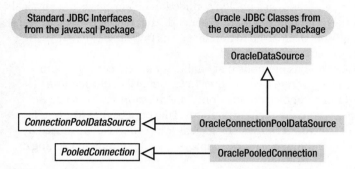

Figure 14-3. *JDBC interfaces that define connection pooling and the Oracle classes that implement them*

The `javax.sql.ConnectionPoolDataSource` interface defines the standard functionality of connection pool data sources. The `getPooledConnection()` method of this interface returns a pooled connection instance and optionally takes a username and password as input in its overloaded version:

```
public javax.sql.PooledConnection getPooledConnection() throws SQLException;
public javax.sql.PooledConnection getPooledConnection(
  String userName, String password ) throws SQLException;
```

As Figure 14-3 indicates, the Oracle class `oracle.jdbc.pool.OracleConnectionPoolDataSource` implements the `ConnectionPoolDataSource` interface. This class also extends the `OracleDataSource` class, so it includes all the connection properties and getter and setter methods described in the section "Connecting to a Database" of Chapter 3. The `getPooledConnection()` method of this class returns an `OraclePooledConnection` class instance, which implements the `PooledConnection` interface.

A pooled connection instance encapsulates a physical connection to the database specified in the connection properties of the connection pool data source instance with which it was created. It implements the following standard `javax.sql.PooledConnection` interface:

```
public interface javax.sql.PooledConnection
{
  public void close() throws SQLException
  public java.sql.Connection getConnection() throws SQLException
  public abstract void addConnectionEventListener(
                     javax.sql.ConnectionEventListener);
  public abstract void removeConnectionEventListener(
                     javax.sql.ConnectionEventListener);
}
```

The getConnection() method of this interface returns a logical connection instance to the application. Calling the close() method on a pooled connection object closes the physical connection—remember, this is performed by the middle-tier code that manages the connection pool. The connection event listeners are used to handle events that arise when an associated logical connection is closed, for example.

The OraclePooledConnection class has methods that enable statement caching (both implicit and explicit) for a pooled connection (see Chapter 13 for details on this feature). All logical connections obtained from a pooled connection share the same cache, since the underlying physical connection is where the caching happens. This implies that when statement caching is enabled, a statement you create on one logical connection can be reused by another logical connection. It follows that you cannot enable or disable statement caching on individual logical connections.

The following are OraclePooledConnection method definitions for statement caching:

```
public boolean getExplicitCachingEnabled();
public boolean getImplicitCachingEnabled();
public int getStatementCacheSize();
public void setExplicitCachingEnabled(boolean);
public void setImplicitCachingEnabled(boolean);
public void setStatementCacheSize(int);
```

Let's move on to look at an example of creating a connection pool data source and getting a pooled connection object.

Example of Creating a Pooled Connection and Obtaining a Logical Connection

In this example, we demonstrate the following concepts:

- Creating a pooled connection

- Getting a logical connection from a pooled connection

- Closing the logical connection

- Closing the pooled connection

To peek behind the scenes, we will run the query that we discussed in the section "Connections and Sessions in Oracle" earlier to list the current physical connections actually made to the database. Note that in this example, there is a one-to-one correspondence between a physical connection and a session.

We need a way to "pause" after each of the four steps in the program, in order to run the query in the database and watch how many connections are created. For this, I wrote a class called InputUtil whose waitTillUserHitsEnter() method pauses until you press the Enter key. Please see the section "A Utility to Pause in a Java Program" of Chapter 1 for more details on this method.

The following program, DemoConnectionPooling, illustrates how to create a pooled connection and retrieve a logical connection from it. First, the necessary import statements and the declaration of the main() method are shown:

```
/* This program demonstrates how to create a pooled connection
* and obtain a logical connection from it.
* COMPATIBLITY NOTE: runs successfully against 9.2.0.1.0 and 10.1.0.2.0
*/
import java.sql.Connection;
import javax.sql.PooledConnection;
import oracle.jdbc.pool.OracleConnectionPoolDataSource;
import book.util.InputUtil;
class DemoConnectionPooling
{
  public static void main(String args[]) throws Exception
  {
```

To create a pooled connection, we first create an instance of OracleConnectionPoolDataSource and set its connection properties:

```
OracleConnectionPoolDataSource ocpds = new OracleConnectionPoolDataSource();
ocpds.setURL ( "jdbc:oracle:thin:@usunrat24.us.oracle.com:1521:ora92i" );
ocpds.setUser("scott");            // username
ocpds.setPassword("tiger");        // password
```

■**Note** Instead of using the setURL() method and so on, you can use the individual setter methods such as setServerName() to set the same properties.

The next step is to obtain the pooled connection from the OracleConnectionPoolDataSource instance as follows (note the pause we give right after, using the InputUtil.waitTillUser➡ HitsEnter() method):

```
PooledConnection pooledConnection = ocpds.getPooledConnection();
InputUtil.waitTillUserHitsEnter(
  "Done creating pooled connection.");
```

We then obtain the logical connection from the pooled connection, followed by another pause:

```
Connection connection = pooledConnection.getConnection();
InputUtil.waitTillUserHitsEnter(
  "Done getting connection from pooled connection object.");
```

After using the logical connection to execute statements, the application can close it:

```
connection.close();
InputUtil.waitTillUserHitsEnter(
  "Done closing logical connection");
```

And finally, to close the pooled connection (thus releasing the actual physical connection), we can use the `close()` method on the pooled connection:

```
    pooledConnection.close();
    InputUtil.waitTillUserHitsEnter("Done closing pooled connection");
  }// end of main
}// end of program
```

Before running the program, I made sure that there was no one connected to my test database. In one session, I connected to my database as SYS user. Then I ran the preceding program and ran the query discussed earlier to list connections as SYS after each of the pauses we introduced. Table 14-1 lists the steps and the query results.

Table 14-1. *Results of Running a Query That Detects Connections After Each "Pause" in the Program* DemoConnectionPooling

Step	Query Results				Notes
After creating a pooled connection	PROGRAM	SERVER	SERVER_PID	USERNAME	A physical connection is created.
	JDBC Thin Client	DEDICATED	22326	SCOTT	
After obtaining a logical connection	PROGRAM	SERVER	SERVER_PID	USERNAME	The physical connection is checked out as a logical connection.
	JDBC Thin Client	DEDICATED	22326	SCOTT	
After closing the logical connection	PROGRAM	SERVER	SERVER_PID	USERNAME	The physical connection remains.
	JDBC Thin Client	DEDICATED	22326	SCOTT	
After closing the pooled connection	No rows selected				The physical connection is closed.

As you can see, the creation of a pooled connection results in an actual physical connection being created. But the retrieval of a logical connection does not result in any new physical connection. Similarly, even after closing the logical connection, the physical connection created is retained for use across other sessions. Finally, when we close the pooled connection, the physical connection is also closed.

In the next section, we'll look at a simple Oracle implementation of a connection cache using the connection pooling framework.

Oracle9*i* Connection Caching

As discussed earlier, a connection cache is a cache of physical connections maintained by the middle tier using the connection pooling framework just discussed. JDBC 2.0 does not specify any API specific to connection cache; it only specifies an API for the underlying connection pooling framework. Thus, the middle tier is free to implement the connection cache in any way. JDBC 3.0 does specify an API along with some connection cache–related properties for implementation of a connection cache at the data source level. As discussed later in the section "Oracle 10*g* Connection Caching," the new Oracle 10*g* caching is compliant with JDBC 3.0 requirements.

■Note The concept of connection caching is not relevant to the server-side internal driver, where you use the default connection.

A connection cache is typically represented by an instance of a connection cache class that caches a group of pooled connection instances (remember, a pooled connection cache is associated with an actual physical database connection). The connection cache class extends the data source API. In Oracle9*i*, for a single connection cache instance, all the associated pooled connections must be physical connections to the same database and schema. In Oracle 10*g*, this restriction has been lifted in the new cache architecture.

■Tip In 10*g*, the restriction that all pooled connections associated with a cache must belong to same schema and database has been removed.

Oracle's Implementation of Connection Cache

Figure 14-4 shows the JDBC standard and Oracle classes related to connection caching.

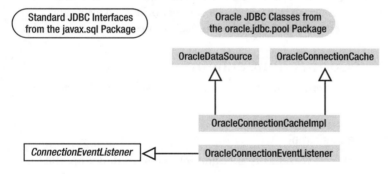

Figure 14-4. *JDBC standard and Oracle-specific connection caching related classes and interfaces*

Oracle provides you with the following classes and interfaces in the `oracle.jdbc.pool` package that implement connection cache functionality for you. In Oracle9*i*, you can use this implementation, or you can code your own using some or all of these classes and interfaces. In Oracle 10*g*, these classes have been deprecated and you should use the implicit connection caching.

- `OracleConnectionCache`: An interface you need to implement if you want to implement your own version of connection caching

- `OracleConnectionCacheImpl`: A class that implements the `OracleConnectionCache` interface

- `OracleConnectionEventListener`: A connection event listener class

As shown in Figure 14-4, the `OracleConnectionCacheImpl` class implements the `Oracle⮞ConnectionCache` interface and extends `OracleDataSource`. It employs `OracleConnection⮞EventListener` class instances for connection events pertaining to cache management scenarios, such as when the application closes the logical connection.

Interaction of the Application and Middle Tier When Using Connection Cache

The following steps occur during a typical interaction of a JDBC application and a middle-tier connection cache. The Oracle implementation is used in our examples.

1. The middle tier creates an instance of a connection cache class with its own data source properties that define the physical connections it will cache.

2. The middle tier may optionally bind this instance to a JNDI source.

3. The JDBC application retrieves a connection cache instance (instead of a generic data source) from the middle tier either by using a JNDI lookup or through a vendor-specific API.

4. The JDBC application retrieves the connection from the connection cache through its `getConnection()` method. This results in a logical connection being returned to the JDBC application.

5. JDBC uses JavaBeans-style events to keep track of when a physical connection (pooled connection instance) can be returned to the cache or when it should be closed due to a fatal error. When the JDBC application is done using the connection, it invokes the `close()` method on the connection. This triggers a connection-closed event and informs the pooled connection instance that its physical connection can be reused.

Steps in Using OracleConnectionCacheImpl

The following sections describe the steps required to instantiate and use the `OracleConnection⮞CacheImpl` class.

Instantiating OracleConnectionCacheImpl

You instantiate an `OracleConnectionCacheImpl` instance and set its connection properties in one of three ways:

- Use the `OracleConnectionCacheImpl` constructor, which takes an existing connection pool data source as input:

  ```
  OracleConnectionCacheImpl occi = new OracleConnectionCacheImpl(cpds);
  ```

- Use the `setConnectionPoolDataSource()` method on an existing `OracleConnection⮞CacheImpl` instance, which takes a connection pool data source instance as input:

  ```
  OracleConnectionCacheImpl occi = new OracleConnectionCacheImpl();
  occi.setConnectionPoolDataSource(cpds);
  ```

- Use the default `OracleConnectionCacheImpl` constructor and set the properties using the setter methods inherited from the `OracleDataSource` class:

```
OracleConnectionCacheImpl occi = new
   OracleConnectionCacheImpl();
occi.setServerName("myserver");
occi.setNetworkProtocol("tcp");
```

Setting Pooled Connection Limit Parameters

The examples in this section assume that `occi` is an initialized `OracleConnectionCacheImpl` variable.

You can set the minimum number of pooled connections by invoking the `setMinLimit()` method as follows:

```
occi.setMinLimit( 3 );
```

The cache will keep three pooled connections open and ready for use at all times.

You can set the maximum number of pooled connections by invoking the `setMaxLimit()` method as follows:

```
occi.setMaxLimit(  10 );
```

The cache will have a maximum of ten pooled connections. What happens when you reach the limit and need another connection? That depends on the cache scheme you set, as discussed next.

Setting Cache Schemes for Creating New Pooled Connections

The `OracleConnectionCacheImpl` class supports three connection cache schemes that come into effect when all three of the following conditions are true:

- The application has requested a connection.

- All existing pooled connections are in use.

- The maximum limit of pooled connections in the cache has been reached.

The three cache schemes are

- *Dynamic*: This is the default scheme. In this scheme, the cache would automatically create new pooled connections, though each of these new connections is automatically closed and freed as soon as the logical connection instance that it provided is closed. You can set this scheme using one of the two overloaded versions of the method `setCacheScheme()`:

```
occi.setCacheScheme( "dynamic" );
occi.setCacheScheme( OracleConnectionCacheImpl.DYNAMIC_SCHEME );
```

- *Fixed return null*: In this scheme, the requests after the maximum limit is exceeded get a null value returned. You can set this scheme using one of the two overloaded versions of the method setCacheScheme():

```
occi.setCacheScheme( "fixed_return_null_scheme" );
occi.setCacheScheme( OracleConnectionCacheImpl.FIXED_RETURN_NULL_SCHEME );
```

- *Fixed wait*: In this case, when the maximum limit of pooled connections is reached, the next request would wait forever. You can set this scheme using one of the two overloaded versions of the method setCacheScheme():

```
occi.setCacheScheme( "fixed_wait_scheme" );
occi.setCacheScheme( OracleConnectionCacheImpl.FIXED_WAIT_SCHEME );
```

Setting Oracle Connection Cache Timeouts

Applications can also time out the physical and logical connections. Oracle JDBC drivers provide following three types of timeout periods for this purpose:

- *Wait timeout*: The maximum period after which a physical connection is returned to the cache. This wait triggers only when all connections are in use and a new connection is requested. A timeout exception, EOJ_FIXED_WAIT_TIMEOUT, is thrown when the timeout expires. You use the getter and setter methods on the property CacheFixedWait➥ Timeout to get and set this timeout.

- *Inactivity timeout*: The maximum period a physical connection can remain unused. When the period expires, the connection is closed and its resources are freed. You use the getter and setter methods on the property CacheInactivityTimeout to get and set this timeout.

- *Time to live timeout*: The maximum period a logical connection can be active. After this time expires, *whether or not the connection is still in use*, the connection is closed and its resources are freed. You use the getter and setter methods on the property CacheTimeToLiveTimeout to get and set this timeout.

Example of Using OracleConnectionCacheImpl

The following DemoOracleConnectionCache class illustrates how to use Oracle connection caching by using the dynamic and "fixed return null" cache schemes. We begin with the imports and the class declaration, followed by the main() method:

```
/* This program demonstrates how to use Oracle connection cache.
* COMPATIBLITY NOTE: runs successfully against 9.2.0.1.0 and 10.1.0.2.0
*/
import java.sql.Connection;
import java.sql.SQLException;
import oracle.jdbc.pool.OracleConnectionCacheImpl;
import book.ch03.JDBCUtil;
```

```
class DemoOracleConnectionCache
{
  public static void main(String args[]) throws Exception
  {
```

We instantiate the cache object and set the properties that define the limits and attributes of the cached connections. We also print the default cache scheme.

```
    OracleConnectionCacheImpl occi = new OracleConnectionCacheImpl();
    occi.setURL ( "jdbc:oracle:thin:@rmenon-lap:1522:ora92" );
    occi.setUser("scott");     // username
    occi.setPassword("tiger"); // password
    occi.setMaxLimit( 3 );     // max # of connections in pool
    occi.setMinLimit( 1 );     // min # of connections in pool
    System.out.println( "By default, the cache scheme is: " +
      occi.getCacheScheme() );
```

We then set the cache scheme to "dynamic" and invoke the method getOneMoreThanMax➥ Connections(). We will see the definition of this method soon, but as the method name suggests, it attempts to get one connection more than the maximum limit of three set previously. This is to see how different cache schemes behave when the limit is exceeded.

```
    occi.setCacheScheme( OracleConnectionCacheImpl.DYNAMIC_SCHEME );
    int maxLimit = occi.getMaxLimit();
    System.out.println( "Max Limit: " + maxLimit );
    System.out.println( "Demo of dynamic cache scheme - the default" );
    _getOneMoreThanMaxConnections( occi, maxLimit );
```

We do the same for the cache scheme "fixed return null":

```
    System.out.println( "\nDemo of fixed return null cache scheme" );
    occi.setCacheScheme( OracleConnectionCacheImpl.FIXED_RETURN_NULL_SCHEME );
    _getOneMoreThanMaxConnections( occi , maxLimit);
  }// end of main
```

The method getOneMoreThanMaxConnections() is defined at the end of the program. It simply loops through and tries to create one more than the maximum limit passed to it as a parameter.

```
  private static void _getOneMoreThanMaxConnections(
    OracleConnectionCacheImpl occi , int maxLimit) throws SQLException
  {
    //Create an array of connections 1 more than max limit
    Connection[] connections = new Connection[ maxLimit + 1 ];

    for( int i=0; i < connections.length; i++ )
    {
      System.out.print( "Getting connection no " + (i+1) + " ..." );
```

```
      connections[i] = occi.getConnection();
      if( connections[i] != null )
        System.out.println( " Successful." );
      else
        System.out.println( " Failed." );
    }
    // close all connections
    for( int i=0; i < connections.length; i++ )
    {
      JDBCUtil.close( connections[i] );
    }
  }// end of getOneMoreThanMaxConnections
}// end of program
```

The following is the output of the program when I ran it on my machine:

```
B:\>java DemoOracleConnectionCache
By default, the cache scheme is: 1
Max Limit: 3
Demo of dynamic cache scheme - the default
Getting connection no 1 ... Successful.
Getting connection no 2 ... Successful.
Getting connection no 3 ... Successful.
Getting connection no 4 ... Successful.

Demo of fixed return null cache scheme
Getting connection no 1 ... Successful.
Getting connection no 2 ... Successful.
Getting connection no 3 ... Successful.
Getting connection no 4 ... Failed.
```

As shown, even though we hit the maximum limit, we still got a connection successfully when the cache scheme was dynamic (which is the default). When the cache scheme was "fixed return null," we got a null object when we tried to get a fourth connection. The "fixed wait" cache scheme isn't shown, but if you modify the program to use it, the program will wait forever when you try to get the fourth connection.

This concludes our discussion of Oracle9*i* connection pooling and caching. It's time now to look at the implicit connection caching of Oracle 10*g*.

Oracle 10*g* Implicit Connection Caching

As mentioned earlier, starting with Oracle 10*g*, the cache architecture just discussed was deprecated. It has been replaced by a more powerful, JDBC 3.0–compliant implicit connection caching. The highlights of implicit connection caching are

- Transparent access to a connection cache at the data source level.

- Support for connections with different usernames and passwords in the same cache.

- Ability to control cache behavior by defining a set of cache properties. The supported properties include ones that set timeouts, the maximum number of physical connections, and so on.

- Ability to retrieve a connection based on user-defined connection attributes (a feature known as *connection striping*).

- Ability to use callbacks to control cache behavior

  - When a connection is returned to the cache.

  - When a connection has been abandoned.

  - When an application requests a connection that does not exist in the cache.

- The new class OracleConnectionCacheManager is provided for administering the connection cache.

With the new cache architecture, you can turn on connection caching simply by invoking setConnectionCachingEnabled(true) on an OracleDataSource object. After caching is turned on, the first connection request to OracleDataSource implicitly creates a connection cache. There is a one-to-one mapping between the OracleDataSource object and its implicit connection cache.

Using the Oracle 10*g* Implicit Connection Cache

The following sections discuss the various steps involved in using the implicit connection cache.

Instantiating OracleDataSource

This step should be familiar to you by now:

```
OracleDataSource ods = new OracleDataSource();
ods.setURL ( "jdbc:oracle:thin:@rmenon-pc:1521:ora10g" );
ods.setUser("scott");          // username
ods.setPassword("tiger");      // password
```

Turning the Connection Cache On

You turn on the connection cache by simply invoking setConnectionCachingEnabled() on the OracleDataSource object:

```
ods.setConnectionCachingEnabled( true );
```

Setting Connection Cache Properties

You can optionally set connection properties listed later in this section by either using the method setConnectionCacheProperties() of the OracleDataSource object, or using the OracleConnectionCacheManager API to create or reinitialize the connection cache as discussed later. For example, the following code sets three properties of the connection cache using the setConnectionCacheProperties() method of the OracleDataSource object:

```
Properties cacheProperties = new Properties();
cacheProperties.setProperty( "InitialLimit", "2" );
cacheProperties.setProperty( "MinLimit", "3" );
cacheProperties.setProperty( "MaxLimit", "15" );
ods.setConnectionCacheProperties(cacheProperties);
```

By setting connection cache properties, you can control the characteristics of the connection cache.

■**Caution** In my tests with 10.1.0.2.0, I found that the JDBC driver silently ignores an invalid (or misspelled) property. Thus, you need to be extra careful in spelling these properties while setting them up. Another problem is that, unfortunately, the property names that Oracle chose in many cases are not the same as the ones mentioned in JDBC 3.0 standard, though their meanings may be the same. For example, the JDBC property InitialPoolSize means the same thing as the Oracle property InitialLimit. This can be confusing.

Let's look at these cache properties in more detail.

Limit Properties

Limit properties control the size of the cache and the number of statements that are cached (see Chapter 13 for details on statement caching), among other things. Table 14-2 lists these properties along with their equivalent JDBC 3.0 standard property (if available), default value, and a brief description.

Table 14-2. *Cache Properties Related to Various Cache Limits Supported by Oracle 10g Implicit Connection Cache*

Property	Equivalent JDBC 3.0 Property	Default Value	Description
InitialLimit	initialPoolSize	0	Determines how many connections are created in the cache when it is created or reinitialized.
MaxLimit	maxPoolSize	No limit	Sets the maximum number of connections the cache can hold.
MaxStatementsLimit	maxStatements	0	Sets the maximum number of statements cached by a connection.
MinLimit	minPoolSize	0	Sets the minimum number of connections the cache is guaranteed to have at all times.
LowerThresholdLimit		20% of maxLimit	Sets the lower threshold limit on the cache. It is used when a releaseConnection() callback is registered with a cached connection. When the number of connections in the cache reaches this limit (LowerThresholdLimit), and a request is pending, the cache manager calls this method on the cache connections (instead of waiting for the connection to be freed).

Timeout and Time Interval Properties

These properties determine when the connections in the cache time out or at what interval Oracle checks and enforces the specified cache properties. Table 14-3 lists each of these properties with its default value and the type of connection it impacts (physical or logical). Only the property PropertyCheckInterval has a JDBC 3.0–equivalent property (propertyCycle).

Table 14-3. *Timeout and Interval Properties of Implicit Connection Cache*

Property	Default Value	Type of Connection Impacted	Description
InactivityTimeout	0 (no timeout)	Physical	Sets the maximum time in seconds a physical connection can remain idle in a connection cache. An *idle* connection is one that is not active and does not have a logical handle associated with it.
TimeToLiveTimeout	0 (no timeout)	Logical	Sets the maximum time in seconds that a logical connection can remain open (or checked out), after which it is returned to the cache.
AbandonedConnectionTimeout	0 (no timeout)	Logical	Sets the maximum time in seconds that a logical connection can remain open (or checked out) without any SQL activity on that connection, after which the logical connection is returned to the cache.
ConnectionWaitTimeout	0 (no timeout)	Logical	Comes into play when there is a request for a logical connection, the cache has reached the MaxLimit, and all physical connections are in use. This is the number of seconds the cache will wait for one of the physical connections currently in use to become free so that the request can be satisfied. After this timeout expires, the cache returns null.
PropertyCheckInterval	900 seconds		Sets the time interval in seconds at which the cache manager inspects and enforces all specified cache properties.

Attribute Weight Properties

Attribute weight properties allow you to set weights on certain attributes of a connection in the connection cache. If the property `ClosestConnectionMatch` is set to `true`, then these weights are used to get a "closest" match to the connection you request. We will look at these properties along with this feature in more detail in the section "Using Connection Attributes and Attribute Weights (10*g* Only)."

The ValidateConnection Property

If you set this property to `true`, the cache manager tests for validity each connection to be retrieved from the database. The default value is `false`.

Closing a Connection

Once an application is done using a connection, the application closes it using the `close()` method on the connection. There is another variant of this method that we will discuss in the section on "Using Connection Attributes and Attribute Weights (10*g* Only)."

An Example of Using Implicit Connection Caching

The following `DemoImplicitConnectionCaching` class illustrates how implicit connection caching works. First, we declare the class and the `main()` method after importing the required classes:

```
/* This program demonstrates implicit connection caching.
* COMPATIBLITY NOTE: runs successfully 10.1.0.2.0
*/
import java.sql.Connection;
import java.util.Properties;
import oracle.jdbc.pool.OracleDataSource;
import book.util.InputUtil;
class DemoImplicitConnectionCaching
{
  public static void main(String args[]) throws Exception
  {
```

Next, in the `main()` method, we instantiate the `OracleDataSource` object, which will hold our implicit cache:

```
    OracleDataSource ods = new OracleDataSource();
    ods.setURL ( "jdbc:oracle:thin:@rmenon-lap:1521:ora10g" );
    ods.setUser("scott");            // username
    ods.setPassword("tiger");        // password
```

We then enable the implicit caching:

```
    // enable implicit caching
    ods.setConnectionCachingEnabled( true );
```

We set the cache properties with an initial and minimum limit of three connections and a maximum limit of fifteen connections. The cache, when first set up, should pre-establish three connections, and it should never shrink below three connections later. Note that in production code, you should use a properties file to set these properties instead of using the setProperty() method in your Java code. This makes it easier to change them during runtime.

```
// set cache properties
Properties cacheProperties = new Properties();
cacheProperties.setProperty( "InitialLimit", "3" );
cacheProperties.setProperty( "MinLimit", "3" );
cacheProperties.setProperty( "MaxLimit", "15" );
ods.setConnectionCacheProperties(cacheProperties);
```

We first establish two connections to the SCOTT user, followed by one connection to the BENCHMARK user. We calculate and print the time it took to establish each of these connections. We also interject pauses using the InputUtil.waitTillUserHitsEnter() method (explained earlier in this chapter) after each connection establishment step. During these pauses, we will examine the database to see the number of physical connections using the query we covered in the section "Connections and Sessions in Oracle."

```
// time the process of establishing first connection
long startTime = System.currentTimeMillis();
Connection conn1 = ods.getConnection("scott", "tiger");
long endTime = System.currentTimeMillis();
System.out.println("It took " + (endTime-startTime) +
  " ms to establish the 1st connection (scott)." );
InputUtil.waitTillUserHitsEnter();
// time the process of establishing second connection
startTime = System.currentTimeMillis();
Connection conn2 = ods.getConnection("scott", "tiger");
endTime = System.currentTimeMillis();
System.out.println("It took " + (endTime-startTime) +
  " ms to establish the 2nd connection (scott)." );
InputUtil.waitTillUserHitsEnter();
// time the process of establishing third connection
startTime = System.currentTimeMillis();
Connection conn3 = ods.getConnection("benchmark", "benchmark");
endTime = System.currentTimeMillis();
System.out.println("It took " + (endTime-startTime) +
  " ms to establish the 3rd connection (benchmark)." );
InputUtil.waitTillUserHitsEnter();
```

At the end of the program, we close all connections, putting a pause after the first close() statement:

```
// close all connections
conn1.close();
InputUtil.waitTillUserHitsEnter("After closing the first connection.");
conn2.close();
```

```
    conn3.close();
  }// end of main
}// end of program
```

I ran this program on my machine, and after every pause, I ran the query to detect connections. Let's look at the output and the query results side by side:

```
B:\> java DemoImplicitConnectionCaching
It took 1015 ms to establish the 1st connection (scott).
Press Enter to continue...
```

The query results executed as the SYS user right after the pause are as follows:

```
sys@ORA10G> select s.server, p.spid server_pid, s.username
  2  from v$session s, v$process p
  3  where s.type = 'USER'
  4    and s.username != 'SYS'
  5    and p.addr(+) = s.paddr;
SERVER          SERVER_PID   USERNAME
--------------- ------------ ----------
DEDICATED       2460         SCOTT
DEDICATED       3528         SCOTT
DEDICATED       3288         SCOTT
```

This tells us that the very first time we establish a connection, the implicit connection caching results in the creation of three connections (equal to the parameter InitialLimit that we set earlier). That also explains why it took 1,015 milliseconds to establish the "first" connection. The program output after I pressed Enter follows:

```
It took 0 ms to establish the 2nd connection (scott).
Press Enter to continue...
```

This shows the main benefit of connection caching. Since we already have three connections established, this call gets one of these from the cache and completes really fast. At this time, if we run the query again, we will see the same output as before, since no new connections have been established. Pressing Enter again results in the following output:

```
It took 266 ms to establish the 3rd connection (benchmark).
Press Enter to continue...
```

Even though we have one more physical connection left in the cache, we cannot use it, since this time the request is to establish a connection to the user BENCHMARK. Hence the connection cache has to create a new connection, which took 266 milliseconds. At this time, the cache has four physical connections (three to SCOTT and one to BENCHMARK) established, as shown by our query results:

```
sys@ORA10G> select s.server, p.spid server_pid, s.username
  2  from v$session s, v$process p
  3  where s.type = 'USER'
  4    and s.username != 'SYS'
  5    and p.addr(+) = s.paddr;
```

```
SERVER          SERVER_PID   USERNAME
---------------  ------------  ----------
DEDICATED       2460         SCOTT
DEDICATED       3528         SCOTT
DEDICATED       3288         SCOTT
DEDICATED       2132         BENCHMARK
```

Finally, we press Enter again and see

```
After closing the first connection.
Press Enter to continue...
```

After the first connection is closed, when we execute the preceding query, we get the same results as before (four connections). This is, of course, because closing the logical connection does not result in a closing of the physical connection.

To manage your implicit caches, Oracle provides you with an API in the form of the class OracleConnectionCacheManager we'll look at it in the next section.

The OracleConnectionCacheManager Class

OracleConnectionCacheManager provides methods for the middle tier to centrally manage one or more connection caches that share a JVM. Each cache is given a unique name (implicitly or explicitly). The OracleConnectionCacheManager class also provides information about the cache, such as number of physical connections that are in use and the number of available connections.

The following sections describe some of the more commonly used methods that this class provides, with short descriptions. For a complete list of supported methods, please refer to *Oracle Database JDBC Developer's Guide and Reference* (for 10g).

createCache()

Using createCache(), you can create a connection cache with a given DataSource object and a Properties object. It also allows you to give a meaningful name to the cache, which is useful when you are managing multiple caches in the middle tier. The second variant listed generates a name for the cache internally.

```
public void createCache(String cacheName, javax.sql.DataSource datasource,
  java.util.Properties cacheProperties );
public void createCache(javax.sql.DataSource datasource,
   java.util.Properties cacheProperties );
```

removeCache()

This method waits timeout number of seconds for the in-use logical connections to be closed before removing the cache.

```
public void removeCache(String cacheName, int timeout);
```

reinitializeCache()

This method allows you to reinitialize the cache with the new set of properties. This is useful in dynamically configuring the cache based on runtime load changes and so forth.

```
public void reinitializeCache(String cacheName, java.util.properties
  cacheProperties)
```

■**Caution** Invoking `reinitializeCache()` will close all in-use connections.

---

enableCache() and disableCache()

These two methods enable or disable a given cache. When the cache is disabled, in-use connections will work as usual, but no new connections will be served out from the cache.

```
public void enableCache(String cacheName);
public void disableCache(String cacheName);
```

getCacheProperties()

This method gets the cache properties for the specified cache.

```
public java.util.Properties getCacheProperties(String cacheName)
```

getNumberOfAvailableConnections()

This method gets the number of connections in the connection cache that are available for use.

```
public int getNumberOfAvailableConnections(String cacheName)
```

getNumberOfActiveConnections()

This method gets the number of in-use connections at a given point of time for a given cache.

```
public int getNumberOfActiveConnections(String cacheName)
```

setConnectionPoolDataSource()

This method sets the connection pool data source for the cache. All properties are derived from this data source.

```
public void setConnectionPoolDataSource(String cacheName,
  ConnectionPoolDataSource cpds)
```

An Example of Using the OracleConnectionCacheManager API

Let's look at the program DemoOracleConnectionCacheManager, which illustrates using some of the methods of the OracleConnectionCacheManager class. First, we import the classes and set up OracleDataSource as usual:

```
/* This program demonstrates using the Oracle connection cache manager API.
* COMPATIBLITY NOTE: runs successfully against 10.1.0.2.0
*/
import java.sql.Connection;
import java.util.Properties;
import oracle.jdbc.pool.OracleDataSource;
import oracle.jdbc.pool.OracleConnectionCacheManager;
class DemoOracleConnectionCacheManager
{
  public static void main(String args[]) throws Exception
  {
    OracleDataSource ods = new OracleDataSource();
    ods.setURL ( "jdbc:oracle:thin:@rmenon-lap:1521:ora10g" );
    ods.setUser("scott");              // username
    ods.setPassword("tiger");          // password
```

We then enable implicit connection caching:

```
    // enable implicit caching
    ods.setConnectionCachingEnabled( true );
```

Next, we set the connection cache properties and print them out:

```
    // set cache properties (use a properties file in production code.)
    Properties cacheProperties = new Properties();
    cacheProperties.setProperty( "InitialLimit", "2" );
    cacheProperties.setProperty( "MinLimit", "3" );
    cacheProperties.setProperty( "MaxLimit", "15" );
    ods.setConnectionCacheProperties(cacheProperties);
    System.out.println("Connection Cache Properties: ");
    System.out.println("\tInitialLimit: 2");
    System.out.println("\tMinLimit: 3");
    System.out.println("\tMaxLimit: 15");
```

We create the connection cache and explicitly give it a name (CONNECTION_CACHE_NAME is a constant defined later in the file):

```
    // create the connection cache
    OracleConnectionCacheManager occm =
      OracleConnectionCacheManager.getConnectionCacheManagerInstance();
    occm.createCache( CONNECTION_CACHE_NAME, ods, cacheProperties );
    System.out.println( "Just after creating the cache, " +
      "active connections: " +
      occm.getNumberOfActiveConnections( CONNECTION_CACHE_NAME ) +
        ", available connections: " +
      occm.getNumberOfAvailableConnections( CONNECTION_CACHE_NAME ) );
```

We print out the number of in-use (or active) connections and available connections:

```
System.out.println( "Just after creating the cache, " +
  "active connections: " +
  occm.getNumberOfActiveConnections( CONNECTION_CACHE_NAME )   +
    ", available connections: " + occm.getNumberOfAvailableConnections(
     CONNECTION_CACHE_NAME ));
```

Next, we get a connection and close it, printing the active and available connections after each step:

```
// get first connection
Connection conn1 = ods.getConnection("scott", "tiger");
System.out.println( "After getting first connection from cache, " +
  "active connections: " +
  occm.getNumberOfActiveConnections( CONNECTION_CACHE_NAME )   +
  ", available connections: " + occm.getNumberOfAvailableConnections(
  CONNECTION_CACHE_NAME ) );
conn1.close();
System.out.println( "After closing first connection, " +
  "active connections: " +
  occm.getNumberOfActiveConnections( CONNECTION_CACHE_NAME )   +
  ", available connections: " + occm.getNumberOfAvailableConnections(
   CONNECTION_CACHE_NAME ));
```

We then get three connections (so that we go beyond the initial minimum of two connections), and close one connection, printing the number of active and available connections after each step:

```
// get 3 connections to go beyond the InitialMinimum limit
Connection conn2 = ods.getConnection("scott", "tiger");
Connection conn3 = ods.getConnection("scott", "tiger");
Connection conn4 = ods.getConnection("scott", "tiger");
System.out.println( "After getting 3 connections, " +
  "active connections: " +
  occm.getNumberOfActiveConnections( CONNECTION_CACHE_NAME )   +
  ", available connections: " +   occm.getNumberOfAvailableConnections(
  CONNECTION_CACHE_NAME ) );
// close one connection - the number of connections should not
// go below 3 since we set a MinLimit value of 3.
conn2.close();
System.out.println( "After closing 1 connection, " +
  "active connections: " + occm.getNumberOfActiveConnections(
  CONNECTION_CACHE_NAME )  + ", available connections: " +
  occm.getNumberOfAvailableConnections( CONNECTION_CACHE_NAME ) );
```

We close the remaining two connections:

```
conn3.close();
conn4.close();
```

Just as an experiment, before ending the program, we disable the cache and try to retrieve a connection from it:

```
// what happens if we disable cache and try to get a connection?
occm.disableCache( CONNECTION_CACHE_NAME );
Connection conn5 = ods.getConnection("scott", "tiger");
conn5.close();
}// end of main
private static final String CONNECTION_CACHE_NAME = "myConnectionCache";
}// end of program
```

The output of this program is as follows:

```
B:\> java DemoOracleConnectionCacheManager
Connection Cache Properties:
        InitialLimit: 2
        MinLimit: 3
        MaxLimit: 15
Just after creating the cache, active connections: 0, available connections: 2
After getting first connection from cache, active connections: 1,
available connections: 1
After closing first connection, active connections: 0, available connections: 2
After getting 3 connections, active connections: 3, available connections: 0
After closing 1 connection, active connections: 2, available connections: 1
Exception in thread "main" java.sql.SQLException: Connection Cache with this
Cache Name is Disabled
        ... <-- trimmed to save space -->
```

In particular, note that the number of connections (available plus active) does not go below the minimum limit of three that we set, even though we close all but two connections, as shown by the last line of the output. Also, if we try to get a connection from a disabled cache, we get an exception as expected.

Let's now look at how we can use connection attributes and attribute weights in Oracle 10*g*.

Using Connection Attributes and Attribute Weights (10*g* Only)

A new feature of Oracle 10*g* JDBC drivers is that you can tag a connection with a label of your choice and use the tag to retrieve the same connection on which the tag was previously set from the connection cache. This feature is also known as *connection striping*.

Typically, you will use connection striping to change the state of the connection (say, setting its transaction isolation level) and then tag it. The next time you retrieve the connection using the tag, its state need not be reinitialized. Thus, you can create "stripes" of connections in your cache, each of which have its state set once to cater to the requirements of different applications sharing the cache.

Applying Connection Attributes on a Connection

We can apply a connection attribute to a connection in the cache in two ways. The first method is to invoke applyConnectionAttributes(java.util.Properties connectionAttribute) on the connection object to set the attributes. Later, when we want to retrieve it, we invoke getConnection(java.util.Properties connectionAttributes) on the connection object. Let's look at an example.

First, we get the connection from the cache (assume ods is initialized properly):

```
OracleConnection conn1 = (OracleConnection)
  ods.getConnection("scott", "tiger");
```

Then, we set the transaction isolation level of the connection to serializable (see the section "Transaction Isolation Levels" of Chapter 4 for details on transaction isolations):

```
conn1.setTransactionIsolation( Connection.TRANSACTION_SERIALIZABLE );
```

Now, we would like to remember this "attribute" of connection throughout its life in the cache, meaning we would like to retrieve a connection with transaction isolation level set to serializable later on. So we would mark this connection object with our own attribute value pair constants (TXN_ISOLATION and SERIALIZABLE are constants defined by us):

```
Properties connectionAttributes = new Properties();
connectionAttributes.setProperty( TXN_ISOLATION, SERIALIZABLE );
conn1.applyConnectionAttributes( connectionAttributes );
```

After using the connection, we close it:

```
conn1.close();
```

Later, we retrieve the same connection back from the cache using the attribute that we set:

```
conn1 = (OracleConnection) ods.getConnection( connectionAttributes );
```

Notice that we use the overloaded version of getConnection() that takes in a set of attributes to get a matching connection. Also note that once we tag a connection, we need to retrieve the connection always using the same tag. If we don't specify a tag (e.g., if we use the getConnection() method without any parameters), we'll get access to only the "untagged" set of connections. This is the intended behavior, since we don't want applications to run into each other's connection states. For example, an application shouldn't inadvertently get a connection with the transaction isolation set to serializable by some other application or module sharing the same cache.

The second method to set these attributes involves using the close(java.util.Properties) method on the connection. This method will override any attributes that we may have set on the same connection using the previous applyConnectionAttributes() method.

> **■Note** For some reason, Oracle treats the "autocommit" attribute of `Connection` as special, in that you can't retain the state of autocommit by setting it to `false` and tagging the connection. Although this looks bad, it turns out that autocommit doesn't involve a round-trip to the database because of the way Oracle JDBC drivers implement it, so tagging it wouldn't have resulted in a performance gain anyway. However, I found this special treatment of autocommit somewhat confusing.

Attribute Weights and the ClosestConnectionMatch Property

Attributes-based connection retrieval can be further refined by specifying attribute weights for each attribute. An attribute weight is a positive integer: the higher the weight, the higher the priority when a match is made for retrieving a connection. When performing a match, the connection cache tries to return a connection that matches all the attributes specified in the `getConnection( Properties connectionAttributes)` invocation. If an exact match is not found, and if `ClosestConnectionMatch` is set to `true`, then the cache tries to return the connection with the maximum number of matching attributes. If there is a tie here as well, then the connection cache returns the connection whose attributes have the highest combined weight.

The attribute weights should usually be specified based on how expensive it is to reconstruct a connection back to its intended state.

The last topic of this chapter is OCI driver connection pooling in 10*g*, which is an OCI driver–specific connection pooling implementation that offers some advantages over the standard connection pooling. This feature is also available in 9*i*.

OCI Connection Pooling

OCI connection pooling allows you to exploit *session multiplexing*, a mechanism in which multiple sessions are created using a low number of physical connections. Recall that in Oracle you can have more than one session on the same physical connection. OCI connection pooling provides better scalability over implicit connection caching, since fewer physical connections are required to support the same number of sessions. As its name suggests, OCI connection pooling requires you to have the JDBC OCI client installed and your environment set up accordingly as explained in Chapter 3.

> **■Note** Although in this section we cover only the Oracle 10*g* implementation of OCI connection pooling, this feature is also available in Oracle9*i*.

To use an OCI connection pool in your JDBC application, you need to take the following steps:

1. Create an OCI connection pool.

2. Configure the OCI connection pool properties.

3. Retrieve a connection from the OCI connection pool.

The following DemoOCIConnectionPooling class looks at these steps in detail. We begin by importing the classes and declaring the main() method:

```
/*
* This program demonstrates explicit statement caching.
* COMPATIBLITY NOTE:
*    runs successfully against 9.2.0.1.0 and 10.1.0.2.0
*/
import java.sql.Connection;
import java.util.Properties;
import oracle.jdbc.pool.OracleOCIConnectionPool;
import book.util.InputUtil;
class DemoOCIConnectionPooling
{
  public static void main(String args[]) throws Exception
  {
```

Creating an OCI Connection Pool

You create an OCI connection pool by initializing an OracleOCIConnectionPool object (OracleOCIConnectionPool extends from the now familiar OracleDataSource class) as follows:

```
    String tnsAlias = "(DESCRIPTION = (ADDRESS_LIST = (ADDRESS =
(PROTOCOL = TCP)(HOST = rmenon-lap)(PORT = 1521))) (CONNECT_DATA =
(SERVER = DEDICATED) (SERVICE_NAME = ora10g.us.oracle.com)))";
    OracleOCIConnectionPool ods = new OracleOCIConnectionPool();
    ods.setURL ( "jdbc:oracle:oci:@"+ tnsAlias );
    ods.setUser("scott");            // username
    ods.setPassword("tiger");        // password
```

Notice how we use the OCI driver–style connection parameters.

Configuring the OCI Connection Pool Properties

The next step is to configure the pool properties that dictate how the pool behaves. Table 14-4 lists the various pool properties we can set and their meanings. Note that all these attributes can be configured dynamically.

Table 14-4. *Oracle OCI Connection Pool Configuration Properties*

Property	Default	Constraints	Getter Method	Description
OracleOCIConnectionPool.CONNPOOL_MIN_LIMIT	1	Is mandatory; must be a positive integer	getMinLimit()	Specifies the minimum number of physical connections in the pool.
OracleOCIConnectionPool.CONNPOOL_INCREMENT	0	Is mandatory; must be a positive integer	getConnectionIncrement()	Specifies the number of additional physical connections to be opened when a request for a connection is pending and all available physical connections are in use.
OracleOCIConnectionPool.CONNPOOL_MAX_LIMIT	1	Is mandatory; must be >(CONNPOOL_MIN_LIMIT +CONNPOOL_INCREMENT)	getMaxLimit()	Specifies the maximum number of physical connections in the pool.
OracleOCIConnectionPool.CONNPOOL_TIMEOUT	0	Must be a positive integer	getTimeout()	Specifies the number of seconds after which an idle physical connection is disconnected.
OracleOCIConnectionPool.CONNPOOL_NOWAIT	false	Must be true or false	getNowait()	When specified, this property implies that the connection pool should return an error if all connections in the pool are busy and another request for a connection comes in.

Continuing the definition of our class, we set the OCI connection pool properties using the `setPoolConfig()` method of the `OracleOCIConnectionPool` class:

```
Properties cacheProperties = new Properties();
cacheProperties.setProperty(OracleOCIConnectionPool.CONNPOOL_MIN_LIMIT, "2" );
cacheProperties.setProperty(OracleOCIConnectionPool.CONNPOOL_INCREMENT, "1" );
cacheProperties.setProperty(OracleOCIConnectionPool.CONNPOOL_MAX_LIMIT, "10" );
ods.setPoolConfig( cacheProperties );
System.out.println("Min Limit: 2");
System.out.println("Max Limit: 10");
System.out.println("Increment : 1");
System.out.println("pool size:" + ods.getPoolSize())
```

The cache gets created when the we invoke the preceding `setPoolConfig()` method.

Retrieving a Connection from the OCI Connection Pool

Once the pool is configured, we can retrieve a connection using the standard `getConnection()` method on the `OracleOCIConnectionPool` object (recall that it extends the `OracleDataSource` class):

```
Connection conn = oocp.getConnection("scott", "tiger");
```

Analyzing Connections and Sessions When OCI Connection Pooling Is in Use

The behavior of OCI connection pooling depends on whether your program is multithreaded or not. For a single-threaded program, the OCI connection pool sets up a connection cache equal to the configured property `OracleOCIConnectionPool.CONNPOOL_MIN_LIMIT`. After that, every connection request results in a *session* being created using one of these cached connections. No new connections are created in the cache above `OracleOCIConnectionPool.CONNPOOL_➡ MIN_LIMIT`. But new sessions are created as requested on top of the connections created initially. As you will learn, this is a case where you can see more than one session being created on top of a connection.

For a multithreaded program, the OCI connection pool sets up a connection cache equal to the configured property `OracleOCIConnectionPool.CONNPOOL_MIN_LIMIT`. After that, every connection request from a new thread results in a new physical connection being created.

Let's look at each of these cases now, beginning with the case of a single-threaded program.

Analyzing OCI Connection Pooling in a Single-Threaded Program

The program `AnalyzeOCIConnPoolSingleThread` described in this section takes as input the number of sessions to open using the OCI connection pool. It has the now familiar pauses introduced for us to run our query listing physical connections and sessions. Let's look at the program piecemeal, starting with the imports and the declaration of the `main()` method:

```
/*
* This program demonstrates use of OCI connection pooling in a single-threaded
program.
* COMPATIBLITY NOTE: tested against 10.1.0.2.0.
```

```
*/
import java.sql.Connection;
import java.util.Properties;
import oracle.jdbc.pool.OracleDataSource;
import oracle.jdbc.pool.OracleOCIConnectionPool;
import book.util.InputUtil;
class AnalyzeOCIConnPoolSingleThread
{
  public static void main(String args[]) throws Exception
  {
```

The function _getNumOfSessionsToOpen(), defined at the end of the program, returns the number of sessions requested as the first command-line parameter value when running the program.

```
    int numOfSessionsToOpen = _getNumOfSessionsToOpen( args );
```

We set up the TNS alias and configure the pool with connection properties to connect to the user SCOTT:

```
    String tnsAlias = "(DESCRIPTION = (ADDRESS_LIST = (ADDRESS =
(PROTOCOL = TCP)(HOST = rmenon-lap)(PORT = 1521))) (CONNECT_DATA =
(SERVER = DEDICATED)(SERVICE_NAME = ora10g.us.oracle.com)))";
    OracleOCIConnectionPool oocp = new OracleOCIConnectionPool();
    oocp.setURL ( "jdbc:oracle:oci:@"+ tnsAlias );
    oocp.setUser("scott");          // username
    oocp.setPassword("tiger");      // password
```

Next we set the pool configuration properties and print them out. We also print out the time it takes to set up the initial pool (which happens when we invoke setPoolConfig()).

```
    // set pool config properties
    Properties poolConfigProperties = new Properties();
    poolConfigProperties.setProperty(
      OracleOCIConnectionPool.CONNPOOL_MIN_LIMIT, "3" );
    poolConfigProperties.setProperty(
      OracleOCIConnectionPool.CONNPOOL_INCREMENT, "1" );
    poolConfigProperties.setProperty(
      OracleOCIConnectionPool.CONNPOOL_MAX_LIMIT, "20" );
    long startTime = System.currentTimeMillis();
    oocp.setPoolConfig( poolConfigProperties );
    long endTime = System.currentTimeMillis();
    System.out.println("It took " + (endTime-startTime) +
      " ms to establish initial pool size of "+ oocp.getPoolSize() +
      " connections." );
    //print config properties
    System.out.println( "min Limit: " + oocp.getMinLimit() );
    System.out.println( "max Limit: " + oocp.getMaxLimit() );
    System.out.println( "connection increment : " + oocp.getConnectionIncrement() );
    System.out.println( "timeout: " + oocp.getTimeout() );
    System.out.println( "nowait: " + oocp.getNoWait() );
```

We can find out the number of physical connections opened by invoking the getPoolSize() method as follows:

```
System.out.println( "num of physical connections: " + oocp.getPoolSize() );
```

Next, we create the number of sessions specified at the command line to the user SCOTT, with a pause before and after. We also measure the time it takes to establish the sessions.

```
InputUtil.waitTillUserHitsEnter( "before establishing scott connections");
for( int i=0; i < numOfSessionsToOpen; i++ )
{
  // time the process of establishing a connection
  startTime = System.currentTimeMillis();
  scottConnections[i] = oocp.getConnection("scott", "tiger");
  endTime = System.currentTimeMillis();
  System.out.println("It took " + (endTime-startTime) +
    " ms to establish session # " + (i+1) + " (scott)." );
  System.out.println( "num of physical connections: "   + oocp.getPoolSize() );
}
InputUtil.waitTillUserHitsEnter();
```

We create and time the same number of sessions for the user BENCHMARK, with a pause at the end:

```
Connection[] benchmarkConnections = new Connection[ numOfSessionsToOpen ];
for( int i=0; i < numOfSessionsToOpen; i++ )
{
  // time the process of establishing a connection
  startTime = System.currentTimeMillis();
  benchmarkConnections[i] = oocp.getConnection( "benchmark", "benchmark");
  endTime = System.currentTimeMillis();
  System.out.println("It took " + (endTime-startTime) +
    " ms to establish the session # " + (i+1) + " (benchmark)." );
  System.out.println( "num of physical connections: " + oocp.getPoolSize() );
}
InputUtil.waitTillUserHitsEnter();
```

Finally, we close all sessions and define the method _getNumOfSessionsToOpen() we invoked earlier to end the program:

```
  // close all connections (or sessions)
  for( int i=0; i < numOfSessionsToOpen; i++ )
  {
    if( benchmarkConnections[i] != null )
      benchmarkConnections[i].close();
    if( scottConnections[i] != null )
      scottConnections[i].close();
  }
}// end of main
private static int _getNumOfSessionsToOpen( String[] args )
{
```

```
    int numOfSessionsToOpen = 3; //by default open 3 sessions
    if( args.length == 1 )
    {
      numOfSessionsToOpen = Integer.parseInt( args[0] );
    }
    System.out.println( "Num of sessions to open for scott and benchmark each = "
      + numOfSessionsToOpen);
    return numOfSessionsToOpen;
  }
}// end of program
```

Let's now look at the program output, and also discuss the output of the query that lists opened physical connections and sessions during the programmed pauses. Consider the case where we request that six sessions be opened each for the SCOTT and BENCHMARK users. The first few lines of program output follow:

```
B:\>java AnalyzeOCIConnPoolSingleThread 6
Num of sessions to open for scott and benchmark each = 6
It took 781 ms to establish initial pool size of 3 connections.
min Limit: 3
max Limit: 20
connection increment : 1
timeout: 0
nowait: false
num of physical connections: 3
before establishing scott connections
Press Enter to continue...
```

Note from the output that it takes 781 milliseconds to establish three physical connections when we use OCI connection pooling. This is slightly better than the 1,015 milliseconds we saw when we used the implicit connection cache. The difference remains even if we use the OCI driver with the implicit connection cache. We also get the number of physical connections by invoking getPoolSize() on the OCI connection pool variable. Our query for listing connections and sessions confirms this:

```
sys@ORA10G> select s.program, s.server, p.spid server_pid, s.username
  2   from v$session s, v$process p
  3   where s.type = 'USER'
  4     and s.username != 'SYS'
  5     and p.addr(+) = s.paddr;

PROGRAM                         SERVER             SERVER_PID    USERNAME
------------------------------  ----------------   ------------  ----------
java.exe                        DEDICATED          3260          SCOTT
java.exe                        DEDICATED          2472          SCOTT
java.exe                        DEDICATED          1896          SCOTT
```

After we press Enter, the program shows the following output after creating six sessions for the user SCOTT:

```
It took 78 ms to establish session # 1 (scott).
num of physical connections: 3
It took 16 ms to establish session # 2 (scott).
num of physical connections: 3
It took 0 ms to establish session # 3 (scott).
num of physical connections: 3
It took 15 ms to establish session # 4 (scott).
num of physical connections: 3
It took 16 ms to establish session # 5 (scott).
num of physical connections: 3
It took 0 ms to establish session # 6 (scott).
num of physical connections: 3
Press Enter to continue...
```

At this point, we have established six *sessions* to SCOTT user. The second-to-last line of our output confirms that we have only three physical connections at this point. Our query results are as follows:

```
sys@ORA10G> /
```

```
PROGRAM                          SERVER            SERVER_PID    USERNAME
------------------------------   ---------------   -----------   ----------
java.exe                         DEDICATED         3260          SCOTT
java.exe                         DEDICATED         2472          SCOTT
java.exe                         DEDICATED         1896          SCOTT
java.exe                         PSEUDO                          SCOTT
java.exe                         PSEUDO                          SCOTT
java.exe                         PSEUDO                          SCOTT
java.exe                         PSEUDO                          SCOTT
java.exe                         PSEUDO                          SCOTT
java.exe                         PSEUDO                          SCOTT
```

We were expecting six rows, but there are nine rows shown by the query! Careful examination shows that only three of them have a server_pid column—those three rows correspond to actual physical connections created by Oracle so far. The remaining six rows that correspond to a null value for the server_pid column (and also have a value of PSEUDO under the server column) are sessions created by Oracle on top of the three physical connections.

When we press Enter once more, we get the following output:

```
It took 78 ms to establish the session # 1 (benchmark).
num of physical connections: 3
It took 16 ms to establish the session # 2 (benchmark).
num of physical connections: 3
It took 0 ms to establish the session # 3 (benchmark).
num of physical connections: 3
It took 15 ms to establish the session # 4 (benchmark).
num of physical connections: 3
It took 16 ms to establish the session # 5 (benchmark).
num of physical connections: 3
```

```
It took 0 ms to establish the session # 6 (benchmark).
num of physical connections: 3
Press Enter to continue...
```

Notice that it took 78 milliseconds to establish a new benchmark session, though the connection pool had all physical connections authenticated as the user SCOTT. This is pretty good compared to the 266 milliseconds we saw when using implicit cache to establish a new connection and session. This is because in this case we are creating a session on an already existing physical connection. Our query confirms that there are three connections, six SCOTT sessions, and six BENCHMARK sessions in the database at this point:

```
sys@ORA10G> /

PROGRAM                        SERVER          SERVER_PID   USERNAME
------------------------------ --------------- ------------ ----------
java.exe                       DEDICATED       3260         SCOTT
java.exe                       DEDICATED       2472         SCOTT
java.exe                       DEDICATED       1896         SCOTT
java.exe                       PSEUDO                       SCOTT
java.exe                       PSEUDO                       BENCHMARK
java.exe                       PSEUDO                       BENCHMARK
java.exe                       PSEUDO                       BENCHMARK
java.exe                       PSEUDO                       BENCHMARK
java.exe                       PSEUDO                       SCOTT
java.exe                       PSEUDO                       SCOTT
java.exe                       PSEUDO                       BENCHMARK
java.exe                       PSEUDO                       SCOTT
java.exe                       PSEUDO                       SCOTT
java.exe                       PSEUDO                       BENCHMARK
java.exe                       PSEUDO                       SCOTT

12 rows selected.
```

We can end the program by pressing Enter once more.

If you try to run the program with an increasing number of sessions using the command-line parameter, you will find that the number of physical connections remains the same, no matter how many sessions you create. As mentioned, this is because in a single-threaded program, the OCI connection pool creates physical connections only at the beginning based on the OracleOCIConnectionPool.CONNPOOL_MIN_LIMIT parameter. Of course, at some point you would run out of resources—there can be only so many sessions created on three physical connections. For example, on my PC, I was able to create 65 sessions each for SCOTT and BENCHMARK on three physical connections. When I tried to bump the number to 66, I got the following exception:

```
Exception in thread "main" java.sql.SQLException: ORA-00604: error occurred at
ecursive SQL level 1
ORA-04031: unable to allocate 4012 bytes of shared memory (
"large pool","unknown  object","session heap","bind var buf")
… <-- trimmed to save space -->
```

The interesting thing is that you can dynamically set this minimum limit by simply passing in the appropriately modified `Properties` object to the `setPoolConfig()` method at runtime, thus controlling the actual number of physical connections used in setting up the sessions in your pool.

What happens if the program is multithreaded? We cover that in the next section.

Analyzing OCI Connection Pooling in a Multithreaded Program

To analyze the case of a multithreaded program, we will first look at the `WorkerThread` class, which executes a query after getting the connection. Since it is a multithreaded program, we can't introduce pauses easily, so we make each worker thread execute a query that we know will take some time to get the output of. In our case, the query is `select object_name from all_objects`. After the necessary imports, the class `WorkerThread` begins with a constructor that takes a connection pool (assumed to be initialized by the calling program) and a thread number.

```
import book.util.JDBCUtil;
class WorkerThread extends Thread
{
  WorkerThread( OracleOCIConnectionPool ociConnPool, int _threadNumber )
  throws Exception
  {
    super();
    this._ociConnPool = ociConnPool;
    this._threadNumber = _threadNumber;
  }
```

The `run()` method of the `WorkerThread` class gets a connection to SCOTT if the thread number is even; otherwise, it gets a connection to BENCHMARK.

```
public void run()
{
  Connection conn = null;
  Statement stmt = null;
  ResultSet rset = null;
  try
  {
    if( _threadNumber % 2 == 0 )
    {
      System.out.println( "connecting as scott" );
      conn = _ociConnPool.getConnection("scott", "tiger");
    }
    else
    {
      System.out.println( "connecting as benchmark" );
      conn = _ociConnPool.getConnection("benchmark", "benchmark");
    }
```

We then execute our query and end the `WorkerThread` class:

```
pstmt = conn.prepareStatement( "select owner from all_objects" );
rset = pstmt.executeQuery();
while( rset.next() )
{
  rset.getString(1);
}
}
catch (Exception e )
{
  e.printStackTrace();
}
finally
{
  JDBCUtil.close( rset );
  JDBCUtil.close( pstmt );
  JDBCUtil.close( conn );
}
} // end of run
private OracleOCIConnectionPool _ociConnPool;
private int _threadNumber = -1;
} // end of class
```

We set up the OCI connection pool and invoke the `WorkerThread` program from the class `AnalyzeOCIConnPoolMultiThread` as follows:

```
/** This program demonstrates the use of OCI connection pooling in a
    multithreaded program.
* COMPATIBLITY NOTE: tested against 10.1.0.2.0.
*/
import java.util.Properties;
import oracle.jdbc.pool.OracleOCIConnectionPool;
public class AnalyzeOCIConnPoolMultiThread
{
  public static void main( String [] args ) throws Exception
  {
    _numOfSessionsToOpen = _getNumOfSessionsToOpen( args );
    String tnsAlias = "(DESCRIPTION = (ADDRESS_LIST = (ADDRESS = (PROTOCOL =
TCP)(HOST = rmenon-lap)(PORT = 1521))) (CONNECT_DATA = (SERVER = DEDICATED)
(SERVICE_NAME = ora10g.us.oracle.com)))";
    OracleOCIConnectionPool cpool = new OracleOCIConnectionPool();
    cpool.setURL ( "jdbc:oracle:oci:@"+ tnsAlias );
    cpool.setUser("scott");              // username
    cpool.setPassword("tiger");          // password
    Properties poolConfigProps = new Properties( ) ;
```

```
poolConfigProps.put(OracleOCIConnectionPool.CONNPOOL_MIN_LIMIT, "2") ;
poolConfigProps.put(OracleOCIConnectionPool.CONNPOOL_INCREMENT, "1") ;
poolConfigProps.put(OracleOCIConnectionPool.CONNPOOL_MAX_LIMIT, "20") ;
cpool.setPoolConfig(poolConfigProps);
System.out.println ("Min poolsize Limit = " + cpool.getMinLimit());
System.out.println ("Max poolsize Limit = " + cpool.getMaxLimit());
System.out.println ("Connection Increment = " + cpool.getConnectionIncrement());
```

Up until this point, this program is the same as the single-threaded program, AnalyzeOCI➥ ConnPoolSingleThread, which we saw in the previous section. After this, we create the number of threads as specified by the command-line parameter and start them.

```
Thread [] threads = new Thread[ _numOfSessionsToOpen ];
for( int i = 0; i<threads.length; i++ )
{
  (threads[i] = new WorkerThread( cpool, i )).start();
}
```

Finally, we wait for all threads to finish in a loop. This ends the main() program, which is followed by the definition of the _getNumOfSessionsToOpen() method at the end:

```
// wait until all threads are done.
for( int i = 0; i<threads.length; i++ )
{
  threads[i].join();
}

cpool.close();
}// end of main

private static int _getNumOfSessionsToOpen( String[] args )
{
  int numOfSessionsToOpen = 6; //by default open 6 sessions
  if( args.length == 1 )
  {
    numOfSessionsToOpen = Integer.parseInt( args[0] );
  }
  System.out.println("Total number of sessions to open for " +
    "scott and benchmark = " + numOfSessionsToOpen);

  return numOfSessionsToOpen;
}

private static int _numOfSessionsToOpen;
}
```

We will run the program and then examine the database while the program is running. For some reason, the only reliable results our original query shows are the number of connections and the number of sessions. I modified the query to print out this information (note that the following query works only for the case in which we know that sessions are being independently created on top of connections, as is the case here). The program output is as follows:

```
B:\> java AnalyzeOCIConnPoolMultiThread 12
Total number of sessions to open for scott and benchmark = 12
Min poolsize Limit = 2
Max poolsize Limit = 20
Connection Increment = 1
connecting as scott
connecting as benchmark
connecting as scott
connecting as benchmark
connecting as scott
connecting as benchmark
connecting as scott
connecting as benchmark
connecting as scott
connecting as benchmark
connecting as scott
connecting as benchmark
```

The program opens six sessions for SCOTT and six more for BENCHMARK.

When I ran the modified query and executed it immediately again and again, it gave the following results:

```
sys@ORA10G> select num_of_conns, (conns_plus_sess -num_of_conns) as num_of_seons
  2  from
  3  (
  4    select count(*) conns_plus_sess,
  5           count( distinct p.spid) num_of_conns
  6    from v$session s, v$process p
  7    where s.type != 'BACKGROUND'
  8      and s.username != 'SYS'
  9      and p.addr(+) = s.paddr
 10  );

NUM_OF_CONNS NUM_OF_SESSIONS
------------ ---------------
           8              12
sys@ORA10G> /
NUM_OF_CONNS NUM_OF_SESSIONS
------------ ---------------
           8              12
sys@ORA10G> /
```

```
NUM_OF_CONNS NUM_OF_SESSIONS
------------ ---------------
          12              12
<-- after some time -->
sys@ORA10G> /
NUM_OF_CONNS NUM_OF_SESSIONS
------------ ---------------
          12              10
<-- after some time -->
sys@ORA10G> /
NUM_OF_CONNS NUM_OF_SESSIONS
------------ ---------------
           0               0
```

This shows that the program had eight connections at the point I executed the query for the first time and 12 sessions. Ultimately, we had 12 sessions created on top of 12 connections. We can also see a stage where the number of sessions goes down to 10, while the number of connections open remains at 12. This experiment proves that each thread had a separate physical connection, in the case of multithreaded programs using OCI connection pooling.

Summary

In this chapter, you learned the difference between connections and sessions in Oracle. You learned why connection pooling is necessary, and you distinguished between connection pooling and caching. You examined how Oracle9*i* implements the connection pooling framework and provides a sample connection caching implementation. As you saw, in Oracle 10*g*, the Oracle9*i* connection caching has been deprecated and replaced by the more powerful implicit connection caching. Finally, you took a look at how Oracle's OCI connection pooling improves scalability and performance by creating lightweight sessions on top of a low number of physical connections.

Summary

CHAPTER 15

■■■

Security-Related Issues

In the previous chapter, we discussed the performance and scalability benefits of using connection pooling. In this chapter, we'll direct our attention to the security issues involved in a three-tier architecture that uses connection pooling. In particular, we'll focus on different alternatives of mapping an application end user to a database end user and different ways in which an application can authenticate to the database on behalf of an end user. We'll cover the following authentication alternatives:

- The application server authenticates to the database by presenting the password of the database user to which the end user corresponds.

- The application server authenticates to the database by using *proxy authentication*, a feature available only in the JDBC OCI driver as of Oracle 10*g* Release 1. It is slated to be supported by the JDBC thin driver in 10*g* Release 2.

Let's begin by discussing two important security principles that all applications should strive to uphold.

The Principle of Least Privilege and Defense in Depth

Two fundamental principles of good security design are the *principle of least privilege* and *defense in depth*. We'll briefly discuss these two principles in this section.

- *Principle of least privilege*: The principle of least privilege states simply that a user should be given the minimum number of privileges possible to enable the user to get his job done. We see this principle being applied routinely in our day-to-day life. For example, only those employees who need access to the rooms in an office building are given access codes (or keys) to those rooms. Similarly, chances are that you and your manager can access part of your company's HR database to see your salary and benefits details, but your peers cannot access your particular information.

- *Defense in depth*: This security principle states that security should be built in using multiple layers such that if an outer layer fails, the inner layers prevent a compromise of security. For example, in a bank the outermost defense layer may begin with the guard on duty. Cameras form the next layer of security. The solid structure of the building's vaults forms a third layer of security, and so on.

You should always strive to design the security in your application keeping the preceding two principles in mind. With these principles in mind, let's now turn our attention to the important design question related to security in an application: "How do we map an application end user to a database user?" In the next section, we'll discuss how this issue can be addressed, especially in the context of a web application.

Mapping an End User to a Database User

An end user ultimately has to connect to the database as some database user to perform operations. This section explores the various alternatives of providing this mapping between the application end user and database end user, and examines the design implications of each alternative. For the discussion in this section, assume that we're designing an HR application that has the following two categories (or roles) of end users:

- clerk_role: This user can generate reports and query data.

- manager_role: This user has the privileges of clerk_role and can also add, update, and delete data.

Also assume that there are 100 clerk end users (clerk1, clerk2, etc., up to clerk100) and 10 manager end users (manager1, manager2, etc., up to manager10).

We have three choices while mapping each of these end users to database users:

One-to-one mapping: The one-to-one mapping implies that you create a database user account for each application user. In our example, this means that we would create 100 clerk user accounts (db_clerk1, db_clerk2, etc.) and 10 manager user accounts (db_manager1, db_ ➥ manager2, etc.). We could, of course, have the same username for the application user and the corresponding database user—we'll choose to prefix the database user with db_ to distinguish between the users in this discussion.

The one-to-one mapping design has the following implications:

- Since each end user is connecting as a separate database user, the user's identity is preserved in the database. This simply means we can trace a given action conducted by a database user back to a single end user (assuming we have proper auditing in place). This is a good thing from a security point of view.

- In the case of a client/server application, the end user can simply present to the application the database user's password to log onto the application. In a web application with a three-tier architecture, this can result in some password management issues. We will examine these issues in more detail in the section "Authenticating an Application End User to the Database."

- If we're using one-to-one mapping in conjunction with connection pooling, then this design can result in performance problems. Here we assume that our connection pool consists of dedicated connection for each database user. Since each connection can be used by only one user, every time a new user logs in, we need to create a new connection for the user (since none of the existing connections in the pool can be reused by this user). Later in the section "Proxy Authentication (N-Tier Authentication)" we'll cover how this problem can be overcome even within the realm of one-to-one mapping.

N-to-M (N > M, M > 1) mapping: In this case, *N* application users are mapped to *M* database users. The mapping is typically done based on the common roles into which the end users can be divided. Thus, in our example HR application, we would create three database users, db_clerk, db_manager, and db_admin. All clerks (clerk1 to clerk100) would connect to the database as the database user db_clerk. Similarly, all managers would use the database user db_manager to connect to the database. This design has the following implications:

- Since multiple end users are mapped to the same database user, the user's identity is no longer preserved natively in the database. For example, if a record is deleted while an end user is connected as db_manager, the database can no longer tell which of the ten managers (manager1, manager2, etc.) actually performed the action, because the action occurred when one of these managers was connected as db_manager. The application has to take specific measures to enable this level of auditing.

- This mapping is amenable to connection pooling in terms of performance and scalability. This is mainly because you need to have only three different types of database connections (corresponding to the three different database users). Since the same connection can be shared across multiple end users (e.g., one connection of db_clerk can be shared at different times among the 100 clerk users), the connection pool can scale for a relatively large end user population.

N-to-1 mapping: This is a special case of the N-to-M mapping just discussed. In this case, all the end users ultimately connect to the database as the same user (say, db_user in our example). This user has the privileges that form the union of privileges associated with different categories of users. The only reason we discuss this case is to point out that it violates both the principle of least privilege and defense in depth. The reason is that all end users have the same privileges when connected to the database. Thus, if the application level security is subverted, then an end user can do things beyond the capabilities of her designed set of privileges. For example, if the end user clerk1 manages to connect to the database by circumventing the application, she can delete records even though she is not supposed to have this privilege at the application level. As is true in the case of N-to-M mapping, the end user's identity is not preserved natively in this case as well.

From the preceding points, we can conclude the following:

- We should avoid using the N-to-1 mapping because it violates both the principle of least privilege and defense in depth.

- Ideally, we should have a separate database account for each end user. This is usually the case when using a client/server application in which each end user has a dedicated connection to the database during an application session. In a three-tier web application, this can present challenges in terms of password management and connection pool scalability. Proxy authentication, a feature available via the JDBC OCI driver that we discuss later, addresses these issues elegantly.

Next, we'll look at another important principle that we should adhere to in order to make our applications more secure.

Separating the End User Database Schema, Data Schema, and Data Access Layer Schema

In this section, we'll examine the need for separating the end user database schema, the data schema, and the data access layer schema. Let's begin by defining these terms.

- The *end user database schema* refers to the database schema to which the end user is mapped.

- The *data schema* is the schema that contains and owns the application data. This is the user that owns the tables in which application data resides. This user would also have the privileges of manipulating table data (i.e., insert, delete, and update privileges on the tables), and creating and dropping objects such as tables.

- The *data access layer schema* is the database account that owns the API through which you access the data. Hopefully, after reading the arguments presented in Chapter 6, you are convinced of the importance of using a PL/SQL API for the database access layer in your JDBC applications. (For a non-Oracle database, you would use the corresponding procedural language layer here—for example, for SQL Server, you would use a Transact-SQL layer API.)

It is vital for your application to not lump all of these schemas into one, otherwise you violate both the principle of least privilege and defense in depth. For example, consider the case where you have just one user for the data (the tables), the data access layer (the procedures and packages that manipulate the data in the tables), and the end user database account. If your application security is compromised and a malicious end user is able to connect to the database using this all-in-one database account, he can potentially delete data from the tables, drop schema objects, and take all kinds of similar destructive actions. Contrast this with the case where you have a design in which the end user account does not own the data or the data access layer, but just has execute privileges on the procedural API that the user indirectly executes when logged in as the application user (through the application). In this case, the user can perform none of the aforementioned destructive actions, simply because he has not been granted the privileges to do so.

Thus, ideally we should have a separate database schema for the end user, data access layer, and data database accounts, as shown in Figure 15-1.

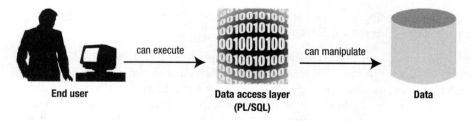

Figure 15-1. *A schema design that separates the end user, data access layer, and data schemas*

As illustrated in Figure 15-1, the data schema owns the tables and the data within these tables. The data access layer contains PL/SQL code to manipulate data. The PL/SQL packages in this schema have privileges to insert, delete, update, and select data as required on appropriate tables they need to work on. The end user accounts are given privileges only to execute the PL/SQL packages they need to execute to get their job done.

In the next section, we'll look at an application example that illustrates the concepts we've covered so far.

An Example Application

Figure 15-2 shows our example application architecture. Application users clerk1 and manager1 map to the database schemas db_clerk1 and db_manager1, respectively. The schema db_data_access_layer consists of PL/SQL code with privileges to manipulate data stored in a third schema called db_app_data. The schema db_clerk1 has the role clerk_role, which can execute the package clerk_pkg. The user db_manager1 has the role manager_role, which can execute the packages clerk_pkg and manager_pkg.

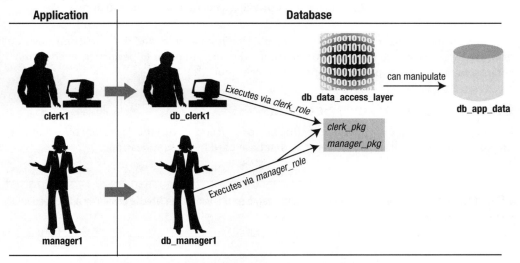

manager_role can execute clerk_pkg and manager _pkg
clerk_role can only execute clerk_pkg

Figure 15-2. *Our example application architecture*

Our rather simplistic HR application consists of two PL/SQL packages that allow a user to perform various actions on the emp and dept tables. The package manager_pkg allows a user to add a department, hire an employee, raise a salary, and so on. The package clerk_pkg allows a user to list the employee and department details.

The architecture shown in Figure 15-2 illustrates the following:

- *Use of database roles to control end user access to the application functionality:* For example, the user db_manager1 has the privileges to execute both packages, manager_pkg and clerk_pkg, via the roles manager_role and clerk_role. However, the user db_clerk1 only needs to report on the data, not modify it, so that user is given the minimum necessary privileges to perform these tasks. This user can execute only clerk_pkg via the role clerk_role.

- *Separation of the data and the application logic that accesses that data into two distinct schemas:* The schema db_app_data contains the application objects (the emp and dept tables) and the application data. The schema db_data_access_layer contains the application API to access data in the schema db_app_data. In our example, this API consists of the two PL/SQL packages clerk_pkg and manager_pkg. As discussed earlier, the main advantage of creating two separate schemas for data and the data access layer code is that we can grant only the minimum required privileges on db_app_data objects to the db_data_access_layer schema. For example, as shown in the design in Figure 15-2, the db_data_access_layer schema cannot drop the tables emp and dept. Thus, we uphold the principle of maintaining the least privileges needed to get the job done.

Let's go ahead and create all the schema objects from scratch, and then we'll demonstrate how the application actually authenticates to the database in order to perform the requested actions, focusing on the proxy authentication technique.

Creating the Database Schemas

Let's begin by logging in as sys and creating an admin account with the dba role. This account's only use is to create other accounts in the database used by our application.

■**Caution** In this example, all passwords are the same as the username. This is obviously a bad idea in a real-life application.

```
sys@ORA10G> create user admin identified by admin default tablespace users;
User created.
sys@ORA10G> grant dba to admin;
Grant succeeded.
```

As discussed, we will have two schemas: db_app_data and db_data_access_layer. The schema db_app_data contains all the application objects (in our case, just tables) used in our application. The schema db_data_access_layer contains all the code (PL/SQL API) that works on the tables in the schema db_app_data. After connecting as admin, we create the db_app_data schema.

```
admin@ORA10G> create user db_app_data identified by db_app_data default
   tablespace users quota unlimited on users;
User created.
```

Note that we need to give some quota on a tablespace for the schema db_app_data to be able to create tables and store some data in them. Next, we grant the privileges to connect to the database (the create session privilege): create table, and create and drop public synonym to db_app_data.

■**Note** See Chapters 5 and 6 of *Oracle Database Security Guide (10*g *Release 1)* if you are not familiar with the concepts of privileges and synonyms.

```
admin@ORA10G> grant create session,
  2         create table,
  3         create public synonym,
  4         drop public synonym
  5         to db_app_data;
Grant succeeded.
```

We now create the db_data_access_layer schema. This user does not need to create any tables, but it needs to connect to the database, create procedures, and create and drop synonyms, so we grant it the corresponding privileges:

```
admin@ORA10G> create user db_data_access_layer identified by db_data_access_layer;
User created.
admin@ORA10G> grant create session,
  2         create public synonym,
  3         drop public synonym,
  4         create procedure
  5         to db_data_access_layer;
Grant succeeded.
```

Creating the Application Data Tables

Next, we connect as db_app_data and create our schema objects. We begin with a table, dept, that contains the department number and name:

```
admin@ORA10G> conn db_app_data/db_app_data
Connected.
db_app_data@ORA10G> -- create schema for the application
db_app_data@ORA10G> create table dept
  2  (
  3    dept_no number primary key,
  4    dept_name varchar2(20)
  5  );
Table created.
```

We create an emp table with various employee-related information:

```
db_app_data@ORA10G> create table emp
  2  (
  3    empno number primary key,
  4    ename varchar2(20),
  5    dept_no references dept,
  6    salary number,
  7    job varchar2(30)
  8  );
Table created.
```

Since we don't want to give the schema name of these two tables each time we refer to them from another schema, we create public synonyms for them. If we now access the table from a different schema (e.g., from the db_data_access_layer schema), we can refer to the synonym emp instead of referring to it as db_app_data.emp:

```
db_app_data@ORA10G> create public synonym emp for emp;
Synonym created.
db_app_data@ORA10G> create public synonym dept for dept;
Synonym created.
```

Granting DML Privileges to db_data_access_layer

We then connect to our admin user and grant select, insert, update, and delete privileges on the tables in the db_app_data schema to the db_data_access_layer user. This is so that the PL/SQL packages that we will create soon in db_data_access_layer can manipulate data in the db_app_data tables emp and dept:

```
db_app_data@ORA10G> conn admin/admin
Connected.
admin@ORA10G> -- need direct privileges on the objects for the procedures to
admin@ORA10G> -- work
admin@ORA10G> grant select, insert, delete, update on emp to db_data_access_layer;
Grant succeeded.
admin@ORA10G> grant select, insert, delete, update on dept to db_data_access_layer;
Grant succeeded.
```

Creating the PL/SQL Packages

We now connect to the db_data_access_layer user and create the PL/SQL API for our application. Our simplistic API consists of just two packages. The first package is called manager_pkg and contains code to add a department, hire an employee, raise an employee's salary, and fire an employee.

```
admin@ORA10G> conn db_data_access_layer/db_data_access_layer
Connected.
db_data_access_layer@ORA10G> create or replace package manager_pkg
  2  as
```

```
 3    procedure add_dept(
 4      p_dept_no in number,
 5      p_dept_name in varchar2 );
 6
 7    procedure hire_emp(
 8      p_empno in number,
 9      p_ename in varchar2,
10      p_dept_no in number,
11      p_salary in number,
12      p_job in varchar2 );
13
14    procedure raise_salary(
15      p_empno in number,
16      p_salary_hike_pcnt in number );
17
18    procedure fire_emp(
19      p_empno in number );
20  end manager_pkg;
21  /
Package created.
```

We explain each of these procedures in our implementation of the package body. The first procedure, add_dept, simply inserts a department's information into the dept table:

```
db_data_access_layer@ORA10G> create or replace package body manager_pkg
 2    as
 3    procedure add_dept(
 4      p_dept_no in number,
 5      p_dept_name in varchar2 )
 6    is
 7    begin
 8      insert into dept( dept_no, dept_name )
 9      values( p_dept_no, p_dept_name );
10    end add_dept;
```

The procedure hire_emp simply inserts an employee record into the emp table:

```
12    procedure hire_emp(
13      p_empno in number,
14      p_ename in varchar2,
15      p_dept_no in number,
16      p_salary in number,
17      p_job in varchar2 )
18    is
19    begin
20      insert into emp( empno, ename, dept_no, salary, job )
21      values( p_empno, p_ename, p_dept_no, p_salary, p_job );
22    end hire_emp;
```

The procedure raise_salary raises the salary of an employee by a given percentage by performing a simple update:

```
24    procedure raise_salary(
25      p_empno in number,
26      p_salary_hike_pcnt in number )
27    is
28    begin
29      update emp
30      set salary = salary * (p_salary_hike_pcnt/100.00)
31      where empno = p_empno;
32    end raise_salary;
```

Finally, the fire_emp procedure deletes a given employee's record from the emp table:

```
33
34    procedure fire_emp(
35      p_empno in number )
36    is
37    begin
38      delete emp
39      where empno = p_empno;
40    end fire_emp;
41  end manager_pkg;
42  /
Package body created.
```

Our second (and final) package, clerk_pkg, simply lists the employee and department details with two functions, list_dept_details and list_emp_details, each of which returns a ref cursor containing relevant details:

```
db_data_access_layer@ORA10G> -- create package that reports schema data
db_data_access_layer@ORA10G> create or replace package clerk_pkg
  2  as
  3    function list_dept_details( p_dept_no in number )
  4      return sys_refcursor;
  5    function list_emp_details( p_empno in number )
  6      return sys_refcursor;
  7  end clerk_pkg;
  8  /
Package created.
db_data_access_layer@ORA10G> create or replace package body clerk_pkg
  2  as
  3    function list_dept_details( p_dept_no in number )
  4      return sys_refcursor
  5    is
  6      l_dept_details sys_refcursor;
  7    begin
  8      open l_dept_details for
```

```
 9          select dept_no, dept_name
10          from dept
11          where dept_no = p_dept_no;
12       return l_dept_details;
13     end list_dept_details;
14
15     function list_emp_details( p_empno in number )
16       return sys_refcursor
17     is
18       l_emp_details sys_refcursor;
19     begin
20       open l_emp_details for
21          select empno, ename, dept_no, salary, job
22          from emp
23          where empno = p_empno;
24       return l_emp_details;
25     end list_emp_details;
26   end clerk_pkg;
27   /
Package body created.
```

We next create public synonyms for these packages so that we can refer to them without having to use the db_data_access_layer schema name:

```
db_data_access_layer@ORA10G> create public synonym manager_pkg for manager_pkg;
Synonym created.
db_data_access_layer@ORA10G> create public synonym clerk_pkg for clerk_pkg;
Synonym created.
```

Creating Database Roles and Schema for End Users

In our sample application, the end users fall into two categories based on their roles.

- The managers use the package manager_pkg to manipulate information stored in the emp and dept tables.

- The clerks use the package clerk_pkg to query information stored in the emp and dept tables.

We will create two database roles, manager_role and clerk_role, which correspond to the two preceding user categories, respectively. A *database role* is a set of privileges that provides a DBA with an alternative to assigning privileges directly to the user. You combine privileges into roles and assign the roles to users. Thus, if you want to add or remove a privilege from a group of users, you can simply grant or revoke it from the corresponding role instead of doing the same for each individual user account. See the section titled "Introduction to Roles" in Chapter 5 of *Oracle Database Security Guide (10g Release 1)* for more details on roles.

First, we create manager_role and grant it privileges to execute both the manager_pkg and clerk_pkg packages after connecting as admin.

```
db_data_access_layer@ORA10G> connect admin/admin
Connected.
admin@ORA10G> -- create manager_role
admin@ORA10G> create role manager_role;
Role created.
admin@ORA10G> grant execute on manager_pkg to manager_role;
Grant succeeded.
admin@ORA10G> grant execute on clerk_pkg to manager_role;
Grant succeeded.
```

Next, we create clerk_role with the privilege of executing only the package clerk_pkg:

```
admin@ORA10G> create role clerk_role;
Role created.
admin@ORA10G> grant execute on clerk_pkg to clerk_role;
Grant succeeded.
```

Finally, it is time to create the database users that correspond to end users of the application in our database. We will create two representative end users. The end user manager1 maps to the database schema db_manager1, which has the roles manager_role and clerk_role. The end user clerk1 maps to the database schema db_clerk1, which is granted only the role clerk_role. Each of these two database users also gets the create session privilege required to log into the database. In a real-life application, we would, of course, have many end users getting mapped to various database roles based on the business functions they perform.

```
admin@ORA10G> create user db_manager1 identified by db_manager1;
User created.
admin@ORA10G> grant create session to db_manager1;
Grant succeeded.
admin@ORA10G> grant manager_role, clerk_role to db_manager1;
Grant succeeded.
admin@ORA10G> create user db_clerk1 identified by db_clerk1;
User created.
admin@ORA10G> grant create session to db_clerk1;
Grant succeeded.
admin@ORA10G> grant clerk_role to db_clerk1;
Grant succeeded.
```

Now, for example, if we try to access the package manager_pkg while connected as db_clerk1, we will get an error because the corresponding access does not exist:

```
db_clerk1@ORA10G> desc manager_pkg
ERROR:
ORA-04043: object "DB_DATA_ACCESS_LAYER"."MANAGER_PKG" does not exist
```

However, the same user can access the package clerk_pkg:

```
db_clerk1@ORA10G> desc clerk_pkg
FUNCTION LIST_DEPT_DETAILS RETURNS REF CURSOR
 Argument Name                  Type                    In/Out Default?
 ------------------------------ ----------------------- ------ --------
 P_DEPT_NO                      NUMBER                  IN
FUNCTION LIST_EMP_DETAILS RETURNS REF CURSOR
 Argument Name                  Type                    In/Out Default?
 ------------------------------ ----------------------- ------ --------
 P_EMPNO                        NUMBER                  IN
```

Now that we have gone through the process of creating all the schema objects required, we will use this sample application for demonstration purposes in the remainder of this chapter. In the next section, we will cover some of the challenges while authenticating an application end user to the database.

Authenticating an Application End User to the Database

In a three-tier architecture typically used by web applications, an end user has to necessarily authenticate herself to the application before carrying out any action. The application in turn has to log into the database on behalf of the end user. For an application to authenticate to the database on behalf of the end user, we will cover the following alternatives:

- *The application supplies the end user's password to the database*. In this case, the end user supplies the database password of her corresponding database user to the application, and the application uses this password to authenticate to the database on behalf of the end user. In our example application, the end user clerk1 would log in as db_clerk1, supplying the database password for the schema db_clerk1.

- *The application uses proxy authentication*. In this case, the application can log into the database using its own account on behalf of the end user *without* supplying the end user's database password. This feature of the Oracle database is called *proxy authentication*. Though this feature may seem not very secure at first glance, you'll soon see that this is a perfectly secure way of connecting to the database.

We'll look at these two alternatives in the sections that follow.

■**Note** Two other alternatives for an application to authenticate to the database are authenticating against a centralized LDAP directory and authenticating using certificates. Coverage of these techniques is beyond the scope of this book.

Authentication Using the End User's Database Password

I discuss this alternative mainly to explain why the proxy authentication feature was invented in the first place. In this approach, the application presents to the database the actual end user's password. This works fine for client/server applications that need to support a small number of dedicated connections for a relatively small user-community. In the context of a three-tier web application, however, this approach has the following drawbacks:

- Most application servers today have built-in authentication mechanisms, such as the use of a central directory service for storing user credentials, which obviate the need for applications to know or use the database password of the end user account.

- It is not uncommon for the same user to access different applications running on the application server. If each application has a different database account for the user, the user would have to sign on separately whenever he wants to switch to a new application. The single sign-on feature available in most application servers today is designed to solve this problem. Using single sign-on, the user authenticates once to the application server and is able to access multiple applications hosted on the application server without logging into each one of them separately. Figure 15-3 illustrates this concept.

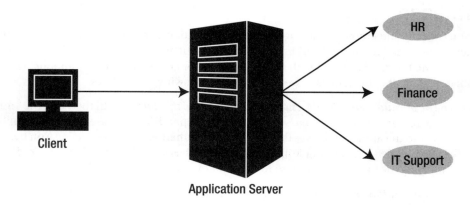

Figure 15-3. *A user accesses multiple applications but authenticates (or signs on) only once to the application server using the single sign-on feature.*

- Security is undermined if the application stores the end user's password. For example, if the application code has the password, then it is trivial to extract the passwords in many cases (e.g., using the `strings` utility found in most UNIX operating system variants).

- Every time there is a change in a user's password in the database, all applications that access the username and password have to be modified as well, leading to maintenance problems.

- Performance and scalability are affected adversely if an application has to authenticate using the end user's database password. Consider an application that uses a connection pool of a maximum 100 connections for a system serving 5,000 end users. Every time a new user logs in, the likelihood of the user's connection not existing in the pool is high, simply because each user connects to a different account. This means that, more likely than not, an existing connection in the pool has to be closed and replaced with a newly created connection. This defeats the purpose of connection pooling to a large extent, especially when you use an implicit connection cache, where each session requires the creation of a physical connection.

Some of the problems just mentioned would be mitigated if all application end users shared a smaller set of database user accounts based on their roles (i.e., an N-to-M mapping). However, this gives rise to new set of problems. One problem is that different application users have to share the same password for the shared database account, leading to poor security. Another problem, as mentioned earlier, is that the user actions cannot be audited effectively.

What we really need is for the application to log into the database using a common database account *on behalf of* an end user *without* requiring it to present the end user's database password. In other words, the account midtier proxies for the end user. This is where proxy authentication (also known as *n-tier authentication*) comes in.

Proxy Authentication (N-Tier Authentication)

Proxy authentication is a feature available only in the JDBC OCI driver as of Oracle 10*g* Release 1.

■**Note** In 10*g* Release 2, this feature is planned to be supported in the JDBC thin driver, too. The examples in this book use an OCI driver on a 10*g* Release 1 database, but the basic concepts should remain the same with a thin driver.

Proxy authentication allows you to connect on behalf of another user without supplying the user's password (provided appropriate privileges have been granted to enable this). The way proxy authentication works is simple. You create an OCI connection pool consisting of connections of the proxy user account. Then you can create sessions on top of these physical connections for the individual database users (as demonstrated in the previous chapter). This solves the problem of password management simply by not requiring the proxied user's password.

For example, assume that the proxy account is called midtier, and you want to create two sessions of db_clerk1 and one session of db_manager1 on top of a single physical connection from the pool of midtier connections. Figure 15-4 shows one such proxy connection carrying three of these sessions.

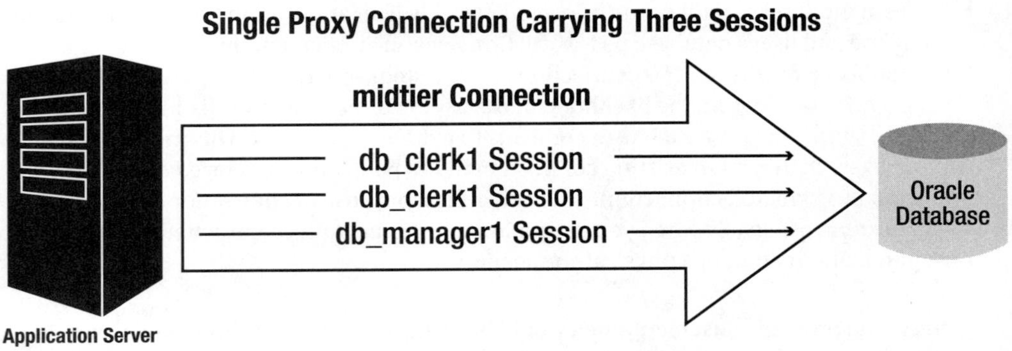

Single Proxy Connection Carrying Three Sessions

Figure 15-4. *A proxy connection carrying three sessions*

We will use our sample application to demonstrate the proxy authentication concept. We first create a database account to connect to the database on behalf of end users. This account is separate from the end user database accounts (db_manager1 and db_clerk1 in our application) and is called midtier in our example:

```
admin@ORA10G> create user midtier identified by midtier;
User created.
```

The account midtier is the proxy account that connects on behalf of all end users to the database from the middle-tier application hosted on an application server. As per the principle of least privilege, we should give it the minimum privilege to get the job done. That privilege is the create session privilege, which allows it to connect to the database:

```
admin@ORA10G> grant create session to midtier;
Grant succeeded.
```

To enable the end user account, db_manager1, to be able to be proxied by the account midtier, we need to alter the db_manager1 account as follows:

```
admin@ORA10G> -- allow connecting through proxy account
admin@ORA10G> alter user db_manager1 grant connect through midtier with
  role manager_role, clerk_role;
User altered.
```

The preceding alter statement in effect says that the user midtier can connect with the privileges of db_manager1 *without* supplying the db_manager1 password, and during this connection it can enable only the roles manager_role and clerk_role. This means that when the application is proxying for db_manager1 via the account midtier, only two specific roles can be enabled: manager_role and clerk_role. Restricting the roles in this manner ensures that the application can enable only the roles with the minimum privileges to do its job.

We issue the same alter statement to the user db_clerk1; however, this time we allow only clerk_role to be enabled during the proxy connection.

```
admin@ORA10G> alter user db_clerk1 grant connect through midtier with
  role clerk_role;
User altered.
```

When a user logs into Oracle, all *default* roles are enabled. A default role means that the role is always enabled for the current session at login without issuing the `set role` statement. To indicate that a role should be set by default on login, you need to issue the `alter user` statement with the following basic syntax:

```
alter user_name default role <role_name>
| all [except role1, role2, ... ] | none ;
```

In the preceding command, `user_name` denotes the name of the user whose role we are setting as the default. `role_name` represents the role that we wish to set as the default. The `all` phrase indicates that all roles should be enabled as the default, except those listed in the `except` phrase. The `none` phrase means that all roles are disabled by default.

For additional security, we want our application roles to be nondefault roles for the end user accounts. We do this by altering the users as follows:

```
admin@ORA10G> -- make all roles default except the ones required
admin@ORA10G> alter user db_manager1 default role all except
  manager_role, clerk_role;

User altered.
```

The preceding statement restricts all roles available to the user `db_manager1` by default, except for the roles `manager_role` and `clerk_role`. In other words, these two roles are not enabled by default for the user `db_manager1`. We do the same to the user `db_clerk1`, only this time we make `clerk_role` the nondefault role:

```
admin@ORA10G> alter user db_clerk1 default role all except clerk_role;

User altered.
```

We will set these roles explicitly when we log in from our Java program in the upcoming section. We can query from the `proxy_users` view to display information about proxy users and their capabilities in our database:

```
admin@ORA10G> select proxy, client, flags from proxy_users;

PROXY       CLIENT           FLAGS
----------  ---------------  ------------------------------------
MIDTIER     DB_MANAGER1      NO PROXY MAY ACTIVATE ROLE
MIDTIER     DB_CLERK1        NO PROXY MAY ACTIVATE ROLE
```

A Proxy Authentication Example

Let's look at an example Java class, `DemoProxyConnection`, in which the account `midtier` proxies for the end user accounts `db_clerk1` and `db_manager1`. After the necessary imports, in the `main()` method, we verify the existence of a single command-line parameter—the end user account to proxy for:

```
/* This program demonstrates proxy authentication.
* COMPATIBLITY NOTE: tested against 10.1.0.2.0, 9.2.0.1.0.
*/
```

```
import java.sql.SQLException;
import java.sql.Connection;
import java.sql.PreparedStatement;
import java.sql.CallableStatement;
import java.sql.ResultSet;
import java.util.Properties;
import oracle.jdbc.pool.OracleOCIConnectionPool;
import book.util.JDBCUtil;
class DemoProxyConnection
{
  public static void main(String args[]) throws Exception
  {
    if( args.length != 1 )
    {
      System.out.println( "Usage: java DemoProxyConnection <end_user>");
      System.exit( 1 );
    }
    String endUser = args[0];
```

Next, we create the OCI connection pool and set the connection URL for connecting using the OCI JDBC driver. We set the credentials to connect as the midtier account:

```
OracleOCIConnectionPool oocp = new OracleOCIConnectionPool();
oocp.setURL ( "jdbc:oracle:oci:@" );
oocp.setUser("midtier");            // username
oocp.setPassword("midtier");        // password
```

To proxy for the end user account, we first set a Properties object in which we set the property OracleOCIConnectionPool.PROXY_USER_NAME to the end user we want to proxy for. The parameter OracleOCIConnectionPool.PROXY_USER_NAME represents one of the four proxy modes that we will discuss in the section "Proxy Authentication Modes" later. The value OracleOCI➡ConnectionPool.PROXY_USER_NAME for this parameter, in particular, indicates that we wish to authenticate by supplying the username:

```
Properties endUserProps = new Properties();
endUserProps.setProperty( OracleOCIConnectionPool.PROXY_USER_NAME,  endUser );
Connection conn = null;
try
{
```

The proxy connection is obtained by invoking the method getProxyConnection():

```
  conn = oocp.getProxyConnection(
    OracleOCIConnectionPool.PROXYTYPE_USER_NAME, endUserProps );
```

The second parameter is the Properties object that we populated earlier with the end user account passed as the command-line parameter. Next, we print a "success" message and invoke the following two functions defined later in the class:

- _displayEnabledRoles(): Displays all roles enabled for a connection

- _enableRole(): Enables a given role or set of roles for a connection

We first display roles that are enabled by default:

```
System.out.println( "successfully connected..." );
_displayEnabledRoles( conn );
```

Next, we invoke _enableRole() with the role all to enable all roles granted to the end user. We invoke _displayEnabledRoles() to verify the enabled roles.

```
_enableRole( conn, "all" );
_displayEnabledRoles( conn );
```

We invoke _enableRole() with the roles clerk_role and manager_role, displaying enabled roles each time. The main() method ends with a finally clause that closes our connection object:

```
    _enableRole( conn, "clerk_role" );
    _displayEnabledRoles( conn );
    _enableRole( conn, "manager_role" );
    _displayEnabledRoles( conn );
  }
  finally
  {
    JDBCUtil.close ( conn );
  }
}// end of main
```

The method _displayEnabledRoles() simply selects all enabled roles for a session from the view session_roles and prints them out:

```
// display enabled roles
private static void _displayEnabledRoles( Connection conn )
throws SQLException
{
  System.out.println( "Displaying enabled roles..." );
  PreparedStatement pstmt = null;
  ResultSet rset = null;
  try
  {
    pstmt = conn.prepareStatement( "select role from session_roles");
    rset = pstmt.executeQuery();
    while( rset.next() )
    {
      System.out.println( "\t" + rset.getString( 1 ) );
    }
  }
  finally
  {
    JDBCUtil.close( rset );
    JDBCUtil.close( pstmt );
  }
}
```

The method _enableRole() enables a given set of roles by invoking the method set_role() of the supplied package dbms_session:

```
// enable a given role or a set of comma-separated roles.
private static void _enableRole( Connection conn, String role )
throws SQLException
{
  System.out.println( "Enabling role(s) " + role );
  CallableStatement cstmt = null;
  try
  {
    cstmt = conn.prepareCall(
      "{call dbms_session.set_role( ? ) }" );
    cstmt.setString( 1, role );
    cstmt.execute();
  }
  finally
  {
    JDBCUtil.close( cstmt );
  }
}
}// end of program
```

Note again that in our program we didn't supply the password for the end user that we will log in as. Let's first see what the output of the program is when we run it with the parameter db_manager1:

```
B:\>java DemoProxyConnection db_manager1
successfully connected...
Displaying enabled roles...
Enabling role(s) all
Displaying enabled roles...
        MANAGER_ROLE
        CLERK_ROLE
Enabling role(s) clerk_role
Displaying enabled roles...
        CLERK_ROLE
Enabling role(s) manager_role
Displaying enabled roles...
        MANAGER_ROLE
```

Note that the first time we didn't have any roles enabled *by default*. When we enabled all roles, the enabled roles were clerk_role and manager_role. This showed us the set of roles that this user can enable. Then we enabled the roles clerk_role and manager_role individually (by replacing the keyword all in the set role command), as shown by the output. Let's now see what the program output is if we invoke the program to proxy for the user db_clerk1:

```
B:\>java DemoProxyConnection db_clerk1
successfully connected...
Displaying enabled roles...
```

```
Enabling role(s) all
Displaying enabled roles...
        CLERK_ROLE
Enabling role(s) clerk_role
Displaying enabled roles...
        CLERK_ROLE
Enabling role(s) manager_role
Exception in thread "main" java.sql.SQLException: ORA-01924: role 'MANAGER_ROLE'
 not granted or does not exist
ORA-06512: at "SYS.DBMS_SESSION", line 124
ORA-06512: at line 1
:125)
        at
… trimmed to save space
```

The main point to note is that this user can only enable clerk_role, as shown by the list of enabled roles immediately after we enabled all roles. This is also proven by the fact that we got an exception when we tried to set the role to manager_role. This is because this role was not granted to the end user db_clerk1. Let's see if we can enable manager_role if we do grant this role to db_clerk1, though:

```
admin@ORA10G> grant manager_role, clerk_role to db_clerk1;
```

```
Grant succeeded.
```

Executing the program again gives us

```
B:\code\book\ch16>java DemoProxyConnection db_clerk1
successfully connected...
Displaying enabled roles...
Enabling role(s) all
Displaying enabled roles...
        CLERK_ROLE
Enabling role(s) clerk_role
Displaying enabled roles...
        CLERK_ROLE
Enabling role(s) manager_role
Exception in thread "main" java.sql.SQLException: ORA-01924: role 'MANAGER_ROLE'
 not granted or does not exist
ORA-06512: at "SYS.DBMS_SESSION", line 124
ORA-06512: at line 1
        at … trimmed to save space
```

We got a different exception this time. This exception tells us that the proxy user midtier cannot enable the role manager_role for the user db_clerk1. This is because, earlier on, we had restricted the universe of roles that can be enabled for db_clerk1 while using the proxy connection via midtier to the role clerk_role as follows:

```
admin@ORA10G> alter user db_clerk1 grant connect through midtier with role
  clerk_role;
```

This demonstrates a technique by which we can restrict the set of roles that can be enabled while using proxy authentication, no matter what roles have been granted to the user for whom we are proxying. This again enables us to apply the principle of least privilege.

One of the questions you may have is, what happens to auditing since all users are now logging in as the proxy user midtier? Won't they lose their identity in the database? We discuss this issue in the next section.

Proxy Authentication and Auditing

A critical difference between the case where we use proxy authentication and the case where we share database accounts between multiple end users without using proxy authentication is that proxy authentication preserves the identity of the end user. We can see this by auditing user connections. To enable auditing, we execute the following alter system command as the system user:

```
alter system set audit_trail=db scope=spfile;
```

We shut down and restart the database for auditing to take effect. Next, we audit proxy connections by issuing the following command as the sys user:

```
sys@ORA10G> audit connect by midtier on behalf of clerk1, manager1;
Audit succeeded.
```

We then execute our program DemoProxyConnection again:

```
B:\>java DemoProxyConnection db_clerk1
successfully connected...
… trimmed to save space
```

We log in as sys and run a select from dba_audit_trail to verify that the connection was audited:

```
sys@ORA10G> select a.username proxied_user, b.username proxy_user,
  2          a.action_name, a.comment_text
  3  from dba_audit_trail a, dba_audit_trail b
  4  where a.proxy_sessionid = b.sessionid;
```

```
PROXIED_USER     PROXY_USER  ACTION_NAM  COMMENT_TEXT
---------------  ----------  ----------  --------------------
DB_CLERK1        MIDTIER     LOGOFF      Authenticated by: PR
                                         OXY;EXTERNAL NAME: R
                                         MENON-LAP\menon
```

To see more details on the database auditing feature, see Chapter 8 of *Oracle Database Security Guide (10g Release 1)*. Next, we briefly examine the various proxy authentication modes available to us.

Proxy Authentication Modes

Four modes are supported in the invocation of the method getProxyConnection():

- We need to provide only the username of the proxied account (db_manager1, clerk1).

- We need to provide the username and password of the proxied account (db_manager1, clerk1).

- We need to provide the end user's distinguished name.

- We need to provide the end user's X.509 certificate.

Let's look at each of these options briefly.

Proxy by Username Only

You've already seen how this works in the class DemoProxyConnection. The main benefit is the fact that you don't need to know the end user's password. Note that the proxy user should itself be set up with minimal privileges (only create session as granted in our setup) for the application to work securely.

Proxy by Username and Password

In this case, you require the username and password of the end user while proxying for it. This is identical to normal authentication and has all the drawbacks of supplying passwords, as discussed earlier. One advantage this mode has over normal authentication is that by using the proxy authentication, it is possible to restrict the set of roles that can be enabled, as demonstrated earlier. This mode should be considered only if there is a way to obtain the end user's password securely.

To require a password while proxying, we have to issue a slightly different alter statement when enabling proxying for an account:

```
admin@ORA10G> alter user db_manager1 grant connect through midtier with role
  manager_role, clerk_role authenticated using password;

User altered.
```

If we now try to run our program DemoProxyConnection to connect as db_manager1, we get an exception:

```
B:\>java DemoProxyConnection manager1
Exception in thread "main" java.sql.SQLException: ORA-28183: proper authentication
 not provided by proxy
        at … trimmed to save space
```

To supply the end user's password, we need to populate another property, OracleOCI↪ConnectionPool.PROXY_PASSWORD, with the end user account's password:

```
endUserProps.setProperty( OracleOCIConnectionPool.PROXY_PASSWORD,
    endUserPassword );
```

Proxy by Distinguished Name

A *distinguished name* is an equivalent of the primary key in the LDAP world. LDAP stands for *Lightweight Directory Access Protocol*. This proxy authentication mode is used by applications using a central LDAP directory as their authentication mechanism. I don't cover this option in this book; please see the section "Oracle Internet Directory" in Chapter 9 of *Oracle Security Overview (10*g *Release 1)* for more details.

Proxy by Certificate

In this mode, you proxy using the X.509 certificate. This option is also not covered in this book. For more details on this topic, refer to Chapter 4 of *Oracle Database Security Guide (10*g *Release 1)*.

Summary

In this chapter, you learned about the security principles of least privilege and defense in depth. You looked at various ways of mapping an application end user to a database user for authentication purposes and each method's pros and cons. You examined proxy authentication (a JDBC OCI driver feature as of Oracle 10*g* Release 1 also known as n-tier authentication) in detail, and you learned how this technique can elegantly solve the problems of authentication and password management for a web application. The proxy authentication feature allows the middle tier to authenticate itself to the database on behalf of an end user database account without supplying the end user database account's password. You also learned how auditing captures the end user identity as well as the proxy user identity.

■ ■ ■

Locking-Related Issues

In this chapter, we'll look at some issues related to locking in Oracle. In particular, we'll discuss the infamous "lost update" problem and various ways to address it. Along the way, we'll examine different strategies to implement two solutions to the lost update problem—namely, optimistic locking and pessimistic locking. We'll also compare these two solutions and determine when to use each strategy.

Locking in Oracle

A *lock* is a mechanism Oracle uses to prevent destructive interaction between transactions accessing the same resource. Here, the resource could be user objects, such as tables; or user data, such as table rows; or internal objects, such as shared data structures in memory. A detailed discussion of locking and concurrency concepts in Oracle is beyond the scope of this book. For that, I refer you to Chapter 13 of *Oracle Database Concepts Guide (10g Release 1)* and Chapter 3 of Tom Kyte's *Expert One-on-One Oracle* (Apress, ISBN: 1-59059-243-3).

In this chapter, I will define what lost updates are and how to deal with them when programming in Oracle. Throughout the chapter, unless otherwise stated explicitly, assume a default transaction isolation level of READ COMMITTED (see Chapter 4 for a discussion of transaction isolation levels).

Lost Updates

In Chapter 2, you learned that the following are true for the Oracle database:

- Reads (selects) don't block writes (inserts, updates, deletes, etc.). For example, a user can be updating a row at the same time as another user is querying the same exact row. The session performing the query would see only the rows that existed at the start of the query.

- Writes don't block reads.

- Writes don't block writes unless the contending writes are "writing" a common set of rows. For example, if two sessions are updating the same table, but update a mutually exclusive set of rows, they don't block each other. Only when they try to update the same row(s) does one of the sessions get blocked until the other session issues a commit or a rollback to end its transaction.

Now consider the following situation, which can occur in any relational database:

1. User1 queries a row.

2. User2 queries the same row in a different session.

3. User1 updates the row and commits.

4. User2 updates the row to a different value and commits.

Unknown to user1, user2 in step 4 overwrote user1's data. This phenomenon is called a *lost update*, since all changes made by user1 in step 3 were lost because user2 overwrote those changes in step 4.

Let's look at an example. Imagine it has been a good sales year for our company, and all salespeople are getting a salary hike. Adam, who is a clerk, is updating the database to reflect this change. One salesperson in particular, Martin, has done well in clinching a mega deal for the company. Martin's boss, Blake, is very happy and decides to give him an additional bonus of $100. The following is how these two transactions occur, presented in the order of time (many of the following examples use hard-coded values; remember to use bind variables in a real-world application).

Blake queries the database to look at Martin's current salary information:

```
blake@ORA10G> select ename, sal from emp where ename='MARTIN';

ENAME          SAL
---------- ----------
MARTIN        1250
```

Blake gets an urgent phone call and leaves his desk to answer it. Meanwhile, Adam has queried records for all employees who are salespeople and is currently looking at Martin's salary details. He updates Martin's record to give Martin a 10% salary hike:

```
adam@ORA10G> select ename, sal from emp where ename='MARTIN';

ENAME          SAL
---------- ----------
MARTIN        1250

adam@ORA10G> update emp set sal = sal * 1.10 where ename='MARTIN';

1 row updated.
```

Being a careful employee, Adam even queries the record back to verify his changes:

```
adam@ORA10G> select ename, sal from emp where ename='MARTIN';

ENAME          SAL
---------- ----------
MARTIN        1375
```

Satisfied that all is well, Adam commits his changes:

```
adam@ORA10G> commit;
```

Blake's phone call is over and he returns to his desk. His screen still shows Martin's old salary information. Unaware of Adam's changes, Blake proceeds to give Martin a bonus of $100 based on his (now old) salary of $1,250, wiping out the changes made by Adam earlier:

```
blake@ORA10G> update emp set sal = 1350 where ename='MARTIN';

1 row updated.

blake@ORA10G> commit;

Commit complete.
```

The final row for Martin's record looks as follows:

```
martin@ORA10G> select * from emp where ename='MARTIN';

    EMPNO ENAME      JOB        MGR HIREDATE        SAL     COMM    DEPTNO
---------- ---------- --------- ---------- --------- ---------- ------- ---------
     7654 MARTIN     SALESMAN  7698 28-SEP-81      1350     1400   30
```

As you can see, the update done by Adam has been overwritten by Blake's changes and is the lost update. Martin expected to see a total salary of $1,475 ($1,250 \times 1.10 + 100$), whereas his salary is only $1,350.

In the preceding example, both updates were changing the same column. The problem can occur even if different columns of the same row are being updated by two different transactions. This happens when the application performing updates is written such that instead of updating only the changed columns of a record (it takes more work to detect which column changed), all (nonprimary key) columns are updated.

For example, let's consider an application screen that allows the end user to update the salary and commission of an employee in our emp table. Adam, in session 1, is updating the comm column of the emp table for Martin's record. In a different session, Blake is changing the sal column of the same record. The application performing the update doesn't detect which column changed, so it happily updates all (nonprimary key) columns that are updateable from the screen (in this case, the sal and comm columns), resulting in a lost update.

First, Blake queries Martin's record:

```
blake@ORA10G> select ename, sal, comm from emp where ename='MARTIN';

ENAME            SAL       COMM
---------- ---------- ----------
MARTIN          1350       1400
```

Next, Adam queries Martin's record:

```
adam@ORA10G> select ename, sal, comm from emp where ename='MARTIN';

ENAME           SAL        COMM
---------- ---------- ----------
MARTIN         1350        1400
```

Blake issues an update of the sal column, but the application doesn't detect whether the sal or comm column changed. It updates the sal column to the new value and "refreshes" the comm column to the old value:

```
blake@ORA10G> update emp set sal = sal*1.10, comm=1400 where ename='MARTIN';

1 row updated.

blake@ORA10G> select ename, sal, comm from emp where ename='MARTIN';

ENAME           SAL        COMM
---------- ---------- ----------
MARTIN         1485        1400

blake@ORA10G> commit;
Commit complete.
```

Meanwhile, another session is issuing an update of the comm column, and this time the sal column is being "refreshed" to its old value, thus wiping out the update to sal done by Blake in the previous session:

```
adam@ORA10G> update emp set comm = comm * 1.10, sal=1350 where ename='MARTIN';

1 row updated.

adam@ORA10G> select ename, sal, comm from emp where ename='MARTIN';

ENAME           SAL        COMM
---------- ---------- ----------
MARTIN         1350        1540

adam@ORA10G> commit;

Commit complete.
```

We'll look at the following three techniques for dealing with lost updates in detail in the following sections:

- *Setting the transaction isolation level to* SERIALIZABLE: When we set the transaction to SERIALIZABLE, we get an error if we issue an update on data that has changed since our transaction began. This can prevent lost updates in some scenarios, as we will discuss shortly.

- *Using pessimistic locking*: This technique involves explicitly locking the row that needs to be updated in advance to prevent lost updates.

- *Using optimistic locking*: This technique involves a mechanism to detect that the row the user is updating has changed, in which case the user typically has to retry her operation.

Setting the Transaction Isolation Level to SERIALIZABLE

As already discussed in Chapter 4, different transaction isolation levels affect a transaction's behavior. In particular, recall that when we set the transaction isolation level to SERIALIZABLE, all queries are read such that retrieved data is consistent with respect to the beginning of the transaction. In other words, the answers to all queries are fixed as of the beginning of the transaction. A side effect of this behavior is that in a serializable transaction, if you attempt to update the same row as some other user, you wait until the user commits and then get an error. Let's look at an example. We'll execute the following two statements from two different sessions:

```
alter session set isolation_level=serializable;
update emp set sal=1450 where ename='MARTIN';
```

The first statement alters the current session to set the transaction isolation level to SERIALIZABLE. If we open two windows and execute the preceding two statements, first in window 1 and then in window 2, we will see that the window 2 session hangs, waiting for the window 1 session to commit or roll back.

Actions in Window 1:

```
scott@ORA10G> alter session set isolation_level=serializable;
Session altered.
scott@ORA10G> update emp set sal=1450 where ename='MARTIN';
1 row updated.
```

Actions in Window 2 (hangs after the second command waiting for the window 1 session to commit or roll back):

```
scott@ORA10G> alter session set isolation_level=serializable;
Session altered.
scott@ORA10G> update emp set sal=1450 where ename='MARTIN';
```

Now if we commit in window 1, window 2 will give an error:

```
scott@ORA10G> update emp set sal=1450 where ename='MARTIN';
*
ERROR at line 1:
ORA-08177: can't serialize access for this transaction
```

If window 1 issues a rollback, though, the window 2 session's update will succeed.

Setting the transaction isolation level just to solve the lost update problem is usually not feasible for the following reasons:

- In most web applications, you grab a connection from a connection pool for each HTTP request. Since the transaction isolation level is associated with a connection, you can use the previous technique only if the select that displayed the record and the update that followed are using the same exact connection. Since the connection may change with each request, and since the query and the update would be performed in two separate requests, setting the transaction isolation level to solve the lost update problem simply will not work. Such an environment, in which you are not maintaining the same database connection across multiple user requests, is termed a *stateless* environment. This is not true in client/server applications where a user has a dedicated database session for the entire user interaction. Such an environment is called a *stateful* environment. Thus, setting the transaction isolation level to SERIALIZABLE is an option only in stateful environments.

- Another important point to note is that changing the transaction isolation level has a huge impact on the way DML statements behave. Most transactions require the use of the default isolation level of READ COMMITTED.

- The third problem with this technique is that the second user has to wait until the transaction of the first user has been committed, only to get an error message asking him to retry. This can be very annoying.

Thus, setting the transaction isolation level can be considered a solution to the lost update problem if

- You are working in a stateful environment (e.g., in a client/server application) where a connection is maintained across multiple user requests.

- There is already a need to use the "serializable" transaction due to other business requirements.

- The number of expected simultaneous updates involving the same row(s) is fairly low. This would ensure that we don't waste the end user's time by giving error messages after making him wait for a long time.

If the preceding criteria are not met, you need to consider the other approaches described in the next sections.

Pessimistic Locking

This locking technique makes the pessimistic assumption that more often than not, the end user will run into a scenario that will result in a lost update. To prevent this from happening, the record being updated is locked, right after the user signals her intent to update it, by issuing a select...for update nowait form of query. The for update nowait clause signals the intent to lock the record being updated. The optional nowait keyword indicates that if the record is already locked by someone else, control should return immediately to the user with an error instead of waiting until the other transaction commits. Typically, the application requirement is to not wait, but to give the control back to the user immediately so that she can perform some other function before returning to try and lock the record again to complete her original transaction. If this is not the case, you can skip the nowait keyword. Note that you can also wait for n seconds before failing by giving the for update wait <n> clause.

Let's revisit the example where we were updating the salary of the salesperson Martin in two conflicting sessions. The application first queries all salespeople and displays them on a screen *without* locking them:

```
blake@ORA10G> select empno, ename, sal from emp where job='SALESMAN';

    EMPNO ENAME             SAL
---------- ---------- ----------
      7499 ALLEN            1600
      7521 WARD             1250
      7654 MARTIN           1350
      7844 TURNER           1500
```

The user navigates to the record containing Martin's data and indicates his intention to update it (say, by clicking an icon in the GUI). At this time, we try to lock the record by issuing a select statement that has

- A for update nowait clause to lock the row so that no one else is able to update the row before we have committed our changes. If the lock cannot be acquired, we want the program to return immediately—hence the nowait clause.

- A where clause criteria to match a row based on the primary key column(s) (in this case, the empno column). This is to ensure we lock only the one record that we want to update.

- A where clause criteria to match a row based on current values of all the columns that can be modified on the screen. In our hypothetical screen, we can potentially modify the ename and sal columns (remember, empno is being displayed but cannot be modified since it is a primary key and hence immutable).

In our example, this would result in the following select being issued to lock Martin's record:

```
blake@ORA10G> select empno, ename, sal from emp where empno=7654
and ename='MARTIN' and sal=1350 for update nowait;

    EMPNO ENAME            SAL
---------- ---------- ----------
     7654 MARTIN          1350
```

The following three scenarios are possible at the point Blake tries to lock the row as shown earlier:

- If Blake's session was able to lock the record, then Blake can proceed to update it safely without worrying about it being overwritten by some other transaction.

- If some other session was able to lock the record before Blake, Blake would get a "resource busy" exception as a result of the previous select indicating that the record is locked, and he needs to try his luck later. In the previous example, Blake has already locked the record, and it is Adam who gets an exception when he tries to lock the same row:

```
adam@ORA10G> select empno, ename, sal from emp
where empno=7654
and ename='MARTIN'
and sal=1350 for update nowait;
select empno, ename, sal from emp
where empno=7654
and ename='MARTIN'
and sal=1350 for update nowait
                                *
ERROR at line 1:
ORA-00054: resource busy and acquire with NOWAIT specified
```

- If between the time Blake looked at the record and signaled his intention to update a record, someone else already changed the underlying data on the screen and committed the changes (thus releasing the lock), then Blake would get zero rows returned by the previous select. This is because Blake included all the columns that could be changed in the where clause of the select that locks the row. At least one of these criteria would not be met due to the changes in the column values performed by the other transaction.

Thus, locking the record before updating it serializes the update and prevents the transactions from stepping over each other. In the previous example, Blake can safely update the salary of Martin:

```
blake@ORA10G> update emp set sal=sal*1.10 where empno=7654;

1 row updated.
blake@ORA10G> commit;
```

Adam, unfortunately, will have to try again.

An advantage of pessimistic locking is that it prevents the situation in which the user has typed in lots of changes on a screen, but when he submits the changes, he is told, "Sorry, someone else has changed the record you have been modifying. Please try again." This can be very annoying. Remember that if someone has locked a row, the user doesn't have to wait until the lock is released: Using the `nowait` option, we can immediately detect this situation and give control back to the user.

Unfortunately, pessimistic locking does have some significant disadvantages:

- *Pessimistic locking can't be used in applications that use a stateless environment, such as a three-tier web application*. Again, this is because typically in such an environment, you don't maintain the same database session across multiple requests. The session that the user used to lock the row while selecting it to display and the session that the user uses to "submit" the changes to update the row may well be different, in which case the lock held by the user is of no use. This is one of the major disadvantages of pessimistic locking, since most applications today are web applications that use connection pooling and don't maintain session state across pages. Thus, pessimistic locking is useful mainly in client/server applications that maintain the same connection across GUI pages. In this respect, this solution is similar to the solution of setting the transaction isolation to `SERIALIZABLE`, as discussed in the previous section.

- *Pessimistic locking can result in a row being locked for relatively long periods of time*. In an application where the chance of users updating the same row is great, the number of users that can get the "Sorry, someone else is changing the record that you want to modify. Please try again." message can multiply rapidly. Also consider what happens if someone locks a row and forgets about it or goes out for lunch. Session timeouts can handle such situations, but this can still be a bottleneck.

The optimistic locking technique discussed next tries to address the problems just outlined.

Optimistic Locking

The philosophy of optimistic locking is to be optimistic in assuming that the underlying data won't get changed by another conflicting transaction. Optimistic locking doesn't lock any records across client requests. Instead, it introduces a mechanism by which the application can detect, during the update, whether or not the record has been modified by another transaction since the user last selected it. If indeed some other transaction has updated the same column(s) that the user was trying to update, the update affects zero rows, and the user is asked to try again. The pseudo code for performing the update looks something like this:

```
If( underlying record has not changed since the user started editing it in UI) then
    Update the record
Else
    Update should affect zero records and the user is asked to retry the operation.
End if
```

There are many ways of implementing optimistic locking, and they differ mainly in the manner in which they detect a lost update scenario. The following sections cover some of these methods. In each of the cases discussed, assume that two users are trying to update

Martin's record. Assume that the UI allows the user to update the name and the salary information. In our example programs, the user actually modifies only the salary, though all the examples should work even if the user modifies the name also.

Optimistic Locking by Saving Old Column Values

Perhaps the simplest way to implement optimistic locking is to save old values of the data to be modified (say, in hidden form fields) when we select the record that needs to be updated. When issuing the actual update, we include the old column values in the where clause, as shown in the following pseudo code:

```
update table_name
set col1 = :new_col1_value,
    col2 = :new_col2_value
    ...
where col1 = :old_col1_value
    and col2 = :old_col1_value
    and primary_key_col1 = :primary_key_col1
    and primary_key_col2 = :primary_key_col2
    ...
```

If the columns being modified have not been changed by any other transaction, the update would successfully change the record. On the other hand, if another transaction updated any of the values that your transaction is modifying, the update would affect zero rows. You can detect this in your application code and ask the user to retry her transaction. For example, if some other transaction changed the value of the column col1 in the preceding pseudo code, then the update would not affect any rows since the where clause criterion col1 = :old_col1_value would not be met.

Let's look at an example. Consider the following package, opt_lock_save_old_val_demo, which demonstrates this technique of implementing optimistic locking:

```
scott@ORA10G> create or replace package opt_lock_save_old_val_demo
  2  as
  3    procedure get_emp_details( p_empno in number, p_ename in out varchar2,
  4      p_sal in out number );
  5    procedure update_emp_info( p_empno in number, p_old_ename in varchar2,
  p_old_sal in number, p_new_ename in varchar2, p_new_sal in number,
  p_num_of_rows_updated in out number );
  6  end;
  7  /

Package created.
```

The definition of the package follows, along with an explanation of the two package procedures. The first procedure, get_emp_details, gets the employee name and salary—the two columns that can be modified by the end user. This query is executed to display the record that the user chose to modify (notice that we don't lock the record):

```
scott@ORA10G> create or replace package body opt_lock_save_old_val_demo
  2  as
  3    procedure get_emp_details( p_empno in number, p_ename in out varchar2,
  4      p_sal in out number )
  5    is
  6    begin
  7      select ename, sal
  8      into p_ename, p_sal
  9      from emp
 10      where empno = p_empno;
 11    end;
 12
```

The procedure update_emp_info updates the salary and the name with the new values. It also has the where clause criteria to compare the existing ename and sal columns with their older values that we obtain using the preceding get_emp_details procedure:

```
 13    procedure update_emp_info( p_empno in number,
          p_old_ename in varchar2, p_old_sal in number,
          p_new_ename in varchar2, p_new_sal in number,
           p_num_of_rows_updated in out number )
 14    is
 15    begin
 16      p_num_of_rows_updated := 0;
 17      update emp
 18      set sal = p_new_sal,
 19            ename = p_new_ename
 20      where empno = p_empno
 21        and ename = p_old_ename
 22        and sal = p_old_sal;
 23      p_num_of_rows_updated := sql%rowcount;
 24    end;
 25  end;
 26  /
```

Package body created.

Notice that the procedure update_emp_info also returns the number of rows successfully updated so that the calling code can detect if the update was successful. We will now demonstrate optimistic locking at work by calling these two procedures from the following Java class, DemoOptLockingBySavingOldValues. We begin the class definition with the required import statements, followed by the main() method that begins with obtaining the database connection:

```
/* This program demonstrates optimistic locking by saving old column values.
* COMPATIBLITY NOTE: tested against 10.1.0.2.0.*/
import java.sql.SQLException;
import java.sql.Connection;
import java.sql.CallableStatement;
import oracle.jdbc.OracleTypes;
```

```
import book.util.JDBCUtil;
import book.util.InputUtil;
class DemoOptLockingBySavingOldValues
{
  public static void main(String args[]) throws Exception
  {
    Connection conn = null;
    Object[] empDetails = null;
    try
    {
      conn = JDBCUtil.getConnection( "scott", "tiger", "ora10g" );
```

We initialize the variable empno with Martin's employee number, and then we invoke the method _displayEmpDetails. The method _displayEmpDetails prints out Martin's salary and name information, and also returns the current employee name and salary in an object array:

```
      int empNo = 7654;
      empDetails = _displayEmpDetails( conn, empNo );
```

We then introduce an artificial pause in our program by invoking InputUtil.waitTill➥ UserHitsEnter() (discussed in section "A Utility to Pause in a Java Program" of Chapter 1) to simulate the time the end user takes to change the employee details before issuing the final update. This enables us to sneak in a conflicting update in our experimental runs:

```
      InputUtil.waitTillUserHitsEnter("Row has been selected but is not locked.");
```

We invoke the _updateEmpInfo() method to update the employee information (we retain the old name but bump up the salary by $100, from $1,350 to $1,450):

```
      String oldEmpName = (String) empDetails[0];
      int oldSalary = ((Integer) empDetails[1]).intValue();
      _updateEmpInfo( conn, empNo, oldEmpName, oldSalary, "MARTIN", 1450 );
    }
    finally
    {
      JDBCUtil.close ( conn );
    }
  }// end of main
```

The _displayEmpDetails method simply invokes the opt_lock_save_old_val_demo.get_➥ emp_details method to retrieve the employee details to be modified:

```
  private static Object[] _displayEmpDetails( Connection conn, int empNo )
    throws SQLException
  {
    Object[] result = new Object[2];
    CallableStatement cstmt = null;
    int salary = 0;
    String empName = null;
    try
```

```
  {
    cstmt = conn.prepareCall(
      "{call opt_lock_save_old_val_demo.get_emp_details(?, ?, ?)}" );
    cstmt.setInt( 1, empNo );
    cstmt.registerOutParameter( 2, OracleTypes.VARCHAR );
    cstmt.registerOutParameter( 3, OracleTypes.NUMBER );
    cstmt.execute();
    empName = cstmt.getString( 2 );
    salary = cstmt.getInt( 3 );
    System.out.println( "empno: " + empNo + ", name: " + empName +
      ", salary: " + salary );
    result[0] = empName;
    result[1] = new Integer( salary );
  }
  finally
  {
    JDBCUtil.close( cstmt );
  }
  return result;
}
```

Toward the end of the class, we define the method _updateEmpInfo() that invokes the
method opt_lock_save_old_val_demo.update_emp_info to update the employee details. Notice
that we print an appropriate message depending on the number of rows successfully updated:

```
private static void _updateEmpInfo( Connection conn, int empNo,
  String oldEmpName, int oldSalary, String newEmpName,
  int newSalary )
throws SQLException
{
  CallableStatement cstmt = null;
  try
  {
    cstmt = conn.prepareCall(
      "{call opt_lock_save_old_val_demo.update_emp_info(?, ?, ?, ?, ?, ?)}" );
    cstmt.setInt( 1, empNo );
    cstmt.setString( 2, oldEmpName );
    cstmt.setInt( 3, oldSalary );
    cstmt.setString( 4, newEmpName );
    cstmt.setInt( 5, newSalary );
    cstmt.registerOutParameter( 6, OracleTypes.NUMBER );
    cstmt.execute();
    int numOfRowsUpdated = cstmt.getInt( 6 );
    if( numOfRowsUpdated <= 0 )
    {
      System.out.println( "Sorry. Someone else changed the data that" +
        " you were trying to update. Please retry." );
    }
```

```
      else
      {
        System.out.println( "You have successfully updated the " +
          "employee information." );
      }
    }
    finally
    {
      JDBCUtil.close( cstmt );
    }
  }
}// end of program
```

To run the program, I opened two windows (you need to use command-line windows in Windows and an xterm or its equivalent in UNIX). I then executed the following command in window 1:

```
B:\>java DemoOptLockingBySavingOldValues
URL:jdbc:oracle:thin:@(DESCRIPTION=(ADDRESS=(PROTOCOL=tcp)
(PORT=1521)(HOST=rmenon-lap))(CONNECT_DATA=(SID=ora10g)))
empno: 7654, name: MARTIN, salary: 1350, checksum: 12858
Row has been selected but is not locked.
Press Enter to continue...
```

With the pause still on in window 1, I executed the same command in window 2:

```
B:\>java DemoOptLockingBySavingOldValues
URL:jdbc:oracle:thin:@(DESCRIPTION=(ADDRESS=(PROTOCOL=tcp)
(PORT=1521)(HOST=rmenon-lap))(CONNECT_DATA=(SID=ora10g)))
empno: 7654, name: MARTIN, salary: 1350, checksum: 12858
Row has been selected but is not locked.
Press Enter to continue...
```

I then pressed Enter in window 1. The update went through successfully, and I got the following message:

```
You have successfully updated the employee information.
```

When I pressed Enter in window 2, though, the update would not work since the same row was changed by the process in window 1 during its pause time. Hence I got the following message:

```
Sorry. Someone else changed the data that you were trying to update. Please retry.
```

This shows that the optimistic locking technique has successfully prevented a lost update.

Optimistic Locking by Maintaining a Shadow Column in the Table

An alternative way for you to detect conflicting changes made by another transaction is to maintain a shadow column, such as a modification timestamp, or a column populated by a sequence in the table, or a GUID column. A GUID is a 16-byte RAW *globally unique identifier*.

After every successful update, you update the shadow column to a new unique value (e.g., a timestamp to the latest timestamp, a sequence to the next sequence value, a GUID column populated by the SYS_GUID() method to a new GUID, etc.). The update statement itself will have a where clause where you compare the shadow column value to the old value that existed when you selected the record to display it to the user. The pseudo code (assuming that the shadow column, shadow_col, is populated by a sequence) would look something like the following:

```
update table_name
set col1 = :new_col1_value,
     col2 = :new_col2_value
     shadow_col = sequence.nextval
where shadow_col = :old_shadow_col_value
     and primary_key_col1 = :primary_key_col1
     and primary_key_col2 = :primary_key_col2;
if( update above updated 0 rows) then
  update failed because someone else changed the underlying
     values - ask the user to retry.
else
  update succeeded
end if;
```

Let's look at an example. We create a copy of the emp table, called emp1, to hold the sample data for our example. We also have a column that we initialize with the value of a sequence. We first create the table emp1 with no data—its structure is that of the emp table except that it has an additional numeric shadow column called row_change_indicator (notice that the table will be created empty since the where clause, where 1 != 1, will always fail):

```
scott@ORA10G> create table emp1 as
  2  select e.*, 1 as row_change_indicator
  3  from emp e where 1 != 1;

Table created.
```

Next, we create a sequence, seq1:

```
scott@ORA10G> create sequence seq1 cache 100;

Sequence created.
```

We now populate the emp1 table with the data from the emp table, along with a different value for row_change_indicator for each row:

```
scott@ORA10G> insert into emp1( empno, ename, job, mgr, hiredate, sal, comm, deptno,
 row_change_indicator )
  2  select e.*, seq1.nextval from emp e;

14 rows created.
```

We next create a package, opt_lock_shadowcol_demo, with two methods, get_emp_details and update_emp_info:

```
scott@ORA10G> create or replace package opt_lock_shadowcol_demo
  2  as
  3    procedure get_emp_details( p_empno in number, p_ename in out varchar2,
  4      p_sal in out number, p_row_change_indicator in out number );
  5    procedure update_emp_info( p_empno in number, p_new_sal in number,
p_new_ename in varchar2,
  6      p_row_change_indicator in number, p_num_of_rows_updated in out number );
  7  end;
  8  /

Package created.
```

The procedure get_emp_details gets the employee name and salary data, along with the row_change_indicator column value:

```
scott@ORA10G> create or replace package body opt_lock_shadowcol_demo
  2  as
  3    procedure get_emp_details( p_empno in number, p_ename in out varchar2,
  4      p_sal in out number, p_row_change_indicator in out number )
  5    is
  6    begin
  7      select ename, sal, row_change_indicator
  8      into p_ename, p_sal, p_row_change_indicator
  9      from emp1
 10      where empno = p_empno;
 11    end;
 12
```

The following procedure, update_emp_info, updates the employee's salary and name information along with row_column_indicator. The where clause ensures that if row_change_indicator is not the same as the one we got when we selected the row using the get_emp_details method, the update will not affect any rows.

```
 13    procedure update_emp_info( p_empno in number, p_new_sal in number,
         p_new_ename in varchar2, p_row_change_indicator in number,
         p_num_of_rows_updated in out number )
 14    is
 15    begin
 16      p_num_of_rows_updated := 0;
 17      update emp1
 18        set sal = p_new_sal,
 19            ename = p_new_ename,
 20            row_change_indicator = seq1.nextval
 21      where empno = p_empno
 22        and p_row_change_indicator = row_change_indicator;
 23      p_num_of_rows_updated := sql%rowcount;
```

```
24     end;
25   end;
26   /
```

Package body created.

Let's now look at the Java class, DemoOptLockingUsingShadowColumn, which invokes the opt_lock_shadowcol_demo package methods in order to demonstrate optimistic locking. The class begins with import statements and gets the connection as scott in the main() method:

```
/* This program demonstrates optimistic locking using ora_rowscn (10g only)
* COMPATIBLITY NOTE: tested against 10.1.0.2.0.*/
import java.sql.SQLException;
import java.sql.Connection;
import java.sql.CallableStatement;
import oracle.jdbc.OracleTypes;
import book.util.JDBCUtil;
import book.util.InputUtil;
class DemoOptLockingUsingShadowColumn
{
  public static void main(String args[]) throws Exception
  {
    Connection conn = null;
    try
    {
      conn = JDBCUtil.getConnection( "scott", "tiger", "ora10g" );
```

At this point, the user is supposed to have indicated that he wants to update Martin's salary. To simulate that we set the variable empNo to Martin's employee number.

```
      int empNo = 7654;
```

Next, we invoke the _displayEmpDetails() method to display Martin's details on the screen that allows the user to modify the details (the ename and sal column values in our example). The method will also return the existing row_change_indicator column value.

```
      long rowChangeIndicator = _displayEmpDetails( conn, empNo );
```

We then pause using our InputUtil.waitTillUserHitsEnter() method (explained in Chapter 1) as before:

```
      InputUtil.waitTillUserHitsEnter("Row has been selected but is not locked.");
```

At the end of the main() method, we invoke the _updateEmpInfo method with the employee number, the new salary, the new name, and the value of the row_change_indicator column we calculated earlier. This method simply invokes opt_lock_shadowcol_demo. update_emp_info to perform the update. We close the statement in the finally clause as usual:

```
      _updateEmpInfo( conn, empNo, 1450, "MARTIN", rowChangeIndicator );
    }
```

```
      finally
      {
        JDBCUtil.close ( conn );
      }
    }// end of main
```

The following definition of the methods _displayEmpDetails() and _updateEmpInfo()
should be fairly self-explanatory. The method _displayEmpDetails() invokes the PL/SQL
package method opt_shadowcol_demo.get_emp_details() to display the employee details
of a given employee:

```
private static long _displayEmpDetails( Connection conn, int empNo )
   throws SQLException
{
  CallableStatement cstmt = null;
  long rowChangeIndicator = 0;
  int salary = 0;
  String empName = null;
  try
  {
    cstmt = conn.prepareCall(
      "{call opt_lock_shadowcol_demo.get_emp_details(?, ?, ?, ?)}" );
    cstmt.setInt( 1, empNo );
    cstmt.registerOutParameter( 2, OracleTypes.VARCHAR );
    cstmt.registerOutParameter( 3, OracleTypes.NUMBER );
    cstmt.registerOutParameter( 4, OracleTypes.NUMBER );
    cstmt.execute();
    empName = cstmt.getString( 2 );
    salary = cstmt.getInt( 3 );
    rowChangeIndicator = cstmt.getLong( 4 );
    System.out.println( "empno: " + empNo + ", name: " + empName +
        ", salary: " + salary + ", checksum: " + rowChangeIndicator );
  }
  finally
  {
    JDBCUtil.close( cstmt );
  }
  return rowChangeIndicator;
}
```

The method _updateEmpInfo() invokes the PL/SQL package method opt_shadowcol_➥
demo.update_emp_info(), passing in the new values along with the row change indicator that
we returned by _displayEmpDetails():

```
private static void _updateEmpInfo( Connection conn, int empNo,
   int newSalary, String newEmpName, long rowChangeIndicator )
   throws SQLException
{
```

```
  CallableStatement cstmt = null;
  try
  {
    cstmt = conn.prepareCall(
      "{call opt_lock_shadowcol_demo.update_emp_info(?, ?, ?, ?, ?)}" );
    cstmt.setInt( 1, empNo   );
    cstmt.setInt( 2, newSalary  );
    cstmt.setString( 3, newEmpName  );
    cstmt.setLong( 4, rowChangeIndicator  );
    cstmt.registerOutParameter( 5, OracleTypes.NUMBER );
    cstmt.execute();
    int numOfRowsUpdated = cstmt.getInt( 5 );
    if( numOfRowsUpdated <= 0 )
    {
      System.out.println( "Sorry. Someone else changed the data that " +
        "you were trying to update. Please retry." );
    }
    else
    {
      System.out.println( "You have successfully updated the employee " +
        "information." );
    }
  }
  finally
  {
    JDBCUtil.close( cstmt );
  }
}
}// end of program
```

To test the program, we can run it exactly like we ran the program DemoOptLockingBy➡
SavingOldValues in two windows in the section "Optimistic Locking by Saving Old Column
Values" earlier.

Optimistic Locking by Using a Checksum of Modified Column Values

Yet another implementation of optimistic locking involves calculating a *checksum* of the column values being modified. A checksum is a mathematical function that computes a single, unique value for any input. No two different inputs should map to the same output value. You can use the owa_opt_lock package's checksum function for this purpose. The owa_opt_lock package comes installed as part of the Oracle's HTTP server's mod_plsql module. The checksum function is defined as

```
function owa_opt_lock.checksum(p_buff in varchar2) return number;
```

■**Note** There is another overloaded version of checksum defined as

function checksum(p_owner in varchar2, p_tname in varchar2,
p_rowid in rowid) return number;

It cannot be used for optimistic locking when being invoked by our JDBC program, since it needs to lock the
row in order to calculate the checksum.

Let's look at an example. Consider the following package, opt_lock_chksum_demo:

```
scott@ORA10G> create or replace package opt_lock_chksum_demo
  2  as
  3    procedure get_emp_details( p_empno in number,
  4      p_ename in out varchar2, p_sal in out number,
  5      p_row_checksum in out number );
  6    procedure update_emp_info( p_empno in number,
  7      p_new_sal in number, p_new_ename in varchar2,
  8      p_checksum in number, p_num_of_rows_updated in out number );
  9    function calc_checksum( p_empno in number,
 10      p_ename in varchar2, p_sal in number ) return number;
 11  end;
 12  /
```

The two methods in the package, get_emp_details and update_emp_info, perform the
same functionality as the methods with same names in the previous sections. The third
method, calc_checksum, calculates the checksum based on the column names that are
being modified and the primary key column. Let's look at their definitions:

```
scott@ORA10G> create or replace package body opt_lock_chksum_demo
  2  as
```

The following get_emp_details procedure performs a select to get the employee information that can be changed by the user (the ename and sal columns of the emp table). In the same
select, it invokes the calc_checksum method to calculate a unique value based on the values of
the two columns that can be changed and the primary key column empno.

```
  3    procedure get_emp_details( p_empno in number,
  4      p_ename in out varchar2, p_sal in out number,
  5      p_row_checksum in out number )
  6    is
  7    begin
  8      select ename, sal, calc_checksum( empno, ename, sal )
  9      into p_ename, p_sal, p_row_checksum
 10      from emp
 11      where empno = p_empno;
 12    end;
```

The procedure `update_emp_info` gets as parameters the checksum calculated previously along with other parameters. We then use an additional check in the `where` clause of the `update` statement to compare the checksum for current values in the row with the one we calculated previously. We return the number of rows updated as an `out` parameter so that the application can detect whether or not its update went through.

```
14    procedure update_emp_info( p_empno in number, p_new_sal in number,
15      p_new_ename in varchar2, p_checksum in number,
16      p_num_of_rows_updated in out number )
17    is
18    begin
19      p_num_of_rows_updated := 0;
20      update emp
21        set sal = p_new_sal,
22            ename = p_new_ename
23      where empno = p_empno
24        and p_checksum = calc_checksum( empno, ename, sal );
25      p_num_of_rows_updated := sql%rowcount;
26    end;
```

Finally, the function `calc_checksum` calculates the checksum by simply invoking the `owa_opt_pkg.checksum` method, passing in the `ename`, `empno`, and `sal` columns of the current row (I will explain the reason for formatting the `empno` and `sal` columns in a moment):

```
27    function calc_checksum( p_empno in number, p_ename in varchar2,
28      p_sal in number )
29    return number
30    is
31    begin
32      return owa_opt_lock.checksum( to_char(p_empno,'0009')
33          ||'/' || p_ename || '/' || to_char(p_sal, '00009.99'));
34    end;
35  end;
36  /
Package body created.
```

The / separators used are required to take care of `null` values. The formatting we used in the `empno` and `sal` columns is required to ensure that the concatenation result is a unique value for any two different rows. Otherwise, we can have a combination where the individual values being concatenated are different, but the concatenated result is the same, eventually resulting in the same checksum. For example, the checksum for two columns whose values are 12 and 34 in one instance but 123 and 4 in another would be the same if we use simple concatenation, as follows:

```
scott@ORA10G> select owa_opt_lock.checksum( 12 || 34)  from dual;
                  25702
scott@ORA10G> select owa_opt_lock.checksum( 123 || 4)  from dual;
                  25702
```

However, if we apply appropriate formatting based on the data, we will get different values, as follows:

```
scott@ORA10G> select owa_opt_lock.checksum( to_char(12, '0009') ||
to_char(34, '0009'))  from dual;
                        58853
scott@ORA10G> select owa_opt_lock.checksum( to_char(123, '0009') ||
to_char(4, '0009'))  from dual;
                        58598
```

Thus, if we have a date column, date_col, we may have to format it with the format string to_char(date_col, 'yyyymmddhh24miss'), for example. The guiding philosophy in formatting the individual columns is that their concatenated value should be unique for any two different combinations of their individual values.

Let's look at the class DemoOptLockingUsingChecksum, which invokes the preceding package opt_lock_chksum_demo and demonstrates optimistic locking. I will explain the class with interspersed comments as usual. The class begins with import statements and gets the connection as scott in the main() method:

```
/* This program demonstrates optimistic locking using checksum
* COMPATIBLITY NOTE: tested against 10.1.0.2.0.*/
import java.sql.SQLException;
import java.sql.Connection;
import java.sql.CallableStatement;
import oracle.jdbc.OracleTypes;
import book.util.JDBCUtil;
import book.util.InputUtil;
class DemoOptLockingUsingChecksum
{
  public static void main(String args[]) throws Exception
  {
    Connection conn = null;
    try
    {
      conn = JDBCUtil.getConnection( "scott", "tiger", "ora10g" );
```

At this point, we again set the variable empNo to Martin's employee number. We invoke the _displayEmpDetails() method to display Martin's details on the imagined UI screen that allows the user to modify the details (the ename and sal column values in our example). The method will return the checksum of the row as well:

```
      int empNo = 7654;
      long rowChecksum = _displayEmpDetails( conn, empNo );
```

We then pause in using our InputUtil.waitTillUserHitsEnter() method, as we did in our earlier examples to simulate a user's think time:

```
      InputUtil.waitTillUserHitsEnter("Row has been selected but is not locked.");
```

At the end of the main() method, we invoke the _updateEmpInfo() method with the employee number, the new salary value, the new name, and the checksum we calculated earlier. This method simply invokes opt_lock_chksum_demo.update_emp_info. We close the connection in the finally clause as usual:

```
    _updateEmpInfo( conn, empNo, 1450, "MARTIN", rowChecksum );
  }
  finally
  {
    JDBCUtil.close ( conn );
  }
}// end of main
```

The following definitions of the methods _displayEmpDetails() and _updateEmpInfo() should be self-explanatory. These methods simply invoke the opt_lock_chksum_demo.get_➥ emp_details and opt_lock_chksum_demo.update_emp_info methods, respectively:

```
private static long _displayEmpDetails( Connection conn, int empNo )
  throws SQLException
{
  CallableStatement cstmt = null;
  long rowChecksum = 0;
  int salary = 0;
  String empName = null;
  try
  {
    cstmt = conn.prepareCall(
"{call opt_lock_chksum_demo.get_emp_details(?, ?, ?, ?)}" );
    cstmt.setInt( 1, empNo );
    cstmt.registerOutParameter( 2, OracleTypes.VARCHAR );
    cstmt.registerOutParameter( 3, OracleTypes.NUMBER );
    cstmt.registerOutParameter( 4, OracleTypes.NUMBER );
    cstmt.execute();
    empName = cstmt.getString( 2 );
    salary = cstmt.getInt( 3 );
    rowChecksum = cstmt.getLong( 4 );
    System.out.println( "empno: " + empNo + ", name: " + empName + ", salary: "
+ salary + ", checksum: " + rowChecksum );
  }
  finally
  {
    JDBCUtil.close( cstmt );
  }
  return rowChecksum;
}
  private static void _updateEmpInfo( Connection conn, int empNo,
int newSalary, String newEmpName, long rowChecksum )
  throws SQLException
```

```
  {
    CallableStatement cstmt = null;
    try
    {
      cstmt = conn.prepareCall(
"{call opt_lock_chksum_demo.update_emp_info(?, ?, ?, ?, ?)}" );
      cstmt.setInt( 1, empNo  );
      cstmt.setInt( 2, newSalary  );
      cstmt.setString( 3, newEmpName  );
      cstmt.setLong( 4, rowChecksum  );
      cstmt.registerOutParameter( 5, OracleTypes.NUMBER );
      cstmt.execute();
      int numOfRowsUpdated = cstmt.getInt( 5 );
      if( numOfRowsUpdated <= 0 )
      {
        System.out.println( "Sorry. Someone else changed the data that you were
trying to update. Please retry." );
      }
      else
      {
        System.out.println( "You have successfully updated the employee
information." );
      }
    }
    finally
    {
      JDBCUtil.close( cstmt );
    }
  }
}// end of program
```

Notice how we again use the number of rows updated to detect whether or not our update was successful. To test the program, we can run it exactly like we ran the program DemoOptLockingBySavingOldValues in two windows in the earlier section titled "Optimistic Locking by Saving Old Column Values."

Optimistic Locking by Using the ora_rowscn Pseudo Column (10*g* Only)

In 10g, Oracle provides you with a pseudo column that allows you to implement optimistic locking without adding a shadow column in your tables or without computing a checksum. The pseudo column ora_rowscn returns the conservative upper-bound *system change number* (*SCN*) of the most recent change to the row. The SCN is a number assigned to a transaction after it is committed. Oracle records this number with the transaction's redo entries in the redo log.

Let's look at a simple example. We create a table, t1, and insert three numbers in it:

```
scott@ORA10G> create table t1 ( x number );
Table created.
scott@ORA10G> insert into t1 values ( 1 );
1 row created.
scott@ORA10G> insert into t1 values ( 1 );
1 row created.
scott@ORA10G> insert into t1 values ( 22);
1 row created.
```

We then select the column x and the pseudo column ora_rowscn from table t1. Since the transaction is not committed yet, the SCN has not been assigned; hence ora_rowscn returns null for all rows.

```
scott@ORA10G> select x, ora_rowscn from t1;

        X ORA_ROWSCN
---------- ----------
        1
        1
       22
```

Let's commit and rerun our query:

```
scott@ORA10G> commit;
Commit complete.
scott@ORA10G> select x, ora_rowscn from t1;
        X ORA_ROWSCN
---------- ----------
        1    4919036
        1    4919036
       22    4919036
```

As you can see, all rows that were committed in this transaction got the same ora_rowscn value. Let's insert another row, issue a commit, and rerun our query:

```
scott@ORA10G> insert into t1 values ( 3 );
1 row created.
scott@ORA10G> commit;
Commit complete.
scott@ORA10G> select x, ora_rowscn from t1;
        X ORA_ROWSCN
---------- ----------
        1    4919036
        1    4919036
       22    4919036
        3    4919038
```

As shown, a different `ora_rowscn` value is set for the last row since it was committed in a different transaction. There is one issue, though. By default, `ora_rowscn` is maintained at a database block level. The problem is that one database block can contain multiple rows. This will not work for us from the optimistic locking point of view, because our pseudo column has to be changed only for the row we update regardless of whether it has other rows in the block it resides in. To demonstrate this issue, we will update one row of table t1 and see how it affects the `ora_rowscn` values selected from the table:

```
scott@ORA10G> update t1 set x = 3 where x =22;
1 row updated.
scott@ORA10G> commit;
Commit complete.
```

We select the `ora_rowscn` values again along with the block number of each row:

```
scott@ORA10G> select x, ora_rowscn, dbms_rowid.rowid_block_number( rowid )
block_number from t1;

         X ORA_ROWSCN BLOCK_NUMBER
---------- ---------- ------------
         1    4919041          508
         1    4919041          508
         3    4919041          508
         3    4919041          508
```

Notice how the `ora_rowscn` value changed for *all* the rows of the table (since they are all in the same database block), even though we updated only one of them. Fortunately, Oracle does provide a way to maintain `ora_rowscn` values at a row level. For this, we need to create the underlying table with the `rowdependencies` option. Let's drop and re-create table t1 and insert some data into it, followed by a select of the `ora_rowscn` values:

```
scott@ORA10G> drop table t1;
Table dropped.
scott@ORA10G> create table t1 ( x number ) rowdependencies;
Table created.
scott@ORA10G> insert into t1 values ( 1 );
1 row created.
scott@ORA10G> insert into t1 values ( 2 );
1 row created.
scott@ORA10G> insert into t1 values ( 22);
1 row created.
scott@ORA10G> commit;
Commit complete.
scott@ORA10G> select x, ora_rowscn from t1;
         X ORA_ROWSCN
---------- ----------
         1    4920043
         2    4920043
        22    4920043
```

All rows have the same ora_rowscn values, since they were inserted in the same transaction. Let's now update one row as before and rerun the select to query ora_rowscn and the block numbers:

```
scott@ORA10G> update t1 set x = 3 where x =22;
1 row updated.
scott@ORA10G> commit;
Commit complete.
scott@ORA10G> select x, ora_rowscn, dbms_rowid.rowid_block_number( rowid )
block_number from t1;
        X ORA_ROWSCN BLOCK_NUMBER
---------- ---------- ------------
        1    4920043          532
        2    4920043          532
        3    4920046          532
```

Notice how the ora_rowscn value of the third row is different from the rest (since it was changed), even though it is in the same block as the other rows. Thus, we can safely use the ora_rowscn column to proxy for the values in our row as long as the underlying tables are created with the rowdependencies option. Note that using the rowdependencies option does cause the row size to increase by 6 bytes due to additional information maintained at the row level.

As of 10*g* Release 1, the use of ora_rowscn has a few restrictions you should be aware of.

- You cannot use ora_rowscn in a query to a view. However, you can use it to refer to the underlying table when creating a view. To understand this, create a view, v1, on table t1:

    ```
    scott@ORA10G> create or replace view v1 as
      2  select x
      3  from t1;

    View created.
    ```

    If you try to select ora_rowscn from it, you will get an error:

    ```
    scott@ORA10G> select ora_rowscn from v1;
    select ora_rowscn from v1
           *
    ERROR at line 1:
    ORA-00904: "ORA_ROWSCN": invalid identifier
    ```

    However, you can refer to ora_rowscn in the view definition itself to overcome this restriction. The view v2 is created with the ora_rowscn pseudo column values as one of its columns:

    ```
    scott@ORA10G> create or replace view v2 as
      2  select x, ora_rowscn
      3  from t1;

    View created.
    ```

The same select should work now:

```
scott@ORA10G> select ora_rowscn from v2;
ORA_ROWSCN
----------
   4920043
   4920043
   4920046
```

- The ora_rowscn pseudo column is not supported for external tables (we covered external tables briefly in Chapter 12).

- You cannot enable rowdependencies for an existing table; you have to drop and re-create the table, which may not be always feasible.

Let's look at an example demonstrating the use of ora_rowscn to implement optimistic locking. The example is similar to the one in the section "Optimistic Locking by Using a Checksum of Modified Column Values," but there are two differences. First, we create another table, my_emp, with the rowdependencies option, and copy into it the data in emp:

```
scott@ORA10G> create table my_emp rowdependencies as select * from emp;

Table created.
```

Next, we create the PL/SQL package opt_lock_scn_demo, which contains the procedure's get_emp_details and update_emp_info methods, this time working on the my_emp table and using an ora_rowscn-based implementation:

```
scott@ORA10G> create or replace package opt_lock_scn_demo
  2  as
  3    procedure get_emp_details( p_empno in number, p_ename in out varchar2,
  4      p_sal in out number, p_ora_rowscn in out number );
  5    procedure update_emp_info( p_empno in number, p_new_sal in number,
  6      p_new_ename in varchar2, p_ora_rowscn in number,
p_num_of_rows_updated in out number );
  7  end;
  8  /

Package created.
scott@ORA10G> create or replace package body opt_lock_scn_demo
  2  as
  3    procedure get_emp_details( p_empno in number, p_ename in out varchar2,
  4      p_sal in out number, p_ora_rowscn in out number )
  5    is
  6    begin
  7      select ename, sal, ora_rowscn
  8      into p_ename, p_sal, p_ora_rowscn
  9      from my_emp
 10      where empno = p_empno;
```

```
11    end;
12
13    procedure update_emp_info( p_empno in number, p_new_sal in number,
p_new_ename in varchar2, p_ora_rowscn in number,
p_num_of_rows_updated in out number )
14    is
15    begin
16      p_num_of_rows_updated := 0;
17      update my_emp
18      set sal = p_new_sal,
19            ename = p_new_ename
20      where empno = p_empno
21        and p_ora_rowscn = ora_rowscn;
22      p_num_of_rows_updated := sql%rowcount;
23    end;
24  end;
25  /
```

Package body created.

The only difference between this package and the package opt_lock_chksum_demo discussed earlier is that here we use the pseudo column ora_rowscn instead of the checksum of modified column values. The Java class that invokes the preceding package to demonstrate optimistic locking would be exactly the same as the class DemoOptLockingUsingChecksum, except that it would use the package opt_lock_scn_demo instead of opt_lock_chksum_demo. Hence, I do not list it here, in order to conserve space.

Comparing Different Optimistic Locking Alternatives

We have covered many alternatives to implement optimistic locking. Which one should you use? Usually the technique that saves the old values and does a simple comparison with the new values is the simplest and generally the best technique. It does make the APIs more complicated, though, since you need to pass the old and new values back and forth. It also adds to the network traffic depending on the number of columns being modified and their size. The technique that calculates the checksum proxies the old column values with a checksum. Checksum calculation can, however, take extra CPU time, and there does exist a tiny chance that the checksum for two different input values is the same. For an existing application, the technique of using a shadow column will work only if it is feasible to change the current tables to add the new columns for an existing application. And using ora_rowscn is feasible only if you are using 10g and you can create (or re-create) your tables with the rowdependencies option.

Pessimistic Locking vs. Optimistic Locking

In most cases, optimistic locking is the best alternative to avoid lost updates for the majority of web applications that use connection pooling. However, it does suffer from the disadvantage that a user may have spent a lot of time making changes, only to be told to try her changes again. Pessimistic locking, on the other hand, is suitable for client/server applications that maintain state across pages.

Summary

In this chapter, you learned about the problem known as "lost updates." You looked at various techniques you can use to solve this problem. Changing the transaction isolation level to SERIALIZABLE can solve the problem in some special cases. The technique of locking the row beforehand (pessimistic locking) solves the problem for cases where you maintain state across pages. Optimistic locking solves the problem by detecting the changes made by another transaction and asking the user to retry his transaction if unsuccessful. In most of the web applications that use connection pooling, optimistic locking is the only real alternative since it does not require the application to maintain connections across pages. You examined several implementations of optimistic locking, and finally briefly compared optimistic and pessimistic locking.

Selected PL/SQL Techniques

In this chapter, we will look at why it is critical for a JDBC programmer working with Oracle databases to learn and master PL/SQL. We will also examine a few PL/SQL techniques that will help you in writing high-performance and more maintainable PL/SQL code.

This chapter is by no means comprehensive in terms of explaining how to exploit PL/SQL fully. For a thorough introduction to PL/SQL, I recommend that you read the excellent Oracle documentation in *Oracle PL/SQL User's Guide and Reference*. For the built-in PL/SQL packages, you can refer to the Oracle documentation in *PL/SQL Packages and Types Reference*. I also highly recommend reading the book *Mastering Oracle PL/SQL* by Connor McDonald (Apress, ISBN: 1-59059-217-4). Chapter 9 of *Effective Oracle by Design* by Tom Kyte (Osborne McGraw-Hill, ISBN: 0-07-223065-7) also gives some very useful PL/SQL techniques.

Further Motivation for Using PL/SQL

In Chapter 2, we looked at an example of why you need to know PL/SQL. We revisited the topic in the section "Where Should Your SQL Statements Reside, in Java or PL/SQL?" of Chapter 6, where you saw ample justification for why you should, in general, encapsulate your database-related logic in PL/SQL and use `CallableStatement` to call the database-related logic from Java (instead of putting your SQL statement strings in your Java code and invoking them using `PreparedStatement`). This strategy implies that you need to be a good PL/SQL programmer if you want to write effective JDBC programs. Note that the underlying philosophy is true even if you don't use Oracle, in which case you need to be proficient in the equivalent procedural language of your database (most prominent database vendors provide such a procedural language). In this section, we will summarize and expand on our list of reasons to use PL/SQL extensively in code.

PL/SQL Is Close to Your Data

PL/SQL is a part of the database. When you access data from PL/SQL you're already connected to the database—you don't need to make separate round-trips for executing multiple SQL statements. PL/SQL and its data structures are also designed up front to be very closely tied with SQL. For example, when you want to declare a variable that stores a value in the column empno of the table emp in the `scott` schema, you can (and should) declare it as follows:

```
l_empno emp.empno%type;
```

This ensures that if in the future you change the data type of the empno column to, say, varchar2(30), your PL/SQL code is insulated from such changes. In the same vein, you can intermingle SQL and PL/SQL freely.

PL/SQL Is Portable

Yes, you heard me right. The reason I make this claim is that if you write your code in PL/SQL, you have ensured that

- Your code can be invoked by any other language that has the ability to connect and talk to Oracle. This includes C, C++, and Java, among other languages.

- Your code is automatically ported to all operating systems to which Oracle is ported (which include most popular flavors of UNIX and Windows).

Those who claim that writing in PL/SQL will tie your code to a database overlook the fact that if you don't exploit a database fully, you're simply not getting your money's worth. If you pursue this strategy, not only does performance suffer but also you'll get code that will give incorrect results when used directly against another database. In most cases, database independence isn't a "real" requirement. Developing code in a database-independent way by restricting developers to use a subset of common features is analogous to a right-handed swordsman fighting a duel with his left hand—odds are that it is a losing fight.

In the relatively rare case you do need to write code that works against different databases, your data access layer should be written using the procedural language of the database (e.g., PL/SQL in Oracle, Transact-SQL in SQL Server, and so on). This way you ensure (among other things) that

- Your code exploits all features of the database and the ones offered by a stored procedure language such as PL/SQL.

- Your Java code is largely independent of the database (assuming you use the SQL92 syntax of invoking procedures from JDBC).

- Your code can be accessed by applications written in any other language and from all the tools that know how to invoke a stored procedure.

PL/SQL Code Is Compact (Fewer Lines of Code)

Compared to code written in Java (or, for that matter, any other language), if a piece of code involves SQL statements, the PL/SQL version is likely to be much more compact. For example, if you want to write a procedure that fetches all employees who have a given job title from the emp table and do some processing on them, in PL/SQL you can write

```
create or replace procedure process_employees( p_job in varchar2 )
is
begin
  for i in ( select * from emp where job = p_job )
  loop
    dbms_output.put_line( 'processing the record of ' || i.ename );
    -- processing code
```

```
   end loop;
end;
/
show errors;
exec process_employees ( 'CLERK' )
```

Notice how the preceding loop implicitly does cursor management for you, such as opening, fetching, and closing the cursor. Try writing the same code in Java—it will require many more lines of code.

Tuning SQL in PL/SQL Is Easier

Tuning SQL written in PL/SQL is quite easy. For example, starting a SQL trace for the PL/SQL code is trivial. For JDBC, you have to have a mechanism to indicate whether or not the code should be traced. Besides, for fixing the code, you need to recompile the Java classes and redeploy them on all your middle-tier machines. In the case of PL/SQL, once you recompile it, the changes are immediately available for every user.

Adding Code to PL/SQL Is Easier

If you want to add another line of code after an insert statement in PL/SQL (say, to log or audit the insert), it is easy. If you were using PreparedStatement, though, you would have to prepare, bind, and execute another statement.

PL/SQL Code May Result in Fewer Round-trips

All related PL/SQL code in a PL/SQL unit involves only one server round-trip. For example, invoking a PL/SQL procedure using a CallableStatement would involve one round-trip no matter how many SQL statements are executed in the PL/SQL procedure. Note that to process any result sets returned, you will still make multiple round-trips based on your fetch size—this is true regardless of the statement class you use in JDBC. If you use PreparedStatement, however, the number of round-trips would be as many as the number of statements you need to invoke (plus any others you need to make to process your result sets).

So far, we've looked at various reasons to use PL/SQL. Let's now look at things that you should watch out for while writing PL/SQL code.

Common Mistakes When Using PL/SQL

Although PL/SQL is a great language, like any language it can be misused. In this section, we'll look at two particularly common scenarios where PL/SQL can be used in a counterproductive manner.

Using PL/SQL When a SQL Solution Exists

SQL must be one of the most underrated and underused tools available to Java programmers in the Oracle database. Most JDBC programmers know how to write simple select, update, delete, and insert statements in Oracle. SQL is much more than that. Over the years and over different versions, Oracle has expanded the capabilities of its SQL engine tremendously. For example, analytic functions are a tremendously powerful feature.

Since the power of SQL is not understood by many JDBC programmers, it is unfortunately a standard practice to code in PL/SQL what can be done in SQL. Almost always, the equivalent code in SQL will outperform that written in PL/SQL. A common example is avoidable row-by-row processing. This happens when, instead of writing a single SQL statement, people write a loop, fetch each record one by one, and process the record. In many cases, the entire loop can—and should—be replaced by a single SQL statement.

Say we want to copy data from one table to another. Let's first create the schema for this example. We create three identical tables—t1, t2, and t3—each with one number column x, which is also the primary key:

```
benchmark@ORA10G> create table t1 ( x number primary key );

Table created.

benchmark@ORA10G> create table t2 ( x number primary key );

Table created.

benchmark@ORA10G> create table t3 ( x number primary key );

Table created.
```

Now we insert 500,000 records into t1 and analyze it to compute statistics for the Oracle optimizer to use:

```
benchmark@ORA10G> insert into t1 select rownum from all_objects,
all_users where rownum <= 500000;

500000 rows created.
```

We gather statistics for table t1 for the Cost Based Optimizer (CBO) to use next:

```
benchmark@ORA10G> begin
  2      dbms_stats.gather_table_stats(
  3          ownname => 'BENCHMARK',
  4          tabname => 'T1',
  5          cascade => true );
  6  end;
  7  /

PL/SQL procedure successfully completed.
benchmark@ORA10G> commit;

Commit complete.
```

Now we need to copy the data in this table to another table. We will look at a PL/SQL solution and a SQL solution. The PL/SQL solution copies table t1's data into table t2 by inserting each row separately:

```
benchmark@ORA10G> -- pl/sql solution
benchmark@ORA10G> declare
  2  begin
  3    for i in ( select x from t1 )
  4    loop
  5      insert into t2 values ( i.x );
  6    end loop;
  7  end;
  8  /

PL/SQL procedure successfully completed.

benchmark@ORA10G> commit;
```

The SQL solution simply uses an insert into select clause to directly perform the insert into t3 with one statement:

```
benchmark@ORA10G> -- sql solution
benchmark@ORA10G> insert into t3
  2  select x
  3  from t1;

38988 rows created.
```

We use the runstats utility to do the comparison as follows. The code begins with marking the start point of a benchmark run by invoking runstats_pkg.rs_start:

```
benchmark@ORA10G> exec runstats_pkg.rs_start;
```

We first invoke our SQL-based solution:

```
benchmark@ORA10G> -- sql solution
benchmark@ORA10G> insert into t3
  2  select x
  3  from t1;

38988 rows created.

benchmark@ORA10G> commit;
```

We mark the middle of the benchmark run and follow it up with the PL/SQL solution. Finally, we invoke runstats_pkg.rs_stop to display the results:

```
benchmark@ORA10G> exec runstats_pkg.rs_middle;

PL/SQL procedure successfully completed.

benchmark@ORA10G> -- pl/sql solution
benchmark@ORA10G> declare
  2  begin
```

```
3    for i in ( select x from t1 )
4    loop
5      insert into t2 values ( i.x );
6    end loop;
7  end;
8  /
```

PL/SQL procedure successfully completed.

benchmark@ORA10G> commit;

Commit complete.

benchmark@ORA10G> exec runstats_pkg.rs_stop(50);
Run1 ran in 5180 hsecs
Run2 ran in 5572 hsecs
run 1 ran in 92.96% of the time

Name	Run1	Run2	Diff
STAT...IMU undo allocation siz	52	0	-52
<-- trimmed to save space -->			
STAT...table scan rows gotten	500,940	3,699,690	3,198,750

Run1 latches total versus runs -- difference and pct

Run1	Run2	Diff	Pct
8,093,305	10,973,079	2,879,774	73.76%

PL/SQL procedure successfully completed.

As you can see, the SQL-based solution took only 93% of the time and consumed only 74% of the latches as compared to the PL/SQL solution. The bottom line is that set operations (i.e., the ones using SQL) are almost always faster than their procedural equivalent in PL/SQL.

■**Note** The preceding benchmark was run against Oracle 10*g*. In Oracle 10*g*, an implicit for loop, such as the one used in the PL/SQL version of the preceding code, uses a technique called *bulk collect* (see the section "Using Bulk Collect") behind the scenes to improve PL/SQL performance tremendously. When I ran the performance benchmark in an Oracle9*i* database, I found that the SQL version ran in 30% of the time and consumed just 3% of the latches in the preceding test case. Of course, you can improve PL/SQL code in 9*i* by explicitly using bulk collect yourself.

Reinventing the Wheel

Another common mistake is to write your own code for what one of the supplied packages or an existing SQL function already does for you. It is well worth the effort to become familiar with the PL/SQL-supplied packages that Oracle provides. Otherwise, you'll end up writing, debugging, and testing code that is already provided by Oracle for you.

Selected PL/SQL Tips

For the remainder of this chapter, we'll look at some useful techniques to improve the performance and maintainability of your PL/SQL code.

Packaging Matters!

You can write your PL/SQL methods as stand-alone functions and procedures, or you can make them part of modular PL/SQL packages. There are several advantages to using PL/SQL packages:

- *Packages break the dependency chain*. This is perhaps the biggest advantage of using packages. In fact, we will go through this benefit in detail in the next subsection.

- *Packages expand the namespace for your procedures and functions*. If you use packages, a method signature has to be unique only within the package. Thus, you have to worry much less about signature clashes with other methods in your application.

- *Packages allow you to hide information and implementation details.* You can declare private methods and variables in a package body. This hides the implementation details from the users of the package and also improves the maintainability of the code tremendously. This is similar to how you declare private variables and define private methods in your Java classes, and declare public interfaces in your Java interfaces.

- *Packages improve the readability and manageability of your code*. Imagine what would happen if all the methods in Oracle's supplied PL/SQL packages were stand-alone. There won't be any decent way to go about looking for a method you need. Fortunately, Oracle supplies its common utility methods in various packages, each catering to a distinct functionality requirement. In this respect, organizing methods in packages is very similar to organizing your files in different directories.

Packages Break the Dependency Chain

Consider three stand-alone procedures, p1, p2 , and p3, such that p2 invokes p1 and p3 invokes p2:

```
benchmark@ORA10G> create or replace procedure p1
  2  as
  3  begin
  4    dbms_output.put_line( 'p1' );
  5  end;
  6  /

Procedure created.
```

```
benchmark@ORA10G> create or replace procedure p2
  2  as
  3  begin
  4    p1;
  5    dbms_output.put_line( 'p2' );
  6  end;
  7  /
```

Procedure created.
```
benchmark@ORA10G> create or replace procedure p3
  2  as
  3  begin
  4    p2;
  5    dbms_output.put_line( 'p3' );
  6  end;
  7  /
```

Procedure created.

The *dependency chain* refers to the fact that p2 depends on p1 and p3 depends on p2. Note that p3 also depends on p1 indirectly. Oracle maintains information in its data dictionary about this dependency chain. Note that this dependency chain may also include schema objects such as tables, views, etc. used by a procedure. Now each time procedure code is changed and recompiled, or a table accessed by the procedure is altered, Oracle makes all the dependent objects invalid in the database. An example will make this clear. Let's first examine the status (valid or invalid) of each of the procedures in the database:

```
benchmark@ORA10G> select object_name, object_type, status
  2  from all_objects
  3  where object_name in( 'P1', 'P2', 'P3' )
  4    and owner = 'BENCHMARK';
```

OBJECT_NAME	OBJECT_TYPE	STATUS
P1	PROCEDURE	VALID
P2	PROCEDURE	VALID
P3	PROCEDURE	VALID

As expected, all three procedures are valid. Let's now make a simple change to the procedure p1 and recompile it:

```
benchmark@ORA10G> -- modify p1 and recompile it
benchmark@ORA10G> create or replace procedure p1
  2  as
  3  begin
  4    dbms_output.put_line( 'p1 modified' );
  5  end;
  6  /
```

Procedure created.

Since p2 and p3 are dependent on procedure p1, Oracle will mark them as invalid in the database, as shown by the following query results:

```
benchmark@ORA10G> select object_name, object_type, status
  2  from all_objects
  3  where object_name in( 'P1', 'P2', 'P3' )
  4    and owner = 'BENCHMARK';

OBJECT_NAME                      OBJECT_TYPE          STATUS
------------------------------   ------------------   -------
P1                               PROCEDURE            VALID
P2                               PROCEDURE            INVALID
P3                               PROCEDURE            INVALID
```

Note that Oracle automatically tries to recompile an invalid procedure (and all other procedures it is directly or indirectly dependent on) the very first time it is invoked. We can see this in action by first executing p2 and rerunning the query to see the status of each procedure:

```
benchmark@ORA10G> exec p2
p1 modified
p2

PL/SQL procedure successfully completed.

benchmark@ORA10G> select object_name, object_type, status
  2  from all_objects
  3  where object_name in( 'P1', 'P2', 'P3' )
  4    and owner = 'BENCHMARK';

OBJECT_NAME                      OBJECT_TYPE          STATUS
------------------------------   ------------------   -------
P1                               PROCEDURE            VALID
P2                               PROCEDURE            VALID
P3                               PROCEDURE            INVALID
```

When we executed p2, Oracle automatically compiled it and ran it. Note, however, that p3 is still invalid. Now, the problem is that if we have a large dependency chain of stand-alone procedures and functions (as may well be the case in a real-life project), then every time a deeply nested procedure is recompiled due to changes, all the procedures depending on it directly or indirectly will become invalid. Oracle will have to recompile each of them as and when they are executed for the first time. Since recompilation is resource-intensive, this can result in performance degradation.

Let's see how packages help mitigate this problem. We re-create the same procedures again, only this time, each of them is in its own package (pkg1, pkg2, and pkg3 contain procedures p1, p2, and p3, respectively):

```
benchmark@ORA10G> -- putting the procedures in a package
benchmark@ORA10G> create or replace package pkg1 as
  2      procedure p1;
```

```
  3  end;
  4  /

Package created.

benchmark@ORA10G> create or replace package body pkg1 as
  2    procedure p1
  3    as
  4    begin
  5      dbms_output.put_line( 'p1' );
  6    end;
  7  end;
  8  /

Package body created.

benchmark@ORA10G> create or replace package pkg2 as
  2    procedure p2;
  3  end;
  4  /

Package created.

benchmark@ORA10G> create or replace package body pkg2 as
  2    procedure p2
  3    as
  4    begin
  5      dbms_output.put_line( 'p2' );
  6      pkg1.p1;
  7    end;
  8  end;
  9  /

Package body created.

benchmark@ORA10G> create or replace package pkg3 as
  2    procedure p3;
  3  end;
  4  /

Package created.

benchmark@ORA10G> create or replace package body pkg3 as
  2    procedure p3
  3    as
  4    begin
```

```
 5        dbms_output.put_line( 'p3' );
 6        pkg2.p2;
 7    end;
 8  end;
 9  /
```

Package body created.

The following query shows that all the packages are valid as expected:

```
benchmark@ORA10G> select object_name, object_type, status
  2  from all_objects
  3  where object_name in( 'PKG1', 'PKG2', 'PKG3' )
  4    and owner = 'BENCHMARK';
```

OBJECT_NAME	OBJECT_TYPE	STATUS
PKG1	PACKAGE	VALID
PKG1	PACKAGE BODY	VALID
PKG2	PACKAGE	VALID
PKG2	PACKAGE BODY	VALID
PKG3	PACKAGE	VALID
PKG3	PACKAGE BODY	VALID

6 rows selected.

Note that in the preceding query results, for each package there are two entries: one for the package specification (the value PACKAGE in the object_type column) and one for the package body (the value PACKAGE BODY in the object_type column). Let's now modify procedure p1 as before and recompile the package body of package pkg1:

```
benchmark@ORA10G> create or replace package body pkg1 as
  2      procedure p1
  3      as
  4      begin
  5        dbms_output.put_line( 'p1 modified' );
  6        pkg1.p1;
  7    end;
  8  end;
  9  /
```

Package body created.

Rerunning our query shows that *none* of the other packages are invalidated:

```
benchmark@ORA10G> select object_name, object_type, status
  2  from all_objects
  3  where object_name in( 'PKG1', 'PKG2', 'PKG3' )
  4    and owner = 'BENCHMARK';
```

OBJECT_NAME	OBJECT_TYPE	STATUS
PKG1	PACKAGE	VALID
PKG1	PACKAGE BODY	VALID
PKG2	PACKAGE	VALID
PKG2	PACKAGE BODY	VALID
PKG3	PACKAGE	VALID
PKG3	PACKAGE BODY	VALID

```
6 rows selected.
```

This is because we only needed to compile the package body of procedure p1. As long as the package specification does not change (and hence is not recompiled), only the objects depending on the package body get invalidated. In this case, package pkg2 is dependent on the package *specification* of pkg1. Similarly, pkg3 is dependent on the package specification of pkg2. Hence, they are both still valid. This exercise demonstrates how packages help break the dependency chain and avoid spending precious Oracle resources on unnecessary compilations.

Next, we will look at some PL/SQL techniques that can help you write high-performance PL/SQL code.

Using Bulk Operations to Boost Performance

In a previous chapter, you learned about collections. You saw in that chapter why using nested table and varrays as columns in a table is not a good idea in general. However, collections can be very useful when implementing array operations in PL/SQL. This section covers some of these techniques.

Using Bulk Collect

The bulk collect clause allows you to fetch more than one row of a table into a collection variable in a single statement. Using bulk collect, you reduce the number of server round-trips because you are fetching more data per round-trip. You will run these examples in Oracle9*i*, since Oracle 10*g* automatically bulk fetches 100 rows at a time when you use an implicit for loop cursor (code that looks like for x in (select * from emp)).

Let's look at an example. In the following code snippet, we first create a nested table of varchar2(30):

```
benchmark@ORA92I> create or replace type object_name_list as table of varchar2(30);
  2  /
```

```
Type created.
```

Next, we select ten object names from all_objects into the collection using the bulk collect clause (highlighted in bold) and print them out:

```
benchmark@ORA92I> declare
  2      l_object_name_list object_name_list;
  3  begin
  4      select object_name
```

```
  5      bulk collect into l_object_name_list
  6      from all_objects
  7      where rownum <= 10;
  8
  9      for i in 1..l_object_name_list.count
 10      loop
 11         dbms_output.put_line( l_object_name_list( i ) );
 12      end loop;
 13   end;
 14   /
DUAL
<-- 9 more rows - results trimmed to save space -->

PL/SQL procedure successfully completed.
```

Be aware that selecting a large number of records into your collection in one shot using the preceding syntax can exhaust server-side memory. In such cases, you can use an explicit cursor syntax with a limit clause as illustrated in the following code snippet. First, we declare a cursor that selects 3,000 object IDs from the all_objects table:

```
benchmark@ORA92I> declare
  2      cursor c_object_ids is
  3        select object_id
  4        from all_objects
  5        where rownum <= 3000;
```

Instead of using a SQL type as we did in the previous example, we use a PL/SQL type (we could have used a SQL type also). We declare the PL/SQL type and a variable of its type followed by a loop counter variable:

```
  6      type number_table is table of number index by binary_integer;
  7      l_object_id_list number_table;
  8      l_counter number := 0;
```

We begin our logic by opening the cursor and bulk collecting the object IDs into the array l_object_id_list. Note that we use the limit clause (shown in bold in the following code) so that at a time, we will only fetch 200 records to avoid straining database memory:

```
  9   begin
 10      open c_object_ids;
 11      loop
 12        fetch c_object_ids bulk collect into l_object_id_list limit 200;
```

The remaining code is straightforward. We loop through the array contents, printing them out. We also increment our loop counter to store the total number of records processed. Finally, we have the exit clause that exits out of the loop when we run out of records:

```
 13        for i in 1..l_object_id_list.count
 14        loop
 15           l_counter := l_counter + 1;
```

```
16        dbms_output.put_line( l_object_id_list( i ) );
17      end loop;
18      exit when c_object_ids%notfound;
19    end loop;
20    dbms_output.put_line( 'total fetched: ' || l_counter );
21  end;
22  /
222
<--   results trimmed to conserve space   -->
6409
total fetched: 3000

PL/SQL procedure successfully completed.
```

The important point to note is that in cases where you expect a large number of records, you should use an explicit cursor and fetch with a `limit` clause to conserve server-side memory.

■**Note** As mentioned earlier, starting with Oracle 10*g*, as an optimization for an implicit cursor loop (e.g., for a x in (select ...) loop), Oracle silently bulk fetches records 100 at a time by default. The bulk collect technique is still very useful for 9*i* systems and even in 10*g*, if the default limit of 100 rows is not optimal for your particular scenario.

Performance Impact of Bulk Collect

Let's see how bulk collect can improve your code's performance. Recall how in the section "Using PL/SQL When a SQL Solution Exists," the PL/SQL solution involved selecting each row one by one and inserting the rows one by one into the table. The correct solution in that case, as you learned, was to use a single SQL statement. But what if the results have to be output to a file instead of a table? In such a scenario, a SQL statement–based solution isn't feasible; you can use bulk collect to improve performance. Let's compare two cases:

- We select 500,000 numbers from table t1 (created and populated as discussed in the section "Using PL/SQL When a SQL Solution Exists") and output them to a file.

- We bulk collect 500,000 numbers, 500 at a time (the number 500 is passed as a parameter), and output them to a file.

We will use the PL/SQL-supplied package UTL_FILE to write the contents into a file (see the section "Alternatives to BFILEs for File Operations" in Chapter 12 for more details on the UTL_FILE package). To use UTL_FILE, we first need to create a directory object that points to a real operating system directory:

```
benchmark@ORA92I> create or replace directory temp_dir as 'C:\TEMP';
Directory created.
```

Next, we create a procedure called no_bulk_collect that will insert 500,000 numbers selected from t1 without using bulk collect into a file called no_bulk_collect.txt in the directory C:\TEMP. Inside the procedure, we first declare a file handle:

```
benchmark@ ORA92I> create or replace procedure no_bulk_collect
  2  as
  3    l_file_handle utl_file.file_type;
  4  begin
```

Then we open the file, retrieving the file handle into our variable l_file_handle:

```
  5    l_file_handle := utl_file.fopen( 'TEMP_DIR', 'no_bulk_collect.txt', 'W' );
```

We loop through the records, outputting the value of the x column into the file. At the end, we close the file handle:

```
  6    for i in( select x from t1 )
  7    loop
  8      utl_file.put_line( l_file_handle, i.x );
  9    end loop;
 10    utl_file.fclose( l_file_handle );
 11  end;
 12  /
```

```
Procedure created.
```

Now let's create a procedure that uses bulk collect into an array a given number of records (passed as a parameter) at a time, and then loops through the array to output the records. The procedure bulk_collect does just that, outputting the data into a file called bulk_collect.txt:

```
benchmark@ ORA92I> create or replace procedure bulk_collect (
p_limit_per_fetch in number default 100)
  2  as
  3    cursor c_x is
  4      select x
  5      from t1;
  6    l_file_handle utl_file.file_type;
  7    type number_table is table of number index by binary_integer;
  8    l_x_list number_table;
  9  begin
 10    l_file_handle := utl_file.fopen( 'TEMP_DIR', 'bulk_collect.txt', 'W' );
 11    open c_x;
 12    loop
 13      fetch c_x bulk collect into l_x_list limit p_limit_per_fetch;
 14      for i in 1..l_x_list.count
 15      loop
 16        utl_file.put_line( l_file_handle, l_x_list(i));
 17      end loop;
 18      exit when c_x%notfound;
```

```
19    end loop;
20    close c_x;
21  end;
22  /
```

Procedure created.

Next, we run the benchmark using the runstats utility:

```
benchmark@ORA92> exec runstats_pkg.rs_start;

PL/SQL procedure successfully completed.

benchmark@ORA92> exec no_bulk_collect;

PL/SQL procedure successfully completed.

benchmark@ORA92> exec runstats_pkg.rs_middle;

PL/SQL procedure successfully completed.

benchmark@ORA92> exec bulk_collect(500);

PL/SQL procedure successfully completed.

benchmark@ORA92> exec runstats_pkg.rs_stop( 50 );
Run1 ran in 1844 hsecs
Run2 ran in 1058 hsecs
run 1 ran in 174.29% of the time
```

Name	Run1	Run2	Diff
LATCH.row cache enqueue latch	60	4	-56
<-- **results trimmed to conserve space** -->			
LATCH.cache buffers chains	1,006,701	6,071	-1,000,630

```
Run1 latches total versus runs -- difference and pct
Run1              Run2            Diff        Pct
1,045,013         7,586       -1,037,427  13,775.55%
```

PL/SQL procedure successfully completed..

As shown in bold in the preceding listing, the code without using bulk collect took almost twice the amount of time to complete. More important, perhaps, it consumed more than 130 times the latches consumed by the code that used bulk collect. In this case, I chose to use a limit of 500 records at a time; you can find a more optimal fetch limit size by trial and error.

In conclusion, you can see that using bulk collect can significantly increase the performance of your PL/SQL code. You should take care, however, to use an appropriate limit on the number of records fetched in one iteration based on the total number of records and size per record.

Using Bulk Binding

Bulk binding allows you to improve performance of inserts, updates, and deletes in a loop. With bulk binding, you insert, delete, or update tables using values from an initialized collection (such as a varray, a nested table, or associative arrays).

Assuming that l_x_coll is a collection variable, without bulk binding a typical for loop processing that involves an insert may look like

```
for i in 1..x.count
loop
  insert into t1(x) values( l_x_coll(i) );
end loop;
```

Of course, if you can replace the preceding code with a single SQL statement, you should. In many cases, though, you may have some complicated processing on the data before inserting it. Bulk binding can be applied in such cases to improve performance significantly.

When using bulk binding, the preceding syntax changes slightly to

```
forall i in 1..x.count
  insert into t1(x) values( l_x_coll(i) );
```

Thus, instead of the keyword for, we use the keyword forall, and we lose the keywords loop and end loop. The reason forall works faster in most cases is that it avoids switching the context back and forth between PL/SQL and SQL.

To elaborate on this concept further, during execution of PL/SQL code, the PL/SQL engine hands over execution of an embedded SQL statement to the SQL engine. When the SQL statement execution is over, the control passes back to PL/SQL engine, and so on. The overhead of this context switch adds up in a loop such as the one without bulk binding shown previously. In the first for loop, with each iteration the loop counter i needs to be incremented (using the PL/SQL context), and then the insert statement needs to be executed (using the SQL context). Bulk binding avoids this by batching the SQL executions with fewer context switches, thus improving performance.

Performance Impact of Bulk Binding

Let's look at an example that demonstrates bulk binding syntax and also showcases its performance impact. We begin by creating two collection types as follows:

```
benchmark@ORA10G> create or replace type object_name_list as table of varchar2(30);
  2  /

Type created.

benchmark@ORA10G> create or replace type object_id_list as table of number;
  2  /

Type created.
```

Next, we create two identical tables, t4 and t5, with each having an object_name and object_id column from the all_objects table (note that the tables are created empty):

```
benchmark@ORA10G> create table t4 as
  2  select object_name, object_id
  3  from all_objects
  4  where 1 != 1;

Table created.
benchmark@ORA10G> create table t5 as
  2  select object_name, object_id
  3  from all_objects
  4  where 1 != 1;

Table created.
```

Now we create two procedures. The first one is called no_bulk_bind. As its name suggests, this procedure inserts a number of records (35,000) into table t4 without using bulk binding in a simple for loop (pretend that the code cannot be written using a single SQL statement):

```
benchmark@ORA10G> create or replace procedure no_bulk_bind(
p_object_name_list in object_name_list,
p_object_id_list in object_id_list )
  2  as
  3  begin
  4    for i in 1..p_object_name_list.count loop
  5      insert into t4( object_name, object_id) values( p_object_name_list(i),
p_object_id_list(i));
  6    end loop;
  7  end;
  8  /

Procedure created.
```

The second procedure, bulk_bind, uses the forall syntax to insert the same number of records using bulk bind, this time into table t5:

```
benchmark@ORA10G> create or replace procedure bulk_bind(
p_object_name_list in object_name_list,
p_object_id_list in object_id_list )
  2  as
  3  begin
  4    forall i in 1..p_object_name_list.count
  5      insert into t5( object_name, object_id) values( p_object_name_list(i),
p_object_id_list(i));
  6  end;
  7  /

Procedure created.
```

To compare the two utilities, we use the `runstats` utility as usual. We first populate a collection variable with values to be populated into tables t4 and t5, respectively:

```
benchmark@ORA10G> declare
  2    l_object_name_list object_name_list;
  3    l_object_id_list object_id_list;
  4  begin
  5    select object_name, object_id
  6    bulk collect into l_object_name_list, l_object_id_list
  7    from all_objects
  8    where rownum <= 35000;
  9
```

We then execute the `runstats` utility and invoke the two procedures to compare them:

```
 10    begin
 11      runstats_pkg.rs_start;
 12    end;
 13    begin
 14      no_bulk_bind( l_object_name_list, l_object_id_list );
 15    end;
 16    begin
 17      runstats_pkg.rs_middle;
 18    end;
 19    begin
 20      bulk_bind( l_object_name_list, l_object_id_list );
 21    end;
 22    begin
 23      runstats_pkg.rs_stop(10);
 24    end;
 25  end;
 26  /
Run1 ran in 190 hsecs
Run2 ran in 11 hsecs
run 1 ran in 1727.27% of the time
```

Name	Run1	Run2	Diff
LATCH.loader state object free	12	0	-12
<-- **results trimmed to conserve space** -->			
STAT...redo size	9,559,460	1,670,356	-7,889,104

```
Run1 latches total versus runs -- difference and pct
```

Run1	Run2	Diff	Pct
375,873	16,893	-358,980	**2,225.02%**

```
PL/SQL procedure successfully completed.
```

As you can see, the performance of our inserts has increased tremendously. The procedure without the bulk bind took 17 times longer and also consumed 22 times more resources than the procedure with the bulk bind!

A limitation of bulk bind as of Oracle 10g Release 1 is that it does not work with an array of objects. For example, in the preceding scenario, if we wanted to use an array of a single object with object_name and object_id as its attributes, the bulk bind will not work:

```
benchmark@ORA10G> create or replace type object_data as object
  2  (
  3    object_name varchar2(30),
  4    object_id number
  5  )
  6  /

Type created.

benchmark@ORA10G> create or replace type object_data_list as table of object_data;
  2  /

Type created.

benchmark@ORA10G> declare
  2    l_object_data_list object_data_list;
  3  begin
  4    select object_data( object_name, object_id )
  5    bulk collect into l_object_data_list
  6    from all_objects
  7    where rownum <= 5;
  8    forall i in 1..l_object_data_list.count
  9      insert into t5( object_name, object_id) values(
l_object_data_list(i).object_name, l_object_data_list(i).object_id);
 10  end;
 11  /
    insert into t5( object_name, object_id) values(
l_object_data_list(i).object_name, l_object_data_list(i).object_id);
                                                             *
ERROR at line 9:
ORA-06550: line 9, column 53:
PLS-00436: implementation restriction: cannot reference fields of BULK In-BIND
table of records
```

Handling Errors in Bulk Binding

Since during bulk bind operations we process many rows at a time, if one or more rows result in an error, the entire operation is rolled back, but the exception information raised does not tell us which rows were at fault. Consider the following table, t6, in which we cannot insert null values in column x. We also have a check constraint such that only values between 1 and 10 (including 10) can be inserted:

```
benchmark@ORA10G> create table t6( x number primary key constraint
check_nonnegative_lt_10 check( x > 0  and x <= 10 )) ;
```

Table created.

We then declare a PL/SQL array of numbers and store ten values in it, three of which (null, -5, and 11) are invalid if inserted into t6. When we insert the array values into table t6, we get a single array message for the first erroneous value (null) in the array:

```
benchmark@ORA10G> declare
  2    type number_table is table of number;
  3    l_number_table number_table;
  4  begin
  5    l_number_table := number_table( 1, 2, 3, null, -5, 6, 7, 8, 9, 11);
  6    forall i in 1..l_number_table.count
  7      insert into t6( x ) values ( l_number_table(i) );
  8  end;
  9  /
declare
*
ERROR at line 1:
ORA-01400: cannot insert NULL into ("BENCHMARK"."T6"."X")
ORA-06512: at line 6
```

Also, none of the records gets inserted, since the entire operation is rolled back, as shown by the following query:

```
benchmark@ORA10G> select * from t6;
no rows selected
```

When you are inserting data in bulk, your requirement may be to successfully insert good records while getting a list of bad records that you can reinsert after incorporating the necessary corrections. Starting with 9*i*, there is a way to save the exceptions raised during a bulk bind operation and print them out later. This is shown in the following code snippet (the code should work the same in both 10*g* and 9*i*):

```
benchmark@ORA10G> declare
  2    type number_table is table of number;
  3    l_number_table number_table;
  4  begin
  5    l_number_table := number_table( 1, 2, 3, null, -5, 6, 7, 8, 9, 11);
  6    begin
  7      forall i in 1..l_number_table.count save exceptions
  8        insert into t6( x ) values ( l_number_table(i) );
  9    exception
 10      when others then
 11        dbms_output.put_line( 'number of exceptions raised: ' ||
sql%bulk_exceptions.count );
 12        for i in 1..sql%bulk_exceptions.count loop
 13          dbms_output.put_line( 'row number : ' ||
```

```
sql%bulk_exceptions(i).error_index );
 14            dbms_output.put_line( 'error code: ' ||
sql%bulk_exceptions(i).error_code );
 15            dbms_output.put_line( 'message: ' || sqlerrm(
-sql%bulk_exceptions(i).error_code ));
 16
 17        end loop;
 18    end;
 19  end;
 20  /
number of exceptions raised: 3
row number : 4
error code: 1400
message: ORA-01400: cannot insert NULL into ()
row number : 5
error code: 2290
message: ORA-02290: check constraint (.) violated
row number : 10
error code: 2290
message: ORA-02290: check constraint (.) violated

PL/SQL procedure successfully completed.
```

We use the save `exceptions` option in the `forall` operation in the preceding code to save the exceptions and continue with inserting other records. This results in PL/SQL storing any exceptions raised in an internal collection called `sql%bulk_exceptions`. From this collection, we can get the culprit row indices as well as the error codes for any exceptions raised during the `forall` operation. Using `sqlerrm`, we can then also print the error message. Since we handled the exception, all the valid records are retained as verified by the following query:

```
benchmark@ORA10G> select * from t6;

         X
----------
         1
         2
         3
         6
         7
         8
         9

7 rows selected.
```

We can conclude that bulk binding can improve the performance of our code tremendously, at the cost of some code complexity. We can also save any exceptions raised using save `exceptions` to achieve a more granular level of error handling.

Preferring Static SQL over Dynamic SQL

Static SQL in PL/SQL is SQL that is embedded in your code and hence is known to the PL/SQL engine at compile time. Dynamic SQL in PL/SQL is SQL in which the SQL statement and its bind value placeholders are contained in a string and are not known to the PL/SQL engine at compile time. For example, the procedure static_proc uses static SQL to count the number of records in table t1:

```
benchmark@ORA10G> create or replace procedure static_proc( p_count in out number )
  2  is
  3  begin
  4    select count(*)
  5    into p_count
  6    from t1 static;
  7  end;
  8  /

Procedure created.
```

And the procedure dynamic_proc does the same thing using dynamic SQL:

```
benchmark@ORA10G> create or replace procedure dynamic_proc( p_count in out number )
  2  is
  3  begin
  4    execute immediate 'select count(*) from t1 dynamic ' into p_count;
  5  end;
  6  /

Procedure created.
```

When you have a choice between using static SQL and dynamic SQL, you should use static SQL. Static SQL tends to be faster, as shown by the following benchmark run:

```
benchmark@ORA10G> declare
  2    l_count number;
  3  begin
  4    begin
  5      runstats_pkg.rs_start;
  6    end;
  7    for i in 1..1000
  8    loop
  9      static_proc( l_count );
 10    end loop;
 11    begin
 12      runstats_pkg.rs_middle;
 13    end;
 14    for i in 1..1000
 15    loop
 16      dynamic_proc( l_count );
 17    end loop;
```

```
18      begin
19         runstats_pkg.rs_stop( 50 );
20      end;
21   end;
22   /
Run1 ran in 4137 hsecs
Run2 ran in 4590 hsecs
run 1 ran in 90.13% of the time
```

Name	Run1	Run2	Diff
STAT...buffer is pinned count	62	0	-62
<-- **results trimmed to conserve space** -->			
STAT...session pga memory	65,536	0	-65,536
STAT...session pga memory max	131,072	65,536	-65,536

```
Run1 latches total versus runs -- difference and pct
Run1                 Run2              Diff        Pct
1,852,564            1,865,552         12,988      99.30%

PL/SQL procedure successfully completed.
```

The static SQL version ran in 90% of the time as compared to the dynamic SQL version.

■**Note** Once again, in 10*g*, there is an optimization due to which code written using dynamic SQL (as in the preceding example) in a loop is soft parsed, in general, only once instead of every time in the loop. Since this optimization was not present in 9*i*, the difference between static and dynamic SQL performance is even more pronounced in favor of static SQL. For example, against my Oracle9*i* Release 2, the static SQL version in the example ran in 77% of time and consumed 67% of latches as compared to the dynamic SQL version.

The following are some reasons besides performance to prefer static SQL:

- Static SQL is checked during compile time, so more errors are caught during compilation time, making the code more robust.

- With static SQL, the code dependency information (e.g., which procedure is dependent on which other procedure or table, etc.) is stored in the data dictionary. With dynamic SQL, this is not the case.

- Code written using static SQL is more readable and maintainable in general than code written in dynamic SQL. It is easier to add to static SQL code as compared to dynamic SQL code.

Thus, in general, you should use dynamic SQL only when you cannot use static SQL to get your job done.

■Note All SQL submitted from JDBC is "dynamic." This is clear from the fact that to find a syntax error in the SQL string, you need to run the program. The only way to take advantage of static SQL from JDBC is to use PL/SQL and invoke it from the `CallableStatement` interface.

Returning Data via a Ref Cursor

When you select multiple records in PL/SQL and return them back to the client (in our case, a JDBC program), generally you have two options:

- Build an array of records, store all the rows in the array, and return the array of records to the JDBC client program.

- Return a ref cursor, which can be retrieved as a `ResultSet` in JDBC.

Out of the two options, using a ref cursor is preferable because

- You need to do less work. Instead of storing all records in an array on the server (requiring memory on the server side), and retrieving it again in another set of records in your JDBC program (requiring memory on the client side), you simply return a pointer to the cursor, which can be retrieved as a result set.

- If you retrieve the data as a result set, it is easy to control the number of round-trips by setting the fetch size, as you learned in the section "Prefetching" of Chapter 7.

- Your JDBC code is simpler when you use a result set.

Understanding the Invoker Rights and Definer Rights Modes

Your PL/SQL code can be written using one of the two modes: definer rights or invoker rights. From a security and performance point of view, it is critical to understand these two modes while designing your PL/SQL code. This section gives an overview of what these modes are and when to use each. The concepts and examples in this section refer only to stand-alone procedures, but they are also applicable to stand-alone functions, as well as to procedures and functions in packages. Let's start by defining some related terms:

- *Object name resolution* is the process by which Oracle determines which schema object (table, view, etc.) you are referring to in your SQL statements. For example, when you refer to the emp object in the scott schema, object name resolution is the process by which Oracle identifies that emp refers to a table owned by scott. Database objects are typically resolved to a schema object owned by the user or to a public synonym.

- The *definer* of a procedure is the database user who defines and owns the procedure.

- The *invoker* of a procedure is the database user who is not an owner of a procedure but invokes (executes) the procedure.

- *Definer rights mode* is the default mode of creating a procedure. In this mode, Oracle uses the security privileges and object name resolution of the definer (or the owner) of a PL/SQL procedure during compilation and execution of your PL/SQL procedure. Under definer rights mode, PL/SQL procedures compile and run with *directly granted privileges* only. This means that any privileges granted to the procedure owner via a role are not available. In other words, all roles are disabled when you compile and execute a procedure that is created with definer rights mode.

- *Invoker rights mode* is the nondefault mode of creating a procedure. In this mode, at compilation time things work as in the case of procedures created in definer rights mode. However, during *execution* time, the database uses the privileges and object resolution of the *invoker* of the procedure.

You may be a little confused at this point, especially if this is the first time you have encountered these definitions. The code example in this section should clarify these concepts for you. In our code example, we will create three users:

- db_app_data: This user will contain a table, t1, along with a public synonym.

- definer: This user will demonstrate definer rights concepts.

- invoker: This user will demonstrate invoker rights concepts.

We begin by connecting as sys, creating the db_app_data user, and granting the appropriate privileges:

```
sys@ORA10G> create user db_app_data identified by db_app_data default tablespace users quota
  2  unlimited on users;

User created.

sys@ORA10G> grant create session,
  2        create table,
  3        create public synonym,
  4        drop public synonym
  5        to db_app_data;

Grant succeeded.
```

We then connect as db_app_data and create table t1, inserting the numbers 1 to 5 in it:

```
sys@ORA10G> conn db_app_data/db_app_data
Connected.

db_app_data@ORA10G> create table t1 ( x number );
```

```
Table created.

db_app_data@ORA10G> insert into t1 select rownum from all_objects where rownum <= 5;

5 rows created.
```

Next, we create a public synonym for this table:

```
db_app_data@ORA10G> create public synonym t1 for t1;

Synonym created.
```

Connecting back as sys, we create a role called demo_role with the select privilege on table t1. We will use this role to demonstrate how roles are disabled for a definer rights procedure.

```
sys@ORA10G> create role demo_role;

Role created.

sys@ORA10G> grant select on t1 to demo_role;

Grant succeeded.
```

We now create a user called definer and grant this user the appropriate privileges:

```
sys@ORA10G> create user definer identified by definer default tablespace users quota
  2  unlimited on users;

User created.

sys@ORA10G> grant create session,
  2         create table,
  3         create procedure
  4         to definer;

Grant succeeded.
```

We also grant demo_role (which has the select privilege on t1) to the user definer:

```
sys@ORA10G> grant demo_role to definer;

Grant succeeded.
```

Let's summarize what we've done so far. We created a user, db_app_data, that owns a table, t1. Table t1 has a public synonym called t1. We have a role called demo_role, which has the select privilege on t1. We also created a user, definer, who has been granted the role demo_role.

Now we connect as `definer` and run an anonymous PL/SQL block that selects and prints the number of rows in `t1`:

```
sys@ORA10G> conn definer/definer
Connected.

definer@ORA10G> -- select from t1 in anonymous block.
definer@ORA10G> declare
  2    l_count number;
  3  begin
  4    select count(*)
  5    into l_count
  6    from t1;
  7    dbms_output.put_line( 'Count is : ' || l_count );
  8  end;
  9  /
Count is : 5

PL/SQL procedure successfully completed.
```

As you can see, the anonymous block ran successfully because the user `definer` has select privileges on `t1` via the role `demo_role`. Let's now try and put the same logic in a procedure, `definer_mode_proc`, and compile it (remember, by default the procedure is created in definer rights mode):

```
definer@ORA10G> create or replace procedure definer_mode_proc
  2  is
  3    l_count number;
  4  begin
  5    select count(*)
  6    into l_count
  7    from t1;
  8    dbms_output.put_line( 'Count is : ' || l_count );
  9  end;
 10  /

Warning: Procedure created with compilation errors.

definer@ORA10G> show errors;
Errors for PROCEDURE DEFINER_MODE_PROC:

5/3      PL/SQL: SQL Statement ignored
7/8      PL/SQL: ORA-00942: table or view does not exist
```

What happened? Apparently, procedure `definer_mode_proc` cannot select from table `t1` even though it has a select privilege on the table. The problem is that in definer rights mode, all roles are disabled for a procedure (which is not the case for anonymous blocks). Remember that the select privilege on `t1` was granted to the user `definer` via the role `demo_role`. Thus, for a procedure created with definer rights to work, requisite privileges on all objects it accesses have to be granted *directly* to the user that defined the procedure.

Let's now grant the select privilege directly to the user definer after connecting as sys:

```
sys@ORA10G> grant select on t1 to definer;

Grant succeeded.
```

If we now compile the same procedure, it should compile just fine:

```
sys@ORA10G> conn definer/definer;
Connected.

definer@ORA10G> -- now the following will compile
definer@ORA10G> create or replace procedure definer_mode_proc
  2  is
  3    l_count number;
  4  begin
  5    select count(*)
  6    into l_count
  7    from t1;
  8    dbms_output.put_line( 'Count is : ' || l_count );
  9  end;
 10  /

Procedure created.
```

To summarize, by default when you create a procedure, it is created in definer rights mode. In this mode, all roles are disabled, hence the privileges on the accessed objects have to be granted directly to the user who owns the procedure.

Let's now look at how to create procedures in invoker rights mode. We first create another user called invoker with the appropriate privileges:

```
sys@ORA10G> create user invoker identified by invoker default tablespace users quota
  2  unlimited on users;

User created.

sys@ORA10G> grant create session,
  2         create table,
  3         create procedure
  4         to invoker;

Grant succeeded.
```

We also grant the role demo_role to the user invoker. Thus, the user invoker has select privileges on table t1 via demo_role:

```
sys@ORA10G> grant demo_role to invoker;

Grant succeeded.
```

We now connect as the user invoker and try to create a procedure, invoker_mode_proc, that prints the number of rows in table t1. The procedure is created in invoker rights mode by specifying the keyword authid current_user as shown highlighted in the following code (authid definer, which is the default, specifies that the procedure be created in definer rights mode):

```
sys@ORA10G> conn invoker/invoker
Connected.
```

```
invoker@ORA10G> create or replace procedure invoker_mode_proc
  2  authid current_user
  3  is
  4    l_count number;
  5  begin
  6    select count(*)
  7    into l_count
  8    from t1;
  9    dbms_output.put_line( 'Count is : ' || l_count );
 10  end;
 11  /
```

```
Warning: Procedure created with compilation errors.
```

```
invoker@ORA10G> show errors;
Errors for PROCEDURE INVOKER_MODE_PROC:
```

```
6/3      PL/SQL: SQL Statement ignored
8/8      PL/SQL: ORA-00942: table or view does not exist
```

The procedure fails to compile again. This is because during *compilation* time, even for a procedure created with invoker rights, roles are disabled. To compile the preceding procedure, we need to use dynamic SQL as follows:

```
invoker@ORA10G> create or replace procedure invoker_mode_proc
  2  authid current_user
  3  is
  4    l_count number;
  5  begin
  6    execute immediate 'select count(*) from t1' into l_count;
  7    dbms_output.put_line( 'Count is : ' || l_count );
  8  end;
  9  /
```

```
Procedure created.
```

When this code is executed, we get the correct answer. This is because, during execution, the roles were enabled, as we had created the procedure with invoker rights. Hence, the procedure runs successfully:

```
invoker@ORA10G> exec invoker_mode_proc
Count is : 5
```

Note that if you use dynamic SQL with the definer rights procedure, you'll be able to compile the code, but you'll get a runtime error if you don't have direct privileges on the accessed object. To demonstrate this, let's connect as sys and revoke the direct select privilege on t1 from the user definer:

```
sys@ORA10G> revoke select on t1 from definer;

Revoke succeeded.
```

If we now connect back as the user definer and try to compile the procedure definer_mode_proc, which now uses dynamic SQL, the compilation will work:

```
sys@ORA10G> conn definer/definer
Connected.

definer@ORA10G

definer@ORA10G> create or replace procedure definer_mode_proc
  2  is
  3    l_count number;
  4  begin
  5    execute immediate 'select count(*) from t1' into l_count;
  6    dbms_output.put_line( 'Count is : ' || l_count );
  7  end;
  8  /

Procedure created.
```

However, when we execute the procedure, since roles are disabled, we will get an error:

```
definer@ORA10G> execute definer_mode_proc
BEGIN definer_mode_proc; END;

*
ERROR at line 1:
ORA-00942: table or view does not exist
ORA-06512: at "DEFINER.DEFINER_MODE_PROC", line 5
ORA-06512: at line 1
```

This example demonstrates how invoker rights procedures differ from definer rights procedures in terms of roles being enabled or disabled during program execution. Let's look at another example to see how these two modes differ in terms of object resolution.

Say we want to write a generic routine that will return the number of rows of a given table or view. We do not want to create this procedure in multiple schemas—we want to create it once and let others share the same code. For such generic code, it is a good idea to create a separate schema. We create one called utils as follows:

```
sys@ORA10G> create user utils identified by utils;

User created.

sys@ORA10G> grant create session,
  2          create procedure,
  3          create public synonym,
  4          drop public synonym
  5          to utils;

Grant succeeded.
```

We now connect as utils and create a function, count_rows(), that takes a table name as a parameter and uses dynamic SQL to return the number of rows:

```
utils@ORA10G> create or replace function count_rows( p_table_name in varchar2 )
  2    return number
  3    is
  4      l_count number;
  5    begin
  6      execute immediate 'select count(*) from ' || p_table_name into l_count;
  7      return l_count;
  8    end;
  9  /

Function created.
```

Since we want this function to be used by other schemas, we create a public synonym and also grant the execute privilege on this function to public:

```
utils@ORA10G> grant execute on count_rows to public;

Grant succeeded.

utils@ORA10G> create public synonym count_rows for count_rows;

Synonym created.
```

We test the function by running it on the dual table and the all_users view:

```
utils@ORA10G> exec dbms_output.put_line( count_rows( 'dual' ) )
1

PL/SQL procedure successfully completed.

utils@ORA10G> exec dbms_output.put_line( count_rows( 'all_users' ) )
51

PL/SQL procedure successfully completed.
```

Now we connect back as the db_app_data user and try to run the same program for table t1:

```
utils@ORA10G> conn db_app_data/db_app_data
Connected.

db_app_data@ORA10G> exec dbms_output.put_line( count_rows( 't1' ) )
BEGIN dbms_output.put_line( count_rows( 't1' ) ); END;

*
ERROR at line 1:
ORA-00942: table or view does not exist
ORA-06512: at "UTILS.COUNT_ROWS", line 6
ORA-06512: at line 1
```

Although db_app_data is able to select from table t1 (recall that t1 is owned by db_app_data), the function count_rows fails to find the table. A careful look at the error message (see the highlighted portion of the code) shows that the function is trying to access table t1 in the schema utils where it was originally defined. This is because when we create a procedure in definer rights mode (which is how we created this function), all objects are resolved within the scope of the definer schema at compile time. The solution is to re-create the function with invoker rights:

```
db_app_data@ORA10G> -- re-create the procedure in invoker rights mode
db_app_data@ORA10G> conn utils/utils
Connected.
utils@ORA10G> create or replace function count_rows( p_table_name in varchar2 )
  2   return number
  3   authid current_user
  4   is
  5     l_count number;
  6   begin
  7     execute immediate 'select count(*) from ' || p_table_name into l_count;
  8     return l_count;
  9   end;
 10  /

Function created.
```

If we now execute the function as db_app_data, it works like a charm:

```
utils@ORA10G> conn db_app_data/db_app_data
Connected.

db_app_data@ORA10G> exec dbms_output.put_line( count_rows( 't1' ) )
5

PL/SQL procedure successfully completed.
```

Invoker rights mode is very useful in creating generic routines that need to resolve the objects with the privileges of the invoker of the routine at runtime.

When to Use Definer Rights Mode

Definer rights mode is the default mode in which procedures are created. The majority of your code should use definer rights mode, which has the following advantages:

- Definer rights mode encourages the use of shared SQL in the shared pool, which leads to better scalability. Recall that all the information that Oracle needs to parse the SQL in a definer rights procedure is available at compile time. For example, if you are logged in as scott and refer to the table emp (e.g., in select * from emp), Oracle *knows* that you are always going to refer to table emp owned by scott; thus, Oracle can share the same SQL for all users in its shared pool, which results in less parsing and improved scalability.

  This is not the case if the procedure is written using invoker rights mode. In this case, if you are executing the procedure as scott, you are referring to scott.emp, and if you are executing as blake, you are referring to blake.emp. Moreover, if you change your environment (e.g., set a different role in the same session), Oracle will have to reparse the SQL statement. This can lead to reduced scalability.

- Definer rights mode enables you to write PL/SQL code that allows end users to manipulate data in tables without having direct access to them. All the users' data manipulations go through your PL/SQL code, and as long as your code ensures data integrity, your data is safe.

When to Use Invoker Rights Mode

You'll commonly use invoker rights mode when you're writing generic routines, as you saw earlier with the example function count_rows.

PL/SQL Debugging

Debugging in PL/SQL gets a lot easier when you follow some of the well-known tenets of defensive programming in any programming language. Two of the important tenets are

- Use good exception handling practices.
- Instrument your code extensively.

This section doesn't go into detail about these practices, which are covered well in many PL/SQL books, including Chapter 10 of Connor McDonald's *Mastering Oracle PL/SQL* (Apress, ISBN: 1-59059-217-4). Instead, we will focus on two related topics:

- How to print an execution stack trace in PL/SQL

- How to instrument your PL/SQL and JDBC code using a custom PL/SQL package such that you can see your Java and PL/SQL instrumentation messages in the same database session, in the order in which they were executed

Printing a Stack Trace in PL/SQL

In Java, it's easy to print a full stack trace of an exception when you catch one. Consider the following program, DemoJavaStackTrace. The main() method simply calls function p1, which in turn calls function p2. Function p2 calls function p3, where we divide 1 by 0 to raise an exception. We handle the exception in the main() method and print the stack trace:

```java
/* This program simply generates a divide-by-zero error and prints the stack
trace.*/
class DemoJavaStackTrace
{
  public static void main(String args[])
  {
    try
    {
      p1();
    }
    catch( Exception e )
    {
      e.printStackTrace();
    }
  } // end of main()
  static void p1()
  {
    System.out.println("in p1" );
    p2();
  }
  static void p2()
  {
    System.out.println("in p2" );
    p3();
  }
  static void p3()
  {
    System.out.println("in p3" );
    int x = 1/0; // will cause an exception
  }
} // end of program
```

The output of the program is as follows:

```
B:>java DemoJavaStackTrace
in p1
in p2
in p3
java.lang.ArithmeticException: / by zero
        at DemoJavaStackTrace.p3(DemoJavaStackTrace.java:29)
        at DemoJavaStackTrace.p2(DemoJavaStackTrace.java:24)
        at DemoJavaStackTrace.p1(DemoJavaStackTrace.java:19)
        at DemoJavaStackTrace.main(DemoJavaStackTrace.java:9)
```

As you can see, we have the entire stack trace, and it is easy to see the exact line number where the original error occurred.

In PL/SQL this was not as intuitive, at least until 10g. Consider the following set of procedures, p1, p2, and p3, which are roughly the equivalent of the functions p1, p2, and p3 in the preceding Java program. We first create p3, which generates the exception, and p2, which invokes p3:

```
benchmark@ORA10G> create or replace procedure p3
  2  is
  3    l_x number := 0;
  4  begin
  5    dbms_output.put_line( 'p3' );
  6    l_x := 1/ l_x; -- divide by zero
  7  end;
  8  /

Procedure created.

benchmark@ORA10G> create or replace procedure p2
  2  is
  3  begin
  4    dbms_output.put_line( 'p2' );
  5    p3;
  6  end;
  7  /

Procedure created.
```

Our first version of p1 does not handle any exceptions raised, so the exception is propagated all the way to the client:

```
benchmark@ORA10G> create or replace procedure p1
  2  is
  3  begin
  4    dbms_output.put_line( 'p1' );
  5    p2;
  6  end;
  7  /

Procedure created.
```

When we execute procedure p1, we get the entire stack trace printed out:

```
benchmark@ORA10G> exec p1
p1
p2
p3
BEGIN p1; END;

*
ERROR at line 1:
ORA-01476: divisor is equal to zero
ORA-06512: at "BENCHMARK.P3", line 6
ORA-06512: at "BENCHMARK.P2", line 5
ORA-06512: at "BENCHMARK.P1", line 5
ORA-06512: at line 1
```

So far, so good. The problem is that many times, we need to handle an exception (e.g., if we want to execute some "cleanup" code) and print the stack trace (as we did in our Java program). Let's do the same in p1. We'll have an exception handler in p1 that simply catches the exception and throws it again by invoking the built-in procedure raise:

```
benchmark@ORA10G> create or replace procedure p1
  2  is
  3  begin
  4    dbms_output.put_line( 'p1 (with "raise"' );
  5    p2;
  6  exception when others then
  7    raise;
  8  end;
  9  /

Procedure created.
```

This time when we execute the procedure, we don't see the entire stack trace; we see only the line number of the code in the procedure where the exception was handled (in this case, p1):

```
benchmark@ORA10G> exec p1;
p1 (with "raise"
p2
p3
BEGIN p1; END;

*
ERROR at line 1:
ORA-01476: divisor is equal to zero
ORA-06512: at "BENCHMARK.P1", line 7
ORA-06512: at line 1
```

This could be a major headache if you're trying to debug a deeply nested routine invoked by many other routines, and you're trying to figure out where the original error occurred. Thankfully, this problem has been resolved in 10*g* with the introduction of the function `format_error_backtrace` in the supplied package `dbms_utility`. This function returns the entire stack trace string, which you can conveniently print at the point where you catch an exception. The following is procedure p1 modified to use this function:

```
benchmark@ORA10G> create or replace procedure p1
  2  is
  3    l_error_backtrace long;
  4  begin
  5    dbms_output.put_line( 'p1' );
  6    p2;
  7  exception when others then
  8    l_error_backtrace := dbms_utility.format_error_backtrace;
  9    dbms_output.put_line( l_error_backtrace );
 10    raise;
 11  end;
 12  /

Procedure created.
```

When we execute p1 now, we get the entire stack trace as shown in bold. Thus, the function `dbms_utility.format_error_backtrace` is the PL/SQL equivalent of Java's `printStackTrace()` in 10*g*:

```
benchmark@ORA10G> exec p1;
p1
p2
p3
ORA-06512: at "BENCHMARK.P3", line 6
ORA-06512: at "BENCHMARK.P2", line 5
ORA-06512: at "BENCHMARK.P1", line 6

BEGIN p1; END;

*
ERROR at line 1:
ORA-01476: divisor is equal to zero
ORA-06512: at "BENCHMARK.P1", line 10
ORA-06512: at line 1
```

In 9*i*, getting the entire PL/SQL stack trace is not feasible. Instead, you can use the `dbms_trace` utility to get the line number where the exception was raised originally. If you do not have the schema required for this utility installed, you need to install it by executing the file `$ORACLE_HOME/rdbms/admin/tracetab.sql` as the `sys` user. Once you have installed the utility, you can create a generic procedure that will print the original line where the error occurred (not the entire stack trace).

The procedure `print_dbms_trace` (adapted from a related thread on `http://asktom`
`.oracle.com`) follows. To compile this procedure, we need to have `select` privileges on the
sequence `sys.plsql_trace_runnumber` and the table `sys.plsql_trace_events` directly granted
to the owner of this procedure (note that we're running on a 9*i* database now with the same
procedures, p2 and p3, created in the schema already):

```
benchmark@ORA92I> create or replace procedure print_dbms_trace
  2  is
  3    l_runid binary_integer;
  4  begin
  5    select sys.plsql_trace_runnumber.currval
  6    into l_runid
  7    from dual;
  8    for x in ( select *
  9             from sys.plsql_trace_events
 10             where runid = l_runid
 11             and event_kind = 52
 12             order by event_seq DESC )
 13    loop
 14      dbms_output.put_line( 'Exception occurred in source ' ||
 15        x.event_unit ||
 16        ' on line ' || x.event_line );
 17      exit;
 18    end loop;
 19  end;
 20  /

Procedure created.
```

We now modify procedure p1 such that it invokes the preceding procedure,
`print_dbms_trace`, from our exception handler:

```
benchmark@ORA92I> create or replace procedure p1
  2  is
  3  begin
  4    dbms_output.put_line( 'p1 (using dbms_trace - trace_all_exceptions)' );
  5    p2;
  6  exception when others then
  7    print_dbms_trace;
  8    raise;
  9  end;
 10  /

Procedure created.
```

To enable the trace, we need to invoke dbms_trace.set_plsql_trace. Note that in 9*i*, for tracing to work as shown in the following code, we cannot invoke dbms_trace.set_plsql_trace from within the PL/SQL procedure itself—we have to invoke it from outside in a separate anonymous block. In 10*g*, this is not an issue.

```
benchmark@ORA92I> exec dbms_trace.set_plsql_trace(
dbms_trace.trace_all_exceptions );

PL/SQL procedure successfully completed..
```

Now when we execute the PL/SQL procedure p1, we get the following output:

```
benchmark@ORA92I> exec p1
p1 (using dbms_trace - trace_all_exceptions)
p2
p3
Exception occurred in source P3 on line 6
BEGIN p1; END;

*
ERROR at line 1:
ORA-01476: divisor is equal to zero
ORA-06512: at "BENCHMARK.P1", line 8
ORA-06512: at line 1
```

The highlighted line is where the exception originated. To disable the trace, we can invoke the procedure dbms_trace.clear_plsql_trace:

```
benchmark@ORA92I> exec dbms_trace.clear_plsql_trace;

PL/SQL procedure successfully completed.
```

For more details on the dbms_trace package, see the Oracle document *PL/SQL Packages and Types Reference (10g Release 1)*.

Seamless Instrumentation of PL/SQL and JDBC Code

Code instrumentation refers to the idea of sprinkling your code with log messages that will help you in debugging afterward. Note that the instrumentation code should be retained in the production code also; it should not be stripped out. This is because contrary to what many people believe, instrumentation of code is *not* an overhead. Code instrumentation plays a critical part in resolving issues during development, and even more so after the software has been released to the customer. Thus, you should instrument your code as much as possible and leave all instrumentation code in the production version of your software.

Of course, from an implementation point of view, you should make sure that you can turn debugging on and off conditionally to improve performance of the code while running in production. Perhaps there is no better example of this fact than the Oracle kernel code itself, which is instrumented very heavily. It is this instrumentation that enables Oracle support and developers to resolve countless issues during the development, testing, and maintenance of software built on Oracle. You encountered the power of this instrumentation in this book when using `tkprof` in several of the examples. Recall that `tkprof` works on trace files generated by the Oracle kernel's instrumented code.

In this section, we'll first look at the limitations of `dbms_output` as a way to instrument PL/SQL code. We'll then look at a custom debug utility and see how by using this utility we can instrument PL/SQL code and the calling Java code in a seamless manner such that we're able to see debug messages in Java and PL/SQL together in the order they were executed.

Limitations of dbms_output As a Way to Instrument PL/SQL Code

A common way of debugging PL/SQL code is to use `dbms_output.put_line` to print out messages on your SQL*Plus prompt. Although `dbms_output` is very useful in doing ad-hoc debugging, it is not a good way of instrumenting your code. This is mainly because, as of Oracle 10*g* Release 1, `dbms_output` suffers from the following limitations:

- The total amount of text that can be output in one session using `dbms_output` cannot exceed 1,000,000 bytes due to an internal buffer size limit.

- Each line can contain a maximum of 255 characters. This limitation can be overcome easily by writing a wrapper routine that breaks each line into chunks of 255 characters.

- The output shown by `dbms_output` comes to your screen only *after* the procedure completes. This can be frustrating if you have a long-running procedure, since you would rather get real-time feedback as it is happening in the procedure than get a whole bunch of log messages after the procedure has completed. Once again, you can overcome this limitation by writing a wrapper routine that logs your messages into a file on the database server using the `util_file` utility. You can then do a `tail` command (on UNIX systems) to see the action inside the procedure in real time.

■**Note** Oracle 10*g* Release 2 is slated to address some of the issues listed in this section.

A Custom Debug Utility

Let's now look at a custom debug utility that can be used to instrument PL/SQL code. This utility was originally written by Christopher Beck of Oracle Corporation, and its original version is available from the Downloads section of the Apress website (http://www.apress.com) for the book *Mastering Oracle PL/SQL*. In its original form, this utility has the following features:

- It is used to instrument your PL/SQL code.

- It does not have a limit on either the amount of debug information you can output or an individual line (recall that these are the limitations of `dbms_output`).

- It can be output to a file writeable by the database server process. This allows you to see your debug messages in real time using utilities such as `tail` in UNIX.

- It prints useful context information such as a timestamp and the code line number where the debug message was printed, along with the message.

- It can easily be turned on and off based on a flag (just like Oracle tracing can be turned on and off at your discretion).

- It allows you to enable debugging to be turned on at a module level.

For a more detailed description of how this utility works, please see Chapter 10 of the book *Mastering Oracle PL/SQL* (Apress, ISBN: 1-59059-217-4) by Connor McDonald. My enhancements to this utility include addition of the following features:

- In the PL/SQL code, I added another flag that allows you to

  - Turn the debugging off for a particular session.

  - Direct the debugging messages to go only to a trace file on the database.

  - Direct the debug messages so that they are retrievable in the middle tier only (if you chose this option, the debug messages are not logged in the trace file on the database server).

  - Direct the debug messages so that they are retrievable in the middle tier as well as logged in a trace file on the database server.

- Through the Java program JDebug I wrote, you can now invoke this utility from your Java code. The PL/SQL code has been modified to store all debug messages in a *global temporary table* (see the following note). This allows you to get these messages in your Java program and also have an API to instrument your Java code using the debug utility. You will see through some examples the advantages of doing this shortly.

■**Note** In Oracle a *temporary table* is created using the syntax create global temporary table <table_name> <other options>. Temporary tables hold information for the duration of a session or a transaction depending on how they are created. The important thing to note is that data in a temporary table is visible only to the *current session*, even if the current session commits the data. *A session can see only its own inserted data in a global temporary table.* Please see Chapter 6 of Tom Kyte's *Expert One-on-One Oracle* (Apress, ISBN: 1-59059-243-3) for further details on temporary tables. You can also read about them in *Oracle Database Concepts (10g Release 1)*.

You can download the enhanced version of this utility from the Downloads section of the Apress website (http://www.apress.com). To install this utility, you should follow the instructions given in the readme.txt file. The utility installs one package called debug and the schema objects used by this package. In the following section, we'll examine the features of this enhanced utility.

Understanding the debug Interface

Let's take a quick look at the debug package's public interface. We'll then go through some examples of using this package in the next section.

The debug package defines the following four constants (added in the enhanced version):

- `DEBUG_OFF`: Indicates to turn debugging off for this session

- `LOG_FOR_MIDDLE_TIER_ONLY`: Indicates that all debug messages should be retrievable from the middle tier but should not be logged in a trace file

- `LOG_IN_TRACE_FILES_ONLY`: Indicates that the debug messages should be logged only in the trace files (they won't be retrievable in the middle tier)

- `LOG_FOR_TRACE_FILES_AND_MTIER`: Indicates that the debug messages should be both retrievable in the middle tier and logged in a log file

Initializing the debug Package

The package debug defines a method, init, which is invoked to initialize the debugging configuration. This method's signature is as follows:

```
procedure init(
  p_debug_flag  in varchar2 default LOG_IN_TRACE_FILES_ONLY,
  p_modules     in varchar2 default 'ALL',
  p_dir         in varchar2 default 'TEMP',
  p_file        in varchar2 default user || '.dbg',
  p_user        in varchar2 default user,
  p_show_date   in varchar2 default 'YES',
  p_date_format in varchar2 default 'MMDDYYYY HH24MISS',
  p_name_len    in number default 30,
  p_show_sesid  in varchar2 default 'NO' );
```

As you can see, it takes the following parameters:

- `p_debug_flag`: A flag indicating whether the debugging is turned off. If debugging is on, then this flag indicates where the debug messages go (trace file only, middle tier only, or both middle tier and trace file). The parameter can take a value of one of the four constants defined earlier; by default, its value is equal to `LOG_IN_TRACE_FILES_ONLY`, which means that the debug messages will go into a trace file.

- `p_modules`: Defines for which modules the debugging should be turned on. The default value `ALL` specifies that all debug messages should be logged. Instead, you can specify a list of comma-separated procedure names to turn on logging selectively for these procedures. For example, if you supply a value of `PROC1, PROC2`, the debug package will log only messages in these two procedures. This is indeed a very powerful feature of the debug utility.

- `p_dir`: Name of the directory object (not the actual directory) where your debug message file will be created.

- `p_file`: Name of your debug file.

- `p_user`: Name of the user for which you want to turn on debugging (the default is the current user).

- p_show_date: Shows the date prefixed with your message in the final output, if it's set to YES.

- p_date_format: Format of the date shown (this is ignored if p_show_date is set to NO).

- p_name_len: Length of the name of the procedure that gets printed as a prefix.

- p_show_sesid: Indicates if the database session ID should be appended to the prefix that gets printed with the message.

For example, the following invocation instructs that we should log messages for all modules, in the directory pointed to by the directory object TEMP in a file called debug.txt:

```
benchmark@ORA10G> exec debug.init( p_debug_flag => debug.LOG_IN_TRACE_FILES_ONLY,
 p_modules => 'ALL', p_dir => 'TEMP', p_file => 'debug.txt')

PL/SQL procedure successfully completed.
```

Printing the debug Configuration

The following procedure, status, prints out the configuration options we set using the previous init method:

```
procedure status(
  p_user in varchar2 default user,
  p_dir  in varchar2 default null,
  p_file in varchar2 default null );
```

The following is example output from invoking this procedure:

```
benchmark@ORA10G> exec debug.status


Debug info for BENCHMARK
------------------------
DEBUG FLAG:           Debugging output in trace files only
USER:                 BENCHMARK
MODULES:              ALL
DIRECTORY:            TEMP
FILENAME:             debug.txt
SHOW DATE:            YES
DATE FORMAT:          MMDDYYYY HH24MISS
NAME LENGTH:          30
SHOW SESSION ID:      NO

PL/SQL procedure successfully completed.
```

Using f() to Log Messages

The following procedure, f(), is one of the two procedures that you can use to log messages in your PL/SQL code. The first parameter is the message itself, and the remaining ten optional parameters enable you to log messages using C-style %s notation.

```
procedure f(
  p_message in varchar2,
  p_arg1     in varchar2 default null,
  p_arg2     in varchar2 default null,
  p_arg3     in varchar2 default null,
  p_arg4     in varchar2 default null,
  p_arg5     in varchar2 default null,
  p_arg6     in varchar2 default null,
  p_arg7     in varchar2 default null,
  p_arg8     in varchar2 default null,
  p_arg9     in varchar2 default null,
  p_arg10    in varchar2 default null );
```

For example, if you execute

```
benchmark@ORA10G> exec debug.f( 'current user is %s, this is a number: %s',
user, 10 )
```

you will generate the following debug message in C:\TEMP\debug.txt given the current configuration:

```
12082004 104635(     BENCHMARK.ANONYMOUS BLOCK     1) current user is BENCHMARK,
this is a number: 10
```

■**Note** The debug utility supports only the format string %s. But as you can see from this section's example, you can use the format string %s to print strings as well as numbers in your debug messages.

The prefix 12082004 104635 is the date and time we logged this message (using the format that we set, namely MMDDYYYY HH24MISS). The expression BENCHMARK.ANONYMOUS BLOCK   1 tells us that this message was logged in line number 1 of an anonymous block. Note that the term ANONYMOUS BLOCK would be replaced by the procedure name in the case of a stand-alone procedure and a package name in the case of a packaged procedure.

The remaining part of the message is our logged message, with substituted parameters for the username and the number. In this case, we passed two parameters, but we can use debug.f to pass up to ten parameters. If you have to pass more than ten parameters, you can use the procedure fa() described next.

Using fa() to Log Messages

Using the procedure fa( ), you can log messages with as many parameters as you like:

```
procedure fa(
   p_message in varchar2,
   p_args    in Argv default emptyDebugArgv );
```

For example, the following message logs 11 numbers in the message file:

```
benchmark@ORA10G> exec debug.fa( 'This message has 11 parameters: %s, %s, %s, %s,
%s, %s, %s, %s, %s, %s, %s', debug.Argv(1,2,3,4,5,6,7,8,9,10, 11))
```

This results in the following output in the debug.txt file:

```
2082004 110510(      BENCHMARK.ANONYMOUS BLOCK       1) This message has 11 parameters:
1, 2, 3, 4, 5, 6, 7, 8, 9, 10, 11
```

Using clear() to Clear Debug Configuration

Finally, the procedure clear clears the debug configuration corresponding to the passed parameters. Once you invoke this procedure, you will not get any debug messages for the corresponding profile:

```
procedure clear(
   p_user in varchar2 default user,
   p_dir  in varchar2 default null,
   p_file in varchar2 default null );
```

Using get_debug_message() to Get Currently Logged Messages

The function get_debug_message() returns a ref cursor to get all messages logged in the current debugging session. You can use this function to get messages logged from your Java code, for example (as you will see shortly):

```
function get_debug_message return sys_refcursor;
```

Using get_debug_message_flush() to Get Currently Logged Messages and Flush

The function get_debug_message_flush() returns a ref cursor to get all messages logged in the current debugging session, and it deletes these messages from the temporary table where they get stored originally. You can use this function if you want to get messages logged but don't want to see them again the next time you invoke this function in the same session:

```
function get_debug_message return sys_refcursor;
function get_debug_message_flush return sys_refcursor ;
```

Using debug to Instrument PL/SQL Code

Let's look at a quick example of invoking this utility once it's installed. First, we need to create a directory object pointing to a directory where our debug file would be generated:

```
benchmark@ORA10G> create or replace directory TEMP as 'C:\TEMP';

Directory created.
```

In our examples, the debug file will be generated in the directory C:\TEMP. We then initialize the debug utility as follows:

```
benchmark@ORA10G> exec debug.init( p_debug_flag => debug.LOG_IN_TRACE_FILES_ONLY,
p_modules => 'ALL', p_dir => 'TEMP', p_file => 'debug.txt')

PL/SQL procedure successfully completed.
```

This code instructs the debug utility that we want debug messages to be generated for all modules, for the currently logged user (benchmark in this case). We should put the messages in a file called debug.txt in the directory pointed by the directory object TEMP (the operating system directory is C:\TEMP in this example). Every time we call init, it prints the configuration information in the debug.txt file as follows:

```
Debug parameters initialized on 08-DEC-2004 11:05:10
       DEBUG FLAG: Debugging output in trace files only
             USER: BENCHMARK
          MODULES: ALL
        DIRECTORY: TEMP
         FILENAME: debug.txt
        SHOW DATE: YES
      DATE FORMAT: MMDDYYYY HH24MISS
      NAME LENGTH: 30
   SHOW SESSION ID: NO
```

Once we've initialized our debug package with a profile, we can instrument our code. The following snippet creates a procedure, demo_debug, with some instrumentation messages using the debug.f procedure:

```
benchmark@ORA10G> create or replace procedure demo_debug
  2  is
  3  begin
  4    debug.f( 'Inside procedure demo_debug ' );
  5    for i in 1..5
  6    loop
  7      debug.f( '%s, my loop counter = %s: ', 'hello', i );
  8    end loop;
  9    debug.f( 'Exiting procedure demo_debug ' );
 10
 11  end;
 12  /

Procedure created.
```

We then initialize the debugging profile:

```
benchmark@ORA10G> exec debug.init( p_debug_flag => debug.LOG_IN_TRACE_FILES_ONLY,
p_modules => 'ALL', p_dir => 'TEMP', p_file => 'debug.txt')
```

and invoke our procedure demo_debug:

```
benchmark@ORA10G> exec demo_debug

PL/SQL procedure successfully completed.
```

This results in the following debug.txt file being generated in the directory C:\TEMP:

```
Debug parameters initialized on 08-DEC-2004 11:21:56
      DEBUG FLAG: Debugging output in trace files only
            USER: BENCHMARK
         MODULES: ALL
       DIRECTORY: TEMP
        FILENAME: debug.txt
       SHOW DATE: YES
     DATE FORMAT: MMDDYYYY HH24MISS
     NAME LENGTH: 30
 SHOW SESSION ID: NO


12082004 112156(              BENCHMARK.DEMO_DEBUG     4) Inside procedure demo_debug
12082004 112156(              BENCHMARK.DEMO_DEBUG     7) hello, my loop counter = 1:
12082004 112156(              BENCHMARK.DEMO_DEBUG     7) hello, my loop counter = 2:
12082004 112156(              BENCHMARK.DEMO_DEBUG     7) hello, my loop counter = 3:
12082004 112156(              BENCHMARK.DEMO_DEBUG     7) hello, my loop counter = 4:
12082004 112156(              BENCHMARK.DEMO_DEBUG     7) hello, my loop counter = 5
```

Using JDebug to Instrument Java Code

The program JDebug discussed in this section invokes selected methods in the debug package. It allows you to log messages from your Java code such that your Java message logging has most of the capabilities of the debug package. This includes your Java code's ability to

- Turn off debugging based on a flag.

- Direct your debugging messages (Java and PL/SQL code) so that they can be retrieved in your Java code only, but not output to any trace files.

- Direct your debugging messages (Java and PL/SQL code) to be output on a trace file in the database server.

- Write C-style messages (using the %s format string), and pass up to ten parameters in your Java code.

JDebug is listed here and interspersed with brief explanations. We begin by importing some classes:

```
/* This class is an interface to invoke the debug package from Java.
   This debug package can be downloaded from the Downloads area
   of the Apress website at http://www.apress.com
 */
package book.util;
```

```
import java.sql.CallableStatement;
import java.sql.Connection;
import java.sql.SQLException;
import java.sql.ResultSet;
import oracle.jdbc.OracleTypes;
import book.util.JDBCUtil;
public class JDebug
{
```

The init() method invokes the debug.init() method (explained earlier) to initialize the debugging session:

```
  public static void init ( Connection connection,
    String debugFlag, String modules, String directory,
    String debugFileName, String dbUserName,
    String showDateFlag, String dateFormat,
    int nameLength, String showSessionIDFlag )
    throws SQLException
  {
    CallableStatement cstmt = null;
    try
    {
      cstmt = connection.prepareCall (
        INIT_DEBUGGING_STMT );
      cstmt.setInt ( 1, Integer.parseInt ( debugFlag ) );
      cstmt.setString ( 2, modules );
      cstmt.setString ( 3, directory );
      cstmt.setString ( 4, debugFileName );
      cstmt.setString ( 5, dbUserName );
      cstmt.setString ( 6, showDateFlag );
      cstmt.setString ( 7, dateFormat );
      cstmt.setInt ( 8, nameLength );
      cstmt.setString ( 9, showSessionIDFlag );
      cstmt.executeUpdate();
    }
    finally
    {
      JDBCUtil.close ( cstmt );
    }
  }
```

The clear() method invokes the debug.clear method (explained earlier) to clear the debugging profile information:

```
  public static void clear ( Connection connection,
   String debugFlag, String dbUserName,
    String directory, String debugFileName )
    throws SQLException
  {
```

```
    if( debugFlag == null ||
        debugFlag.equals(DEBUG_OFF) ||
        !_isValidDebugOutputOption ( debugFlag ) )
      return ;
    CallableStatement cstmt = null;
    try
    {
      cstmt = connection.prepareCall ( CLEAR_DEBUGGING_STMT );
      cstmt.setString( 1, dbUserName );
      cstmt.setString( 2, directory );
      cstmt.setString( 3, debugFileName );
      cstmt.executeUpdate();
    }
    finally
    {
      JDBCUtil.close ( cstmt );
    }
}
```

The getDebugMessageAndFlush() method invokes the debug.get_debug_message_flush
method (explained earlier) to get debugging messages logged so far in this session and to
delete them so that they are not retrieved again in the next invocation of this method:

```
public static String getDebugMessageAndFlush ( Connection connection,
  String debugFlag )
  throws SQLException
{
  if( debugFlag == null ||
      debugFlag.equals(DEBUG_OFF) ||
      !_isValidDebugOutputOption ( debugFlag ) )
    return "";

  return _getDebugMessageAndFlush ( connection );
}
```

The printDebugMessage() method invokes the debug.f method (explained earlier) to log
a debugging message from the Java code. It appends the debugging messages from the Java
code with the constant MIDDLE_TIER_DEBUG_MESSAGE_PREFIX defined later in the program. This
allows us to easily distinguish between messages logged in the middle tier and messages coming from our PL/SQL code. Note that we can pass up to ten parameters in messageArguments; if
we pass more, the additional parameters are ignored.

```
public static void printDebugMessage ( Connection connection,
  String debugFlag, String message, String[] messageArguments )
  throws SQLException
{
  if(debugFlag == null ||  debugFlag.equals(DEBUG_OFF) )
    return ;
```

```
   int numOfArgs = 0;

   if( messageArguments != null )
   {
     numOfArgs = messageArguments.length;
     if( numOfArgs >= 10 )
       numOfArgs = 10; // only 10 args supported
   }

   CallableStatement cstmt = null;
   try
   {
     cstmt = connection.prepareCall (
      PRINT_DEBUG_MESSAGE_STMT   );
     cstmt.setString ( 1, MIDDLE_TIER_DEBUG_MESSAGE_PREFIX + message );
     for( int i=0; i < numOfArgs; i++ )
     {
       cstmt.setString ( i+2, messageArguments[i] );
     }
     for( int i=numOfArgs; i < 10 ; i++ )
     {
       cstmt.setString ( i+2, "" );
     }
     cstmt.executeUpdate();
   }
   finally
   {
     JDBCUtil.close ( cstmt );
   }
   return;

}
```

The method `printDebugMessage()` is a convenience function to log messages without any parameter. It invokes the first version of the `printDebugMessage()` function described earlier.

```
public static void printDebugMessage ( Connection connection,
   String debugFlag, String message)
   throws SQLException
{
   if( debugFlag == null ||
       debugFlag.equals(DEBUG_OFF) ||
       !_isValidDebugOutputOption ( debugFlag ) )
     return ;

   printDebugMessage ( connection, debugFlag, message,
     (String[]) null );
}
```

We then define public and private constants that are used by this program. Please see the comments for further explanation of how the constant is used.

```
////////////////  PUBLIC CONSTANTS //////////////////////////
/* the debug flag in the URL should be set to the following value
 * to turn the debug OFF
 * from the URL as a string - wanted to avoid converting to int.
 */
public static final String DEBUG_OFF = "0";
/*
 * enable debugging so that you see the output only in the URL
 * displayed - don't do any trace file generation in the trace
 * file directory.
 */
public static final String  LOG_FOR_MIDTIER_ONLY = "1";
/*
 * enable debugging so that you see the output only in the trace
 *  file directory - don't display the output in the URL.
 */
public static final String  LOG_IN_TRACE_FILES_ONLY = "2";
/*
 * enable debugging so that you see the output the trace
 * file as well as on the URL.
 */
public static final String LOG_FOR_TRACE_FILES_AND_MIDTIER = "3";
/*
 * constant that indicates that debugging is on for all modules.
 */
public static final String ALL_MODULES = "ALL";
/*
 * default directory
 */
public static final String DEFAULT_DEBUG_DIRECTORY = "TEMP";
/*
 * default directory
 */
public static final String DEFAULT_DEBUG_FILE_NAME = "debug.txt";
/*
 * YES
 */
public static final String YES = "YES";
/*
 * NO
 */
public static final String NO = "NO";
/*
 * default date format
 */
```

```
public static final String DEFAULT_DATE_FORMAT = "MMDDYYYY HH24MISS";
/*
 * default name length
 */
public static final int DEFAULT_NAME_LENGTH = 30;
```

The private method _getDebugMessageAndFlush() simply invokes the PL/SQL method
debug.get_debug_message_flush():

```
  private static String _getDebugMessageAndFlush ( Connection connection )
    throws SQLException
{
  StringBuffer result = new StringBuffer ("");
  CallableStatement cstmt = null;
  ResultSet res = null;

  try
  {
    cstmt = connection.prepareCall (
      GET_DEBUG_MESSAGE_AND_FLUSH_STMT );
    cstmt.registerOutParameter( 1, OracleTypes.CURSOR);
    cstmt.execute();
    res = (ResultSet) cstmt.getObject( 1 );
    while ( res != null && res.next () )
    {
      result.append ( res.getString (1) );
      result.append ( HTML_BREAK_TAG );
    }
  }
  finally
  {
    JDBCUtil.close ( res );
    JDBCUtil.close ( cstmt );
  }

  return result.toString();
}
```

The following method validates that the debug flag being used has a valid value:

```
private static boolean _isValidDebugOutputOption ( String debugFlag )
{
  return debugFlag != null &&
    (
      debugFlag.equals( LOG_FOR_MIDTIER_ONLY ) ||
      debugFlag.equals( LOG_IN_TRACE_FILES_ONLY ) ||
      debugFlag.equals( LOG_FOR_TRACE_FILES_AND_MIDTIER ) ||
      debugFlag.equals( DEBUG_OFF )
    );
}
```

The following code defines some private constants with interspersed explanatory comments. The constant HTML_BREAK_FLAG is used to put a line break in the HTML output we generate for our UI pages (as you'll see soon). We use this to separate out different debug statement lines when displaying them in an HTML page being generated by JSP, for example.

```
private static final String HTML_BREAK_TAG = "<br>";
```

The following constant is the SQL statement to invoke the method that gets the debug information emitted by procedures in the debug package (debug.f and debug.fa) and deletes them from the temporary table (where they get stored for a particular database session) after retrieving them:

```
private static final String GET_DEBUG_MESSAGE_AND_FLUSH_STMT =
  "begin ? := debug.get_debug_message_flush; end;";
```

The following constant is the SQL statement to invoke the method that enables debugging:

```
private static final String INIT_DEBUGGING_STMT =
  "begin debug.init ( ?, ?, ?, ?, ?, ?, ?, ?, ? ); end;";
```

The following constant is the SQL statement to invoke the method that disables debugging:

```
private static final String CLEAR_DEBUGGING_STMT =
  "begin debug.clear( ?, ?, ? ); end;";
```

The following constant is the SQL statement to invoke debug.f with the passed message from the middle-tier code. This is useful if you want to get middle-tier layer messages also in the UI screen, for example. Please note that you should invoke this procedure only in debug mode, otherwise the database round-trips can cause performance problems. This version can take a maximum of ten arguments. It supports simple C-style messages.

```
private static final String PRINT_DEBUG_MESSAGE_STMT =
  "begin debug.f( ?, ? ,?, ? ,?, ? ,?, ? ,?, ?, ? ); end;";
```

The following constant defines a prefix to distinguish between messages coming from PL/SQL and messages coming from the middle tier. The messages in the URL that have the following prefix should be coming from the middle tier.

```
private static final String MIDDLE_TIER_DEBUG_MESSAGE_PREFIX =
  "MIDDLE TIER: ";
private static final String MESSAGE_PARAM_ARRAY_NAME = "DEBUG.ARGV";
}// end of program
```

To demonstrate how to use the program JDebug, I wrote another sample program called DemoJDebug, which is as follows with some interspersed comments:

```
/*
 * This class demonstrates how to use the JDebug class
 */
package book.util;
import java.sql.Connection;
```

```
import java.sql.CallableStatement;
import oracle.jdbc.OracleTypes;
import oracle.jdbc.OracleCallableStatement;
import oracle.jdbc.OracleConnection;
import book.util.JDBCUtil;

import java.sql.SQLException;
import java.sql.ResultSet;

public class DemoJDebug
{
  public static void main( String[] args ) throws SQLException
  {
    Connection conn = null;
```

In this program, we direct our output to the trace file and the middle tier, as indicated by the following variable, debugFlag. This means that we will be able to retrieve these messages in the Java code as well as in the trace file on the database server:

```
String debugFlag = JDebug. LOG_FOR_TRACE_FILES_AND_MIDTIER;
```

The default parameters for the init() method are declared and initialized:

```
String dbUserName = "BENCHMARK";
String directory = JDebug.DEFAULT_DEBUG_DIRECTORY;
String debugFileName = JDebug.DEFAULT_DEBUG_FILE_NAME;
try
{
  conn = JDBCUtil.getConnection( "benchmark", "benchmark", "ora10g" );
```

After getting the connection, we initialize the debugging profile by invoking JDebug.init():

```
JDebug.init( conn, debugFlag, JDebug.ALL_MODULES,
  directory,
  debugFileName,
  "benchmark", JDebug.YES, JDebug.DEFAULT_DATE_FORMAT,
  JDebug.DEFAULT_NAME_LENGTH, JDebug.YES );
```

We then log our first message in the middle tier:

```
JDebug.printDebugMessage( conn, debugFlag,
  "Before invoking PL/SQL Code" );
```

We call the method _callDemoDebug(), which in turn will invoke the PL/SQL procedure demo_debug that we discussed earlier. Remember that the procedure demo_debug has been instrumented with debug messages as well using the package debug:

```
_callDemoDebug( conn );
```

Next we log our second (and final) debug message from the middle tier:

```
JDebug.printDebugMessage( conn, debugFlag,
   "Before invoking PL/SQL Code" );
```

We then print out the logged debug messages using JDebug.getDebugMessageAndFlush(). Note that this function would have been a no-op (a null operation) if we had not configured it to retrieve the messages in the middle tier (e.g., if we had configured our debugging package with a debug flag value of JDebug.LOG_IN_TRACE_FILES_ONLY).

```
System.out.println( JDebug.getDebugMessageAndFlush( conn, debugFlag ) );
```

Finally, we clear the debugging configuration—no more debug messages will be generated or output after this line in our program:

```
   JDebug.clear( conn, debugFlag, dbUserName, directory, debugFileName );
   }
   catch (SQLException e)
   {
     // handle the exception properly - we just print the stack trace.
     JDBCUtil.printException ( e );
   }
   finally
   {
     // release the JDBC resources in the finally clause.
     JDBCUtil.close( conn );
   }
 }
```

At the end of the program, the private method _callDemoDebug() is used to invoke the procedure demo_debug:

```
 private static void _callDemoDebug( Connection conn ) throws SQLException
 {
   CallableStatement cstmt = null;
   try
   {
     cstmt = conn.prepareCall( "{call demo_debug()}" );
     cstmt.execute();
   }
   finally
   {
     JDBCUtil.close( cstmt );
   }
 }
} / / end of program
```

When we invoke the program DemoJDebug, we get the following output:

```
B:\>java book.util.DemoJDebug
URL:jdbc:oracle:thin:@(DESCRIPTION=(ADDRESS=(PROTOCOL=tcp)(PORT=1521)
(HOST=rmenon-lap))(CONNECT_DATA=(SID=ora10g)))
MIDDLE TIER: Before invoking PL/SQL Code<br></br>Inside procedure
demo_debug <br></br>hello, my loop counter = 1: <br></br>hello, my
loop counter = 2: <br></br>hello, my loop counter = 3:
<br></br>hello, my loop counter = 4: <br></br>hello, my loop counter
= 5: <br></br>Exiting procedure demo_debug <br></br>MIDDLE TIER:
Before invoking PL/SQL Code<br></br>
```

The messages from both the Java code and the PL/SQL code can be seen in a formatted HTML output. The message logged from Java is prefixed with the string MIDDLE_TIER:.

I have found this technique extremely useful in debugging any UI code written in Java, say, using JSP technology. For example, if your Java code is getting or manipulating data from the database using PL/SQL, you can use JDebug to log messages in your middle tier code while using the debug package to log messages in your back-end PL/SQL code. Then with a URL-based parameter, you can dump your log messages into your page. For example, say your web page looks as shown in Figure 17-1.

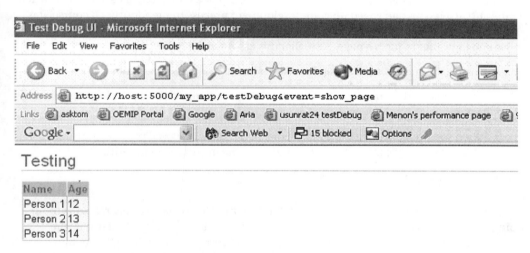

Figure 17-1. *A web page that has debugging turned off*

The URL of the page shown in Figure 17-1 is http://host:5000/my_app/testDebug&↩
event=show_page.

We can now add another parameter in the URL that takes a value of our debug flag (debug=2 implies that all debug messages should be shown in the middle tier only). Our URL now becomes http://host:5000/my_app/testDebug&event=show_page&debug=2. The page looks as shown in Figure 17-2.

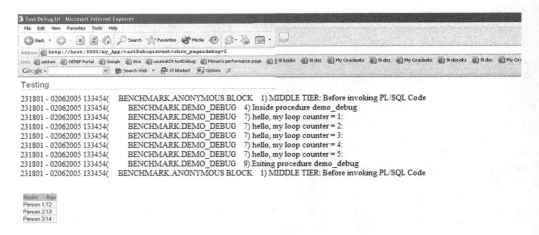

Figure 17-2. *A web page that has debugging turned on*

Notice how all the messages in the middle tier and PL/SQL are shown in the web page itself. The messages with the prefix MIDDLE TIER are coming from the middle-tier code. Using this method, you can instrument your PL/SQL and Java code and debug it easily with a switch in the URL itself. This can speed up your development process tremendously. Of course, it is also very useful when debugging any logical problem, or even performance bottlenecks in the back-end logic that renders a page. Note that this assumes the following:

- You are using the same connection when rendering a page. This is normally true.

- You invoke init() in your code with the right parameters to begin the logging at the beginning of your UI logic.

- When you are done with the UI rendering logic, you retrieve all your log messages using JDebug.getDebugMessageAndFlush() and print the messages on the URL.

- As a final step, you invoke JDebug.clear().

Note that if debugging is off, then all methods in the JDebug class simply return without doing anything, so you don't incur any noticeable performance penalty. Similarly, if your debugging is off (you pass JDebug.DEBUG_OFF), then the corresponding PL/SQL program's debug.f() method also becomes a no-op, thus incurring a negligible performance penalty.

■**Caution** Although the idea of showing debug messages as part of the web page is extremely useful during development, it can unfortunately create security problems if this feature is exposed in production. This is because any end user can turn the debug message on and read the logged messages, which could potentially contain proprietary information or information that can be used to compromise the security of the system. Note that this is not an issue if you use the option where your messages are logged in a file since files can and should be protected by using appropriate OS permissions. Hence I strongly recommend that the method of turning debug messages to be dumped into the web page itself should be disabled permanently before shipping the product. In other words, it should be usable only during the development stage. This can, of course, be achieved by using a separate configuration flag in your code.

One disadvantage of debugging is that when it is turned on, each Java-side debug message incurs a server round-trip. However, this issue is mitigated by the fact that during debugging and diagnosing problems (which is when debugging would be turned on), performance is not a major concern.

Summary

In this chapter, you learned why PL/SQL is such an important tool for a JDBC developer. You examined some PL/SQL techniques to increase the performance and maintainability of your code. These techniques included putting your code in packages, using bulk operations to improve performance, and preferring static SQL to dynamic SQL when you have a choice. You also learned about invoker rights and definer rights modes in PL/SQL, and when to use each mode. You then looked at PL/SQL debugging techniques and enhanced a custom PL/SQL package called debug, using which you can instrument your Java and PL/SQL code.

Appendix

Table A-1 shows the default mappings between SQL types and Java types.

Table A-1. *Default Mappings Between SQL Types and Java Types**

SQL Data Types	JDBC Typecodes	Standard Java Types	Oracle Extension Java Types
CHAR	java.sql.Types.CHAR	java.lang.String	oracle.sql.CHAR
VARCHAR2	java.sql.Types.VARCHAR	java.lang.String	oracle.sql.CHAR
LONG	java.sql.Types.LONGVARCHAR	java.lang.String	oracle.sql.CHAR
NUMBER	java.sql.Types.NUMERIC	java.math.BigDecimal	oracle.sql.NUMBER
NUMBER	java.sql.Types.DECIMAL	java.math.BigDecimal	oracle.sql.NUMBER
NUMBER	java.sql.Types.BIT	boolean	oracle.sql.NUMBER
NUMBER	java.sql.Types.TINYINT	byte	oracle.sql.NUMBER
NUMBER	java.sql.Types.SMALLINT	short	oracle.sql.NUMBER
NUMBER	java.sql.Types.INTEGER	int	oracle.sql.NUMBER
NUMBER	java.sql.Types.BIGINT	long	oracle.sql.NUMBER
NUMBER	java.sql.Types.REAL	float	oracle.sql.NUMBER
NUMBER	java.sql.Types.FLOAT	double	oracle.sql.NUMBER
NUMBER	java.sql.Types.DOUBLE	double	oracle.sql.NUMBER
RAW	java.sql.Types.BINARY	byte[]	oracle.sql.RAW
RAW	java.sql.Types.VARBINARY	byte[]	oracle.sql.RAW
LONGRAW	java.sql.Types.LONGVARBINARY	byte[]	oracle.sql.RAW
DATE	java.sql.Types.DATE	java.sql.Date	oracle.sql.DATE
DATE	java.sql.Types.TIME	java.sql.Time	oracle.sql.DATE
TIMESTAMP (see Note)	java.sql.Types.TIMESTAMP	javal.sql.Timestamp	oracle.sql.TIMESTAMP

Note For database versions, such as 8.1.7, that do not support the TIMESTAMP datatype, this is mapped to DATE.

(Continued)

Table A-1. *Default Mappings Between SQL Types and Java Types* (Continued)*

SQL Data Types	JDBC Typecodes	Standard Java Types	Oracle Extension Java Types
STANDARD JDBC 2.0 TYPES			
BLOB	java.sql.Types.BLOB	java.sql.Blob	oracle.sql.BLOB
CLOB	java.sql.Types.CLOB	java.sql.Clob	oracle.sql.CLOB
User-defined object	java.sql.Types.STRUCT	java.sql.Struct	oracle.sql.STRUCT
User-defined reference	java.sql.Types.REF	java.sql.Ref	oracle.sql.REF
User-defined collection	java.sql.Types.ARRAY	java.sql.Array	oracle.sql.ARRAY
ORACLE EXTENSIONS			
BFILE	oracle.jdbc.OracleTypes.BFILE	N/A	oracle.sql.BFILE
ROWID	oracle.jdbc.OracleTypes.ROWID	N/A	oracle.sql.ROWID
REF CURSOR type	oracle.jdbc.OracleTypes.CURSOR	java.sql.ResultSet	oracle.jdbc.OracleResultSet
TIMESTAMP	oracle.jdbc.OracleTypes.TIMESTAMP	java.sql.Timestamp	oracle.sql.TIMESTAMP
TIMESTAMP WITH TIME ZONE	oracle.jdbc.OracleTypes.TIMESTAMPTZ	java.sql.Timestamp	oracle.sql.TIMESTAMPTZ
TIMESTAMP WITH LOCAL TIME ZONE	oracle.jdbc.OracleTypes.TIMESTAMPLTZ	java.sql.Timestamp	oracle.sql.TIMESTAMPLTZ

* *Table information courtesy of Oracle Database JDBC Developer's Guide and Reference (10g Release 1), Table 4-3.*

Table A-2 shows the mapping between Oracle database types and the standard JDBC data types. You should use standard JDBC data types if you want to make your code portable across databases.

Table A-2. *Valid SQL Data Type–Java Class Mappings**

These SQL Data Types:	Can Be Materialized As These Java Types:
CHAR, VARCHAR, LONG	oracle.sql.CHAR java.lang.String java.sql.Date java.sql.Time java.sql.Timestamp java.lang.Byte java.lang.Short java.lang.Integer java.lang.Long java.lang.Float java.lang.Double java.math.BigDecimal byte, short, int, long, float, double
DATE	oracle.sql.DATE java.sql.Date java.sql.Time java.sql.Timestamp java.lang.String
NUMBER	oracle.sql.NUMBER java.lang.Byte java.lang.Short java.lang.Integer java.lang.Long java.lang.Float java.lang.Double java.math.BigDecimal byte, short, int, long, float, double
OPAQUE	oracle.sql.OPAQUE
RAW, LONG RAW	oracle.sql.RAW byte[]
ROWID	oracle.sql.CHAR oracle.sql.ROWID java.lang.String
BFILE	oracle.sql.BFILE
BLOB	oracle.sql.BLOB java.sql.Blob
CLOB	oracle.sql.CLOB java.sql.Clob
TIMESTAMP	java.sql.Date, oracle.sql.DATE, java.sql.Time, java.sql.Timestamp, oracle.sql.TIMESTAMP, java.lang.String, byte[]
TIMESTAMP WITH TIME ZONE	java.sql.Date, oracle.sql.DATE, java.sql.Time, java.sql.Timestamp, oracle.sql.TIMESTAMPTZ, java.lang.String, byte[]

(Continued)

Table A-2. *Valid SQL Data Type–Java Class Mappings* (Continued)*

These SQL Data Types:	Can Be Materialized As These Java Types:

`TIMESTAMP WITH LOCAL TIME ZONE`	`java.sql.Date, oracle.sql.DATE, java.sql.Time,`
	`java.sql.Timestamp, oracle.sql.TIMESTAMPLTZ,`
	`java.lang.String, byte[]`

Object types	`oracle.sql.STRUCT`
	`java.sql.Struct`
	`java.sql.SqlData`
	`oracle.sql.ORAData`

Reference types	`oracle.sql.REF`
	`java.sql.Ref`
	`oracle.sql.ORAData`

Nested table types and `VARRAY` types	`oracle.sql.ARRAY`
	`java.sql.Array`
	`oracle.sql.ORAData`

* *Table information courtesy of* Oracle Database JDBC Developer's Guide and Reference (10*g* Release 1), Table 25-1.

Index

forums.apress.com

JOIN THE APRESS FORUMS AND BE PART OF OUR COMMUNITY. You'll find discussions that cover topics of interest to IT professionals, programmers, and enthusiasts just like you. If you post a query to one of our forums, you can expect that some of the best minds in the business—especially Apress authors, who all write with *The Expert's Voice*™—will chime in to help you. Why not aim to become one of our most valuable participants (MVPs) and win cool stuff? Here's a sampling of what you'll find:

DATABASES
Data drives everything.

Share information, exchange ideas, and discuss any database programming or administration issues.

INTERNET TECHNOLOGIES AND NETWORKING
Try living without plumbing (and eventually IPv6).

Talk about networking topics including protocols, design, administration, wireless, wired, storage, backup, certifications, trends, and new technologies.

JAVA
We've come a long way from the old Oak tree.

Hang out and discuss Java in whatever flavor you choose: J2SE, J2EE, J2ME, Jakarta, and so on.

MAC OS X
All about the Zen of OS X.

OS X is both the present and the future for Mac apps. Make suggestions, offer up ideas, or boast about your new hardware.

OPEN SOURCE
Source code is good; understanding (open) source is better.

Discuss open source technologies and related topics such as PHP, MySQL, Linux, Perl, Apache, Python, and more.

PROGRAMMING/BUSINESS
Unfortunately, it is.

Talk about the Apress line of books that cover software methodology, best practices, and how programmers interact with the "suits."

WEB DEVELOPMENT/DESIGN
Ugly doesn't cut it anymore, and CGI is absurd.

Help is in sight for your site. Find design solutions for your projects and get ideas for building an interactive Web site.

SECURITY
Lots of bad guys out there—the good guys need help.

Discuss computer and network security issues here. Just don't let anyone else know the answers!

TECHNOLOGY IN ACTION
Cool things. Fun things.

It's after hours. It's time to play. Whether you're into LEGO® MINDSTORMS™ or turning an old PC into a DVR, this is where technology turns into fun.

WINDOWS
No defenestration here.

Ask questions about all aspects of Windows programming, get help on Microsoft technologies covered in Apress books, or provide feedback on any Apress Windows book.

HOW TO PARTICIPATE:

Go to the Apress Forums site at **http://forums.apress.com/**.
Click the New User link.